AMERICAN ERAS

EARLY AMERICAN CIVILIZATIONS AND EXPLORATION TO 1600

AMERICAN ERAS

EARLY AMERICAN CIVILIZATIONS AND EXPLORATION TO 1600

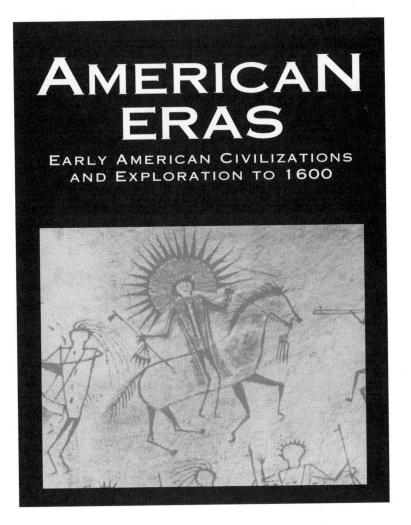

EDITED BY

GRETCHEN D. STARR-LeBEAU

A MANLY, INC. BOOK

GALE

DETROIT LONDON

AMERICAN ERAS

EARLY AMERICAN CIVILIZATIONS AND EXPLORATION TO 1600

Matthew J. Bruccoli and Richard Layman, Editorial Directors
Karen L. Rood, Senior Editor

CONTENTS

INTRODUCTION VII

ACKNOWLEDGMENTS XI

Chapter 1:
WORLD EVENTS. 3

Chapter 2:
AMERICAS: THE PEOPLE. 21

Chapter 3:
THE ARTS 55

Chapter 4:
COMMUNICATIONS 77

Chapter 5:
EDUCATION 103

Chapter 6:
GOVERNMENT & LAW. 115

Chapter 7:
LIFESTYLES, SOCIAL TRENDS, & RECREATION. . . 155

Chapter 8:
RELIGION 175

Chapter 9:
SCIENCE, MEDICINE & TECHNOLOGY. 203

Chapter 10:
TRADE & COMMERCE. 237

Chapter 11:
WARFARE 253

GENERAL REFERENCES 281

CONTRIBUTORS 285

GENERAL INDEX. 287

INDEX OF PHOTOGRAPHS 293

INTRODUCTION

Diversity of Native Populations. From the first contacts between Europeans and North American Indians to the present day, the area which today is the United States and Canada has been home to thousands of indigenous populations. Although most researchers have concluded that Native Americans came to the Western Hemisphere via a land bridge from Asia, this does not mean that all indigenous peoples shared a common language or culture. Differences in climate and history created marked distinctions among native groups. In the northern reaches of the continent, in what is today much of eastern Canada and northern New England, the climate was too cool to permit much agriculture or permanent settlement. Instead these populations were nomadic, traveling from place to place to keep ahead of the weather and to find food in summer and winter. Plains Indians in the western part of the continent also led largely nomadic lives, a trend that was heightened by the introduction of the horse after the arrival of the Spanish. In other parts of North America such as southern New England and the Mid-Atlantic states, Native Americans alternated settled communities with periods of mobility. American Indians such as Hurons and Iroquois built settled communities but relocated when fields were exhausted or climate dictated. Hunters also tended to take extensive trips away from the community to hunt or to fight with other tribes in the area. Finally some indigenous groups maintained a much more settled, or sedentary, existence. The mesa-dwelling Pueblos of the southwest and Mississippian chiefdoms of the southeast both established more permanent communities with larger populations. These distinctions, of course, are just one way of distinguishing among the many Indian groups. For example, the Pueblo Indians spoke (and still speak) a radically different language from the Choctaw and other Mississippian tribes and used different agricultural techniques, dwellings, and ceremonies.

Indigenous Societies in Transition. Even before Europeans arrived Native American societies were in a period of transition. In the northeastern United States tribes began to form larger confederations for the purpose of mutual defense. The greatest example of this were the Mohawks, Oneidas, Onondagas, Cayugas, and Senecas, who formed the League of the Iroquois in the fifteenth century. Shifts in political and military power, which are often easiest for archeologists, anthropologists, and historians to detect, were also apparent in the southeast and west. The impressive rise and decline of Cahokia, a large Native American city near what is now St. Louis, is only one example. It cannot be denied, however, that even in this period, when Europeans numbered at most one thousand among the millions of indigenous people, the presence of western European traders, fishermen, soldiers, and a few settlers had a profound impact upon indigenous life in North America. Trade with Europeans, usually Basque or Breton fishermen, increased the demand for beaver pelts far beyond what Native Americans had hunted for themselves. As a result new conflicts arose among native populations over who would control the best trapping regions and who would trade with these foreigners. Europeans also introduced new items into the trade routes. Beads, buttons, and metal implements such as axes have been found far from early European settlement sites, and it is clear that many Indians knew of such goods long before they ever met a European. Most devastating for Native Americans, though, was a more dangerous European import: disease. Native Americans had little natural resistance to European diseases, which often spread along trade routes and, like axes and beads, made their presence felt before Europeans actually arrived on the scene. Indeed the population losses due to these epidemics may well have precipitated some of the other political and military conflicts among Indians in the sixteenth century. The slower pace of change among indigenous societies in the sixteenth century was soon overtaken by change caused, directly or indirectly, by Europeans.

Western Europe: A Changing Society. Like Native American societies, European societies were also changing in the decades before 1600. The fifteenth century not only witnessed Christopher Columbus's historic voyage to the Caribbean but also the height of the Renaissance. From its origins on the Italian peninsula the Renaissance brought together new trends in art, science, and technology and witnessed the production of some of the most impressive art Western Europe ever produced. Leonardo da Vinci, who in many ways exemplified the Italian Renaissance, was a brilliant painter, an inventor, and an author of treatises on waterworks and military technology. As Europe moved into the sixteenth century, though, the wealth and artistic endeavor of the Renaissance was superceded by decades of religious, economic, and political upheaval. Martin Luther and John Calvin rewrote Europe's religious boundaries, creating new alternatives to Catholicism. For more than a century Protestantism and Catholicism contested for the souls of Europeans, sometimes in armed conflict. Gold and silver from Spain's colonies, together with the poor monetary policies of some European leaders, created an extended period of inflation which decreased the ability of the population to support itself. Wars further impoverished the continent. The long Hapsburg-Valois wars between Spain and France were the most prominent of a series of conflicts that stretched from one end of Europe to the other. Threats from outside Europe also grew in the sixteenth century. The Ottoman Turks marched on Europe from the Balkans, taking Serbia, Bosnia, Croatia, and Hungary before they were stopped just beyond Vienna. In short the period between 1492 and 1600 was one of great turmoil in the so-called Old World.

First Contacts. Columbus was the first person to bring knowledge of North America to Europe, but he was not the first European to reach the Western Hemisphere. Northern Europeans had been aware of good fishing on both sides of the North Atlantic for centuries. Some twentieth-century readers think that Irish legends may tell of travel to America, but the first clear evidence of contact between Europeans and American Indians comes from the Vikings. In the tenth and eleventh centuries Vikings led by Leif Ericson set up a small colony in what are now the maritime provinces of Canada, but cold weather, difficult traveling, and hostility from the "skraelings," or Native Americans, forced the Vikings to abandon their site. Contact did continue over the years, however, by means of fishermen from the Atlantic coasts of Spain and France. Fishermen and traders brought European products to the Americas and in return received furs, which were both valuable back home and easily portable in the small boats fishermen used. These contacts were consistent enough that a pidgin developed, a rudimentary mixture of two or more languages used in trade. In the early sixteenth century explorers who thought that they were the first Europeans to see this land were astonished to be greeted by the natives in French, Basque, and English. It is important to remember, however, that while these contacts were relatively frequent, they were not well-known, nor did they occur on a large scale. The total number of European fishermen who traveled as far as the eastern coast of Canada and New England was quite small, and their deeds were little known or recognized in the wider world.

Motivations. After Columbus's fateful trip Europeans began to seek out the Western Hemisphere as a destination in its own right. Even Columbus's journey was motivated by a larger purpose than that of the fishermen who preceded him. For Columbus, as for many who followed him, financial rewards were a powerful motivation. Columbus sought a route to the lucrative trade centers of Asia which would not require him to travel through Portuguese-held territory. If he had been successful, Columbus would have gained himself and his sponsors immense wealth. Later, when it became clear that America, too, was a rich land, many explorers and colonists went in search of the "next Mexico" or the "next Inca Empire." Much of the exploration of the southeast and southwest of the United States in this period was for the express purpose of discovering untold wealth in legendary sites such as the "Seven Cities of Gold." Money was not the only motivator, however. Religious beliefs, just as much as financial standing, moved Europeans to extend their reach into the rest of the globe. Columbus, for instance, hoped to use his new route to Asia to spearhead a crusade. More important than money was the opportunity to retake Jerusalem for western European Christians. One out of every eight people sent by the Spanish government to their various holdings in the Americas was a religious figure—either a priest or one of the groups of friars and monks dedicated to converting the indigenous population. Many of these men believed that the world was coming to an end and that they needed to convert the world so that Jesus Christ could return to earth. Other Europeans arrived besides the Spanish, but their motivations were often closely linked to Spanish aims. In fact, French and English explorers such as Sir Francis Drake worked hard both to copy Spanish success and to defeat their European rivals.

Settlements. Europeans came to what is now the continental United States and Canada in the sixteenth century, but few intended to stay. Most arrived looking for trade, easy wealth, or souls for conversion, but some explorers created more-permanent settlements. Trade posts were the least permanent settlements created by Europeans because trade was usually seasonal, especially in northern climes. Military outposts were the first permanent homes that Europeans created for themselves. These sites, known among the Spanish as presidios, were designed to protect local settlers and to maintain control over hostile territory. Presidios were scattered across the southern United States, from Arizona and New Mexico in the southwest to Florida and South Carolina in the southeast. They marked the outer frontier of Spanish colonial territory. The presidios not only protected Spaniards from Indians who resented their intrusion, but they also protected Spanish claims from other European powers. In the southeast, for example, Spaniards often spent as much time fighting the French as they did fighting indigenous peoples. European settlement, however, was not limited to military garrisons. The explorers also set up missions to begin the conversion of Native Americans in the Spanish territory of the southwest and southeast and in the French-controlled lands of what is now eastern Canada. These housed missionaries, usually Jesuits or Franciscans, and some native peoples. Missions in the sixteenth century achieved mixed results. Some missionaries did succeed in converting and baptizing Indians, but others failed in the face of active native resistance and were forced to leave. The difficulty of the missionaries' task is apparent in much of their building; the fortresslike churches resemble military fortifications more than peaceful sites of religious education. Indeed, since missionaries were often among the first Europeans to visit an area, their buildings had a military purpose as well as a religious one. By the end of the sixteenth century a few Europeans had tried to create more permanent, stable communities in North America. The English built Roanoke, a community designed both to challenge Spanish claims to North America and to serve as a base for British military operations. Nearby, in what is now South Carolina, French Huguenots constructed Fort Caroline, a refuge from attacks by Catholics in France as well as a base of operations from which to harass the Spanish. In what is now Florida the Spanish had survived attacks from both the French and local indigenous people to maintain St. Augustine, a military fortification that became the first permanent settlement by Europeans in what is now the United States. This should not suggest that Europeans had successfully colonized North America. Except for St. Augustine and Santa Fe, New Mexico, all European settlements founded in North America before 1607 were abandoned by 1625. Moreover, of the approximately 10,000 Spanish, French, English, and Dutch colonists who had migrated to the Atlantic coast of North America by 1625, only about 1,800 remained.

Range of Exploration. Much more common than permanent settlements were exploratory trips designed to help Europeans understand the breadth of the landmass that Columbus had stumbled upon. These men led their expeditions through unknown territory, far beyond European settlement, in an attempt to understand the region and where its wealth lay. Some, such as Ponce de Leon, encountered fierce resistance from the Florida natives he encountered. Others, such as Hernando de Soto and Francisco Vásquez de Coronado, were remembered by generations of American Indians for their vicious treatment of native peoples. On occasion individuals not formally sent by the government provided useful information. Alvaro Nuñez Cabeza de Vaca survived shipwreck and the collapse of his superior's expedition, and with three other survivors traveled around the Gulf of Mexico in search of Spanish settlements. The book which he wrote on his return provided detailed knowledge of the region for the Spanish government.

Discovery, Encounter, or Invasion? For many years historians, anthropologists, and archaeologists have debated what to call these activities by Europeans in North and South America. Since 1992 and the Colombian Quincentennial this debate has moved into the public arena. Previously most Americans called this period "The Age of Discovery"; now most scholars have rejected this phrase. After all, the first discoverers of North and South America were the Native Americans who crossed the Bering Land Bridge millennia ago, and to call Europeans "discoverers" implies that no one else was here. Some people have responded that it was a discovery to Europeans and so call it the "European discovery" of the Americas. By the 1970s some people began calling this era "The Invasion of America." This clearly identified Europeans as aggressors, but it implied a conscious, well-formulated plan of attack which did not adequately explain the ad hoc nature of much European activity in North America. Another group of scholars tried calling what happened an "encounter." This term avoided describing European intentions at all, which made the century sound like a series of friendly meetings rather than the armed conflict that usually took place. The authors of this volume tend to use other terms. "Exploration" is used to describe the activities of men such as Coronado and de Soto, and "conquest" describes successful European attacks on native societies.

Indian or Native American? Another term to come under fire lately is the word "Indian." Columbus, who insisted to the end of his life that he had reached Asia, called the people he had found Indians since he assumed that they were natives of the East Indies. Today some people find the word "Indian" offensive, and other terms are coming into use. "Native American" is one frequently used phrase. It distinguishes native Americans from European, African, or Asian Americans, but some people avoid using it since any person born on the continent, whatever his or her ancestry, is technically a native American. Other people use the phrase "indigenous peoples," which is more accurate but cumbersome to use. In Canada the official term is "First Nations." Most of the authors in this book use a variety of phrases to describe the peoples living here before the arrival of Europeans.

North America in 1600. By 1600 most attempts at permanent settlement had been disastrous, and native populations had successfully repulsed several European military forays. Had they wished, North American Indians could have virtually eliminated Europeans from the continent. Few people would have foretold the incredible success of European colonization only a few short decades later. Yet the seeds of that success were already present. The growing trade between Europeans and Indians had already changed indigenous society and made it more dependent on European goods. European diseases were already taking their toll on the population, with other epidemics still to come. And local leaders saw in the Europeans a new advantage in local conflicts which had long been at a stalemate. For all these reasons few indigenous people were willing to completely expel Europeans, even if such a move had been possible. Native Americans still held the balance of power in 1600, but their dominance on the continent was coming to an end.

ACKNOWLEDGMENTS

This book was produced by Manly, Inc. Anthony J. Scotti was the in-house editor.

Production manager is Philip B. Dematteis.

Office manager is Kathy Lawler Merlette.

Administrative support was provided by Ann M. Cheschi. Bookkeeper is Joyce Fowler.

Copyediting supervisor is Samuel W. Bruce. The copyediting staff includes Phyllis A. Avant, Charles Brower, Patricia Coate, Christine Copeland, Thom Harman, and Nicole M. Nichols.

Editorial associate is Jeff Miller.

Layout and graphics staff includes Janet E. Hill and Mark McEwan.

Photography editors are Margaret Meriwether and Paul Talbot. Photographic copy work was performed by Joseph M. Bruccoli.

Systems manager is Marie L. Parker.

Typesetting supervisor is Kathleen M. Flanagan. The typesetting staff includes Pamela D. Norton and Patricia Flanagan Salisbury.

Walter W. Ross and Steven Gross did library research. They were assisted by the following librarians at the Thomas Cooper Library of the University of South Carolina: Linda Holderfield and the interlibrary-loan staff; reference-department head Virginia Weathers; reference librarians Marilee Birchfield, Stefanie Buck, Stefanie DuBose, Rebecca Feind, Karen Joseph, Donna Lehman, Charlene Loope, Anthony McKissick, Jean Rhyne, Kwamine Simpson, and Virginia Weathers; circulation-department head Caroline Taylor; and acquisitions-searching supervisor David Haggard.

AMERICAN
ERAS
BEFORE 1600

AMERICAN ERAS

EARLY AMERICAN CIVILIZATIONS
AND EXPLORATION TO 1600

WORLD EVENTS:
SELECTED OCCURRENCES OUTSIDE NORTH AMERICA

MAJOR POWERS AND LEADERS

China—Ming Hong Zhi, born Zhu You-Tang (1488–1505), Ming Zheng De, born Zhu Hou-Zhao (1506–1521), Ming Jia Jing, born Zhu Hou-Cong (1522–1566), Ming Long Qing, born Zhu Zai-Hou (1567–1572), Ming Wan-Li, born Zhu Yi-Jun (1573–1619).

Denmark and Norway—John (1481–1513), Christian II, "the Cruel" (1513–1523), Frederick I (1523–1533), Christian III, "Father of the People" (1534–1558), Frederick II (1558–1588), Christian IV (1588–1648).

England—Henry VII (1485–1509), Henry VIII (1509–1547), Edward VI (1547–1553), Mary (1553–1558), Elizabeth I (1558–1603).

France—Louis XII (1498–1512), Francis I (1515–1547), Henry II (1547–1559), Francis II (1559–1560), Charles IX (1560–1574), Henry III (1574–1589), Henry IV (1589–1610).

Holy Roman Empire—Maximilian I (1493–1519), Charles V (1519–1556), Ferdinand I (1556–1564), Maximilian II (1564–1576), Rudolph II (1576–1612).

Hungary and Bohemia—Ladislas II (Hungary, 1490–1516, Bohemia, 1471–1516), Louis II (1516–1526), Ferdinand I, Holy Roman Emperor (1526–1564), Maximilian II, Holy Roman Emperor (1564–1576), Rudolph II, Holy Roman Emperor (1576–1612).

Ottoman Empire—Bayezid II (1481–1512), Selim I, "the Inexorable" (1512–1520), Suleiman the Magnificent or the Lawgiver (1520–1566), Selim II, "the Sot" (1566–1574), Murad III (1574–1595), Mehmed III (1595–1603).

Papacy—Alexander VI (1492–1503), Pius III (1503), Julius II (1503–1513), Leo X (1513–1521), Adrian VI (1521–1523), Clement VII (1523–1534), Paul III (1534–1549), Julius III (1550–1555), Marcellus II (1555), Paul IV (1555–1559), Pius IV (1559–1565), St. Pius V (1566–1572), Gregory XIII (1572–1585), Sixtus V (1585–1590), Urban VII (1590), Gregory XIV (1590–1591), Innocent IX (1591), Clement VIII (1592–1605).

Poland—John Albert (1492–1501), Alexander (1501–1506), Sigmund I (1506–1548), Sigmund II (1548–1572), Interregnum (1572–1573), Henry (1573–1574), Interregnum (1575–1576), Stephen (1575–1586), Interregnum (1586–1587), Sigmund III (1587–1632).

Portugal—Emanuel the Fortunate (1495–1521), John II, "the Perfect Prince" (1521–1557), Sebastian I (1557–1578), Philip I, who was also Philip II of Spain (1580–1598), Philip II, who was also Philip III of Spain (1598–1621).

Russia—Ivan III, "the Great" (1462–1505), Basil III (1505–1533), Ivan IV, "the Terrible" (1533–1584), Theodore I (1584–1598), Boris Godunov (1598–1605).

Spain—Isabel of Castile (1474–1504), Ferdinand of Aragon (1479–1516), Charles I, who was also Charles V of the Holy Roman Empire (1516–1556), Philip II (1556–1598), Philip III (1598–1621).

Sweden—Gustav Vasa (1523–1560), Eric XIV (1560–1568), John III (1568–1592).

United Provinces of the Netherlands—William I, "the Silent" (1572–1584), Maurice of Nassau (1585–1621).

MAJOR CONFLICTS

1519–1522—Conquest of Mexico

1521–1529—Turkish invasion of southern Europe

1522–1559—Hapsburg-Valois Wars

1524–1525—Peasants' War

1546–1547—Schmalkaldic War

1557–1582—Livonian War

1562–1598—French wars of religion

1585–1589—War of the Three Henries

1492

- Alonso de Nebrija publishes his grammar of Spanish, the first grammar of any vernacular language in Europe. In his introduction he writes that "language is the companion of empire."

1 Jan.   Ferdinand and Isabella conquer the kingdom of Granada, ending eight hundred years of Muslim rule on the Iberian peninsula.

31 Mar.   The decree of expulsion is issued in Spain, requiring all Jews to leave or convert to Christianity within three months.

12 Oct.   After six weeks at sea Christopher Columbus makes landfall in the Caribbean.

1493

- Maximilian I is the first to take the title of "Holy Roman Emperor elect."

1494

- Pope Alexander VI approves the Treaty of Tordesillas between Spain and Portugal. The treaty specifies that Spain can claim all territory west of a line in the Atlantic while Portugal can claim all territory east of that line, including its current holdings in Africa and Asia.

1495

- The Diet of Worms attempts to modernize the Holy Roman Empire through various administrative reforms.

1496

- The decree of expulsion is issued for the Jews of Portugal. When the Jewish population is assembled at the docks, they are not permitted to leave but instead are forced to convert. New converts are given a fifty-year period to assimilate into Christian society.

1497

- The Jews of Navarre, the last Jews of Iberia, are forced to leave the kingdom.
- John Cabot, in the service of the English Crown, explores Newfoundland.
- Amerigo Vespucci makes his first voyage to the Western Hemisphere, exploring the Caribbean.
- Portuguese navigator Vasco da Gama sails around the southern tip of Africa and reaches India; he returns to Portugal in 1499.

1498

- John Cabot is lost at sea while exploring the western Atlantic.

1499

- The Turks defeat a Venetian fleet at Sapienza.

1500

- The Treaty of Granada is signed between Ferdinand and Isabella and the Muslim population of Granada. The treaty guarantees that Muslims in Granada can maintain their religious faith under Spanish authority.
- The African kingdom of Monomotapa, centered in present-day Zimbabwe, is formed.

1501

- The first African slaves are brought to Hispaniola. Spaniards hope that they will help alleviate the labor shortage caused by the death of much of the indigenous population.

1502

- The Spanish consolidate their power in Naples through a combination of force and diplomacy.

1503

- The humanist scholar Erasmus of Rotterdam publishes his *Enchiridion*, a handbook of Christian virtues.
- Cesare Borgia, illegitimate son of Pope Alexander VI and tyrannical ruler of the Papal States, falls from power.
- Leonardo da Vinci paints the *Mona Lisa*.

1504

- Isabella of Castile dies, and her husband, Ferdinand, rules as regent of Castile for their daughter, Juana the Mad.

1505

- Czar Ivan III, "the Great," of Russia, dies after forty-three years on the throne. He is succeeded by his son, Basil III.

1506

- Christopher Columbus dies.
- The Jewish community in Lisbon is massacred.
- Construction of the new St. Peter's basilica is begun in Rome under the orders of Pope Julius II.

1507

- To help pay for the building of St. Peter's, Pope Julius II begins to sell indulgences. It is this practice that later incites Martin Luther to speak out against him.
- The Martin Waldseemüller map is the first to label the South American continent "America."

1508

- The League of Cambrai is formed against Venice.

1509

- Henry VIII succeeds his father as king of England.
- Erasmus writes *In Praise of Folly,* his best-known and most popular work.
- Michelangelo paints the ceiling of the Sistine Chapel in the Vatican.

1510

- The Portuguese acquire Goa, a port on the west coast of India.

1511

- The Portuguese seize the city of Malacca on the Malay peninsula in order to protect their spice trade.

1512

- Ferdinand of Aragon conquers Navarre.
- Henry VIII invades France.

1513

- Niccolò Machiavelli writes *The Prince,* an analysis of the responsibilities of rulers, and dedicates it to the new pope, Leo X.

1514

- Hungarian peasants led by George Dózsa revolt.

1515

- Francis I ascends the throne of France.

1516

- Ferdinand of Aragon dies and is succeeded by his grandson, Charles V.

- Thomas More publishes *Utopia*.

- Erasmus of Rotterdam publishes a new edition of the Greek New Testament using his knowledge of Greek and of the early texts still available.

1517

- The Ottoman Turks conquer the Mamluk Sultanate of Syria and Egypt, thus gaining control of the Red Sea.

31 Oct.   Martin Luther publishes his Ninety-five Theses in Wittenberg, listing criticisms of the Catholic Church and marking the start of the Protestant Reformation.

1518

- Hernando Cortés lands at present-day Vera Cruz, Mexico.

- The Peace of London ends fighting between England and France.

1519

- Charles V Hapsburg of Spain is crowned Holy Roman Emperor.

- Huldrych Zwingli begins preaching in Zurich. Like Martin Luther he protests abuses of the church; unlike Luther he challenges the real presence of Jesus Christ in the Eucharist (transubstantiation and consubstantiation). Zwingli ultimately begins the Swiss Reformation.

- Ferdinand Magellan begins his circumnavigation of the globe. Nineteen members of his crew return three years later, but Magellan himself is killed in the Philippines.

1520

- Raphael, one of the great painters of the Renaissance, dies.

- Martin Luther is threatened with excommunication by the papal decree (bull) *Exurge Domine*.

- The Swede Gustav Vasa leads a rebellion against Christian II, "the Cruel," of Denmark. By 1523 Sweden and Finland will be independent of Denmark and Norway.

1521

- After several setbacks Cortés succeeds in conquering Tenochtitlan, capital city of the Aztecs of central Mexico and site of present-day Mexico City.

- An army under Suleiman the Magnificent takes Belgrade.

- Calusa warriors thwart Juan Ponce de León's attempt to colonize Florida for Spain, kill him, and drive the invaders back to Cuba.

10 Jan. Martin Luther is excommunicated from the Roman Catholic Church. Luther then begins his own movement, later known as Lutheranism.

1522

- The first Hapsburg-Valois War begins in Italy, pitting the Holy Roman Empire, Spain, and England against France.

- Francisco Jiménez de Cisneros directs the publication of the Complutensian Polyglot Bible, which provides the text of the Bible in six parallel columns. Because Erasmus had recently published his own new edition of the Greek New Testament, however, the Complutensian Bible never achieves great popularity.

Nov. Luther's New Testament is published in German, leading to a wave of Bible translation into the vernacular.

- Rhodes falls to the Ottoman Turks as a part of their advance across the Mediterranean.

1523

- Christian II of Denmark is deposed; in Sweden, Gustav Vasa becomes king.

- The Knights' Revolt in Germany is suppressed.

1524

- The Peasants' War begins in the Holy Roman Empire. Under the leadership of Thomas Müntzer the peasants take several cities.

- Francis I conquers Milan.

- The Council of the Indies is formed in Spain to oversee colonization of the New World.

- Sailing under the French flag, Giovanni da Verrazzano explores the east coast of North America.

1525

- The German peasants are defeated, and their leader, Thomas Müntzer, is executed.

- The first Hapsburg-Valois War ends when the Spanish defeat the French at the Battle of Pavia.

1526

- The Ottoman Turks take the city of Mohács in Hungary and continue advancing on central Europe.

- William Tyndale's translation of the New Testament into English arrives in England from the Holy Roman Empire and immediately becomes popular.

1527

- The army of Charles V sacks Rome, and Pope Clement VII becomes a virtual prisoner.
- Castiglione writes *The Courtier* about the ideal virtues of courtly life.

1528

- Albrecht Dürer, one of the greatest artists and engravers of the Holy Roman Empire, dies.
- The Spanish explorer Panfilo de Narváez attempts to explore the Florida interior, but attacks by the Apalachee Indians force him to retreat. He and all but four of his men disappear somewhere in the Gulf of Mexico.

1529

- Vienna is besieged by the Turks but is able to fend off the invaders.

1530

- Martin Luther and his assistant, Philip Melanchthon, write the Augsburg Confession, a statement of basic Lutheran belief.

1531

- The Schmalkaldic League of Protestant princes is formed in the Holy Roman Empire.
- Parliament recognizes King Henry VIII as Supreme Head of the Church in England.

1532

- Following the example set by Hernando Cortés, Francisco Pizarro leads an invasion against the Inca Empire. Because the Inca are in the midst of civil war, he is able to gain control of the empire in only two years.
- Machiavelli's *The Prince* is published posthumously.
- The Turks invade Hungary.

1533

- Basil III of Russia dies, and Ivan IV, "the Terrible," of Russia ascends to the throne. Ivan's mother, Helena Glinskaia, rules as regent until 1538.
- Francisco Pizarro captures and kills the Inca ruler Atahualpa.

1534

- Henry VIII of England wishes to divorce his wife, Catherine of Aragon, and marry Anne Boleyn. To circumvent the opposition of the Roman Catholic Church he signs of the Act of Supremacy, making himself head of the English church.

- St. Ignatius of Loyola, a Spanish noble and soldier, undergoes a conversion to a more devout form of life. To help others achieve this same conversion and to aid the poor, he establishes the Society of Jesus (Jesuits).

- The Iroquoian Indians of Stadacona and Hochelaga welcome French explorer Jacques Cartier in the first of his three voyages of exploration up the St. Lawrence River. His efforts to build a colony come to naught, and his kidnapping of several Indian youths angers the Iroquoians.

1535

- After a long siege the Anabaptists of Münster in the Holy Roman Empire are massacred.

- Sir Thomas More is executed in England for refusing to recognize Henry VIII's authority over the church in England.

1536

- John Calvin writes and publishes the first edition of his *Institutes of Christian Religion*. In laying out his detailed description of Reformed theology he emphasizes the doctrine of predestination: that some individuals are destined to be saved while others are destined for damnation.

- France signs a peace treaty with the Ottoman Empire.

- Michelangelo paints *The Last Judgment* in the Sistine Chapel.

1537

- A civil war erupts in Peru between rival conquistadors.

1538

- John Calvin, expelled from Geneva, settles in Strasbourg.

1539

- Over the course of the next three years thousands of North American Indians encounter the expeditions of Hernando de Soto in the southeast and Hernando Vásquez de Coronado in the Southwest. Native resistance and a lack of provisions force both exploring parties to beat hasty retreats to Mexico.

1540

- The Society of Jesus, more commonly known as the Jesuits, is recognized by the Pope and formally sanctioned as a new order. Under their founder, Ignatius of Loyola, the Jesuits will travel as missionaries and educators throughout the globe.

1541

- John Calvin returns to Geneva and begins to institute reforms of city life based on his reading of the Scriptures. His *Ecclesiastical Ordinances,* published this year, becomes the model for Reformed Protestant communities throughout Europe.

- Francisco de Orellana explores the Amazon, returning the following year.

- The Ottoman Turks conquer Transylvania in Romania and Budapest in Hungary.

1542

- The Roman Inquisition starts.

1543

- Nicholas Copernicus dies, and one of his students publishes *De Revolutionibus,* Copernicus's explanation of the heliocentric theory of the universe.

- Charles V, Holy Roman Emperor, and Henry VIII of England form an alliance against Francis I of France.

- Portuguese sailors introduce firearms to the Japanese.

1544

- The University of Königsberg is founded.

1545

- In response to the rapid growth of Protestantism the Roman Catholic Church calls the first of three sessions of the Council of Trent; this first session lasts until 1547.

- Silver deposits are discovered at Potosí in present-day Bolivia.

1546

- The Schmalkaldic War begins.

1547

- Henry VIII of England dies and is succeeded by his son, Edward VI, who moves the country toward a more thorough acceptance of Protestantism.

1548

- St. Ignatius of Loyola's *Spiritual Exercises* is published for the first time.

1549

- The Book of Common Prayer is published in England.
- St. Francis Xavier arrives in Japan.

1550

- Michelangelo paints *Deposition from the Cross*.

1551

- The second session of the Council of Trent meets and focuses on reform of the clergy and stricter standards of education for priests.
- The Ottomans take the city of Tripoli.
- The Hapsburg-Valois Wars resume.

1552

- St. Francis Xavier dies in China. In his journeys for the Society of Jesus, Francis Xavier traveled in India, Southeast Asia, China, and Japan.
- Henry II of France allies with German Protestants.
- Ivan IV, "the Terrible," starts the conquest of Astrakhan and Kazan.

1553

- Edward VI of England dies and is succeeded by his half sister Mary. Daughter of Catherine of Aragon, Mary is a devout Catholic and tries to move the country back to Catholicism.

1554

- Mary Tudor, queen of England, marries Philip II of Spain.

1555

- The Peace of Augsburg, negotiated by Charles V and his princes, mandates that each prince in the Holy Roman Empire can choose Lutheranism or Catholicism to be the religion of his principality. This ends an extended period of religious war in the empire.

1556

- Charles V abdicates as Holy Roman Emperor and king of Spain and is succeeded in Spain by his son, Philip II. Charles retires to a monastery in Yuste, Spain, where he dies two years later.
- Akbar the Great becomes the Mughal emperor of India and rules until 1605.

1557

- The Livonian War begins when Russia, Sweden, Denmark, and Poland vie for control of the Baltic territories.

- The first Index of Prohibited Books is issued by Pope Paul IV.

- Europe undergoes a widespread financial crisis as banks fail.

- A Portuguese settlement at Macao is established.

1558

- Mary of England dies and is succeeded by her half sister, Elizabeth I, who is the daughter of Anne Boleyn. Elizabeth advocates a *via media*, or middle ground, between Catholicism and radical Protestantism.

1559

- The Treaty of Cateau-Cambresis creates peace between France and Spain after decades of fighting in the Hapsburg-Valois Wars. France gives up any claims to land in Italy. At the festivities marking the conclusion of the war, King Henry II of France is fatally wounded in a tournament, and his son Francis II succeeds him.

1560

- Catherine de Medici begins a five-year term as regent for her son Charles IX of France. Her attempts to placate the Huguenot minority ultimately succeed in further dividing the country.

1561

- The Colloquy of Poissy, designed to reconcile Huguenots and Catholics, takes place in France.

1562

- The French wars of religion begin between Catholics and Huguenots. Although the Protestants comprise only about 10 percent of the population, sporadic fighting continues until 1598.

- Chief Saturnia welcomes Frenchman Jean Ribault's Charlesfort colony in Florida. The site is abandoned two years later.

- The third and final session of the Council of Trent begins. Unlike the first two sessions, which dealt primarily with reform of the clergy, this session addresses doctrinal questions raised by Protestants. French bishops, in attendance for the first time at Trent, urge those present to work harder to confront Protestantism.

1563

- A general outbreak of plague occurs in Europe and kills more than twenty thousand people in London.
- The first printing presses begin operations in Russia.
- The Peace of Amboise grants limited toleration to Huguenots.

1564

- Michelangelo, last of the great Renaissance artists, dies.
- The Peace of Troyes settles the conflict between England and France.
- Ivan IV, "the Terrible," battles with his *boyars,* or noblemen, for power.
- Saturnia helps Réné de Laudonnière build a second French colony in Florida, Fort Caroline, but grows angry with the Frenchman's unwillingness to uphold certain promises he had made.

1565

- The Ottoman Turks launch a major expedition against Malta in the western Mediterranean but fail to capture the island.
- Pedro Ménendez de Avilés's Spanish force destroys the French settlement at Fort Caroline and builds the city of St. Augustine in Florida.

1566

- Open resistance to Spanish rule in the Netherlands begins.
- Suleiman the Magnificent dies and is succeeded as sultan by Selim II, "the Sot."

1567

- An estimated two million Indians die of typhoid fever in South America.
- The duke of Alba becomes the Spanish military governor of the Netherlands and begins a reign of terror.
- In Japan, Nobunaga deposes the shogunate and centralizes the government.

1568

- Spanish territories in the Low Countries (present-day Holland and Belgium) revolt, protesting taxes, religious oppression, and the foreign rule of Philip II.
- Muslim *moriscos,* or converts, revolt against Spanish rule in Granada.

1569

- Approximately forty thousand inhabitants of Lisbon die from an epidemic of carbuncular fever.
- A public lottery is held in London to finance repairs to port facilities.
- Sigismund II of Poland unites Poland and Lithuania in the Union of Lublin.

1570

- The morisco rebellion in Granada is thwarted by the Spanish.
- Japan begins to permit visits by foreign ships.
- The Ottoman Turks attack Cyprus and begin a war with Venice.

1571

- Ottoman Turks take Cyprus as part of their advance across the Mediterranean.

7 Oct. In the greatest naval battle since Actium in 31 B.C., a Spanish-Venetian fleet defeats a Turkish fleet in the Battle of Lepanto. Out of 230 Ottoman galleys only 40 escape destruction or capture.

1572

- Exiled Calvinist privateers from the Netherlands known as "Sea Beggars" seize fifty towns in the Low Countries.
- The Peace of Constantinople ends Turkish attacks on Europe.

24 Aug. After a botched assassination attempt against the Protestant Gaspard de Coligny, Catholics kill at least thirty thousand Huguenots in Paris. The St. Bartholemew's Day Massacre spreads to other cities in France, where more French Protestants are killed.

1573

- Venice makes peace with the Ottoman Empire.

1574

- The Ottoman Turks conquer Tunisia.
- Torquato Tasso completes *Jerusalem Liberated*.

1575

- Philip II of Spain declares bankruptcy.
- Spanish traders arrive in Canton, China.

1576

- The French Catholic League is formed by rural nobles who want to resist the Huguenots.

1577

- Sir Francis Drake begins his circumnavigation of the globe.

1578

- The catacombs of Rome are discovered.
- John III of Sweden secretly converts to Catholicism.
- One of the chief rulers of Japan, Otomo Yoshishige, converts to Christianity.

1579

- The Union of Utrecht is established, uniting the northern Low Countries (present-day Netherlands) in opposition to Spanish rule. Under William of Nassau, prince of Orange, Dutch resistance is further organized.

1580

- When the king of Portugal dies without an heir, Philip II of Spain annexes the country; Portugal and Spain will remain united until 1640.
- Michel de Montaigne publishes the first two books of his *Essays,* which comment on the human condition.
- Sir Francis Drake returns from his voyage around the world.

1581

- Thomas Kyd's *The Spanish Tragedy* is performed. It is the first romantic tragedy—a play mingling love, betrayal, and revenge.
- Akbar the Great of Mughal India conquers Afganistan.

1582

- Pope Gregory reforms the calendar; the Gregorian calendar is still in use today.

1583

- Galileo discovers the principle of the pendulum.

1584

- Ivan IV, "the Terrible," of Russia dies, and his son, Theodore I, becomes czar.
- Prince William of Orange is killed on orders of Philip II of Spain.

1585

- The War of the Three Henries begins in France, a religious conflict involving Henry III of Valois, Henry of Navarre, and Henry Guise.

- William Shakespeare arrives in London.

- Chief Wingina allows the English to build the Virginia colony on Roanoke Island, but relations between him and the colonists deteriorate, and the colonists flee back to England the following year.

1586

- Mary, Queen of Scots, is implicated in a plot to kill Elizabeth I; she is tried and convicted of treason. Meanwhile, Mary recognizes Philip II of Spain as her heir.

1587

- Mary, Queen of Scots, is executed.

- Christopher Marlowe's play *Tamburlaine the Great* is performed in London.

- A second attempt to found a Virginia colony is undertaken, but it too fails, and the colonists vanish in 1590.

1588

- Boris Godunov, brother-in-law to Czar Theodore I, becomes the effective head of Russia.

- Michel de Montaigne publishes his third and final book of *Essays*.

- Christopher Marlowe's *Doctor Faustus* is performed in London.

7 Aug. A British fleet defeats the Spanish Armada.

1589

- Henry III, king of France, on his deathbed recognizes Henry of Navarre, a Protestant, as his successor.

- Christopher Marlowe's *The Jew of Malta* is performed in London.

- The head of the Russian Church is elevated to the level of a Patriarch, the highest rank in the Orthodox Church. As a result the Russian Church gains new prestige and strengthens its organization.

- A mutiny of the elite soldiers of the Ottoman sultan, known as janissaries, occurs; they kill the grand vizier and other officials.

1590

- Theodore de Bry and his sons begin publication of the first of ten volumes of the lavishly illustrated series *Great Voyages*. Publication will continue for the next twenty-eight years.

- Edmund Spenser's *The Faerie Queen* is published.

1591

- The Songhay Empire along the Niger River in Africa collapses.

1592

- Hideyoshi of Japan fails in his attempt to invade China via Korea.
- The Portuguese settle Mombasa, an island off the east coast of Africa.
- The ruins of Pompeii, a Roman city destroyed by a volcanic eruption in 79 A.D., are discovered.

1593

- Japan attacks the Korean peninsula, which is controlled by China, and succeeds in taking some coastal fortifications.

1594

- After converting to Catholicism the previous year, Henry IV enters Paris and is crowned the king of France.

1595

- The Dutch begin colonization of the East Indies.
- Henry IV of France declares war on England.

1596

- Shakespeare's play *Romeo and Juliet* is performed in London.

1597

- A second Spanish Armada leaves for England but is scattered by storms.
- The Dutch found Batavia, Java.
- The English Parliament approves the transportation of criminals to the colonies as a means of punishment.

1598

- Philip II of Spain dies and is succeeded by his son, Philip III.
- Henry IV of France decrees the Edict of Nantes, which grants limited rights to Huguenots.
- Theodore I of Russia dies and is succeeded by his brother-in-law, Boris Godunov.
- War between Japan and China ends when the former sues for peace.
- Tycho Brahe publishes *Astronomiae instauratae mechanica*, a description of his astronomical experiments and calculations.
- Juan de Oñate settles among the Pueblo Indians.

1599

- Shakespeare's *Julius Caesar* is performed in London.

1600

- The English East India Company is formed to develop overseas trade.
- Shakespeare's *Hamlet* is performed in London.
- Tokugawa Ieyasu ends decades of civil war in Japan at the battle of Sekigahara. Having defeated his enemies, this shogun (military leader) brings peace to Japan and moves the capital to Edo (known today as Tokyo).

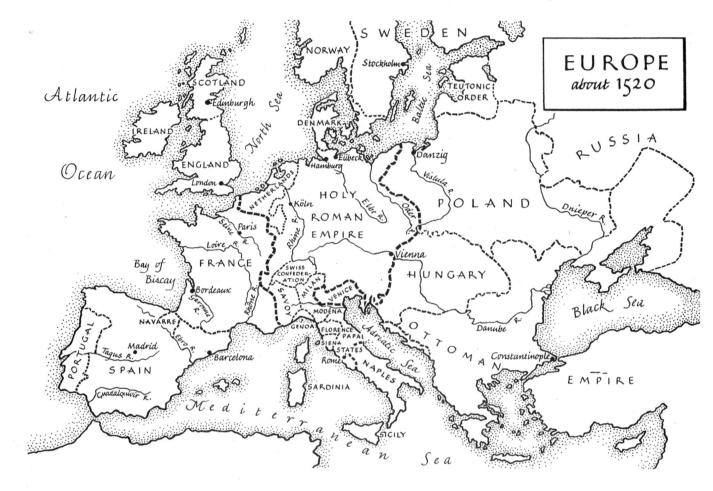

Atlantic

Ocean

SCOTLAND
Edinburgh

IRELAND

ENGLAND

London

NORWAY

North Sea

DENMARK

Lübeck

Hamburg

NETHERLANDS

Köln

Seine R.

Paris

Loire R.

FRANCE

Bay of
Biscay

Bordeaux

Garonne R.

NAVARRE

Ebro R.

PORTUGAL

Tagus R.

Madrid

SPAIN

Barcelona

Guadalquivir R.

SWEDEN

Stockholm

Baltic Sea

TEUTONIC
ORDER

Danzig

Vistula R.

POLAND

Elbe R.

HOLY
ROMAN
EMPIRE

Rhine R.

Oder R.

Rhône R.

SWISS
CONFEDER-
ATION

SAVOY

MILAN

MODENA

GENOA

FLORENCE

SIENA

Rome

NAPLES

SARDINIA

Mediterranean Sea

VENICE

PAPAL
STATES

Adriatic Sea

Vienna

HUNGARY

Danube R.

OTTOMAN

Constantinople

RUSSIA

Dnieper R.

Black Sea

EMPIRE

SICILY

EUROPE
about 1520

CHAPTER TWO

AMERICAS: THE PEOPLE

by JAMES CARSON

CONTENTS

CHRONOLOGY
22

OVERVIEW
24

TOPICS IN THE NEWS

Ancient America,
40,000–1500 B.C. 25
*Prehistory, Protohistory,
and History* 26
The Atlatl 27
Classical America: The East: Midwest
and Great Lakes Region...... 27
Classical America: The East:
Northeast 29
The Three Sisters 30
Classical America: The East:
South 31

Classical America: The West:
California 33
Classical America: The West:
Great Basin 34
Classical America: The West:
Great Plains 34
Classical America: The West: Pacific
Northwest.................... 35
Classical America: The West:
Southwest.................... 36
The Colonization of Vinland,
986–1014 A.D. 38
Early Exploration of America..... 39
Rights of Discovery and Conquest .. 39
Early Settlement of the Americas by
Spain........................ 40
Early Settlement of the Southeast by
Spain 41
Luis de Velasco and the Jesuits..... 42
Early Settlement of the Southwest by
Spain 43

France and the New World 45
French Settlement of the
Southeast................... 46
Imperial England and the
New World 47
Imperial England Settles the
Southeast 48
Tobacco 49

HEADLINE MAKERS

Alvar Núñez Cabeza de Vaca 50
The Lady of Cofitachequi......... 51
Thomas Harriot 52

PUBLICATIONS
54

Sidebars and tables are listed in italics.

40,000–10,000 B.C.	• Paleolithic Asians migrate to North America across a land bridge in the Bering Strait.
8000–1500 B.C.	• Native Americans invent basketry and the atlatl (a device for throwing a spear), which sparks the formation of Archaic culture hunting-and-gathering bands.
1500 B.C.–**1492** A.D.	• Several Archaic cultures develop pottery and adopt horticulture. The changes produce some of the largest and most complex native societies in the Americas.
986–1014	• Vikings explore and settle Newfoundland.
1492	• Christopher Columbus lands in the Caribbean and mistakes the region for Asia. His landfall marks the beginning of the Age of Discovery.
1497	• John Cabot, in the service of the English Crown, explores Newfoundland.
1521	• Calusa warriors thwart Juan Ponce de León's attempt to colonize Florida for Spain and drive him and his followers back to Cuba.
1524	• Sailing under the French flag, Giovanni da Verrazano explores the east coast of North America.
1528	• The Spanish explorer Pánfilo de Narváez attempts to explore the Florida interior, but attacks by the Apalachee Indians force him to retreat. He and all but four of his men disappear somewhere in the Gulf of Mexico.

1534–1542

- The Iroquoian Indians of Stadacona and Hochelaga welcome French explorer Jacques Cartier's three voyages of exploration up the St. Lawrence River. Cartier's efforts to build a colony come to nought, and his kidnapping of several Indian youths angers the Iroquoians.

1539–1542

- Thousands of North American Indians encounter the expeditions of Hernando de Soto in the Southeast and Francisco Vásquez de Coronado in the Southwest. Native resistance and a lack of provisions force both exploring parties to beat hasty retreats back to Mexico.

1562

- Chief Saturnia welcomes Frenchman Jean Ribault's Charlesfort colony in Florida (present-day Port Royal, South Carolina). The site is abandoned two years later.

1564

- Saturnia helps René Goulaine de Laudonnière build a second French colony in Florida, Fort Caroline, but grows angry with the Frenchman's unwillingness to uphold certain promises he had made.

1565

- Pedro Menéndez de Avilés's Spanish force destroys the French settlement at Fort Caroline and builds the city of St. Augustine.

1585

- Chief Wingina allows the English to build the Virginia colony on Roanoke Island, but relations between him and the colonists deteriorate, and the colonists flee back to England the following year.

1587

- A second attempt to found a Virginia colony is undertaken, but it too fails, and the colonists vanish in 1590.

1598

- Juan de Oñate settles among the Pueblo Indians of the Southwest.

OVERVIEW

Ancient North America. North America has been home to humans for tens of thousands of years. The first people came from Asia, and they brought with them a Stone Age culture called Clovis that they spread from coast to coast and from pole to pole during their pursuit of the giant mammals that roamed the continent. Thousands of years after the first settlement of North America, the common Clovis culture that the immigrants had brought from Asia splintered into hundreds of different Archaic cultures based on hunting and gathering. The Archaic cultures reflected the particular demands of the different environments in which the people lived. For example, in the arid Southwest, Archaic peoples hunted the fauna of the desert and gathered roots to feed themselves while the inhabitants of the forests of the East subsisted on white-tailed deer and various berries, fruits, and roots. Over time the gathering of wild plants developed into a rudimentary form of horticulture that enabled Archaic societies to grow larger and larger. Horticulture ultimately gave rise to many of the Classical cultures of North America that the first Europeans encountered during their voyages of exploration. In the Southwest, Classical Indians developed methods of irrigation to grow corn and other crops, and they invented the adobe tradition of home construction to shelter them from the hot days and keep them warm during the cool nights. The Classical Mound Builders who lived east of the Mississippi River grew corn on river floodplains and built great ceremonial mounds to honor the sun god. On the plains people combined farming with buffalo hunting in a lifestyle attuned to the seasons, and in the Pacific Northwest salmon, not corn or buffalo, was the native inhabitants' staff of life.

First Contacts. There are several theories as to who actually discovered North America. Questionable evidence has put navigators from Polynesia, sailors from ancient Egypt and Phoenicia, fishermen from China and Japan, and priests from Ireland in touch with the native population. A more substantial case can be made for fishermen from the Basque region of Spain, who, while dipping their fishing nets into the waters off the coast of Newfoundland, may have traded with the local inhabitants for furs. While it may be interesting to speculate about such early undocumented visits, the first verifiable landfall by nonnatives was made by the Vikings at the end of the eleventh century A.D.

The Age of Exploration. Not until the fifteenth century, however, did oceanic exploration and the building of overseas colonies capture the imagination of Europeans. How historians have approached the so-called Age of Discovery has changed over time, and the terms historians have used to describe the colonization of North America have undergone substantial revision over the past several decades. The voyages of Christopher Columbus and John Cabot as well as the overland expeditions of Francisco Vásquez de Coronado and Hernando de Soto were once lauded as milestones in an age of epic adventure. But the recent commemoration of the quincentenary of Columbus's landfall has reoriented scholars' and the public's appreciation of the pivotal events in the early history of what Europeans called the "New World."

The New World. The Europeans who first visited the shores of North America in the decades following Columbus's landfall were as diverse as the native inhabitants. The Spanish had built on earlier advances in sailing and navigation made by their neighbors the Portuguese and gradually worked their way west across the Atlantic Ocean until Columbus found land in the Caribbean in October 1492. While he had not been the first European to set foot in the New World, Columbus was the first to make a case through various published books and pamphlets that Europeans could open regular channels of contact and colonization with the land he believed to be Asia. France also sought to participate in the rush for colonies, but religious strife and an inability to colonize successfully the St. Lawrence River Valley militated against the creation of a strong French presence in North America before 1600. Unwilling to allow the Pope and his secular agents to dominate the New World, the English brought the might of Protestantism to bear on the race for colonies. Their decisions on where to explore and settle and when to do it were as much dictated by what their Spanish and French counterparts were doing as they were by their own needs. Nevertheless, England's initial forays in colonization were no more successful than France's efforts.

Consequences of Spanish Colonization. The Spanish attempted to pattern their colonies in North America on organizational models developed in the conquest of Central and South America. Stiff resistance from the native population as well as the inability of Spain to finance and outfit adequately its colonial enterprises frustrated the Crown's ambitions. While explorers chased after the mythic lands of Chicora, Cíbola, and Quivira, friars and settlers eked out a life in the harsh environments of Florida and New Mexico. Despite their lack of success they did exert a profound influence on the Native Americans who prayed in the missions and who labored on the estates of the Spanish landowners. By far the greatest impact of Spanish colonization, however, was the spread of European diseases among the native populations. On the island of Hispaniola, where Columbus established the first permanent Spanish colony, the native Arawak population plummeted from eight million in 1492 to two hundred in 1550. In Florida, Indian populations declined by 95 percent between 1565 and the mid 1600s. Among the Pueblo Indians of New Mexico, the story was no different; in four decades of contact with the Spanish, their numbers declined by one-half. Spanish North America, to borrow a phrase from one historian, was "a widowed land."

Consequences of French Colonization. Fears that Spain might replicate the success of its southern colonies in North America caused France to enter the Age of Discovery. Early exploration of the North American coast and several ill-fated attempts to settle the St. Lawrence River Valley and Florida laid the foundations of what became in the 1600s a far-flung and profitable empire. Still, as of 1600 there was no permanent French presence in North America. But if they had failed to fulfill their imperial ambitions, their presence in the New World, unlike that of the Spanish, was not associated with the catastrophic Native American population losses that characterized Florida and New Mexico.

Consequences of English Colonization. It is easy to assume that the English beat the Spanish and the French in the race to colonize North America because the history of colonization after 1600 is largely the story of English growth and expansion. Before the founding of Jamestown, Virginia, in 1607, however, the English experienced the same problems as the Spanish and the French. They were unable to build viable colonies, and they could not overcome native resistance. Although the two attempts to settle Roanoke Island off the coast of present-day North Carolina were dismal failures, they nevertheless only whetted the English appetite for the gold, silver, and other riches that they believed they would discover in the New World.

The People of North America in 1600. By the end of the Age of Discovery, North America was still firmly in native hands. Neither the French nor the English had been able to found a permanent settlement. The Spanish had been more successful, but only barely. Roughly six hundred soldiers, priests, and settlers and a handful of slaves lived in Florida, and a little more than one thousand colonists maintained a tentative grip on the Pueblos in New Mexico. Native North America, however, contained hundreds of different cultures. Some groups had witnessed firsthand European attempts to settle the continent, but most others had only experienced contact with Europeans through word of mouth or through the new diseases that raced inland along indigenous trade routes. The total native population north of the Rio Grande at the time of Columbus's landing has been a topic of great debate. Early estimates made by anthropologists in the 1920s and 1930s placed the figure at around one million, which fit well with the population of Native Americans living at that time. Subsequent revisions, however, have suggested that the number was somewhere between seven and eighteen million around 1500. How many natives died of disease, starvation, and war-related causes between 1500 and 1600 is impossible to determine.

TOPICS IN THE NEWS

ANCIENT AMERICA, 40,000–1500 B.C.

Land Bridge. The first immigrants to North America came to the continent between 40,000 and 10,000 B.C. in two large movements timed to the rhythmic shrinking and expanding of the world's seas. Between what is today Alaska and Siberia a land bridge sixty miles long and a thousand miles wide emerged periodically as ocean waters receded to allow passage overland from Asia to America. The migration route into North America ran between glacial ridges to the northeast and southwest, and the first peoples worked their way south along the Canadian Rockies into the American Great Plains and

When historians and archaeologists discuss early North America, they employ three terms to characterize different periods of time, all of which are predicated on a definition of history as the written record of the human past. North America's prehistory goes back at least twenty thousand years and encompasses all time that came before the first European landings in North America. The period is called prehistory not because nothing happened but because none of the native peoples left behind written records of what happened. Protohistory occupies that fuzzy space between prehistory and history, and it is usually meant to describe the early contact period when natives and Europeans first met but had little sustained contact with one another. Written records describing contact existed, but the bulk of what happened to native peoples went unseen by European eyes and unrecorded by European scribes. History starts after prolonged interaction between natives and Europeans and is characterized by the voluminous writings left behind by colonists, soldiers, officials, and even a handful of natives who learned to read and write.

Source: Glyn Edmund Daniel, *The Idea of Prehistory* (Edinburgh, Scotland: Edinburgh University Press, 1988).

from there to all points of the compass. The migrants came in three waves. The first consisted of what archaeologists call the Amerinds, the ancestors of most Native American peoples and the progenitors of most Native American languages. Second were the Na-Déné, a cultural and linguistic group that gave rise to the Athapaskans of Canada and the American Southwest. Last were the Inuit, who populated the Arctic and moved eastward until they collided with the Vikings in Greenland.

Paleolithic Culture: 40,000–8000 B.C. What we know of the first North Americans is what archaeologists have been able to determine from examinations of the stone tools they made, the garbage pits they left behind, and the sites they chose for their homes. Remarkable more for the similarities in their cultures across the continent than for the differences, the first people have come to be known as Paleo-Indians. In spite of the ice that covered much of the continent when they first arrived, the area encompassing Siberia and Alaska consisted of flat, grassy plains that supported large animals such as the woolly mammoth and giant sloth and smaller creatures such as the ancestors of today's horses. The Paleo-Indians followed the herds of beasts and hunted them for food, clothing, and the materials with which they made many of their tools. Over time their culture evolved into four distinct traditions, the most important and most widespread of which is called Clovis. Socially and politically, the Paleo-Indians were organized in band societies, small groups of extended kin that had little or no allegiance to other bands. Band leaders were in charge of or-

A map of the New World, made in 1507 by Martin Waldseemüller

THE ATLATL

As big game died out, Paleo-Indians needed to develop technologies and strategies for hunting smaller mammals such as white-tailed deer and mule deer. The large, heavy thrusting spears that they had tipped with Clovis points needed to be replaced. During the transition to the Archaic period, spears were made smaller and lighter, but hunters made an even more important technological advance that enabled them to hurl their new spears with greater force and accuracy. The atlatl consisted of a throwing stick with a notch on one end that held the spear in place. To improve the throwing action of the stick, a craftsman drilled a hole through a specially carved stone and slipped the stone over the throwing stick. As the hunter hurled the stick, the stone shifted its weight from back to front and added additional force to the thrust of the hunter's arm. The new weapon worked well, and hunters used it for several thousand years before adopting the more accurate, more efficient, and more deadly bow and arrow in the early centuries A.D.

Sources: Robert L. Bettinger, *Hunter-Gatherers: Archaeological and Evolutionary Theory* (New York: Plenum Press, 1991);

Lynda Shaffer, *Native Americans before 1492: The Moundbuilding Centers of the Eastern Woodlands* (Armonk, N.Y.: M. E. Sharpe, 1992).

ganizing the hunt and leading the people in a nomadic pursuit of big game.

Changes. By 8000 B.C. the Paleo-Indians had replaced their relatively dull stone blades and projectile points with much sharper ones made by chipping flint or chert. They also developed the atlatl, a sort of lever used to extend the length of the arm while throwing a spear. The device improved the velocity, accuracy, and penetrating power of spears and increased Paleo hunters' efficiency. Two thousand years later the earth began to warm, and the ice melted. As the oceans rose once again, the land bridge disappeared beneath the waves, and the Paleo-Indian population was cut off from its Asian homeland. When coupled with the natives' increased proficiency in hunting, the climatic changes triggered an important change in the Paleo environment. Between 9000 and 5000 B.C. the big game animals that had dominated the landscape vanished.

Archaic Culture: 8000–1500 B.C. The demise of the woolly mammoths, mastodons, giant sloths, and giant bison and the retreat of the great North American icecap forced Paleo-Indians to change the ways in which they fed, clothed, and organized themselves. They began to hunt smaller mammals and to supplement their diets with fruits, nuts, and grains that the women gathered. Moreover, the invention of basketry enabled people to

store quantities of food for later use as they moved from site to site in pursuit of seasonally available resources. The culture that had structured Paleo-Indian societies gave way to a new cultural configuration archaeologists call Archaic. The Archaic hunter-gatherer societies were the last cultural tradition that was ubiquitous throughout most of the continent. As different Archaic groups developed techniques for hunting and gathering in their local environments, however, their cultures began to diverge from one another. Competition for land also grew more fierce, and people developed more sedentary lifestyles in order to avoid the constant conflict with other groups that seasonal migrations caused.

Horticulture. If the atlatl and basketry were important technological innovations, then the impact of horticulture—the cultivation of plants—can only be characterized as a revolution in lifestyle. Indeed, horticulture emerged out of the increased sedentarism that characterized the late Archaic period and gave rise to the variety of unique Classical cultures that arose across North America beginning about 1000 B.C. The green revolution dates back more than nine thousand years to when Mesoamericans began experimenting with wild varieties of corn, beans, and squash. Between 3400 and 2300 B.C. horticultural Mesoamerican societies began to flourish, and, owing to the trade networks that connected natives in the Americas, it was not long before the plants spread into North America. Although the rate of their spread varied from region to region, by the ninth century corn, beans, and squash had developed into staple crops from the Southwest to the Northeast. Horticulture changed things because it provided a regular and relatively predictable source of food that enabled groups to stay in one place. To store the food some groups used baskets while others developed the ability to make pottery. With the technology to raise and store crops, hunting-and-gathering societies grew into larger and more-complex units anthropologists call tribes, which were characterized by more differentiation between leaders and commoners and by more-complex forms of social, political, and economic organization.

Sources:
James E. Dixon, *Quest for the Origins of the First Americans* (Albuquerque: University of New Mexico Press, 1992);

Carl Waldman, *Atlas of North American Indians* (New York: Facts on File, 1985).

CLASSICAL AMERICA: THE EAST: MIDWEST AND GREAT LAKES REGION

Old Copper Culture: 4000–1500 B.C. Between 4000 and 1500 B.C. an Archaic culture peculiar to the Great Lakes region developed out of the Clovis-type people that originally had settled the area. Although the Old Copper people depended on hunting, gathering, and fishing for their livelihoods and made tools of a wide array of materials to exploit the forest and lake environments, their ability to work copper set them apart from their Archaic counterparts across the continent. Initially

Copy of a daguerreotype of the Big Mound, St. Louis, made in 1852 by Thomas Easterly
(Missouri Historical Society)

they chipped at it like stone in order to fashion items, but over time they learned to heat the metal, which enabled them to make more elaborate and delicate decorative pieces. The value of copper goods to the region's trade is evident in the number of copper artifacts that turn up in other archaeological sites in the East.

Adena and Hopewell: 500 B.C. to 550 A.D. South of the Old Copper people lived numerous groups of Archaic Indians who developed stratified societies and who built earthen mound centers. Around 500 B.C. the Adena culture appeared in present-day southern and central Ohio, and three hundred years later another mound-building culture, Hopewell, arose in Ohio and spread much farther south. The Adena and Hopewell mounds were built in relation to the movements of the stars and the sun, and they were often designed in the shapes of birds, snakes and symbols of the sun, sky, moon, and earth. The Adena people and the Hopewellians lived adjacent to rivers so they could easily control the flow of trade goods up and down the Ohio River. Seashells from the South and minerals from the North flowed through the mound centers, and Adena and Hopewell traders linked native peoples from Florida to the Rocky Mountains. For subsistence the Mound Builders relied for the most part on the same animals and wild plants that had fed their Archaic ancestors. The ceremonial importance they attached to the dead, however, distinguished them from their Archaic predecessors. The people of

Hopewell and Adena regularly buried important individuals in the mounds, usually with prestige goods such as copper jewelry, shell gorgets, ornate pipes, and so forth. The veneration accorded the dead as evidenced by the quality of the burial goods has led archaeologists to surmise that the dead bodies were those of chiefs or priests. If such special attention was lavished only on political and religious leaders, perhaps the populations of the Adena and of the Hopewell cultures were divided into classes. By 550 A.D. Hopewell and Adena had vanished. Changes in climate and trade or the availability of foodstuffs may have caused the collapse, but no one is certain.

The Upper Ohio Country: 550–1600 A.D. After the disappearance of Adena and Hopewell, the populations of present-day Ohio, Indiana, northern West Virginia, and western Pennsylvania gathered in small towns and lived lifestyles typical of what archaeologists call Eastern Woodland culture. In many ways Woodland cultures were similar to Archaic ones: Woodland people blended hunting and gathering for subsistence purposes, often lived in tribes, and often followed seasonal migration patterns. Unlike Archaic people, however, Woodland people made pottery, farmed to various extents, interred the dead in elaborate burials, and often comprised large tribes that demanded a more complex social and political organization than was present in the Archaic cultures. The Foley-Farm culture, for example, was a Woodland culture that developed between 900 and 1500. These people made pottery, and they inhabited towns where the houses were positioned around central town plazas and were guarded by palisades and moats. Storage houses and bone houses, where the bones of the dead were stored, also characterized the urban landscape of the Woodland Indians of the upper Ohio. Over time the Foley-Farm culture evolved into a people Europeans called Monongahelas. What separated the historic Monongahelas from their prehistoric predecessors was their adoption of horticulture.

Fort Ancient: 1000–1600 A.D. Between 1000 and 1600 the Fort Ancient people of present-day Ohio and Indiana carried on much of the Mound Builders' traditions. They buried many of their dead in mounds with prestige goods, and they built fortifications to protect their towns. The intensive cultivation of corn, beans, and squash separated Fort Ancient most clearly from Adena, Hopewell, Foley-Farm, and the contemporaneous Monongahelans. The historic Shawnees were most closely linked to the Fort Ancient culture because they practiced the same typical Woodland subsistence techniques and shared a similar material culture. They also hunted and gathered and lived in semipermanent towns in the summer and in scattered hunting camps in the winter.

Sources:

James L. Phillips and James A. Brown, eds., *Archaic Hunters and Gatherers in the American Midwest* (New York: Academic Press, 1983);

Louise Robbins and Georg K. Neumann, *The Prehistoric People of the Fort Ancient Culture of the Central Ohio Valley*, Anthropological Papers, Museum of Anthropology, University of Michigan (Ann Arbor: University of Michigan Press, 1972).

CLASSICAL AMERICA: THE EAST: NORTHEAST

Early Prehistory: 10,500–1600 B.C. Around 10,500 B.C. Paleo-Indians migrated into the present-day northeastern United States. The big-game hunters gave way to hunters and gatherers around 6000 B.C., and slowly over time the hunting-and-gathering-cultures diversified and developed according to the limits and the possibilities of the physical environments in which they lived. Between 1600 and 1000 B.C. a hunting-and-gathering society from the South, the Iroquoians, and a hunting-and-gathering society from the West, the Algonquians, drove the original Archaic inhabitants of the Northeast out of the region.

Abenaki: 1600 B.C. to 1600. A.D. The Abenakis were an Algonquian group that lived in present-day Maine, New Hampshire, and Vermont. They probably situated their settlements adjacent to rivers and lakes, where they fed themselves by hunting deer and bear, by gathering berries and nuts, and by fishing. As a rule they did not practice horticulture, but from time to time, when the weather allowed, they may have cultivated small gardens. Although their language bound the several Abenaki tribes together, there is no evidence that the groups were politically linked. The Abenakis on the coast probably had contact with English or Basque fishermen, but substantive evidence linking them to the European presence in North America is first seen in their use of Old World trade goods in the early 1600s. They incorporated clay pipes and triangular pieces of copper or brass that they cut from kettles and pots and used as projectile points.

Narragansett: 1600 B.C. to 1600 A.D.. The Narragansetts were situated in present-day Rhode Island, and although they too spoke an Algonquian tongue, their way of life was quite different from their Abenaki neighbors to the North. The Narragansetts farmed and lived in villages for much of the year. Also, their political organization united several villages under the leadership of two hereditary sachems, one old and one young. The Narragansetts were quite powerful within the region because they grew surpluses of corn which they traded to northern hunting groups such as the Abenakis for meat which they then traded farther south to various horticultural peoples. Oral history suggests the Vikings may have visited the Narragansetts, but most scholars believe their first contact with Europeans came during Giovanni da Verrazano's voyage in 1524.

Powhatan: 1570–1600 A.D. One of the southernmost Algonquian societies was the Powhatan confederacy, which was formed by Chief Powhatan in the latter decades of the sixteenth century A.D. Situated in the tidewater regions of Virginia and Maryland, the Powhatans lived in several towns characterized by large, round, bark-covered houses and, frequently, by stockades built for their protection. In winter the inhabitants vacated their towns and dispersed into smaller hunting camps, but the majority of their time was spent inside the walls of their towns. Their technology was comparable to other Woodland groups because they made tools of bone, antler, shell, and wood, but they were also skilled in the cold-hammering of copper into thin sheets that ar-

An Iroquois wampum belt (circa 1600 A.D.) celebrating the friendship between colonists and Native Americans (New York State Museum)

At roughly the same time that Asians began experimenting with domesticated wheat, Indians in south central Mexico began growing teosinte, a type of grass. Over the next several millennia teosinte began to evolve into a plant similar to modern corn. The breeding experiments led to testing other strands and seeds as well as the development of chili peppers, avocados, cotton, and other plants. For North American Indians, however, corn, beans, and squash were by far the most important native cultigens. Because women were the primary farmers in prehistoric North America, the plants were always associated with the feminine powers of fertility. In fact, the Iroquois called them the "Three Sisters." Squash was the first of the Mesoamerican crops to infiltrate North America, and by 1000 B.C. the plant had reached the East. Also known as cucurbits, the squashes were similar to present-day pumpkins and summer squashes. Around 200 B.C. corn and beans had diffused from their ancestral home in Mexico to the Southwest, and by 800 A.D. the new crops had reached the East. How they got into the Indians' hands is unknown, but it is reasonable to speculate that the elaborate trade networks that carried obsidian, skins, and other goods back and forth across the Rio Grande also carried a few dried kernels of corn, beans, and squash seeds, and the knowledge of how to plant them. The new crops' spread, however, was limited. The cultivation of corn, for example, was restricted to below the so-called corn line that stretches across the United States just below the border with Canada. Above the line the growing season is generally too short to allow for substantial horticulture. As important as the "Three Sisters" were, it is not surprising that they should figure prominently in Native American mythology. Iroquois oral tradition, for example, relates a story in which the Good Twin who created the earth made corn, but his antagonist, Sky Woman, fixed the kernels so that they had to be parched and ground in a mortar in order to be eaten. The Mississippian Choctaws told that corn had been dropped by a bird from the South and that it had been found by a little girl whose mother told her of the value of the plant. The Cherokees, however, believed corn and beans came from a woman named Selu. Her two sons had killed her, and wherever a drop of her blood fell a corn plant grew. And another historic Mississippian society, the Tunicas, believed beans had been given to a boy by his deceased sister.

The important links between women and plants probably originated in Paleo-Indian times, but as horticulture developed and became more complex, so too did the important roles women played in the subsistence of their societies. Europeans who saw native gardens marveled at how messy they were, at least to European eyes. Accustomed to well-defined rows of crops and fields devoted entirely to one plant, explorers and colonists were bewildered by how natives mixed their plants together. For example, women planted corn in small mounds and around the base of the mound they placed beans and squash seeds. As the corn grew taller the beans spiraled around the cornstalk and rose above the ground. Squash stayed close to the ground, and its broad leaves sheltered the other plants' roots from the harsh sun and helped prevent soil erosion. The technique also helped the soil because just as corn leeches nitrogen from the soil, beans fix new nitrogen into it. In terms of diet the plants must also go together. On their own, corn and beans are less nutritious than when combined in the same diet because each plant possesses amino acids that complement the acids of the other. When native peoples relied solely on corn, archaeologists have found that their teeth rotted rather quickly, their bones grew more slowly, and over time their societies diminished in size and vigor. The most typical breed of corn Indians grew is called "tropical flint" and was characterized by the small size of its ears and the ten to fourteen rows of kernels that covered the ears. The corn we eat today is a hybrid of the original flint corn and a breed called dent corn, which also was developed in Mesoamerica. One of the most striking things about the prehistory of corn is that it virtually disappeared from the archaeological record, save for the Southwest, between 400 and 900 A.D. The gap may be attributable to changes in the climate because corn requires a certain number of days of sunlight and inches of water. When the plant reappeared it was important to many societies, including the Mississippians, the Pueblos, and the Algonquians of the Northeast. Because squash remains are hard to find in archaeological sites, we still have a poor knowledge of the plant's importance, but Indians probably ate both the seeds and the flesh of the fruit. The bean varieties Indians ate included kidney beans, pinto beans, green beans, and other kinds that are still with us today.

Sources: R. Douglas Hurt, *Indian Agriculture in America: Prehistory to the Present* (Lawrence: University Press of Kansas, 1987);

Francis Jennings, *The Founders of America* (New York: Norton, 1993).

tisans turned into ornamental bands and flat gorgets. Women planted large fields of corn, beans, and squash and provided 25 percent of the Powhatan diet. They grew tobacco for ritual purposes as well. The remainder of the diet came from white-tailed deer, which men hunted by using fire to frighten the animals into open spaces, where archers could fell them. They also fished, hunted small mammals, and gathered shellfish. The Powhatans developed a polity more complex than the sachems to the north. The paramount *wereowance* or chief, oversaw subchiefs who governed the individual towns of the chiefdom. Copper headbands and ornaments distinguished the chiefly class from commoners, and the accumulation of wealth further distanced the chiefly class from their subjects. Like the peoples of the Pacific Northwest, however, Powhatan leadership was predicated on redistribution, so the chiefs periodically dispensed food, tools, and other items to solidify the ties that bound chiefs and commoners together as one society.

Iroquois: 1600 B.C. to 1600 A.D.. The ancestors of the people we know today as the Iroquois, a people archaeologists call the Frost Island culture, first migrated into the northwestern portion of present-day New York state sometime around 1600 B.C. The Frost Island culture made the shift from nomadic to semipermanent settlements, developed their own ceramic tradition, buried their dead with prestige goods, and became dependent on native plants for much of their subsistence. Around 1000 A.D. the introduction of corn revolutionized their culture and sparked the development of a full-fledged Woodland culture archaeologists call Owasco, which characterized the groups that Europeans recognized as the Five Nations—the Mohawks, Senecas, Onondagas, Oneidas, and Cayugas. Because of horticulture, over time their populations grew larger, and competition for land grew more intense. In response the Owascans moved their towns from river bottomlands to defensible hilltops around which they built elaborate palisade fortifications. The Owascans also developed what has come to symbolize the social organization of Five Nations: the longhouse. Built out of wood and bark, the long rectangular dwellings housed many families, all of which belonged to the same clan.

Sources:

Robert S. Grumet, *Historic Contact: Indian People and Colonists in Today's Northeastern United States in the Sixteenth through Eighteenth Centuries* (Norman: University of Oklahoma Press, 1995);

Bruce G. Trigger, ed., *Handbook of North American Indians: Northeast* (Washington, D.C.: Smithsonian Institution, 1978).

CLASSICAL AMERICA: THE EAST: SOUTH

Moundbuilding Tradition. Beginning around 2300 B.C. the Archaic inhabitants of the South domesticated the bottle gourd from which they made light and sturdy containers that did not break like ones made of pottery. They also domesticated sunflowers and added native squash and chenopodium to their diets. The horticul-tural bounty as well as the countless stocks of white-tailed deer, bear, and other small mammals that roamed the forests provided the Archaic societies of the region with the food supply necessary to increase their populations rapidly. In fact, the environment was so rich that the Archaic bands that had evolved into tribes developed further into chiefdoms, a form of organization archaeologists consider the pinnacle of political and social organization in Native North America. The chiefdoms were characterized generally by nucleated settlement patterns, mound building, and strong lines of social stratification between chiefs and commoners.

Poverty Point: 1500–700 B.C. Poverty Point, located in present-day northeastern Louisiana, flourished between 1500 and 700 B.C. and was the first of the southern mound-building societies. The site covered nearly three square miles, and the pathways that crisscrossed the mounds and other earthworks marked the trajectories of the summer and winter solstices. Emblematic of the people's high regard for the sun and the sky, one large mound was crafted in the shape of a bird. Perhaps two thousand people lived at Poverty Point, and their diet had changed little from that of their Archaic predecessors—they still hunted and gathered. But their capacity for trade was much more developed. Located near the Mississippi River, traders imported chert, soapstone, and other minerals from northern regions in exchange for locally produced finished goods such as figurines, bowls, pipes, and tools. By about 500 B.C. Poverty Point's preeminence in the native economy of the South had started to decline, but their influence had spread up the rivers through the Mississippi and Ohio River valleys.

Coles Creek: 700–1100 A.D. After the collapse of the Poverty Point culture several societies in the South began to bury the dead with prestige goods, build mounds, and farm for the bulk of their sustenance. In 700 A.D., for example, the Coles Creek people emerged in Arkansas, Louisiana, and Mississippi, and they built impressive civil and ceremonial mound centers. They placed houses on top of the mounds presumably to house the chiefs, a pattern that suggests that Coles Creek societies may have been stratified. Unlike the Poverty Point culture, however, Coles Creek people depended on plants more so than animals for their subsistence, but kernels of corn are conspicuously absent from the sites archaeologists have excavated. Instead they raised local plants for consumption. By 1100 A.D. contact with the Mississippian society of Cahokia in Illinois ended the Coles Creek culture and produced a new one archaeologists call Plaquemine.

Cahokia: 1000–1250 A.D. The third generation of Mound Builders in the South continued the trajectory apparent in the archaeological records of Poverty Point and Coles Creek but differed in one respect. With few exceptions the people archaeologists call Mississippians grew corn. The crop's bounty enabled them to produce more food and thus support more people than in any other native culture in precontact America. The first and

Theodor de Bry's engraving of two Virginia *weroans* or chiefs, from Thomas Harriot's *Briefe and True Report of the New Found Land of Virginia* (1588)

largest Mississippian site, Cahokia, developed in the bottomlands of the Mississippi River near present-day East St. Louis, Illinois, sometime around 1000 A.D. Cahokia's chiefs supervised the building of the largest earthen structures in prehistoric North America, and they coordinated the production and exchange of a wide range of prestige goods in addition to enormous quantities of foodstuffs. What kept the chiefdom going was trade, and so long as the goods flowed, the chiefdom prospered. The population of Cahokia probably peaked at about twelve thousand people. By 1250 A.D., however, Cahokia was declining. Competition with other chiefdoms, climatic change and a breakdown in the subsistence economy or internal strife may have triggered the decline, but archaeologists still are not sure why a society as well developed as Cahokia disappeared. Nevertheless, the spirit of Cahokia persisted in the religious and political imagery of its art and the tools of its material culture that had been traded throughout the South and in the several Mississippian societies that arose after Cahokia's decline.

Mississippians in the South. How the Mississippian culture of Cahokia diffused into the South is something of a mystery. Some archaeologists theorize that migrants from Cahokia carried their culture down the Mississippi River and into the region. Others argue that through trade the ideology and material culture of Cahokia made its imprint on the other indigenous cultures of the South. The Coles Creek culture, in particular, suggests the latter argument because it clearly shows in its later phases the grafting of a foreign Mississippian culture onto the preexisting one. Regardless, Mississippian societies depended on regular surpluses of food to support their growing populations and sprawling political boundaries.

Groups in the interior relied much more heavily on corn, however, than those on Gulf and Atlantic coasts where fishing and gathering shellfish remained important.

Coosa: 1500–1560 A.D. In the early 1500s Coosa was the largest Mississippian chiefdom in the Southeast. It stretched nearly 250 miles from near present-day Knoxville, Tennessee, down the Appalachian Mountains nearly to modern Montgomery, Alabama. Women raised corn, the chiefdom's most important source of food, on the several floodplains that ran through the chiefdom, and sunflower, squash, beans, nuts, and fruits such as persimmons rounded out the people's vegetable diet. White-tailed deer and bear provided the bulk of meat calories, but men hunted other smaller animals as well. The chiefdom's dependence on corn led to nutritional disorders that archaeologists have found in their examinations of the bones of the Coosa population. A high percentage of corn in the daily diet led to protein deficiencies and anemia. The population lived in small towns that were clustered around one of several mound centers scattered regularly between the northern and southern ends of the chiefdom. Coosa's total population was nearly four thousand, but it declined precipitously in the aftermath of Hernando de Soto's visit to the area in 1540.

Calusa: 1500–1600 A.D. Calusa was one of the few southern chiefdoms that was not Mississippian. What separated it from the rest was a lack of horticulture and a dependence on an Archaic economy. The chiefdom of Calusa was populous and powerful. By combining efficient hunting-and-gathering strategies with fishing they were able to produce enough food to preclude any dependence on horticulture. A hereditary chief who also acted as a priest sat atop the social and political hierarchy and governed the subchiefs, who presided over the individual villages of the chiefdom. To ensure his or her power the chief oversaw the intermarriage of close relatives and used military force to exact tribute from neighboring societies not completely under his or her control.

Sources:

Charles Hudson, *The Southeastern Indians* (Knoxville: University of Tennessee Press, 1976);

Timothy R. Pauketat and Thomas E. Emerson, eds., *Cahokia: Domination and Ideology in the Mississippian World* (Lincoln: University of Nebraska Press, 1997).

CLASSICAL AMERICA: THE WEST: CALIFORNIA

Environment and Early Settlement. The present-day state of California encompasses a wide range of environments. In the North are large, wet forests situated between steep mountains. In the center of the state run several large, well-watered valleys, and in the South one finds desert climates typical of the Southwest. The coast varies as well; some stretches are rocky and inaccessible while others have sandy beaches. Little archaeological work has been carried out in California, and piecing together the region's prehistory is difficult. What little digging has been done, however, confirms patterns typical of the rest of the continent. Clovis people entered the state approximately nine thousand years ago, and between 6000 and 3000 B.C. they made the transition from big-game hunting to hunting and gathering. By 3000 B.C. the Archaic inhabitants had developed diversified subsistence strategies that initiated a prolonged period of regional cultural diversification.

Pomo: 3000 B.C. to A.D. 1600. The Pomos lived on the north coast and divided their time between coastal redwood forests, where they erected seasonal camps and fished and hunted marine mammals such as seals, sea lions, and sea otters, and the foothills of the interior where they built semipermanent villages. They lived in small groups of several hundred, but chiefs belonged to a ruling elite differentiated from commoners by their control of prestige goods such as shells, ornamental finery, and other goods the people held in high esteem. Their most important source of food was the acorns they collected in the fall. Women pounded them into meal and soaked the meal overnight in water to leech out the bitter tasting tannins before preparing it in breads and soups. Women also used stone mortars to grind seeds, and they dried seaweed for consumption. Men hunted small game. A lack of pottery marks the Pomos as a decidedly Archaic people, and their culture changed little from its Archaic roots before 1600 A.D..

Yokut: 4000 B.C. to 1600 A.D. At least eight thousand years ago the first humans moved into the present-day San Joaquin Valley in central California. After six thousand years the roots of the Yokut culture appeared, and over time two groups emerged—the Southern Yokuts and the Northern Yokuts. The Southern Yokuts lived in

Corn grown by Native American farmers in Mexico. By 1000 B.C. the tiny cob and the loose-husked ear shown at top were crossed to produce the hybrid shown at bottom.

a more arid climate than their northern counterparts, and acorns were scarce. Instead they fished and hunted in the marshes that characterized the reaches of the lower valley. They migrated little and tended to live in permanent villages, and like the Pomos they never developed an indigenous pottery tradition. The Northern Yokuts enjoyed a milder climate, foraged for acorns, and fished for salmon. They also lacked pottery but traded for earthen containers with nearby tribes. Like the Pomos, the Yokuts underwent little cultural change in the millennia before 1600 A.D.

Chumash: 1000 B.C. to 1600 A.D. One of the richest environments in California included present-day Santa Barbara, where a narrow channel separates the mainland from offshore islands and is home to a diverse sea-life population. Sometime around 5000 B.C. the first humans settled the area, and by 1000 B.C. the distinct Chumash culture appeared in the archaeological record. Although they lacked pottery, Chumash women made basins and bowls from steatite, a mineral that can be chipped and ground into a variety of shapes. For fishing and for hunting seal and porpoise in the channel, men made canoes out of planks. When not at sea, hunters pursued deer and rabbits while women collected acorns in baskets. The culture retained its basic form well into the historic period.

Sources:

Robert F. Heizer, ed., *Handbook of the North American Indians: California* (Washington, D.C.: Smithsonian Institution, 1978);

Heizer and Mary A. Whipple, eds., *The California Indians: A Sourcebook* (Berkeley: University of California Press, 1971).

CLASSICAL AMERICA: THE WEST: GREAT BASIN

Environment. Trapped between the Sierra Nevada and the Rocky Mountains, the Great Basin is an arid expanse of terrain that includes present-day Nevada, Utah, western California, and southern Oregon. Temperatures fluctuate wildly. The summers are brutally hot while the winters can be bitterly cold. The area's inhabitants depended primarily on the Archaic hunting-and-gathering strategy. Rabbits, antelope, snakes, pine nuts, roots, berries, and other wild plants contributed the bulk of the people's diet. The scarcity of food inhibited the development of large, settled communities, and band structures persisted here well into the contact period.

Early Prehistory: 8000 B.C. to 1000 A.D. Clovis people moved into the Great Basin more than ten thousand years ago, and their culture transformed into what archaeologists call the Western Archaic tradition. Between 8000 B.C. and contact with Europeans in the early nineteenth century, the Archaic culture of the inhabitants changed little. Tools and artwork may have become more elaborate, but their basic forms remained. If the culture

A black-on-white painted pottery bowl, circa 1050–1150 A.D., Treasure Hill site, New Mexico, Mogollon culture (Maxwell Museum of Anthropology University of New Mexico, Albuquerque)

remained stable, however, the population did not. Around 1000 A.D. new populations moved into the area and displaced the original inhabitants. From southern California came the forerunners of the people known as Shoshones and Paiutes. The two groups spoke Numic languages that belonged to the Uto-Aztecan family, a language group that originated in the Amerind populations of Mesoamerica.

Shoshone: 1000–1600 A.D. The Shoshones were hunters and gatherers who migrated into the region to take advantage of the environment. Plant foods contributed the bulk of their diets although antelope and big-horn sheep were important sources of protein. They lived in temporary dwellings because of their migratory lifestyle, and large groups gathered only during the winter months to pass the time. Basketry was crucial for the storage of dried meat, roots, and berries, and they also made pottery which, because it was too heavy and fragile to carry, they left behind at various sites so that when they returned the following year they would have a ready source of food. Leaders had little authority in Shoshone society because the groups were widely dispersed and focused on feeding themselves rather than fighting with neighbors. The form of social organization changed in the early 1600s, however, when the Shoshones began to move to the Great Plains to hunt buffalo. Inhabitants of the Plains resented the newcomers, and periodic warfare occurred that led the Shoshones to choose leaders who could organize a defense against the raiding of the Plains' tribes.

Paiute: 1000–1600 A.D. Like the Shoshones, the Paiutes were divided into small bands and lived much in the Archaic tradition. Women gathered a variety of plants, including pine nuts, and men hunted rabbits, gophers, and other small mammals. Paiutes spent the winters in higher elevations where firewood was more plentiful, and when their winter stores of food ran out they moved into lower elevations to begin again the cycle of hunting and gathering. Some bands made pottery but others did not. Basketry was a far more important technology for storing and transporting food and other items because of its light weight and sturdiness.

Sources:

Warren L. D'Azevedo, ed., *Handbook of North American Indians: Great Basin* (Washington, D.C.: Smithsonian Institution, 1986);

Pamela Bunte and Robert Franklin, *The Paiute* (New York: Chelsea House, 1990).

CLASSICAL AMERICA: THE WEST: GREAT PLAINS

Semi-Sedentary Cultures. When we think of the Indians of the Great Plains, we think of riders mounted on horses pursuing endless herds of buffaloes. The horses they used, however, came from Europeans, and the new animals were not common on the Plains until the mid 1600s. Life before the horse was completely different for Plains peoples because most groups lived on the fringes of the great grasslands that were home to the buffaloes. In the spring they lived in settled villages along rivers and sowed crops of corn, and in the summer they left their homes on foot to hunt buffaloes. They returned to their villages in the fall, laden with dried meat and hides, and before the onset of winter the women harvested the corn they had planted the previous spring.

Prehistory: 1500 B.C. to 1500 A.D. The Great Plains were home to several Archaic cultures. Inhabiting portions of present-day western Saskatchewan, Canada, Montana, Wyoming, and the Dakotas, the Pelican Lake people emerged around 1500 B.C. They made their living gathering plants and hunting buffaloes with stone-tipped spears hurled by atlatls. They also developed the buffalo jump, a cliff over which hunters chased the animals to kill them. The Pelican Lake people's tenure on the Plains was short, however, because a new culture from the East moved into the region. The Besant people also hunted buffaloes with atlatls, but unlike Pelican Lake people, they possessed a more stratified social order as evidenced by their burial of the dead in mounds with prestige goods. Over time the Plains climate became hotter and drier, which diminished the buffalo population and put a stress on the Besant culture. The climatic change also sparked the Athapaskan migration to the Southwest that introduced another culture archaeologists call Avonlea to the region. Armed with bows and arrows, the Avonlea people were better suited to exploit the new environment, and they displaced the atlatl-armed Besant people by the ninth century A.D. A century later, however, the Avonlea culture disappeared from the archaeological record. Whether or not this reflected the Athapaskans' continued movement to the Southwest or the evolution of the original Avonlea culture into an unidentifiably Athapaskan one is unclear. Whatever the case may be, around 1200 A.D. another group migrated onto the Plains, the Old Woman's people, who shared the culture of the Mound Builders of the East. Whether or not they pushed the Avonlea people out of the region or coexisted with them is hard to say because archaeologists have investigated only a few archaeological sites that date between 1000 and 1500 A.D.

Protohistory: 1500–1600 A.D. When Columbus landed in the Caribbean the descendants of the Old Woman's people had developed a culture centered on the communal hunting of bison. But as the prehistory of the Plains suggests, the area was in constant demographic turmoil because other groups consistently moved into and out of the region over time. Shoshonean peoples from the Great Basin, for example, headed east and began hunting buffaloes. Archaeologists know they were present because they left behind the tell-tale flat-bottomed pottery that was unique to their culture. The Shoshoneans probably pushed Athapaskan speakers such as the Kiowas and Apaches farther south to the Rio Grande valley. Other Algonquian groups such as the Blackfeet, Arapahos, and Cheyennes migrated from the East onto the Plains in response to population pressures in their homelands and to the availability of resources on the Plains.

Cheyenne: 1000 B.C. to 1600 A.D. The Cheyennes are an example of one of the Algonquian-speaking cultures that migrated onto the Plains around 1500 A.D. Their early ancestors, the Lake Forest Archaic people, lived north of the Great Lakes before 1000 B.C. and depended on hunting and gathering. After about 300 B.C. horticulture had reached its northern limit in the Great Lakes area, and it is unknown whether or not the proto-Cheyennes participated in this green revolution. Sometime after 1000 A.D., however, it is clear the proto-Cheyennes had moved into present-day Minnesota, where they lived in semisedentary towns protected by fortifications. The women practiced horticulture and gathered wild plants, especially wild rice, while the men hunted buffaloes in the spring and fall. From here the proto-Cheyennes moved in response to population movements in the East that pushed them farther south and west where they became more and more enmeshed in the dual subsistence strategy of farming and hunting that was characteristic of most Plains peoples at the time of contact.

Sources:

John H. Moore, *The Cheyenne* (Cambridge, Mass.: Blackwell, 1996);

Karl H. Schlesier, ed., *Plains Indians, A.D. 500–1500: The Archaeological Past of Historic Groups* (Norman: University of Oklahoma Press, 1994).

CLASSICAL AMERICA: THE WEST: PACIFIC NORTHWEST

Early Prehistory: 8000–400 B.C. The Pacific Coast was home to some of the most complex Archaic hunter-gatherer societies in the prehistoric world. Clovis sites are scarce in the region, but the first settlers drifted into the area around 8000 B.C. By 1500 B.C. an expansive coastal trade in obsidian, a volcanic glass used to make knife blades and other sharp tools, and other goods linked the disparate coastal communities to other far-flung societies. Around 400 B.C. improvements in hunting and, more particularly, fishing technology led to a large growth in population. Like most coastal Indians and like all hunter-gatherer peoples, the Salishes and the Nootkas migrated from place to place depending on the season. In the summer they lived by the ocean and spent the bulk of their time fishing. In the fall they moved inland by rivers and streams and poised themselves to harvest salmon. Winter drove them into sheltered bays, where they rode out the cold weather. They did not raise plants or vegetables for their own use, but their hunting-and-gathering economy worked well in the rich coastal environment and enabled them to enjoy a considerable amount of free time. Potlatch ceremonies were particularly important occasions in which wealthy chiefs and elites shared their food and other resources with less-fortunate members of the population.

Indigenous Slavery. The inhabitants of the Pacific Northwest, like other indigenous groups, incorporated war captives into their societies. However, whereas other groups considered captives as kinsmen, the Pacific Coast peoples held them as slaves. Masters had power of life and limb over their bondsmen, and slave adults passed their status on to their children. Taboos on marriage between slaves and free people further reinforced social boundaries and ensured the maintenance of a permanent laboring class.

Salish: 1200 B.C. to 1600 A.D. The Salishes lived on the present-day border of British Columbia and Washington State, an area first settled around 4500 B.C. The first distinct non-Clovis culture, which archaeologists call Locarno Beach, emerged around 1200 B.C., and it established the basic outlines of precontact Salish culture. Indeed, there is a great continuity between the early cultures who depended heavily on fishing for their livelihood and later periods. What changed, however, was the degree to which the society was stratified. Whereas there is little evidence the Locarno people were divided between elites and commoners, by the early centuries A.D. prestige burials and a high degree of socio-economic stratification mark the Salish culture as typical of the Pacific Northwest.

Nootka: 400 B.C. to 1600 A.D. The Nootkans lived on Vancouver Island and were famous whale hunters. Each summer they gathered at prime whale spots and took to the seas in red-cedar dugout canoes. Like the Salishes, their culture underwent little substantive change over the centuries. As they improved their subsistence techniques they developed into an increasingly more stratified society characterized by wealthy elites, commoners, and slaves. The potlatch, however, helped smooth over social tensions by providing for the redistribution of foodstuffs and other material items.

The Columbia Plateau: 10,000 B.C. to 1600 A.D. The Columbia River drains much of the hinterland of the Pacific Northwest, and the Columbia Plateau is, in general, arid because the Cascade Mountains, which run parallel to the coast, block most of the rainfall from reaching the interior. The Plateau's first inhabitants migrated into the region around ten thousand years ago and gave rise to the Nez Percés, so named by the French for their habit of wearing bits of shell or stone pierced through the nostrils. Life was hard on the Plateau, and its inhabitants had to move about to find adequate supplies of food. The Nez Percés built permanent towns that consisted of clusters of pithouses in which they lived during the winter. At other times of the year they moved from site to site in small bands to look for food. In the spring, before heading for the river valleys, they congregated at sites along the Columbia River where they met with members of tribes who lived on the Great Plains, the Great Basin, and the coast. The fairs enabled the groups to trade for items that they could neither manufacture nor find for

themselves. Cultural exchange also occurred at the fairs as the Nez Percés learned specific basket designs and the practice of flattening children's heads for aesthetic reasons. After the fairs they moved in to cool mountain valleys where they erected pole lodges and awaited the annual spawning runs of the salmon. The Nez Percés did not grow crops for their own use but instead relied heavily on starchy roots and bulbs that women pried out of the ground with digging sticks.

Sources:

Robert H. Ruby, *Indians of the Pacific Northwest: A History* (Norman: University of Oklahoma Press, 1981);

Wayne Suttles, ed., *Handbook of North American Indians: Northwest Coast* (Washington, D.C.: Smithsonian Institution, 1990).

CLASSICAL AMERICA: THE WEST: SOUTHWEST

Cochise: 8000–300 B.C. In the desert regions of the American Southwest the Paleo-Indians adapted their big-game hunting techniques to the pursuit of the smaller mammals native to the region. The hunting-and-gathering Desert culture, also known as the Cochise tradition, developed during the Archaic period, and when corn entered the region after 3000 B.C., the Cochise people began to adopt a more sedentary lifestyle. Still, the growing of domesticated crops did not restrict the Cochise to any one particular site, for they continued to follow a pattern of migration that was tied to changes in the seasons. With the development of pottery around 300 B.C., the Desert culture developed further into three distinct traditions: the Mogollon, Hohokam, and Anasazi.

Mogollon: 300 B.C. to 1100 A.D. The Mogollon culture emerged out of the Archaic Cochise tradition, and their archaeological sites can be found throughout present-day Arizona and New Mexico. The use of pottery and the continued evolution of horticulture set the Mogollons apart from the more general Desert culture and marked them as the first truly sedentary people in the region. They lived in pithouses, structures built partially into the earth, which were clustered in small villages, and they relied upon innovations such as the bow and arrow, which first appeared among them around 1 A.D., to supplement their vegetable diet. For reasons unknown the Mogollon began to disappear around 1100 A.D. when their sites gave way to sites identifiable with the Anasazi tradition.

Hohokam: 300–1400 B.C. The Hohokams also evolved out of the Cochise tradition, but they originated farther south than the Mogollons, in the Sonora Desert. In time they moved into present-day Arizona and settled the area around Phoenix and Tucson. The Hohokams were far more adept than their Mogollon counterparts at growing corn because they constructed elaborate systems of canals to irrigate the arid land. They also built large earthen mounds for religious ceremonies which attested to their high level of sociopolitical organization. Around

The ruins of Pueblo Bonito in Chaco Canyon, New Mexico, built circa 961 A.D. Covering more than three acres, the pueblo housed approximately one thousand people.

1400 B.C., however, the Hohokam culture began to show signs of Anasazi influence, and shortly thereafter it disappeared altogether from the archaeological record.

Anasazi: 1000–1300 A.D. Around 1000 A.D. the Anasazis emerged as the preeminent elaboration of the Cochise tradition. Located in present-day Utah, Colorado, New Mexico, and Arizona, the Anasazis built on many of the developments made by the previous cultures. They made and used both baskets and pots; they irrigated their fields to supplement the periodic flooding of the region's rivers; and they retained the pithouse style of the Mogollons. But they also innovated. For instance, the Anasazis constructed special structures called *kivas* for their religious ceremonies. Kivas were built underground, and men and women climbed through the roof and descended on a ladder to pay homage to the *sipapu*, a hole in the floor that led to the center of the earth from whence the Anasazis, so their legends told, came. If their religion took them into the earth, their habitations climbed higher and higher. The Anasazis were famous for their cliff dwellings and their adobe villages situated on top of the mesas, flat-topped mountains, that are common in the desert country. Capacious and multistory pueblos contained the Anasazis' burgeoning population, and they continued to flourish until 1300 A.D. when a cycle of droughts and raids by neighboring peoples dispersed them into the dozens of scattered, small pueblos that greeted the arrival of the Spanish conquistadors in the 1540s.

Athapaskan: 800–1540 A.D. The raiders who decimated the Anasazis were Athapaskans who were descended from the Na-Dénés, the second wave of Asian immigrants. The nomadic group had migrated from the Rocky Mountain region in present-day Canada to the desert Southwest between 800 and 1500 A.D., where they set themselves up as middlemen in the trade that went on between the pueblo people and the inhabitants of the Great Plains. One branch of the Athapaskans adopted local traditions, particularly horticulture and irrigation technology, and became known as the Navajos. Other groups, however, retained the nomadic ways of the original early Archaic Athapaskans. The Apaches, for example, raised a little corn, but on the whole remained di-

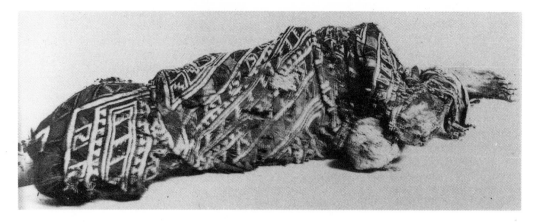

A mummy wrapped in a diamond twill tapestry cotton blanket, 1132–1135 A.D., found in Grand Gulch, Utah, Anasazi culture (American Museum of Natural History, New York)

vided up into small bands and scoured the dry countryside for food.

Sources:

Linda S. Cordell, *Prehistory of the Southwest* (New York: Academic Press, 1984);

Alfonso Ortiz, ed., *Handbook of North American Indians: Southwest*, 2 volumes (Washington, D.C.: Smithsonian Institution, 1979, 1983).

THE COLONIZATION OF VINLAND, 986–1014 A.D.

First Sightings. In 986 A.D. Bjarni Herjolfsson was on his way to Greenland from Iceland when he and his ship got lost in a storm. After the sky had cleared he saw "a country that was not mountainous, but was well wooded and with low hills. . . ." Thus was made the first recorded European sighting of North America. As new arrivals in Greenland, the Norse were hardly prepared to expand yet again to the west, and only after the population grew and land became scarce did the Vikings begin to calculate the benefits of colonizing the land Herjolfsson had spotted. In 1001 Leif Ericsson bought Herjolfsson's ship, outfitted it with some of the former owner's crew, and sought out the mysterious land in the west they called Vinland, where they built a small settlement called Leifsburthir.

First Contact. After Ericsson and his men had returned to Greenland, Thorvald Ericsson set out in 1006 for Leifsburthir. On the beach they saw three bumps that upon closer inspection proved to be skin boats under which several Indians were sleeping. Thorvald killed eight of the frightened men, and his crew retreated to their ship. Much to their surprise scores of skin boats full of Indians appeared offshore, and the Vikings took up a defensive position. The so-called Skraelings let loose several barrages of arrows, one of which struck Thorvald dead. After the Indians had retreated, the remaining crewmen buried their leader nearby and holed up in Leifsburthir for the winter. In the spring they collected wood, harvested some grapes, and returned to Greenland with a less rosy picture of the New World.

The Vinland Colony. Three years later Thorfinn Karlesefni, his wife, and 160 other settlers located Leifsburthir, repaired the dilapidated houses, and built several new buildings to house the rest of the colonists. Subsequent dealings with the local population, however, convinced Karlesefni that they not only outnumbered the Vikings but also had the potential to destroy the tiny settlement.

War with the Skraelings. The native inhabitants were intrigued by the cattle the Vikings had brought with them and confined their first swaps of goods to furs and skins for fresh milk. Later they added red cloth to the list of goods they desired, and they were always intrigued by the Vikings' metal weapons. During one trade visit to the settlement, a native man tried to get hold of a sword, and its owner immediately killed him. The rest of his companions fled, and Karlesefni warned his men to prepare for a battle. Weeks later the assault came. Were it not for the heroics of Freydis, Leif's half sister, who charged headlong into the attackers, the Vikings would have been vanquished. After having spent three winters in Vinland, Karlesefni and the colonists retreated to Greenland. Freydis made a subsequent voyage to Vinland, but Karlesefni's failure ended the attempt to colonize the region. By 1014 sustained contact between Greenland and Vinland had stopped, but over the next few centuries an occasional ship was blown off course into the waters first sailed by Herjolfsson.

Sources:

Helge Ingstad, *Westward to Vinland: The Discovery of Pre-Columbian Norse House-Sites in North America* (New York: St. Martin's Press, 1969);

The Vinland Sagas: The Norse Discovery of America (New York: New York University Press, 1966).

EARLY EXPLORATION OF AMERICA

Portugal. The country responsible for opening the Age of Exploration was Portugal. Positioned on the west coast of the Iberian peninsula and lying at the crossings of the Mediterranean and Atlantic shipping lanes, the country was well situated to lead a revolution in European navigation. Under the sponsorship of King John I, Dom Henrique, also known as Prince Henry the Navigator, sent sea captains out into the ocean to find passageways to Africa and India so that seaborne Portuguese merchants might undercut the land caravans of Arab traders. Borrowing hull and sail designs and navigational equipment from their Arab rivals, Portuguese sailors soon acquired mastery of the seas and explored the coast of Africa. The trade they opened with the African kingdoms revolved around gold and slaves and stirred the interest of other nations. Building supply stations along the coast of Africa, Portuguese sailors such as Bartholomeu Días and Vasco da Gama gradually worked their way around the Cape of Good Hope, up to the Horn of Africa, and over to the Indian mainland, where they entered the spice trade. To the west they reached Newfoundland in 1500 and attempted to found a colony on Cape Breton Island, Nova Scotia, in 1520.

Spain. While the Portuguese focused on Africa and the Indian trade, the Spanish turned their attention westward. The first step in what would culminate in

RIGHTS OF DISCOVERY AND CONQUEST

When Europeans arrived in the New World, they had to establish and maintain a claim to the land they had seen that would be respected by the other European powers. One legal doctrine, the Right of Discovery, conveyed to European monarchs the right to claim lands discovered in his or her name so long as they had not already been claimed by another Christian people. As such the Pope was an important adjudicator of disputes between Christian peoples, such as happened in the Treaty of Tordesillas (1494). When the French began exploring the New World, they challenged the Iberian kingdoms' Rights to Discovery and claimed that the right did not pertain to land that had not actually been explored. The French and the English proposed an alternative theory called the Right of Conquest. Only by conquering native populations and by building permanent settlements, they argued, could a monarch receive a rightful claim to the land. Legal principles based on use of the land rather than discovery of the land fundamentally changed the game of imperialism because they forced Europeans to colonize their holdings and to attack the colonies of their rivals in order to protect their imperial interests.

Sources: Colin M. MacLachlan, *Spain's Empire in the New World: The Role of Ideas in Institutional and Social Change* (Berkeley: University of California Press, 1988);

Patricia Seed, *Ceremonies of Possession in Europe's Conquest of the New World, 1492–1640* (Cambridge: Cambridge University Press, 1995).

Christopher Columbus's voyage was the conquest of the Canary Islands and the extermination of the Guanche natives in the early 1400s. But before money could be spent on further overseas exploration and colonization, the Catholic kingdoms of what would become Spain had to expel the Moors from Africa who had invaded and occupied their land. When in the late fifteenth century Ferdinand and Isabella united the crowns of Castile and Aragon and laid the foundations for the modern nation of Spain, they set into motion the final phase of the *reconquista,* the expulsion of the Moors. The last Moorish stronghold in Grenada fell in 1492, and that year Columbus set sail for the West.

New World. Columbus was born in Genoa, a port on the Italian peninsula that produced many of the finest sailors of the day. He had been employed in the Portuguese slave trade and, based on his experiences, believed he could find a route to India by sailing west across the Atlantic Ocean. He sought royal patronage in several courts before finding a sympathetic ear in Queen Isabella, who agreed to finance his expedition. His ships set sail in August 1492, and two months later Columbus made landfall on an island he named San Salvador. Thinking at the time that he was in Asia, he and his crew spent the next several months exploring the nearby islands in search of the emperor of China. Needless to say they never found the emperor, but they did acquaint themselves with two native tribes whom they erroneously called Indians—the Arawaks and the Caribs. Columbus left behind a small settlement he called Navidad on the island of Hispaniola, but upon his return the next year the site had been abandoned. In 1499 he and his brothers, who had governed the newfound lands, were arrested for mismanagement and sent back to Spain in irons. Columbus died in 1506, still firm in the belief that he had found Asia.

First Contact. Columbus's experience with the people he believed were Indians shaped much of the subsequent history between Europeans and Native Americans. Welcomed by the friendly Arawaks on the island of Hispaniola, Columbus deemed them *indios pacíficos,* friendly Indians who were kind, trustworthy, and generous to their Spanish visitors. In contrast the Carib Indians who had a reputation for cannibalism and perfidy were *indios bravos,* bad Indians. In the narratives sent back to Spain by Columbus and others the dichotomy between the good and bad Indians shaped European expectations and justified all the more easily the brutal subjugation of Indians who were deemed innately bad and children of the devil.

Treaty of Tordesillas. A year after Columbus's landfall, Pope Alexander VI issued a bull that divided the New World between the two Catholic powers, Spain and Portugal. In 1494 the two nations refined the papal decree in the Treaty of Tordesillas, so named after a small outpost in South America. According to the treaty's stipulations the Portuguese received a title to all unclaimed lands east of Tordesillas, present-day Brazil, and

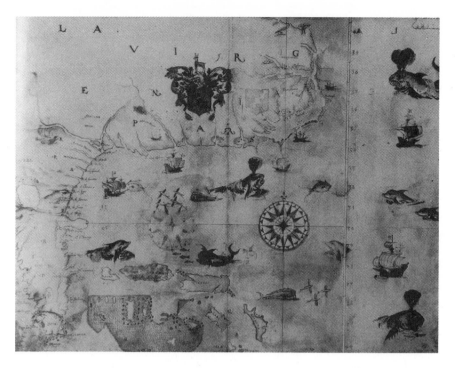

John White's 1585 map of the east coast of North America from Florida to the Chesapeake Bay (British Museum, London)

Africa. The Spanish received title to the rest of the Americas.

Sources:

David Traboulay, *Columbus and Las Casas: The Conquest and Christianization of America, 1492–1566* (Lanham, Md.: University Press of America, 1994);

John Ure, *Prince Henry the Navigator* (London: Constable, 1977).

EARLY SETTLEMENT OF THE AMERICAS BY SPAIN

Expansion. The land grant in the Treaty of Tordesillas (1494) opened up a whole range of possibilities for Spaniards, and in the following decades thousands of adventurers, petty nobles, and colonists set out for Cuba, Jamaica, and Hispaniola. They brought with them horses, cows, pigs, European crops and diseases, and ap-

A German's view of Europeans meeting inhabitants of the New World (engraving from Sebastian Münster's *Cosmographia*, 1550)

petites for wealth that could not be satisfied by the islands' native societies. The fanatic quest for mineral wealth led the Spanish from island to island, and they decimated the Caribs, Arawaks, and other native populations. Early in the 1500s conquistadors headed for the Central and South American mainlands to search for the treasure that had not been found in the islands. Between 1519 and 1522 Hernando Cortés conquered the Aztecs, the descendants of America's first horticulturalists. His army of four hundred men relied on smallpox and the support of various tributary chiefdoms that had chafed at Aztec rule to subjugate the hundreds of thousands of Aztecs. The gold and silver he pillaged made him wealthy and filled the Crown's treasury. Meanwhile, Francisco Pizarro searched for a wealthy native society in the Andes about which rumors had circulated for years. Smallpox had already exacted a terrible toll on the eight to twelve million Incas, and Pizarro was able to exploit quarrels among the leaders to subjugate the empire for Spain in 1531–1533.

Stratification. To govern their new lands and the native populations, the Spanish implemented a strategy for colonization best described as stratification. Officials raised in the hierarchical culture of Spain conceived of the New World in similar terms, and they organized colonists and Indians as two distinct social orders, or republics. The first republic was the order of Spaniards—the gentlemen who supervised the land and who ran the mines, the lawyers and soldiers who staffed the colonial administrations, and the artisans who provided the colonies with skilled labor. The second order, *la republica de los indios,* consisted of the Native Americans who provided the backbreaking labor that fed, housed, and clothed the Spanish; in return the Indians received instruction about the saving grace of the Christian faith.

Implementation. In order to implement their colonial vision the Spanish had to shift local Indian populations in order to make them more manageable and amenable to the stratification doctrine. Priests and soldiers gathered far-flung bands together and settled them on *rancherias* while nomadic hunters–gatherers were united into *congregaciones*. *Doctrinas*, missions with churches and friars to instruct native peoples in Catholicism, were the cornerstone of the resettlement policy, and the Crown chartered them for a limited number of years. After the charter expired, the Crown assumed that the Indians would be converted and ready to assume their own government. Alongside the missions were the *presidios*, military outposts of fifty to one hundred soldiers who protected the two republics from outside invasion.

Enforcement. The Spanish enforced the system of stratification through three institutions: the *requerimiento*, the *encomienda*, and the *repartimiento*. When soldiers first contacted native peoples, they read aloud in Spanish the requerimiento, which required the natives either to submit to the authority of the Spanish crown or be put to the sword. Once a measure of control had been established, the Crown dispensed native land to nobles and officers who, through the encomienda, received tribute in the form of goods or labor from Indian villages for nine months of the year. In exchange the Indians received military protection and Catholic indoctrination. Missionaries decried the exploitation of the encomienda, particularly because of the landlords' brutal methods of extracting labor and their refusal to provide the Indians with religious instruction. Changes to the policy came slowly. In the early 1600s missionaries persuaded the king to end the encomienda and replace it with the repartimiento, an annual levy of labor and goods payable to the colonial government rather than to individual landlords. Although the New Laws of 1542 outlawed the encomienda, it continued in operation in North America in order to attract Spanish settlers.

Sources:
Colin M. MacLachlan, *Spain's Empire in the New World: The Role of Ideas in Institutional and Social Change* (Berkeley: University of California Press, 1988);

Donald W. Meinig, *The Shaping of America: A Geographical Perspective on 500 Years of History, Volume 1: Atlantic America, 1492–1800* (New Haven: Yale University Press, 1986).

EARLY SETTLEMENT OF THE SOUTHEAST BY SPAIN

La Florida. After the conquest of the Aztecs and the Incas, opportunities for fame and fortune in Central and South America were limited. To the north, however, lay what many people thought was an island where they expected to find quantities of gold and silver comparable to what Hernando Cortés and Francisco Pizarro had found. In 1513 Juan Ponce de León sighted a peninsula he named La Florida, and in 1521 he returned to try to build a settlement. The Calusas, however, resisted the invasion and drove Ponce de León and his men back to their ships. León died of his wounds in Cuba, but his death did not diminish interest in the unexplored land. Seven years later the one-eyed, red-haired adventurer Pánfilo de Narváez attempted to settle the Gulf Coast of Florida. His expedition set out for the interior to find food and gold, but the local Mississippians attacked the party. The men retreated to the coast only to find that their support ships had not arrived to meet them. Desperate to escape, they built crude boats and set sail for Mexico. After the fleet washed up on the shore of present-day east Texas, only Alvar Núñez Cabeza de Vaca and three others survived to reach Mexico on foot in 1536. In 1541 Tristán de Luna y Arellano attempted to build another Spanish settlement in Florida on the Gulf Coast near present-day Pensacola, but a hurricane destroyed his supplies.

Chicora. In June 1521 Pedro de Quejo and Francisco Gordillo were scouring the Bahamas for Indians they could seize as slaves for sale in Havana. Finding none, they ventured northwest and landed at what is today the mouth of the present-day Santee River in Georgia. For several weeks the Spanish crews traded with the local inhabitants for food and small pearls, and then they seized two dozen Indians for presentation to the governor in Havana. One of the patrons of the slave raid, Lucas Vázquez de Ayllón, was impressed by their find as well as the rumors of silver, gold, and pearls that swirled around the land the slavers called Chicora. Ayllón journeyed to the court of King Charles V to claim the rich province for himself, and to interest a king distracted by wars raging on the European continent, he portrayed the sandy soils and scrubby forests as a sylvan paradise teeming with grapevines, rich fields, stout forests, and untold sources of mineral wealth. Charles granted him permission to undertake a colony, and in 1525 Ayllón set out with six ships carrying several hundred colonists. Because the soils at the first landing site were poor, Ayllón moved south to present-day Sapelo Sound, Georgia, where he established a town he called San Miguel de Gualdape. The delay in establishing the settlement prevented the Spanish from planting their crops before cold weather came, and their demands for food alienated the local Mississippians. Sickness spread among the settlers as well, killing Ayllón and demoralizing the colonists further. After weeks of bickering, the 150 survivors abandoned the colony and fled to Spain. Despite the terrible experience of the Ayllón colony the legend of Chicora as a rich land of agricultural wealth and teeming mines endured in the published reports of adventurers, geographers, and mapmakers.

De Soto. Hernando de Soto had served under Pizarro during the conquests of Panama, Nicaragua, and Peru. Having heard of the legend of Chicora and having seen the fortune Pizarro had made for himself, he asked the king for permission to lead an expedition into the Southeast to search for gold and silver. In 1539 he landed near

LUIS DE VELASCO AND THE JESUITS

Early European explorers typically seized members of the native groups they encountered to take back to Europe where the Indians could learn Spanish, French, or English and serve as interpreters on later voyages. Usually the kidnapped Indians died of disease, starvation, and homesickness, but the few who survived played interesting roles in the colonization of the New World. In the sixteenth century the most famous kidnapped Indian was Don Luis de Velasco, who had been taken by the Spanish from his home among the Algonquians of the Virginia Tidewater in 1560. He was baptized in Mexico City and named after his patron Luis de Velasco. In 1566 he participated in an ill-fated attempt by the Spanish to explore Chesapeake Bay, and in 1570 he persuaded the Jesuit priest Father Segura to undertake a second attempt to missionize the region. Led by Don Luis, the Jesuits set out for Velasco's homeland, where they built a mission they called Ajacán. In addition to converting the Indians who lived in the vicinity they hoped to map a route to China. In the meantime Don Luis had rejoined his people, taken several wives, and lived, in the eyes of his Jesuit companions, in sin. Tiring of the priests' criticism of his indigenous lifestyle, in 1571 Don Luis led a party of warriors that destroyed the mission and killed the priests. When word of the attack reached Pedro Ménendez de Avilés in St. Augustine, he dispatched a punitive expedition that killed forty of Don Luis's fellow tribesmen.

Sources: Frederic W. Gleach, *Powhatan's World of Colonial Virginia: A Conflict of Culture* (Lincoln: University of Nebraska Press, 1997);

Helen Rountree, ed., *Powhatan Foreign Relations, 1500–1722* (Charlottesville: University Press of Virginia, 1993).

present-day Tampa Bay with more than 650 men, a few women, 250 horses, a pack of trained war dogs, scores of pigs, and plenty of chains to shackle Indian slaves. Between 1539 and 1543 the party traveled throughout the region and encountered several Mississippian chiefdoms such as the Apalachee, Cofitachequi, and Coosa. De Soto typically seized hostages in each town to inform him where he could find treasure and food and to lead him to the next town. He also seized hundreds of slaves to carry the party's luggage and supplies, which only exacerbated poor relations with the native inhabitants. Frequently his men found themselves trapped in ambushes, and several Spaniards were killed. In pitched battles, however, their armor, steel swords, trained war horses, Irish wolfhounds, and firearms were too much for the bows and arrows of the Indians. When the party reached the banks of the Mississippi River in 1542, de Soto caught a fever and died. The surviving members of his force attempted to find an overland way to Mexico, but finding no such easy route, they holed up in a village and built several boats to sail down the Mississippi to the Gulf of Mexico. A powerful chiefdom located on the Mississippi River harassed the bedraggled survivors and killed several before the tiny fleet hit open water and made its way to Mexico. Having seen the lack of wealth to be found and exploited in the interior, the conquistadors focused their efforts back onto the Florida coast.

St. Augustine. The French wanted to settle Florida because their privateers could use the sheltered inlets of the Atlantic coast as bases for raids on the Spanish treasure fleets. In order to block French expansion into the area, King Philip II dispatched a Spanish force under the command of Pedro Menéndez de Avilés to explore the coast, capture any Frenchmen they might find, and build a permanent outpost. In 1565 Avilés's force located and destroyed a French settlement called Fort Caroline near present-day Jacksonville, Florida, and his men built a fort they called Santa Elena. Turning south, the Spanish carved a permanent settlement out of the sawgrass and mangrove swamps of the coast, which they named St. Augustine. The city, like all others in Spanish America, was built in a grid pattern centered on a civic plaza where the church, public buildings, and governor's home were located. Poised to check French and English intrusions into Chicora and to help defend the treasure fleets as they lumbered up the Bahama Channel back to Spain, the city was a minor but nevertheless important outpost.

Contact with the Indians. Unlike other conquistadors, Avilés endeavored to win the favor of local inhabitants rather than try to intimidate and conquer them. He was particularly solicitous of the Calusas who had driven Ponce de León back into the sea half a century earlier. The Spanish leader met with the chief whom he called Carlos in the Calusas' capital located near present-day Fort Myers. Carlos, hoping to enlist Avilés as a subordinate chief, urged the Spaniard to marry his sister. With a wife back in Spain, Avilés was uncomfortable with the arrangement, but he needed the Calusas if his endeavor was to succeed, so he agreed to take the sister's hand in marriage. The soldiers and settlers who had come with Avilés, however, shared none of their commander's spirit of cooperation. Tired of being insulted, threatened, and victimized by the abusive colonists, local Indians revolted with French assistance in 1568 and destroyed a Spanish outpost. Shocked by the attack, Avilés denounced the "infamous people, Sodomites, sacrificers to the devil" and pressed the Crown for permission to wage a war of extermination on the Indians of Florida. He died before the orders came through, and over the next few decades Indian raids, pirate attacks, and periodic English assaults forced the abandonment of Santa Elena in 1587 and the contraction of the colony to within the walls of St. Augustine.

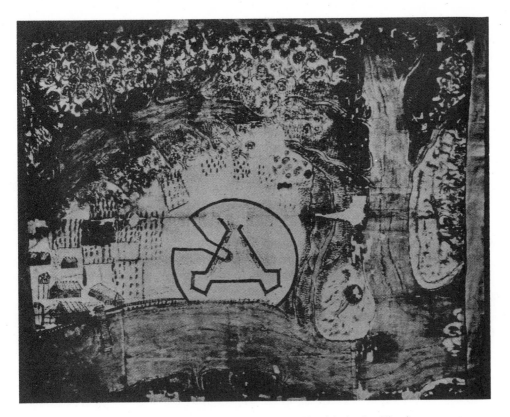

The earliest map of St. Augustine, Florida, circa 1565, with the fortifications at center
(Archives of the Indies, Seville)

Mission Indians. The Jesuits who had accompanied Avilés to Florida opened several missions along the southeastern coast and in the interior of Florida, but their attempts to end polygamy and other indigenous traditions doomed their mission. Troubles with a Muskhogean-speaking chiefdom known as Guale near Santa Elena and hostilities with the other Indians of Florida forced the Jesuits to abandon their project in 1572, but the Franciscans came the following year to resume the missionary effort. Empowered by the Royal Orders of 1573 that encouraged missionaries to persuade rather than to force Indians to convert, the Franciscans built several doctrinas and settled native populations around them. The priests sought to Hispanicize the Indians, but the native population resented criticism of their marriage patterns, rules of inheritance, economic life, and religious beliefs. In 1597 the Guales revolted and drove the Franciscans southward. Not until the mid 1600s did the Spanish return to the Georgia coast, but even then, in spite of the near collapse of native populations, they faced rebellions and native intransigence and enjoyed little success in enforcing the doctrine of stratification.

Sources:

Paul E. Hoffman, *A New Andalucia and a Way to the Orient: The American Southeast during the Sixteenth Century* (Baton Rouge: Louisiana State University Press, 1990);

Bonnie G. McEwan, ed., *The Spanish Missions of La Florida* (Gainesville: University Press of Florida, 1993).

EARLY SETTLEMENT OF THE SOUTHWEST BY SPAIN

Explorations by Land. Persistent rumors of rich silver lodes north of Mexico set in motion the Spanish exploration of the American West. In 1539 Fray Marcos de Niza set out to search the region, and he heard stories of seven cities of gold and silver, named Cíbola. Between 1540 and 1542 Francisco Vásquez de Coronado followed up Niza's effort, and his men traveled throughout the West in search of the elusive cities and the treasure they were reputed to contain. In the meantime Coronado also heard of another magical city, Quivira, that lay to the east, so he roamed into present-day Kansas and Arkansas, where he found several villages of semisedentary Indians but no gold and silver. The Coronado expedition was based among the Pueblo Indians, and relations between the two groups were initially peaceful, but the Spaniards' exorbitant demands for food and land turned the local population against them. The Pueblos' lack of gold and silver, however, may have saved them from further depredations because Coronado retreated into Mexico and reported to his superiors that the region did not possess enough wealth to justify its colonization. For missionaries in search of souls rather than ores, however, the West remained an enticing destination. In the early 1580s two Franciscan friars, Agustín Rodríguez and Antonio Espejo, visited Pueblo country to lay the groundwork for later missionary efforts. The favorable reports

Cliff Palace, a pueblo village built by the Anasazi in 1175-1273 A.D. (Mesa Verde National Park, Colorado)

they circulated upon their return to Mexico revived official interest in settling the Southwest.

Explorations by Sea. In 1542, when Hernando de Soto died and Coronado returned to Mexico, Juan Rodríguez Cabrillo sailed up the California coast, made the first maps of what the Spanish called Alta California, and may have made contact with the Archaic Chumash Indians living in the area. For the next fifty years, however, no one followed up on Cabrillo's findings. Not until 1578, when the English pirate Sir Francis Drake touched ground at the thirty-eighth parallel near present-day San Francisco and claimed California for his sovereign, Queen Elizabeth I, did the Spanish redouble their efforts to establish a claim to the Pacific coast. Over the next few years a series of expeditions carried the Lion and Castle standard of Spain further and further north up the coast, ending with Juan de Fuca's landing among the Nootkas of Vancouver Island. The charts the navigators made were important, but their efforts failed to start the colonization of Alta California.

Colonization of the Southwest. Because of the glowing reports circulated by the Franciscan priests, in 1595 Juan de Oñate asked for and received permission from King Philip II to colonize the Pueblos that Coronado had visited. In 1598 he and his party of 129 soldiers and their wives and children reached the Pueblos, who had developed a resentment of the Spanish after their experiences with Coronado. Relations between the Spaniards and Indians were tense, and because the Spanish were ill equipped to produce enough food for themselves, they imposed themselves on the local population as Coronado's men had done. The Pueblos, however, barely man-

aged to store enough surplus corn to last them through the famines that were common in the arid Southwest. Oñate and his soldiers ruled with an iron fist, and revolts, starvation, and distrust came to characterize life in early San Juan de Yunque.

Conflict. Within the first year of colonization the Acoma pueblo revolted and killed several Spanish soldiers. In retaliation Oñate dispatched a small party of soldiers who made their way atop the mesa and into Acoma. In three days they destroyed the pueblo and executed nearly eight hundred men, women, and children. They also captured nearly six hundred people who were tried and found guilty of murder. Oñate sentenced all captives between the ages of twelve and twenty-five to twenty-five years of servitude, and he ordered his soldiers to sever one foot of each man older than twenty-five years. The brutal tactics temporarily repressed native discontent, but the puny Spanish force was never able to cower entirely the other Pueblo Indians.

Mission Indians. The small contingent of Franciscan friars who had accompanied Oñate to New Mexico immediately set about building churches and doctrinas. Moving slowly up the Rio Grande, the missionaries met with relatively little resistance, and their efforts produced many converts. The number of new Catholics, however, were misleading. Whereas the Jesuits accepted converts only after they had mastered the intricacies of Christian theology, the Franciscans were content to give the Indians only the barest outlines of their faith before immersing them in water. Indians who learned to sing hymns, who received a rudimentary education, who mastered Castillian Spanish, and who accepted the new Hispanic

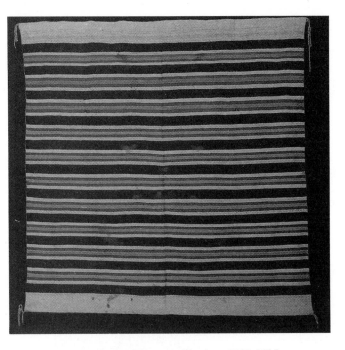

Anasazi striped twill cotton blanket, 1132–1135 A.D.
(private collection)

way of life were counted among the members of the new republic of Indians. With the priests' help the Pueblos learned how to raise sheep and how to cultivate new crops such as wheat, peach trees, and watermelon. Priests also challenged the powers of native healers and shamans and managed to persuade many Pueblos that they and not the indigenous spiritualists had access to the wondrous powers of the heavens.

Sources:

David Hurst Thomas, ed., *Columbian Consequences, Volume One: Archaeological and Historical Perspectives on the Spanish Borderlands West* (Washington, D.C.: Smithsonian Institution, 1989);

David J. Weber, *The Spanish Frontier in North America* (New Haven: Yale University Press, 1992).

FRANCE AND THE NEW WORLD

Imperial Rivalries. The enormous wealth that the Spanish had extracted from their Central and South American colonies impressed the French and stirred them to action. After capturing several treasure-laden Spanish galleons during a war with Spain, the French king Francis I, with the support of silk merchants and other businessmen who were anxious to find the "Passage to the Orient," commissioned the Florentine navigator Giovanni da Verrazano in 1524 to explore the New World. Starting roughly at present-day Florida, Verrazzano sailed north and believed he saw the Pacific Ocean just behind the outer banks of what is today North Carolina. The find proved illusory, but the charts and maps he made of the east coast of North America provided a useful store of information for later French explorers.

St. Lawrence River. Subsequent voyages to North America overturned Verrazzano's proposed route to Asia. French navigators, however, reasoned that if the passage did not lie in the Southeast it must lie to the north. Jacques Cartier undertook two voyages to search the waters of Canada for the passage. On his first voyage in 1534 he sailed up the St. Lawrence River, which seemed to him a likely choice for a route to Asia. In the process he made contact with Iroquoian Indians who lived at Stadacona, near present-day Québec City. Cartier kidnapped two young boys from the town to take back to France, where they could learn French and act as interpreters on the next voyage. When he returned in 1535, he proceeded farther up the St. Lawrence River to the Iroquoian town Hochelaga, present-day Montreal, but Lachine (The China) Falls blocked any further exploration by water. He and his crewmen returned to Stadacona, where they barely survived the frigid winter temperatures and scurvy. Cartier returned a third time in 1541 to set up a base camp at Cap Rouge, west of Stadacona, in preparation for Jean-François de La Rocque de Roberval's plans to build a permanent colony. Cartier and his men survived the bitter winter but decided to abandon the site. On their way back to France, they met with Roberval's small fleet, which was carrying two hundred men, women, and children and livestock to Cap Rouge. Despite the hardships Cartier's men had suffered, Roberval refused to turn back, and he continued on to Cap Rouge, where he founded the colony Charlesbourg Royal. One-fourth of the settlers died during the first winter, and the survivors packed up their belongings and set sail for France in 1543. Caught in a war with the Italian city-states, King Francis I had no interest in continuing the fruitless efforts to settle the cold climes of what was called New France on maps. Occasional fur-trading expeditions visited the region over the years, but no further attempt to colonize the St. Lawrence River valley was made prior to 1600.

Religious Strife. In 1547 King Henry II succeeded his father, Francis I, and during his twelve-year reign he dedicated himself to driving Protestantism out of France. The Huguenots, followers of John Calvin, had gained a substantial following among the artisanal and professional classes of the cities, and in spite of the repression, they managed to wield considerable economic and political clout. In 1559, when the Huguenots held their first national meeting, Henry II died and was succeeded by his mentally handicapped son, Francis II. The day-to-day government of the kingdom fell to Francis II's advisors, and they continued the persecution of the Protestants. Upon Francis II's death his mother and Henry's widow Catherine de Medici acted as regent to the ten-year-old King Charles IX, and she sought to reconcile Catholics and Protestants and to extend religious toleration to the Huguenots. The end of official persecution, however, hardly put an end to the violence and bloodshed. The Crown saw in the Americas an opportunity both to defuse sectarian tension and challenge Spanish power overseas. The first attempt to plant the Hu-

René de Laudonnière meeting the Florida Indian chief Saturnia in 1564 (engraving by Theodor de Bry, after a painting by Jacques le Moyne)

guenots in the New World was made in Brazil in 1555, but difficulties there forced the Crown to train its eyes on Florida.

Sources:

Paul E. Hoffman, *A New Andalucia and a Way to the Orient: The American Southeast during the Sixteenth Century* (Baton Rouge: Louisiana State University Press, 1990);

Donald W. Meinig, *The Shaping of America: A Geographical Perspective on 500 Years of History, Volume 1: Atlantic America, 1492–1800* (New Haven: Yale University Press, 1986).

FRENCH SETTLEMENT OF THE SOUTHEAST

Florida. Warfare between Spain and France had spilled over into South America and the Caribbean, and both nations turned their attentions to the Southeast because it lay parallel to the route Spanish galleons followed on their return to Spain. French leaders knew of the legend of Chicora, and they zeroed in on the southern low country as the site for their next attempt to build a colony. In 1562 the Protestant leader Jean Ribault departed the port of Le Havre with two ships, a crew of experienced sailors, veteran soldiers, and a few noblemen. When they sighted Florida, they saw a land that had not been visited by Europeans for almost twenty years. Turning north, Ribault landed his party near present-day Jacksonville, where the region's Mississippian population welcomed the newcomers. In return Ribault presented their chief with a blue robe decorated with the French fleur-de-lis. Seeing the gold jewelry worn by the Indians, which they had scavenged from shipwrecks, and mistaking tent caterpillars for silk worms, the French believed they had at last found the rich land of Chicora. Ribault spent the next several weeks coasting northward,

trading with local people, and mapping the various bays and rivers. Charged with only exploring the region, he and his men nonetheless decided to build a settlement that they called Charlesfort at present-day Port Royal, South Carolina. When Ribault embarked for France, he left thirty men to guard the Huguenot paradise. The settlers, however, did not know how to feed themselves, and they soon became enmeshed in a relationship with a nearby chiefdom whereby they received food in exchange for goods such as beads, mirrors, cloth, and metal. But it was not enough. Famine begat internal strife, and the colonists were soon squabbling. By 1564 the men had had enough, and they decided to build a boat and sail back to France. The journey was hard; food ran low; and they cannibalized a crew member to survive, but just when the coast of France came into sight an English ship drew alongside the leaky vessel, and the captain seized the prisoners in the name of Queen Elizabeth I.

Voyage of Laudonnière. When Ribault returned to France, he found the Catholics and Huguenots once again at war, so he went to England to solicit support for Charlesfort. Queen Elizabeth I was sympathetic to the Protestant cause, but she decided to jail the Frenchman. Meanwhile, in France, René Goulaine de Laudonnière assumed charge of the Huguenot effort to found colonies, and in 1564 he and his crew set out for Florida. He sailed with three ships and a group of Huguenot gentlemen, common laborers, artisans, a few women, and a few free Africans. Laudonnière's group landed near the site of Charlesfort, and a group of four hundred Indians came out to meet them. The train of conversation, one Frenchman wrote, centered on making an alliance:

The French sailing into the mouth of the St. John's River, Florida (1564), initially called the River of May because it was discovered on the first of that month (engraving by Theodor de Bry, after a painting by Jacques le Moyne)

"They sat down together and made signs expressing to Mr. de Laudonnière how happy they were that we had come . . . and that he should go to war with them against their enemies. . . ." The local Chief Saturnia, however, grew suspicious of the French, held negotiations with Laudonnière, and true to Native American diplomacy, persuaded the Frenchman to make the Fort Caroline settlement a tributary to his chiefdom and to provide it with military support should the need arise. Saturnia did not wait long to call on his new allies for their support in a war against a neighboring chiefdom, but Laudonnière dragged his feet and reneged on the deal he had made. Estranged from their native allies, unable to find any treasure, and lacking adequate food, the colonists grew dissatisfied. Three mutinies dissipated the colony's resources and gave notice to the Spanish that the French were settled in their own backyard. Ribault, after his release from England, returned to the colony with several soldiers and an order to relieve Laudonnière, but he was unable to restore order to the colony. Shortly after his arrival the sails of a Spanish force led by Pedro Menéndez de Avilés appeared on the horizon. In late 1565 his troops exterminated the Huguenots, destroyed Fort Caroline, and continued their efforts to colonize Florida.

Sources:

Charles E. Bennett, *Laudonnière and Fort Caroline: History and Documents by Charles E. Bennett* (Gainesville: University of Florida Press, 1964);

David B. Quinn, comp. and ed., *New American World: A Documentary History of North America to 1612, Volume 2: Major Spanish Searches in Eastern North America: Franco-Spanish Clash in Florida* (New York: Arno, 1979).

IMPERIAL ENGLAND AND THE NEW WORLD

Religious Struggles. While Portugal and Spain claimed Roman Catholicism as the one true faith, the English, like the French, engaged in a bitter national debate over state religion and religious toleration. Moreover, the rulers of Europe regarded the Tudor family that ruled England for much of the fifteenth century as uncouth pretenders to the throne. Henry VIII, however, made the Tudors' mark on the international scene when in 1534 he broke away from the Pope and initiated the English Reformation. The issue of the official faith, however, was far from settled because Mary Queen of Scots, wife of Philip II of Spain, reigned between 1553 and 1558 and restored Catholicism as the established church of England. Upon the accession of Elizabeth I in 1558, the Crown reestablished Protestantism, and the Queen entered into a protracted war with King Philip of Spain. After the defeat of his armada in 1588, Elizabeth I assumed the mantle of protector of Protestantism, and she looked to the New World as a battleground where the forces of her faith could do battle with those of the Pope and of Spain.

The Voyage of John Cabot. Following on the heels of Christopher Columbus's three voyages to the New World, the English decided to get involved in the Age of Discovery in order to find a quick route to the Spice Islands. In 1497 the Venetian seaman John Cabot sailed the *Mathew* due west in search of the "Northwest Passage" to Asia. He reached Newfoundland, saw snares and fishing nets on the island's shore, and was struck by the abundance of cod, but he did not find a shortcut to Asia.

The Northeast. A long period of inactivity followed Cabot's voyage. Sebastian Cabot, his son, scouted the icy Arctic Sea, and John Rut returned to explore Newfoundland in 1527, but their findings stirred little interest at home. Not until 1576 did the English regain their interest in the New World, when Martin Frobisher set out to find the Northwest Passage. Like Cabot he failed in his original goal, but he returned with samples of shiny gold rocks that English geologists declared to be gold. After a second fruitless search for the passage, he brought back more of the golden mineral, which was on a second test deemed to be iron pyrite, or "fool's gold." Investment in subsequent voyages plummeted, but the Crown grew interested in building colonies to provide markets for England's burgeoning industrial economy and a home for the country's booming population. Sir Humphrey Gilbert led the first of the new colonizing expeditions, and

he offered tracts of land in North America, sight unseen. He claimed Newfoundland for England in 1583, but his ship disappeared shortly thereafter, and nothing came of the speculative enterprise.

The Southeast. Having read in several published volumes about the Spanish and the French search for a passage to Asia, the English figured that the elusive route must lay somewhere between the Florida peninsula and the St. Lawrence River. According to leading English geographers the Chesapeake Bay marked the way to the Orient as well as to the legendary land of Chicora. In 1584 Queen Elizabeth granted Sir Walter Raleigh, Humphrey Gilbert's half brother, title to any lands he might claim in the region "not actually possessed of any Christian prince, nor inhabited by Christian people." Within a month Raleigh sent Arthur Barlowe to explore the coast and to select a site for a colony. After two months Barlowe reached the Outer Banks of present-day North Carolina and reported to Raleigh that the land was "the most plentifull, sweete, fruitful and wholsome of all the world." In addition to his glowing reports he brought back to England two Indians, Manteo and Wanchese.

Sources:

Paul E. Hoffman, *A New Andalucia and a Way to the Orient: The American Southeast during the Sixteenth Century* (Baton Rouge: Louisiana State University Press, 1990);

Donald W. Meinig, *The Shaping of America: A Geographical Perspective on 500 Years of History, Volume 1: Atlantic America, 1492–1800* (New Haven: Yale University Press, 1986).

IMPERIAL ENGLAND SETTLES THE SOUTHEAST

The Lane Colony. Arthur Barlowe's description of the settlement site thrilled Sir Walter Raleigh, so in April 1585 he put his cousin Sir Richard Grenville and another man, Ralph Lane, in charge of the 108 men who would build the first English colony of Virginia, so named after Queen Elizabeth I, the Virgin Queen. Manteo and Wanchese also went along to provide translation skills and practical advice. Lane supervised the construction of Fort Raleigh and several frame houses, and he and the other men quickly began searching for gold and the passage to Asia. Supplies soon ran out, however, and relations with the local Algonquians were terrible.

Chief Wingina. The Roanoke colonists encountered three groups of Algonquians: the Roanokes, Croatoans, and Secotans, who together amounted to about seven thousand people. In terms of culture they lived in a fashion similar to the Powhatan Indians of the Virginia Tidewater. Verrazzano may have had contact with the groups during his voyage, and there is scattered evidence to suggest that the Secotans from time to time rescued shipwrecked Spanish sailors. The *wereowance*, or paramount chief, of the Roanokes, Wingina, assigned the colonists a portion of Roanoke Island for their colony, and he attempted to position himself so that he controlled their movements and their trade with the rival

A seventeenth-century engraving of an Algonquian priest and his family; the daughter is carrying an English doll
(British Museum, London)

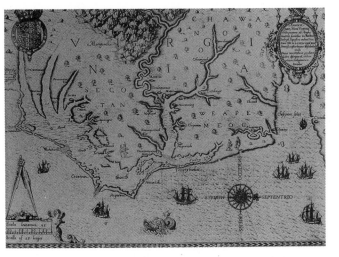

John White's map of Sir Walter Raleigh's Lost Colony
"Roanoac," circa 1585

Native societies from the Mogollons to the Algonquians smoked a wide variety of plants in their ceremonies and healing rituals, but of all of the various plants, tobacco was by far the most common, and, given the course of colonization, the most important for both natives and newcomers. Tobacco, a Spanish corruption of the Arawak word for cigar, grows in several different species, the most common of which was *Nicotiana rustica,* which came originally from the Andes region of South America. How it got to North America is unknown, but like corn and other plants it probably was carried over such great distances by traders. The frequency with which pipes are found in archaeological sites suggests the importance of the plant, but it was also used as snuff and was eaten. Notwithstanding the stimulant properties of tobacco, its smoke was considered to unite the earth on which the Indians lived with the spirits and gods of the skies. Whenever Indians wanted Europeans to enter into an alliance with them they shared with the newcomers a calumet, or pipe, stuffed with the weed. The tobacco that gained later fame as the staple of the Jamestown colony was not indigenous to North America but was imported from the Orinoco Valley of Brazil.

Sources: Wilbert Johannes, *Tobacco and Shamanism in South America* (New Haven: Yale University Press, 1987);

V. G. Kiernan, *Tobacco: A History* (London: Hutchinson, 1991).

Croatoans. Twice he fell sick and requested that the English pray for him. When his health improved he and many others began to express a great interest in the English god, but their curiosity soon gave way to resentment. Short of food, the English demanded of Wingina's people supplies of corn they were not prepared to surrender. English frustrations came to a head when an Indian allegedly stole a silver cup from a colonist's home. Unable to reclaim the missing object, the settlers burned a town and destroyed its cornfields. Later, after hearing of a conspiracy organized by Wingina to drive the English off the island, one of the military commanders assassinated the chief and his advisors. The murders hardly settled things, and the colonists settled in for a period of protracted hostility. By chance Sir Francis Drake, who had just sacked St. Augustine, arrived in 1586, and he hauled the surviving colonists back to England. The bags of pearls that they brought back nevertheless confirmed to many the existence of the elusive Chicora.

The "Lost Colony." In spite of Lane's failure, Raleigh had faith that a colony could be built, so in 1587 he sent John White, who had belonged to the first Roanoke expedition, to try again, only this time the target was Chesapeake Bay. The following year White led eighty-four men, including Manteo; seventeen women; and nine children across the Atlantic, but problems with food and dissension among the settlers forced him to land at Roanoke, where he at least knew the ground and what to expect. Continued hostility with the Roanokes threatened the new colony, and White began drawing up plans to relocate among the friendly Croatoans where Manteo's mother was chief. When supplies ran short White returned to England to collect more provisions. He planned to return with a supply ship the following summer, but Philip II's Spanish armada cut off English naval traffic in 1588. Not until 1590 did White make it back to Roanoke, where he found "the houses taken down [and] things throwen here and there, almost overgrown with grasse and weedes." He also found the word "CROATOAN" carved on a tree. No one knows what happened to the so-called Lost Colony, but most scholars agree that the colonists probably headed inland to live with the Croatoans. Evidence suggests that the Powhatans killed the colonists in 1606, one year before the founding of Jamestown, in order to forestall further English settlement of the area.

Sources:
David B. Quinn, comp. and ed., *The Roanoke Voyages, 1584–1590,* 2 volumes (London: Hakluyt Society, 1955);
David B. Quinn, *Set Fair for Roanoke: Voyages and Colonies, 1584–1606* (Chapel Hill: University of North Carolina Press, 1985).

HEADLINE MAKERS

ALVAR NÚÑEZ CABEZA DE VACA

1492?-1559?
SPANISH SOJOURNER IN NORTH AMERICA

Early Life. Alvar Núñez Cabeza de Vaca was born around 1492 in Andalusia, a region of Spain. His parents died while he was young, so he moved in with an aunt and uncle, and he probably had a fairly comfortable early life. During his teenage years he was appointed chamberlain for the house of a noble family, and he later served the household in a war in Italy where he fought with distinction. He returned to Spain in 1521 and enlisted as an officer in the crown's army.

Narváez's Expedition. What happened next in Cabeza de Vaca's life is unclear, but in the summer of 1527 he embarked with six hundred other men Pánfilo de Narváez had assembled to explore Florida. Because of a hurricane and logistical problems Narváez landed in present-day Tampa Bay with only half of his original force and a handful of supplies. When he asked his leading men what to do next, he received two responses. Cabeza de Vaca urged him to stay close to the coast and to his ship so that the party could return to Cuba in a moment's notice. Others, however, appealed to the aspiring conquistador to march inland and to search for treasure. Emboldened by the last option, Narváez led most of his men into the interior while the others remained on the ship and were ordered to sail along the coast. The party soon met with some Indians whom they forced to locate a supply of corn for the hungry Spaniards. The amount of gold the explorers saw in the village surprised them, and the inhabitants informed them that in a nearby land called Apalachee they would find all the riches they could want. The local chief also hoped to use the Spaniards to attack the rival chiefdom, but something happened to change the Indians' minds. One evening they ambushed a group of Spaniards, and the next morning the Indians abandoned their village. Forced to rely on captured guides, Narváez set out to find Apalachee, a place he hoped would rival the Aztecs in splendor and riches. When they reached the chiefdom they were immediately caught in an ambush. After the Spaniards beat the Apalachees back, they found forty houses and large quantities of corn but no gold. In the next town they were not as lucky because the Indians had burned everything to the ground. Disease, starvation, and ambushes had taken a toll on the party, and they returned to the coast to link up with the supply ship. For whatever reason, the ship was nowhere to be seen, so Narváez elected to build boats to carry the men to Mexico. Two months later the motley fleet set sail.

Sailing the Gulf. The crude ships drifted in the Gulf of Mexico for months. On one occasion Indians invited the men ashore for a feast, but while they slept an attack awakened them. After several attacks and counterattacks the Spaniards demanded the return of the men who had been captured. The Indians refused to return the captives, so the survivors headed back out to sea where a storm broke up the fleet. Some boats sank or crashed on the shore of East Texas, and the starving crews were either drowned, killed by Indians, or reduced to cannibalism before dying of exposure. Cabeza de Vaca's weary crew washed up on a beach and surrendered to a large group of Coahuilticans armed with bows and arrows and bearing gifts of food. "They are a very generous people," Cabeza de Vaca wrote, "sharing whatever they own with others."

Slave and Healer. The Archaic hunting-and-gathering Coahuilticans enslaved Cabeza de Vaca and made him gather roots, work done customarily by the women. He resented his treatment and planned to run away to a neighboring tribe. Gradually he met with three other survivors of the expedition, all of whom lived as slaves in different bands. Their scattered situation as well as their lowly status made it hard to plan an escape, and on several occasions they were frustrated in their efforts. Finally they escaped to a nearby tribe that welcomed the four men as healers. Their reputation spread, and they made their way slowly to the South and to the

West, staying with different tribes and working their miraculous cures.

Encounter with the Spanish. In late winter 1536 Cabeza de Vaca encountered four Spaniards mounted on horseback. They were stunned by the sight of the bedraggled wanderer, but they took him and the others to a small town, New Galicia. At the urging of the local military commander, Cabeza de Vaca called together the Indians with whom he had been living, not suspecting the commander's motives. "After this," he wrote, "we had many great altercations with the Christians, because they wanted to make slaves of the Indians we had brought. . . ." An angry Cabeza de Vaca sent the Indians home, and he and his men were in turn sent under guard into Mexico. The stories they told amazed the imperial officials.

Return to Spain. Cabeza de Vaca rested in Mexico for several months before returning to Spain in 1537. Upon his arrival he began composing and editing his memoirs. Based on his experience King Charles V put him in charge of an expedition to explore the Rìo de la Plata in South America. His tenure as governor of the region reflected the lessons he had learned from his travels, for he immediately sought to end the settlers' abuse of the Indians. Such measures, however, were unpopular, and the colonists revolted in 1544 and put Cabeza de Vaca on a ship back to Spain, where he faced several lawsuits and the open hostility of the royal government. In 1551 the Crown forbade him to return to the New World, and he died a broken and vilified man sometime around 1559. His memoirs, however, are one of the most important documents in early American history, for Cabeza de Vaca recorded what life was like in a region that would not be colonized for another three centuries.

Sources:

Alvar Núñez Cabeza de Vaca, *Castaways: The Narrative of Alvar Núñez Cabeza de Vaca*, edited by Enrique Pupo-Walker, translated by Frances M. López-Morillas (Berkeley: University of California Press, 1993);

David J. Weber, *The Spanish Frontier in North America* (New Haven: Yale University Press, 1992).

THE LADY OF COFITACHEQUI

FLOURISHED MID 1500s
CHIEF OF COFITACHEQUI

Native American Biography. Uncovering the histories of Native American individuals in North America before 1600 is difficult. Since few natives wrote, scholars have to depend on the descriptions recorded by Europeans of the Native Americans they encountered. Part of the problem with such sources is that Europeans often misconstrued the motives to which they attributed the behavior of the Indians. To compensate for such biases historians attempt to match what they can discern about the culture of the individual in question with what the Europeans actually wrote about him or her. In so doing it is possible to uncover some of what the individual might have thought as he or she tried to cope with European explorers, soldiers, colonists, and priests.

Early Life. One of the most interesting leaders in early North America was the Lady of Cofitachequi. From sources written by the Spanish, we know a bit about her adult life but absolutely nothing about her childhood. Based on archaeological investigations and later sources it is nevertheless possible to put together a rough sketch of how she might have grown up. In Mississippian societies such as Cofitachequi, women farmed, so the Lady of Cofitachequi probably had experience clearing fields, planting seed, weeding rows of corn, and harvesting crops. Women also made pottery, so she was probably a skilled artisan. The fact that she belonged to a chiefly lineage, however, may have restricted her from participating in such activities. Instead, she may have been raised by temple priests who taught her the myths and sacred powers that enabled her and her people to prosper. It is also probable that she grew up in a matrilineal society, where infants traced their ancestry and family through the mother rather than through the father. As chief she probably inherited the title from her mother and then passed it on to either a son or a daughter.

Contact with De Soto. In 1539 Hernando de Soto started out on his long trek through the Southeast. Having failed to find gold among the same Apalachees that Narváez had visited, he headed for Cofitachequi, a chiefdom in present-day South Carolina rumored to be teeming with wealth and to be governed by a woman. When the Spaniards reached the riverbank across from the chiefdom's principle town, six delegates came out and inquired of de Soto "Sir, do you wish peace or war?" He assured them that the former was his goal, and he requested rafts to carry his men across the river and food to feed them. The delegates deferred any final decision to their chief, "a young marriageable woman," who had just inherited her office.

An Alliance Is Made. Nearly every time a Mississippian chief met a European explorer, he or she tried to enlist the newcomers in a military alliance aimed at a rival chiefdom. The Lady of Cofitachequi was no different. Across the river from de Soto she boarded a canoe over which an ornamented awning was stretched. Eight women accompanied her while several men in another canoe towed the royal vessel ashore. She seated herself before de Soto and offered to do what she could to help the expedition, opening a large storehouse of corn to the Spaniards, vacating her own home for de Soto, and ordering that the newcomers be given use of half of the residences in the town. She also provided rafts and canoes for the Spaniards to cross the river. As a final gesture she took off a great length of pearls "as large as hazelnuts" and handed it over to de Soto, and he returned the favor with a ruby ring. Acutely aware of the importance of generosity, the Lady of Cofitachequi constantly apologized that she could not help more. What the Spanish did not understand was that by accepting her hospitality they had entered into an alliance with Cofitachequi.

Opposition. Because the Cofitachequans were matrilineal, mothers had a considerable amount of power. When the Lady of Cofitachequi's mother learned of the alacrity with which her daughter had made an alliance with de Soto, the woman expressed her hearty disapproval and refused to come to "see a people never seen before. . . ." De Soto wanted to see her, however, so he dispatched his accountant, Juan de Añasco, to convince the elderly woman of his noble intentions. On the way to her house, however, Añasco's Indian guide committed suicide because he did not want to displease the widow by leading the Spanish to her, and she, having gotten word of the suicide, moved to a house farther away. Añasco decided to call off the expedition and returned to the main town of Cofitachequi.

End of the Alliance. De Soto wanted gold and silver, so he asked the Lady of Cofitachequi to bring out samples of the minerals her people had. They presented beautiful copper objects that the Spanish admired, and they showed de Soto a chunk of mica, neither of which satisfied his appetite for riches. Gold and silver, not copper and mica, were the ores of fame and fortune. To retain the Spaniard's interest the Lady of Cofitachequi pointed them in the direction of a temple where the bodies of former chiefs were kept and told them to take "as many [pearls] as you like. . . ." The Spaniards took from the temples bags of pearls and bundles of skins, but it was not enough to warrant a longer stay. Having consumed nearly all of the food in the town, de Soto and his men asked the Lady of Cofitachequi about the location of other nearby chiefdoms where they might find more treasure.

Escape. De Soto typically captured the chiefs he visited and forced them to lead him to the next chiefdom whereupon he would either kill them or turn them loose. In May 1540 the Spanish left Cofitachequi and forced the chief to accompany them. Rather than let her ride on a horse, de Soto forced her to walk with the party's Indian slaves. The party headed for the Appalachian Mountains where de Soto hoped to find Chiaha, a tributary town of the Coosa chiefdom. As they marched, "the governor ordered," one of the Spaniards wrote, "a guard to be placed over [the Lady of Cofitachequi] not giving her such good treatment as she deserved. . . ." Just before the expedition entered the adjoining province of Xuale, which the Lady of Cofitachequi also governed, she "stepped aside from the road and went into a wood saying that she had to attend to her necessities." After a brief search the Spaniards failed to find her. They continued on their way, but they never forgot the remarkable welcome they had received from the Lady of Cofitachequi.

Sources:

Lawrence A. Clayton, Vernon James Knight Jr., and Edward C. Moore, eds., *The De Soto Chronicles: The Expedition of Hernando de Soto to North America in 1539–1543*, 2 volumes (Tuscaloosa: University of Alabama Press, 1993);

Charles Hudson and Carmen Chaves Tesser, eds., *The Forgotten Centuries: Indians and Europeans in the American South, 1521–1704* (Athens: University of Georgia Press, 1994).

THOMAS HARRIOT

1560-1621
ENGLISH ETHNOGRAPHER

Youth. Little is known about Thomas Harriot's early life. He was born in Oxford in 1560, and at the age of seventeen he enrolled at university, where he studied science and mathematics. After graduation he joined Sir Walter Raleigh's household staff and worked as a tutor. Raleigh was fascinated by Harriot's lessons in astronomy, navigation, and math and enlisted his aid when in 1584 Raleigh received a charter to colonize the New World. At his patron's request Harriot drew up the plans for Arthur Barlowe's exploratory voyage, and with a textbook he had written he taught the pilots and crewmen how to apply their nautical navigational skills to the exploration of land.

The Lane Expedition. When Barlowe returned with glowing reports of the future site of the colony, Harriot decided to join the Ralph Lane expedition. His job was to record astronomical observations, aid in navigation, and with John White observe the native inhabitants as well as their natural environment with the aim of mapping and surveying the colony. He was well prepared to undertake an ethnographical investigation of the Algonquian population because he had spent a full winter with two Indians, Manteo and Wanchese, who had been captured by Barlowe during his visit to the area. Harriot learned the Algonquian tongue spoken by the Indians while he taught his two charges English; he also began to develop a phonetic alphabet to aid in recording their speeches and vocabulary. Upon their arrival at Roanoke, Harriot spent the next several months recording his observations of Indian life while White painted what he saw.

A Briefe and True Report. Harriot published his observations upon his arrival back in England in 1588. He began *A Briefe and True Report of the New Found Land of Virginia* with a chapter on Virginia's "Marchantable Commodities." What caught his eye first were tent caterpillars he took to be silkworms. With careful cultivation of mulberry trees, the plant on which silkworms fed, Harriot predicted "there will rise as great profite in time to the Virginians, as there of doth now to the Persians, Turkes, Italians and Spaniards." Other economic endeavors for which he thought the colony was well suited included the cultivation of sassafras, used as a treatment for venereal disease, and wine grapes. Cedar, a valuable wood, was plentiful, and the great walnut and oak trees provided nuts and acorns from which a "good and sweete oyle" could be made. The colony also held out great potential for miners and hunters. He had found iron deposits in two areas, and the copper ornaments worn by the wereowances suggested that the mineral would not be hard to find. Deer, bears, and wildcats could provide hunters with enough furs to make a "good profite."

Assessment of the Natives. Having outlined where and how colonists could extract a living from the Carolina coast, Harriot went to great pains to describe the Algonquian groups already resident in the area. He first assured the readers they had nothing to fear: the Indians had "no edge tooles or weapons, of yron or steele to offend us with." They also lacked any defenses for English weapons, having only shields made of bark and armor made of woven twigs. Their towns were small, with only ten to twelve homes on average, and they were organized as chiefdoms under the command of various wereowances. "In respect of us," Harriot informed his English audience, "they are a people poore, and for want of skill and judgement. . . ." And the fact that they believed their god had created woman first, Harriot implied, was further evidence of their inferiority. In conclusion he reminded readers that were it not for certain English provocations, which were nonetheless justifiable to his mind, the colony might have survived. The Indians, he asserted, gave what they got, and future settlers ought, he believed, to take the lesson into consideration.

Impact. *A Briefe and True Report of the New Found Land of Virginia* sold perhaps two or three hundred copies. However, it was republished two years later complete with engravings of the detailed and naturalistic paintings made by White. The second edition, undertaken by the Flemish printer and engraver Theodor de Bry, was translated into Latin, French, German, and reissued in English. With the addition of the drawings and the accessibility that different translations offered, the book became incredibly popular and was reissued for several decades. Indeed, the story of the first Roanoke colony became standard reading among a literate European population that was fascinated by the New World. One of the most avid readers was John Smith, who later governed the Jamestown colony. Not only did he prefigure his behavior based on what Harriot wrote, but also he took the volume as a model and patterned his own writings about Virginia after it. Harriot's small book also transformed the way Europeans wrote about the New World. Instead of simply describing native behaviors and the flora and the fauna, those who followed Harriot began to rationalize native cultures and to develop scientifically based interpretations of the land and its human, animal, and vegetable inhabitants in order to calculate the wealth that they might extract from their colonies.

Later Years. Unlike White, Harriot did not return for the second Roanoke colony. Instead he became a favorite in the household of Henry, earl of Northumberland. Although he corresponded with Johannes Kepler, the famous German astronomer and mathematician, Harriot failed to make any further contribution to the sciences. He died of cancer of the nose in 1621.

Sources:

Thomas Harriot, *A Briefe and True Report of the New Found Land of Virginia: The Complete 1590 Theodor de Bry Edition* (New York: Dover, 1972);

David Beers Quinn, *Set Fair for Roanoke: Voyages and Colonies, 1584–1606* (Chapel Hill: University of North Carolina Press, 1985).

PUBLICATIONS

Charles E. Bennet, *Laudonnière & Fort Caroline: History and Documents* (Gainesville: University of Florida Press, 1964)—in addition to a brief history of Fort Caroline by the author, the book consists of René de Laudonnière's journal, which describes his relations with Saturnia as well as various depositions given by certain colonists that reflect the bitter divisions and conflicts that debilitated the colony;

Henry S. Burrage, ed., *Early English and French Voyages Chiefly from Hakluyt, 1534–1608* (New York: Scribners, 1906)—this collection of narratives from various voyages of discovery includes reports of Jacques Cartier's voyages and exploration of the St. Lawrence River, records of Humphrey Gilbert's and Arthur Barlowe's voyages, and accounts of the two Roanoke colonies by Ralph Lane and John White;

Lawrence A. Clayton, Vernon James Knight Jr., and Edward C. Moore, eds., *The De Soto Chronicles: The Expedition of Hernando de Soto to North America in 1539-1543,* 2 volumes (Tuscaloosa: University of Alabama Press, 1993)—brings together the narratives of de Soto's expedition written by the Gentleman of Elvas, Luys Hernandez de Biedma, Rodrigo Rangel, and Garcilaso de la Vega, which present not only the first historic glimpse of the Mississippians of the southern interior but also conflicting accounts of the same events witnessed by the various authors;

Christopher Columbus, *The Diario of Christopher Columbus's First Voyage to America, 1492–1493* (Norman: University of Oklahoma Press, 1989)—includes entries from Columbus's journal that describe the ocean voyage and relations with and among the crew, as well as detailed accounts of his encounters with various islands and Indians of the Caribbean;

Thomas Harriot, *A Briefe and True Report of the New Found Land of Virginia: The Complete 1590 Theodor de Bry Edition* (New York: Dover, 1972)—a published account of observations made by Harriot during the brief tenure of Ralph Lane's colony that outlines both the resources that colonists could exploit as well as the lifeways of the Indians who lived on and around Roanoke Island;

Bartholomé de Las Casas, *In Defense of the Indians,* translated and edited by Stafford Poole (De Kalb: Northern Illinois University Press, 1992)—Las Casas was a Dominican priest who believed, unlike many of his contemporaries, that Indians were human beings. Written between 1548 and 1550, the *Defense* cites incidences of abuse, murder, and exploitation by Spanish colonists and officials and argues for a humane policy toward the Crown's native subjects;

Alvar Núñez Cabeza de Vaca, *Castaways: The Narrative of Alvar Núñez Cabeza de Vaca,* edited by Enrique Pupo-Walker, translated by Frances M. López-Morillas (Berkeley: University of California Press, 1993)—a translation of Cabeza de Vaca's original *Relación,* which tells of his experiences as an explorer, slave, trader, and healer among several native groups in the American Southwest and justifies his actions;

André Thevet, *André Thevet's North America: A Sixteenth-Century View,* edited by Roger Schlesinger and Arthur P. Stabler (Kingston: McGill-Queen's University Press, 1986)—Thevet was the Royal Cosmographer of France, and the book includes translations of his writings on the exploration and discovery of North America with an emphasis on Canada, Florida, and Mexico;

The Vinland Sagas: The Norse Discovery of America (London: Penguin, 1965)—includes translations of the two sagas "Graenlandinga Saga" and "Eirik's Saga," which discuss the politics and motivations behind the various attempts to settle Vinland and include fairly detailed descriptions of the Indians the Vikings encountered.

THE ARTS

by CHARLENE VILLASEÑOR BLACK

CONTENTS

CHRONOLOGY
56

OVERVIEW
58

TOPICS IN THE NEWS

American Indian Art in the Northeast and Plains 59
American Indian Art of the Southwest 61

Indo-Christian Art and Terminology 61
British Colonial Art 63
French Colonial Art 63
New Mexico 65
Mexican Mission Precedents 66
Pecos Mission 66
Quarai Mission 68
Open Chapels and Architectural Hierarchies 68
St. Steven of Ácoma 69
Secular Spanish Colonial Architecture 70
Spanish Colonial Painting 71

Spanish Colonial Sculpture 72
Spanish St. Augustine 73

HEADLINE MAKERS

Theodor de Bry 74
Jacques le Moyne de Morgues 74

PUBLICATIONS
76

Sidebars and tables are listed in italics.

1500 B.C.

- The ability to make ceramic pottery appears in the coastal regions of South Carolina, Georgia, and Florida. The ceramic vessels resemble flowerpots and are similar to the earlier steatite (soapstone) bowls of the area.

1000 B.C.

- Techniques for carving stone and hammering copper are developed among Eastern Woodlands tribes. Ceramic pottery-making is also widespread, and animal symbols (owls, eagles, frogs, snakes, and turtles) decorate the vessels.

200 B.C.

- The Hohokam people of the southern Arizona desert create distinct pottery styles and use shells to make jewelry and turquoise mosaics. Meanwhile the Mogollon people of southwest New Mexico start to fire their clay pots to make them smooth and then paint them with long brushes made from the yucca plant. Decorations include complex geometric designs, animals, and human figures.

500 A.D.

- The Anasazi culture of Arizona, New Mexico, Colorado, and Utah arises. Over time these people construct cliff dwellings and use a dry fresco technique to paint murals on the walls. Typical images include supernatural beings, plants, and natural phenomena such as clouds and lightning. These people also develop unique pottery styles, basketry, textiles, and personal adornments.

800

- Southeastern Native Americans use a symbolic system of art that has links to South and Central America. Many vessels and jars resemble Aztec ones, and common motifs are winged serpents and eagle warriors.

900

- Tribes in the Southwest use wooden dolls known as kachinas in their religious ceremonies.

1528

- The European print artist Theodor de Bry, famous for his images of the "New World," is born in Liège.

1550s

- Franciscan friars direct the building of the mission of St. Michael the Archangel at Huejotzingo, Puebla, Mexico, which will later influence architectural designs of missions built in the southwestern United States.

1564
- The French traveler-artist Jacques Le Moyne de Morgues arrives in Florida with an expedition led by the Huguenot explorer René Goulaine de Laudonnière.

1585
- The English artist and cartographer John White accompanies an expedition to North America.

1587
- John White accompanies a second English expedition and executes a map of the east coast of North America.

1590
- Over the course of the next twenty-eight years, Theodor de Bry and his sons publish ten volumes of the series *Great Voyages,* detailing with copious illustrations the European colonization of the Americas.

1598
- Franciscan missionaries begin building missions throughout New Mexico, utilizing Native American labor.

1600
- The Micmac Indians of northeastern North America start to apply quillwork to bark in order to exchange it for European trade goods.

OVERVIEW

Colonial Cultural Contact. During the age of discovery, from 1492 to 1600, European explorers, traders, and religious dissenters ventured to the so-called New World. As a result the cultures of Europe, the Americas, Africa, and Asia experienced sustained contact with each other for the first time. The encounters of these different worlds produced not only new cultures, races, and political structures but also new art and architectural forms. These colonial works of art, which fulfilled both practical and creative functions, illuminated European colonial ideologies as well as the experiences of colonizers and indigenous people in what is now the United States. In short, colonial artworks in the Americas are unique visual documents of the age of exploration and colonization.

European Art. European explorers and settlers brought a variety of artistic styles to the New World during the age of discovery. In Europe the period from 1492 to 1600 witnessed the Renaissance, a self-conscious return to the classical values of Greece and Rome. Various artistic advances occurred during this period, including the refinement of mathematical perspective systems, the perfection of the representation of human anatomy, and the development of classical architectural forms such as the column, pediment, and dome. Armed with these new technical and stylistic advances artists attempted to represent realistically the world around them. In addition to Renaissance modes, Europeans imported various other styles to the Americas. Spanish art served as a particularly rich source of artistic ideas. Indeed Spanish art was the syncretic product of centuries of cultural mingling between Christians, Muslims, and Jews in Spain. Spanish artistic styles that transferred to America included Medieval, Romanesque, and even Islamic styles. In contrast to Renaissance art, which attempted to re-create the appearance of the real world, these other Spanish approaches appeared more abstract and symbolic. In place of realistic representation they often favored nonfigural forms such as interlace and geometric designs. These styles traveled directly from Europe to North America or arrived from Mexico, where they had acquired additional indigenous or African influences.

Native American Art. During the period of European contact North America was home to about one thousand different tribes. The first European-indigenous contact occurred along the Atlantic Coast in the sixteenth century, followed by encounters in the southwestern United States in the late sixteenth and early seventeenth centuries and in the Great Lakes region in the seventeenth century. Relations between colonizers and natives were at times peaceful, and some Native Americans eagerly sought trade with Europeans. At other times, of course, European-indigenous relations were hostile and destructive. Eventually European colonists usurped native land, pushing the indigenous population west. Few Native American artifacts survive from the early years of colonial contact. With the exception of pottery most were made of perishable materials. Furthermore, because of the functional nature of many objects in native society, Indians did not take special measures to preserve them. In fact, no word comparable to "art" in the Western European sense exists in any native North American language.

Permanent Settlements. Initial Northern European excursions to the Americas were primarily for trading purposes or to escape religious persecution in Europe. With few exceptions Northern Europeans expressed little interest in indigenous cultures, chose to live in separate and isolated settlements, and rejected intermarriage. In contrast the Spanish arrived in the Americas practicing a policy of settling among, learning about, and intermarrying with the indigenous populations. They were not only searching for riches and new lands to govern but also seeking to convert the indigenous peoples to Catholicism. As a result the Spanish built mission complexes and attempted to establish permanent settlements amongst the native populations, in sharp contrast to French, English, and Dutch approaches to colonialism in the New World. Monumental architecture and art became important by-products of Spanish and later French colonization and conversion. Indeed art acquired a vital role in Spanish and French Catholic missionary enterprises. In contrast to Protestantism, Judaism, or Islam, which all emphasized text over image, the visual arts were central to Catholic culture. Not surprisingly the image served as the major means of Catholic conversion in the New World.

Hybrid Artistic Styles. Colonial contact forever changed European, indigenous, and African art. New artistic styles emerged that combined traits of both the mother countries and the colonized peoples. These new syncretic or hybrid colonial styles testified to the act of colonialism. Such hybrid styles enjoyed especially high visibility in areas of Spanish colonization. To facilitate conversion Spanish missionary friars often encouraged the combining of native and Spanish art forms and techniques in the creation of new Catholic art. Specifically Franciscan missionaries, the order responsible for proselytizing the Spanish frontier regions of New Mexico, Texas, California, and parts of Arizona, facilitated the creation of hybrid Indo-Christian art and architecture.

TOPICS IN THE NEWS

AMERICAN INDIAN ART IN THE NORTHEAST AND PLAINS

Woodlands Culture. From 1492 to 1600 the Woodlands region of North America, a vast area ranging from the St. Lawrence River and the Great Lakes in the North to the Gulf of Mexico in the South, and from the Atlantic Ocean in the East to the Mississippi River in the West, was home to hundreds of different Native American groups, most of whom lived by hunting and agriculture. The Woodlands populations produced a range of functional artworks, most significantly birch-bark canoes, birch-bark architecture, pottery, quillwork, beadwork, animal-skin clothing, woodcarving, stone sculpture, and basketry.

Sculpture. The Woodlands Indians created a particularly rich tradition of wood, stone, bone, and shell sculpture. Most carvings were small and transportable, suitable to seminomadic hunting cultures. Representative Woodlands objects include wooden bowls, spoons, ladles, pipes, war clubs, and ritual face masks. Carved three-dimensional wood sculptures with human or animal head decoration appeared frequently.

Basketry. Although native basketry has prehistoric roots, the oldest surviving Woodlands baskets only date from the seventeenth and eighteenth centuries. Geometric designs and "false embroidery" were common. To create false embroidery, native women dyed moose hair or porcupine quills and applied them to the baskets, twisting them around the twined hemp.

Quillwork. The most unique native North American art form was decorative quillwork. Woven quillwork was commonly applied to leather objects such as shirts, bags, or moccasins. This technique utilized plucked quills from porcupines or birds which native women dyed and used to create dense mosaic-like patterns. The designs,

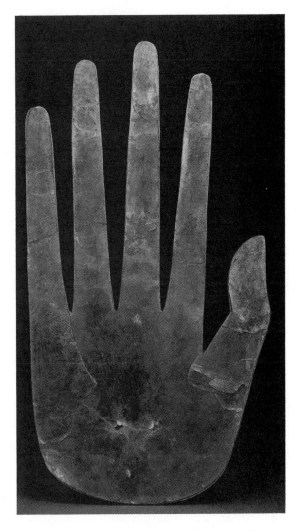

A hand-shaped cutout made of sheet mica, Ohio Hopewell culture, Middle Woodland period, 200 B.C.–400 A.D. (Ohio Historical Society, Columbus)

A ceramic bear-effigy bottle, Mississippian period, 1200–1500 A.D. (University of Arkansas Museum, Fayetteville)

usually abstract as opposed to figural, often took the form of geometric or curvilinear patterns in a variety of colors, including black, red, yellow, and occasionally blue. The earliest examples of quillwork came from the Micmac area north of Lake Huron. In the late sixteenth century Micmac women began to apply quillwork to bark, creating the first tourist art for European traders. The Hudson Bay Cree also produced notable examples.

Wampum Belts. The Eastern Woodlands Indians produced a type of beadwork referred to as wampum belts which consisted of bands woven from purple and white beads made of clam or conch shells from the northeast Atlantic coast. They displayed a variety of abstract and representational designs and had a variety of uses. The Iroquois and Delaware used wampum to keep records. Wampum was also exchanged in treaties or other political or ceremonial transactions. After colonial contact and the introduction of European iron tools, production of wampum increased, and it came to constitute an important form of exchange.

Clothing and Adornments. Clothing and personal adornment attained the status of art among many of the native North Americans. Woodlands Indians in particular created elaborate animal-skin clothing. Women sewed deerskin garments such as breechcloths and coats for men and kiltlike skirts or strap dresses for themselves. Native women ornamented the leather clothing with quill embroidery or pigments. Face or body painting and elaborate hairstyles completed the effect, serving as indicators of the wearer's social status or to commemorate a special event. The paint was temporary in nature and usually employed mineral pigments, charcoal, and pollen mixed with water or grease. Simple linear tattoos provided permanent bodily decorations. They were created by tattoo specialists who pricked the skin and then rubbed black charcoal paste into the wounds to create a design. Indigenous Woodlands clothing and personal adornments are seen in the sixteenth-century prints by the Flemish engraver Theodor de Bry. Woodlands Indians preserved traditional forms of dress well into the late eighteenth century, when wool began to replace animal-hide garments.

Plains Hide Art. The Plains Indians, nomadic tribes who followed the buffalo herds in the central United States, are known for their buffalo-hide art. The Plains tribes lived in portable epees, conical structures of poles covered with decorated buffalo pelts. Plains men executed paintings on epee linings and robes that recorded their war exploits. Although the Spanish documented the existence of these hides in the sixteenth century, the earliest extant buffalo-hide painting, the *Mandan Robe*, dates from 1797 to 1805. Despite its late date it is thought to reflect accurately the earlier Plains hide-painting style. The robe depicts a battle scene between the Mandan of North Dakota and the Lakota. Warrior figures, drawn in outline, are depicted in twenty-two separate battle episodes. Significant attention has been paid to the warriors' costumes and weapons. In addition, the artist elaborated the hide with natural pigments and quillwork embroidery. The pictographic style, while clearly recording the important battle, is rather abstract. In other words, the artist did not wish to re-create accurately the appearance of the visible world. As a result many warrior figures combine multiple views. For example, a figure's head may be presented frontally while his body appears in profile. These pictorial strategies, which are common to many indigenous traditions throughout the Americas, increase visibility for the viewer. The painted and embroidered robe was worn by the warrior-artist on his shoulders as a proclamation of his valor. Plains hide painting had a strong influence on certain forms of Spanish colonial painting in the Southwest.

Source:
Christian F. Feest, *Native Arts of North America* (New York: Oxford University Press, 1980).

AMERICAN INDIAN ART OF THE SOUTHWEST

Pueblo Culture. Key among Southwestern Native American cultures are the Pueblo Indians, prolific Desert culture artists and architects. The Pueblo people are famous for their multistoried dwellings, the only permanent indigenous architecture of the precontact period. In addition, Pueblo artists produced the only known fresco paintings and weavings in North America as well as notable examples of pottery, basketry, and ritual art and architecture.

Adobe Architecture. The New Mexican Pueblo people have lived for centuries in permanent adobe dwellings

in agricultural communities. Taos Pueblo in northern New Mexico maintains traditional indigenous building techniques in its two-house blocks. Although the current buildings date from around 1700, having been rebuilt after a 1690 fire, they preserve precontact adobe building techniques. To create these structures indigenous builders formed hand-shaped adobe bricks and laid them in horizontal courses to build walls, which were finished with a coating of plaster. They placed *vigas*, or beams,

Petroglyphs at the Village of the Great Kivas in New Mexico; Anasazi, circa 1100 A.D.

A decorated Hohokam pottery bowl (circa 600–900 A.D.) found along the banks of the Santa Cruz River in southern Arizona (Arizona State Museum, University of Arizona, Tucson, Arizona)

across the walls to form the framework for flat roofs. On top of the vigas Pueblo builders layered smaller branches, grasses, and mud to form the roof. Typically, the vigas projected on the exterior beyond the walls, a distinctive hallmark of Pueblo architecture which Spanish colonial builders would appropriate and which can be seen today in many contemporary New Mexican buildings. Using these techniques Pueblo builders erected one- to four-story apartment-like structures. Traditionally the dwellings had no doors and few windows, and entrance was gained via an opening in the roof reached by a ladder. Although adobe structures have to be replastered

due to weathering, they are extremely well insulated. Traditionally Pueblo women oversaw the replastering, a custom that Spanish women would imitate in colonial New Mexico.

The Kiva. Pueblo multistoried housing blocks were typically arranged around a main plaza, which included a kiva, or round semisubterranean ceremonial room. The kiva, the interior of which was reached through an opening in the roof accessed by a ladder, was the heart of the community and served both sacred and social functions. Pueblo painters decorated kivas with dry fresco wall paintings of deities and religious symbols executed in a flat style with strong outlines. Famous examples can be found in Awatovi, Arizona, and Kuauá, New Mexico.

Kachinas. Desert culture Indians, including the Pueblos, are known for their kachina dolls. Because of the great religious significance of these wooden sculpted dolls, the Spanish repeatedly tried to suppress their creation during the colonial period. Unfortunately, because kachinas were not collected or studied until the 1850s, no contact era kachinas exist. It has been posited that early kachinas originated in the tenth or eleventh century A.D. and were extremely simple carved cottonwood sticks or boards. The earliest dolls were unclothed and probably hung from the walls of dwellings by strings. Usually carved by men, they represent the spirits of natural elements such as animals, clouds, or mountains and act as intercessors between humans and the gods, bringing rain and curing disease. Carved kachina dolls also replicate the masked dancers who impersonate the invisible spirits represented by the kachinas in religious ceremonies. Clothed kachinas began to appear in the nineteenth century, and today's figures are freestanding sculptures. Elders traditionally gave these small carved figures to children. Young men also presented them as gifts to young women.

A pottery bowl of the Mogollon culture, circa 900–1100 A.D., deliberately broken in the center ("killed") before it was placed in the grave of its owner (Arizona State Museum, University of Arizona, Tucson, Arizona)

Sources:

Bainbridge Bunting, *Early Architecture in New Mexico* (Albuquerque: University of New Mexico, 1976);

Christian F. Feest, *Native Arts of North America* (New York: Oxford University Press, 1980);

Trent Elwood Sanford, *The Architecture of the Southwest: Indian, Spanish, American* (New York: Norton, 1950).

BRITISH COLONIAL ART

Before 1600. Little British colonial art exists from the period of 1492 to 1600 in North America because there were few permanent settlements. Furthermore dissenters such as the Puritans had little need for art, building only the simplest buildings for religious worship. Not until after 1650 did English colonial art and architecture become visible.

White. An exception can be found in the work of John White, an English artist and cartographer who accompanied two expeditions to North America in 1585 and 1587. White, one of the first European traveler-artists in the Americas, executed some of the first visual representations of North America. His watercolor *Map of the East Coast from Florida to Chesapeake Bay* (1585) features the coat of arms of Sir Walter Raleigh, the expedition's initiator. The map depicts the detailed coastline and ocean, six ships, plus fantastic fish. White executed additional watercolor maps, views of fortifications, as well as images of local flora and fauna. For example, one 1585 watercolor represents an exotic "flamenco," or flamingo, bird. Other remarkable sketches depict indigenous villages, customs, and portraits. The European printmaker Theodor de Bry used White's sketches as sources for print illustrations in several volumes of his ten-volume work on the Americas, the *Great Voyages* (1590–1618). White's sketches provided European audiences with their first glimpses of native North American culture.

Sources:

John Wilmerding, *America Art* (Harmondsworth, U.K. & New York: Penguin, 1976);

Hugh Honour, *The New Golden Land: European Images of America from the Discoveries to the Present Time* (New York: Pantheon, 1975).

FRENCH COLONIAL ART

Arrival. The French arrived in the New World in the sixteenth and seventeenth centuries. Most early explorers were Huguenot traders and fur trappers, French Protestants who had left France to escape religious persecution. Before 1650 the population of New France, the area of eastern Canada, included only a few hundred settlers. In 1663, however, the French king Louis XIV declared New France a royal province, and immigration increased.

Early French Forts. Upon their arrival in North America, French explorers built forts, most of which were fairly simple structures built to geometric plans. Two of the earliest were erected in the sixteenth century in the southeastern United States. Charlesfort or Fort Charles, near present-day Beaufort, South Carolina, marked the short-lived French settlement founded by the Huguenot Jean Ribault. Theodor de Bry memorialized the fort in a 1591 engraving. French Huguenots established a similar fort, Fort Caroline, in upper Florida in 1564. Although a flood destroyed the original in 1880, a replica has been built ten miles east of Jacksonville, Florida. In 1565, one year after it was built, the Spanish took control of it.

Fort Rémi. In the seventeenth century several forts were built in what is now Quebec, Canada. Fort Rémi in Lachine, Quebec, demonstrated the typical French colonial fort plan of palisaded walls with stone bastions in the corners. Inside was situated a residential complex of houses, church, and granary, all built of timber. The fort, which was begun in 1671, guarded the city of Montreal, playing a key role in the Iroquois wars. In the eighteenth century the French abandoned it. The 1689 plan is thought to reflect earlier-sixteenth-century French fort architecture.

French Settlements. The first permanent European settlement north of St. Augustine, Florida, was the Port Royal Habitation in Lower Granville, Nova Scotia, built in 1605 on an inlet of the Bay of Fundy by Samuel de Champlain. In 1613 Samuel Argall, the English leader of the Virginia expedition, destroyed the original settlement. The French rebuilt it two additional times and later abandoned it, and finally the English destroyed it in 1777. In 1939 archaeologists completed a reconstruction based on such seventeenth-century descriptions of the settlement as Samuel de Champlain's *Voyages* (1613), Marc Lescarbot's *History of New France* (1609), and the Jesuits' *Relations* (1610–1791). In the style of a sixteenth-century French manor house, the buildings are arranged around an open court. They include living quarters, the governor's residence, storerooms, workshops, a kitchen, and a gatehouse. The architecture demonstrates a late Medieval style, the preferred building style in New France. The structures have steep roofs, tall chimneys, and a few small windows. In a typical Medieval approach, the buildings openly acknowledge their structure, with exposed half timbering in the rooms' interiors.

Missionary Activity. In the seventeenth century French missionaries began serious attempts to convert the northern Woodlands tribes in what is now eastern Canada. They collected groups of native peoples at various mission sites. One such place was Fort de Buada (present-day Saint-Ignace, Michilimackinac Island). Antoine Laumet de la Mothe, Sieur de Cadillac's mid-seventeenth-century description of the village notes the main architectural form as the cabin, built of curved poles and covered with bark.

Native Influences. In building their mission villages the French missionaries sought inspiration in native architecture and art, just like the Spanish did in the South-

Reconstructed Huron village of the seventeenth century, complete with a palisade wall, at the University of Western Ontario's Museum of Indian Archaeology and Pioneer Life

Bird-claw-shaped cutout made of sheet mica, Ohio Hopewell culture, Middle Woodland period, 200 B.C.– 400 A.D. (Ohio Historical Society, Columbus)

west. In the 1635 Jesuit *Relations* a priest described the mission in Trois-Rivières, Quebec: "Our first house was nothing but some saplings bent together, the cracks stopped up with mud, and covered with grass; we had in all about twelve square feet for the chapel and our dwelling together. . . ." In imitation of indigenous architecture, the chapel was built of a framework of poles covered with bark. As in areas of Spanish colonization, French missionaries in New France employed art in the Catholic conversion process. No examples of this early colonial art, however, have survived. Textual sources relate that the priests used small images on leather and prints to instruct native neophytes. These leather paintings must have been similar to the hide paintings used by Spanish missionaries in New Mexico.

Art and Conversion. Extant drawings, prints, and paintings depict the missionary process in New France. The most famous work of New French art is an anonymous painting titled *France Bringing the Law to the Hurons of New France,* dating from the 1660s. This monumental oil painting shows the Huron Indians before an allegorical figure of France, in the guise of the French queen Anne of Austria, requesting that the Queen commemorate their conversion to Christianity. In response Anne of Austria presents a kneeling Indian figure with a painting of the Holy Family as she points to the celestial Trinity above in the heavens. The scene is set against the landscape of Canada. On the left appear simple, rustic wood missions while on the right a European ship approaches in the water. Although the author

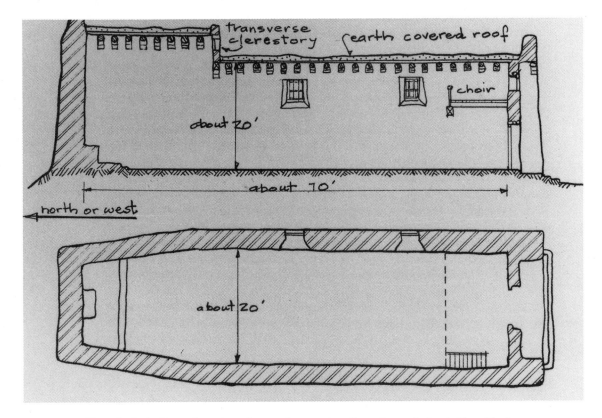

Hypothetical plan and section of an early-seventeenth-century mission in New Mexico
(Arthur LaZar, Albuquerque)

remains anonymous, the painting's imposing size and high quality indicate that a French artist executed it in the 1660s, and it arrived in Quebec in 1670.

Martyrdom. Another seventeenth-century painting, *The Martyrdom of Jesuit Missionaries,* illustrates the dangers faced by the Jesuits in New France. The painting dates from the second half of the seventeenth century since in 1664 the *Historiae Canadensis* published its compositional source, an engraving by Grégoire Huret. Both compositions are based on an earlier 1650 print of the Iroquois torturing missionaries in Canada. The various tortures and martyrdoms represented in the painting occurred between the years 1646 and 1650.

Sources:

Alan Gowans, *Building Canada: An Architectural History of Canadian Life* (Toronto: Oxford University Press, 1966);

Gowans, *Looking at Architecture in Canada* (Toronto: Oxford University Press, 1958);

Luc Noppen and René Villeneuve, *Le trésor du Grand Siècle: l'art et l'architecture du XVIIe siècle à Québec* (Quebec: Musée du Québec, 1984).

NEW MEXICO

Spanish Conquest. Nowhere is the Spanish colonial cultural legacy more visible than in New Mexico, the first area of the southwestern United States colonized by the Spanish. Although the conquistador Francisco Vásquez de Coronado claimed the territory for the Spanish monarchy in 1542, permanent settlements were only established there after persistent indigenous resistance to colonization. The first Spanish explorers arrived in 1540, led by Coronado, followed by another Spanish expedition in 1581 and a third in 1582. Finding little mineral wealth, these explorers quickly abandoned the desolate area.

Oñate's Expedition. The Spanish king, Philip II, officially authorized settlement of New Mexico in 1583. He was interested in establishing missions to convert the Indians and in protecting Mexico's northern mines. He chose Juan de Oñate as the official leader and financier of the colonizing expedition. Oñate's group, including ten Franciscan missionary friars, left Zacatecas, Mexico, in 1598. On 30 April, Oñate officially took possession of New Mexico at modern-day El Paso. In that same year Oñate chose San Gabriel (today Chamita), the second permanent European settlement in North America, as New Mexico's capital. In the course of the seventeenth century, between two and three thousand Spaniards arrived to settle New Mexico. The region, however, proved difficult to colonize due to harsh conditions. In 1609 Oñate's successor as governor, Pedro de Peralta, founded a new capital, La Villa Real de la Santa Fe (The Royal City of the Holy Faith), present-day Santa Fe, New Mexico.

Early Missions. The Franciscan friars immediately began converting the native population to Catholicism. During the initial period of 1598 to 1609 the missionaries built temporary, provisional churches. In 1609, however, King Philip III made New Mexico a royal colony and henceforth the pace of mission building accelerated. The self-taught architect-friars directed the building projects, utilizing Native American labor. By 1617 friars and Native Americans had built eleven churches which purportedly served fourteen thousand new Catholic converts in New Mexico. The missionaries also directed native production of Catholic works of art. These artworks combined native techniques and styles with European content and form, resulting in hybrid or syncretic works of art. Like these works of art and architecture, Pueblo Catholicism was also syncretic. Many Pueblo Indians even today combine Catholic beliefs with traditional native practices. Undoubtedly many of the initial conversions were nominal at best, for during the Pueblo Revolt of 1680–1692 the Pueblos eagerly returned to their original native religion.

Permanent Missions. The period from 1620 to 1680 witnessed the building of larger, more monumental

A seashell decorated by the first known etching process, developed between 1000 and 1200 A.D. by the Hohokam, who probably used an acid made from fermented cactus juice (Arizona State Museum, University of Arizona, Tucson, Arizona)

churches. These missions extended from old El Paso (now Ciudad Juárez in Mexico) north to Taos, New Mexico, and from Pecos in the east to Zuñi in the west. Although located on the fringes of the Spanish Empire, these churches demonstrate innovative plans, window arrangements, and roofing designs. In addition, the architecture displays a unique Indo-Christian style which features Pueblo Indian influence. This style was distinctive from Spanish colonial architecture in New Spain (Mexico), California, Texas, Arizona, or Florida. Mission development came to an end with the 1680 Pueblo Revolt, the most successful native uprising in North America.

Sources:

Bainbridge Bunting, *Early Architecture in New Mexico* (Albuquerque: University of New Mexico Press, 1976);

Mary Grizzard, *Spanish Colonial Art and Architecture of Mexico and the U.S. Southwest* (Lanham, Maryland: University Press of America, 1986);

George Kubler, *The Religious Architecture of New Mexico in the Colonial Period and since the American Occupation* (Albuquerque: University of New Mexico Press, 1990);

Trent Elwood Sanford, *The Architecture of the Southwest: Indian, Spanish, American* (New York: Norton, 1950);

David J. Weber, *The Spanish Frontier in North America* (New Haven & London: Yale University Press, 1992).

PECOS MISSION

Our Lady of the Angels. The mission of Our Lady of the Angels (*Nuestra Señora de los Ángeles de Porciúncula*) at Pecos has a history that illustrates the vicissitudes of

---

MEXICAN MISSION PRECEDENTS

During the age of exploration the Spanish destroyed countless indigenous temples in order to build thousands of Catholic missions throughout the Spanish empire. The purpose of this vast building program was to create a new Christian utopia in the New World. Most Spanish missions followed the pattern established by Mexico's first viceroy, Antonio de Mendoza, in the sixteenth century. Thus all missions included a church, friary, atrium, and some type of outdoor chapel. Often missions were intentionally constructed on top of preexisting native religious structures.

The Franciscan mission of St. Michael the Archangel at Huejotzingo, Puebla, Mexico, is typical. Built in the 1550s by Native Americans under the direction of friar-architects, it defines the fortress church type. Fortress churches tower over the landscape in order to impress the native population with the power of Christianity. They may have also served as refuges in the event of attack. Fortress churches may have additionally contributed to the friars' notions of themselves as soldiers of Christ in a spiritual conquest in the Americas. These monumental churches, with their massive, bare walls, platformlike roofs, towers, high windows, and powerful buttresses, seem more like fortresses than churches.

Sources: James Early, *The Colonial Architecture of Mexico* (Albuquerque: University of New Mexico Press, 1994);

George Kubler, *Mexican Architecture of the Sixteenth Century* (New Haven: Yale University Press, 1948);

Kubler and Martin Soria, *Art and Architecture in Spain and Portugal and Their American Dominions, 1500 to 1800* (London & Baltimore: Penguin, 1959).

mission building in New Mexico. The magnificent ruins of the current adobe church, the fourth structure on the site, date from the early eighteenth century. Parts of two of the three earlier churches are still visible today, however. Examination of their remains illuminates the history of church building in New Mexico.

First Church. Although Francisco Vásquez de Coronado visited Pecos in 1540–1541, the first church was not built until the early 1600s, with the arrival of Franciscan friars. Like most early-seventeenth-century New Mexican churches, this temporary single-nave structure, situated north of the pueblo, was built of adobe with a dirt floor. The nave is the main vessel of a Christian church, usually long, narrow, and rectangular. Single-nave churches are simple and easy to build and therefore appropriate in frontier areas such as New Mexico. Furthermore, the single-nave vessel was not just functional but also symbolic. In the friars' minds this simple type seemed to recall the uncomplicated piety of the early Christian church, to which they endeavored to return. This desire was related to church reform ideals of the sixteenth and seventeenth centuries, a period called the Counter-Reformation, or Catholic Reformation.

Second Church. Building began on the second church, located south of the pueblo, in 1622. It has been attributed to friar Andrés Suárez, the head of the mission. Remains of this second church are visible today. In the seventeenth century this was not only the largest church north of the present-day Mexican border but also the largest European structure in North America. One may glean information about the original state of the second church from the ruins as well as from a 1625–1629 report compiled by a visiting friar, Alonso de Benavides. In contrast to the simple first church, the second church was built to a cruciform plan. Two sacristies, or priests' vestment rooms, formed the crossing. The cruciform plan, which has a long history in Western architecture, is symbolic in nature since the cross shape refers to the central event of Christianity, the crucifixion of Jesus Christ. The apse, or altar end of the church, was polygonal, or multisided. The polygonal apse, in contrast to the semicircular or flat apse, is more complex in nature and indicates the ambitious nature of this second church. Similarly, instead of packed-dirt floors the Pecos church floors were formed of whitewashed adobe bricks. The nave walls, which were an impressive 133 feet long, measured ten feet thick. According to a 1664 document, the church even had an organ, a luxury in this isolated region of the northern Spanish frontier.

Fortress Church. Seventeenth-century descriptions of the church exterior recall fortress missions in Mexico. The church's fortresslike structure was probably designed to have a psychological impact on the recent Indian converts. Fortress churches may have also served as bastions of defense in hostile territories. Forty-five-foot, massive rectangular wall buttresses, which transferred the walls' weight to the ground, propped up the Pecos church's exterior walls. The parapet, a fortified section on the top of the building, was punctuated by crenellations, or openings, from which to shoot at enemies below. Six towers served as lookout posts. In addition, two bell towers flanked the central portal of the facade, creating an entrance porch, or narthex. Above the main portal the friars constructed an exterior balcony, a type of elevated open chapel, for outdoor preaching. Elevated open chapels were typical features of both New Mexican and Mexican missions. Attached to the church was a large friary, or cloister, a square courtyard consisting of rooms organized around an interior patio marked by arcades. It contained the friars' living quarters as well as classrooms, a library, a kitchen, storerooms, and stables. The mission burned in the 1680 Pueblo Revolt, and today only the foundations are visible.

Third and Fourth Churches. After the Spanish reconquest of New Mexico in 1692–1693, a third church positioned parallel to the burned second church was built in 1694. Little is known of this church, except that it must have been a temporary structure since a fourth and final church was erected in 1706 on top of the burned foundations of the second church. These are the impressive ruins visible today.

Reading the Ruins. Analysis of the ruins provides today's viewer with clues to the fourth church's original state. It was smaller than the monumental second church on the site but more lavishly decorated. The cruciform church had a seventy-six-foot-long nave, shallow transepts or crossing arms, and a polygonal apse. The walls, which partially remain today, were made of adobe brick and measured between five and one-half to seven and one-half feet thick. Further information about the church found in the 1776 report on New Mexican missions authored by friar Atanasio Domínguez reveals that the interior was truly impressive. In imitation of Pueblo architecture, the church had a flat roof held up by squared pine *vigas* (beams) resting on decorative carved corbels or brackets. The roof of the transept was elevated above the nave roof to allow for the insertion of a window (called a transverse clerestory window) through which light streamed onto the altar. This window provided a hidden source of light, a dramatic effect in tune with the latest developments in seventeenth-century Baroque architecture in Europe. The dramatic light flooding the altar would have also been symbolic in nature, representing the "new light" or "new day" of Christianity. Five wooden steps separated the nave from the restricted sacred altar space in the apse. Two paintings hung above the altar, one of the Assumption of the Virgin, the other of the titular madonna, Our Lady of the Angels, the latter of which survives today in the Pecos church of St. Anthony of Padua. Two buffalo-hide paintings of St. Anthony of Padua and the Virgin of Guadalupe, as well as a wooden pulpit for preaching, were located in the transept. In addition, the Pecos church boasted unique adobe arches near the transept. Arches, curved elements that span space, had been a mainstay of Western architecture since Roman times. They were nonexistent, however, in native adobe architecture and were utilized only rarely in Spanish colonial adobe structures.

Sources:

Bainbridge Bunting, *Early Architecture in New Mexico* (Albuquerque: University of New Mexico Press, 1976);

Mary Grizzard, *Spanish Colonial Art and Architecture of Mexico and the U.S. Southwest* (Lanham, Md.: University Press of America, 1986);

John L. Kessell, *Kiva, Cross, and Crown: The Pecos Indians and New Mexico, 1540–1840* (Tucson: Southwest Parks and Monuments Association, 1987);

George Kubler, *The Religious Architecture of New Mexico in the Colonial Period and since the American Occupation* (Albuquerque: University of New Mexico, 1990);

Trent Elwood Sanford, *The Architecture of the Southwest: Indian, Spanish, American* (New York: Norton, 1950).

QUARAI MISSION

Our Lady of the Immaculate Conception. The largest stone—as opposed to adobe—mission church in New Mexico is Our Lady of the Immaculate Conception of Cuarác, now called Quarai (*Nuestra Señora de la Purísima Concepción de Cuarác*), which dates from the seventeenth century. Franciscan missionaries built the first chapel on this Pueblo site in 1615–1620. Today one may still see fragments of its stone walls. With its single-nave design, polygonal apse, and dirt floor this small church was typical of other New Mexican missions built between 1598 and 1630. The structure was razed to the ground in 1625 when building began on a new, more monumental stone church. In 1632 this church became the seat of the Inquisition in New Mexico. In 1678 the inhabitants abandoned the site due to Apache attacks, and the church was left unfinished. Today the remains of a one-hundred-foot-long nave with walls rising thirty to forty feet and the friary still stand. In comparison to other New Mexican missions, Quarai was unusual because it was built of stone.

Hybrid Structure. Quarai is a richly syncretic monument, combining traditional European traits with Islamic and indigenous influences. The basic structure was European. The second church was cruciform in plan, with chapels forming the transept. Northeast of the nave could be found the sacristy. The church's massive walls consisted of flagstone courses, or horizontal layers, enclosing rubble fill. The floor was made of finished flagstone. On the 1625 Quarai facade one may see remains of two towers as well as a lintel and window above the main door. Indo-Christian frescoes finished the original interior walls. The roof was also inspired by Pueblo architecture. Vigas, resting on corbels, with *latías,* or thin wood branches, filling the interstices, formed the flat roof. These branches were arranged in herringbone patterns, a ceiling design unique to New Mexican colonial architecture. The friars based their herringbone design on geometrically patterned wooden ceilings in Mexico and Spain which have their ultimate roots in Spanish Islamic

OPEN CHAPELS AND ARCHITECTURAL HIERARCHIES

Open chapels, which appear in missions throughout the Spanish empire, are the most significant architectural form created after the conquest. These structures, built to encourage open-air religious worship, take several forms. The type most frequently built in New Mexican missions is the elevated open-air chapel. At Ácoma, Pecos, and Quarai builders incorporated open-air balconies into the church or cloister facade. Friars preached from these balconies to the Indian converts gathered below in the atrium, or church yard, which served as an outdoor church nave. Scholars have advanced many theories to explain the creation of such chapels. Open chapels may have consciously imitated indigenous open-air temples, a fact which the friars hoped would facilitate conversion to Christianity. They also functioned to create and maintain social and racial hierarchies. For example, in sixteenth-century Mexico only Spaniards were allowed to worship inside the main churches. Native Americans and mestizos prayed in the open air. According to the friars, this was to keep the naive, childlike Indian converts away from the corrupting influences of the worldly Spaniards.

Sources: John McAndrew, *The Open-air Churches of Sixteenth-Century Mexico: Atrios, Posas, Open Chapels, and Other Studies* (Cambridge, Mass.: Harvard University Press, 1965);

James Early, *The Colonial Architecture of Mexico* (Albuquerque: University of New Mexico Press, 1994).

art and architecture. Thus, Quarai combined traits of European, indigenous, and Islamic architecture.

Baroque Effects. The lighting effects of Quarai indicate familiarity with the latest European developments in window solutions. The Quarai church had an unusual number of windows on the facade and the west nave wall, and as a result it must have been well lit. In addition, a transverse clerestory window created dramatic lighting effects on the altar. This window was placed at the roofline facing the altar where the sanctuary roof raised two to three feet above the nave, as in the Pecos church. It created a hidden light source of the type fashionable in seventeenth-century European Baroque churches which allowed light to stream dramatically and symbolically onto the altar.

Indo-Christian Cloister. The Quarai mission complex, like other Spanish missions throughout the Americas, also included a cloister or friary, a *portería* (porter's lodge), and a baptistry where new converts or babies were baptized. The portería was located east of the church facade on the cloister exterior, an arrangement seen in Mexican missions. It probably functioned as a waiting room for Indians wishing to consult with the friars. Behind the portería was the square friary, which was probably two stories in height. Fragments of Indo-Christian frescoes, consisting of an orange band framed by black lines, have been found within the friary. Surprisingly, two indigenous kivas also have been located within the cloister compound. Kivas, which are round-roofed indigenous structures often built underground or partially underground, are sacred sites for the performance of native ceremonies and rituals. Earlier scholars assumed that these two kivas were pre-Hispanic structures and that the Franciscans built their mission on top of them as an act of domination, a common practice in Mexican mission building. A recent theory, however, challenges this interpretation. Archeological evidence indicates that the kivas were built at the same time as the cloister and thus must have been intentionally planned by the Franciscans. How these kivas were incorporated into Catholic ritual, however, remains unknown.

Sources:

Bainbridge Bunting, *Early Architecture in New Mexico* (Albuquerque: University of New Mexico Press, 1976);

Mary Grizzard, *Spanish Colonial Art and Architecture of Mexico and the U.S. Southwest* (Lanham, Md.: University Press of America, 1986);

George Kubler, *The Religious Architecture of New Mexico in the Colonial Period and since the American Occupation* (Albuquerque: University of New Mexico Press, 1990);

Trent Elwood Sanford, *The Architecture of the Southwest: Indian, Spanish, American* (New York: Norton, 1950).

ST. STEVEN OF ÁCOMA

Ácoma Mission. The mission of St. Steven of Ácoma (*San Esteban del Rey*), built from 1629 to 1642, is one of the best preserved and most representative prerevolt churches in New Mexico. It still functions today as a parish church atop Ácoma Pueblo's mesa. Loosely based on Mexican mission plans, Ácoma demonstrates clear evidence of indigenous Pueblo influence in both its structure and decoration. It was named after a Hungarian saint famous for converting the Magyars to Christianity.

Mexican Influences. Dramatically sited on the mesa top in an eminently defensible position, the majestic adobe church is based on sixteenth-century fortress mission churches in Mexico such as St. Michael the Archangel in Huejotzingo, Puebla. Like its Mexican precedents, Ácoma mission includes a large, single nave church with a fortresslike exterior, an adjoining cloister, an atrium or open church yard, and elevated open balcony chapels. Franciscan friars, many of whom had trained at Huejotzingo, a major religious center in Mexico, brought Mexican architectural influences with them to New Mexico. The major differences between New Mexican and Mexican missions is the use of indigenous adobe building techniques.

Adobe Architecture. The use of adobe exemplifies the syncretic nature of Indo-Christian art and architecture in New Mexico. It has been suggested that adobe was employed in colonial buildings because the Pueblo Indians refused to learn European architectural techniques. In fact, Native Americans in New Mexico did strongly resist Spanish colonization. Two additional factors, however, may have conditioned the choice of adobe. First, New Mexico did not have enough trees to build stone architecture, which requires extensive wooden scaffolding. Second, the Franciscans may have intentionally employed local building techniques to facilitate native conversion to Catholicism. In any case, Ácoma retains many traits of traditional Pueblo architecture. Whatever its genesis, the use of adobe to build Spanish Colonial churches was an innovation unique to New Mexico. Never before had indigenous construction techniques been retained to such an extent in the colonial era. Its use in New Mexican missions is a significant example of the survival of indigenous building techniques after the Spanish conquest.

Influence. The use of adobe dramatically influenced the form and style of Ácoma's church. First, the structure is simple and stark, with no arches or domes, standard traits of classical European stone architecture. Nor does the church have buttresses since adobe walls are lighter than stone and therefore do not require such support. Because of their lightness, though, adobe walls cannot support vaulted stone ceilings. As a result, the church has a flat wooden roof built on a framework of vigas, cut from tree trunks, in the style of traditional Pueblo architecture. Accordingly, the nave measures only forty feet in width, the maximum length of a viga. Due to their adobe and viga construction, New Mexican churches are generally narrower and smaller than their Mexican counterparts. They also have few windows since adobe walls cannot withstand extensive fenestration. The fortresslike whitewashed adobe church measures 150 feet long and 40 feet wide, with walls sixty feet tall and ten feet thick.

Typical Adobe Style. The simple cubic design of *San Esteban del Rey* is typical of New Mexican adobe mission style. The facade, with a simple portal flanked by two massive adobe towers, is plain and unadorned. A single choir window above the entrance may have originally functioned as an elevated balcony chapel for preaching, similar to Quarai and Pecos. The facade has no additional windows, no decorative columns, no cornice, and no pediment. Its massive, simple contours and lack of windows recall fortress architecture.

Interior. The church's interior mirrors the exterior in its stark simplicity. It preserves its original packed-dirt floor. The church has few windows, and those that it does have are strategically placed to light the sanctuary. Because window glass was unavailable in seventeenth-century New Mexico, translucent native selenite stone was used, creating soft, subdued lighting effects. The windows are located just below the flat ceiling, which sits upon a framework of vigas resting on decoratively carved corbels or brackets. The sacred space of the sanctuary, where the altar is located, is separated from the nave by a series of steps. The sanctuary's walls slant backward, a

Southeast view of San Esteban del Rey, Acoma, New Mexico, built between 1629 and 1642

dramatic strategy to heighten the optical illusion of spatial recession. Like the Pecos church, Ácoma also once had a dramatic hidden window to light the altar area.

Decoration. The original interior decoration was typical of early New Mexican missions in its minimalism. All early New Mexican missions, like their Mexican counterparts, had frescoed walls, although few of these paintings still exist. At Ácoma one can still detect fragments of the stations of the cross. Undoubtedly, these frescoes were syncretic in nature. The *retablo,* wooden altar screen, visible today in the church dates from the late seventeenth century. It has been attributed to the Laguna Santero, one of New Mexico's most famous (although still unidentified) Spanish colonial artists. The retablo was extensively repainted in the 1920s and has lost its original aspect. The church was probably also originally decorated with buffalo-hide paintings.

Mission Complex. In addition to the church, the Ácoma missionary complex includes an atrium, cloister, portería, and elevated open balcony chapels, just like Mexican missions. Because of the siting of the church near the side of the mesa, the enclosed atrium (or church yard) is irregular in shape. It measures about two hundred square feet. Like other New Mexican mission atria, it functioned as a *campo santo,* or burial ground, for Christianized Indians. It also served as a large outdoor churchyard, complete with atrial cross. Indian neophytes listened to the preacher standing in one of the elevated open chapels, one originally found on the church facade, the other located in the lookout tower on the northeast corner of the cloister's exterior face. A one-story friary or cloister, the friars' residence, is located on the north side of the Ácoma church. A portería, a vestibule which al-

lows access into the friary, is located on the exterior. Modeled on similar porterías found in Mexican missions such as Acolman, the portería was a type of waiting room for Native Americans wishing to consult the friars.

Revolt. Ácoma's *San Esteban del Rey* was one of the only New Mexican churches to survive the Pueblo Revolt. According to letters written by Diego de Vargas, the leader of the expedition to reconquer New Mexico, the church was still standing in 1692. Thus, with the exception of the revolt period of 1680 to 1692, the Ácoma church has been in continuous use from the seventeenth century to the present. It is in many ways the quintessential example of New Mexican mission style.

Sources:

E. Elizabeth Boyd, *Popular Arts of Spanish New Mexico* (Santa Fe: Museum of New Mexico Press, 1974);

Bainbridge Bunting, *Early Architecture in New Mexico* (Albuquerque: University of New Mexico Press, 1976);

Mary Grizzard, *Spanish Colonial Art and Architecture of Mexico and the U.S. Southwest* (Lanham, Md.: University Press of America, 1986);

George Kubler, *The Religious Architecture of New Mexico in the Colonial Period and since the American Occupation* (Albuquerque: University of New Mexico Press, 1990);

Trent Elwood Sanford, *The Architecture of the Southwest: Indian, Spanish, American* (New York: Norton, 1950).

SECULAR SPANISH COLONIAL ARCHITECTURE

Style. In addition to building Indian missions, the Spanish colonists in New Mexico also built permanent settlements for themselves. The Palace of the Governors in Santa Fe, New Mexico, is the oldest public building in the United States. A classic example of Spanish-Pueblo style, it was built in 1610–1611 shortly after the governor of the colony, Pedro de Peralta, founded Santa Fe as the capital, replacing Juan de Oñate's first capital in San Gabriel. Located on the main plaza of the colony's capital, the palace became the official seat of the New Mexican government and governor's residence. The organization of the walled town around a main plaza had its origins in Spanish city-planning designs. During the 1680 Pueblo Revolt the palace served as a fortress to protect the Spanish settlers.

Palace of the Governors. Like the New Mexican missions, the Palace of the Governors was built of adobe by Native American labor. A series of wings organized around interior patios, its block-long facade, originally four-hundred-feet long, faced the plaza. A covered walk supported by wooden columns and brackets ran the length of the south portal. Typical of adobe architecture, it had few windows. In its original state residential rooms and the chapel were located in the east end. The west end housed the soldiers' guardroom, stables, armory, and a jail. From 1912 to 1914 the building was extensively remodeled. A new portal and corner *torreones,* or towers, were added. Nevertheless, the Palace of the Governors is one of the best preserved Spanish colonial buildings in the United States and retains much of its original aspect.

Mexico City. Although located on the fringe of the Spanish empire, Santa Fe's governor's palace adheres to the standard Spanish plan for palace architecture of wings organized around open patios. A similar arrangement can be seen in the monumental Governor's Palace of Mexico City, which dates from the same period. In contrast to this classical stone structure Santa Fe's Palace of the Governors displays the hybrid Pueblo-Spanish architectural style typical of New Mexico.

Rebellion. The Palace of the Governors is most famous for its role in the Pueblo Indian Revolt of 1680, the most successful indigenous uprising in North America. This well-organized rebellion, led by the San Juan medicine man Popé, united nearly all the Pueblos in a well-orchestrated attack on the Spanish colonizers. When the revolt began on 10 August 1680, more than one thousand Spanish fled to the palace and were besieged once inside. When it was over, six days later, not a single living Spaniard was left in New Mexico. All Spanish settlers and friars were killed or were forced to retreat to El Paso del Norte (today Ciudad Juárez, Mexico). The Indians destroyed all Spanish homes and most churches (Ácoma being the most significant exception), killed all the friars, and firmly rejected Catholicism. Popé declared all Catholic marriages dissolved, ordered all baptisms to be "washed off," and rejected all Christian names. Spanish ceased to be spoken. The Pueblo Indians then assumed control of the palace and occupied it for twelve years, turning it into living quarters. They made the chapel into a kiva.

The Reconquest. The Spanish were kept out of the region for twelve years, until 1692, when the reconquest of New Mexico began under the leadership of Diego de Vargas Zapata Luján Ponce de León. He and his forces arrived in Santa Fe in September 1692 to find the Pueblos living in the palace. The Spanish besieged the palace, forcing the Pueblos to evacuate. The Spanish reconquest of the rest of New Mexico was accomplished quickly, largely due to Native American infighting. The Pueblos had suffered severe drought and Apache raids in the preceding twelve years.

Sources:

E. Elizabeth Boyd, *Popular Arts of Spanish New Mexico* (Santa Fe: Museum of New Mexico Press, 1974);

Bainbridge Bunting, *Early Architecture in New Mexico* (Albuquerque: University of New Mexico Press, 1976);

Mary Grizzard, *Spanish Colonial Art and Architecture of Mexico and the U.S. Southwest* (Lanham, Md.: University Press of America, 1986);

Trent Elwood Sanford, *The Architecture of the Southwest: Indian, Spanish, American* (New York: Norton, 1950);

Marcus Whiffen and Frederick Koeper, *American Architecture, 1607–1860,* volume 1 (Cambridge, Mass.: MIT Press, 1983).

SPANISH COLONIAL PAINTING

Hide Paintings. Although New Mexican mission churches were eminently simple in design and decoration, most churches were decorated with paintings and sculptures. In addition to wall frescoes, fragments of which have been detected by archeologists, most churches were adorned with animal-hide paintings, a syncretic Indo-Christian art form unique to New Mexico. Scholars have identified close to sixty extant colonial New Mexican hide paintings. These paintings, executed by Native Americans under the direction of Franciscan missionaries, employed natural pigments on tanned buffalo, elk, and deer skins. They combined Christian iconography with Native American form and technique. These portable paintings, which rolled up easily to transport, played a central role in missionary activities. Friars used them to instruct native catechumens and to adorn the simple churches. Recent research indicates that Spanish settlers also purchased hide paintings. Although the earliest extant hide paintings date from the late seventeenth and early eighteenth centuries, the use of hide paintings in New Mexico can be documented in the early seventeenth century. Presumably, earlier examples were destroyed during the Pueblo Revolt of 1680.

Syncretic Origins. The hide paintings demonstrate a syncretic mix of indigenous and European styles and forms. Painting on animal skin appears to have both European and indigenous roots. During the Middle Ages, European manuscript illuminators painted on vellum, or animal hide. Native Americans throughout North America had an established tradition of buffalo hide painting. Indeed the natural pigments used on colonial hides were the same as those employed in Native American art. On the other hand, the subject matter—the Passion of Christ, the life of the Virgin Mary, and saints—was certainly European in origin. Indeed, artists often used European prints as inspiration for the compositions.

Christian Imagery. Indo-Christian hide paintings most frequently depicted the Virgin Mary, the crucifixion of Christ, and various saints. The Crucifixion of Christ is the central image of Christianity. It depicts the source of human salvation, the sacrifice of Christ's life for the sins of humanity. Thus it is not surprising that the subject appears frequently in conversion art. The scene of the *Crucifixion* by an anonymous late-seventeenth- or early-eighteenth-century painter is typical. Christ on the cross is flanked by his mother, Mary, and St. John the Evangelist. Below, Mary Magdalene, the reformed prostitute and follower of Christ, outwardly expresses her grief as she clutches the cross's base. A small angel appears at Christ's side, catching the saviour's blood in a chalice. The composition seems loosely based on a 1616 print designed by the Flemish Baroque artist Peter Paul Rubens. Prints of the scene could be found in New Mexican colonial books and specifically in the Roman missal.

The Virgin Mary. The most frequent subject matter of extant New Mexican hides is that of the Virgin Mary, the mother of Christ. She is the major intercessor of Catholicism. Most commonly she appears as the Mexican Virgin of Guadalupe. This Virgin, also called *La Guadalupana*, appeared to a native convert to Catholicism, Juan Diego, on the hill of Tepeyac outside Mexico City on 8 December 1531. She instructed Juan Diego to inform the archbishop to build a church in her honor. Juan Diego dutifully complied and reported this request to the high-ranking archbishop, who refused to believe that Mary would appear to such a lowly person. To prove the veracity of the vision, the Virgin gave Juan Diego two signs: she filled his *tilma,* or clock, with Castillian roses and left imprinted on the garment her image. This is the image venerated in the Basilica of the Virgin of Guadalupe outside Mexico City today. New Mexican hide paintings closely copy the iconography of the original Mexican painting. Mary is rendered as a Mexican Madonna, with long, straight black hair and dark skin. Despite her indigenous aspects, however, her iconography derives from the Bible and from European artistic sources. The major literary source for her depiction is the Book of Revelation (12:11), which describes St. John the Evangelist's vision of the apocalyptic woman clothed with the sun, with the moon at her feet, and stars crowning her head. Thus the Virgin of Guadalupe appears with the crescent moon at her feet, an ancient symbol of chastity, while the sun surrounds her in a hallow of light. Although today the Virgin of Guadalupe is recognized as the patron of indigenous peoples in the Americas, mestizos, and Chicanos in the United States, in the colonial period she was an emblem of creole Spanish pride. Her major following during the colonial period was among the Spanish settlers. As a result it is not surprising that her image appeared frequently in colonial New Mexico.

Images of Saints. The two most frequently represented saints in New Mexican hide paintings, and indeed in later New Mexican *santero* art of the eighteenth and nineteenth centuries, were St. Joseph and St. Anthony of Padua. St. Anthony was a friar saint famous for his preaching whose cult was promoted by the Franciscans. He was also the patron of women facing fertility problems or searching for husbands. In hide painting he usually appears as a single devotional figure wearing the Franciscan tonsure and habit, holding the infant Christ child in his arms. St. Joseph, the earthly husband of the Virgin Mary and foster father of Jesus, appears in a similar guise in hide paintings, usually holding the Christ child by the hand. In this and similar images St. Joseph holds his main attribute, the flowered staff, an emblem of his chastity, and clutches the hand of his foster son, Jesus. While artists intended these images to present emblems of perfect fatherhood, they also underscored the source of Joseph's conversion to Christianity from his natal Judaism: it was his daily, physical contact with Jesus. Missionaries advocated this intimate approach to Catholicism to Native Americans. In fact, Joseph played an especially important role in the conversion of the indigenous populations of the Americas. Hernando Cortés brought Joseph's image to Mexico in 1519. In 1555 Joseph became both patron of the Americas and of the conversion. Until 1746 he reigned as sole patron of the Spanish empire in the Americas, at which time the Church declared the Virgin of Guadalupe his copatroness. Evidence indicates that he was the most important saint throughout the Spanish Empire from the sixteenth to eighteenth centuries.

Sources:

E. Elizabeth Boyd, *Popular Arts of Spanish New Mexico* (Santa Fe: Museum of New Mexico Press, 1974);

Bainbridge Bunting, *Early Architecture in New Mexico* (Albuquerque: University of New Mexico Press, 1976);

Kelly Donahue-Wallace, "Print Sources of New Mexican Colonial Hide Paintings," *Anales del Instituto de Investigaciones Estéticas,* 68 (Spring 1996): 46–64;

Mary Grizzard, *Spanish Colonial Art and Architecture of Mexico and the U.S. Southwest* (Lanham, Md.: University Press of America, 1986);

James Hall, *Dictionary of Subjects and Symbols in Art* (New York: Harper & Row, 1974);

Jeanette Favrot Peterson, "The Virgin of Guadalupe: Symbol of Conquest or Liberation?," *Art Journal,* 51 (Winter 1992): 39–47.

SPANISH COLONIAL SCULPTURE

The "Conquering Virgin." The most famous sculpture in Spanish colonial New Mexico was *La Conquistadora*, the Conquering Virgin, reputed to be the oldest image of the Virgin Mary in the United States. In 1625 the friar Alonso de Benavides brought the small polychromed or painted-wood statue from Mexico to Santa Fe and placed it in the parish church of the Assumption of the Virgin. Today she resides in her own chapel in Santa Fe's Cathedral of St. Francis. Because she holds the rosary in her hands, she is regarded as a Virgin of the Rosary.

Sculptural Technique. Because the painted and gilded wood statue was a collaborative work, it typifies Spanish and Spanish-colonial sculptural production. A sculptor carved the wood, which he then gessoed, filed, and smoothed. After the carving was finished, one painter executed the *encarnación* (flesh tones) of the figure while another painted the draperies, enriching them with gold leaf designs. Images such as this one, which was intended to be carried in procession, are called *pasos*. Because this image wears real clothing, it is also an *imagen de vestir,* or dressing image. Both are typical of Spanish and Mexican sculpture. Small processional Virgins dressed in elaborate gowns date back to the Spanish Middle Ages.

Popular Processions. After Friar Benavides brought the statue to Santa Fe, it became the focus of a Marian devotional confraternity, or religious brotherhood. During the Pueblo Revolt of 1680 the Spanish took the statue with them when they fled to the Guadalupe Mission at El Paso del Norte (now Ciudad Juárez). In 1692–1693 the Spanish returned her to Santa Fe. Diego de Vargas, leader of the expedition to reconquer New Mexico, claimed to have won back Santa Fe with her protection. In 1694 the Spanish held a procession in appreciation of her aid during the reconquest. She was processed from her new shrine in the new parish church to the site of the Spanish military encampment outside the walls of the city. This procession, the oldest festival in honor of Mary in the United States, is re-enacted yearly in Santa Fe by descendants of the Spanish colonists.

Source:
David J. Weber, *The Spanish Frontier in North America* (New Haven & London: Yale University Press, 1992).

SPANISH ST. AUGUSTINE

Florida. Founded on the northern Atlantic coast of Florida in 1565 by Pedro Menéndez de Avilés, San Agustín de la Florida was the first Spanish settlement and the oldest European city in the United States. As the capital of Spain's colony of Florida for more than 250 years, the city was the site of important military fortifications. The colony had an adventurous history. In 1763 Florida became the property of England, passing back to Spain in 1783, to be ceded to the United States in 1819. The Spanish colonial city was loosely organized into a grid of streets centered on a main plaza, a type of urban planning popular in sixteenth-century Spain, with its roots in ancient Rome. The Spanish relocated the city twice, in 1566 and in 1572, and in the seventeenth century its population grew dramatically.

Castle of St. Mark. Because of its position on the coast, the city required fortifications to protect it from British pirates and military attacks. The Spanish fortress *Castillo de San Marcos* (Castle of St. Mark), which was moved and rebuilt on three separate occasions (1572, 1595, and 1672), is truly unique in the history of architecture. The 1672 fortification visible today was the only city structure to survive a devastating fire in 1702. Attributed to the Cuban military engineers Juan Síscara and Ignacio Daza, it was built entirely of local shell limestone. Although parts of the star-shaped structure were still under construction as late

as 1756, most of the fortification was built between 1672 and 1687. The fortress features triangular bastions, a form invented in sixteenth-century Italy by Antonio and Giuliano Sangallo and perfected in the seventeenth century by the French military engineer Sébastien Le Prestre de Vauban, whose influence can be seen in the structure. The fortress is a rare example of a masonry fortress. Because most stone fortresses shatter when hit by cannon fire, many fortresses were built of earth works. What is unusual here is the soft limestone used in the fortress's construction. When struck by cannon fire, it did not shatter. Cannon balls seemed to bounce right off. As the oldest stone fortress in the United States, the *Castillo* is an enduring monument to the Spanish presence in Florida. Whereas the various northern Florida missions collapsed in the years 1680 to 1706, St. Augustine's fortifications still stand today, having withstood three British sieges in 1702, 1728, and 1740.

Sources:
David J. Weber, *The Spanish Frontier in North America* (New Haven & London: Yale University Press, 1992);

Marcus Whiffen and Frederick Koeper, *American Architecture, 1607–1860*, volume 1 (Cambridge, Mass.: MIT Press, 1983).

A four-legged effigy urn, circa 250–800 A.D. (Indian Temple Mound Museum, Fort Walton Beach, Florida)

THEODOR DE BRY

1528-1598
ARTIST, ENGRAVER, PUBLISHER

Refugee. Many Europeans first glimpsed the wonders of the New World in prints executed by the engraver Theodor de Bry. De Bry, a Lutheran originally from Spanish-controlled Flanders, fled to the Protestant city of Strasbourg, Germany, in 1570 due to Spanish persecution of non-Catholics. In Strasbourg, which was the European center of the book trade, he worked and studied with the French Huguenot engraver Etienne Delaune. During a twenty-eight-year period, from 1590 to 1618, de Bry and his sons published in Europe ten illustrated volumes titled *Great Voyages* which depicted the conquest of the Americas by English, French, Dutch, and Spanish colonists. The purpose of these volumes was to encourage colonization of the New World.

The Invention of America. The lavishly illustrated *Great Voyages* circulated widely and were published not only in German and Latin but also in English and French. The texts were an instant success among both the European aristocracy and merchant classes. Furthermore, the printed illustrations were sold on the streets of European cities, thus reaching an even larger audience. Although de Bry himself never ventured to the New World, he was responsible for shaping many Europeans' notions of it. As explorers discovered America, de Bry and others were busy inventing it in the minds of the masses.

The Engravings. De Bry's engravings relied on life drawings by such artist-explorers as John White and Jacques Le Moyne de Morgues, as well as on textual descriptions by adventurers such as Hans Staden or Jean de Léry. The first volume of the *Great Voyages,* published in 1590 with engravings after sketches by White, described the English expedition to Virginia.

A second volume followed in 1591 detailing the French Huguenots' experiences in Florida in 1565 with engravings after Le Moyne de Morgues's sketches. A fourth volume on the Spanish colonization focused on the mistreatment of the indigenous population, betraying de Bry's decidedly anti-Spanish bias. After the artist's death his two sons took over production of the *Great Voyages,* ensuring that European audiences would have access to these fanciful descriptions of the Americas throughout the colonial period.

Technique and Style. The engraving process itself, which allows for the dissemination of multiple copies of an image, was partly responsible for the success of de Bry's *Great Voyages.* The process is complex. Using a sharp implement called a burin, the artist scratches the image onto a metal plate, which is then inked in order to print the image on paper. De Bry's engravings demonstrate his great artistic talents. They are executed in the Mannerist style current in the late sixteenth century, as demonstrated by the elongated, muscular, and idealized figures, and reveal his talent for drawing and composition.

Sources:

Bernadette Bucher, *Icon and Conquest: Structural Analysis of the Illustrations of de Bry's* Great Voyages (Chicago: University of Chicago Press, 1981);

Hugh Honour, *The New Golden Land: European Images of America from the Discoveries to the Present Time* (New York: Pantheon, 1975).

JACQUES LE MOYNE DE MORGUES

?-1588
ARTIST, CARTOGRAPHER

Travels. The French artist Jacques le Moyne de Morgues, a draftsman, painter, and engraver, accompanied a 1564 French Huguenot expedition to Florida led by the explorer René Goulaine de Laudonnière. Le Moyne's remarkable watercolor studies, unusual due to their rich ethnographic detail, are among the first European depictions of North America. Upon his return to Europe these sketches served as the basis for engravings to illustrate a history of his voyage. Thus le

Moyne de Morgues was instrumental in the spread of American imagery in the Old World.

Artistic Training. Le Moyne de Morgues trained as a cartographer in the great French mapmaking tradition. He learned not only how to execute maps but also the skills of drawing and painting. In contrast to modern conceptions of cartography, early modern maps included not just geographical information but depictions of the region's flora, fauna, and inhabitants. Thus le Moyne de Morgues was the perfect traveler-artist to accompany an expedition to North America. The abstraction and preciousness of his style reveal the influence of the French Mannerist school, as does the primarily pastel palette. After the 1564 expedition to North America the artist returned to Europe, dying in London in 1588.

Extant Sketch. Despite the importance of le Moyne de Morgues's work for the history of North America, only one original painting by his hand seems to have survived. Scholarly assessment of his artwork has been necessarily based on study of the copies after his work in the forms of prints and sketches. The only extant original painting by the artist probably dates from after his return to Europe. It depicts the 1564 encounter between the French explorer Laudonnière and the Na-

tive American chief Athore of the Timucua in northern Florida. Both figures stand before a column at the mouth of the St. John River near present-day Jacksonville, having just exchanged gifts. The column, which displays the arms of France, was erected by Jean Ribault in an earlier 1562 expedition. Native Americans kneel before it reverently, having adorned it with flowers and leaves. The political message of the image is clear: the indigenous population seems to have eagerly embraced French colonial rule. Within a year of the 1564 encounter, however, the Spanish arrived in the area, murdering all the French colonists. They claimed the land for Spain, founding the city of St. Augustine, and French colonization of Florida came to an end.

Sources:

E. Bénézit, ed., *Dictionnaire critique et documentaire des Peintres, Sculpteurs, Dessinateurs et Graveurs de tous les temps et de tous les pays par un groupe d'écrivains spécialistes français et étrangers* (Paris: Librairie Gründ, 1976);

Bernadette Bucher, *Icon and Conquest: A Structural Analysis of the Illustrations of de Bry's* Great Voyages (Chicago: University of Chicago Press, 1981);

Hugh Honour, *The New Golden Land: European Images of America from the Discoveries to the Present Time* (New York: Pantheon, 1975);

John Wilmerding, *American Art* (Harmondsworth, U.K. & New York: Penguin, 1976).

Kiva mural decoration, circa 1400 A.D., from Awatovi, Arizona

PUBLICATIONS

Alonso de Benavides, *Fray Alonso de Benavides' Revised Memorial of 1634,* edited and translated by Frederick W. Hodge, George P. Hammon, and Agapito Rey (Albuquerque: University of New Mexico Press, 1945)—an extremely valuable description of the missions in New Mexico written in the early seventeenth century by a visiting Franciscan friar;

Theodor de Bry, *Grands voyages,* 10 volumes (Frankfurt am Main, 1590–1618)—copiously illustrated volumes detailing the European conquests of the Americas;

Friar Atanasio Domínguez, *Missions of New Mexico, 1776: A Description by Fray Atanasio Domínguez,* edited and translated by Eleanor B. Adams and Angélico Chávez (Albuqerque: University of New Mexico Press, 1956)—a Franciscan friar's detailed description of the New Mexican missions;

Francisco Pacheco, *El arte de la pintura,* edited by Bonaventura Bassegoda i Hugas (Madrid: Cátedra, 1990)—a major treatise written by an Inquisition art censor in the early 1600s which includes the Inquisition's guidelines for the production of religious art throughout the Spanish Empire;

Gaspar Pérez de Villagrá, *Historia de la Nueva México, 1610,* edited and translated by Miguel Encinias, Alfred Rodríguez, and Joseph P. Sánchez (Albuquerque: University of New Mexico Press, 1992)—an epic poem of the Spanish conquest of New Mexico.

Human-effigy pipe made of hermatitic stone, Dallas culture, late Mississippian period, 1300–1500 A.D. (Frank H. McClung Museum, University of Tennessee, Knoxville)

COMMUNICATIONS

by NANCY L. HAGEDORN

CONTENTS

CHRONOLOGY
78

OVERVIEW
81

TOPICS IN THE NEWS
Communication in Native
   North America.............83
Historical Linguistics 84
Rituals of Possession.............85

First Contacts along the
   East Coast.................85
Jargons and Pidgins 87
Coastal Algonquians 88
First Contacts: The Early
   Explorers 89
Interpreters 90
First Contacts: Penetration of
   the Interior 91
Indian Slavery 93
First Contacts: The Roanake
   Venture 94
The Transformation of Communica-
   tion in Early America 95

HEADLINE MAKERS
Donnacona 96
Estévanico the Moor 98
Messamouet 99

PUBLICATIONS
101

Sidebars and tables are listed in italics.

40,000–10,000 B.C.

- Paleolithic peoples migrate from Asia to North America and spread through unglaciated regions.

7000 B.C.–700 A.D.

- Free-wandering Paleolithic peoples settle into more-regular patterns of movement within restricted territories as they adapt to local conditions and exploit their new environments, giving rise to a variety of Archaic cultures throughout the continent. Increasing cultural differentiation among these Archaic peoples leads to increasing linguistic diversity.

1480s?

- Bristol fishermen from the west coast of England begin fishing for cod in the waters off Newfoundland in the North Atlantic. Rudimentary trade begins with the native inhabitants.

1501

- Portuguese captain Gaspar Côrte-Real kidnaps some fifty Indians from the northeastern coast of North America and sends them to his king in Lisbon as slaves.

1519

- Alvarez de Pineda completes a survey of the Gulf Coast for Spain.

1520s?

- Basque fishermen from southwestern France and the western Pyrenees of Spain begin fishing and whaling off the Newfoundland and Labrador coasts and establish good relations and trade with the local natives. A Basque-based pidgin begins to develop.

1524–1525

- Portuguese explorer Estevâo Gomes surveys the Newfoundland and New England coasts beyond Cape Cod for Spain.

1525

- Spaniard Pedro de Quejo maps the southeastern coastline of North America as far north as Delaware.

1526

- Lucas Vázquez de Ayllón takes Indian interpreter Francisco de Chicora and several other native translators with him on his colonizing venture to South Carolina. Francisco and the others had been kidnapped from the area of Winyaw Bay, South Carolina, five years earlier.

1528

- Pánfilo de Narváez attempts to explore Florida and the Gulf Coast but is forced to retreat. The entire expedition is lost except for four men, including Alvar Núñez Cabeza de Vaca and Estévanico the Moor.

1529–1536

- Cabeza de Vaca, Estévanico, and the other two survivors of the Narváez expedition wander Texas and northern Mexico as captives, traders, and shamans, learning the languages and customs of the local inhabitants.

1530s

- Discovery of Grand Banks leads to increased European fishing off the Maine coast and the beginning of more intensive contacts with the native peoples living there.

1534

- Jacques Cartier explores the Gulf of St. Lawrence and the St. Lawrence River, contacting Iroquoian Indians living at Stadacona and Hochelaga. He kidnaps two sons of Stadaconan chief Donnacona and takes them to France to be trained as interpreters.

1535–1536

- Cartier and his Stadaconan interpreters return to the St. Lawrence. Over the winter relations sour between the French and the St. Lawrence Iroquoians. When Cartier leaves for France, he takes ten captives with him, including Donnacona and his two sons. All are dead by the time Cartier again sails for New France in the early 1540s.

1536

- Cabeza de Vaca, Estévanico, and the other two survivors of the Narváez expedition reach Culiacán, Mexico, in early April.

1538

- Mexican viceroy Antonio de Mendoza sends Franciscan Fray Marcos de Niza on a reconnaissance to the north. Estévanico the Moor accompanies him as guide and interpreter and is killed by Zuni Indians in the spring of 1539.

1539–1542

- Hernando de Soto explores the interior southeast for Spain and is the first European to encounter the Indians of the Mississippi River valley. De Soto finds a survivor of the Narváez expedition, Juan Ortiz, living among the natives of Florida and takes him along as an interpreter.

1540-1542

- Conquistador Francisco Vásquez de Coronado, with Fray Marcos as his guide, coordinates several expeditions to explore the interior southwest.

1542

- The first allusion to the existence of Basque pidgin appears in the historical record.

1561

- A Spanish crew captures a young Indian from the York River in Virginia and takes him to Spain to be trained as an interpreter. During his nine years in Europe he is baptized and given the name Don Luis de Velasco.

1570s?

- Micmac chief Messamouet visits Bayonne, France, and lives with the mayor of the southwestern port during his stay.

1570

- Don Luis returns to the York River with a small group of Jesuits to establish a mission. He runs off shortly after his arrival and later leads an Indian attack on the priests in which all of them are killed.

1580

- English explorer John Walker lands at Penobscot Bay and finds an Indian building containing more than two hundred moose hides. His discovery is the earliest evidence of an indigenous fur trade conducted by native Souriquois middlemen between the Indians of the Maine coast and Europeans in the Gulf of St. Lawrence.

1584

- The English adventurer Sir Walter Raleigh sends the first reconnaissance voyage to the Outer Banks in preparation for establishing a colony. The explorers encounter local Algonquian Indians and bring two, Wanchese and Manteo, back to England to be trained as interpreters.

1585

- Raleigh's first colony is established, under Ralph Lane, on Roanoke Island. Difficulties in obtaining provisions lead to worsening relations with the local Roanokes, and the colony is abandoned in June of the next year. Manteo returns to England with them.

1587

- Raleigh sends a second group of colonists, with Manteo, to the Carolina coast under John White. The group fails to reach their intended destination in the Chesapeake Bay and again settles at Roanoke Island. White leaves in the fall to obtain more supplies in England but is delayed in returning. By 1590 the colonists have vanished.

OVERVIEW

Communication. Although the word "communication" may be used to identify activities that do not involve people—animals or even machines can be said to communicate—it is usually defined as the means through which people exchange feelings and ideas with one another. Communication is a process rather than a thing; it begins when a person feels a need to express an idea, a message, or a feeling. In other words, it begins with a purpose: to convey information, to express feelings, to imagine, to influence, or to meet social or cultural expectations. Unlike objects, feelings and ideas are difficult to exchange because they have no physical substance. Since they have no concrete existence, they cannot be handed directly to another person. Instead they must be exchanged, or communicated, through the use of symbols—things that represent or stand for other things. In order for meaningful communication to take place, people must share the same symbol system or language.

Oral Communication. The earliest form of human communication was probably spoken, or oral, communication. In oral communication, sound patterns represent other things, whether objects, ideas, or feelings. Early humans made contact with the outside world and with each other through their five senses—through sound, sight, touch, smell, and taste—and they used sounds, gestures, and touch as symbols to convey information. Over time, a language developed that stood for the objects and actions common to their daily lives and necessary for survival. In addition to words and phrases, however, oral communication also involves the vocal characteristics of rate, pitch, loudness, and inflection (sometimes called paralanguage) and nonverbal elements such as facial expression, gestures, and eye contact. Even pauses and silences carry meaning in spoken communication. For example, a pause makes a difference between *careless* and *care less*. Finally, to communicate effectively, people must share not only a symbol system and paralanguage but also knowledge about how to use a language properly in various social situations or contexts. Communication contexts consist of a blend of the audience being addressed and the social settings in which the communication occurs, and social expectations can differ greatly from culture to culture. Humor is especially difficult to translate across cultural and linguistic boundaries

because without clear understanding of the cultural and social context of the joke or faux pas the source of merriment will not be apparent or make sense. Choice of language can also have social meaning. Informal language or slang that might be appropriate at a party or among friends would be inappropriate in a more formal setting and would normally be replaced by standardized language. Among many American Indian groups, council oratory, which is heavily laced with metaphor and allusion, is completely different from ordinary conversational speech, and few natives mastered it. Those who did held a special position as orators and were respected for their talent.

Language. Above all language is meaning. Meanings are attached to pieces of words, entire words, or groups of words as well as to the spoken signals of languages and to the shifts and changes of grammar and the way in which words are put together to form phrases and sentences (syntax). The sounds of words have no intrinsic meaning to begin with; people attach meaning to them, thereby creating language. Written language is a substitute for spoken language. The various symbols, or letters, stand for the main sounds in the language. When combined, sound patterns representing words are formed, which can in turn be used in combination to form phrases and sentences. In addition to using letters to represent sounds, punctuation marks convey information about the paralanguage required to clarify a particular meaning. Commas, for example, indicate a slight pause; question marks signal a rise in pitch or inflection; and an exclamation point represents an increase in volume or intensity. Although the nonverbal aspects of oral communication cannot be represented by written language, the infinite variety of combinations allows for great flexibility and complexity of communication.

Translation. Languages, paralanguages, nonverbal symbols, social contexts, and rules regarding usage vary from culture to culture. In order to communicate across cultural boundaries, then, some form of translation or interpretation of meaning is necessary. Since the words of one language seldom mean exactly the same as the words of another, however, translation is, at best, an approximation of meaning. Translation requires that the translator attain at least rudimentary bilingualism, or knowledge of both languages. Mastery of two languages is difficult and time-consuming, so in many contact situations specialized substitutes, called contact languages, often evolve. Some, such as sign language, are completely nonverbal while others are hybridized combinations of the two languages in contact. In early North America a variety of contact languages were in use both before and after European contact.

Linguistic Diversity. Paleolithic peoples migrated from Asia to North America and spread through unglaciated regions of the continent sometime between 40,000 B.C. and 10,000 B.C. The final retreat of the ice sheets, which began about 7000 B.C., created a mosaic of new, rapidly evolving environments and ecosystems and initiated a period of migration into previously inaccessible interior regions of North America. Paleolithic groups, as they encountered these new environments and changing ecosystems, were forced to readjust their subsistence patterns and lifestyles. Eventually the new environments stabilized, and by about 700 A.D. these free-wandering peoples settled into regular patterns of movement within more-restricted territories. As they adapted to specific local conditions and exploited their new environments, a variety of Archaic cultures arose throughout the continent. Increasing cultural differentiation and specialization among these peoples, in turn, led to increasing linguistic diversity. By the eve of contact some four hundred distinct languages were spoken in native North America.

Intercultural Communication. Most native North American languages can be grouped into families of similar languages that apparently evolved from a common ancestral language stock, or protolanguage, in the distant past. Within these language families there is often some degree of mutual intelligibility between pairs or small groups of closely related languages. Still, the languages of native North America are extraordinarily diverse. They do not belong to a single family or conform to a single type; there were at least 221 mutually unintelligible languages in precontact North America. Despite the existence of such language barriers, however, the discovery of exotic, nonlocal goods and materials at precontact archaeological sites and associated with prehistoric burials make it clear that long-distance, intercultural trade occurred before the arrival of Europeans. Neighboring groups that engaged in such exchanges undoubtedly shared at least a limited amount of bilingualism. Intermarriage probably helped promote bilingual communication while also fostering the formation of trade and military alliances. At greater distances, native middlemen skilled in a variety of languages or knowledgeable in a shared lingua franca, or common language, may have specialized as long-distance traders. These native trade and communication networks later formed the basis for intercultural trade and communication between Europeans and the indigenous inhabitants of North America.

Nonspeech Communication. In addition to bilingualism and the use of linguae francae, Native Americans also employed several nonspeech communication systems. At least one of these, sign language, apparently facilitated intercultural communication among precontact native North Americans. Sign language is not a secondary system based on a particular language or languages but a completely independent system for communicating ideas directly. Since Indian sign language is often used by people speaking different languages, the signs cannot stand for words; instead the signs themselves have meaning. Each person translates the meaning of the hand signals into the words of his own language. Similarly, various kinds of picture writing and long-distance signaling may also have served as the basis for intercultural communication across linguistic boundaries.

Postcontact Communication. When Europeans and Native Americans first confronted each other on the North American continent, they faced communication problems similar to those faced by Europeans of different linguistic backgrounds in Europe or by precontact native groups speaking different languages in America. Despite linguistic differences, however, all Europeans shared similar material lives, religions, economies, gender roles, polities, and worldviews that could serve as the foundation for the development of communication across language boundaries. Similarly, all Native Americans experienced certain common underlying features of North American life. The difficulty of finding a common basis for meaningful intercultural communication between Europeans and Native Americans was considerably magnified by the vast differences between the lifestyles, economies, kinship systems, belief systems, worldviews, and cultural systems on either side of the Atlantic. To make matters worse, Indian languages bore little syntactic, morphological, or phonological resemblance to European tongues. At first, then, communication between Europeans and native North Americans probably took the form of rudimentary gestures and signs, leaving a great deal of room for misinterpretation and misunderstanding. As contact between European explorers and the indigenous inhabitants increased, specialized jargons and pidgins emerged. Unfortunately these specialized contact languages, while useful in limited exchanges focusing on trade, were ill-suited to communication of abstract concepts and ideas. Finally, by about 1600, more intensive, long-term contact had led to the use of linguae francae and some European-American bilingualism, at least in certain areas.

Effects of Contact. Although postcontact intercultural communication bore many similarities to pre-1492 communication among native North Americans and among Europeans, contact wrought many changes in North American communication systems. Most obvious, perhaps, were the many new and borrowed words and phrases that appeared in both Native American and

European languages to describe the unfamiliar peoples, places, flora, and fauna encountered by both sides as a result of transatlantic contact and exchange, such as *canoe, moccasin,* and *toboggan.* Less obvious, though more significant, were the entirely new language communities that formed as refugee and remnant groups combined in the wake of devastating epidemics and warfare. In other cases the sharp decline in indigenous populations resulted in the extinction of some native North American languages following contact. Finally, as Europeans slowly came to dominate regions of the continent in the seventeenth and eighteenth centuries, their languages and modes of communication assumed dominance, too, displacing older, indigenous systems.

TOPICS IN THE NEWS

COMMUNICATION IN NATIVE NORTH AMERICA

Language Development. As the Paleolithic ancestors of native North Americans spread across the continent in the wake of retreating ice fields after 7000 B.C., they encountered a vast array of new environments and ecosystems. During the next eight millennia free-wandering bands adapted to these new environments, and their movements became increasingly restricted to well-defined territories. As language communities migrated and grew, portions of them split off and moved on. Over time, physical separation, combined with adaptation to different environments and contact with new and unrelated bands, led to increasing linguistic and cultural divergence between subgroups of formerly unified language communities. Together these evolutionary linguistic descendants of a single, common protolanguage constitute a language family and are said to be genetically related to one another. The more closely related two languages are and the higher the degree of mutual intelligibility, the more recent the split between them. Historical linguists, who study and compare languages as they change through time, have grouped native American languages into thirty-four multilanguage families; another thirty or so seem to stand alone without demonstrable genetic relation to any other language. In total, some four hundred distinct languages were spoken in North America on the eve of European contact, at least half of them mutually unintelligible to each other.

Oral Culture. All precontact North American languages were spoken only, without any written elements. Native North American societies, therefore, were almost completely dependent on the collective memory of their members for cultural knowledge. All environmental, historical, political, religious, and social knowledge necessary to ensure a group's survival lived only in the memories of its living members and was passed to future generations by word of mouth. As a result, in most of these oral cultures the spoken word assumed great importance, and the act of speaking took on special significance. To aid memory, cultural information was often transmitted through stories and songs. In formal settings words were not spoken thoughtlessly or in haste but rather with gravity and deliberation. Oratory, laced with meaningful metaphors and allusions, often assumed a central role in political and diplomatic exchanges, where great courtesy and respect were shown to both speakers and listeners to guarantee that all involved could hear, understand, and remember. Finally, without a written record to freeze the spoken word for all time, words took on a life of their own. Consequently, most native peoples focused on the nature of a relationship and the ongoing process of maintaining it through the exchange of words and gifts rather than on a finite, static agreement between two people or groups. The underlying truth or meaning of an ever-changing repertoire of stories, histories, and songs was more important than the specific words through which it was conveyed. Speech, like all of life, was a process, and words, in a real sense, became deeds of great significance and power.

Ritual. An important aspect of the act of speaking and of the significance of the spoken word in native North America was the ritual surrounding them. Rituals are a specialized kind of nonverbal communication. Often rituals legitimize, validate, or solemnize the messages and speech acts they frame. They give the words and acts they accompany special weight and meaning and reinforce the collective cultural identity of those who participate. In addition, rituals usually engage the senses. Instead of merely hearing the words being spoken, the listeners also see accompanying gestures or dances and frequently smell special incense or smoke, taste particular

HISTORICAL LINGUISTICS

Languages change constantly in form, pronunciation, syntax, vocabulary, and meaning. The study of these changes through time, and it is called historical linguistics. As they analyze variations in a language between two or more points in time, historical linguists often discover differences across space. Both are of concern to the historical linguist, whose ultimate task is not merely to describe the nature and direction of change within a language but to try to explain it. Migration or isolation of populations, contact with other cultures and languages, and alterations in lifestyle or circumstances can all cause languages to change. Native American languages present special challenges for the historical linguist because knowledge of the precontact history of many groups is incomplete and because the languages had no written component until contact with Europeans. Even after contact, written examples of native languages recorded by European observers were usually fragmentary and influenced by nonnative cultural perspectives and misconceptions. Still, by combining these sources with knowledge gained from archaeology about early American cultures and lifestyles, historical linguists have been able to establish family relationships between many native North American languages and have had some success in reconstructing the hypothetical parent forms, or protolanguages, from which they evolved. This information, speculative as it may be in some instances, when combined with more-recent data on the distribution of Native American languages across the continent, provides important clues to migration patterns, trade and communication networks, and intercultural contact before the arrival of Europeans.

Sources: Ives Goddard, ed., *Handbook of North American Indians*, volume 17: *Languages* (Washington, D.C.: Smithsonian Institution, 1996);

Winfred P. Lehmann, *Historical Linguistics: An Introduction*, third edition (London & New York: Routledge, 1992).

foods or drinks, hear music and singing, and touch each other or significant objects related to the message being conveyed. These sensory experiences make both the experience and the message more memorable—an important consideration in oral cultures. For Native Americans an orator's pacing and somber visage signaled his gravity and deliberation while emphasizing the importance of his speech; the taste and smell of tobacco reminded partakers of the agreements discussed over a calumet or pipe; and the smoke wafting skyward visually carried the words and prayers of the people to the powerful beings who lived there. Without such rituals and sensory cues speech remained mere discourse, suitable for exchanging information or expressing views and opinions but lacking the force and legitimacy of the more formal speech acts used to solicit and control spiritual power or to establish and maintain advantageous relationships.

Nonverbal Communication. Native North Americans employed a variety of nonspeech communication systems in addition to ritual. By far the most sophisticated was sign language, which probably originated in the communication needs of deaf or mute individuals or in the impromptu signing necessary in particular circumstances such as war or hunting, where silence was required. Whatever its origins, a native sign language was clearly in use in the extreme southern plains by the time of contact as a means of communication between groups speaking different languages. Trade undoubtedly stimulated its spread throughout the plains following European contact and the introduction of the horse. Although sign language was the most sophisticated and complex of native nonverbal communication systems, it was not the only one in use. For long-distance communication, when speech was impossible, American Indians employed other kinds of audible or visual signals. Audible signals were simple and limited primarily to the imitations of birdcalls and animal cries used by war parties and scouts to communicate when stealth was required. When terrain permitted, smoke and fire as well as body, arm, or blanket signaling could convey limited kinds of information regarding the presence of game or enemies across long distances. In such cases, however, meanings had to be either conventional and obvious or quite specific and assigned by prior agreement to particular signals. Finally, Native Americans made widespread use of the physical representation of ideas. Some of these representations were largely symbolic and somewhat stereotypical, such as totems representing clan or tribal affiliation. Others were much more flexible and complex, such as pictography, where anyone capable of recognizing the pictures could deduce at least the subject of the message or representation, though specific details might remain unintelligible outside the cultural context of the artist. All of these nonverbal or nonspeech systems are independent from a particular language. The symbols employed do not stand for particular words but are themselves representations of particular meanings and convey information and ideas directly. As a result these nonverbal communication systems are particularly well suited to communication across linguistic and cultural boundaries.

Intercultural communication. Prior to European contact, native North Americans did not live in isolation from each other. They traded and raided extensively, and by the time the first European explorers arrived on the continent extensive trade, transportation, and communication networks were in place. Given the wide diversity of Native American languages in North America, much of this precontact trade and communication occurred between native groups who spoke different, often mutually

Europeans, like native North Americans, relied on nonverbal rituals to legitimize and reinforce their words and actions in public contexts. Despite the fact that European languages had written components, in the fifteenth and sixteenth centuries the ability to read and write was restricted to the nobility, the higher clergy, and an emerging class of educated professionals and government officials. These groups made up a small, elite portion of the population. The majority of Europeans remained illiterate and lived out their lives within predominantly oral cultures. As a result rituals and ceremonies assumed great importance as nonverbal modes of communicating with the general population. Religious services, for example, were conducted in Latin, and few in the congregation "understood" the words of the priest or the responses they themselves uttered by rote. Most, however, comprehended the meaning of the rituals that accompanied communion, baptism, and prayer. Similarly, the royal courts of Europe were steeped in pomp and ceremony that symbolized and legitimized the sovereignty and power of monarchs over their subjects. European states created their own authority and communicated it through language and gestures derived from everyday life. Similarly, in America, European powers initiated colonial rule through ceremonies of possession—planting crosses, banners, and coats of arms; marching in processions; picking up dirt; drawing maps; and reading proclamations. The specific symbolic actions for instituting authority varied dramatically from nation to nation, for every European power defined possession, dominion, lordship, and sovereignty differently and experienced a distinctive lifestyle and language. These symbolic enactments of possession, however, were directed predominantly at the newcomers' own countrymen and political leaders in an effort to convince them of the legitimacy of their rule over the new territory and its inhabitants. Such rituals, while strange and incomprehensible to native onlookers, communicated legitimacy and power to countrymen back home and, though perhaps less clearly, to European rivals.

Source: Patricia Seed, *Ceremonies of Possession in Europe's Conquest of the New World, 1492–1640* (Cambridge, U.K. & New York: Cambridge University Press, 1995).

---

unintelligible, languages. Initial contacts undoubtedly involved the use of relatively crude gestures to convey basic information surrounding barter of material goods and regarding local landscapes and peoples. As the nature of contact changed and intensified, however, simplistic gestural systems had to be replaced by more sophisticated means of communicating abstract ideas and the subtleties of diplomacy and alliance. Sign language clearly evolved sufficiently to fill the need for a more advanced communication system on the southern plains. Much more common was the emergence of people knowledgeable in the language and customs of both groups, usually through intermarriage, captivity, slavery, or the intentional exchange of children as hostages and bilingual trainees. These individuals often served as translators and interpreters, facilitating communication at the highest, most complex levels. If interaction between the groups became regular, sustained, and stable, the groups sometimes came to share a common language, or lingua franca, in the sense of general mutual intelligibility among the population. After European contact the newcomers exploited these existing communication networks, and the development of intercultural communication between Europeans and Native Americans followed a similar pattern.

Sources:

Michael Coe, Dean Snow, and Elizabeth Benson, *Atlas of Ancient America* (New York & Oxford: Facts on File, 1986);

Ives Goddard, ed., *Handbook of North American Indians*, volume 17: *Languages* (Washington, D.C.: Smithsonian Institution, 1996);

Susan Wurtzburg and Lyle Campbell, "North American Indian Sign Language: Evidence of Its Existence before European Contact," *International Journal of American Linguistics*, 61 (April 1995): 153–167.

FIRST CONTACTS ALONG THE EAST COAST

Newfoundland Fisheries. The first Western Europeans to reach North America in the late fifteenth century may have been fishermen from Bristol in western England. Certainly Christopher Columbus spoke with Bristol fishermen and gathered information from them before sailing across the Atlantic for the first time in 1492. Drawn to the fish-laden waters off the Newfoundland coast, fishing fleets from the Atlantic ports of England, France, Spain, and Portugal sailed yearly in search of cod, the inexpensive "beef of the sea." Their cargo filled the bellies of Europe's armies, navies, and poor and stocked the tables of obedient Catholics on the 165 meatless days in the Church's liturgical calendar. By the early sixteenth century more than one hundred ships frequented Newfoundland's coastal bays and inlets, processing and drying their catch for shipment to European markets at the close of the season. The discovery of the rich fishing grounds of the Grand Banks in the 1530s only increased the traffic between America's North Atlantic coast and Europe. These regular seasonal visits to northeastern North America initiated the first sustained contacts between Europeans and the indigenous inhabitants of the region surrounding the Gulf of St. Lawrence.

The Basques. The Basques of southwestern France and the western Pyrenees of Spain were among the first

Native American petroglyphs inscribed on a boulder in Utah, 900–1700 A.D.

to frequent the fishing grounds of the North American coast. Well known as accomplished seafarers, whalers, and fishermen in medieval Europe, their shipbuilding techniques were among the most advanced in Europe. Whaling in the Gulf of Biscay was crucial to their economy as early as the eleventh century, and by the early fifteenth century they were apparently engaged in fishing and whaling in Icelandic waters. Basques reached Newfoundland and Canada in the first decades of the sixteenth century, making seasonal summer voyages for cod and frequently staying well into the winter for whaling. While French Basques focused their efforts on the cod fishery, those from Spain sent much larger ships for whaling. At the height of the Newfoundland trade in the sixteenth century twenty to thirty ships brought two thousand Basques to work out of the ports of Labrador and Newfoundland each season. Although they came to the area primarily for whales and cod, they also established a thriving trade with the local natives.

Sixteenth-century Trade. Most fishermen engaged in the cod fishery practiced "dry fishing," which required that the fresh catch be flayed and dried upon stages ashore before being packed for shipment. Many also brought along winter crews of boatbuilders and scaffold-men who remained in the area during the winter months preparing for the arrival of the next season's fish-

ing fleet. In addition nearly all European ships had to put ashore every few weeks for repairs and provisioning. If the arrival of large "floating islands" peopled by strangely dressed men did not sufficiently arouse native curiosity, their presence on shore certainly merited investigation, and a cautious exchange of goods and information—as well as the occasional arrow or musket ball—soon began. As familiarity grew, a regular trade in furs and European goods and foodstuffs was quickly established. Furs and hides made welcome additions to cargoes of cod and whale products for fishermen and merchants trying to maximize profits, particularly when they could be purchased with items of little value to Europeans. Most commonly mentioned as items desired by the Indians are metal tools and utensils, clothing, bread, ship's biscuits, liquor, and decorative trinkets and beads. Apparently, individual seamen unofficially conducted much of this early trade in furs, but by the mid sixteenth century fishing vessels regularly left Europe stocked with merchandise taken for the express purpose of trading with the natives. In the early seventeenth century French fishing crews were notorious for practically selling their ships out from under their captains in attempts to accumulate private cargoes of furs for sale in European markets on their return home.

JARGONS AND PIDGINS

Jargons and pidgins are languages that emerge in the special circumstances found during the early stages of intercultural contact. They arise as makeshift adaptations, usually in response to specific communication needs such as those surrounding trade. As a result most are short-lived, quickly replaced by true bilingualism if the contact continues and intensifies. Basically, a pidgin is a greatly reduced or simplified form of a language that is typically used between speakers of different languages who do not share a tradition of bilingualism. All areas of the base language are reduced: inflection is eliminated; vocabulary is limited; and pronunciation is simplified. Pidgins are also hybrid, or mixed, languages. While the grammar, syntax, and morphology (rules of word formation) may generally be a simplified version of one language, the lexicon, or vocabulary, often includes words and parts of words taken from all of the languages in contact. Ultimately, a true pidgin is not the native language of any of its speakers and usually is unintelligible to speakers of the languages from which it is derived; in other words, it must be learned. Three stages of pidginization can be distinguished. Jargons (nor-mally trade jargons) have very small vocabularies, almost no grammar, and are suitable for communication on only a very limited range of topics. Pidgins are jargons that have been fleshed out. They have rules of grammar and syntax and greatly expanded vocabularies, often consisting of loan words from the parent languages, and can be used to discuss almost any topic. Pidgins that become the native language of a speech community are called creoles. Europeans and native North Americans developed several pidgins during the sixteenth and seventeenth centuries, among them the Basque-Algonquian Pidgin used in Nova Scotia and Newfoundland; the Pidgin Unami Delaware used throughout the Hudson and Delaware Valleys; Pidgin Massachusetts, used among the Indians of southern New England; and Pidgin Virginia Algonquian, used by the early settlers of Virginia.

Sources: Ives Goddard, "The Delaware Jargon," in *New Sweden in America,* edited by Carol E. Hoffecker and others (Newark: University of Delaware Press, 1995), pp. 137–149;

John A. Holm, *Pidgins and Creoles,* volume 1: *Theory and Structure,* Cambridge Language Surveys (Cambridge, U.K. & New York: Cambridge University Press, 1988).

Basque-Indian Relations. Among the various European groups engaged in the sixteenth-century fishing and fur trades, the Basques seem to have enjoyed particularly good relations with the native inhabitants of the area surrounding the Gulf of St. Lawrence. In addition to trading, natives apparently occasionally worked side-by-side with Basque fishermen. Montagnais along the banks of the St. Lawrence River helped them "exploit the fish on the coast in exchange for a little cider and a piece of bread." Basque whalers found the Beothuks of Newfoundland "ready to assist them with great labour and patience" in the killing, cutting, and boiling of whales "without expectation of other reward, then [*sic*] a little bread, or some such small hire." Basques and Native Americans also apparently shared other common activities, including feasting and possibly playing games. According to several European sources, Basques also occasionally took natives home to Europe with them. Messamouet, a Micmac chief from the region east of the St. John River, visited Bayonne, a seaport in southwestern France just north of the Spanish border, sometime before 1580 as the houseguest of the French Basque mayor. Another Micmac chief claimed to have been baptized in Bayonne before 1611. Most of these sojourns were apparently voluntary and temporary and fostered rather than impeded the growth of a stable, friendly relationship between the Basques and the coastal inhabitants.

Basque-American Indian Pidgin. Trade between Europeans and native North Americans required communication. Finding themselves without a shared language, they first resorted to "body language" in the form of signs, gestures, and facial expressions. Since such corporeally demonstrative tongues are as open to cultural interpretation and influence as are spoken ones, misunderstandings no doubt occurred. For trade, which involved concrete objects, pointing, counting, and nodding probably sufficed most of the time. Similarly, facial expressions undoubtedly conveyed basic human emotions quite clearly. As contact intensified, however, more sophisticated methods were required to express ideas and abstractions less closely tied to the material world. Perhaps as a result of the particularly close relations between the Basques and the natives of the St. Lawrence area, Basque formed the basis of the oldest known trade language in eastern North America. The earliest allusion to the existence of this pidgin, which was used for more than a century, dates to 1542. According to Basque fishermen questioned in 1710, this Basque-American Indian pidgin was "composed of Basque and two different languages of the Indians," predominantly Micmac and Montagnais. The grammar of this language consisted of simplified Basque rules for word formation and syntax while the vocabulary, or lexicon, contained words from Basque, Portuguese, French, and several Algonquian languages. The first French settlers on the St. Lawrence

COASTAL ALGONQUIANS

European fishermen and explorers of the eastern North American coast encountered a great variety of indigenous peoples who spoke a babel of different languages. Most of these distinct tongues, however, belonged to just four or five language families, or groups of related languages: Eastern Algonquian, Iroquoian, Siouan-Catawba, Timucuan, and Muskogean. Along the coast and immediately inland, from the Canadian Maritimes to North Carolina, the native inhabitants spoke Eastern Algonquian languages. Consequently they are often referred to collectively as Coastal Algonquians. Although the languages of the Coastal Algonquians exhibit considerable diversity, each shared features with its immediate neighbors and often a certain amount of mutual intelligibility. In addition, neighboring groups often had cultural traits in common, which also fostered intergroup communication. The primary languages included within this eastern branch of the larger Algonquian family are Micmac (Canadian Maritimes); Maliseet-Passamaquoddy (western New Brunswick and eastern Maine); Etchemin (Maine coast between the Kennebec and St. John rivers); Eastern Abenaki (central and western Maine); Western Abenaki (probably the upper Connecticut River Valley); Massachusetts (southeastern New England coast and islands); Narragansett (southern Rhode Island); Mohegan-Pequot (Connecticut, east of the Connecticut River); Mahican or Mohican (upper Hudson River Valley); Munsee (western Long Island and southeastern New York); Unami (southern New Jersey and eastern Pennsylvania); Nanticoke (Chesapeake coast of Maryland); Powhatan (James and York River drainages in Virginia); and Carolina Algonquian (northeastern North Carolina). Once Europeans moved farther inland, they encountered other eastern language families, predominantly Iroquoian speakers in the northeast and Siouan-Catawba speakers in interior Virginia and North Carolina. In the Southeast the surviving evidence is less clear, but at least two language families have been identified: Timucuan in central and eastern Florida and Muskogean along the northeastern gulf coast of Florida, the interior of Alabama, northwestern Georgia, and eastern Louisiana.

Sources: Ives Goddard, ed., *Handbook of North American Indians*, volume 17: *Languages* (Washington, D.C.: Smithsonian Institution, 1996);

Bruce Trigger, ed., *Handbook of North American Indians*, volume 15: *Northeast* (Washington, D.C.: Smithsonian Institution, 1978).

during the early seventeenth century learned this pidgin from the natives and continued to employ it for trade for many years. Marc Lescarbot, who encountered the Micmacs in Acadia in the early years of the century, noted that in addition to "a language of their own, known only to themselves," they spoke to the French in "a language which is more familiar to us, with which much Basque is mingled." In fact, in Lescarbot's opinion, the language of the coast tribes was "half Basque." Another French observer, Jesuit missionary Paul Le Jeune, who worked among the Montagnais in the 1630s, reported that in studying their language he had discovered "a certain jargon between the French and the Savages, which is neither French nor Indian." To further confuse matters for this early linguist, "when the French use it, they think they are speaking the Indian tongue, and the Savages, in using it, think that they are speaking good French." The facts that the pidgin words *orignal* (moose) and *tabagie* (tobacco store) found their way into Québecois French and that a number of Canadian place-names have a Basque etymology are further indications that the early settlers used the pidgin. Such survivals were not one-sided, however, since two words of Basque origin, *atlai* (shirt) from Basque *atorra* and *elege* (king) from Basque *errege,* are still used in Micmac.

Native Middlemen. European trade goods, trade practices, and, apparently, variants of Basque pidgin spread down the coast of Maine and into the interior of North America along the St. Lawrence and Great Lakes waterways during the sixteenth century. Archaeologists have discovered metal tips from belaying pins, spiral brass earrings worn by Basque sailors, and ship's bolts and rigging rings on sixteenth-century Seneca sites on the southern shores of Lake Ontario, items apparently carried there by native travelers or traders long before Europeans penetrated the interior of the continent. By the early seventeenth century and probably before, Algonquian entrepreneurs bartered furs for European goods in the Gulf of St. Lawrence and in turn traded them for more furs along the coast of Maine. In 1580 English explorer John Walker landed in Penobscot Bay and took from an unattended building on shore more than two hundred dried moose hides. Such a large store concentrated in a single structure probably indicated that the hides were intended for trade with the Europeans fishing to the northward rather than for the local inhabitants. Twenty years later a member of explorer Bartholomew Gosnold's company recorded an encounter with several Micmacs off the coast of Cape Neddick, Maine. The party included "six Indians in a baske [Basque] shallop [whaling boat] with a mast and saile, an iron grapple, and a kettle of copper [who] came boldly aboard us, one of them apparrelled with a waistcoat and breeches of black serge [woolen cloth], made after our seafashion, hose and shoes on his feet." In addition to their European appearance and accoutrements these Indians "could name Placentia of the New foundland" and "spoke divers

A fanciful 1550 French map of the New World with pygmies attacking flamingoes while a unicorn stands in the foreground (British Library, London)

Christian words." During the next decade other explorers in the area recorded similar encounters with shallop-sailing Indians, clothed in bits and pieces of European apparel, speaking Basque pidgin, and desiring to barter their stores of skins for European food and trade goods. As these native middlemen carried European merchandise along indigenous trade routes, knowledge of the newcomers spread, laying the foundation for future intercultural encounters and communication along the eastern coast of North America.

Sources:

James Axtell, "At the Water's Edge: Trading in the Sixteenth Century," in his *After Columbus: Essays in the Ethnohistory of Colonial North America* (New York & Oxford: Oxford University Press, 1988), pp. 144–181;

Emerson W. Baker and others, eds., *American Beginnings: Exploration, Culture, and Cartography in the Land of Norumbega* (Lincoln: University of Nebraska Press, 1994);

Peter Bakker, "'The Language of the Coast Tribes Is Half Basque': A Basque-American Indian Pidgin in Use between Europeans and Native Americans in North America, ca. 1540–ca. 1640," *Anthropological Linguistics*, 31 (1989): 117–143;

Ives Goddard, ed., *Handbook of North American Indians*, volume 17: *Languages* (Washington, D.C.: Smithsonian Institution, 1996).

FIRST CONTACTS: THE EARLY EXPLORERS

Motives. During the fifteenth and sixteenth centuries European exploration was motivated primarily by economic necessity. The growing demand for the exotic and expensive luxury goods brought overland from Asia and increasing European dependence on Muslim and Venetian middlemen in this spice trade compelled western and northern merchants and monarchs to begin searching for alternate routes to the riches of the East. The Portuguese, strategically located on the Atlantic coast and drawing on a long history of maritime endeavors,

were first to begin the quest for an ocean passage to the Orient. They sailed down the west coast of Africa and eventually monopolized the eastern waterway to Asia. Portugal's success left its European neighbors with little choice but to look to the west for a water route to the Indies. Following in the wake of Christopher Columbus, sixteenth-century explorers came to North America with the overriding purpose of locating a Northwest Passage through the continent to the ocean beyond and then to the East Indies. Not until the seventeenth century did political, imperial, and religious aspirations or scientific curiosity play a significant role in motivating exploration and settlement of North America.

Early Communication. Most of the early explorers viewed North America largely as an obstacle to be overcome rather than a source of wealth or profit in its own right. Consequently they showed little, if any, interest in initiating trade with natives. Much more important to these European adventurers was knowledge about the new land: its harbors and waterways, resources and geography, flora and fauna, and native peoples. The latter were crucial to their search for profits, whether in the Far East or in North America, for only the indigenous inhabitants knew the land, how to travel through it, and what riches it had to offer. The collection of usable, trustworthy information required the establishment of reliable communication between natives and newcomers. In the absence of clear understanding, wishful thinking often took the place of actual translation in early explorers' accounts. Each new arrival created his own "silent rhetoric," but most found that, beyond the basics, ad hoc gestures and signs did not suffice. Since the explorers rarely stayed long in one place, quickly moving on to investigate the next section of coastline, these early con-

Euro-Americans and Indians brought not only different languages but also different cultural perceptions, expectations, meanings, and values to their encounters on the shores of North America. Once the focus of contact began to shift away from initial greetings and barter toward more intensive exchanges of goods and detailed information, both natives and newcomers found ad hoc gestures and even jargons and pidgins to be inadequate means of communication. The subtleties and complexities of the emerging relationship between the European explorers and America's indigenous inhabitants required more subtle and complex communication. The best solution, though not necessarily the easiest to achieve, was to train Indians or Europeans as interpreters—individuals who could speak both languages with some proficiency and who were at least familiar with the customs of each group. At the most basic level an interpreter had to command two languages, and even a rudimentary level of linguistic skill could be difficult to attain since Indian languages bore little syntactic, morphological, or phonological resemblance to European tongues. In addition, as interpreters translated and explained disparate languages and rituals infused with culturally based meanings and values, they acted as brokers, mediating the confrontation of European and Indian cultures. As cultural brokers, interpreters inhabited the cultural frontiers of North America. Of necessity the most accomplished became repositories of two or more cultures and used their multicultural knowledge and understanding to forge bonds across the cultural divide. By virtue of their specialized skills, these cultural intermediaries often gained prestige and influence in both worlds as long as they maintained the fine balance between the two worlds and performed satisfactorily. By the time permanent settlement began, neither the Europeans nor their native neighbors could safely do without interpreters.

Source: Nancy L. Hagedorn, "'A Friend to Go between Them': Interpreters among the Iroquois, 1664–1775," Ph.D. diss., College of William and Mary, 1995.

tacts remained haphazard and brief and rarely provided the opportunity for the development of jargons or pidgins. As the newcomers searched for alternative solutions, they quickly focused on native North Americans as potential interpreters.

Kidnapping. Following the example set by Christopher Columbus, many European explorers carried human booty home from the shores of North America. For some, contemplating an empty-handed return to their sponsors without news of gold, silver, or the coveted Northwest Passage, native slaves seemed the most readily available source of profit. Portuguese captain Gaspar Côrte-Real forcibly kidnapped some fifty Indians from the northeastern coast in 1501 and sent them to his sovereign in Lisbon, where they were judged to be "excellent for labor and the best slaves that have hitherto been obtained." Although the cargo pleased the king, it did Côrte-Real little good since his ship was lost before he could return home to reap his reward. Other explorers sent natives home as exotic curiosities, which, like other specimens of American flora and fauna, might amuse or impress European officials and investors. For many, however, kidnapping Indians fulfilled another goal: the bridging of the language chasm between native North Americans and Europeans. On board sailing vessels and in the capitals of Europe, Native American minds and tongues were soon bent to learning Old World languages and customs in hopes that they would become useful guides and intermediaries in their captors' further explorations of the American coast. More often than not, however, such plans backfired. Jacques Cartier, who captured two sons of Stadaconan chief Donnacona during his first voyage to the Gulf of St. Lawrence in 1534, found them of limited use during his subsequent two voyages. He took them to France, where they learned to speak French. On the return to Canada the following year they served as pilots and guides as the second expedition made its way inland toward their home village, Stadacona (Quebec), on the St. Lawrence River. Once reunited with family and friends on their home ground, however, they quickly began to show dissatisfaction with the French and were undoubtedly behind the deterioration of Cartier's relationship with the Stadaconans during the remainder of the expedition. Later explorers reaped even greater disasters from seeds they sowed in kidnapping Indians. In 1561 a Spanish crew captured a young Indian from the York River in Virginia. Nine years later, having received instruction in Spanish language and the Catholic religion, this Hispanicized native, Luis de Velasco, led a small group of Jesuits back to the land of his birth. Shortly after his arrival Don Luis ran off and only returned to lead an attack on the mission in which all the priests were killed. If Luis was, as many historians believe, Opechancanough, his anger against the European invaders smoldered for many years. In 1622 and 1644 Opechancanough led two devastating uprisings against the English colonists of early Virginia.

Native Americans in Europe. Native North Americans who found themselves cast upon European shores as living, breathing audiovisual aids for their captors' stories about the wonders of America learned a great deal more than new languages. As they were schooled in European language, manners, and religion, they also received some harsh lessons in European civility. The newcomers were exhibited as objects of curiosity before crowds of courtiers and commoners, who poked, prodded, laughed, and pointed at them. Once the novelty wore off, other concerns came to the fore, and the efforts of their hosts to civilize them began. Forced to abandon native hairstyles and dress, they spent much of their time in religious and linguistic instruction and rarely escaped the cramped, dirty, alien environment of European cities and towns. Far from home among strangers, undoubtedly uncomfortable and unhappy, and at the mercy of European diseases to which they had no immunity, many died and were buried in alien soil before they could return to their native land. The lessons their captors taught did not always have the desired effect. Exposure to the power, might, and wonders of European society did not seem to make native peoples more submissive to their betters or desirous of accepting civilization and its trappings. Yet those who survived and went home took valuable knowledge and skills with them which shaped the relationship between Europeans and Native Americans for decades to come.

Reciprocal Learning. Knowledge flowed both ways between native North American visitors to Europe and their hosts. The exhibition of Indians as exotic curiosities throughout the continent gave a broad spectrum of the European population their first glimpse of America and often left an indelible impression. The appearance of native North Americans was captured in portraits, which were copied in woodcuts and engravings that circulated widely in books and as broadsides. Tales of their homeland inspired songs, ballads, and books, which joined the growing literature of explorers' accounts during the sixteenth century. European interpretations of their clothing and culture were depicted in court pageants and tableaux. Fascination with America and the New World's hold on the European imagination rested largely on these early vicarious encounters. On a more practical level, as these exiled Indians received instruction in things European, they also provided their captors with valuable information about America and gave lessons in their native tongues. Both sides benefited and suffered as a result of the European practice of kidnapping native North Americans. Ultimately, however, the linguistic and cultural knowledge gained by each of the partners to this educational exchange laid the foundation for future advances in intercultural communication in eastern North America.

Sources:

James Axtell, "At the Water's Edge: Trading in the Sixteenth Century," in his *After Columbus: Essays in the Ethnohistory of Colonial North America* (New York & Oxford: Oxford University Press, 1988), pp. 144–181;

Axtell, "Babel of Tongues: Communicating with the Indians in Eastern North America," in *The Language Encounter in the Americas, 1492–1800,* edited by Edward G. Gray and Norman Fiering (Providence, R.I.: Berghahn Books, forthcoming);

Emerson W. Baker and others, eds., *American Beginnings: Exploration, Culture, and Cartography in the Land of Norumbega* (Lincoln: University of Nebraska Press, 1994);

David Beers Quinn, ed., *New American World,* volume 1: *America from Concept to Discovery. Early Exploration of North America* (New York: Arno Press & Hector Bye, 1979).

FIRST CONTACTS: PENETRATION OF THE INTERIOR

Early Voyages. The completion of the conquest of Mexico by Hernando Cortés spurred Spanish conquistadors to look elsewhere in the Americas for sources of wealth. Some were already exploring the Pacific coast of South America and would soon add the Incan Empire to Spain's dominions in the New World. For others North America seemed to hold more promise. During the late 1510s Spanish explorers mapped much of the eastern and southern coastline of the continent. In 1513 Juan Ponce de León scanned most of the eastern and southern coasts of Florida, and Alvarez de Pineda completed a survey of the Gulf Coast six years later. During the early 1520s the continent's outlines became even clearer as Estevâo Gomes sailed along the Newfoundland and New England coast beyond Cape Cod (1524–1525), and Pedro de Quejo mapped the southeastern coastline as far north as Delaware (1525). As knowledge of the edges of the continent increased, so did contact with the indigenous inhabitants and rumors of the riches to be found in the interior. In response to these rumors several unsuccessful expeditions attempted to penetrate the interior, and a Spanish colony was established on Sapelo Sound in present-day Georgia for a short time in 1526.

Narváez Expedition. Within two years of the failure of the colony on the Atlantic coast, Pánfilo de Narváez, a veteran conquistador, received a license from the Crown "to explore, conquer, and settle" lands along the northern Gulf Coast. The conquistador's second in command was Alvar Núñez Cabeza de Vaca. The Narváez expedition, which included some four hundred men, eighty horses, and several ships, was impressive when it arrived at Tampa Bay in April 1528, but it proved no more successful in achieving its ends than its predecessors. Within seven months the straggling survivors found themselves stranded without horses, weapons, ships, or food among the Karankawas of coastal Texas near Galveston Island. Having the advantages of numbers and familiarity with the region, the Karankawas enslaved the starving Spaniards.

Cabeza de Vaca and Estévanico. Among the enslaved survivors of the Narváez expedition was Cabeza de Vaca. Over the next several years most of his companions died or were scattered as their captors moved about the countryside, and he lost track of them. Eventually, Cabeza de Vaca gained a measure of freedom from his captors and began traveling about the interior as a shaman, or medi-

An Algonquian pictograph on a cliff overlooking Hegman Lake, Minnesota, circa 1600, of a man, moose, puma, and canoes

cine man, and merchant. In his travels he encountered many of the indigenous inhabitants of Texas and northern Mexico and learned their customs and languages. He also managed to locate three other survivors of the expedition: Alonso del Castillo, Andrés Dorantes, and Dorantes's Moorish slave, Estévanico. In 1534 the four comrades set out to return to Mexico. Their journey took them two years, during which time they learned six Indian languages. They also adopted, of necessity, native clothing and lifestyles and became familiar with Indian religions and customs. This knowledge allowed them to pose effectively as holy men, which garnered them food, lodging, and escorts to lead them from place to place as they made their way toward Spanish Mexico. In fact, when they finally encountered a Spanish party hunting slaves in northwestern Mexico in the spring of 1536, Cabeza de Vaca and Estévanico had become so thoroughly "Indian" that the two were hardly recognized as fellow Spaniards by the slavers. The four mounted Spaniards were "thunderstruck to see me so strangely dressed and in the company of Indians. They went on staring at me for a long space of time, so astonished that they could neither speak to me nor manage to ask me anything." Spanish reticence did not last long, however, and as word

of the survivors' six-year odyssey spread, enthusiasm for further exploration to the north again mounted.

Early Spanish-Indian Communication. Although the Narváez expedition was a failure, the intelligence gleaned from the survivors had a significant influence on Spanish penetration of the North American interior. Cabeza de Vaca and his companions provided Spanish colonial officials with the first reliable information about New Spain's northern frontier. They were the first Europeans to cross the continent north of Mexico and saw more of its inhabitants than any of their predecessors. The cultural and linguistic knowledge acquired by Cabeza de Vaca, and particularly Estévanico, also shaped future communication between the Spanish and native North Americans. In the earliest stages of contact the Spaniards followed precedents established in the conquest of Mexico. Local native inhabitants either voluntarily or through force became interpreters for the European invaders. Once communication was established, the conquistadors relied on the relatively widespread bilingualism of neighboring groups to form chains of translation, one speech sometimes passing through several interpreters and languages before emerging in a form understandable to its intended recipient. As they moved into the interior, the invaders added new native translators to their retinues as they entered new speech communities. The system worked quite well in Mesoamerica because of the widespread intelligibility of Nahuatl, the language of the Aztecs, as an indigenous lingua franca.

Spanish Borderlands. The situation in North America was more complex. Linguistic diversity was greater, and the less sedentary village and band cultures that predominated made the development of widespread precontact native linguae francae unlikely. Early European explorers of North America often brought accomplished linguists knowledgeable in a variety of European and Mediterranean languages with them in the vain hope that these men would prove useful as translators. After the conquest of Mexico, Spanish explorers often took Mesoamerican translators with them, expecting that Nahuatl or another Mesoamerican language might be familiar to native North Americans. When they failed to discover recognizable languages among native North Americans, kidnapping and forcibly educating native interpreters seemed the easiest solution. Lucas Vázquez de Ayllón, for example, took some Indian interpreters with him on his colonizing venture to South Carolina in 1526. One of them, Francisco de Chicora, had been among the natives captured by Spanish slavers at Winyah Bay in South Carolina in 1521 and transported to Spain. Francisco charmed the Spanish court with stories of his homeland, convincing them of its wealth and beauty. Once Ayllón's ships anchored in Winyah Bay, however, Francisco's true feelings about the Spaniards surfaced. As soon as he and the other Indians got ashore, they fled into the swamps. Cabeza de Vaca and Estévanico gave Spanish explorers of the interior an alternative to un-

INDIAN SLAVERY

For most Americans of European descent "slavery" means the use of African peoples as forced laborers in plantation agriculture. In the European system slaves were property that could be bought or sold, and they had economic value. For Native American peoples it can mean something quite different: the native practice of holding war captives, the European practice of capturing or purchasing Indians for use in plantation agriculture, or the similar use of African Americans by southern Indians for their own farms and plantations. For most native North Americans in precontact America, there was no equivalent to the European practice of slavery. War captives served social rather than economic purposes. Deaths through torture served as revenge and an emotional release for their captors. Adopted captives, on the other hand, enabled a bereaved family to replace members who had died or been killed. An adoptee became a member of the kinship network of the family and assumed all the privileges and obligations of any other birth relative. Those few captives who remained on the fringes of society, without benefit of adoption, were kinless. These individuals had an anomalous status in Indian societies, where kinship determined an individual's status and social role. These marginal individuals often performed menial tasks and were called "slaves" by early European observers. While they contributed to the economic survival of the group, however, they were not a capital investment; precontact native societies did not value or depend on slave labor. The arrival of Europeans in the sixteenth century changed the aboriginal institution of slavery. Spanish slave raiding on the Atlantic coast depleted indigenous populations and introduced peoples in the southeast to the European concept of slavery. Hernando de Soto impressed Indians into service as pack carriers. Later, European colonists in the southeast employed local Indians to capture other natives for sale as slaves and to capture and return runaway Africans. By the eighteenth century some American Indians in the southeast began to adopt European attitudes toward Africans and began to purchase them for use on native farms and plantations.

Source: Theda Purdue, "Slavery," *Encyclopedia of North American Indians*, edited by Frederick E. Hoxie (Boston & New York: Houghton Mifflin, 1996), pp. 596–598.

---

trustworthy native translators. They were, after all, from the Old World; they had been eyewitnesses to the lands and peoples north of Mexico; and they spoke a variety of their languages. Their abilities did not eliminate the need for native interpreters or the practice of kidnapping and training unwilling Indians for the post, but for a while Cabeza de Vaca and Estévanico could serve as a source of information and inspiration for those who followed.

Fray Marcos. In the autumn of 1538 Viceroy Antonio de Mendoza of Mexico sent the Franciscan Fray Marcos de Niza on a reconnaissance to the north. Mendoza hoped to convince one of the white Spanish survivors of the Narváez expedition to serve as Fray Marcos's guide, but all three declined. Instead Mendoza turned to the Moor, Estévanico, to accompany the Franciscan as guide and interpreter. Also with Fray Marcos were several Indians, probably Pimas, who had accompanied Cabeza de Vaca on his return to Mexico two years earlier. Fray Marcos was thus well equipped to gather information from the inhabitants of the interior. Estévanico's multilingual abilities were well known since he had often served as interpreter for Cabeza de Vaca's party. Estévanico was also adept in the use of the sign language that served as a kind of lingua franca among many of the Indians of the southern plains. As Cabeza de Vaca noted, though he and his companions had "passed through many and dissimilar tongues," the people "always understood us, and we them. We questioned them, and received their answers by signs, just as if they spoke our language and we theirs." In addition, the Pima language, according to Cabeza de Vaca, was in use from south of the Gila River stretching inland one thousand miles.

Coronado and De Soto. When Fray Marcos arrived back in Mexico City about one year later, he brought such favorable reports that Mendoza authorized an extensive exploration of the interior under the direction of Francisco Vásquez de Coronado. This time Fray Marcos served as guide since Estévanico had died during his service with the Franciscan. With the Franciscan's help and the backing of the viceroy, Coronado pushed far into the interior southwest between 1540 and 1542. About the same time another ambitious Spaniard, Hernando de Soto, penetrated much of the Southeast, relying on the aid of yet another survivor of the Narváez expedition, Juan Ortiz, whom de Soto found living among the Indians of Florida. Ortiz pierced the language barrier separating the expedition from the Apalachees and other Muskogean-speaking peoples. As de Soto noted, "This interpreter puts new life into us, for without him I know not what would become of us." So providential was Ortiz's appearance that the commander took it as a sign that God had "taken this enterprise in His especial keeping." By 1542 Spaniards had covered a vast portion of North America. While Cabeza de Vaca's and Estévanico's approach to the inhabitants of the interior differed greatly from that of Coronado or de Soto, the two survivors paved the way for their successors' deeper penetration of the continent. Circumstances forced Cabeza de Vaca and Estévanico to learn Indian languages and adopt native lifeways—to understand the Indians on their own terms. The Spanish under de Soto and Coronado, however, had little reason to adapt or learn. Instead, backed by large, well-equipped expeditions, they were able to use the knowledge and experience of Cabeza de Vaca and his companions to impose their will on the native North Americans they encountered. Neither de Soto's nor Coronado's expeditions returned triumphant, and a legacy of hatred and distrust lingered after them, but the information they gathered paved the way for more-permanent ventures in the Spanish borderlands.

Sources:

Alvar Núñez Cabeza de Vaca, *Castaways*, edited by Enrique Pupo-Walker, translated by Frances M. López-Morillas (Berkeley: University of California Press, 1993);

Carroll L. Riley, "Early Spanish-Indian Communication in the Greater Southwest," *New Mexico Historical Review*, 46 (1971): 285–314;

David J. Weber, *The Spanish Frontier in North America* (New Haven: Yale University Press, 1992).

FIRST CONTACTS: THE ROANOKE VENTURE

Roanoke. In March 1584 the English adventurer Sir Walter Raleigh obtained a patent to discover and settle lands in North America in the name of the English Crown. The voyages and colonizing experiments that followed during the next six years marked the first attempts of English men, women, and children to settle any part of the new continent. Although all their attempts failed, the colonists' experiences shaped later English ventures at Jamestown and elsewhere on the Atlantic coast in the early years of the seventeenth century. The first voyage in the spring of 1584 surveyed the coastal region along the Outer Banks of present-day North Carolina, selected a site for the proposed colony at Roanoke Island, and gathered information about the landscape and its inhabitants. The next two ventures, in 1585 and 1587, sent groups of English colonists to try to establish a toehold on the coast. The first colony at Roanoke had difficulty getting supplies from England and turned to the nearby Algonquians to provide them with needed corn instead. Relations quickly soured, and when ships arrived from England the following year, the survivors returned to England. The second attempt at colonization also failed. They, too, settled at Roanoke despite intentions to establish themselves farther north in the Chesapeake Bay among friendly Indians encountered by the earlier colonists on an exploratory trip to the north. After experiencing difficulties with food supplies and problems with the local Indians, the leader of the colony, John White, sailed for England to get additional provisions. Before he could return to Roanoke, all English shipping was halted and pressed into service against the Spanish Armada (1588). By the time White sailed back to the Outer Banks in 1590, the colonists had vanished.

Establishing Relations. Three groups of coastal Algonquians inhabited the area chosen by the English for the Roanoke Colony: the Roanokes, the Croatoans, and the Secotans. These Indians, like other Algonquian-speaking peoples farther north, had little in common with the European colonists who invaded their lands. Still, mutual curiosity and the desire to learn enabled the English to establish friendly relations with their non-European neighbors through the use of simple non-linguistic gestures, signs, and exchanges of goods. When the first exploratory expedition prepared to leave for home with the knowledge they had gained, they took steps to ensure future success. Following the practice of their predecessors farther north, they took two "lustie" young men along with them to England to be trained as interpreters: Wanchese (a Roanoke) and Manteo (a Croatoan).

Wanchese and Manteo. Wanchese and Manteo arrived in England in September 1584 and, in the following months, learned much about English society and culture. Thomas Harriot spent the winter with them teaching them English and learning some Algonquian from them. When the first colonizing voyage left England for Roanoke the following spring, Thomas Harriot, Wanchese, and Manteo accompanied the colonists. Harriot was placed in charge of making a study of the "naturall inhabitaunts," no doubt because of his familiarity with their language and the knowledge he had gained from his native charges. Both Wanchese and Manteo put their newfound expertise to good use, too, though each chose a different path. Wanchese reacted against English control and may have used his knowledge of their language and culture to undermine the colonists' position and contribute to the increasingly hostile relations between his people and the settlers. Manteo, on the other hand, took a more favorable view of the colonists. He attempted to maintain good relations between the Croatoans and the English and insisted on returning to England with the colonists when they abandoned their colony in 1586. One year later Manteo accompanied the final venture back to Roanoke, where John White appointed him the queen's deputy in Roanoke Island and Croatoan and baptized him a Christian.

Demise of the Colony. Despite the best efforts of Manteo, Thomas Harriot, and John White, maintaining good relations between the English and the Roanokes proved impossible. Long-term occupation of Indian land by the colonists brought tensions and strains. The English expected the Native Americans to continue producing food to support the colonists throughout the year though this placed a heavy burden on the Indians' cyclical, fragile economy. In the face of continual demands for food tempers flared, and hostility erupted on both sides. By the time the first colony left in June 1586, relations had soured beyond redemption. The next group of colonists posed an even greater threat to the local natives, for it contained not merely military men but also women and children. The implication was clear: the English intended to establish permanent homes within Roanoke territory. Under White's direction they hoped to become self-sufficient and avoid imposing on the Indians for food. In spite of his good intentions, however, a series of mishaps destroyed most of their provisions, and they were forced to look to the local inhabitants for assistance. Violence again broke out, and, at the time of White's departure, the colonists were making preparations to move north to Chesapeake Bay to settle among the friendlier Indians there. Whether they made it to their intended destination is unknown.

Sources:

Karen Ordahl Kupperman, *Roanoke: The Abandoned Colony* (Totowa, N.J.: Rowman & Allanheld, 1984);

David Beers Quinn, *Set Fair for Roanoke: Voyages and Colonies, 1584–1606* (Chapel Hill: University of North Carolina Press, 1984);

Quinn and Alison M. Quinn, eds., *The First Colonists: Documents on the Planting of the First English Settlements in North America, 1584–1590* (Raleigh: North Carolina Department of Cultural Resources, 1982).

THE TRANSFORMATION OF COMMUNICATION IN EARLY AMERICA

Effects of Contact. European contact permanently altered the nature of communication in early America. While the intruders often found existing native systems and networks of exchange essential in establishing communication with native North Americans, in adopting them for their own use they also manipulated and changed them. Initial short-term relations were relatively easy to establish by allowing human nature and natural mutual curiosity between disparate peoples to forge basic understandings and connections. Once encounters became prolonged, however, deeper, more sophisticated communication was necessary to navigate the potentially treacherous waters of coexistence and cooperation on common ground. The explorers needed accurate, trustworthy information in order to penetrate the continent and establish effective control over the newly discovered territories, resources, and peoples. Language, like the gun, horse, smallpox, and influenza, became a tool of conquest.

New Communication Methods. As the explorers' needs changed, so did the methods of communication. Ad hoc gestures proved inadequate for the expression of subtle, detailed, and abstract concepts, so the intruders sought other, more reliable techniques. In contacts focused on trade, jargons and pidgins often emerged to fill the requirement for better communication. Elsewhere, Europeans turned to kidnapping and the forcible education of natives as translators. Frequently such measures failed to achieve the desired results since coerced interpreters could prove untrustworthy, and many ran away at the first opportunity. Eventually Europeans who spent time among the Indians as captives or traders, as well as missionaries and natural philosophers interested in learning native languages, provided a supply of Europeans who could serve as interpreters.

New Speech Communities. The presence of explorers who traveled along the coasts and into the interior of North America transformed existing speech communities and created new ones. The spread of trade jargons and pidgins along native trade routes and into new areas forged larger speech communities as these contact languages served, at least briefly, as new linguae francae among both natives and Europeans. Where shared languages for trade and diplomacy existed, their use was geographically broadened by European explorers and traders who adopted them and carried them beyond established speech communities into the interior. Such was the case in the Southwest and the southern plains, where Pima, Nahuatl, and sign language served this purpose. Indian interpreters accompanying European explorers encountered new peoples and languages and established additional links and networks in the process. Finally, as warfare and disease ravaged native communities and bands, survivors regrouped or moved into new areas, forming new speech communities. In the process some native languages became extinct.

Tool of Conquest. As Europeans made ever greater inroads along the coasts of North America in the seventeenth and eighteenth centuries, their numbers grew, and their superior weaponry, arrogance, and diseases enabled them to begin imposing the use of European tongues on the natives in surrounding areas. English, French, Spanish, Portuguese, and Dutch, the languages of the American colonial societies, eventually supplanted native tongues as the languages of Indian relations. In addition, written language assumed greater authority than the spoken word in the literate culture that dominated the North American colonies, devaluing the spoken word and prompting interested colonial officials and missionaries to sponsor efforts to capture native languages in written form. By the mid nineteenth century many American Indian languages had disappeared from daily use.

Source:

Ives Goddard, ed., *Handbook of North American Indians*, volume 17: *Languages* (Washington, D. C.: Smithsonian Institution, 1996).

HEADLINE MAKERS

DONNACONA

1485?-1539?
STADACONAN LEADER

The Stadaconans. In July 1534, while exploring the Baie de Gaspé, the French explorer Jacques Cartier established the first European relations with Iroquoian-speaking Indians from the St. Lawrence River. Little is known about these native North Americans beyond Cartier's early descriptions. These St. Lawrence Iroquoians vanished from the historical record after the abandonment of Jean-François de La Roque de Roberval's colony in 1543. When Samuel de Champlain arrived in the St. Lawrence Valley in 1603, he found no trace of them. Still, with careful use of surviving accounts and archaeological evidence, it is possible to describe certain aspects of their culture. The St. Lawrence Iroquoians consisted of at least two distinct groups: the Hochelagans, who lived on Montreal Island, and the Stadaconans, who lived in the vicinity of present-day Quebec City. Although they spoke similar if not identical Iroquoian languages, the Hochelagans and Stadaconans differed in patterns of subsistence and settlement and appear to have been rivals for control of indigenous trade along the St. Lawrence. The Hochelagans lived in a large, palisaded village of about fifteen hundred people and relied quite heavily on agriculture, supplementing their diet seasonally by fishing at nearby camps. The Stadaconans, on the other hand, occupied seven to ten unfortified villages, sited along the north bank of the St. Lawrence upriver from the Ile d'Orléans, each numbering no more than five hundred inhabitants. Residing farther downriver and to the north, these Iroquoians followed a less sedentary lifestyle than their upriver neighbors and depended primarily on fishing, gathering, and hunting and only marginally on agriculture. During the winter male hunting parties were absent for long periods. In the summer large groups of men, women, and children moved down the river to the Gaspé Peninsula to fish for mackerel. It was one of these fishing parties that Jacques Cartier encountered in July 1534.

Encounter. Donnacona, leader of the Stadaconans, greeted Cartier and his crew with gaiety and merriment, but the cordial relationship soon soured. On 24 July Cartier erected a thirty-foot cross bearing the arms of France, rais-

ing Donnacona's suspicions that his "guests" apparently had more in mind than trade and friendship. Accompanied by three of his sons and his brother, Donnacona approached Cartier's ship in a canoe. He spoke vehemently to the Frenchman, "pointing to the cross and making the sign of the cross with two fingers; then he pointed to the land all around us, as if to say that all the land was his, and that we should not have planted the cross without his leave." To pacify them Cartier offered to give Donnacona an axe in exchange for the skin robe he was wearing. When the Indians moved closer to make the trade, the crew seized their canoe and forced the occupants aboard the ship.

Sons Kidnapped. Once aboard, Cartier attempted to reassure the Stadaconans. After a feast he explained that the cross was intended only as a landmark to aid the French in their intended return to the area. He also indicated that he wished to take two of Donnacona's sons, Domagaya and Taignoagny, with him to France, promising to return them on his next visit and bring iron wares and other goods for the Indians. Cartier then dressed Donnacona's two sons in "shirts and ribbons and in red caps, and put a little brass chain round the neck of each, at which they were greatly pleased." Outnumbered and outmaneuvered, Donnacona reluctantly agreed to the plan, and he, his brother, and remaining son were given a hatchet and two knives and departed from the French on seemingly good terms. Actually, such an exchange of children to serve as hostages for good behavior and to be trained as interpreters was not unfamiliar to Donnacona. Native Americans frequently exchanged the progeny of important leaders to cement alliances and secure good relations as well as to provide future interpreters. These hostages, however, were generally taken into the household of the respective chiefs and treated well. Donnacona may very well have had some misgivings about the care his sons would receive and the sincerity of Cartier's promise to return them to their friends and families.

Tales of Riches. On the voyage back to France, Domagaya and Taignoagny filled Cartier's head with tales of a great river that flowed from their country and of Saguenay, a kingdom from which they received copper. Whether the story was based in fact or legend, or merely a ploy to ensure the greedy Frenchman would want to return to their native country with them as guides, is unclear. Whatever their intentions, their enticing stories had the latter effect. Within nine months of their arrival in France, Domagaya and Taignoagny were on their way home to the St. Lawrence with Cartier. As they approached familiar territory, the two Stadaconans served as guides and pilots, imparting their knowledge of the coast and the St. Lawrence interior in the French they had learned during the months spent with Cartier.

Homecoming. On 7 September 1535 Cartier's ships anchored near the Ile d'Orléans, and he went ashore with Domagaya and Taignoagny to meet the inhabitants. Wary of these strangers and not at first recognizing their compatriots, who were probably attired in European dress, the Indians fled. Once Domagaya and Taignoagny revealed their identity, the local inhabitants returned, and the feasting and celebrations began. The next day Donnacona was reunited with his sons and renewed his acquaintance with Cartier. Once the courtesies were disposed of, Cartier became eager to visit Hochelaga and Saguenay, of which Domagaya and Taignoagny had told him and to which they had promised to guide him. Both seem reluctant to fulfill their pledge, however, now that they were back among family and friends. Their father, anxious to preserve his privileged position as intermediary between the French and the Indians farther upriver, had no desire to help Cartier make direct contact with the Hochelagans. Consequently the three conceived a plan to protect their interests while maintaining good relations with the Europeans.

The Plan. As Cartier's preparations for a trip upriver continued, Taignoagny informed him that he would not accompany the party because Donnacona was angry about the proposed expedition. The next day the chief himself appeared and offered Cartier a little girl and two boys (a niece and sons of Donnacona). Acting as interpreter, Taignoagny indicated that Donnacona intended them as presents on the condition that Cartier did not go to Hochelaga. Domagaya then intervened, saying that the children were instead given "out of pure affection and in sign of alliance" and offering to accompany Cartier. After a heated exchange between the brothers—which Cartier was unable to understand—Cartier accepted the children and presented Donnacona with two swords and a brass bowl. Apparently Domagaya intended to pretend to side with Cartier and salvage the relationship while leaving Taignoagny free to spread rumors and stir up trouble behind the scenes. The next day the brothers revealed their true intentions by staging a demonstration of witchcraft and relating evil portents about Cartier's proposed journey in another attempt to dissuade him from going. When Carter remained undaunted, Donnacona made one last try at resistance, offering to send both guides if Cartier would leave a hostage at Stadacona, but Cartier refused to compromise. When the explorers sailed upriver, none of the Stadaconans went along; Cartier no longer trusted them. After a brief but cordial visit to Hochelaga, Cartier returned to his anchorage near Stadacona and proceeded to build a fort.

Relations Deteriorate. Cartier's refusal to follow Donnacona's wishes, along with his overtly hostile actions on his return, permanently ended friendly relations with the Stadaconans. The Indians tried to obtain the return of their three children but secured the escape of only the little girl, further angering Cartier. Having second thoughts about antagonizing the Frenchman, they made a fresh approach and cordial, though tense, relations were restored during the winter. The change probably resulted at least in part from the serious hardships the French suffered during the long, severe Canadian winter. The tables were temporarily turned as Cartier found himself playing out a bluff to hide the Europeans' weakened, vulnerable condition from the Stadaconans; his company was in dire straits. Once spring arrived, however, relations again deteriorated, and mutual distrust revived. Donnacona and the other Stadaconans began to avoid the French, and, on one occasion, Donnacona feigned sickness to avoid meeting with Cartier.

Kidnapped Again. As Cartier prepared to depart again for France, he learned that an internal dispute had erupted among the Stadaconans and that an Indian named Agona headed the opposition against Donnacona. Playing on Donnacona's weakness, Cartier offered to take the recalcitrant Iroquoian with him to Newfoundland and leave him stranded there on an island. The Stadaconan chief would have preferred that Agona be taken to France, but Cartier lied and told Donnacona the French king had forbidden him to take any adult natives back to Europe. Having lulled Donnacona into a false sense of security, Cartier seized his opportunity to remove the troublesome, untrustworthy chief and his leading men and replace them with the potentially more amenable Agona and his supporters. Cartier invited the Stadaconans to a feast, and when Donnacona, Domagaya, Taignoagny, and the headmen appeared at the fort, the French seized them, scattering the other Indians "like sheep before a wolf." When Cartier sailed for France, he took ten captive Iroquoians with him: old chief Donnacona, his two sons, three other headmen, the little girl and two little boys given to him by Donnacona, and a little girl he had received from another chief upriver. None of the Iroquoians ever saw their homeland again. In France, Donnacona had an audience with the king, but as time passed and Cartier made plans to return to Canada, it became clear that the Frenchman had no intention of taking the Stadaconans with him as promised. The ten captives lived at the king's expense after their arrival in France in 1536. Three males were baptized in March 1539, possibly as they lay dying. About this time Donnacona disappears from the records. According to one account he spoke French and was a Christian at the time of his death. By the spring of 1541 all were dead but one little girl; she apparently never returned to Canada, and what became of her is unknown.

Sources:

H. P. Biggar, ed., *The Voyages of Jacques Cartier*, Publications of the Public Archives of Canada, no. 11 (Ottawa: F. A. Acland, 1924);

Bruce G. Trigger and James F. Pendergast, "Saint Lawrence Iroquoians," in *Handbook of North American Indians*, volume 15: *Northeast*, edited by Bruce G. Trigger (Washington, D.C.: Smithsonian Institution, 1978), pp. 357–361;

Marcel Trudel, *The Beginnings of New France, 1524–1663*, The Canadian Centenary Series (Toronto: McClelland & Stewart, 1973).

ESTÉVANICO THE MOOR

1500?-1539
SPANISH SLAVE, EXPLORER, AND INTERPRETER

Early Life. Estévanico the Moor was born at the beginning of the sixteenth century in the small town of Azamor (today Azemmur) on Morocco's western coast. Raised in the Islamic world of northwestern Africa, at some point in his young life the black Moor was taken from his homeland and transported to Christian Spain as a slave. He might have been captured by slave raiders who worked the African coast or been taken captive in one of the military clashes between Spain and Morocco that followed the final reconquest of Spain from the Moors in 1492. He became nominally Christian under the tutelage of his Spanish owners and was baptized and given the name "Estévanico." By 1527 he was in the Caribbean as the property of Andrés Dorantes, commander of a company of infantry in the expeditionary force being formed to accompany Pánfilo de Narváez on his exploration of the northern Gulf Coast.

The Narváez Expedition. As the slave of Dorantes, Estévanico's initial duties on the Narváez expedition probably involved acting as the personal servant of his master, and Cabeza de Vaca makes little mention of him during the early months. Once the shipwrecked survivors of the disastrous expedition washed ashore near Galveston Island in the fall of 1528, however, Estévanico began to assume a more prominent role. By the following spring only sixteen of the eighty men cast ashore remained alive on their "island of misfortune," among them Cabeza de Vaca, Alonso del Castillo, Andrés Dorantes, and Estévanico. In April 1529 Dorantes, Estévanico, Castillo, and ten others crossed to the mainland, leaving behind Cabeza de Vaca and two others who were ill. On the mainland they fell into the hands of the hostile Karankawas and were enslaved. Within eighteen months all but Dorantes, Estévanico, and Castillo had died from hard labor, exhausting travel, and harsh treatment by their captors.

Reunion. In the spring of 1533 an Indian informed the three captives that he had heard news of another white man living with a neighboring band, and shortly thereafter they were reunited with Cabeza de Vaca. Dorantes and his companions were "very astonished" to see the leader they had left ailing on the island years before, "for they had thought me dead for many a day," remembered Cabeza de Vaca. "That day was one of the happiest we had had in our lives." Together again, the four began planning their escape to Mexico. While awaiting a suitable opportunity, Dorantes and Cabeza de Vaca became slaves of the same family while Estévanico and Castillo were traded to a neighboring band. After some months apart the four again met and made good their escape. On their long route to Mexico the intrepid, resourceful travelers made good use of the knowledge and talents each had acquired during their ordeal. Cabeza de Vaca had traveled extensively as a trader and healer and had garnered considerable knowledge of the natives' customs and languages. They assumed the role of healers, or medicine men, and as their fame spread, the Indians welcomed them and treated them kindly. The three Christians usually posed as the principal shamans, and Estévanico acted as their interpreter and go-between. This role, though subordinate, suited the Moor, who apparently had an easygoing manner and an aptitude for languages. He "talked with them constantly, found out about the ways we wanted to go and what towns there were and the things we wished to know." In addition to spoken language, Estévanico had also mastered their sign language, for as Cabeza de Vaca recalled, "even though we knew six languages we could not make use of them everywhere." Eventually the wayfarers reached Culiacán on Mexico's west coast, where Spanish officials welcomed them warmly.

Fray Marcos. As news of the survivors' adventures spread throughout New Spain, officials began planning further explorations of the region to the north. In 1538 the viceroy of Mexico, Antonio de Mendoza, organized a reconnaissance mission under Fray Marcos de Niza, a Franciscan brother. Mendoza hoped to convince Cabeza de Vaca, Castillo, or Dorantes to assist the expedition as guide, but when they refused, he settled on Estévanico instead. Also among the group were a number of the Indians who had accompanied the four survivors to Mexico two years earlier. Once the party passed beyond the reach of the Spanish military and entered "unknown" territory, Estévanico began to take on a more prominent role, much to the chagrin of Fray Marcos. Both the territory and the people were familiar to Estévanico, as he was to them. The Moor became the de facto leader of the expedition, talking and negotiating with the natives and providing information and advice to his Franciscan "masters."

Franciscans. As Estévanico moved among the Indians, he acquired considerable personal baggage and a large entourage suitable for the leader of an expedition. The Moor acquired a harem of native girls, who followed in his wake to the consternation of the friars, and two greyhounds accompanied him everywhere. He adorned himself with clusters of bright feathers and wore a crown of plumes on his head. Small bells fastened around his ankles chimed as he walked, and coral and turquoise ornaments presented to him by the Indians decorated his chest. Described as a large, strong man, Estévanico must have made an impressive sight, particularly in comparison to the frugal clothing and effects of the Franciscans. Although Fray Marcos was honored as the emissary of the Spaniard's God, Estévanico received much more attention and willingly joined in native ceremonies and festivities. Not surprisingly, the Moor "did not get along well with the friars because he took the women that were given him and collected turquoises" and other goods. The Indians got along better with Estévanico because they had seen him before and because he seemed to accept them and understand them.

Death. Probably because of his exasperation with the Moorish guide, Fray Marcos decided to send Estévanico on ahead of the main body in the spring of 1539 "to see whether, by that route, information could be obtained of what we were seeking." Fray Marcos ordered Estévanico to go no more than 150 miles, and if he learned of "some inhabited and rich country" to stay put and send word. Within four days Estévanico sent a messenger with news that he had met people who told him of seven great cities to the north. Fray Marcos sent word to the coast and waited for additional information. By the time the Franciscan moved out to rejoin Estévanico, the Moor had already advanced. For more than two weeks Fray Marcos chased his disobedient guide. Although declining to await the rest of the expedition, Estévanico did prepare the natives along his route for the Franciscans' arrival, and Indians welcomed the friars warmly when they appeared. Word of Estévanico continued to filter back to Fray Marcos. He was apparently still hot on the trail of the seven magnificent cities and had acquired an entourage of more than three hundred Indians who traveled with him. By this time Estévanico had entered unknown territory and had to rely on his Indian escorts. As Estévanico's party approached the first Zuni village, which he called Cíbola, the confident Moor followed his normal procedure and sent messengers ahead to tell of his arrival. The Zunis did not react as expected; instead of welcoming the traveler, they admonished him to stay away or be killed. Unfortunately, Estévanico ignored their warning. When he entered the pueblo, he and his entire escort were confined without food until the next day, when most were killed. Word of Estévanico's demise was carried back to Fray Marcos by a few of the survivors. The Franciscan prudently declined risking his own life and returned to Mexico with news of Estévanico's discovery. The following year Fray Marcos served as Francisco Vásquez de Coronado's guide on a renewed quest for the Seven Golden Cities of Cíbola.

Sources:

Anne B. Allen, "Estévanico the Moor," *American History* (August 1997): 36–41;

Alvar Núñez Cabeza de Vaca, *Castaways*, edited by Enrique Pupo-Walker, translated by Frances M. López-Morillas (Berkeley: University of California Press, 1993);

John Upton Terrell, *Estevanico the Black*, Westernlore Great West and Indian Series XXXVI (Los Angeles: Westernlore Press, 1968).

MESSAMOUET

?-1610?
SOURIQUOIS HEADMAN

The Souriquois. Among the native North American groups encountered by early European fishermen in the Gulf of St. Lawrence were the Micmacs of Nova Scotia and New Brunswick. The Basques developed a particularly close relationship with these Indians, whaling, fishing, and trading with them during the yearly visits to the Newfoundland fishing grounds. One result of Basque interaction with the Micmacs was the development of a Basque-based pidgin that spread throughout the Gulf of St. Lawrence and down the coast of Maine. The French, who learned the pidgin and used it to communicate and trade with the inhabitants of the area, came to call the Micmacs the Souriquois, apparently adopting as the Indians' name the pidgin word for the trade language. The term came from the Basque *zurikoa* (pronounced "surikoa") meaning "that of the whites." It may also refer to the Souris River in New Brunswick where the Basques had a trading place, in which case the *-koa* ending would be a Basque suffix denoting geographic origin and giving the word the meaning "people from Souris." By the turn of the seventeenth century the Souriquois were heavily engaged in a brisk though short-lived trade in furs and European goods between the Gulf of St. Lawrence and the Maine coast.

Messamouet Visits France. The Basques sometimes took their Micmac or Montagnais trading partners back to Europe with them at the end of the fishing season. Invitations were generally extended to chiefs or other influential natives, presumably to forge closer trading relationships and increase native cooperation with the French Basques in the Gulf of St. Lawrence. At least some of the Indians thus favored willingly accepted the opportunity to visit the foreigners' homeland. Sometime during the third quarter of the sixteenth century Messamouet, a sagamore, or headman, of the Souriquois living at La Have on Nova Scotia's southern coast, embraced his chance to see the Old World and accompanied some French Basques returning to Bayonne, a seaport in southwestern France. Little is known about Messamouet's sojourn among the Basques, except that he "stayed at the house of M. de Grandmont, Mayor of Bayonne," which places his visit sometime before Grandmont's death in 1580. Messamouet may, in fact, have been one of the first natives from the area to visit France. His later activities in northeastern North America make it clear that he observed and absorbed something about European commercial practices and seamanship from his hosts. He may also have adopted certain habits of European dress at this time.

Champlain. Messamouet reappears in the historical record in Samuel de Champlain's record of his third voyage down the New England coast in September 1605. Just off the mouth of the Ste. Croix River, Champlain encountered several Indians, among whom he identified Messamouet and Secoudon, an Etchemin sagamore from Ouigoudi, at the mouth of the St. John River. When Champlain sailed from Ste. Croix, the two Indians, in their own boat, accompanied the French as far as Saco, Maine, "where they wished to go to make an alliance with those of that country by offering them sundry presents." At Saco, Messamouet met with Onemechin of Saco and Marchin of Casco Bay, both chiefs of the local Armouchiquois Indians. He gave Onemechin "kettles, axes, knives and other articles," receiving Indian corn, squash, and Brazilian beans in return. According to Champlain, the Souriquois chief left "much displeased" because he had not been "suitably repaid" for his gifts. The French captain feared that Messamouet intended to make war on the Armouchiquois before long, "for these people give only with the idea of receiving something."

Fur Trade. Marc Lescarbot's account of Jean de Biencourt, sieur de Poutrincourt's voyage down the New England coast from Port Royal, Nova Scotia, in the fall of 1606 throws a different light on Messamouet's activities in Maine and on the reasons for his dissatisfaction with Onemechin the year before. Upon their arrival at the Saco River, Marchin and Onemechin brought Poutrincourt a Souriquois prisoner, "their enemy whom they had captured in the river at Port La Have." A couple of hours later Messamouet and his partner Secoudon arrived in a sailing shallop with "much merchandise, gained by barter with the French, which they came thither to sell," including kettles of all sizes, hatchets, knives, dresses, capes, red jackets, peas, beans, and biscuits worth more than three hundred crowns (a type of coin) in cash. While the two entrepreneurs were displaying their wares, Onemechin's Indians arrived in full war regalia, which, according to Lescarbot, was their custom when they wished "to appear at their best." The next hour was occupied by Messamouet's harangue to the assembled Armouchiquois, recounting their past "friendly intercourse together" and requesting that they join the Souriquois and Etchemin to work with the French. The advantages to be gained, according to Messamouet, were significant. The alliance would allow the Souriquois "in future to bring merchandise to them and to aid them with their resources, whereof he knew" because of his sojourn in Bayonne twenty-five years before. At the conclusion of his speech Messamouet threw all of the goods into Onemechin's canoe, as if making him a present of them as a sign of friendship.

War. Messamouet's attempt to reestablish friendly relations and trade with the Armouchiquois failed. The following day Onemechin rejected the Souriquois offer by neglecting to give Messamouet a similar speech and presents in return. As Lescarbot explained, the Indians had the "noble trait" of giving freely, but it was done "with the hope of receiving some honourable return." Again disappointed in his aspirations for trade and alliance on the western coast of Maine, Messamouet began planning revenge. That winter, tension rose between the Souriquois, their allies the Etchemins, and the Armouchiquois. In June 1607 a large party of Souriquois under the direction of the chief sagamore of the eastern Souriquois, Membertou, gathered at Port Royal in order to go to war against their foes to the southwest. Messamouet participated in the raid as one of Membertou's war captains. In early August they returned from their raid at Saco, where they killed twenty Armouchiquois, among them Onemechin and Marchin.

Inroads on Trade. In their dealings with the Souriquois of western coastal Maine, Messamouet and his Etchemin ally Secoudon employed European shallops, presented themselves in European clothing, and exhibited quasi-European attitudes toward the exchange of goods. Messamouet was in an excellent position to exploit such techniques, having been exposed to them firsthand many years earlier in Bayonne. His long-standing close ties with the French Basques also apparently enabled him to communicate more easily with the French and quickly establish cordial relations with Champlain and Poutrincourt. The arrival of the French in Nova Scotia and on the New England coast was a double-edged sword, however. On one hand, they provided a ready source of supply for the European goods Messamouet desired. By taking advantage of his favorable location near the French and controlling the flow of European trade goods down the New England coast, he could increase Souriquois power over the Armouchiquois. At the same time he could expand his influence with the French by serving as the conduit for the furs they coveted. On the other hand, the French seemed determined to explore the coast themselves and to establish direct trade with Messamouet's customers, undermining his position and cutting him out of the trade. During the first half of the seventeenth century Messamouet and other native middlemen steadily lost ground to European traders in New England. Because of the region's proximity to the French, this process occurred much more rapidly in the Gulf of Maine. When Captain John Smith explored the Maine coast in 1614, he reported that the French already dominated the trade in the eastern part of the gulf. Direct French contact also brought the ravages of European diseases. In 1610 an epidemic among the Souriquois at La Have claimed sixty persons, "the great part of those who lived there." Messamouet may have died in this epidemic; he is not mentioned after 1607.

Sources:

Peter Bakker, "'The Language of the Coastal Tribes Is Half Basque': A Basque-American Indian Pidgin in Use between Europeans and Native Americans in North America, ca. 1540–ca. 1640," *Anthropological Linguistics*, 31 (1989): 117–147;

Bruce J. Bourque and Ruth H. Whitehead, "Trade and Alliances in the Contact Period," in *American Beginnings: Exploration, Culture, and Cartography in the Land of Norumbega*, edited by Emerson W. Baker and others (Lincoln: University of Nebraska Press, 1994), pp. 131–147;

Marc Lescarbot, *The History of New France*, translated and edited by W. L. Grant, introduction by H. P. Biggar, 3 volumes (Toronto: The Champlain Society, 1907–1914;

David Beers Quinn, ed., *New American World*, volume 4: *Newfoundland from Fishery to Colony. Northwest Passage Searches* (New York: Arno Press, 1979).

PUBLICATIONS

Alvar Núñez Cabeza de Vaca, *Castaways: The Narrative of Alvar Núñez Cabeza de Vaca,* edited by Enrique Pupo-Walker, translated by Frances M. López-Morillas (Berkeley: University of California Press, 1993)—a translation of Cabeza de Vaca's original narrative of the 1528 Narváez expedition and his experiences among the natives of the Southwest;

Jacques Cartier, *The Voyages of Jacques Cartier: Published from the Originals with Translations, Notes, and Appendices,* edited by H. P. Biggar (Ottawa: F. A. Acland, 1924)—includes annotated accounts of all three of Cartier's voyages. The Frenchman was the first European to explore the St. Lawrence River Valley, and his texts include the earliest descriptions of the St. Lawrence Iroquoians, who had vanished by the time of Samuel de Champlain's arrival some seventy years later;

Cartier, *Two Navigations to Newe Fraunce,* The English Experience, no. 718 (Amsterdam: Theatrum Orbis Terrarum; reprinted, Norwood, N.J.: W. J. Johnson, 1975)—a facsimile reprint of the original English edition (1580) of Cartier's accounts of his first two voyages;

Samuel de Champlain, *Voyages of Samuel de Champlain, 1604–1618,* edited by W. L. Grant, Original Narratives of Early American History (New York: Scribner's, 1907)—this contains the accounts of Frenchman Samuel de Champlain's voyages to plant a French colony in the early seventeenth century, describing the local inhabitants of the St. Lawrence and New England coastal region and their relations with the French;

Lawrence A. Clayton, Vernon James Knight Jr., and Edward C. Moore, eds., *The De Soto Chronicles: The Expedition of Hernando de Soto to North America in 1539–1543,* 2 volumes (Tuscaloosa: University of Alabama Press, 1993)—includes firsthand narratives of the de Soto expedition, which contain accounts of the interior southeast and the native peoples dwelling there;

Richard Hakluyt, *The Principal Navigations, Voiages and Discoveries of the English Nation [1589],* edited by David B. Quinn and Raleigh A. Skelton, 2 volumes (Cambridge: Cambridge University Press, 1965)—a facsimile edition of the original publication by the foremost promoter of English colonization in America, it contains the collected accounts of many sixteenth-century North American voyages;

Marc Lescarbot, *The History of New France,* translated by W. L. Grant, 3 volumes (Toronto: Champlain Society, 1907–1914)—a translation of the expanded 1618 Paris edition of Lescarbot's 1609 account of Acadia. It is the earliest published history of New France and includes a great deal of information about sixteenth-century French ventures in the Gulf of St. Lawrence region and the interactions with the native peoples there;

Lescarbot, *Nova Francia, or a Description of Acadia [1609],* edited by Henry P. Biggar (London: George Routledge & Sons, 1928)—the first edition of Lescarbot's account of the voyages of Sieur de Monts and Jean de Biencourt de Poutrincourt to Acadia (Nova Scotia and New Brunswick) in 1606–1607. Lescarbot accompanied de Poutrincourt and was an eyewitness to many of the events and peoples depicted;

Samuel Purchas, *Hakluytus posthumus, or, Purchas his Pilgrimes: contayning a history of the world in sea voyages and lande travells by Englishmen and others,* 20 volumes (Glasgow: J. MacLehose & Sons, 1905–1907)—reprint edition of Purchas's 1625 edition, which contains many early exploration and travel narratives, several of them taken from Hakluyt. Several of them deal with the fifteenth- and sixteenth-century European voyages to North America;

David Beers Quinn, ed., *New American World: A Documentary History of North America to 1612* (New York: Arno Press, 1979)—a five-volume compilation of contemporary fifteenth-, sixteenth-, and early-seventeenth-century publications, letters, and documents describing all aspects of European exploration and colonization, from the first conceptualization of America to the planting of the first colonies. Excellent coverage of all of North America, including the Northeast, Southeast, Gulf Coast, and Spanish borderlands and interior southwest.

A 1593 plan of the fort at St. Augustine, Florida (Archives of the Indies, Seville)

C H A P T E R   F I V E

EDUCATION

by JAMES CARSON

CONTENTS

CHRONOLOGY
104

OVERVIEW
106

Sidebars and tables are listed in italics.

TOPICS IN THE NEWS

America before Columbus......106
European Scholarship and the
 Exploration of the New
 World...................108
Scholasticism and Humanism.....109
New World Colonies 110
Franciscans 111
Jesuits.......................111

PUBLICATIONS
114

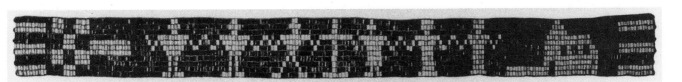

A 1683 Huron wampum belt commemorating the erection of the first Jesuit church on tribal lands (McCord Museum, Notman Photographic Archives, University of New Mexico, Albuquerque)

IMPORTANT EVENTS TO 1600

1486

• King Ferdinand of Aragon and Pope Innocent VIII sign the *Real Patronato* treaty, which makes Ferdinand the patron of Catholicism abroad.

1493

• Pope Alexander VI issues the bull (edict) *Inter Catera Divinae,* which declares that Indians are capable of converting to Christianity.

1498

• The University of Alcalá de Henares is founded in Spain.

1504

• In the bull *Illius fulciti praesidio* Pope Julius II asserts that the Roman Catholic Church will Christianize the Indians.

1530

• Peter Martyr's *De Orbe Novo* and Francisco López de Gómara's *Historia general* are published.

1537

• Two papal bulls, *Sublimis Deus* and *Veritas ipsa,* reaffirm the principles of *Inter Cetera Divinae* and *Illius fulciti praesidio.*

1539

• The College of Santa Cruz de Tlaltelolco is founded in Mexico to educate Indian men for the clergy.

1555

• Richard Eden's book *Decades of the Newe Worlde* is published in England.

1556

• André Thevet's book *La France Antarctique* is published in France.

1565

• The Jesuits begin to build missions in Florida.

1572
- The Guale chiefdom revolts against the Jesuits, and the Crown withdraws them from Florida.

1573
- Franciscan missionaries arrive in Florida to help pacify and convert to Roman Catholicism the region's native population.

1582
- Richard Hakluyt's books *Divers Voyages* and *Principall Navigations . . . of the English Nation* are published in England.

John White's *A Camp-Fire Ceremony,* 1585–1587

OVERVIEW

Native Americans. In October 1492 Christopher Columbus landed on an island he named San Salvador and set in motion the creation of the New World. How Native Americans educated themselves and their children before his arrival is difficult to say. In the absence of sufficient archaeological evidence scholars have attempted to piece together how prehistoric Americans taught their children by assuming that the practices used in the centuries after Columbus were similar to the ones used before. This method is problematic because it does not take into account the cultural discontinuity that resulted from the devastating epidemics spread by European explorers and settlers.

The Renaissance. European explorers comprehended and explained what they saw and the people they met in North America in terms of their own intellectual and educational traditions. The years of the fifteenth and sixteenth centuries were part of the Renaissance, a general movement across Europe that affected everything from the arts to politics to religion. Although the encounter with the New World forced European scholars to revise what they had known before with what they learned afterward, it nevertheless took several centuries for the importance of Columbus's discovery to make its full impact on European scholarship.

European Education in America. Upon their arrival in North America, Spanish, French, and English colonial officials and settlers attempted to replicate the social structures and political systems that had formed their home societies. The French and English, however, were unable to found permanent colonies in North America before 1600. French settlements in present-day Florida and Canada lasted less than a year, and the English experiment on Roanoke Island in present-day North Carolina failed twice. Without colonies neither power faced the need to educate colonists and their children, nor, for that matter, did they have to educate Native American populations that might have threatened their interests. The Spanish, however, founded two colonies that lasted beyond 1600, one in present-day Florida and the other in present-day New Mexico. As part of Spanish imperial policy the Crown sent out missionaries to convert the Indians to Catholicism and to subjugate them politically. Education ranked among the missionaries' tasks, and they opened schools to educate Indians in the new faith as well as in the various technological and social skills required for survival in a Spanish society. During the latter decades of the 1500s Franciscan missionaries made a strong start in this direction in Florida, but their counterparts in the Southwest did not open their first missions until 1598.

TOPICS IN THE NEWS

AMERICA BEFORE COLUMBUS

Early Prehistory. More than forty thousand years ago the Paleo-Indians began migrating into North America across the great land bridge that connected the continent to Asia. How they taught their children the skills necessary for survival in the Ice Age environment is unknown.

Based on studies of ancient stone tools, refuse sites, and skeletons, archaeologists have forwarded several suggestions about the kind of culture the earliest immigrants had. It is fairly certain, for example, that men and perhaps women hunted in large groups mammals such as mammoths and giant sloths. Extending such inferences to the care and rearing of children, however, is quite difficult.

Archaic America. Over time changes in the climate of North America and improvements in Paleo-Indian hunting skills decimated the continent's large mammal population. In the absence of big-game animals, Paleo-Indian groups had to adapt to the various local environments across the continent. Some of the groups, whom archaeologists call Archaic Indians, hunted deer or bison while others fished; foraged for roots, berries, and seeds; or killed small game. The methods parents used to teach their children in this phase of American prehistory are as murky as for the Paleo-Indians.

Classical America. The Indians of North America learned how to cultivate crops from the Indians of the central Valley of Mexico. By approximately 1500 B.C. the knowledge and skills to cultivate plants such as corn, squash, and beans had spread over much of North America, and the innovation sparked a transformation from Archaic to Classical cultures. The Classical cultures that arose with horticulture shared remarkably similar lifestyles with the Indian tribes that formed after the diseases introduced by Europeans to North America killed approximately 90 percent of the continent's aboriginal population. For this reason it is possible to infer how Classical Indians might have educated their children based on records left by later European observers.

The Southeast. The Southeast was home to the Mississippians, whose culture was characterized by the construction of ceremonial mounds, the production of agricultural surpluses, and the occupation of towns and small villages. In Mississippian society kinship was traced through the mothers and not the fathers, so the mother's clan had the responsibility of teaching her children. A boy's maternal uncles would provide him at an early age with a blowgun to practice hunting squirrels, birds, and other small game. Mothers and aunts likewise showed young girls how to sow seed, to weed gardens, to manufacture pottery and clothing, and to prepare food. The most important dates in young people's lives involved the shedding of blood. When a boy killed his first enemy, he was accorded the titles and privileges that separated men from boys. When a girl had her first menses, she was taken to one of several menstrual huts that stood on the outskirts of Mississippian settlements. Here she probably learned the lore and magic that distinguished women from girls.

The Northeast. Horticulture was common among many of the native groups that inhabited the Northeast. The ancestors of groups we know as the Iroquois, the Narragansetts, and the Powhatans shared a division of labor and, presumably, a method of education that was similar to that of the Mississippians. There were, however, important differences. Mississippian societies were more stratified than northeastern ones, so whereas the children of Mississippian chiefs may have been excluded from mundane chores or privileged to learn more sacred

A Hopewell Indian wooden figurine of a mother carrying a child, circa 400 B.C.–400 A.D., discovered in western Illinois (Milwaukee Public Museum)

arts, northeastern children probably shared a more common educational experience. Warfare and menstruation were also equally important as markers for the transition from adolescence to adulthood. One northeastern group, the ancestors of the Abenakis, did not farm. Young girls instead probably learned how to gather nuts, berries, and plants from their mothers just as their female counterparts in horticultural societies learned to farm.

The Great Plains. Early Plains peoples mixed aspects of settled and migratory lifestyles. They grew crops in permanent villages but left them during the summer months to hunt buffalo on the plains. Just as among the horticultural southern and northeastern societies, women farmed and probably instructed young girls to do the same. Boys probably followed their fathers on the hunt and sought by feats of bravery to slay their first bison or their first enemy. Because of their mobile pattern of residence, Plains groups may not have had the same institutionalized method of isolating menstruating

Products of Native American craftsmen and farmers of the Southwest, circa 700 A.D.: pottery, a sandal made of yucca fiber, jewelry, a basket of beans, corn, and squash (Southwest Museum, Santa Fe, New Mexico)

women, so much of what women had to teach girls was probably passed on in the fields, in the homes, and on the migratory hunt.

The Southwest. Southwestern ceremonial life revolved around earthen sweat lodges called *kivas*. Here religious leaders and medicine men honored their gods and spirits and probably taught young boys the secrets of the sacred world. Because women oversaw the crops that grew in their irrigated fields, they probably spent a lot of time with their daughters and nieces and instructed them not only how to grow corn but also how to ensure through magic their crops' success. Among the nonhorticultural Indians of California sweat lodges were also important places in the education of males. Elders also taught boys how to make bows, arrows, and arrowheads. Menstruation marked an important transition in the lives of young females. They were secluded at this time, prohibited from eating meat, and visited by their female relatives, who lectured them on the responsibilities of being women.

The Northwest. The Indians of the Pacific Northwest subsisted on fishing, hunting, and gathering. Maternal uncles took their nephews to fish and hunt around age seven or eight. Uncles also toughened boys with icy baths, sweating ceremonies, and hard work. After their first successful hunt boys were feasted and accorded the respect of adults. Girls' lives centered on their first menses, at which point they were confined for perhaps two years. During their seclusion female relatives taught

them everything they needed to know to enjoy a prosperous home life and a beneficial relationship with the spiritual world. Among the inhabitants of the drier Great Basin, families foraged together for food, and perhaps children learned how to collect plants and hunt for animals. Parents did not differentiate their children by sex; however, a female's first menses ended her existence as a gender-neutral person and made her socially and culturally a woman.

Sources:

Michael S. Nassaney and Kenneth E. Sassaman, eds., *Native American Interactions: Multiscalar Analysis and Interpretations in the Eastern Woodlands* (Knoxville: University of Tennessee Press, 1995);

William Sturtevant, ed., *Handbook of North American Indians*, volumes 7, 8, 9, 11 (Washington, D.C.: Smithsonian Institution, 1978, 1979, 1986, 1990).

EUROPEAN SCHOLARSHIP AND THE EXPLORATION OF THE NEW WORLD

The Renaissance. After Europe recovered from the blight of plague, different commercial routes to Asia opened; new centralized political states formed; and disgruntled subjects began to challenge the hegemony of the Roman Catholic Church. As scholars, governors, kings, and clergy grappled to understand the changes they witnessed around them, they together produced an intellectual, artistic, and cultural movement called the Renaissance which first started in the thirteenth century in the prosperous commercial city-states of the Italian peninsula. Today the vibrancy of this important move-

SCHOLASTICISM AND HUMANISM

The Renaissance transformed European thinking. During the Middle Ages scholasticism was the dominant mode of religious scholarship. It emphasized the rationality of the individual, and its practitioners sought to understand how faith and rationality could coexist. By questioning the Bible and other religious texts, scholastics attempted to render in systematic ways rational justifications for faith in God. Humanism, which arose in the fourteenth century, challenged scholasticism. To humanists faith did not need to be justified because it was an inherent part of an individual's makeup. Humanists such as Petrarch in Italy and Desiderius Erasmus in northern Europe sought to understand the innate qualities of people by collecting, translating, criticizing, and publishing works of Greek and Roman antiquity as well as Christian religious texts. By comparing sources they hoped to reproduce ancient texts in a pristine form that would enable them to get closer to the spirit and intellect of the ancient Classical world which they took for their inspiration.

Source: Alistair E. McGrath, *Reformation Thought: An Introduction* (Cambridge, Mass.: Blackwell, 1993).

ment can be seen in the artwork of Michelangelo, the inventiveness of Galileo, and the literary work of Dante.

Scholarship. Two distinct intellectual traditions battled for the minds of Europeans during the Renaissance. Scholastics and humanists argued about the central questions that preoccupied the professors at Europe's leading universities. Above all, they debated the relationship between humans and God and about how religion and reason coexisted to make humans rational and spiritual beings. By the early 1500s the humanists had won the battle for the European mind, and they turned their attention to the New World that Columbus and others had explored.

Writing about America. Writing about North America typically involved translating, transcribing, and editing the accounts of explorers. Building on the humanists' tradition of criticism of sources, Peter Martyr, Francisco Lopez de Gómara, Richard Eden, and André Thevet put their scholarship into print and created some of the first best-sellers. The New World posed serious problems for scholars. Clergy and professors wondered if the biblical flood had reached North America, puzzled over Adam's relationship to Native Americans, and debated the Indians' humanity. Others, such as Lucas de Heere, used a study of reports on Indians to piece together what ancient Europeans might have been like. But before 1600 the New World had only made a dent in European historiography. It would not be until the late 1600s and early

1700s that the early questions generated by the discovery of America sparked systematic thought and study. In the words of one writer in 1512, the opening of the New World "matters not at all or very little to the knowledge of . . . [our] History."

Spain. When Cardinal Francisco Jiménez de Cisneros founded the University of Alcalá de Henares in 1498, humanists established a strong grip on education in Spain, and the university played an important role in the publication of research about the New World. One scholar, Martyr, who worked in the service of the duke of Milan, had interviewed several Spaniards involved with the exploration and settlement of the American Southeast and wrote an account of the ill-fated Lucas Vázquez de Ayllón colony in present-day South Carolina. Although Martyr questioned his sources, he unwittingly perpetuated many of the original lies and exaggerations about the wealth of the region made by Ayllón when he had persuaded the king to approve the founding of the colony. In effect Martyr popularized the myth of Chicora, a tale of the fabulous wealth and bounty that other explorers who read Martyr's account also hoped to find in the American South. In 1530 the university published Martyr's notes with his writings on Christopher Columbus's and Amerigo Vespucci's voyages as *De Orbe Novo* (The New World). The book went through several translations and new editions and inspired French and English attempts to settle the South. Despite Spain's considerable success in colonizing and in publicizing the New World, however, Spanish authors made only a small contribution to the growing body of printed material on the New World. Gómara was by far the most famous native-born scholar. His book, *Historia general* (General History), was published in 1530 as the first comprehensive Spanish account of Spain's activities in North and South America. The book sold widely and influenced later explorers' initial impressions of North America.

France. A late entry in the race for America was France. Giovanni da Verrazano's voyage in 1524 along the coast of eastern North America marked the country's first attempt to gain information about the New World. In 1556 the Italian author Giovanni Bautista Ramusio published *Navigationi et Viaggi* (Navigations and Voyages), which collected documents related to Verrazzano's voyage and subsequent report to the French king Francis I. One year later André Thevet's *La France Antarctique* (Antarctic France) appeared and marked the first major French contribution to the growing body of scholarship about America. Thevet had visited various spots along the east coast on a return trip to France from Brazil. By reporting his own rather than others' findings Thevet established a French claim to the land that other powers had to at least acknowledge if not respect. The optimistic report he gave of the southeastern coast in particular dovetailed with Martyr's and Gómara's work on the same area and also influenced the choice that the Huguenot

Title page for Gregor Reisch's *Margarita philosophica* (1503), with representations of the seven liberal arts and philosophy

leader Jean Ribault made to locate his Protestant colony near present-day Jacksonville, Florida.

England. Like the French, the English in the sixteenth century were intermittent colonizers at best, and several of the nation's leading scholars hoped that through their published work they could stimulate the Crown to devote more money and energy to the exploration and settlement of the New World. Richard Eden's *Decades of the Newe Worlde* (1555), a version of Martyr's book that drew on Gómara as well, provided a well-rounded picture of North America. Unlike the other two authors, however, Eden focused a good deal of his attention on the northern sea and the great fisheries off present-day Newfoundland. Eden had hoped to build on the pioneering legacy of John and Sebastian Cabot, the father and son who had explored the area four decades before the book's publication, but his book failed to spark English interest in the New World. In the 1580s Richard Hakluyt resumed Eden's project. As a humanist Hakluyt compiled a variety records related to various explorations and published them in two books: *Divers Voyages Touching the Discovery of America* (1582) and *Principall Navigations . . . of the English Nation* (1589). By highlighting the various English voyages of exploration, Hakluyt created the impression that England had exerted an important influence in the creation of the New

World and hoped that his message would spur Queen Elizabeth I to action.

Sources:

Jacob Ernest Cooke, ed., *Encyclopedia of the North American Colonies*, 3 volumes (New York: Scribners, 1993);

Karen Ordahl Kupperman, ed., *America in European Consciousness, 1493–1750* (Chapel Hill: University of North Carolina Press, 1995).

NEW WORLD COLONIES

France and England. The French and the English considered education a vital part of their imperial missions. When Francis I commissioned Jacques Cartier's third voyage to Canada in 1540, he ordered the explorer to collect information about "savage peoples who live without knowledge of God and without use of reason . . . [and] . . . to have them instructed in the love and fear of God and of the holy Christian law and doctrine." The English colonizers of Roanoke Island in the 1580s carried with them a similar missionary imperative to collect information about Native Americans and to begin the process of converting them to Christianity. But neither the French nor the English founded permanent settlements in North America before 1600, and their attempts to build colonies were so short-lived that they neither built schools for colonial children nor fulfilled their mission to instruct Indians in Christian doctrine.

Spain. Unlike France and England, during the sixteenth century Spain developed an enormous colonial enterprise in the New World. New Spain (present-day Mexico) was the heart of the Crown's American empire, and the Spanish made substantial inroads into South America as well. They were less successful in North America. Although explorers such as Juan Ponce de León, Hernando de Soto, and Francisco Vásquez de Coronado had provided a wealth of information about the geography and population of the continent, the lack of large deposits of gold and silver, such as the Spanish had found further to the south, militated against a substantive and systematic effort to plant colonies in North America. Nevertheless attempts were made to build centers of Spanish settlement in North America, and education emerged as an important part of the extension of the Spanish dominion northward.

Florida. As the Spanish treasure fleets lumbered back to Spain laden with New World riches, they stayed close to the Florida coast before picking up the gulf current to Europe. For this reason the Florida coast became a haven for pirates, and the Spanish government decided to build a permanent settlement that would serve as a base for warships that could protect the unwieldy galleons. Despite several earlier failures to build colonies in Florida, in 1565 Pedro Menéndez de Avilés founded St. Augustine, and the outpost became the center of a far-flung Spanish presence in the American South.

New Mexico. Although Coronado's expedition in the 1540s had shown that the Southwest lacked precious

FRANCISCANS

In 1209 the man who became known as St. Francis of Assisi decided to dedicate his life to living in poverty and to preaching the Christian word. Two years later Pope Innocent III recognized Francis and his followers as an official Roman Catholic order, and the Pope prohibited the Franciscans from owning property to enforce their vow of poverty. The order worked tirelessly to educate the poor, and its members survived on what they could obtain through begging and menial labor. Franciscans entered the New World following Hernando Cortés's conquest of the Aztecs in 1523. Two years later royal regulations mandated that Franciscan friars accompany each exploration party so that, in the words of the bishop of Mexico, the subjugation of and conversion of Native Americans would be "a Christian apostolic [event] and not a butchery."

Source: David J. Weber, *The Spanish Frontier in North America* (New Haven, Conn.: Yale University Press, 1992).

metals, forty years later two Franciscan friars, Agustín Rodríguez and Antonio Espejo, revisited the Pueblo country to scout out opportunities for missionizing the Indians. They wrote glowing reports of the region, and in 1595 Juan de Oñate asked for and received permission from King Philip II to colonize the area Coronado had written off as too arid and too impoverished for Spanish settlement. In 1598 his party of colonists arrived among the Pueblos, and despite tensions with the local inhabitants as well as the threat of drought and starvation, the small group managed to build an outpost they called San Juan de Yunque.

Converting the Indians. Neither the Florida nor the New Mexico colony developed enough of a population of children to justify the creation of day schools. However, the goal of converting and subjugating the Indians required that Spaniards instruct them in Christianity as well as Spanish language and technology so that the Hispanicized Indians could be incorporated into the stratified social order that colonial officials envisioned. Without an educated Indian peasantry to work for the Spanish upper class the colonies would not have survived because royal officials rarely enlisted enough colonists to make self-contained viable settlements. Two groups undertook the task of converting the Indians, the Jesuits and the Franciscans, and they relied on several legal and religious precedents to guide their efforts.

Papal Proclamations. The papacy had a tremendous influence on the education of native North Americans by Spanish missionaries. Six years before Columbus's first voyage, King Ferdinand of Aragon, who married Isabella of Castile to form the core of the modern Spanish nation, negotiated with Pope Innocent VIII a treaty called *Real Patronato,* which made Ferdinand the official patron of Catholicism abroad. In exchange for such control over Catholicism, Ferdinand promised the Pope that his government would tolerate no other religions. In 1493 Alexander VI issued a papal bull, or policy statement, called *Inter Catera Divinae,* which decreed that Indians were capable of converting to Christianity. Pope Julius II's bull *Illius fulciti praesidio* (1504) further clarified the relationship between the Church, the Crown, and the Indians. It defined the Crown's duties in the New World as "[to] preach the word of God, convert the . . . infidels and barbarous peoples, instruct and teach the converts in the true faith." In 1537 the bull *Sublimis Deus* clarified matters further by asserting that "Indians are truly men capable of understanding the catholic faith." Another bull issued the same year, *Veritas ipsa,* reinforced *Inter Catera Divinae* and ended an ongoing debate among Spanish intellectuals about the essential humanity of the Indians. If they could convert, so the argument went, then they were capable of rational thought and were, therefore, human.

Spanish Education. The Spanish church, financed by the War Ministry, undertook the education of native North Americans and drew upon historical, pedagogical, and institutional influences from Spain as well as upon certain aspects of precontact native education. Humanism was important in this respect because its practitioners valued the essential humanity of all people as decreed by *Inter Catera Divinae* and *Veritas ipsa.* In addition, the incorporation into Spanish society of conquered peoples that had begun when Ferdinand and Isabella reconquered the Iberian peninsula from its Arabic occupiers was simply extended to the native

JESUITS

In 1534 Ignatius of Loyola, a former soldier, met at the University of Paris six other men who shared his interest in Christianity and humanitarianism. Together the group founded the Society of Jesus and dedicated themselves and their order to charitable work, educating the poor, and working as missionaries abroad. New members took vows of poverty and of celibacy and agreed to work in the service of the Pope. Given Spain's responsibility to spread Roman Catholicism throughout the New World, the Pope provided hundreds of Jesuit missionaries for the conversion of Indians in the Americas. By 1556 there were more than one thousand "black robes," as the Jesuits were called, serving as missionaries around the world.

Source: William J. Bangert, *A History of the Society of Jesus* (St. Louis: Institute of Jesuit Sources, 1972).

An Apache bison-skin cloak (circa 1600) with instructions for carrying out magical cures (from *The Ninth Annual Report of the Bureau of American Ethnology,* 1887–1888)

inhabitants of the New World. The center of the Spanish educational universe was the University of Alcalá de Henares, where clergymen educated the poor and trained young men for service to the church. The spirit of Alcalá de Henares was transplanted to the New World in 1536 when the College of Santa Cruz de Tlaltelolco was founded in Mexico to train Indian converts as clergymen. At the school Indian men learned reading, writing, theology, Latin, rhetoric, logic, and medicine, but the program was not popular. In 1555 a religious council closed the school and forbade the further ordination of either Indians or mestizos, children of Indian and Spanish parents. In spite of the closure, Spanish professors continued to believe in the importance of educating Indians. Two scholars in particular recommended to the Crown that all Indians be taught religion and the liberal arts because, they reasoned, "who are we to show discrimination that Christ never showed[?]"

Jesuit Missions in Florida. A few Jesuits had accompanied Pedro Menéndez de Avilés to Florida, and they opened six missions along the southeastern coast of the peninsula and in the interior. Their unwillingness to accept native traditions of polygamy and inheritance and their practice of kidnapping and sending to Cuba the children of prominent chiefs, however, doomed their missions. A revolt by the Guale chiefdom in present-day Georgia forced the Society of Jesus to abandon its project in 1572.

Franciscan Missions in Florida. In 1573 several Franciscans arrived in Florida to resume the project of converting the Indians to Roman Catholicism. Empowered by the Royal Orders of 1573, which encouraged missionaries to persuade rather than to force Indians to convert, and informed by the traditions of humanism, which valued individuals' inherent goodness, the Franciscans built several *doctrinas,* mission settlements, where they gathered the populations of nearby native villages. Although more tolerant than the Jesuits, the Franciscans' unwillingness to allow the Indians to dictate the pace and scope of cultural change got them in trouble. In 1597 the Guales again revolted and drove the Franciscans back to St. Augustine. The Franciscans enjoyed better success among the Timicuans who inhabited much of the peninsula. Fathers Francisco Pareja and Gregorio de Movilla even translated Christian texts into the Timucuan language in order to facilitate their conversion. Franciscan missions were spread far and wide, and at no one time were there more than seventy missionaries in the region.

Franciscan Missions in New Mexico. When Juan de Oñate founded San Juan de Yunque, he divided New Mexico into seven missionary districts, but only two missions were built before 1600: San Juan de los Caballeros and San Gabriel. As in Florida, the Franciscans first tried to gather native populations into their missions. With the priests' help the Pueblo Indians learned various new skills. Priests also challenged the powers of native healers and shamans and managed to persuade many Pueblos that they and not the indigenous spiritualists had access to the wondrous powers of the heavens. In spite of such achievements, nearly one century later the Pueblos, like the Guales, decided they were better off without the Franciscans, and the Pueblo Revolt of 1680 drove the missionaries and the Spanish colonists out of New Mexico.

The Missions. The construction of missions and the education of the Indians were the first two steps in the Spanish colonial plan to pacify new regions and to prepare them for later settlement by Spaniards. Not only did Indians have to be incorporated into the colonizers' faith, but they also had to learn the skills necessary to keep the colonial outposts functioning. Jesuit and Franciscan missionaries took as their model for instruction the Aztec Calmecac school, which, before Columbus, had trained the children of elites to be responsible and intelligent governors.

The Pupils. The children the missionaries selected for their pupils, the *catecumenos,* played important roles in mission education because they worked as translators and explained to the other students and to their parents the meaning of the Roman Catholic faith. Once the catecumenos had demonstrated a sufficient proficiency in reciting the catechism, a short book that consisted of questions and answers about the Christian faith, they were baptized by the friars and became known as *cristianos.* Some who were particularly adept at the Spanish language and trades earned the right to be called *muy españolado* (very Spanish). The priests also renamed the children after baptism to conform to Christian practice.

The Lessons. Whether in New Mexico or in Florida, the catecumenos and cristianos learned many of the same things. In an attempt to transform the native diet into one the Spanish could recognize as their own, the priests introduced sheep and pigs to the missions and taught the children as well as their parents how to care for the animals and how to grow nonnative crops such as wheat, grapes, peaches, and watermelons. The New Mexican missionaries also instructed their charges in new methods of irrigation and introduced women to the virtues of growing, spinning, and weaving cotton. Whereas only a handful of students learned to read and write, most males at least learned a trade. Spanish artisans would take on native apprentices to learn skills such as shoemaking, carpentry, blacksmithing, and tailoring. Over time the students emerged to play important roles in the lives of the colonies and of their tribes, but by 1600 the mission schools in Florida and New Mexico were only beginning to accomplish their goals.

Sources:

David Hurst Thomas, ed., *Columbian Consequences, Volume One: Archaeological and Historical Perspectives on the Spanish Borderlands West* (Washington, D.C.: Smithsonian Institution, 1989);

David J. Weber, *The Spanish Frontier in North America* (New Haven: Yale University Press, 1992).

PUBLICATIONS

Pietro Martiere d'Anghiera, *De Orbe Novo: The Eight Decades of Peter Martyr d'Anghera,* translated by Francis MacNutt, 2 volumes (New York: Putnam, 1912)—the original classic study of the New World by Peter Martyr. The book exerted a formative influence not only on how Europeans thought about the New World but also how subsequent scholars wrote about it;

Jacques Cartier, *A Shorte and Briefe Narration of the Two Navigations . . . to Newe France,* translated by John Florio (London: H. Bynneman, 1580)—published reports of Cartier's first two voyages to the New World;

Richard Hakluyt, *The Original Writings and Correspondence of the Two Richard Hakluyts,* edited by Eva G. R. Taylor, 2 volumes (London: Hakluyt Society, 1935)—includes Hakluyt's books, which attempted to stir English interest in colonizing the New World;

André Thevet, *André Thevet's North America: A Sixteenth-Century View,* edited by Roger Schlesinger and Arthur P. Stabler (Kingston: McGill-Queen's University Press, 1986)—Thevet, the royal cosmographer of France, translated various documents associated with the exploration of the New World as well as reported his own observations of North America.

An engraving of an astronomer teaching a theologian about the stars, from Pierre d'Ailly's *Concordantia astronomiae cum theologia* (1490)

CHAPTER SIX

GOVERNMENT AND LAW

by TIMOTHY GARRISON

CONTENTS

CHRONOLOGY
116

OVERVIEW
124

TOPICS IN THE NEWS

Civil Law 129
Natural Law 129
English Common Law........ 130
European Parliamentary
    Government.................. 131
European Perceptions of
    Native Government......... 132
*Observations on Native American
    Government* 132

*Tomas Ortiz's Description
    of Indians* 133
Before Europeans 134
Native American Government:
    First Origins 134
Native American Government:
    Eastern Woodlands 136
Population Centers............ 136
Native American Government:
    Mississippian Chiefdoms 137
Native American Government:
    The Southeast............ 138
Native American Government:
    The West 140
The Rattlesnake's Revenge 140
Petrine Mandate 142
Native American Law: Blood
    Revenge 142

Spanish Conquest of the Americas:
    The Treaty of Tordesillas 144
The Spanish Defense:
    Legal Justifications for
    Conquest 145
Spanish Government in the
    Americas 147

HEADLINE MAKERS

Deganawidah and Hiawatha....151
Franciscus de Victoria.......... 152

PUBLICATIONS
154

Sidebars and tables are listed in italics.

80,000-10,000 B.C.

- The Wisconsin glaciation periodically exposes the Alaskan-Siberian land bridge and opens a path for human entrée into North America.

9000 B.C.

- Paleolithic peoples devise large-scale cooperative hunting efforts such as stampeding bison over cliffs or into arroyos. Native political activity is limited to informal leadership among families and bands.

8000 B.C.

- Archaic era begins and lasts until 1500 B.C.
- Peoples in the Columbia River region increasingly exploit the salmon; some scholars contend that dominant groups charge other peoples a toll to fish the river.

5000 B.C.

- The domestication of plants begins in Central and South America.

3500 B.C.

- The domestication of plants starts in North America.

2600 B.C.

- Expansive trade networks develop in southeast North America. The remains of shells suggest that native groups used trade as a way to develop and maintain diplomatic relations.

2000 B.C.

- The Chumash people of southern California devise a system of exchange based on shell beads.
- Four plants—squash, sunflowers, marsh elder, and chenopodium—are domesticated in eastern North America, leading to the development of larger community populations. Many cultures become more sedentary.

1500-700 B.C.

- Mound-building societies emerge.

1500 B.C.

- Southwestern cultures begin cultivating corn.

1000 B.C.

- The people of the lower Mississippi River reside in ordered communities and build large mounds.

500-100 B.C.

- Adena culture develops in the Ohio River valley.

500 B.C.

- Eastern Woodlands and Plains Woodlands cultures begin to build burial mounds.

300 B.C.

- Hohokam culture emerges in the Southwest.
- Eastern Woodlands societies begin cultivating corn.

100 B.C.-400 A.D.

- The Anasazi culture emerges in the Southwest.

100 B.C.-600 A.D.

- The Hopewell culture flourishes in the great river valleys of the Ohio and Mississippi.

100 B.C.

- Native peoples in present-day Ohio construct the Serpent Mound, a massive public-works project that is more than a thousand feet long and varies in height from three to twenty feet.

1 A.D.

- Eastern Woodlands cultures begin to develop elaborate political hierarchies with increasingly stratified social statuses.

200-900

- The Mogollon culture develops in present-day New Mexico; some people of the area become more sedentary.

300	• Hohokam cultures begin construction of large-scale irrigation systems.
400	• Great Basin cultures become more sedentary and begin practicing horticulture.
500	• Pacific Northwest cultures begin to recognize the possession of wealth as significant for social status.
700-1500	• The Mississippian culture develops and thrives in the Ohio and Mississippi River valleys.
800	• Northern Athapaskan peoples, the forerunners of the Navajos and Apaches, migrate into the Great Plains and the Southwest.
800-1100	• Spiro, a site on the Arkansas River in present-day Oklahoma, becomes a major Mississippian trade center; other cultures in places such as Kincaid, Ohio, emerge around the same time.
950	• Ancestors of the Hidatsas and Mandans migrate from the area of present-day Minnesota and Iowa to the Missouri River valley on the Great Plains.
1001-1014	• Leif Ericson explores and settles Newfoundland, making contact with Native Americans.
700-1150	• The Anasazi culture is replaced by Pueblo culture.
1200-1300	• The Mississippian community of Cahokia declines.

1300-1600
- Temple Mound civilizations develop in the Mississippi, Missouri, and Ohio River valleys and other riverine areas of eastern North America.

1325-1500
- The Aztecs acquire dominance in Mexico.

1400-1500
- The League of the Iroquois develops.

1488
- Bartholomeu Dias sails to the Cape of Good Hope.

1492
- Christopher Columbus's first voyage instigates the continuous European settlement of the Americas.

1493-1496
- Columbus makes his second voyage and founds Isabella (in present-day Dominican Republic), the first European settlement in the Americas.

1493
- Pope Alexander VI issues the *Inter Caetera Divinae,* granting to Spain all lands discovered one hundred leagues west of the Azores.

1494
- The Treaty of Tordesillas between Portugal and Spain assigns the previous year's demarcation line 270 leagues to the west of the Cape Verde Islands.
- Columbus enslaves several hundred Indians and transports them to Spain.

1496
- Bartolomé Columbus, brother of Christopher, establishes Santo Domingo on the island of Hispaniola, the oldest continuous European settlement in the Americas.

1497
- John Cabot reaches Newfoundland and Nova Scotia, claiming North America for England; he also makes contact with the Micmac Indians.

1498-1500

- Columbus makes his third voyage to the Americas.

1501

- Gaspar Corte Real of Portugal kidnaps fifty Indians and sells them into slavery.

1502-1504

- Columbus conducts a fourth voyage to the Americas.

1508

- Sebastian Cabot enters Hudson Bay while searching for the Northwest Passage.

1511

- The Dominican priest Bartolomé de las Casas criticizes Spanish treatment of Indians.

1512

- Spain enacts the Laws of Burgos, which place restrictions on Indian labor.
- Pope Julius II declares that Indians are the descendants of Adam and Eve, thereby implying equality with Europeans.

1512-1521

- Juan Ponce de León explores Florida.

1513

- Vasco Núñez de Balboa crosses the Isthmus of Panama and views the Pacific Ocean.
- Spain issues the *Requerimiento* (Requirement), a document justifying the conquest of native peoples.

1519-1521

- Hernando Cortés conquers the Aztecs and Mexico.
- Ferdinand Magellan's expeditionary fleet circumnavigates the globe.

1524

- Giovanni da Verrazano explores the north Atlantic coast.

1526
- Lucas Vázquez de Ayllón establishes San Miguel de Gualdape on the Atlantic coast in present-day Georgia.

1528-1536
- Pánfilo de Narváez explores the Gulf Coast from present-day Florida to Texas.

1532
- Spanish lawyer Franciscus de Victoria writes that Native Americans are "the true owners of the New World."

1534-1542
- Jacques Cartier explores eastern Canada and the St. Lawrence River valley in the name of France.

1537
- Pope Paul III declares that Indians are humans and can be converted to Christianity.

1539
- Franciscus de Victoria lectures at the University of Salamanca and declares that Indians have the same natural rights as Europeans.

1539-1542
- Hernando de Soto explores the Southeast.

1540-1542
- Francisco Vásquez de Coronado explores the Southwest and the Great Plains.

1541-1543
- Jacques Cartier and the Sieur de Roberval make a futile effort to establish a French colony along the St. Lawrence River at Stadacona.

1542
- Juan Rodríguez Cabrillo explores the coast of California.

1549
- Spain adopts the *Repartimiento* as a way to reform the *encomienda,* a system of forced Indian labor.

1559
- Spanish explorer Tristán de Luna y Arellano visits Coosa in present-day Alabama and finds it depopulated by disease. The main center of Coosa has been reduced from five hundred to fifty houses since de Soto's visit twenty years earlier.

1563
- A group of French Huguenots attempt to establish a colony along the Atlantic coast. The French artist Jacque le Moyne provides some of the earliest drawings of Native Americans. Spanish warships destroy the colony two years later.

1565
- Pedro Menéndez de Avilés of Spain establishes St. Augustine on the Atlantic coast of present-day Florida.

1570
- Spanish Jesuits establish a mission in the Chesapeake region.

1576-1578
- English admiral Martin Frobisher conducts three expeditions to the Atlantic coast.

1577-1579
- Francis Drake sails around the world and explores the coast of California.

1578
- Humphrey Gilbert obtains a patent to establish a colony in North America.

1582
- Spanish begin the settlement of New Mexico.

1585-1587
- Sir Walter Raleigh fails in his attempt to establish an English colony on Roanoke Island.

1587-1590

- Raleigh's second attempt at colonization on Roanoke Island (the famous Lost Colony) also fails.

1597

- Spain puts down a Guale rebellion in Florida.

1598

- Spanish explorer Juan de Oñate establishes the colony of New Mexico.

A small seated human figure carved in wood, circa 1480, found near the Tomoka River, Florida (Tomoka State Park, Ormond Beach, Florida)

OVERVIEW

Government. The history of government in North America begins with the coming together of two drastically different political traditions. The Europeans who first came to the Western Hemisphere were the agents of centralized monarchies that regulated the behavior of hundreds of thousands of national citizens. By the time of Christopher Columbus the governments of Spain, England, Holland, and France were powerful enough to tax, regulate, and defend the people living within the boundaries of thousands of square miles of national domain. In the Americas, European explorers and colonists encountered thousands of different Native American communities that ordered their social and political affairs in a manner that was quite different from the kings, parliaments, and courts of Europe. In fact, many anthropologists object to the use of the word "government" to describe the way that Indians regulated their societies. Government evokes images of judges in robes, politicians debating in grand halls, and kings and queens sitting on elevated thrones of absolute power. These conceptions, however, were not representative of Native American government in the period before 1600. Perhaps then it is more appropriate to think of native government in terms of patterns and regulations of behavior. An American anthropologist of the twentieth century named E. Adamson Hoebel described Native American methods of behavioral regulation as "law-ways" to demonstrate that they essentially met the same objectives as western governments but were at the same time quite distinct from the courts and laws and governments of Europe. Rather than being produced by a coercive, centralized government and imposed on the people of the society from above, Indian law-ways emerged organically in response to the needs of the community. Although Native American cultures were not literate before the European discovery, their communities maintained social mechanisms that served the same purpose as a written code of law. Individuals always knew the boundaries of appropriate or acceptable behavior in native communities, and each Indian society maintained practices that provided for order and the common good.

Religion. While the European nations were in the process of differentiating or separating their religious, social, and political institutions from each other in the centuries before their explorations of America, the Native American peoples continued to maintain almost completely synergetic societies during this time. In other words, the legal and political institutions of Indian communities were indivisibly integrated with their spiritual beliefs and their kinship networks. These cultures harbored no concept of a separation between religion and government. Religious prescriptions and family relationships, not governments, determined most legal rights and duties for Native Americans. Therefore it is impossible to understand how Native American government worked without taking into account the intertwining nature of politics, kinship, and religion in their societies. Although the substantive religious beliefs of Native Americans varied widely from culture to culture, there were some common characteristics among Indian groups that influenced the way that they ordered their communities. Most native religions were grounded on the belief that all beings in the universe hold spiritual power. Contrary to European Judeo-Christians, Indians did not believe that God had given them dominion over the earth. Instead Native Americans believed they were part of a dynamic, spiritual world. Indians believed that the forces of the natural world had to be recognized and respected and that it was incumbent on humans to help maintain the universe in a state of balance. An important process that promoted balance was reciprocity, the idea that an individual act calls for an appropriate and equivalent response. Many native societies practiced extensive gift-giving rituals that were intended to promote social balance and interdependence between peoples holding different levels of power and prestige. At the same time Indians felt they had a responsibility to preserve a reciprocal relationship with nature. This worldview dissuaded natives from thinking of land as something that could be owned and exploited by one person. Native American religion also stressed the importance of access to spiritual power. The council meetings of native cultures were marked by ceremonial rituals that were intended to provide individuals with the ability to tap into the spiritual power that would lead them to decisions. Since there was no true separation between government and religion, spiritual considerations often guided or influenced political decisions. Consequently, priests such as shamans and medicine men played an important role in native governments. These spiritual leaders healed the sick, interpreted dreams and natural signs, and were the conduit between the community and the spirit world. Because of their spiritual power, the opinions of a community's religious leaders carried considerable weight in many native councils.

The Clan. The family and the clan were the institutions primarily responsible for maintaining order and security in Native American communities. A clan is a group of kin who claim descent from a common ancestor. Clan members often believed that the original ancestor possessed the characteristics of an animal that was indigenous to their culture's environment. For example, the bear clan and the wolf clan were common clan names throughout North America. Depending on the society, clan membership passed down from the mother (matrilineal descent) or the father (patrilineal descent) to the children. Some groups recognized bilateral membership. In other words, children in a bilateral society could claim membership in the clans of their mother and their father. Membership in a clan provided individuals with important rights, obligated them to specific duties, and ordered their relationships with other people. For example, clan membership determined rights to land use, identified who an individual could or could not have sexual relations with, and provided mechanisms such as the law of blood revenge that inhibited violent behavior. The clan also played a role in providing judicial, political, and military leadership for a native community. For instance, clan leaders or elders often mediated quarrels between family members. In many societies the elders of the clan were also the most influential members of village and tribal councils. In short, the political structures of Native Americans were clearly founded upon kinship relations. Political leadership or government beyond the clan network only emerged when circumstances required unrelated bands to cooperate with each other for food production and for extensive public projects such as irrigation systems, ceremonial earthworks, and defensive structures.

Consensus. Although there were societies with leaders of paramount power, most native societies were basically egalitarian. An egalitarian society is one in which most or all adults have an equal voice in community decisions. However, these groups did not vote or decide questions on the basis of majority rule. Instead decisions in these societies emerged through consensus after long consultation and considerable oratory and debate. Individuals in Indian societies learned to conform to the social mores and to cooperate with other members of their communities at an early age. They learned to be reflective, to respect the opinions of the others, and to abide by the consensual decisions of their elders and council. Among some peoples individual leaders emerged to take a more influential role than others. Depending on the culture, leaders achieved their position by their skill in oratory, wisdom in judgment, achievements in war, facility in administration, or generosity. Leaders, however, generally did not have the power to coerce other members of the community to follow their will. Instead they moved people to action by persuasion and worked to form agreement and consensus in the community. When leaders lost the ability to form or maintain consensus in the community, their communities replaced them with another. Those who disagreed with the consensus were not obligated to follow the decisions of their councils. Occasionally dissenters from an important community decision departed the village or town and established new bands or villages. In some cases Europeans who dealt with native peoples were often confused by this practice. They often believed that Indians had difficulty reaching decisions or were duplicitous. For example, representatives of a European nation sometimes made peace with a native people and then suffered an attack from what they thought to be the same group. In reality what had happened was that a dissident minority of the native society had refused to accept a decision of peace, left the council, and instigated its own war on the Europeans. Disturbances such as these encouraged many native peoples in the seventeenth and eighteenth centuries to begin centralizing their own governments so that they could respond more effectively to the European invasion.

The European State. By 1600 agents of Spain, France, and England had all visited parts of the Atlantic coast of North America. While France and England did not establish a lasting settlement on the American mainland until the early decades of the seventeenth century, Spain had by that time constructed a vast empire in Mexico and Central and South America and had explored and established missions, presidios, and plantations throughout the southern third of the present-day United States. These three European powers had only developed in the few centuries before their American expeditions. Their emergence as imperialistic nation-states was the culmination of a long period of political and legal evolution that began in the Middle Ages. In the ninth century the people of Europe lived under the authority of the Christian church, the empire of Charlemagne, and various local kings, princes, and chieftains. After the death of Charlemagne in 814 centralized government collapsed, and feudalism became the primary system of legal and political order in western Europe. Feudalism was a private form of social and political organization based on the ownership of land. During the early stages of the development of the feudal structure the kings of Europe rewarded favored chieftains with vast parcels of land in appreciation for their military leadership. This grant was called a fief, and it gave the chieftain noble status. He also obtained a feudal title. In exchange for the fief these overlords promised fealty, or fidelity, to the king. Effectively this meant that the overlords would provide men and arms to fight the king's wars. With this agreement the overlord became what was called a vassal of the king.

The overlords divided up their own estates into smaller tracts and gave possession of them to their own set of vassals in exchange for certain services and fees. These tenants also had the power to divide up their land and enter into feudal arrangements with subordinate lords. Local men agreed to this relationship because it was the only legal way to acquire an estate in land. In exchange for the land these local lords offered their allegiance, their service, and their military support. They also safeguarded their lord's family, sat in judgment of their peer vassals, and offered financial assistance and advice to their overlord. Consequently, a powerful overlord could expect several vassal lords to provide him with soldiers for his army. In sum the feudal system was a vast and complicated pyramid of contractual relationships between people of varying degrees of wealth, influence, and power. This hierarchy was never implemented by a king or legislature. Instead it developed over time through contracts of necessity between families of differing levels of economic and military power.

The Manor. Under feudalism local political and legal authority had collapsed into the hands of hundreds of landholding lords. At the lowest levels of feudalism lived the lord on his manor or estate. The right to this land passed down the hereditary line from the father to his eldest son. This system of succession to land is called primogeniture. The local lord held authority over the landless tenants who lived on the farms and in the villages on his estate. These people were called peasants or serfs. They were legally bound to the land of their lord and could only leave with his permission. Serfs were required to work their lords' land for a certain number of days each week and were obligated to provide him with a portion of their crop as rent. In exchange the lord ostensibly provided protection, a system of justice, a common mill, and a church for the residents of his estate. The manor was thus a self-sustaining community that supported the status and welfare of the lord. On some manors the lord appointed special officers from the peasantry to protect his property. For example, some lords maintained foresters who were responsible for limiting the amount of wood that the peasants could cut. The foresters also punished poachers who hunted on the lord's land without his permission. These foresters were the forerunners of local law enforcement officers. Feudalism provided a system of law and order for the manor in a time when coercive state authority was absent in Europe. At the apex of the feudal hierarchy sat the hereditary king.

The Feudal King. The kings of western Europe continued to claim dominion over their lands during the Middle Ages; however, their powers were limited. Although the kings of Europe claimed their authority as the supreme overlords of their realms, they were dependent on their vassals for their military and financial support. The king held direct authority only over his immediate vassals and could only claim jurisdiction over the people of his realm by virtue of this relationship. Feudal monarchs did not have the support of national courts and legislatures. They did not possess a coercive system of national taxation beyond the feudal scheme of rents and fees. The monarchs of Europe were also unable to raise national armies except through the feudal system. The king did hold the supreme title to the land of his nation; and all of his vassals, and all of their vassals, claimed possession of their land through the king. The king expected his underlords to pay him fees from the income earned on his lands to provide for the expenses of government. He also demanded military service from his underlords, who in turn provided their own vassals and subvassals as soldiers and knights in the king's army. While the king could not issue laws that bound all of the people of the nation, he could order his vassals to require their subjects to abide by his edicts. Moreover, the king did not hold legal jurisdiction over his country as we now understand it. Instead he held the legal power to decide disputes between his immediate underlords. The power of government held by the king was thus based on the feudal contract. As a result the crown heads of Europe were constantly in competition and conflict with their vassals for control of their kingdom. The king's vassals often challenged his authority if he demonstrated weakness or violated his feudal obligations. If the monarch violated these obligations, his vassals had a legal right to demand that he fulfill his duties. If the king failed to do so, his underlords could ask him to release them from the arrangement. Overall the European kings during the age of feudalism held extremely limited powers. Between the tenth and sixteenth centuries, however, the monarchs of western Europe slowly reacquired the authority that they had surrendered under the feudal system. By 1600 several of the royal families of Europe had vanquished the competing power of the nobility and were on their way to acquiring absolute power over their kingdoms.

Church and State. During the Middle Ages, the Pope, the head of the Roman Catholic Church, held powerful influence over the governments of Europe. Pope Gregory VII, who governed the church from 1073 to 1085, had dreamed of a Christian world government in which the papacy controlled the crown heads of Europe. For centuries the Church attempted to realize this dream. The popes of Rome intervened in European internal affairs, mediated disputes between nations, and apportioned newly discovered lands among the Catholic monarchs of Europe. Many of the rulers of Europe, such as the Holy Roman Emperor Henry IV, who ruled from 1056 to 1106, bridled at the Church's efforts to control secular as well as spiritual affairs. Henry co-opted the Pope's right to invest the bishops of the Church with their symbols of office and thus challenged the Holy See's authority to control the clergy in the empire. For that act Pope Gregory excommunicated Henry from the Church. The threat of excommunication, or expulsion from the Church, persuaded many European rulers to abide by the wishes of the Pope. Ultimately, though, the Church's influence over the European governments waned dramatically in the fourteenth and fifteenth centuries. The corrupt practices of a series of popes and bishops tarnished the Church's position as the spiritual and moral authority of Europe. In addition, many of the monarchs of Europe followed Henry's precedent and repudiated the Church's demands for a say in the secular affairs of their governments. England, for example, refused to accept Pope Alexander's division of the Western Hemisphere between the Catholic nations of Spain and Portugal in 1493. The English nationalist Richard Hakluyt declared that the Pope did not have the right to cede undiscovered lands to whomever he liked. Finally, the Protestant Reformation ended the Church's monopoly over the European spiritual world. In 1517 a German professor of theology named Martin Luther posted a devastating critique of the Church on the door of a sanctuary in Wittenberg, Germany. The Ninety-five Theses, as his statement was called, initiated a general religious, social, and political upheaval in Europe. Luther criticized the trappings of the Church and called for an end to the dispensation of indulgences, a practice in which officials of the Church offered forgiveness for sins in exchange for cash payments. More importantly Luther set forth a radical new interpretation of Christianity that challenged the existing dogma of Catholicism. Among other things, he argued that the Pope in Rome did not have the authority to define appropriate beliefs for Christians, that all individuals should be able to read the Bible and interpret it according to their own conscience, and that Christians did not acquire grace or eternal life from their works but from their faith. These assertions had a powerful impact on the relationship between Christianity and government in Europe. Luther urged the monarchs of Europe to seize control of the faith in their countries. He wrote that people owed their spiritual allegiance to God but that they should devote all of their worldly interests to their king. Some of the rulers followed Luther's directive and extended their power over the often troublesome clergy in their kingdoms. Another Protestant wave swept through much of Europe when John Calvin published his *Institutes of the Christian Religion* in 1536. Calvin expanded upon Luther's ideas on several theological issues. In particular Calvin preached that there were a certain elect group of people who were predestined by God to enter the kingdom of heaven. No act or degree of faith could change one's destiny if God had not created the individual as one of the elect. Calvin also differed with Luther on the proper relationship between the church and the state. While Luther had contended that the church should be subordinate to the state on secular matters, Calvin preached that Christians should seize control of their governments and create Christian theocracies. Calvin created such a community in Geneva, Switzerland. In 1620 English Puritans established a Calvinist theocracy in America at Plymouth, Massachusetts. The emergence of Luther's Protestant-

ism and Calvinism, and the concomitant repudiation of the Catholic Church's authority, opened up the Americas to colonization by England and Holland in the seventeenth century.

The City and Commercial Law. Another dramatic process that influenced the nature of government in America was the decline of feudalism and the rise of the absolute monarch. An important intermediate step in this transition was the rise of municipal government and the development of a common commercial law. Throughout medieval Europe merchants and artisans living in towns and villages chafed at the restrictions imposed by the feudal lords. Unlike the peasant farmers on the manors, they were able to retain much of the wealth they produced. Accordingly they wanted to have a greater voice in the regulation of their businesses. Consequently they moved to construct their own legal and political institutions so that they could free themselves from the overbearing restraints and fees of feudalism. The governments of these emerging cities were typically managed by a council of merchants and administered by one or more magistrates. The magistrates, chosen by the citizens of the community, were responsible for collecting taxes and tolls, building public-works projects, and providing for the city's defense. These governments also developed their own codes of commercial dealing. They devised laws that regulated borrowing and lending and the sale and transfer of goods. These regulations limited individual rights for the good of the citizenry and the local economy. For example, they mandated that farmers only sell their produce in the town market, required artisans and craftsmen to ply their trades within the city walls, and implemented protective tariffs on goods brought into the city from other places. Artisans in many towns also established guilds, associations of craftsmen that regulated the activities of their members and protected them from competition from other towns. The guilds oversaw production practices, preserved the quality of the local product, regulated prices and wages, and provided a system of instruction for apprentices. In short the governments of the cities actively worked to protect local producers from economic competition from other towns. The nation-states of early modern Europe later emulated this practice on a much broader scale. Over time the laws of commerce became quite standardized as traveling merchants spread the knowledge of their effectiveness in promoting economic growth across the continent. Early modern cities also established special merchant courts that applied the commercial law. These courts provided speedy trials for traveling commercialists and ensured that the property rights of local producers were being protected.

The Free City. Most of the cities of Europe remained nominally subject to the authority of the feudal kings; however, around the twelfth century several cities established themselves as free cities or independent republics. Cities such as Venice, Florence, Milan, Bruges, and

Ghent became the beneficiaries of the Renaissance economic expansion and developed into formidable commercial powers. The governments of these cities offered personal liberty to their residents. The peasants of the manor often abandoned the estates of their lord and their feudal obligations for the freedom and economic opportunity offered by the free cities. In other areas of Europe towns joined together into formal leagues or confederations to deal with problems of security, piracy, and robbery. The political independence of the free cities and leagues and their economic prosperity helped to bring on the decline of feudalism. The feudal structure was not capable of administering and allocating the new sources of wealth that were coming in from around the world during the Renaissance. These pressures, and the reinvigoration of the monarchies, finally destroyed the feudal system and left in its place modern, capitalistic nation-states.

Rise of the Nation-State. The political and economic power that flowed from the manors to the cities also had the effect of strengthening the monarchies of Europe against the feudal nobility. Since the cities were producing considerable wealth, the crown heads of Europe could tax the cities and their residents and avoid appealing to the nobility for revenue. In addition the merchant class preferred a strong, central government that could provide order and security for commerce throughout the nation. Therefore, the cities and the commercial classes willingly turned to the monarchy for that protection. As part of this process many post-Renaissance cities relinquished regulatory control of manufacturing and commerce to the national governments. In other cases the kings of Europe simply seized control of the cities within their realm. The monarchs of Europe also slowly acquired the allegiance of a national populace tired of overbearing and warring feudal lords. A powerful king or queen offered the promise of national law and order, and as a general rule, the people preferred the authority of the Crown over that of the nobility. To facilitate the expansion of their power, the monarchs of Europe sent out administrative superintendents and legal officers to exert their authority and presence throughout the country. These agents expanded the royal judicial system throughout the land and enforced the nation's law over the people of their kingdoms. As the commercial economy became more important in early modern Europe, rulers also created national armies and navies to protect their kingdoms and their economic interests. The professionalization of the military required enormous outlays of capital, and the monarchs of the continent developed innovative taxes to increase their revenues. In particular monarchs expanded their tax base by transforming feudal duties into personal tax obligations. For example, under the feudal system an underlord owed a period of military service each year to his overlord. The English crown transformed this obligation into a payment called a scutage, a fee that nobles could pay to avoid military service. These new taxes dramatically enhanced a king's treasury and his authority over the nation. In this cycle of empowerment and taxation the ruler also used the new revenues to expand into new geographical areas. Other factors beyond the strengthening of the monarchy helped generate the large, centralized nation-states of western Europe. The development of a national culture helped bring the people of a nation together. The invention of the printing press helped standardize a nation's language. Improved roads and expanding commerce brought the people of a country into closer communication, and the great wars of the fourteenth and fifteenth centuries promoted a nationalistic spirit among the citizens of warring nations. By the end of the fifteenth century the emerging national powers of Europe were prepared to exert their authority beyond their borders.

Mercantilism. These European governments followed an economic policy called mercantilism. Under the theory of mercantilism, economic philosophers held that a finite amount of wealth existed in the world and that a nation achieved power in relation to its rivals by building up its supply of gold and silver bullion. In order to do this a nation ideally produced a favorable balance of trade and made its economy self-sufficient. To obtain this mineral wealth and independence, proponents of mercantilism argued that a nation should establish overseas colonies that would provide the nation with valuable natural resources. In the case of Spain, it sought to draw as much gold and silver out of the Western Hemisphere as possible. At the same time mercantilists also recommended that a nation use its colonies as a place of relocation for its citizens in times of overpopulation. The colonies theoretically would provide a productive class of consumers for homeland manufacturers. Hence mercantilist governments also encouraged industrial production and commerce. The theory further inflamed the rivalries that already existed between the European nations, and the governments of these emerging imperial powers sent agents out in all directions to seize the wealth of the world. The economic policy of mercantilism, more than anything else, persuaded the governments of Europe to colonize North America in the sixteenth, seventeenth, and eighteenth centuries.

TOPICS IN THE NEWS

CIVIL LAW

Legal Heritage. When Europeans began coming to America in the late fifteenth and sixteenth centuries, they brought with them two major legal traditions. Continental European nations had developed the civil law system while the English had formulated their own form of justice called the common law. The foundations of civil law can be found in the *Corpus Juris Civilis*, the code of Justinian. In the sixth century Justinian, the emperor of the eastern half of the Roman Empire, ordered his officials to reform and codify the law. These lawyers accumulated all of the existing laws, purged the obsolete ones, and revised the remainder into a comprehensive legal code. In the eleventh century Catholic legal scholars revived the *Corpus Juris Civilis* and made it the fundamental basis of law in continental Europe. The code provided clearly enunciated laws and procedures that judges used to resolve legal conflicts. Theoretically the responsibility of the judge in a civil system was to determine the

NATURAL LAW

Natural law is a legal philosophy that emerged in classical times. The theory became the most important element of legal thought during the Enlightenment. The advocates of natural law contend that there exists in nature a system of rules and principles that guide human conduct. These rules and principles exist independently of laws created by governments. Proponents of natural law believe that the elements of natural law can be identified by rational thought. Ideally, according to natural-law theorists, governments should attempt to identify the principles of natural law and codify them into their political systems and legal codes. While some jurists only admitted that these laws existed in nature, several Christian legal philosophers of the medieval period argued that God created natural law at the beginning of time.

Source: Francis Stephen Ruddy, *International Law in the Enlightenment: The Background of Emmerich de Vattel's "Le Droit des Gens"* (Dobbs Ferry, N.Y.: Oceana, 1975).

facts of the case, identify the relevant principle of the civil code, and apply it to the case at hand. Practically speaking, then, the judges of continental Europe historically had less discretion to construe the law than did their counterparts in England.

Charlemagne. The Holy Roman Emperor Charlemagne also contributed some important concepts to the Continental legal tradition. Charlemagne divided his empire into a number of jurisdictional units called counties. He appointed counts, administrators of the noble class, to govern the counties. In particular the counts were responsible for providing justice for the people within their jurisdiction. Thus the emperor's county courts provided justice from the royal throne at the local level. Charlemagne's court, the *curia regis,* served as the highest court of appeal over these county courts. In addition Charlemagne sent out administrative officers to ensure that the local courts were functioning properly. He also authorized these officials to decide cases in areas that did not have permanent judges. These agents of the Holy Roman Emperor were the antecedents for three important European civil-law traditions: the assizes or assemblies of knights that served as an investigative judicial body; the circuit courts, in which judges rode from town to town dispensing justice; and the theory of royal judicial supremacy, in which the king sat as the ultimate arbiter of the law of the land.

Parlement. After the breakup of Charlemagne's empire, the nations of Europe gradually adopted a similar scheme of hierarchical and centralized legal authority. For example, the Parlement, the chief judicial body of France, developed out of Louis IX's *curia regis* in the thirteenth century. The Parlement, a permanent court located in Paris, heard legal cases and reviewed the decisions of the bailiffs and seneschals, the royal representatives at the local level. In the fourteenth century the French king established parlements throughout all of the provinces of France. Effectively then the crown asserted its control over the judicial administration of the country. From time to time the monarchs of Europe reformed specific aspects of the Continental system. Louis IX, for instance, ended the ancient practice of trial by combat. Under this system of justice the parties to a dispute battled to death or submission. Trial by combat was grounded on the presumption that God would intervene in the battle and ensure that the right party emerged victorious. Louis ended trial by combat because he believed it a barbaric way of resolving disputes. However, the idea that God was an active agent in the judicial process remained an integral element of European justice for centuries to come. Continental courts also used the inquisitorial method of criminal justice. Under that system a criminal defendant did not have the right to a trial by jury. Whereas the English judge developed into an impartial umpire in a trial, the Continental trial judge took an active role in finding evidence and questioning witnesses. The inquisitorial method allowed the court to use torture to coerce confessions from criminal defendants. Torture, of course, prompted thousands of innocent defendants to admit to crimes that they did not commit.

Ecclesiastical Law. By the late medieval period the people of western Europe were subject to a potpourri of laws, courts, and customs derived from the Germanic tribal traditions, the decrees of the kings and the Holy Roman Emperor, the feudal contract, and the commercial laws of the free cities. In addition the ecclesiastical courts of the Catholic Church claimed jurisdiction over areas of the law that are now considered strictly secular. The bishops of the Church presided over the ecclesiastical courts and applied the canon law, the principles of the Christian church as pronounced by the Pope. These courts claimed jurisdiction over priests, monks, theological students, and widows, orphans, and other wards of the Church. The courts also held jurisdiction over moral or religious questions. This claim of jurisdiction was broad and included not just cases of Church dogma but disputes involving marriage, commercial transactions sanctioned by oath, and criminal cases. The decisions in these cases could ultimately be appealed to the Pope. The sanctions applied in criminal cases in the Church courts tended to be less severe than those in the king's secular courts. In particular the Church preferred not to issue sentences that required corporal punishment. Therefore, in some cases the legal systems of the Catholic Church and the monarchy worked together to torture and punish suspected violators of the law. In 1233 Pope Gregory IX sanctioned the creation of special inquisitorial courts for the purpose of locating and punishing heretics. The Church endowed these special courts with broad powers, including the authority to use torture to obtain confessions. Those found guilty of heresy were subject to penalties that ranged from penance to imprisonment. In extreme cases the inquisitorial courts turned convicted heretics over to the state to be burned at the stake. In all but the most serious of offenses, however, the ecclesiastical courts imposed monetary fines. These fines were a substantial source of revenue for the Church. Over time the kings of Europe recognized the potential income and coercive authority that attached to the institution holding the judicial power, gradually seized control over criminal jurisdiction from the Church, and transferred it

to their royal courts. Despite this assertion of royal criminal jurisdiction, the Catholic Church continued to retain considerable judicial power well into the colonial period.

Sources:
John H. Langbein, *Torture and the Law of Proof: Europe and England in the Ancien Regime* (Chicago, Ill.: University of Chicago Press, 1977);

Susan Reynolds, *Kingdoms and Communities in Western Europe, 900–1300* (Oxford, U.K.: Clarendon Press, 1997).

ENGLISH COMMON LAW

Origins. Between the reign of William I in the eleventh century and Elizabeth I in the sixteenth century, the government of England was transformed into a constitutional monarchy grounded on the rule of law. Although the Roman Empire had conquered much of the island of Britain, their civil law system did not leave the lasting influence that it did on the continent of Europe. Instead, until 1066, English legal institutions were influenced more by the customary traditions of the Germanic Angle and Saxon tribes. Consequently, unlike the civil law nations, the parliamentary code was not a prominent source of law in precolonial England. Rather than being written down into a comprehensive code, English law was the accumulation of legal customs and traditions. This law became known as the "common law" because it became common throughout England. The mechanism that produced the common law was the rule of *stare decisis,* which informally requires judges to follow past decisions on the same questions of law and fact. Stare decisis encouraged both uniformity and flexibility in the law as judges followed precedent, or carved out distinctions from those precedents, when issuing rulings. Over time the common law developed into a complex system of rules and principles that could only be understood after considerable study and experience in court. The men who became knowledgeable in the common law and represented individuals with legal problems in English courts became known as lawyers.

The Jury. In 1066 William the Conqueror, a Norman, invaded England and began a new age in English history. William greatly enhanced royal political authority during his reign. He created and collected a national tax and insisted that all feudal lords owed their ultimate allegiance to the king. William also diminished the legal authority of the feudal lords by encroaching on the jurisdiction of the manorial courts. He retained the Anglo-Saxon jurisdictional framework of shires that English kings had devised in the eleventh century. Under the shire system administrative and legal authority was held by a royal officer called the shire reeve (sheriff). William also integrated the jury into English justice. Under the jury system a royal minister or justice, who was usually a clergyman, would go out into the country to determine the wealth of the manorial estates for the purpose of taxation. The minister summoned a group of twelve free men together and asked them to testify under oath about the alue of each estate. This assembly of free men was called jury. Eventually the jury also became the body responsible for finding facts and issuing verdicts in civil and criminal cases. While the Continental nations continued to follow the inquisitorial method of justice, the English gradually developed an adversarial system. Under the adversarial process the parties to a dispute argued their cases in front of a judge and a jury of their peers. During the early centuries of the jury system the judge and jury were actively involved in looking for evidence. The jury could even ask questions of the parties and witnesses in a trial. Gradually, however, the judge and jury became more independent and left trial strategy and the location of evidence to the parties and their lawyers. The judge took on the role of an umpire who decided questions of law. The jury became primarily responsible for deciding factual questions. In the twelfth century Henry II expanded the use of the jury to identify and indict persons suspected of committing criminal acts. The king required these "grand juries," which were comprised of several members of the community, to report every case of robbery, murder, and arson that had occurred since their last meeting with the circuit justice.

Magna Carta. By the thirteenth century the monarchy had seized a considerable amount of political and legal power from the feudal lords and transferred it to royal courts and councils. Henry I, for example, established a permanent council called the Court of the Exchequer. This group of royal advisors was responsible for collecting taxes, paying for the expenses of government, and auditing the minor officials who handled the nation's money. The Court of the Exchequer was the first of several special councils or departments created to deal with specific affairs of the state. During the late twelfth and thirteenth centuries several groups began to chafe at the trend toward centralized monarchical authority. In 1215 nobles, clergymen, and commoners rose up against King John and forced him to accept and seal what has come to be known as the Magna Carta (Great Charter). In this agreement John promised that he and his successors would follow the rule of law in dealing with their vassals and subjects. The Magna Carta implied that there was a law higher than that of the king's will and that the nobility had a legal right to force the king to abide by the law of the nation. Article 39 of the charter also established the principle of due process, the idea that the state cannot take away an individual's property or freedom without a fair and impartial hearing. The English would come to conceive of the Magna Carta as the foundation of liberty and constitutional government.

Courts. By the time of Edward I, English legal jurisdiction was divided into several separate courts with special areas of jurisdiction. The Court of Common Pleas was responsible for hearing civil cases between commoners. The Court of King's Bench was responsible for trying civil and criminal cases and became the highest court of appeal in the nation. The Court of the Exchequer handled the financial affairs of the nation and had exclusive jurisdiction over cases involving unpaid taxes. Edward I also established the Court of Chancery to take over the civil cases in equity (cases that involved disputes outside of the established common law) so that the king's council could devote its time to purely administrative and governmental affairs. During this same period a new judicial office emerged at the local level to handle civil functions and minor criminal offenses. This official was called the justice of the peace. The justices were usually large landowners or knights who had acquired popular respect and prominence among their communities. By 1600 the English judicial system had reached its modern form; and when English men and women began coming to settle in America, they brought with them the traditions of constitutionalism and the English common law.

Sources:

John Hamilton Baker, *An Introduction to English Legal History,* third edition (London: Butterworths, 1990);

Arthur R. Hogue, *Origins of the Common Law* (Bloomington: Indiana University Press, 1966).

EUROPEAN PARLIAMENTARY GOVERNMENT

Beginnings. The evolution of parliamentary government in Europe directly influenced the political structures that emerged in North America. Parliaments, or legislative assemblies, developed out of the feudal monarchies during the medieval period. The kings of Europe during that era often turned to their vassal underlords and court clergy for advice and counsel. These discussions between the king and his advisors were called parleys. In these meetings the king asked his vassals to support his policies for the country, requested their financial support, and listened to grievances from around the realm. In the twelfth and thirteenth centuries some European monarchs began inviting representatives from the towns and villages of their kingdom to important parleys. These assemblies of local representatives, noblemen, and clergy developed into formal parliaments, assemblies devoted to representing the interests of the different estates of a nation. During the early stages of parliamentary government, these different classes of representatives consulted as separate group. The monarch often called these assemblies together for the purpose of imposing new taxes on the people of the realm. Kings recognized that taxes would be easier to collect if they were approved by the representatives of the people. Eventually in England the parliament acquired enough power to force the king to obtain its consent before he imposed new taxes.

Representatives. The origins of the English Parliament can be traced to the Witenagemot, a body of men who performed important administrative, legislative, and judicial functions for the Anglo-Saxon kings. This body was replaced by the *curia regis,* or great council, when William the Conqueror invaded England in 1066. In the late thirteenth century the king of England called a meeting of national representatives. He ordered his sheriffs to "cause two knights from [each] county, two citizens from each city in the same county and two burgesses from each borough . . . to be elected without delay, and to cause them to come to us at the aforesaid time and place." This was perhaps one of the earliest meetings of the modern English Parliament. At the early stages of parliamentary government in England, the individual representatives did not have the right to take part in the consultations about the king's course of action. Instead they could only respond to questions from the royal court or announce their consent through their representative. This man was called the speaker of the house. The English Parliament was originally composed of four major social classes: the feudal lords and high clergy, the lower clergy, the knights, and the burgesses. The Parliament thus represented a wide range of political, military, and economic interests and could often force the king to abide by its wishes. These four estates originally sat in groups in different parts of the assembly hall in London. Each estate provided its own grant of money to the king for the expenses of the national government. Over time the lower clergy ended its participation in the Parliament. In addition the knights and the burgesses joined together to form a single house of Parliament. This body became known as the House of Commons because it represented the interests of the common people. The House of Commons became the body of government responsible for initiating legislation. The feudal lords and the high clergy also united, as the House of Lords. Thus, by the end of the fourteenth century, the English Parliament had reached its modern form. Occasionally, English monarchs attempted to ignore or overpower the national assembly. By the eighteenth century, however, Parliament had become the most influential base of political power in Britain.

Estates General and Cortes. Parliaments had also developed in France and Spain by the thirteenth century. In France the national assembly was known as the Estates General. Like the English Parliament, the Estates General developed out of the king's council. In 1302 King Philip IV began calling representatives of the city merchant classes, the clergy, and the nobility to Paris to obtain their consent and advice on decisions of national consequence. The Estates General did not initiate laws; it simply gave its consent to the monarch's wishes or provided him with grievances from the public or the nobility. The Estates General never accumulated as much political power as the English Parliament. Essentially this is due to the fact that the French assembly never acquired control over the financial affairs of the nation. The Estates General also never held any official authority (like the Magna Carta) to force a king to abide by its wishes, but it was able by unofficial means to draw royal attention to local problems. Unlike the English Parliament, which met fairly regularly, the French monarchs only called the Estates General into session in times of war or

when they wanted to impose extraordinary taxes. In fa the Estates General did not meet between 1614 an 1789. Since this representative body was relatively wea the monarchy and nobility retained formal politic power far longer than they did in England. The politic situation in Spain was quite similar to that of France. I that Catholic state the parliamentary assembly wa known as the Cortes. The Cortes originated in the king dom of Castile and was comprised of representatives the upper and middle classes. Like the French Estate General, the Cortes only occasionally limited the pow of the monarchy during the age of European exploratio In sum the national assemblies of Europe varied in the power relative to the monarch. In England Parliamer obtained considerable political power and limited th authority of the Crown. The rulers of France and Spai however, did not suffer from an intrusive parliament. A a result, by the end of the sixteenth century these latte two nations were moving toward an age of absolute mon archy.

Sources:

R. G. Davies and J. H. Denton, eds., *The English Parliament in t Middle Ages* (Philadelphia: University of Pennsylvania Press, 1981

J. R. Strayer, *On the Medieval Origins of the Modern State* (Princeto N.J.: Princeton University Press, 1970).

EUROPEAN PERCEPTIONS OF NATIVE GOVERNMENT

Land of Anarchy. When Europeans first encountere Native American communities in the late fifteenth an sixteenth centuries, they often commented that Indian lived without government in a state of nature much lik the animals of the forest. To Europeans, Indians did no seem to have parliaments, courts, or laws. Tomas Ortiz Dominican priest from Spain, wrote in 1525, "There i no justice among them. . . . They are unstable." Th Spanish jurist Juan Ginés de Sepúlveda wrote that th Indians observed no written laws. Instead, he said, the maintained "barbaric institutions and customs." Sinc the native cultures in America did not appear to hav

---

OBSERVATIONS ON NATIVE AMERICAN GOVERNMENT

Bartolomé de las Casas rejected the Spanish depiction of Indians as atheistic, uncivilized savages devoid of political, social, or legal institutions:

They are not ignorant, inhuman, or bestial. Rather, long before they had heard the word Spanish, they had properly organized states, wisely ordered by excellent laws, religion, custom. They cultivated friendship and, bound together in common fellowship, lived in populous cities in which they wisely administered the affairs of both peace and war justly and equitably, truly governed by laws that in many points surpass ours.

Source: Marvin Lunenfeld, ed., *1492: Discovery, Invasion, Encounter* (Lexington, Mass. & Toronto: D. C. Heath, 1991).

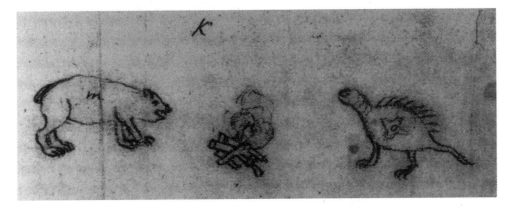

A French drawing of an Iroquois pictograph of the bear and turtle clans in council, circa 1666
(Archives Nationales, Paris)

these familiar legal and political institutions, many Europeans presumed that Indians lived in anarchy, that is, in a state of society without a working system of security and order. Some Europeans even suggested that In-

dians were intellectually incapable of organizing governments. Other European observers often attempted to apply their own political terminology and experience to what they observed in America. These commentators tended to look for monarchs and judges among the native societies because these were offices and institutions of government with which they were familiar. Consequently European officials often described particular Indians who appeared to be more influential than others as kings or emperors, even though Native American groups did not maintain European-styled monarchies. Some, such as Pietro Martire, an Italian historian, were astonished that native societies could survive without these institutions of government. In 1511 he wrote, "They deal truly with one another, without laws, without books, without judges." Since Europeans believed their civilization was the most advanced in the world, some of their political and religious leaders felt an obligation to convert Indian people to their way of life, including their legal and political concepts. George Peckham of England wrote in 1583 that Indians needed to be converted from their "disordered riotous riots and companies to a well governed common wealth." In particular Europeans believed that the natives held a flawed conception of land ownership. Indians did not think of land as something that could be divided up and sold to individuals. Peckham and other Europeans, on the other hand, believed that private ownership was an essential step toward civilization. Consequently European governments, and later the United States, would go to great lengths to convince Indians to embrace private property ownership.

Native Reality. People come together and form political institutions for basic purposes. They want to improve their ability to obtain food, shelter, and other necessities of life. In addition they seek to provide security for themselves and a sense of order for their community. In reality Indian communities on the eve of the European discovery of the Americas maintained functioning systems of law and order that were as effective in providing for the welfare and security of their communities as the centralized governments of Europe. Most native societies encouraged behavior that was in the best interest of the commonweal and maintained social mechanisms that provided clear parameters of acceptable and unacceptable behavior. Over the thousands of years before Christopher Columbus, the native peoples of the Americas had constructed forms of government that adequately responded to the unique demands of their environments and subsistence methods. As such Native American government had become quite diverse across the continent by the age of Columbus. In the Arctic and Subarctic, in the Great Basin, and throughout the Great Plains native people depended on hunting and gathering for the preponderance of their food. These peoples were necessarily nomadic and lived in small, mobile bands. As a result these peoples maintained governments that were informal and limited in organization and scope. Their governments were not structured in a hierarchical fashion. Instead the people of these communities spread the power of making decisions to most of the adult population. In the river valleys and flood plains of arable North America, Indian peoples usually occupied specific territories and produced their own food through sophisticated agricultural techniques. Agricultural production on these lands tended to support more people than a hunting and gathering existence. These societies required greater planning to organize the planting, harvesting, and distribution of food. Quite naturally the governments of these sedentary peoples were more complicated and centralized than those that continued to live by hunting and gathering. By the time of the European discovery of America, Native American governments ranged in complexity from the small groups led by family or clan patriarchs in the Great Basin to the powerful chiefdoms of the Southeast to the multitribal alliance of the Iroquois confederacy.

European Objectives. A few Europeans such as the Spanish friar Bartolomé de las Casas, recognized that Native Americans possessed effective and functional systems of government and admired the relative stability of their societies. However, views such as those of las Casas were exceptions to the norm of ethnocentrism. Throughout the European colonial period in America, European lawyers and rulers that did recognize the existence of Indian government tended to act on the presumption that native governments were illegitimate, inferior to those of Europe, and not worth preserving. The leaders of the European nations used these ill-founded presumptions about Indian political and legal organization to justify their actions when they took the lands of Native American peoples. Since the Indians did not seem to occupy all of their land or maintain national borders, the kings of Europe and their legal counselors often argued that Indians did not have the right to own the large tracts of land on which they lived. Over time European legal philosophers developed theories that their kings or queens could use to justify the seizure of the Americas and the extension of their sovereignty over the people who lived there.

BEFORE EUROPEANS

A Native American song that described Mexico before the coming of Europeans:

There was then no sickness.

They had then no aching bones.

They had then no high fever.

They had then no smallpox.

They had then no burning chest.

They had then no abdominal pains.

They had then no consumption.

They had then no headache.

At that time the course of humanity was orderly.

The foreigners made it otherwise when they arrived here.

Source: John Mack Faragher, and others, *Out of Many: A History of the American People* (Englewood Cliffs, N.J.: Prentice-Hall, 1994).

In many cases these Europeans simply misrepresented the existence and nature of native government and land use as a convenient means to justify their end of acquiring native land. Unfortunately for Native Americans these arguments would become precedents that the United States would later use in its own conquest and acquisition of Indian land.

Sources:

James Axtell, *The European and the Indian: Essays in the Ethnohistory of Colonial North America* (Oxford, U.K.: Oxford University Press, 1981);

Robert F. Berkhofer Jr., *The White Man's Indian: Images of the American Indian from Columbus to the Present* (New York: Knopf, 1978);

Robert A. Williams Jr., *The American Indian in Western Legal Thought: The Discourses of Conquest* (Oxford, U.K.: Oxford University Press, 1990).

NATIVE AMERICAN GOVERNMENT: FIRST ORIGINS

Paleolithic Era. Based on archeological evidence, students of Indian culture have drawn some limited conclusions about the origins of Native American government. During the Paleolithic or Paleo-Indian period, the era of Indian social development before 8000 B.C., Indian peoples lived a nomadic lifestyle that centered around the hunting of large game. Paleolithic Indians lived and hunted in very small groups and roamed over a widespread geographical area. Their political structure was, of necessity, limited and informal. In the earliest Native American societies the family was the primary social unit. Occasionally kinship groups or extended families joined together into bands, autonomous social and political units that lived, subsisted, and survived on their own. Bands were essentially egalitarian, meaning that most or all adult members participated in the process of making decisions for the group. Generally an adult male

Timucuan tribal leaders meeting while women prepare *casina,* an emetic used to purify individuals on important occasions (engraving from Nicholas Le Challeux, *Discours de l'historie de la Floride,* 1566)

informally led the band. These leaders probably acquired their influence because of their proficiency as hunters. They did not have, however, any coercive authority over the rest of the members of the group.

Archaic Period. With the extinction of the mammoth, the subsistence methods of people became more diversified. Instead of relying solely on the large mammals for food, some native groups turned to the hunting of smaller animals or the gathering of plants, seeds, and fruits. Since flora and fauna varied across the continent, the lifestyles of people became more varied as groups adapted to subsist in the environment in which they lived. This period of diffusion and variation is known as the Archaic era (8000–1500 B.C.). Many groups during this period became somewhat less nomadic. Although most Archaic Indians continued to migrate from place to place, many settled into regional patterns of movement or tended to remain primarily in one specific area. Some groups, particularly in California and the Pacific Northwest, did establish permanent settlements because of the reliability and availability of the local food sources.

Cooperation. In some areas Archaic Indians began to reside together in greater numbers. They also began to exhibit sophisticated coordination in their hunting and gathering expeditions. For example, archeologists have discovered evidence of the jump-kill technique of hunting, in which large numbers of hunters worked together as a unit to force large game over cliffs to their deaths. Similarly, in the Southwest groups of hunters con-

structed corrals to trap game. Some groups in the eastern half of North America also used the technique of controlled burning to revive the plants and deer population of the forests of their environment. The new growth that emerged after a clearing fire provided fresh supplies of fruits, berries, nuts, leaves, and roots. Not only did this new growth augment the Archaic peoples' vegetable diet, it also attracted deer. As a result the deer population expanded in the areas recently cleared by the controlled burning. These processes, which made hunting more productive, was another indication that the relationships between unrelated Indian peoples were becoming more complicated. Several other cooperative efforts emerged during this era. For instance, as Archaic people became more sedentary in some areas, they demonstrated a greater interest in how they disposed of the corpses of the deceased. In other words some Archaic peoples began to spend more time and effort on group mortuary rites. Coordinated trade efforts throughout many parts of North America also began during this period. The development of trade routes between native groups allowed innovations, ideas, and methods to be spread around the continent. Individual native groups developed distinctive religious beliefs, and traders spread these beliefs along the trade networks. Knowledge about agricultural production also began to be passed up from Mexico into North America during the late Archaic era. Social organization was thus becoming somewhat more complicated than it had been during the Paleolithic period. However, formal political organization continued to be quite limited. Archaic Indians apparently did not make class or status distinctions between themselves for political or social purposes. They also did not centralize political power into the hands of dominant leaders. Instead decisions probably continued to be made with the participation of the entire adult community through consultation and consensus.

Source:

Alice Kehoe, *North American Indians: A Comprehensive Account* (Englewood Cliffs, N.J.: Prentice-Hall, 1981).

NATIVE AMERICAN GOVERNMENT: EASTERN WOODLANDS

Adena cultures. The social organization of native cultures became more complex in eastern North America during the Woodlands era (1500 B.C. to A.D. 700). The climate of the eastern portion of the continent was mild, moist, and lush and capable of supporting communities with large populations. The Woodlands peoples lived in temporary settlements near rivers and tributaries in groups of 25 to 150 people. Most of the Woodlands Indians continued to pursue the same lifestyle and maintained the same informal political structure as their ancestors had done during the Archaic period. However, in one area of eastern North America, Indians developed a distinctive way of life called the Adena culture. The Adena peoples emerged about 500 B.C. and were concentrated in the upper Ohio River valley. While the Adena societies had begun to cultivate a few plants, they primarily continued to obtain the preponderance of their food supply by hunting and gathering. Like the rest of the Woodlands peoples, the Adena Indians lived in small temporary villages and continued to migrate from spot to spot within a broad geographical area. However, the Adena peoples were distinct from their neighbors in that they were evolving toward a more complicated pattern of sociopolitical organization. The best evidence of this increasing complexity were the physical structures they left behind. In an area within about 150 miles of present-day

POPULATION CENTERS

The following is a list of the estimated populations of Cahokia and some major European cities during the thirteenth century:

City	Population
Cahokia	30,000–40,000
Cologne	30,000
Florence	90,000
Ghent	40,000–50,000
London	40,000
Milan	100,000
Paris	100,000
Venice	100,000

Chillicothe, Ohio, the Adena people built hundreds of burial mounds.

Burial Practices. The Adena societies practiced a sophisticated religion that placed considerable significance on death, funeral ceremonies, and burial practices. Occasionally Adena societies met in large gatherings to honor and bury beloved or respected members of their society. After death the people placed the body of the deceased into a burial lodge. They allowed the corpse to decompose in the lodge until only the skeleton remained. At that point they buried the bones and began depositing baskets of dirt over the grave until they formed a small mound. In some cases the community constructed massive mounds over the gravesite. These mounds were the earliest major public-works projects in North America. These prominent burials suggest that the Adena societies had begun to elevate certain people to a special status. The burial sites of these individuals contained rare and valuable goods that were not indigenous to the region.

Engraving of an Iroquoian longhouse, circa 1720 (Newberry Library, Chicago)

These unusual goods were obtained through trade networks that ranged across much of the continent. Some Adena graves contained obsidian and the teeth of sharks and alligators, items that were not natural to the Ohio Valley. Archeologists generally did not find these trade items in the graves surrounding these special individuals. Scholars have concluded that a small group of people held a monopoly over the access to these goods and used them while they were alive to signify or validate their elevated status in the society. Archeologists have also found that Adena cultures sometimes accorded different types of burial to different individuals. The Adena people cremated some bodies and placed them in clay urns. They buried others rather simply, without grave goods. They coated some corpses with the red mineral hematite. Some of the deceased were buried in elaborate tombs. Many of these differences can probably be attributed to simple local variations in custom. However, these distinctions in burial goods and mortuary methods are also evidence of the existence of stratified societies, that is, cultures in which the community divides people into different levels of social importance or value. Social stratification is important in examining the development of government because it suggests that a society's political structure is becoming more complex and hierarchical.

Hopewell. While the Adena peoples lived in a rather limited area, their culture influenced a region that extended from the Gulf of Mexico to the Great Lakes and from the lower Missouri River to the Appalachian Mountains. In some areas the Adena culture continued to evolve toward greater social and political complication. Around the first century A.D., some of these Adena societies developed into what archaeologists refer to as the Hopewell culture. These scholars have identified Hopewell sites in the Ohio and Mississippi River valleys and along the Gulf Coast and in Florida. Hopewell societies carried larger populations than those of the Adena type and were spread over a larger geographical area. The burial mounds of the Hopewell societies tended to be larger and higher and were often formed in the shape of an animal or a geometric figure. Works such as these required community cooperation, engineering skills, and close management. Clearly some individuals during this period were developing specialized leadership abilities beyond those required for hunting and other subsistence activities. Hopewell mounds also included a wider variety of status goods. Some of the Hopewell graves included pearls, mica, quartz, bear teeth, copper, and other sacred minerals. Burial sites contained intricately designed pottery, statuettes, and clay or stone pipes that symbolized animals and spiritual beings. Apparently Hopewell societies cremated most of their deceased and reserved burial for only the most important or influential people. In some archeological sites it appears that hunters received a higher status in the community because their graves were more elaborately constructed and contained more status goods. Again, these distinctions in the way Hopewell societies treated their deceased demonstrated a trend toward social hierarchy. More than likely these cultures accorded certain families a special place of privilege. Some scholars suggest that these societies were marked by the emergence of "big-men." These leaders acquired their position because of their ability to persuade others to agree with their positions on important matters. They also perhaps were able to develop influence by the clever creation of reciprocal obligations with other important members of the community. Whatever the source of their status and power, the emergence of "big-men" was another step toward the development of the highly structured and stratified sociopolitical organization called the chiefdom.

Sources:

Patricia Galloway, *Choctaw Genesis, 1500–1700* (Lincoln: University of Nebraska Press, 1995);

Alice Kehoe, *North American Indians: A Comprehensive Account* (Englewood Cliffs, N.J.: Prentice-Hall, 1981).

NATIVE AMERICAN GOVERNMENT: MISSISSIPPIAN CHIEFDOMS

Emergence of Agriculture. Between 200 B.C. and A.D. 700 the native people of eastern North America began to adopt agricultural techniques and increased the prominence of harvested plant food like squash and sunflowers in their meals. Between 700 and 1200 the Woodlands cultures began to add cultivated corn and beans to their diets. By 1200 Indians in the east were growing corn almost everywhere that the climate would allow, from the present American border with Canada to the Gulf of Mexico. The availability of a reliable source of vegetable food allowed the population of Woodland communities to expand dramatically. As the population grew, these societies required more complicated systems of government. In some locations these societies developed severely stratified social classes and a hierarchical political structure. These societies were called chiefdoms.

The Chiefdom. In a chiefdom a paramount chief of great authority required the population of his adherent villages to provide him with a portion of their crop. Some chiefs also took a percentage of each individual's kill from hunting. This offering to the paramount chief is called tribute. The paramount chief then redistributed some of the tribute to his family. He also redirected the tribute to the towns of the chiefdom through his underchiefs. These subordinates to the chief were often related to the paramount chief by blood or marriage. The chief also used tribute for public purposes. He conveyed it to other peoples in diplomatic ceremonies or redistributed it to members of the society who could not provide for themselves. The larger chiefdoms were capable of organizing, collecting, and redistributing sustenance for thousands of people. Between the eighth and fifteenth centuries large and powerful chiefdoms dominated many areas of eastern North America. The period of the great chiefdom is called the Mississippian era because most of these societies were located on the major river ways of the Mississippi River watershed. The largest and most powerful chiefdom, Cahokia, was located along the Mississippi itself, just outside of present-day St. Louis. Cahokia's population climbed as high as thirty thousand to forty thousand by the thirteenth century, making it the largest settlement in North America and one of the largest cities in the world at the time. Cahokia was so large and influential that it attracted tribute from towns and villages from several miles away. The hierarchical structure of the chiefdom brought a system of social order to thousands of adherents living in dozens of villages around the central residence of a chief. However, this order originated out of the authoritarian rule of the paramount chief. Consequently, chiefdoms were fragile sociopolitical structures that could collapse from various internal and external forces. Droughts, disease epidemics, and war always had the potential to bring on an implosion of the chiefdom.

Southeastern Ceremonial Complex. The chief held the power of life or death over every member of his chiefdom and over prisoners captured in wars against neighboring tribes. The Mississippian societies were characterized by a similar set of religious beliefs, burial rites, and symbolic artwork that archeologists refer to as the Southeastern ceremonial complex. Most Mississippian societies worshiped a sun god and maintained a fertility cult. Many of the paramount chiefs, such as those of the Natchez, often claimed to be descendants of the sun. The people of the chiefdom therefore treated the chief and his family as divine beings. When the paramount chief died, the people of the chiefdom often killed his wives, children, and servants so that they could join him in the afterlife. Since food production was organized by the chief and his subordinates, some people were free to become specialized potters, artists, and sculptors. At the same time organized agricultural production allowed these societies to use available labor and technological ability to build massive public-works projects such as the temple mounds of Cahokia, Moundville, and Etowah. The largest mound in North America, Monks Mound in Cahokia, covered more than eighteen acres and was over one hundred feet tall. The mounds were used as temples and residences for the chiefs and priests of Mississippian societies. The temple mound was built as a place to honor the god of the sun and was symbolic of the divine power of the paramount chief.

Decline and Collapse. By the time the Spanish began widespread colonization in the sixteenth century, almost all of the major chiefdoms had collapsed and splintered into remnant groups. The specific reasons for the decline and fall of the great chiefdoms is still unclear. Some scholars argue that the populations of the chiefdoms were decimated by diseases brought to the Americas by European explorers, fishermen, and castaways. Depopulation by disease, combined with devastating civil wars, could have caused the collapse of the tributary system of

food production and distribution. Other students of chiefdoms suggest that some of them failed because of a crisis in the succession of leadership from one paramount chief to another. Other theorists contend that the simple structure of a chiefdom was inherently unstable and that chiefdoms often developed, disintegrated into smaller groups, and then reemerged again in a natural cycle. Whatever the cause of their demise, the disappearance of the chiefdom resulted in a political and social leveling of the peoples of the Woodlands region.

Sources:

Patricia Galloway, *Choctaw Genesis, 1500-1700* (Lincoln: University of Nebraska Press, 1995);

Charles Hudson, *The Southeastern Indians* (Knoxville: University of Tennessee Press, 1976).

NATIVE AMERICAN GOVERNMENT: THE SOUTHEAST

The Region. After the decline of the great Mississippian chiefdoms, the native population of the southeastern part of the present-day United States was dispersed into dozens of different bands and villages. Occasionally these small groups coalesced into larger cultural units called tribes. Through this process several large and powerful tribes, comprised of thousands of people, emerged about the same time that Europeans were beginning to colonize the Southeast. The Creek Indians were an example of this process of amalgamation. They were a conglomeration of formerly autonomous villages and peoples such as the Alabamas, Euchees, and Hitchitis. These peoples had their own cultural traditions and spoke different languages and dialects. Over time, though, these combinations of smaller groups developed common cultures and systematic methods of regulating behavior and preserving order. Although the Creeks, Choctaws, Chickasaws, and other southeastern Indians maintained their own unique political traditions, some aspects of their governments were common throughout most of the region. These customary practices facilitated the preservation of the social and spiritual state of balance and harmony that was essential to native life.

Localized Government. As was the case with many native peoples, the clan was the primary form of social organization and the main source of institutional order among the southeastern tribes. However, some matters involved all members of a community. These concerns were managed by the town or village council. Generally speaking, the villages of the southeastern tribes in the precolonial period were self-governing and autonomous. Before 1600 they rarely united in combined council for concerted action. There were no national governments to speak of at this time. The center of political activity in a southeastern village was the council house. In most of these groups the entire adult community met to decide important political or diplomatic questions. The villages reached decisions through a process of prolonged discussion and debate. The objective of the council was to reach a consensus, a course of action that most or all of

John White's rendering of Pomeioc, a typical Algonquian village surrounded by a defensive palisade, 1585

the community agreed upon. Although the town councils were comprised of the entire population of the village, they were usually particularly influenced by three groups—the priests, the clan elders, and a group of "beloved men" who had achieved great deeds as warriors or civil leaders. Although these men held considerable sway, all men and women were allowed to express their opinions. Some women, such as the "beloved women" of the Cherokees, held a particularly strong voice among the civil councils of their communities. Of course the process of consensus required individual members of the council to compromise their positions in order to reach agreement. Debates over the appropriate course of action might continue for days, and the development of a consensus would often require entrenched dissenters to withdraw from the debate.

Leadership. Although southeastern communities were predominantly egalitarian, there were certain individuals of office or influence who were able to persuade others to follow a proposed course of action. These leaders usually achieved their position from their past success in war, administration, oratory, or diplomacy. Most of the villages selected a principal chief. Among some tribes the post historically belonged to a particular clan. In those cases the office was hereditary, and under the mat-

rilineal system succession fell to the chief's nephew, his oldest sister's son. If this nephew was ill-suited for leadership, however, he could just as easily be passed over for a more capable man. The chief held his position at the will of the community. If he lost the confidence of the people, he could be removed from leadership. The principal chief was assisted by a professional speaker who articulately presented the chief's positions and thoughts for him at council meetings. The chief rarely spoke in council. Therefore, it was up to the speaker to persuade the council to follow his chief's proposed course of action.

Moieties. Southeastern Indians conceived of the oversight of war and civil government as distinctly separate functions that required different groups of leaders. This had the effect of preventing one individual or one group from acquiring an unhealthy monopoly of power, a circumstance that native people feared. These social divisions of responsibility were called moieties; the term implies the division of a society into halves. The white or peacetime moiety was strongly influenced by a group of sage and experienced clan elders and was responsible for all governmental activities except war. The red moiety, dominated by younger warriors, ascended to leadership when the village became involved in hostilities with other villages or tribes. Among the Creeks a civil chief presided as head of a council of clan elders. These men were experts in diplomacy and administration. The white council was responsible for divvying up agricultural lands between clans, for accumulating and distributing the town's food surplus, and for maintaining trade and diplomatic relations with other peoples. The red moiety was divided into rigid ranks of military leadership. In times of war the red moiety would ascend temporarily to almost an authoritarian leadership of the nation. Upon a decision to go to war by the white moiety, the highest ranking military man, the big or great warrior, as he was called, would take over the reins of government. When peace was restored, the white government returned to national leadership.

The Green Corn Ceremony. Southeastern societies celebrated a particularly important annual event, the Busk, or Green Corn, Ceremony, that functioned to clear the air of all ill feelings in the community. During this harvest festival all animosities, conflicts, and offenses (except murder) were symbolically exorcised. Over several days each community would ignite a new ceremonial fire, conduct rituals of spiritual cleansing, give thanks for its harvest, hear from its priests a recitation of the laws and history of the people, and receive admonitions from the spiritual leaders about the importance of forgiveness and renewal. The Green Corn Ceremony allowed each individual to begin the year untainted and revived, and it signified a return to the precious and fragile state of natural balance and harmony.

Sources:
Michael D. Green, *The Politics of Indian Removal: Creek Government and Society in Crisis* (Lincoln: University of Nebraska Press, 1982);

Charles Hudson, *The Southeastern Indians* (Knoxville: University of Tennessee Press, 1976);

Rennard Strickland, *Fire and the Spirits: Cherokee Law from Clan to Court* (Norman: University of Oklahoma Press, 1975);

John R. Swanton, *The Indians of the Southeastern United States* (Washington, D.C.: Smithsonian Institution Press, 1946).

NATIVE AMERICAN GOVERNMENT: THE WEST

Great Basin and Great Plains. Archeological evidence suggests that the methods of acquiring food and shelter for the native people of the Great Basin and Great Plains became more diversified during the Archaic period. However, the political structures of these societies apparently changed little. These societies continued to exist in bands or small groups of extended families. Only occasionally during the winter or for the purpose of gathering a specific food did several families come together to form a temporary village. Most of the time, though, these small groups pursued their own patterns of movement. This seasonal roaming had the effect of limiting the development of settled societies in large numbers and kept social organization centered around the kinship group. There were no hierarchies of leadership. Instead the family and social pressure provided order

within these small communities. Government continued to be egalitarian and decentralized. An older and experienced man likely directed the activities of the band and organized hunting expeditions, planned migratory movements, and mediated disputes between individuals. The men who became leaders in these societies were probably industrious, generous, eloquent, and skilled in hunting and acquiring food. Most bands also recognized a priest, or shaman, who served as a conduit between the community and the spirit world.

Southwest. Societies in the Southwest developed quite differently from those in the Great Basin and Great Plains. In the early stages of the Archaic period, native peoples in the Southwest continued to move from one region to another in seasonal patterns. Like the people of the Great Basin and Great Plains, they continued to live in small groups with a similarly uncomplicated political structure. However, between 3500 and 2500 B.C. some southwestern societies began to farm and domesticate animals such as dogs and turkeys. As the farming of corn, beans, squash, and pumpkins replaced hunting and gath-

THE RATTLESNAKE'S REVENGE

Cherokee parents told their children the following story to illustrate how the clan law of blood revenge functioned. The story begins with a man who hears a strange sound as he is coming home from a hunting trip:

Looking about he found that he had come into the midst of a whole company of rattlesnakes, which all had their mouths open and seemed to be crying. He asked them the reason of their trouble, and they told him that his own wife had that day killed their chief, the Yellow Rattlesnake, and they were just now about to send the Black Rattlesnake to take revenge. The hunter said he was very sorry, but they told him that if he spoke the truth he must be ready to make satisfaction and give his wife as a sacrifice for the life of their chief. Not knowing what might happen otherwise, he consented. They then told him that the Black Rattlesnake would go home with him and coil up just outside the door in the dark. He must go inside, where he would find his wife awaiting him, and ask her to get him a drink of fresh water from the spring. That was all. He went home and knew that the Black Rattlesnake was following. It was night when he arrived and very dark, but he found his wife waiting with his supper ready. He sat down and asked for a drink of water. She handed him a gourd full from the jar, but he said he wanted it fresh from the spring, so she took a bowl and went out of the door. The next moment he heard a cry, and going out he found that the Black Rattlesnake had bitten her and that she was already dying. He stayed with her until she was dead, when the Black Rattlesnake came out from the grass again and said his tribe was now satisfied.

Source: John Phillip Reid, *A Law of Blood: The Primitive Law of the Cherokee Nation* (New York: New York University Press, 1970).

ering as the primary means of subsistence, the peoples of the Southwest, like those in the East, became more sedentary. Unlike the Eastern Woodlands peoples, though, the communities of the Southwest did not have a plentiful water supply. Thus, over time the Southwestern Indians developed sophisticated irrigation techniques to water their crops. Remarkably they constructed canals, aqueducts, reservoirs, dikes, and dams without the wheel or beasts of burden. (The Spanish did not reintroduce the horse into North America until the sixteenth century.) Irrigation required community planning and effort, and the increasing importance of controlling the flow of water demanded a stable and effective political system.

Hohokams and Anasazis. Some Southwestern Indians, such as the Hohokams, who lived in the Salt and Gila River valleys, were so successful in their water management skills that they were often able to grow two separate crops in a growing season. The Hohokams lived in permanent villages of up to several hundred people. Most of these villages remained politically independent. However, some of them merged into large confederations that were tied together by the irrigation canals. A central village controlled important aspects of life in these confederations. For example, the council of the central village conducted trade and diplomatic negotiations, planned and assigned work responsibilities for the irrigation works, and organized religious ceremonies and ball games for the people of the confederation. Northeast of the Hohokams, around the Four Corners area, lived the Anasazi people. *Anasazi* is a Navajo word that means "the ancient ones." Sometime after the fifth century the Anasazis moved into pueblos, interconnected multifamily apartments of stone or adobe that were located under the cliffs or on the high mesas of the southwestern desert. The Anasazis collected water in reservoirs and then transferred it to their terraced agricultural fields through long canals, some of which extended for up to four miles. The Anasazis became powerful in the Southwest, and their culture left a lasting influence in the region. In the Chaco canyon in New Mexico several Anasazi villages united into a powerful confederation of about fifteen thousand people. From this site they built roads out of the canyon to affiliated pueblos as far as sixty miles away. They built these roads in straight lines directly over cliffs and boulders. On these roads the outer pueblo peoples of the Anasazi came to Chaco for religious ceremonies and trade. Because of their effective irrigation system, the people of Chaco were usually capable of producing enough food to provide for these outlying pueblos in harsh times. In the twelfth and thirteenth centuries, however, the Anasazi culture declined, the great confederations at Chaco and Canyon de Chelly disintegrated, and the Anasazi peoples dispersed throughout the Southwest.

Pueblo Government. The descendants of the Anasazis continued to live in adobe pueblos under their own unique form of sociopolitical structure. Pueblo communities held land in common. While village decisions required the unanimous consent of all of the adult men, women held an influential voice in the councils of government. Pueblo societies developed specialized offices for the unique responsibilities required by their lifestyle and environment. The people of the Isleta pueblo, for example, were governed by a chief, a war priest, and a hunting chief. Perhaps the chief's greatest responsibility was his selection of the individuals who were responsible for maintaining and managing the irrigation facilities. The Isleta people expected their chiefs to be gentle men who had never injured or killed a living being. The chief was required to remain within the pueblo at all times and was responsible for performing the agricultural rituals that ensured that the crops and irrigation works would receive adequate rain. Because his duties were so important to the preservation of the community, the public supported the chief by planting and harvesting his crops for him. The war priest, who was appointed by the chief, was responsible for obtaining meat, firewood, and clothing from the residents of the pueblo for the chief. The war priest was also the leader of a society of warriors that maintained internal order and protected the community and its farmland from invasion by outsiders. The hunting chief was responsible for leading the hunt and performing rituals that ensured that an adequate supply of game would be provided for the community. The pueblo communities also had specialized shamans who were responsible for the specific tasks of regulating the weather and healing. In short the Isleta people maintained an effective system of specialized leaders who oversaw every aspect of pueblo life.

Pacific Northwest. On the Pacific coast in the Northwest the people of the Archaic period resided in settled villages and took advantage of their rich marine environment. The abundant fish and plant life of the region supported large and stable villages and allowed the peoples of the coast to devote their time and effort to activities other than procuring food. Some clans distinguished themselves from others by producing elaborate totem poles or canoes carved from wood. By portraying a link between the family and a spiritual ancestor, the clan used the totem pole as a way to claim social superiority over other families. Like most native cultures, the only sense of responsibility and duty for individuals was to their families and their own villages. While the people of a northwestern community may have felt some sense of familiarity with the people of another village who spoke a related language or dialect, for the most part they did not recognize a political relationship to their neighbor villages. There were no great chiefdoms or confederations as there were in other parts of the continent. Each village maintained its own territory and claimed possession of distinct hunting grounds, fishing holes, meeting spots, and sacred locations. In some societies visitors who used these territorial spots were considered guests. In others, such as the Kutenai, visitors who used the resources of the people were considered trespassers. Consequently, the peoples of the Northwest occasionally warred with each other over particular fishing areas. Each village had a chief, a subchief, and a council who were responsible for governing and for encouraging harmony and peace in the community. While the chiefs were almost always men, women did have the right to express their opinions at council meetings of the village. All members of the village, men and women, could attend and speak at council meetings. The chief was responsible for settling disputes in the village, hosting the councils, counseling people of the community, and handling diplomatic affairs with other villages. As with most other native societies, however, the chief could only take action that conformed with the consensus of the village. The chief usually inherited his position from his father or brother. Ultimately, though, his authority had to be recognized by the council. The chief was considered to be an equal to all of the other members of the village. The community expected him to be honest, of great character, and a good mediator of disputes. With the council's support the chief selected a subchief and assigned him duties to perform. Many of the societies in this region also selected a speaker. At council meetings the chief whispered his thoughts into the ear of the speaker and the speaker delivered them on the chief's behalf. When a prospective chief attempted to gain a following among his community, he invited his village to a great feast called a potlatch. In the potlatch ceremony the aspiring leader would either give away to his neighbors or destroy almost all of the property that he owned. Throughout the ceremony the potlatch host would deliver chants pronouncing his abilities and ridiculing his rivals to the chieftainship. By giving away his possessions the prospective chief acquired a following of villagers who would be obligated to him in the future. Some Columbia River societies, such as the Sanpoil, selected a special officer called the Salmon Chief. The Salmon Chief held authority only during the fishing season and was usually a shaman or an individual who had the salmon as a guardian spirit. He determined who would build the fishing traps, decided when and where they would be set, and performed rituals that encouraged the fish to swim into them. He was also responsible for ensuring that the taboos and regulations regarding fishing were enforced and led the community in the First Salmon Ceremony, the most important event in the Sanpoil culture. After the catch the Salmon Chief decided how it would be distributed to the people of the village. As demonstrated by this sample of the varied forms of government in Native America, the political structure of a society was a product of the peoples' relationship with their environment.

Sources:
Alice Kehoe, *North American Indians: A Comprehensive Account* (Englewood Cliffs, N.J.: Prentice-Hall, 1981);

Alfonso Ortiz, *Handbook of North American Indians: Southwest*, volumes 9 and 10 (Washington, D.C.: U.S. Government Printing Office, 1979–1983).

PETRINE MANDATE

In the medieval period officials in the Catholic Church claimed that the Pope held supreme authority over all spiritual and secular matters by virtue of this passage from the sixteenth chapter of the book of Matthew:

13. When Jesus came into the coasts of Caesarea Philippi, he asked his disciples, saying, "Whom do men say that I the Son of Man am?"

14. And they said, "Some say that thou art John the Baptist; some Elias; and others, Jeremias, or one of the prophets."

15. He saith unto them, "But whom say ye that I am?"

16. And Simon Peter answered and said, "Thou art the Christ, the Son of the living God."

17. And Jesus answered and said unto him, "Blessed art thou, Simon Barjona; for flesh and blood hath not revealed it unto thee, but my Father which is in heaven.

18. And I say also unto thee, That thou art Peter, and upon this rock I will build my church; and the gates of hell shall not prevail against it.

19. And I will give unto thee the keys of the kingdom of heaven; and whatsoever thou shalt bind on earth shall be bound in heaven; and whatsoever thou shalt loose on earth shall be loosed in heaven."

NATIVE AMERICAN LAW: BLOOD REVENGE

Retaliation. Blood revenge was a process that many Native American groups used to resolve the animosities that resulted when one individual killed another. Blood revenge was, as one scholar called it, "the foundation of most [Indian] legal systems, the solder which holds together the social structure." This practice has also been called the *lex talionis*, Latin for the law of retaliation. In the Mosaic law of the Old Testament blood revenge was described as an "eye for an eye and a tooth for a tooth." However the lex talionis was far more complicated than the scripture implies. The law of blood revenge was grounded in the clan structure of a Native American society. In other words, the killing was not an act against the public but a private matter between the clans of the victim and the assailant. The killing created in the clan of the deceased both a legal right and a societal duty to enforce lethal revenge on the clan of the manslayer. At the same time the killer's kin had a sacred obligation to produce a life in exchange for the original victim and a duty to be indifferent or unresponsive when the victim's clan came for revenge. If this principle was respected by the society, then the second killing generally ended the retaliation process. Of course there were instances when the system did not work, and blood feuds developed between clans. However, for the most part the retaliatory killing returned the conflicting clans to the state of balance that so many native societies tried to main-

A 1494 woodcut of Christopher Columbus's arrival in the New World, showing imaginary
European-style houses on the islands

tain. The lex talionis also took on spiritual significance, for some tribes believed that the soul of the deceased could not enter the spirit world until his kinsmen had avenged his death. Blood revenge thus allowed a society to channel the despair and hatred spawned by a violent killing into a customary process that had the effect, if sufficiently ingrained in the society, of inhibiting a potentially dangerous feud between clans.

The Practice. The principles of blood revenge were quite unforgiving. If a nonrelative exacted the revenge, clan law considered this killing to be a separate death requiring another round of retaliation. The killing by the nonrelative also did not wipe out the debt of blood created by the first assault. The lex talionis also did not make a distinction between an accidental death or a premeditated homicide. The questions of intent or negligence were irrelevant under the practice. Moreover, blood revenge did not excuse a killing that resulted from self-defense. Some scholars suggest that blood revenge was so fundamental to some native groups that they even applied the law to their hunting. The Cherokees believed that after killing a deer, the game's ghost would follow the hunter back to his village in an effort to obtain blood revenge. The Cherokees feared that the ghost could retaliate by infecting the hunter and his kin with misfortune or a deadly disease. Therefore, native hunters performed special incantations over the game that they killed to pacify these spirits.

Mourning War. Though blood revenge had the potential to spawn endless bloodlettings between clans, the law was so ingrained as a way of life and justice that this was rarely the case. Each individual learned at an early age to respect the law of blood revenge. If one boy accidentally injured another, the latter child would look for an opportunity to retaliate. Retaliation was a mortal problem, however, on the intertribal level. Unlike Europeans, Indians did not usually fight wars for land, wealth, or religion. For young men war was a pathway toward social distinction. Consequently, wars sometimes began as young men set out to acquire acclaim and respect; the casualties that resulted often led to long wars of vendetta. Long conflicts, described as mourning wars, doomed some neighboring groups to almost interminable wars of blood revenge. Mourning wars between the different Iroquois tribes, for example, may have convinced those peoples to confederate in the fifteenth century and renounce the use of blood revenge against each other.

Compensation. Where legal systems are rigid in theory, as in blood revenge, they are often countered by practical exhibitions of flexibility. In other words there were probably many instances where the involved clans leavened the strict rule of revenge and allowed a killing to go unavenged. More than likely many accidental deaths went unpunished. Additionally, in various native societies the family of the victim could accept compensation payments in wampum, furs, or other goods instead of retaliating against the killer. The tender and acceptance of compensation, or the renunciation of revenge in particular situations, evidenced the perception among Native Americans that the law was functional. The law was strict; its adherents occasionally bent it.

Sources:

Charles Hudson, *The Southeastern Indians* (Knoxville: University of Tennessee Press, 1976);

John Phillip Reid, *A Law of Blood: The Primitive Law of the Cherokee Nation* (New York: New York University Press, 1970);

Daniel K. Richter, *The Ordeal of the Longhouse: The Peoples of the Iroquois League in the Era of European Colonization* (Chapel Hill: University of North Carolina Press, 1992).

America on a world map drawn by Alberto Catino in 1502
(Biblioteca Estense, Modena)

SPANISH CONQUEST OF THE AMERICAS: THE TREATY OF TORDESILLAS

Henry the Navigator. In the middle of the fifteenth century Prince Henry of Portugal subsidized several expeditions down the western coast of Africa. In 1455 Henry, who was known as "the Navigator," appealed to Pope Nicholas V to confer the title to all of the countries that his agents discovered on these voyages to Portugal. In return Henry promised to spread the Christian faith to nonbelievers and bring them under the authority of the Church. Nicholas, anxious to expand the religion beyond Europe, issued a papal bull called the *Romanus Pontifex*. This decree gave Portugal title to those African "provinces, islands, ports, districts and seas . . . which have already been acquired and which shall be acquired in the future." The Pope warned that any European monarch who encroached upon or interfered with Portugal's rights would be excommunicated from the Church. Excited by the stories of the Portuguese discov-

eries in Africa, other explorers set out in their wake. One of those adventurous entrepreneurs was Christopher Columbus, who persuaded King Ferdinand of Aragon and Queen Isabella of Castile to bankroll an excursion to locate a western route to Asia. By opening up trade to Asia, Columbus hoped to enrich both himself and the coffers of Spain. Like the Navigator before him, Columbus also believed that the Spanish could fulfill their Christian duty by taking the Gospel to the people of Asia and ultimately conquer Jerusalem. After considerable debate Isabella and Ferdinand sanctioned Columbus's plan and instructed him to stake a claim for Spain to all lands that he discovered on his voyage.

Inter Caetera Divinae. Reports of Columbus's landfall in the Caribbean immediately provoked questions about the title to the newly discovered lands. Portugal suggested that it held title to the territory under the Romanus Pontifex. In 1493, however, Spanish lawyers convinced Pope Alexander VI to issue the *Inter Caetera Divinae*, a series of papal bulls that confirmed Spain's title to the lands discovered by Columbus. The first bull declared that Columbus had discovered a new land and a new people and recognized Ferdinand and Isabella's title to all of the land in the area. The second bull directed Spain to convert the native inhabitants of this land to Christianity. In the decree Alexander declared: "Among other works well pleasing to the Divine Majesty and cherished of our heart, this assuredly ranks highest, that in our times especially the Catholic faith and the Christian religion be exalted and everywhere increased and spread, that the health of souls be cared for and that barbarous nations be overthrown and brought to the faith itself." The second bull also established a line that ran from pole to pole, one hundred leagues west of the Azores. The Inter Caetera Divinae endowed Portugal with dominion over all of the undiscovered lands east of the imaginary line and gave Spain title to the lands west of the boundary.

Treaty of Tordesillas. A few months later, in the Treaty of Tordesillas, Spain and Portugal agreed to move the line of demarcation to 270 leagues to the west of the Cape Verde Islands. Pope Alexander approved of this amendment. Despite this concession to Portugal, the Spanish later discovered that the treaty conveyed to them almost all of North and South America while Portugal received only a small portion of what is now eastern Brazil. In the sixteenth century the Spanish moved out from Columbus's bases in the Caribbean islands and colonized Central America, South America, and Mexico. In addition they established mission and military outposts in the southern region of North America from Florida around the Gulf of Mexico and westward across the present states of Texas, New Mexico, Arizona, and California. In expanding their imperial dominion over the Indian tribes of the region, the Spanish left a lasting legacy of the Christian faith, Iberian culture, and the Spanish language. However, in totality, the Spanish conquest was a tragedy for the native inhabitants of North America. Spanish lawyers devised a legal precedent that Europeans and Americans would use to justify the wholesale taking of the continent from the Indians. The Inter Caetera Divinae and the Treaty of Tordesillas were essential elements of the legal argument for the European conquest of the Americas. In perfecting their title Spanish conquistadores ruthlessly exerted their claim over the native peoples of the Americas. They annihilated whole communities of Indians and attempted to coerce the survivors of the Spanish conquest to renounce their traditional religion and culture. In their place the agents of Spain moved to impose their own system of social and political order over the lands and peoples of the Americas.

Sources:

Wilcomb E. Washburn, *Red Man's Land, White Man's Law: The Past and Present Status of the American Indian* (Norman: University of Oklahoma Press, 1971);

Robert A. Williams, *The American Indian in Western Legal Thought: The Discourses of Conquest* (Oxford, U.K.: Oxford University Press, 1990).

THE SPANISH DEFENSE: LEGAL JUSTIFICATIONS FOR CONQUEST

Papal Donation. Spain proffered three arguments to justify their seizure of the American continents and their subjugation of the native inhabitants: papal donation, discovery, and conquest. Under papal donation the Spanish crown's lawyers noted that Jesus Christ had given St. Peter the keys to the kingdom of heaven. According to the officials of the Catholic Church, this bequest, called the Petrine Mandate, gave Peter's successors, the Catholic popes in Rome, the right to convey title to and dominion over lands that had been, or might be, discovered by a Christian nation. With the Inter Caetera Divinae, Pope Alexander VI conveyed title to most of the Americas to Spain. This papal donation was a significant argument for title so long as the Catholic Church remained the only spiritual authority in Europe. After the Protestant Reformation, however, the Protestant nations of Europe rejected the idea that the Pope could convey title of undiscovered lands to favored kings.

Discovery. The doctrine of discovery, the second prong of Spanish title, was devised by Church officials during the time of the Crusades. Under this theory a nation acquired the right to exclusive possession of newly discovered lands that were not previously claimed or possessed by a Christian monarch. Usually the discovering nation left a memento—a cross, plaque, or perhaps a coat of arms—to signify its claim. Thus Spanish officials contended that when Christopher Columbus made landfall on San Salvador he established a superior claim for their nation to the entire Western Hemisphere. In the sixteenth century England, Holland, and France would object to this Spanish argument as well.

Conquest. Papal donation and discovery were based on the presumption that the lands of non-Christians were open to seizure by Christian nations. However, to many legal theorists of the time, papal donation and discovery alone did not confer sovereignty and title. Rather, some legal philosophers contended that the Christian nation was required to perfect its title by purchase, colonization, or conquest. The doctrine of conquest held that a victorious nation in war acquired sovereignty over the conquered nation and could exert its legal and political jurisdiction over its residents. The doctrine of conquest dates back at least to Roman law, and in the fifth century A.D., St. Augustine made the concept of a Christian war of conquest a principle of Catholic law. Augustine believed that such a war had to be for a "just" cause, that it could only be just for one side, and that the only just causes of war were self-defense and the recovery of stolen

A 1598 engraving of Spanish cruelty to Caribbean Indians

property. In the eleventh century Pope Gregory expanded upon this doctrine and proclaimed that God sanctioned wars against nonbelievers and enemies of the Church. English nationalists, on the other hand, who could not claim that their nation held title by papal donation or original discovery, saw the theory of conquest as a separate doctrine that they could use to trump the claims of Spain.

The Rights of Non-Christians. In the thirteenth century Pope Innocent IV suggested that non-Christians possessed the same rights as Christians under natural law. He then asked rhetorically, "[I]s it licit to invade a land that infidels possess, or which belongs to them?" In answering that question, Innocent IV argued that violations of natural law by nonbelievers, such as Christian conceptions of sexual perversion or idolatry, created a duty in the Pope to force the miscreant peoples to admit missionaries into their lands. If the nonbelievers did not convert to Christianity, Innocent argued, he could then authorize secular governments to declare war on the nonbelievers and force them to accept the faith. Out of Innocent IV's theory emerged two competing lines of authority. One recognized that non-Christian peoples held property rights and sovereignty under the theory of natural law, and the other maintained that under certain conditions Christian nations could encroach upon and extinguish those rights. This ambiguity, which essentially gave non-Christians natural rights with one hand and took them back with the other, controlled philosophical discussions of Native American rights for the next five hundred years. Thus, even before Columbus set sail for the West, Christian European governments possessed legal theories that they believed gave them the right to seize the lands of Native Americans. These doctrines were based on the premises that western culture was sanctioned by God and that Europeans were spiritually and culturally superior to peoples of other lands and faiths. Under that flag of cultural arrogance Europeans could invade and conquer the lands of non-Christians, and they could by right sanctioned by God take the lands of the conquered and make them their own. Ultimately, though, the title conferred by these doctrines was only as good as the military power behind it. Consequently, the parties to disputes over the sovereignty and ownership of newfound lands settled them on the battlefield or at the diplomatic table. For the non-Christian inhabitants of those lands, the same rule applied. For the European nations to enforce their claims over them by papal donation or discovery, they had to be militarily powerful enough to perfect them by conquest. As long as Native Americans successfully resisted the European military threat, they retained their title and autonomy.

Sources:

L. C. Green and Olive P. Dickason, *The Law of Nations and the New World* (Edmonton, Canada: University of Alberta Press, 1989);

Robert A. Williams, *The American Indian in Western Legal Thought: The Discourses of Conquest* (Oxford, U.K.: Oxford University Press, 1990).

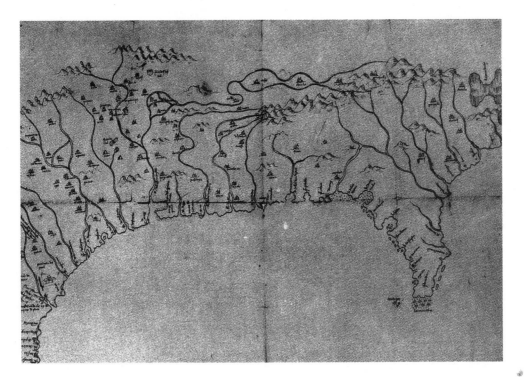

An unusually accurate sixteenth-century map of the region explored by Hernando de Soto

SPANISH GOVERNMENT IN THE AMERICAS

Silver and Gold. The earliest Europeans in the Americas were the Spanish conquistadores (conquerors). The conquistadores were adventurous minor nobles and military officers fresh from the *Reconquista* of Spain from the Moors. After word of the discovery of silver in Mexico reached Spain, hundreds of these men rushed to America solely for the purpose of procuring the mineral wealth of the continent. Their demand for gold and silver was insatiable. As Hernando Cortés began his attack on Mexico, he admitted, "I and my companions suffer from a disease of the heart which can be cured only with gold." The government of Spain profited greatly from this gold lust. Between 1500 and 1650, historians estimate that Spain carried more than 180 tons of gold and 16,000 tons of silver back to Europe. The extraction of gold during this period was perhaps as much as ten times more than the amount drawn from all of the rest of the world's mines put together. These precious metals made Spain the wealthiest and most powerful nation in the world during the sixteenth century. However, this enrichment came at a terrible cost for the native peoples of the Americas. The conquistadores left a horrible trail of mayhem, murder, plunder, and disease across the lower third of the North American continent. By 1600 the population of Mexico alone declined from about fifteen million to less than a million. Some historical demographers estimate that 90 to 95 percent of the Indian population of North America was wiped out during the first 150 years of the European colonial period in America. Most of this decimation was caused by diseases such as smallpox, typhus, measles, and influenza. However, the Spanish conquistadores also simply slaughtered thousands of native people in their furious search for gold and silver.

The *Requerimiento*. When Pope Alexander VI conveyed title of the Americas to Spain, he instructed Ferdinand and Isabella to convert the native inhabitants of the continents to Christianity. After considering the problem, Spanish policy makers concluded that it was essential for Indians to adopt Hispanic culture before they would be ready to accept the teachings of the Catholic Church. In other words Spanish missionaries first tried to teach Indians to dress, speak, and work like the people of Spain before they attempted to convert them. In 1513 Ferdinand issued a decree called the *Requerimiento* (the Requirement). The purpose of the law was to ensure that the conquistadores gave Indians a reasonable opportunity to convert to Christianity and peacefully submit to Spanish rule. In the event that a conquistador came upon a group of Indians, the decree required a Spanish notary to read a prepared statement to the natives before the conquistador and his army commenced hostilities. The statement declared that the Indians could either accept Christianity and Spanish rule or be annihilated. Native Americans were advised, in Latin or Spanish, of the Christian conception of the creation, that they had an obligation under God's law to hear the Gospel, and that God had given authority over the earth to Saint Peter, the first pope. Peter's successors, the Requerimiento explained, had recently given the Indians' lands to Spain. Consequently, the king and queen of Spain now ex-

A 1595 engraving by Theodor de Bry of Spanish treatment of runaway slaves

pected the Indians to submit to their rule. Juan López de Palácios Rubios, who prepared the Requerimiento, believed that it was a genuine effort on the part of the Spanish to meet their legal duty to convert the Indians to Christianity. Palácios Rubios, explaining the purpose behind the Requerimiento, wrote that "Indians must be treated like tender new plants, worthy of loving care and protection of the Crown." However, the Requerimiento held that those plants could be trampled underfoot if they stood in the way of Spanish will. In reality the Spanish conquistadores either ignored the Requerimiento decree or mechanically read the statement without interpreting and explaining it to the Indians. The Requerimiento was "read to trees and empty huts when no Indians were to be found. Captains muttered its theological phrases into their beards on the edge of sleeping Indian settlements, or even a league away before starting the formal attack, and at times some leather-lunged Spanish notary hurled its sonorous phrases after the Indians as they fled into the mountains. . . . Ship captains would sometimes have the document read from the deck as they approached an island." In many cases Spanish records reveal that armies led by conquistadores would discover an Indian village, read the Requerimiento outside of the earshot of its residents, and ride in and mercilessly destroy them. Bartolomé de las Casas, a missionary to the Indians, wrote that he did not know whether to laugh or cry after reading the Requerimiento.

Presidios and Missions. The presidio and the Catholic mission were the visible demonstrations of Spanish authority in America. A presidio was a military post or fort. Some presidios were small and were manned by only a few soldiers of the Spanish army. Some, however, were powerful outposts protected by hundreds of cavalry and infantrymen. The presidios were responsible for protecting the Spanish population from hostile Indian attack. They were also the military arm for enforcing the Spanish will over Native Americans. The Catholic Church was also an important and powerful weapon that Spain used to extend its influence over the Indians. Throughout the sixteenth century groups of Catholic missionaries came to America for the purpose of converting the native population to Christianity. The most important mission orders who came to spread the Gospel were the Franciscans, Dominicans, Augustinians, and Jesuits. These orders established missions throughout Florida, Mexico, and the American Southwest. Since the Catholic Church was so closely affiliated with the Spanish government, the missionaries in America served a dual role. They represented the Church and the Spanish Crown. Their responsibilities were therefore broader than simply converting the Indians to Christianity. The missionaries also wanted to convince native people to adopt what they felt was the superior civilization of Catholic Spain. Many early Spanish conquistadores, however, cared little about the Christian mission and civilization duty. They were more concerned with acquiring wealth and generally thought of Indians as either obstacles to their economic aggrandizement or as a potential labor force that they could ruthlessly exploit. In the early stages of the Spanish entrée into the Americas, the conquistadores and their armies brutally attacked and annihilated thousands of

Indians who stood in the way of their material objectives. Some members of the Dominican order of Catholic missionaries in Spanish America strongly censured the actions of the conquistadores. They urged King Ferdinand to issue regulations to prevent further atrocities and to fulfill the responsibility given to him in the Inter Caetera Divinae to convert the Indians to Christianity.

The *Encomienda*. The conquistadores needed a cheap supply of labor to work in the mines and on the farms and plantations of America. The *encomienda* system seemed to satisfy both of these objectives for the Spanish colonists. The encomienda was a forced system of labor that distributed Indian workers to certain favored Spanish colonists. Upon request the Crown "commended" a group of Indian villages to a Spanish individual called an *encomendero*. The people of these villages provided a set period of labor for their encomendero. Moreover, the system required the laborers to provide tribute in the form of corn, blankets, animals skins, and other items to their encomendero. In return for the grant the encomenderos agreed to provide military service to the Crown and pay a head tax for each Indian worker. He also promised to protect his Indians and indoctrinate them into Christianity and Spanish civilization. The Spanish established encomiendas wherever they went in the Americas. At first only conquistadores or military officers possessed encomienda rights. Over time, though, the government expanded the system and gave encomienda grants to wealthy civilians and officials of the Spanish government. The enslavement of Indians pro- duced a great deal of wealth for the encomenderos and the Spanish government. Consequently, the government was at first reluctant to impose restrictions on the encomenderos when members of the Dominican order of missionaries criticized the system. In 1511 a Dominican friar named Antón Montesino rebuked the encomenderos: "[Y]ou are in mortal sin . . . you live and die in it, for the cruelty and tyranny you use in dealing with these innocent people. Tell me, by which right or justice do you keep these Indians in such a cruel and horrible servitude? On what authority have you waged a detestable war against these people? Are these not men? Have they not rational souls? Are you not bound to love them as you love yourselves?" The defenders of the encomienda system argued that they were not enslaving Indians. However, in practice it was difficult to distinguish the encomienda from slavery. Encomenderos often bought and sold Indians as if they were property. They ruthlessly overworked thousands of Indians to death, kept them in line with brutal beatings, and refused them freedom of movement.

The Laws of Burgos. In response to the criticism of missionaries such as Montesino and Las Casas, the Spanish made occasional efforts to reform the system. For example, in 1512 King Ferdinand issued the Laws of Burgos. The laws limited the number of months out of every year that a laborer could work for his encomendero and required the encomendero to pay his workers a wage. The laws also provided that Indians working in the mines be given periods of rest and that they be supplied

Theodor de Bry's 1566 engraving of Timucuan men dredging a Florida river bottom for gold nuggets

with adequate food. In addition the statutes imposed restrictions on the Indian laborers. They prohibited polygamy, required Indians to learn the sacraments of the Catholic Church, and exhorted the natives to act in accord with what Spanish Christians deemed to be proper behavior. When King Charles came to the throne in 1516, he also worried that the encomenderos were becoming too powerful and were challenging his authority in America. The Spanish government was thousands of miles away and incapable of overseeing the activities of the encomenderos. Thus, in most cases, the encomenderos simply ignored royal reforms and continued to repress their Indian laborers. The king therefore moved to restrict the rights of the encomenderos. In 1542 Charles limited the inheritance of encomienda rights and sent visitadores to America. The visitadores were government officials who were responsible for ensuring that the encomenderos were abiding by Spanish law. At the end of the sixteenth century, the Spanish crown supplemented the encomienda with the *repartimiento*. Under the repartimiento system Spanish law required Indian villages unaffiliated with an encomienda to supply a set number of male laborers for a specific time period to work on Spanish buildings, in Spanish mines, and in Spanish fields. As the Indian labor supply dwindled from disease and overwork, the Spanish also began bringing Africans to America to serve as slave labor. By 1560 the Spanish had already transported more than 100,000 Africans to the Americas.

Native Resistance. At times Indian people violently resisted Spanish efforts to subjugate them. Those who opposed the Spanish conquest, however, were either annihilated by the forces of the presidios or placed into the forced labor of the encomienda system. When Hernando de Soto was exploring the Southeast in 1539, a group of Mabila Indians refused to submit to his demands. In response de Soto's cavalry rode in and killed more than three thousand Mabilas. Similarly in 1597 the Guales, a native group located in what is now Georgia and Florida, were destroyed by the Spanish invaders. The Guales despised the proselytization efforts of the Spanish missionaries and tired of their constant demands for food. Eventually the Guales and other groups revolted against the Spanish. They attacked the Spanish missions and killed several friars. In response the missionaries requested support from the presidio in St. Augustine. Spanish troops attacked the native rebels, burned down their villages, and seized their grain supplies. In New Mexico a year later, the people of the Acoma pueblo also learned what could happen if they opposed Spanish plans to seize control of the continent. In 1598 the Spanish government ordered Juan de Oñate to occupy the vast area drained by the Rio Grande River. Oñate led an expeditionary force of 129 soldiers along with some missionaries and civilians to claim and settle the region. Oñate sent representatives out to all of the pueblos of New Mexico. These agents told the pueblo peoples that they were now under the authority of the Spanish king, that their lands would be seized and distributed under Spanish law, and that the Indians should immediately renounce their tribal religion and convert to Christianity. Most of the pueblo peoples accepted their fate. However, the people of Acoma rejected the Spanish message and violently resisted the Spanish army's attempts to subdue them. The Spanish then sent Oñate a larger force to attack Acoma in 1599. After a three-day battle Oñate's army finally conquered Acoma. Oñate ruthlessly punished the Acoma people for their resistance. Along with killing almost one thousand Indians, Oñate issued harsh sentences for the survivors that were intended to deter any future native group from resisting Spanish expansion. Oñate ordered his men to amputate one foot from each man more than twenty-five years old and sentenced the victims to slave labor for twenty years. The Spanish conqueror also sentenced young men between twelve and twenty-five and all women over twelve to twenty years of forced servitude. The children of Acoma did not escape punishment; they were taken away from their families and placed into the hands of the missionaries. Incidents such as these and other atrocities throughout the Americas demonstrated that the Spanish desire to seize land and wealth overrode their espoused desire to convert Indians to Christianity.

Sources:

L. C. Green and Olive P. Dickason, *The Law of Nations and the New World* (Edmonton, Canada: University of Alberta Press, 1989);

Lewis Hanke, *The Spanish Struggle for Justice in the Conquest of America* (Philadelphia: University of Pennsylvania Press, 1949);

Charles Hudson, *Knights of Spain, Warriors of the Sun: Hernando de Soto and the South's Ancient Chiefdoms* (Athens: University of Georgia Press, 1997);

Robert A. Williams, *The American Indian in Western Legal Thought: The Discourses of Conquest* (Oxford, U.K.: Oxford University Press, 1990).

HEADLINE MAKERS

DEGANAWIDAH AND HIAWATHA

FLOURISHED 1570
FOUNDERS OF THE IROQUOIS CONFEDERACY

Union. The Iroquois Confederacy was perhaps the most complicated governmental organization among the native peoples of North America. The League of the Iroquois, as it was also called, dates back to sometime in the late fourteenth or fifteenth century. The Iroquois peoples lived in the area of present-day Pennsylvania and New York. During this period five Iroquoian tribes—the Mohawks, Senecas, Onondagas, Oneidas, and Cayugas—joined together into a political and military alliance. (A sixth tribe, the Tuscaroras, joined the confederacy in 1722.) Before the construction of the confederacy the individual tribes lived in clusters of self-sufficient villages that were separated by large tracts of fishing or hunting territory. Before they confederated, the separate tribes of the Iroquois often engaged in bitter wars of blood revenge. With the creation of the confederation the Iroquois renounced the practice of blood revenge. Several forces probably pulled the Iroquois peoples into this alliance. Trade enhanced communication and cooperation between the Iroquois. In addition the Iroquoian tribes may have come together to ward off enemies such as the Hurons from the north. However, most anthropologists agree that the five tribes confederated in order to end the animosities caused by the law of blood revenge. The Iroquois oral tradition about Hiawatha and Deganawidah corroborates this theory.

Endless Wars. According to this tradition there once lived a man named Hiawatha who became discouraged by the seemingly endless cycle of war and violence that plagued the Iroquois. "Everywhere there was peril and everywhere mourning," one version of the story goes. "Men were ragged with sacrifice and the women scarred with the flints, so everywhere there was misery. Feuds with one another, feuds with other nations, feuds with brother nations, feuds of sister towns, and feuds of families and of clans made every warrior a stealthy man who liked to kill." Hiawatha in vain tried to convince his peo-

ple to renounce the law of blood revenge. A witch, who despised the proposition of peace among the Iroquois, killed Hiawatha's seven daughters in an effort to spur him into a fit of revenge. Distraught over this tragedy, Hiawatha wandered through the forest of his homeland for days. For sustenance he ambushed and ate innocent travelers. One day, while sitting by the shore of a lake, Hiawatha had a series of visions. In his dreams Hiawatha met a holy man named Deganawidah the Peacemaker.

Creating Stability. Deganawidah told Hiawatha that he was also horrified by the endless wars and violence between the Iroquoian peoples, and he told Hiawatha that the Iroquois tribes needed to join together and create a council of the wisest men to govern them. Deganawidah then presented Hiawatha with a string of wampum. (The Iroquois historically presented wampum, strings of quahog clams and whelk shells, when they concluded treaties to demonstrate their sincerity.) Deganawidah told Hiawatha that the beads were intended to wipe the tears of grief from Hiawatha's eyes. The holy man presented another string of wampum and told Hiawatha that it was to open his ears to hear his message of peace and reconciliation. Finally Deganawidah gave Hiawatha a third strand of beads to restore his voice and revive his ability to speak with patience, reason, and peace. The two then took the strings of wampum to the warring Iroquois nations and taught them the ceremony that Deganawidah had performed with Hiawatha. (In some versions of the story Deganawidah was only visible to Hiawatha.) Each nation, they said, was a longhouse just like the homes in which the Iroquois lived. Although each nation possessed a separate land, the Iroquois tribes had all descended from the same mother. It was therefore wrong for them to feud and war with each other. Ultimately Hiawatha and Deganawidah persuaded the Iroquois nations to reconcile their differences and come together as one people.

Sacred Fire. Since Hiawatha was an Onondaga, the delegates selected his people to maintain the tribal fire at the first council meeting. They thus became responsible for calling the other tribes in for the annual councils that were intended to reaffirm the peace and sanctity of the confederacy. The Onondagas were also entrusted with the sacred wampum strand, the beads of which represented the important events in the history of the confederacy and the points of agreement that held the tribes together. The confederacy outlawed war among the five nations and replaced the law of blood revenge with a system of compensation. (The Iroquois only suppressed blood revenge between the nations of the confederacy. They continued the practice of blood revenge with other tribes such as the Hurons and Eries.) The confederation council consisted of fifty men from the five tribes of the confederacy. The women of the tribes confirmed the selection of these men and thus held a considerable veto power over their actions. Primarily the confederacy dealt with problems of a diplomatic and military nature that affected all of the member tribes. It had no control over the internal policies or government of the member tribes. However, the confederation council could act as a decision-making body in disputes that tribal leaders had been unable to resolve independently. Separately, the Mohawks, Senecas, Onondagas, Oneidas, and Cayugas could not adequately defend themselves from enemy attack. United as the Iroquois Confederacy, they were the most powerful military force in North America during the colonial period.

Sources:

Daniel K. Richter, *The Ordeal of the Longhouse: The Peoples of the Iroquois League in the Era of European Colonization* (Chapel Hill: University of North Carolina Press, 1992);

Anthony F. C. Wallace, *The Death and Rebirth of the Seneca* (New York: Knopf, 1970).

FRANCISCUS DE VICTORIA

1480-1546
DOMINICAN SCHOLAR

Dominican Protests. The atrocities committed by the Spanish during their conquest of the Americas provoked vehement protests from the Dominican order of Catholics. The most effective of these critics of Spanish policy was Bartolomé de las Casas. Las Casas urged Charles V, the Holy Roman Emperor and king of Spain, to completely reform Spanish policies toward the Indians. He argued that Indians possessed the same natural rights as Europeans. Consequently, Las Casas said, the justifications of conquest devised by Spanish lawyers were illegitimate; the Spanish taking of Indian land, labor, and property was wrongful; and the conquistadores and encomenderos had a duty to restore Indians to their natural rights. Moreover the Spanish, as demonstrated by the Requerimiento, attempted to impose Christianity on the Indians by force. Potential converts to Christianity, according to Las Casas, had to have the liberty of conscience to choose their faith. If they did not, their conversions were meaningless in the sight of God. Spain therefore did not have the right to conquer the Indians because they were not Christians and did not have the

right to enslave, assault, and murder Indians for the purpose of coercing them to accept their religion. Las Casas went so far as to declare those who disagreed with these assertions as heretics, and he encouraged Charles to intercede and return the Americas to the Indians.

Legal Opinion. The criticism of Las Casas disturbed King Charles, and in 1532 he asked Franciscus de Victoria, one of his legal advisers, to counsel him on Spain's rights to the Indian lands in America. Victoria, a Dominican professor of theology at the University of Salamanca, used the opportunity to prepare a series of lectures on the rights of nations. These lectures were published posthumously in 1557 and represented one of the earliest attempts to construct a comprehensive code of international law. In 1551, between the public pronouncement and publication of Victoria's thoughts, King Charles, still concerned about the legality of the Spanish claim, ordered a court debate about the morality of Spain's Indian policy. Charles asked Las Casas and other critics of Spanish policy to present their views before a board of royal advisers. The humanist scholar Juan Ginés de Sepúlveda presented the argument supporting the legality of the Spanish title and the morality of the Indian labor system. Sepúlveda, unlike Las Casas, had never been to America and based his conclusions about Indians on the writings of the Spanish historian Fernández de Oviedo. Indians, Sepúlveda said, were uncivilized barbarians intellectually incapable of self-government. As such, under natural law Spain had a paternalistic duty to instruct them in the ways of Spanish civilization and convert them to Christianity. Sepúlveda also contended that Indians practiced human sacrifice and idolatry and were sexually promiscuous. As a Christian nation Spain therefore had an obligation to end, by force if necessary, these "unnatural" practices. Sepúlveda concluded that Spain had a natural right to conquer the Indians, enslave them, and force them to convert to Christianity.

Conclusions. When Victoria's lectures were published a few years after the debate, it was clear that he had attempted to reconcile the positions of Las Casas and Sepúlveda. As a student of natural law, Victoria began his study with Las Casas's presumption that indigenous non-Christian peoples possessed the same natural rights as all other free and rational peoples. Native Americans could therefore claim the same sovereign powers and legal entitlements as the people and states of Christian Europe. Victoria declared that Alexander VI's conveyance of the Americas to Spain was "baseless" and did not impact the national and individual rights of Native Americans. Roman civil law declared that "what belongs to nobody is granted to the first occupant." Consequently Victoria concluded that Native Americans theoretically retained absolute ownership of their property. In short Victoria rejected the doctrines of discovery and papal donation. He also repudiated Sepúlveda's argument that Indians forfeited their rights when they refused to accept Christianity. Despite these seemingly firm convictions, Victoria awkwardly approved the Spanish conquest. Indians, he wrote, were required to abide by the natural law of nations. He accepted Sepúlveda's argument that practices such as cannibalism, idolatry, and human sacrifice were abhorrent to natural law. When Indians performed acts such as these, they did, as Sepúlveda had argued, forfeit their rights under natural law. Victoria added that Christians had a natural duty to civilize the Indians and convert them to their faith. Though the Pope could not capriciously hand out title to native lands to secular monarchs, he could grant Spain an exclusive guardianship over Indians for the purpose of converting them to Christianity. Indians, on the other hand, were obligated, under what Victoria called the doctrine of "natural society and fellowship," to admit Christian missionaries into their lands, to listen to their message, and to provide them with the facilities to assist in their own conversion. If a native group failed to admit or listen to the Pope's emissaries, they again violated natural law. Natural law, according to Victoria, also required Indians to treat the agents of "civilized" nations hospitably, to allow them free access into their lands, and to protect them from harm. This implied that Indians could not legally interfere with the "free and open commerce" of Spain. Victoria concluded that though Indians were rational human beings, they were intellectually inferior to Europeans. This inferiority at times resulted in a political structure that was so debased that an Indian people could not administer their own affairs. This offered another opportunity for a civilized nation to take sovereignty over the Indian people in question and teach them the benefits of Spanish civilization. The refusal to accept the benefits of Spanish Catholic civilization—its economic system, culture, and religion—negated the presumption of native rationality and created a right of guardianship in Spain over the recalcitrant natives. If Indians opposed or infringed upon a Christian nation's rights or refused to remedy their reprobate activities, Victoria wrote, then the Christian nation could summarily "enforce against them all the rights of war, de-spoiling them of their goods, reducing them to captivity, deposing their former lords and setting up new ones."

Surrender of Rights. In sum Victoria agreed with Las Casas that Indians maintained national and individual rights under natural law. At the same time, though, Victoria agreed that Christians had a duty to try to convert all of mankind to their religion. When these two concepts came into conflict, the natural law sacrificed the inherent rights of Native Americans to the Christian mission. Arguably Victoria did not really attempt to deduce law from nature; he worked backwards to achieve a particular result. More than likely the ambiguity of Victoria's doctrine resulted from a surrender to the royal will. In the early 1530s Victoria, following Las Casas's lead, had brazenly lectured on the sanctity of the natural rights of Indians. His rationalizations for the Spanish conquest, however, appeared only in the lectures from around 1539. Later Victoria explained that Charles V "took exception" to his early pronouncements in favor of Indian rights and that his subsequent lectures were an effort to moderate his original position. This royal dissatisfaction brought two disparate lines of authority together into a murky equivocation, and these two clearly incongruous threads of argument remained bound together in the writings of the legal theorists that followed. Although the Spanish never formally adopted Las Casas's humanitarian ideas, advocates of British and French colonization in America used his criticism of Spanish policy to justify their own claims to North America. By violating the natural rights of Indians, they argued, Spain had forfeited the rights to the Americas that they had claimed under the theories of papal donation and discovery.

Sources:

L. C. Green and Olive P. Dickason, *The Law of Nations and the New World* (Edmonton, Canada: University of Alberta Press, 1989);

Robert A. Williams, *The American Indian in Western Legal Thought: The Discourses of Conquest* (Oxford, U.K.: Oxford University Press, 1990).

PUBLICATIONS

Jean Bodin, *On Sovereignty: Four Chapters from the Six Books of the Commonwealth* (Cambridge: Cambridge University Press, 1992)—selections from Bodin's 1576 work on international law, *Six Livres de la Republique*;

Mary T. Clark, *An Aquinas Reader* (New York: Fordham University Press, 1988)—includes Thomas Aquinas's discussion of natural law and Christianity;

John Dillenberger, ed., *John Calvin: Selections from His Writings* (Garden City, N.Y.: Anchor Books, 1971);

Dillenberger, ed., *Martin Luther: Selections from His Writings* (Garden City, N.Y.: Anchor Books, 1961);

D. C. Douglas and G. W. Greenway, eds., *English Historical Documents*, 10 volumes (London: Oxford University Press, 1953; reprinted, London: Routledge, 1996)—a multivolume collection that chronicles the development of English political and legal institutions;

Richard Eden, *The First Three English Books on America*, edited by Edward Arber (New York: Kraus Reprint, 1971)—in the second half of the sixteenth century Eden collected and published excerpts from the writings of Amerigo Vespucci, Fernández de Oviedo, Martire, and other early commentators on America;

B. G. Kohl and R. G. Witt, eds., *The Earthly Republic: Italian Humanists on Government and Society* (Philadelphia: University of Pennsylvania Press, 1978)—a collection of Renaissance writings on politics;

Niccoló Machiavelli, *The Prince* (New Haven: Yale University Press, 1997)—the classic statement of Renaissance politics;

Michel de Montaigne, *Essays,* translated by J. M. Cohen (New York: Penguin, 1993)—Montaigne's essays urged skepticism toward and toleration from government;

Thomas More, *Utopia* (Cambridge: Cambridge University Press, 1993)—*Utopia* included justifications for the taking of Indian land;

James Muldoon, ed., *The Expansion of Europe: The First Phase* (Philadelphia: University of Pennsylvania Press, 1977)—Muldoon's work contains some of the writings of Pope Innocent IV;

E. G. R. Taylor, ed., *The Original Writings and Correspondence of the Two Richard Hakluyts,* 2 volumes (London: Hakluyt Society, 1935)—writings of the sixteenth-century English advocate of American colonization;

Lewis G. M. Thorpe, ed., *Two Lives of Charlemagne* (Harmondsworth, U.K.: Penguin, 1983)—translation of the chronicles by Einhard and Notker the Stammerer;

Brian Tierney, *The Crisis of Church and State, 1050–1300* (Englewood Cliffs, N.J.: Prentice-Hall, 1964)—includes a collection of primary source documents;

Francisco de Vitoria, *De indis et de iure belli relectiones* (Buffalo: William S. Hein, 1995)—the Spanish legal philosopher's law of nations;

H. R. Wagner and Henry Raup Parish, eds., *The Life and Writings of Bartolomé de Las Casas* (Albuquerque: University of New Mexico Press, 1967)—contains excerpts from the Dominican critic of Spanish policy in the Americas.

LIFESTYLES, SOCIAL TRENDS, AND RECREATION

by GREG O'BRIEN

CONTENTS

CHRONOLOGY
156

OVERVIEW
159

TOPICS IN THE NEWS

Daily Work....................161
*Gendered Work and the Raising
    of Children* 161
The Importance of Agriculture . . 163

The Uses of Corn at Hochelaga 163
The Iroquois Longhouse 164
*Champlain Shoots Two
    Mohawk Chiefs* 165
Kinship 165
Mississippian Chiefdoms........166
Pueblos of the Southwest.......167
Pueblo Architecture and Clothing. . . 167
Rites of Passage.................168
Isolated Women 168
San Agustín: Europeans
    Come to Stay 170
Sickness 170

*"The People Began to Die
    Very Fast"* 171
Sports and Recreation 171

HEADLINE MAKERS

Don Luis 172
Manteo 173

PUBLICATIONS
173

Sidebars and tables are listed in italics.

1000?

- The Mississippian mound-building societies, such as Cahokia in present-day Illinois, develop in the Mississippi River valley and the Southeast.

1492-1502

- Christopher Columbus voyages to the West Indies and uses the term "Indians" to describe the native inhabitants of the region.

1497-1498

- John Cabot explores the Atlantic coast, encountering Beothuks, Abenakis, Massachusetts, and Powhatans and kidnapping three Micmacs.

1513-1521

- Juan Ponce de León makes contact with Calusas, Timucuans, and other Indians in Florida.

1523-1524

- Giovanni da Verrazano sails from the Carolinas to Newfoundland and meets various native peoples.

1526

- Lucas Vásquez de Ayllón sails up the Atlantic coast and kidnaps more than one hundred Indians for slaves.

1528-1536

- Alvar Núñez Cabeza de Vaca encounters several tribes as he travels overland through Texas and Mexico to the Gulf of California.

1534-1542

- Jacques Cartier sails up the St. Lawrence River and meets Beothuks, Micmacs, Montagnais, Algonkins, and Hurons. He takes a tribal leader named Donnacona and several other Hurons to Europe.

1539

- The Franciscan missionary and explorer Fray Marcos de Niza claims to have seen the "Seven Cities of Cíbola" in the Southwest.

1539-1543

- Hernando de Soto visits several Mississippian societies during his expedition through the Southeast.

1540-1542

- Francisco Vásquez de Coronado leads an expedition that reaches the Grand Canyon. In the process he makes contact with the Hopi, Zuni, Apache, Wichita, and Pawnee tribes.

1541

- Tristán de Luna y Arellano explores the Alabama River and encounters Mobiles, Napochis, and Tohomes.

1551-1562

- Hernando de Escalante Fontaneda is held prisoner by Calusa Indians in Florida.

1562

- Jean Ribault attempts to form a settlement on Parris Island, South Carolina, called Charlesfort. He also explores the Florida coast and makes contact with Cusabos, Saturiwas, Tactacuras, and Timucuas.

1564-1565

- René Goulaine de Laudonnière and Jacques le Moyne establish a settlement on the St. Johns River on the Atlantic coast of Florida, and le Moyne paints pictures of the local Timucuans.

1565

- Pedro Menéndez de Avilés seizes Laudonniere's post and establishes St. Augustine.

1566-1567

- Juan Pardo journeys inland from the Atlantic coast to the Blue Ridge Mountains, making alliances with several native groups in the process.

1570

- Spanish Jesuits attempt to settle in the Chesapeake Bay area, while returning the Powhatan Indian Don Luis, kidnapped a decade earlier. Powhatans kill the Jesuits but suffer at the hands of a Spanish punitive expedition three years later.

1578-1579

- Sir Francis Drake sails up the California coast and encounters Miwoks.

1582–1583

- The Antonio Espejo expedition travels through Pueblo settlements in the Rio Grande and New Mexico area.

1586

- Richard Grenville with Sir Walter Raleigh's backing establishes the Roanoke Island, North Carolina, settlement. He treats local Algonquian Indians roughly and burns one village over suspicion that the residents stole a cup.

1587

- John White at the Roanoke settlement draws highly detailed pictures of the Algonquian Indians there.

1590–1591

- Gaspar Castaño de Sosa visits the Pecos River, New Mexico, area and encounters Tiwa Pueblos.

1592

- Juan de Fuca sails to the northwest coast of North America and makes contact with Cowichans, Nootkas, Songish, and Stalos.

1598

- Juan de Oñate massacres inhabitants of the Acoma Pueblo.

OVERVIEW

Diversity. By the time Europeans first encountered North America, there existed hundreds of Native American groups. Each people had its own history, culture, and language. The type of physical environment in which they lived largely determined their day-to-day lives. Every region of what is now known as the United States provided subsistence for groups of native people who adapted to their physical settings in practical and ingenious ways. Whether building canals in the arid Southwest or constructing fishing weirs in the streams and rivers of the rest of the continent, Indians altered their environments to provide the necessities of daily existence. Native Americans constantly adjusted to changing surroundings by developing new methods of acquiring sustenance. The manner of their adjustment decided the size of their settlements, the varieties of shelter in which they lived, the clothing they wore, the extent of their seasonal movements, and the types of familial and interpersonal relationships they maintained.

Subsistence. No group relied on a single source of food. A varied diet made up of meat, fish, berries, nuts, and plants provided the basis of Indian menus. All tribes hunted some animals and gathered plant products found in their territory. For example, California Indians relied primarily on acorns as a gathered food, whereas Eastern Woodlands people hunted deer, cultivated corn, and collected berries to supplement their diets. For those living in the Great Plains, the hunting of buffalo and other large mammals furnished the bulk of their nutritional needs. For those who lived on the northwest coast or on the southern tip of Florida, fish and other marine products provided the mainstay of the food supply. The Powhatan Indians near the Chesapeake Bay grew crops; hunted deer, bear, and other animals; and gathered oysters, fish, and other seafood. Many groups planted and harvested vegetables in addition to hunting and gathering. Those tribes who practiced horticulture lived in areas where the growing season was sufficiently long and rainfall amounts were adequate. Corn, beans, and squash were the principal crops for horticultural Indians. But even in the areas where gardens produced abundantly, natives relied to some degree on hunting, gathering, and fishing.

Maize Agriculture. Cultivation of corn originated in Mesoamerica (present-day Mexico) around six thousand years ago. From Mexico the techniques of maize agriculture spread northward, and corn became the dominant crop in the Southwest, in the Missouri and Mississippi River valleys, and along the Atlantic coast. In nearly every native society where horticulture existed, women did the bulk of planting, harvesting, and preparing of crops into a variety of tasty foods. The role of women in bringing corn and other vegetables out of the earth was associated with their ability to reproduce and sustain society through childbirth. By the time of European contact in the 1500s, corn had become so important that Indian peoples performed elaborate annual ceremonies, such as the Green Corn Ceremony in the Southeast, to give thanks and to ensure a successful harvest. Requesting spiritual sanction reflected Native American beliefs and values, in which they recognized their dependence upon the bounties of nature for their survival. The cultivation of corn (along with tomatoes, potatoes, squash, peanuts, and beans) originated in America and remains a principal source of food around the world.

Hunting. All Native American societies hunted a variety of animals for food and utilitarian purposes. In the Plains region buffalo hunting predominated, greatly facilitated by the introduction of horses and guns beginning in the seventeenth century. Buffalo supplied meat, shelter, clothing, and tools to Plains Indians. Throughout North America deer, elk, bear, beavers, turkeys, dogs, rabbits, and other small animals provided meat, clothing, and tools. Communal hunting parties tracked large game animals and traveled for weeks or months killing game. Because Indians traveled great distances while hunting, Europeans often called them "nomads," meaning that they had no fixed home or village. Except for some of the Plains groups, this label was grossly inaccurate. In the East, Southwest, and Northwest Coast, Indians lived in villages that stayed in the same place for years, moving only to plant new fields once the old ones wore out. Many Indian pueblos of the Southwest exist where they have for centuries. Americans of the late twentieth century, especially college students, move more often and for greater distances than did most Native Americans of the pre-1600 era.

Shelter. Geography determined to a large degree in what type of home an Indian person lived. In mainstream American consciousness Native Americans are universally portrayed as living in buffalo-hide tepees, but that form of housing only existed among some cultures in the Plains area. More typically, Indians lived in dome-shaped earth lodges (prevalent on the Upper Plains among groups such as the Mandans and Hidatsas), hogans (circular above-ground dwellings typical among the Navajos), or wickiups (temporary brush shelters). Many native peoples were distinctive for the type of shelter they utilized: the Iroquois and Hurons of the Great Lakes region built large, rectangular, wooden longhouses that held several nuclear families; most southwestern groups created apartment-style adobe or stone pueblos; northwest coast Indians constructed cedar plank houses; and southeastern peoples erected wattle and daub circular dwellings with thatched roofs. Many Indian societies occupied different residences in winter and summer; summer homes allowed breezes to pass through while winter structures remained airtight. Native Americans also constructed buildings for specialized purposes. These included the kivas of the Pueblo Indians in the Southwest—underground ceremonial chambers, usually round and with entrances through the roof. Mississippian peoples in the Southeast raised hundreds of immense temple mounds during the few centuries before European contact. Additionally, nearly all native societies utilized the sweathouse—either small temporary structures or large communal lodges built partially underground—for ritual sweating and purification.

Clothing. As with housing, the prevailing image of Native American clothing is that of Plains Indians, consisting of leather, beadwork, and war bonnets. Like diet and shelter, however, the clothing an Indian wore depended upon local plant and animal resources as well as climate and season. All native peoples used animal skins as clothing, especially those living in the Plains and Great Lakes regions, but many also utilized woven fibers when grasses and other plants were available. Some southwestern peoples, for example, made woven plant-fiber sandals and cotton garments, and southeastern women fabricated skirts out of grass reeds. In the summer Indians wore as little as possible, perhaps only a breechcloth covering their midsection, which resulted in Europeans deeming them to be "naked." It made little sense to native people to wear unneeded clothing in the hot summers, however, and they in turn made fun of Europeans sweating in their woolen pants and shirts. To combat cold winters, Native Americans covered themselves in thick buffalo, deer, elk, or bear skins.

Community Organization. Settlement size and location depended on availability of resources. Where horticulture was practiced and other resources were abundant, settlements tended to be larger and more permanent. This is particularly true among the southwestern Pueblos and the southeastern Mississippian chiefdoms. In both cases, large-scale farming produced societies with permanent villages, immense multifamily buildings, and large populations. Where hunting of migratory animals was important, such as on the Plains, settlements moved and often rotated between small winter camps and large summer sites. Native Americans looked to the family group as the most important social relationship. Each household (or kinship group) maintained its own fields and owned the products grown there. Except in rare cases such as the southwestern Pueblos and southeastern Mississippian societies, a family fed itself first before contributing to the wider group's resources. The animals that men killed were likewise distributed to the members of their immediate family before being offered to more-distant relatives. After the immediate family, other members of the same clan formed an individual's next closest relatives. Members of a clan, generally speaking, recognized a common ancestor and considered themselves related to each other. Most Native American groups consisted of several clans, with each clan having members in many villages. Leaders of each clan usually formed a village or tribal council responsible for certain political decisions such as war and diplomacy.

Land and Migration. Across North America, Indians held usufruct rights to the lands that they used and occupied, or, in other words, no group owned a particular area of land, but they maintained rights to its use based upon a history of residing in that particular area. Indian societies were not static. They moved to new territories when they exhausted an area's resources and sought better living conditions elsewhere. Indian peoples migrated to new areas before contact with Europeans, although European contact greatly increased the frequency of such movements. Navajos and Apaches, to furnish one example, migrated south away from their Athapaskan relatives in western Canada to present-day New Mexico and Arizona before 1500. The Lakota Sioux, the quintessential Plains Indians, moved onto the Upper Plains after Europeans arrived in North America, in order to monopolize access to natural resources and to control the flow of European trade to the Plains. Migrations impacted social conditions and lifestyles in various ways, such as sparking wars with groups already living in the area and transforming cultural beliefs to match new environmental conditions.

European Invasion. Europeans traveled through and around North America with increasing frequency in the sixteenth century. Three areas of the continent received the most intrusive contact: the Southwest (present-day Arizona, New Mexico, and Texas), the Southeast (Louisiana, Mississippi, Alabama, Florida, Georgia, the Carolinas, and Virginia), and the Northeast (particularly Maine, the Hudson River valley of New York, and the eastern Great Lakes). Spanish, French, and English expeditions to North America sought to find riches, establish colonies, convert Indians to Christianity, and discover an all-water route through the continent to Asia.

Such expeditions were overwhelmingly military in character. Violence between Indians and Europeans arose immediately as whites sought slaves, rare minerals, and food from native populations. Despite the prevalence of violence, mutually beneficial trade between Europeans and Indians also occurred and served to introduce new items and technology into native societies. Another legacy that Europeans brought to America proved to be far more devastating than either trade or violence: disease.

TOPICS IN THE NEWS

DAILY WORK

Allocation of Tasks. Division of labor by age, gender, and talent was as universal among Native Americans as it was elsewhere in the world. Children were incapable of performing most adult activities and lacked the knowledge and experience of those who were older. The old lacked the strength of younger adults, but they became respected elders who advised the village or group on matters of diplomacy, warfare, spirituality, and history. Few Indians became full-time craft specialists, such as pottery makers or basket weavers, but those who had special talents engaged more often than others in that particular activity. Other part-time specialists included political leaders, shamans, and war chiefs. Although age was important in determining the jobs that sixteenth-century Indians performed, gender provided the main dividing point in the allocation of labor.

GENDERED WORK AND THE RAISING OF CHILDREN

In the early seventeenth century French missionary Gabriel Sagard described how Hurons trained boys and girls to do adult tasks:

[I]f a mother asks her son to go for water or wood or do some similar household service, he will reply to her that this is a girl's work and will do none of it . . . Just as the little boys have their special training and teach one another to shoot with the bow as soon as they begin to walk, so also the little girls, whenever they begin to put one foot in front of the other, have a little stick put into their hands to train them and teach them early to pound corn, and when they are grown somewhat they also play various little games with their companions, and in the course of these small frolics they are trained quietly to perform trifling and petty household duties.

Source: James Axtell, ed., *The Indian Peoples of Eastern America: A Documentary History of the Sexes* (New York: Oxford University Press, 1981), pp. 35–36.

Division of Labor. As with cultures the world over, Native Americans separated work according to gender. In most cases women farmed and gathered, while men hunted, warred against enemies, and traveled far and wide on trade missions. Some important exceptions to

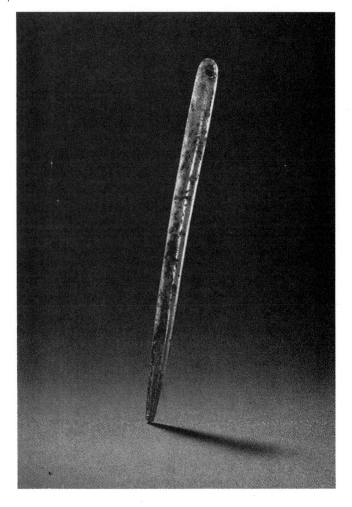

An Ice Age needle made from bone (American Museum of Natural History, New York)

Florida Indians drying meat and fish (engraving by Theodor de Bry, after a painting by Jacques le Moyne, 1564)

this general rule existed. Among the Pueblo peoples men did most of the farm labor, while women owned the fields and produce; and in nearly all Indian societies some women fought enemies as readily as men. Usually everyone, regardless of gender, contributed to planting crops in the spring and helped with the harvest in the autumn. At such crucial times the demands of village survival outweighed the rules of a gendered separation of labor. Nevertheless, among some groups men would never be caught performing "women's work" such as hoeing fields or gathering nuts and berries. Other areas in which a gendered division of labor was maintained included the construction of shelters. Where buildings were small, women tended to build them; where they were large, men most likely did the work. Almost universally women cured animal skins, fashioned clothing, and made pottery and baskets while men assembled bows, arrows, knives, and clubs.

The Work of Children. As soon as children could walk and carry small items they began to help in daily chores. For boys this meant hunting small game animals and birds while learning how to use the bow and arrow and developing the physical fortitude necessary for warfare. Girls accompanied their mothers into the fields and helped in household chores. They learned to plant and weed corn, gather firewood, fetch water, make clothes, weave mats and baskets, and fashion pottery. Indian parents let children have a relatively free rein and offered positive reinforcement to shape their behavior. Unlike the European custom of negative reinforcement by cor-

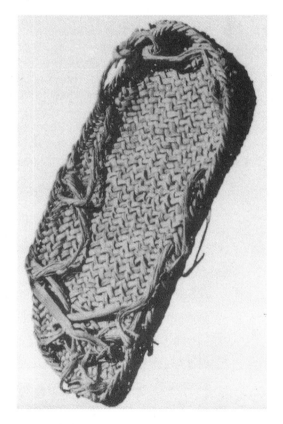

A nearly intact woven yucca-fiber sandal, made circa 1100 A.D. and found at Mesa Verde, Colorado (Mesa Verde National Park)

Seneca ornamental combs of the mid-sixteenth and late-seventeenth centuries (New York State Museum, Albany)

poral punishment, native cultures used public shame and ridicule on children who misbehaved.

Sources:
James Axtell, ed., *The Indian Peoples of Eastern America: A Documentary History of the Sexes* (New York: Oxford University Press, 1981);

Gretchen M. Bataille and Kathleen Mullen Sands, eds., *American Indian Women: Telling Their Lives* (Lincoln: University of Nebraska Press, 1984).

THE IMPORTANCE OF AGRICULTURE

Three Sisters. Corn or maize, beans, and squash were the most important food resources for nearly all Indians residing in the present-day United States. Called the "three sisters" by the Iroquois because they naturally grew well together, corn, beans, and squash provided the nutritional base and chief source of subsistence for most Indians until the twentieth century. Cornstalks supplied the climbing surface for bean vines, while beans and squash restored nitrogen to the soil depleted by mineral-hungry corn. By 1000 A.D., Indians living in the Southwest, along the Missouri and Mississippi Rivers, and in eastern North America grew all three crops. Many varieties of corn were utilized by different Indian groups, depending on the particular climate in their area. Corn that needed comparatively little water flourished in the semiarid Southwest, whereas quick-growing corn varieties suited the short growing season of the Canadian border area.

Origins. Maize formed such an important part of the diet among some tribes that they credited its origin to su-

pernatural forces or people. Almost everywhere in native America, the creative powers of women became associated with the abilities to grow corn. Women found the original maize or were shown the secrets of its cultivation by supernatural powers according to many native societies, particularly those in the Southeast, where corn constituted the primary foodstuff. In Cherokee oral tradi-

THE USES OF CORN AT HOCHELAGA

In September 1535 Frenchman Jacques Cartier sailed up the St. Lawrence River until reaching the Huron town of Hochelaga. While there he commented on the many uses of corn:

There are lofts in the upper part of their houses, where they store the corn of which they make their bread. This they call *carraconny,* and they make it in the following manner. They have wooden mortars, like those used in France for braying hemp, and in these wooden pestles they pound the corn into flour. This they knead into dough, of which they make small loaves, which they set on a broad hot stone and then cover them with hot pebbles. In this way they bake their bread for want of an oven. They also make many kinds of soup with this corn, as well as with beans and pease [sic], of which they have a considerable supply.

Source: David Beers Quinn, *New American World: A Documentary History of North America to 1612,* 5 volumes (New York: Arno, 1979), I: 315.

Bird ornaments with golden eyes made by south Florida tribesmen using silver and gold salvaged from Spanish shipwrecks, circa 1500 (South Florida Museum and Bishop Planetarium, Bradenton)

tions the wife of *Kanati* (the Lucky Hunter) was named *Selu* (which means "Corn"), and she introduced the Cherokees to maize, which she generated by rubbing her stomach or through her blood. After her death cornstalks sprouted wherever her blood hit the ground. In Creek mythology a woman first produced corn by washing her feet and rubbing them; she then instructed other Creek women how to grow corn and process it into bread and other dishes. These traditions helped to explain why women were responsible for agricultural production, as well as why women possessed inherent supernatural powers of creation.

Seasonal Ceremonies. Public events revolving around the first seasonal harvest of corn supplied the most important part of the ceremonial calendar for Indians east of the Mississippi River. In the Southeast the Green Corn Ceremony occurred among all groups in August or September. The Creek term for the ceremony, *poskita,* or *busk,* means "to fast". By denying themselves food for the duration of the ritual, lasting several days, and drinking emetics (concoctions that induced vomiting), they sought purity through ridding their bodies of pollutants. Similarly, southeastern Indians threw away their old belongings and clothing and sometimes tore down and built new homes and other structures as part of the

Green Corn Ceremony. They extinguished old cooking and sacred fires and replaced them with new ones started by elders and religious officials. They also forgave all offenses except murder committed during the prior year. Such purging meant that a new year could begin without the burdens of the prior one being carried over into the next. The Green Corn Ceremony provided a time of renewal and community solidarity, as well as a time for Indians to offer thanks to nature for giving them food and life.

Sources:

Charles Hudson, *The Southeastern Indians* (Knoxville: University of Tennessee Press, 1976);

John R. Swanton, ed., *Myths and Tales of the Southeastern Indians* (Norman: University of Oklahoma Press, 1995).

THE IROQUOIS LONGHOUSE

Home to Many. As an example of the distinctive ways in which many Indian groups adapted their housing to fit their physical environment and social needs, the Iroquois longhouse stands out. In every Iroquois village stood thirty or more longhouses. Positioned side by side in parallel rows, longhouses were about twenty feet wide and stretched from forty to two hundred feet in length. Their framework consisted of saplings anchored in the ground and arched into a roof about fifteen feet tall. Sheets of elm bark formed the walls and roof. Inside the longhouse a central corridor, interspersed with fireplaces every twenty or so, traveled the length of the building. Living compartments, one on each side of a hearth, housed separate but related nuclear families. Each dwelling represented a particular matrilineage. Everyone living in a longhouse, except for husbands who moved into their wives' apartments, belonged to a lineage traced through the female line. The oldest generation of women, the matrons, in each longhouse dominated its domestic affairs and united the families.

Symbol for a People. The five tribes of the Iroquois (the Mohawks, Oneidas, Onondagas, Cayugas, and Senecas) identified themselves collectively as the *Haudenosaunee,* meaning the "Extended House" or the "Longhouse." The five central council fires of the member tribes stretched across Iroquoia, what is today upstate New York, just like the fires of a longhouse extended the length of its walls. The *Haudenosaunee* was also called the League of Peace to represent the amicable relations between the Iroquois groups. The culture heroes Deganawidah and Hiawatha established the League of Peace sometime around 1400 A.D. to end a destructive civil war among the Iroquois tribes. They adopted the Longhouse as a metaphor that all Iroquoians would recognize and understand. Just as the longhouse roof united all families living under it to care for one another, the *Haudenosaunee* joined the Iroquois tribes under one connection of peace. Thus the shelter that Iroquoian people selected as befitting their natural environment developed into the symbol for their identity as a distinct people.

CHAMPLAIN SHOOTS TWO MOHAWK CHIEFS

Native Americans were astounded at the power of firearms when they first encountered them. This excerpt was written by Samuel de Champlain in 1609 as he accompanied Montagnais and Algonkin warriors down the Richelieu River into the lake that bears his name. The goal of the party was to war against the Iroquois, and the battle that resulted changed forever the face of Indian warfare in northern New England. Mohawks had no experience with guns, and after their encounter here the traditional rituals, defensive tactics, and woven shields were forgotten in favor of guerrilla warfare. Mohawks and Frenchmen became inveterate enemies from this point onward. Champlain described the battle:

I marched on until I was within some thirty yards of the enemy, who as soon as they caught sight of me halted and gazed at me and I at them. When I saw them make a move to draw their bows upon us, I took aim with my arquebus and shot straight at one of the three chiefs, and with this shot two fell to the ground and one of their companions was wounded who died thereof a little later. I had put four bullets into my arquebus. . . . The Iroquois were much astonished that two men should have been killed so quickly, although they were provided with shields made of cotton thread woven together and wood, which were proof against their arrows. This frightened them greatly.

Source: Colin G. Calloway, ed., *Dawnland Encounters: Indians and Europeans in Northern New England* (Hanover, N.H.: University Press of New England, 1991), pp. 137–141.

Source:

Daniel K. Richter, *The Ordeal of the Longhouse: The Peoples of the Iroquois League in the Era of European Colonization* (Chapel Hill: University of North Carolina Press, 1992).

KINSHIP

The Basis of Society. Kinship provided the base for any Native American society's structure, including economics, politics, and social relations. Whom one was related to determined where one lived, whom one married, where one's crops grew, and how one stood in relation to others in the society. Groups who depended to a significant degree upon horticulture tended to practice matrilineal kinship, meaning that one's relatives were traced through the mother's side of the family. The Northwest Coast groups who depended upon fishing also exercised this form of kinship. A smaller number of groups, such as some Plains Indians, practiced patrilineal descent, tracing relatives through the father's line. Tracing ancestors and relatives through only one parent is an alien concept to most contemporary citizens of the United States, who usually see both of their parents' families as relatives. Societies that were matrilineal did not necessarily give women a role in politics or diplomacy, but they often granted women the rights of home and land ownership. This is a significant recognition of the importance of women to the society; women in matrilineal systems generally owned the crops that they grew and thus contributed as much as (if not more than) their husbands to the subsistence economy. Moreover, women in such societies, and indeed in most Indian groups, exercised the autonomy to choose their own mates and divorce them if they desired.

Clans. Among many North American Indians, particularly the larger and more sedentary groups in the East, the Southwest, and the Northwest coast, clans were a leading, or perhaps the most important, unit of social organization. People of the same clan recognized some sort of common ancestor; that is, they were relatives. Although clans were frequently named for an animal, there was no belief that the people actually descended from such an animal. Generally, people of the same clan could

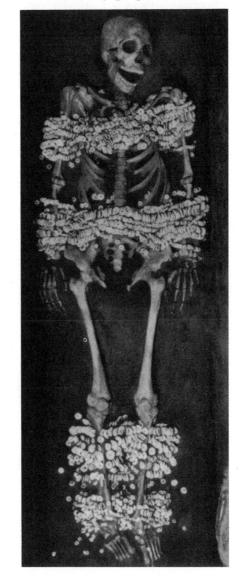

The skeleton of a Mississippian woman adorned with strands of two thousand shell beads (Milwaukee Public Museum)

not marry one another, and a child belonged either to the clan of his mother or father. Members were spread out over several villages, and an individual could almost always find shelter and food from a member of the same clan in a different village. Where they existed, clans had different functions. In some Indian societies they owned personal names and titles, which made a particular clan responsible for certain ceremonies and political positions. Among the Creeks, for example, the Wind Clan supplied village leaders. Clan members enacted revenge upon the members of another clan who murdered one of their own. Such acts of vengeance put all members of the offending clan in danger; any relative of the murderer qualified as an appropriate target for retaliation.

Source:
Charles Hudson, *The Southeastern Indians* (Knoxville: University of Tennessee Press, 1976).

MISSISSIPPIAN CHIEFDOMS

The Southeast before 1600 A.D. Native American societies varied greatly across the continent. One of the most distinctive cultures developed in the precontact Southeast and is called Mississippian by anthropologists and historians. Mississippian societies arose around 1000 A.D. and lasted until about 1600. Several European expeditions, most notably the one led by Hernando de Soto in the 1540s, encountered Mississippian peoples. Although groups speaking several different languages produced Mississippian societies, they shared many cultural traits. The most spectacular features of these societies were the temple- and burial-mound centers they constructed. The largest such site is at Cahokia in what is now Collinsville, Illinois, just east of St. Louis, Missouri; the village area extended for six miles along the Illinois River, contained eighty-five temple and burial mounds, and sustained a population perhaps as high as seventy-five thousand persons. Being master farmers allowed the Mississippians to develop such large societies, although most chiefdoms were much smaller than Cahokia. All Mississippian sites utilized maize or corn as a primary staple and supplemented it with other plants and meats.

Chiefdoms. Mississippian societies are called chiefdoms because they were governed by small groups of elites or even by a single individual, called a paramount chief. Commoners and outlying satellite villages paid tributes of corn, deer meat, animal skins, and prestige items to the principal town. In some cases new towns joined a chiefdom by military conquest. The labor of commoners built the mounds and suggests that elites held the power to assemble large bodies of people to do their bidding. Leadership passed through hereditary lines in at least some of these chiefdoms, but high status was most likely based upon command of spiritual forces. The general population recognized the large amounts of power that leaders manipulated and honored them with positions of prestige. Matrilineal kinship characterized Mississippian culture, and female paramount chiefs greeted Spanish expeditions,

Section of a wall made circa 1050–1300 A.D. by the Anasazi culture, showing the sophisticated masonry of the period (Pueblo Bonito, Chaco Canyon, New Mexico)

such as the "Lady of Cofitachequi" from the chiefdom of Cofitachequi in present-day South Carolina who welcomed Hernando de Soto in the 1540s.

Decline. Mississippian chiefdoms still existed in the mid 1500s when de Soto and others traveled through the Southeast, but just a century later the mound sites were abandoned. Because of this timing, scholars looked to the de Soto campaign as the cause of this phenomenon. It is probable that some of de Soto's men, or maybe the horses and pigs that accompanied them, carried diseases to which the Indians had no immunity. Pandemics may have wiped the Mississippians from the map, replacing them with refugee groups of survivors who banded together for protection but lacked the numbers to maintain the mounds. Many Mississippian sites became vacant before European contact, however, which suggests that local reasons contributed to abandonment. Perhaps Mississippians overused their resources, depleting the soil for corn and cutting down trees necessary for their buildings and fires. Possibly climatic changes resulted in drought or a shorter growing season, thus reducing the food supply. Political conflict and war between chiefdoms could have weakened some to the point of being unsustainable. Likely, all of the above factors contributed to the abandonment of the mound sites. The Choctaws, Creeks, Chickasaws, Cherokees, and Seminoles descended from the Mississippian peoples and held many traits in common with their ancestors.

Sources:

Paul E. Hoffman, *A New Andalucia and a Way to the Orient: The American Southeast during the Sixteenth Century* (Baton Rouge: Louisiana State University Press, 1990);

Charles Hudson and Carmen Chaves Tesser, *The Forgotten Centuries: Indians and Europeans in the American South, 1521–1704* (Athens: University of Georgia Press, 1994);

Jon Muller, *Mississippian Political Economy* (New York: Plenum Press, 1997).

PUEBLOS OF THE SOUTHWEST

General Characteristics. Pueblo peoples constituted a distinctive culture in present-day Colorado, New Mexico, and Arizona. Although speaking languages of diverse affiliation, all Pueblo Indians typically lived (and live) in multistoried stone or adobe buildings, sometimes

---

PUEBLO ARCHITECTURE AND CLOTHING

Pedro de Castañeda accompanied Francisco Vásquez de Coronado's expedition in search of gold and gems at the fabled Seven Cities of Cíbola (actually the Zuni Pueblos). They traveled throughout the Pueblo country of present-day New Mexico from 1540 to 1542. Castañeda left the most complete account of that exploration and the often violent encounters between the Spanish and Pueblo peoples. Moreover, he described the multistory buildings and some of the clothing worn by Pueblo men and women, which stand in stark contrast to Iroquoian styles:

Cíbola is composed of seven pueblos, the largest of which is called Mazaque. The houses, as a rule, are three and four stories high, but at Mazaque there are houses of four and seven stories. The natives here are intelligent people. They cover the privy and immodest parts of their bodies with clothes resembling table napkins, with fringes and a tassel at each corner, tying them around the hips. They wear cloaks made with feathers and rabbit skins, and cotton blankets. The women wear blankets wrapped tightly around their bodies, and fastened or tied over the left shoulder, drawing the right arm over them. They also wear well-fashioned cloaks of dressed [animal] skins, and gather their hair over their ears in two wheels that look like coif puffs.

Source: David Beers Quinn, *New American World: A Documentary History of North America to 1612*, 5 volumes (New York: Arno, 1979), I: 392.

---

on the top of high mesas. Each town contained anywhere from fifty to five hundred houses grouped around a central plaza. In the sixteenth century Pueblo society generally had matrilineal kinship patterns, and women owned the plots on which corn and other foodstuffs grew. Women owned the homes also, requiring men to move in with their wives upon marriage. Large portions of a mother's day were spent preparing meals for her household. As with other horticultural peoples, corn, beans, and squash were the main staples. Together, these crops

A Hohokam child's poncho made of cotton, circa 1100–1400 A.D. (Arizona State Museum, University of Arizona, Tucson, Arizona)

contributed more than 50 percent of the Pueblo diet. The male domain existed outside the home. Aside from engaging in warfare, men conversed with the spirit world inside their kivas.

Life in the Pueblos. Because of the semiarid condition of the American Southwest, Pueblo peoples concerned themselves first and foremost with getting enough food and water. They stored as much corn and other agricultural products as they could spare to prepare for times of drought. They also collected wild plants and traded agricultural products for game with the Apaches, Navajos, and other neighbors. The mid-sixteenth-century Spanish explorer Francisco Vásquez de Coronado reported that Pueblo Indians subsisted on maize, beans, and game, including rabbits and deer. Although Pueblo Indians domesticated the turkey, they insisted that the birds were a source of ceremonial feathers rather than food. Coronado found their corn tortillas delicious, and he noted that Indians ate them daily. Pueblos often relied on each other for assistance in hard times. Likewise, individuals often found marriage partners among members of a neighboring pueblo. Periodically, ceremonial specialists also traveled from one group to another offering assistance in rituals and ceremonies. Pueblo Indians maintained (and still do to this day) a rich and complex ceremonial life centered on the agricultural cycle and dominated by maize rituals. They worshiped the water, Coronado thought, because it made the corn grow and sustained all life.

Arrival of Spaniards. In July 1540 Coronado's expedition from Mexico City reached the Zuñi Pueblo of Hawikuh. They came in search gold and silver, but they found little of either. Ignorant of Pueblo customs, Coronado's force trespassed on Zuñi lands, which prompted an attack from the village's defenders. The Zuñis were no match for the Spanish military, however, and several died, while the rest tried to flee. Coronado spent nearly two years terrorizing and demanding tribute from Pueblo Indians until returning to Mexico City in 1542. For half a century the Spanish in Mexico largely ignored their northern territory until Juan de Oñate journeyed north in 1598 with a large force intent on settling the New Mexico region. Once there, he led a punitive expedition against Acoma Pueblo in response to the killing of thirteen Spanish soldiers. When the battle finally subsided after three days, more than eight hundred Acoma residents lay dead; eighty men and five hundred women were taken prisoner. The prisoners over the age of twelve were sentenced to twenty years of servitude, and all men over the age of twenty-five had one foot cut off. After this massacre large-scale Pueblo resistance against the Spanish did not resurface until the 1680s, when the Pueblos united to eject the Spanish from New Mexico.

Sources:
Ramón A. Gutiérrez, *When Jesus Came, the Corn Mothers Went Away: Marriage, Sexuality, and Power in New Mexico, 1500–1846* (Stanford, Cal.: Stanford University Press, 1991);

Elizabeth A. H. John, *Storms Brewed in Other Men's Worlds: The Confrontation of Indians, Spanish, and French in the Southwest, 1540–1795* (Norman: University of Oklahoma Press, 1975).

RITES OF PASSAGE

Types of Rituals. In all Native American societies, rituals marking transitions from one stage of life to another were observed. Such occasions included birth, naming ceremonies, marriage, girls' puberty rites at first menstruation, boys' conversion to men, and death. In some regions, notably the Plains, a vision quest undertaken by boys served as a puberty rite. The vision quest undertaken by both boys and men obtained power from the supernatural for use as a personal protector in times of war and as a spiritual guide throughout life. Among most native groups, rites at death included some ceremonial component designed to keep the deceased's spirit away from the living. Pregnant and menstruating women almost universally had to observe certain taboos, especially to avoid contact with the opposite sex. Men, too, sequestered themselves before leaving on a war party and performed elaborate rituals to ensure the success of their missions. In both cases isolation from the rest of the community enabled an individual to gather spiritual power.

Selection of Leaders in New England. Political, religious, and other formal leaders often had to undergo rites of purification as part of their training for office. According to accounts from the early seventeenth century, New England Algonquian Indians chose promising adolescent boys for specialized training. Forced to abstain from eating meat and made to drink concoctions

---

ISOLATED WOMEN

French missionary Gabriel Sagard offers an early-seventeenth-century account of the rituals surrounding menstruation among the Ottawas and Hurons:

The [Ottawa] women live very comfortably with their husbands, and they have this custom, like all other women of wandering peoples, that when they have their monthly sickness [menstruation] they leave their husbands, and the girl leaves her parents and other relatives, and they go to certain isolated huts away from their village; there they live and remain all the time of their sickness without any men in their company. The men bring them food and what they need until their return, if they have not themselves taken provisions enough as they usually do. Among the Hurons and other settled tribes the women and girls do not leave their house or village for such occasions, but they cook their food separately in little pots during that period and do not allow anyone to eat their meats and soups.

Source: James Axtell, ed., *The Indian Peoples of Eastern America: A Documentary History of the Sexes* (New York: Oxford University Press, 1981), p. 59.

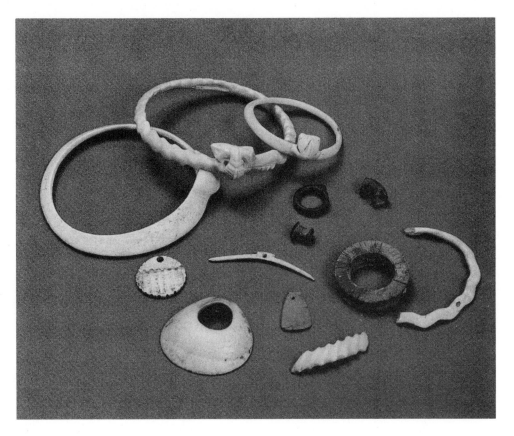

Hohokam jewelry made of red argillite, shell, stone, and turquoise (Arizona State Museum, University of Arizona, Tucson, Arizona)

that caused them to vomit, these young men experienced severe physical deprivation. After purging their stomachs of all food and liquid, they were beaten and turned outdoors in the middle of winter. While in this emaciated and delirious condition a spirit, or manitou, appeared to those boys worthy of spiritual support. The manitou endorsed the individual's claims to supernatural power. When that happened, other Indians viewed the young men with awe and granted them the authority to act on behalf of the tribe as political or war leaders.

Menstruation. Nearly all Native American societies observed certain taboos concerning menstruating women. Many tribes forced women to live in a separate house during their monthly discharge and to have no contact with men, whereas other groups insisted only that such women eat their meals separately from men while continuing to live in the same house. European observers interpreted these actions as an attempt to avoid the "pollution" that menstruating women supposedly embodied. More likely, however, women experienced the peak of their spiritual powers during menstruation. While in isolation, women sought spiritual visions, fasted, meditated, and ritually bathed themselves. Many Native American cultures viewed women as the creators of the first humans or as the originators of vital substances such as corn. The Cherokees associated blood with creation and reproduction. They believed that corn sprang from Selu, the first woman. Thus women and

their blood held mystical significance, and women reconnected with their mythical past through the ceremonies observed during menstruation.

Naming Patterns. All North American Indians received a name at birth. Usually females held the same name from birth to death. In matrilineal societies the mother usually bestowed the name on babies since the child belonged to her family. Often the birth name reflected the particular clan to which the mother belonged. For boys to become men in matrilineal societies they performed certain tasks, such as killing an enemy in war, in order to gain a new name bestowed by prominent men in the community. Once that was accomplished, an elaborate ceremony was held at which male elders gave the boy a new name reflecting his exploits. At that point he became a man. As a man continued to move up the social ladder, he earned new titles reflecting the positions he held.

Becoming a Man in the Southeast. Southeastern Indian boys trained throughout their entire childhoods to be strong, agile, and capable of enduring tremendous physical exertion. After killing a large game animal or an enemy, a boy became a man when warriors and religious specialists held a ceremony and bestowed a title on him reflecting the exploit. The name, actually a title, reflected either the accomplishments of the boy or some personal characteristic. Choctaw and Chickasaw war names often ended in *-tubby*, signifying "killer." Having

A Hohokam sunken ball court at Snaketown, Arizona, originally constructed between 600 and 900 A.D.

proved his adult status, a man then acquired other titles based on new deeds, thus increasing his stature within his society. The highest rankings denoted success in war and command over spiritual powers, such as *Mingo Hopaii* (War-Prophet King) among the Choctaws and Chickasaws. Each time that a man performed notable actions, a naming ritual ensued, thus making it possible to hold several titles at once.

Source:

John R. Swanton, "Source Material for the Social and Ceremonial Life of the Choctaw Indians," in *Smithsonian Institution, Bureau of American Ethnology Bulletin no. 103* (Washington, D.C.: U.S. Government Printing Office, 1931), pp. 119–124.

SAN AGUSTÍN: EUROPEANS COME TO STAY

Spanish Settlement. In 1565 Spain established the earliest permanent European settlement in North America at San Agustín (present-day St. Augustine) on the Atlantic coast of the Florida peninsula. The first order of business for the new colony and its leader, Pedro Menéndez de Aviles, consisted of routing a fledgling French colony that arrived in Florida at the same time. Marching overland to the French fort, La Caroline, while the French ships and forces lay stranded south of San Agustín because of a hurricane, Menéndez slaughtered the fort's remaining defenders, including the leader of the colony, Jean Ribault. With the French threat crushed, Menéndez established a garrison system by rebuilding the fort of La Caroline (renamed San Mateo) and strengthening San Agustín.

Daily Life. As the founding of San Agustín suggests, it served as a military garrison and was staffed primarily by soldiers. Under Menéndez's tutelage, however, the colony grew to include several garrisons strung along the coast north and south of San Agustín. Spain intended these fortifications to protect against French intrusion, though they also proved useful in limiting attacks by Indians. In the first few years single men made up the whole population at San Agustín. Later, soldiers sent for wives, and army families characterized life in the colony. Other people contacted the colony on a daily basis; these included Dominican and Jesuit friars, a smattering of African slaves employed in the administrators' households, and various Indian peoples native to Florida. Although the Spanish found it impossible to work Indians as slaves because they ran away to rejoin their communities, they forced nearby Indian communities to pay tributes of corn and other foodstuffs or risk attack. Adequate supplies of all kinds remained a problem for the colony for years, because they depended on sporadic shipments from Spain or Mexico. To be a Spaniard, or African, living in San Agustín during the 1500s meant isolation from the outside world, inadequate supplies, constant threat of attack from Indians or the French (which occurred in 1568), and a lack of female companionship.

Source:

Jerald T. Milanich, *Florida Indians and the Invasion from Europe* (Gainesville: University Press of Florida, 1995).

SICKNESS

No Resistance. Native Americans had no natural resistance against deadly European diseases such as smallpox, measles, bubonic plague, influenza, and whooping cough. Diseases spread like wildfire in the "virgin soil" conditions of the Americas. Epidemics occurred in the New World in 1520–1524, 1564–1570, 1586, 1588, and 1592–1593. In the Americas, Indians generally enjoyed a better diet and healthier surroundings than did the average European. But because they encountered these diseases for the first time when Europeans touched American shores (and therefore had built up no immunities), they died quickly and in large numbers. Native people who never saw any Europeans still encountered diseases as infected Indians from other groups traveled around the countryside in the course of everyday life. As Europeans arrived in America, they often settled in unoccupied areas that Native Americans had cleared. In many cases these Indians had died from diseases, thus leaving a "widowed" land for Europeans to occupy.

Social Impact. Indian populations plummeted in the face of European diseases. For example, the area of present-day Florida contained as many as one million Timucuan-speaking Indians in the early 1500s; by 1700 they were nearly all dead, most from pandemic diseases. That statistic repeated itself throughout the continent. Diseases rarely attacked in solitary fashion; usually a combination of different illnesses debilitated Indians at the same time. Even the common cold proved deadly when added to other diseases such as smallpox. The young and the old were most vulnerable to illness. Thus even if some of the population survived, the children (the future) and the elders (the keepers of the past) perished. Often entire villages got sick at once, leaving no one to care for the sick and causing many to die of simple neglect and starvation. Even the survivors of a pandemic faced extreme danger. Because of their reduced numbers and state of shock, they could offer little resistance to attacks from other Indian groups or from Europeans. These refugee communities often joined together and formed new societies out of the ashes of several old ones. In addition their entire cosmological world turned upside down. Shamans who normally healed the sick could do little against smallpox, and the people lost faith in the

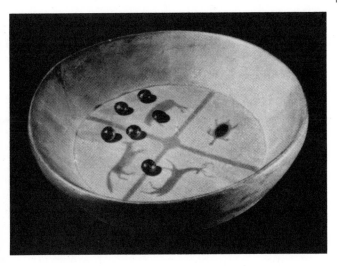

An Iroquoian bowl game made circa 1600. The object of the game was to rap the bowl on the ground and get all the peach pits (one side of each was black, the other white) to turn up the same color (National Museum of Man, National Museums of Canada, Quebec)

"THE PEOPLE BEGAN TO DIE VERY FAST"

In 1588 Thomas Harriot accompanied Sir Walter Raleigh's settlers establishing a colony on the North Carolina coast. The English inadvertently brought diseases with them. Hariot described the impact of smallpox on the Algonquian Indians of North Carolina:

There was no town where we had any subtile [sic] device practiced against us, we leaving it unpunished or not revenged (because we sought by all means possible to win them by gentleness) but that within a few days after our departure from every such town, the people began to die very fast, and many in short space, in some towns about twenty, in some forty, and in some six score [120], which in truth was very many in respect to their numbers. This happened in no place that we could learn but where we had been. . . . The disease also was strange, that they neither knew what it was, nor how to cure it, the like by report of the oldest men in the country never happened before, time out of mind. . . . All the space of their sickness, there was no man of ours known to die, or that was specially sick.

Source: Thomas Christensen and Carol Christensen, eds., *The Discovery of America & Other Myths: A New World Reader* (San Francisco: Chronicle Books, 1992), pp. 131–132.

ability of their religious leaders to protect them from evil outside forces.

Sources:

Henry F. Dobyns, *Their Number Become Thinned: Native American Population Dynamics in Eastern North America* (Knoxville: University of Tennessee Press, 1983);

Ann F. Ramenofsky, *Vectors of Death: The Archeology of European Contact* (Albuquerque: University of New Mexico Press, 1987);

Neal Salisbury, *Manitou and Providence: Indians, Europeans, and the Making of New England, 1500–1643* (New York: Oxford University Press, 1982).

SPORTS AND RECREATION

Leisure Pursuits. Native American peoples engaged in a variety of leisure activities. Heavy betting accompanied most games and contests. Warriors of all tribes competed in swimming and running matches to test their strength and endurance. A less rigorous activity was the hand game. Approximately eighty-one Plains and western tribes played this guessing game in which a person concealed objects in each hand. Another person would then guess which object was marked. If he chose correctly, the guesser won a counting stick; if he guessed wrong, he would lose one. The hand game was played by two teams with individuals from each side taking turns at guessing. Elaborate hand gestures, singing, and drumming marked the event, and it ended when one side won all the counting sticks.

Stickball Games. At the time of European contact in 1492, the native inhabitants of North America played several different stickball games. *Toka,* the forerunner of field hockey, was a traditional women's game among the Tohono O'odhams (more commonly known as Papagos) of northern Mexico and southern Arizona. A similar game was called *shinny.* Probably the most well known stickball game was lacrosse, played by tribes in the eastern portion of North America from the Great Lakes to the Gulf of Mexico.

Lacrosse. The origins of lacrosse are uncertain, but some anthropologists maintain it evolved from a Mesoamerican rubber-ball game. Early French colonists called it lacrosse because its curved stick (crosse) looked like a bishop's staff. The Onondagas called it *dehuntshigwa'es* (men hit a rounded object) while the Cherokees referred to it as *da-nah-wah'uwsdi* (little brother of war). Usually a male team sport, lacrosse differed from *toka* and *shinny* in that it used a netted racket by which a player threw and caught a ball. The object was to get the ball, usually made of deerskin or animal guts, past a goal. The ball could not be touched with the hands. Game equipment varied by regions. Southeastern players used two sticks (each 2.5 feet in length), while northern tribesmen had only one stick (3 or more feet long). Teams ranged in size from a few players to several hundreds, and events could last all day. The competition was occasionally fierce, with broken limbs, concussions, and even death resulting for some contestants. Aside from its worth as a recreational activity, lacrosse served a more important role in native society by bringing communities together. Ceremony surrounded the game, and holy men ritually prepared players and equipment before each match. Also tribes sometimes used it as an alternative to war by settling their disputes on the lacrosse field.

Sources:

Stewart Culin, "Games of the North American Indians," in *Twenty-fourth Annual Report of the Bureau of American Ethnology, 1902–1903* (Washington, D.C.: U.S. Government Printing Office, 1907);

Thomas Vennum Jr., *American Indian Lacrosse: Little Brother of War* (Washington, D.C. & London: Smithsonian Institution Press, 1994).

HEADLINE MAKERS

DON LUIS

FLOURISHED 1560s
POWHATAN TRIBAL LEADER

Kidnapped. In 1561 a Spanish ship commanded by Pedro Menéndez de Avilés journeyed into the Chesapeake Bay and seized an adolescent boy. The Spanish named the boy Don Luis, and he stayed under the care of Menéndez, who became commander of Spanish Florida in 1565. Don Luis viewed Spanish colonial society firsthand for ten years. He was taught the Spanish language and the intricacies of Catholicism. Menéndez hoped to use Don Luis as an interpreter and missionary for a Spanish colony to be established in the Chesapeake region. Since Don Luis was related to a Powhatan chief, Menéndez treated him well; he lived in Cuba, Mexico, and Spain at different times and even met King Philip II.

Return to the Chesapeake. In 1570 Don Luis returned home accompanied by two Jesuit priests and seven assistants, but with no military support. Don Luis directed the Jesuits to settle in an area away from any native village, and he then left them to rejoin his people. Quickly he asserted his elite status and took several wives, in direct repudiation of his Christian education. After six months the Jesuits pestered Don Luis and his people incessantly for food, and Powhatan religious leaders viewed the missionaries as a threat. Having reached the end of his patience, Don Luis led a war party that killed all of the Jesuits except for one boy.

Aftermath. Menéndez soon learned what happened to the Jesuits he had helped finance, and he dispatched a punitive expedition to the Chesapeake. The Spanish rescued the boy and killed several Powhatans, but Don Luis refused to deliver himself over to them. In retaliation for the killing of the Jesuits and Don Luis's refusal to cooperate, the Spanish hanged some Powhatan captives from the yardarms of their ship and let them die of starvation and exposure. "After seeing the opposite of what the fathers were, they tremble," wrote a member of the punitive force, "this chastisement has become famous throughout the land." The fate of Don Luis is uncertain. It is possible that he was related to the Powhatan leaders Wahunsonacock and Opechancanough, who confronted John Smith and the English after 1607. Some speculate that Don Luis and Opechancanough may have been the same person. Regardless, Don Luis certainly shaped his people's perceptions of Europeans by telling them of all the things he had seen in Europe, Cuba, and Mexico.

Source:
Clifford M. Lewis and Albert J. Loomie, *The Spanish Jesuit Mission in Virginia: 1570–1572* (Chapel Hill: University of North Carolina Press, 1953).

MANTEO

FLOURISHED 1580S
CROATOAN TRIBAL LEADER

Journey to England. Manteo traveled voluntarily to England in 1584 with the initial ships sent to North Carolina by Sir Walter Raleigh. He learned English rapidly while living in London. He accompanied the first settlement attempt by the English on North Carolina's Outer Banks in 1585 as an interpreter and guide. In June 1586, however, he returned to England where he worked closely with Thomas Harriot and John White to complete a vocabulary of the Algonquian language. Both groups of men learned much about the other's culture. Knowledge of the English language and ways enabled Manteo to take a dominant position among his people when he returned for good in 1587.

Return to the Outer Banks. Manteo's mother ruled a small chiefdom in the area of present-day Cape Hatteras. When he returned to Roanoke Island once again with John White in 1587, he built upon his noble lineage and his intimate connections with powerful outsiders to assume a leadership position in the tribe. After being home a couple of months, the English baptized Manteo, who probably received at least the rudiments of Protestant education while in England. Manteo used such connections with the English to seize control over the Roanoke Island peoples after the English killed the previous leader, Wingina. When Raleigh's ships returned to Roanoke Island in 1590, they discovered that the English colonists had disappeared. The only clue to the fate of these people was the word CROATOAN carved on a tree. What actually happened to the settlers remains uncertain to this day, but it is probable that many stayed with Manteo, who could communicate with them and teach them how to survive. In the early seventeenth century Indians reported English survivors living far inland, and other accounts suggested that the Powhatans killed English people living among their enemies the Chesapeakes, but no official confirmation ever surfaced.

Source:
David Beers Quinn, *Set Fair for Roanoke: Voyages and Colonies, 1584–1606* (Chapel Hill: University of North Carolina Press, 1985).

PUBLICATIONS

David Beers Quinn, *New American World: A Documentary History of North America to 1612*, 5 volumes (New York: Arno, 1979)—all of the known early travel accounts and reports by Spanish, French, Dutch, and English explorers of North America. Included are documents from the expeditions of Jacques Cartier, Francisco Vásquez de Coronado, Hernando de Soto, Juan de Oñate, Samuel de Champlain, Thomas Harriot, and others. An indispensable source of information on the native groups of the continent;

James Axtell, ed., *The Indian Peoples of Eastern America: A Documentary History of the Sexes* (New York: Oxford University Press, 1981)—conveniently divided into chapters such as Birth, Love and Marriage, Work, and Death, this collection of documents provides an in-depth look at Native American daily life.

Native American hunters, disguised in deerskins, stalking prey (engraving by Theodor de Bry, after a painting by Jacques le Moyne, 1564)

CHAPTER EIGHT

RELIGION

by RACHELLE E. FRIEDMAN

CONTENTS

CHRONOLOGY
176

OVERVIEW
180

TOPICS IN THE NEWS

Religion in Europe:
   Catholicism...................183
Religion in Europe: Catholicism: The
   Inquisition................184
The Return of the Lord........185
Religion in Europe: Catholicism:
   Missionaries 186
Religion in Europe: Catholicism:
   Missionaries: Efforts in
   St. Augustine 188
Religion in Europe:
   Protestantism 189

Religion in Europe:
   Protestantism: Calvinism 189
Religion in Europe: Protestantism:
   The Huguenots............190
Religion in Europe:
   Protestantism: Luther's
   Ninety-five Theses 190
Religion in Europe: Religious
   Conflict...................191
Religion in Europe: Women 191
A Woman Speaks Out........191
Religion in the New World: America as
   "Virgin Land".............192
"The People from Heaven".......193
Religion in the New World:
   The Huguenots in
   South Carolina..............194
Religion in the New World: Native
   American Myths 194
Aztec Myth 194
Religion in the New World: Native
   American Spirituality.......194

Iroquoian Creation Myth.....197
Religion in the New World:
   Native American Spirituality:
   Shamans 198
Religion in the New World:
   Requierimento............199

HEADLINE MAKERS

Pierre Biard.....................199
John Calvin 200
Christopher Columbus 200
Teresa of Ávila.................201

PUBLICATIONS
202

Sidebars and tables are listed in italics.

660 B.C.

- The mound-building culture with ceremonial areas and temples begins to flourish in the Mississippi Valley, near present-day St. Louis.

1000? A.D.

- Leif Ericsson's father, Eric the Red, an early explorer of Greenland, sets forth the idea that the New World is a virgin land and earthly paradise. This theme is picked up by other explorers and especially articulated by the New England Puritans six centuries later.

1454

- Johannes Gutenberg's Bible is printed. Despite suspicion toward any human-made version of the Scriptures, the Church soon recognizes its value in spreading the Gospel.

1473

- Nicholaus Copernicus is born and later overturns the ancient Ptolemaic and Christian notion that humans are at the center of the universe; rather, he shows that the Earth revolves around the sun.

1491

- Ignatius Loyola, founder of the Order of the Society of Jesus, or Jesuits, is born. Jesuits are tremendously influential in education and missionary efforts.

1499

- Amerigo Vespucci makes his second voyage to the New World and notes that natives lack religion.

1500

- Franciscans begin arriving in the Americas.

1510

- The first Spanish Dominicans arrive in the Americas.

1513

- Juan Ponce de León explores the Florida coast and takes possession of the area in northern Florida which he believes to be the Fountain of Youth.

1517 • Martin Luther draws up his Ninety-five Theses attacking the sale of indulgences by the Church and helps begin the Reformation.

1531 8 Dec. Juan Diego, a recent native convert to Catholicism, claims that the Virgin Mary appeared to him on the hill of Tepeyac in what is now Mexico City.

1534 • Henry VIII signs the Act of Supremacy, making him head of the Church of England.

1536 • John Calvin publishes *The Institutes of the Christian Religion* and moves to Geneva, Switzerland, a city amenable to Protestant beliefs.

1537 9 June In Peru the Dominican monk Bernadino de Minaya obtains a papal bull from Paul III titled *Sublimus Deus*. It rejects the idea that the Indians "should be treated as dumb brutes created for our service, pretending that they are incapable of receiving the Catholic faith."

1539 • Three Franciscans accompany Francisco de Ulloa's expedition to the Gulf of California.

1540 • Six priests make the journey with Francisco Vásquez de Coronado into the Southwest.

1541 • King Charles I of Spain requires that hospitals in the Americas be open to Spaniards and Indians alike, for caring for the sick is seen as part of doing God's work. Catholic brothers are sent to operate the facilities.

1553 • Catholic Mary Tudor ascends the English throne, driving many Protestants into exile.

1555
- Peter Martyr, an Italian cleric in Spain who was acquainted with many explorers, publishes a systematic account of their findings in *The Decades of the New World or West India*.

1558
- Elizabeth I ascends the throne and allows Protestantism to return to England.

1562
- Huguenots found a colony at Fort Caroline in what is present-day Jacksonville, Florida.

1565
- The Spanish defeat the Huguenots in Florida and found St. Augustine.

1570
- A mission is established in Maryland by seven Jesuits. They are guided by the converted Indian Don Luis Velasco but are ultimately killed by members of the Powhatan tribe.

1572
- The last of the Jesuits leave Florida after they are unsuccessful in gaining converts.
- St. Bartholomew's Day Massacre occurs in France. Twelve thousand French Protestants are killed, one of the bloodiest events in the Catholic-Huguenot conflict.

1578
- Queen Elizabeth I gives Sir Humphrey Gilbert power to seize "remote heathen and barbarous lands."

1580s
- For the next twenty years an English uncle and nephew, each named Richard Hakluyt, urge exploration and colonization of the far side of the Atlantic, in part to effect the conversion of native peoples to Protestantism.

1580
- French author Michel de Montaigne publishes *The Essays*, in which he concludes that explorers are too biased against native peoples and assume, unfairly, that they lack civility and the spiritual superiority of the Europeans.

1585

- Queen Elizabeth I of England sends six thousand troops to assist the Dutch Protestants, under attack by Phillip II of Spain's Catholic armies.

1588

- England defeats the powerful Spanish Armada and emerges as a stronghold of Protestantism.

- Thomas Harriot's *A Brief and True Report of the New Found Land of Virginia* is published, arguing that natives would wish to learn about the Protestant faith, the "true religion," and thus "be brought to civilitie."

1595

- Franciscan efforts at converting Native Americans in Florida begin to show signs of success.

1597

- Guale Indians living in missions on the Georgia coast revolt. Soldiers from St. Augustine are called to help put rebellion down.

A late-sixteenth-century Seneca antler comb with human visages that reflect the Iroquois preoccupation with the spirit world (Rochester Museum and Science Center, Rochester, New York)

OVERVIEW

Heathens. In popular thought, the introduction of religion to America began with the Pilgrims' arrival in Plymouth in 1620. The Native Americans, the argument continues, were heathens who lacked any religion, not only Christianity. Even the other English who arrived earlier, those who settled in Virginia, came for riches and were notoriously godless. In fact the first Americans, the Native Americans, did have a religion and possessed a well-developed sense of spirituality, albeit one unrecognizable to the Europeans. Christianity arrived in the Americas not with the Pilgrims or, a decade later, the Massachusetts Bay Puritans but with the explorers who began arriving in the late fifteenth century. Indeed, in part, exploration was prompted not only by economic and political goals but also to spread faith to the "ignorant masses." Priests and missionaries were present on the ships bound for the New World. To understand religion in the sixteenth-century Americas and what occurred when Native American and European systems of faith encountered one another, one must consider the two very different ways of belief.

Universal System. Throughout history every culture and people have had religion. Though varying in whom or what is believed, how faith is expressed and practiced, religion has universally offered comfort and explanation. To people living in worlds in which mysteries of nature seemed unknowable and undiscoverable and in which tragedy and hardship seemed to abound, faith provided answers. Despite common reasons for religious belief, religions varied widely in the sixteenth century. The philosopher Huston Smith has divided religion into two broad categories: historical religion and primal religion. Adherents to historical religions (such as Judaism, Christianity, and Islam) hold certain texts to be sacred. Historical religions also tend to change over time. In contrast, followers of primal religions, such as Native Americans, do not have a sacred text, nor do their belief systems tend to be in flux. They are often nature-based.

Changes. The sixteenth century witnessed much change in the practice of religion in Europe. The Protestant Reformation and the Catholic response, the Counter-Reformation, not only affected how many individuals practiced their religion but also had far-reaching effects on government, economy, and society. These changes led to further alterations in religious belief and practice. Such changes did not only affect Europe; exploration, fueled in part by new interest in religion and the missionary impulse, brought Europeans to the New World and into (often disastrous) contact with indigenous peoples.

Emergence of Protestantism. Until the late sixteenth century the vast majority of Europeans were Catholics, adhering to the idea that one church existed, governed on Earth by the Pope as the Vicar of Christ. Several reasons led to the emergence of Protestantism: nationalism (movements in various countries to strengthen their own governments and cultures and a lessening of the Pope's authority); the emphasis on individualism during the Renaissance (the belief that individuals were capable of self-education and self-direction); and the growth of political economies. Another factor was the abuse of ecclesiastical authority. Local parish priests enjoyed riches at the expense of their parishioners, who were starving both physically and spiritually. Such discontent led to the rapid growth of Lutheranism and especially Calvinism. In contrast to the Catholic Church's emphasis on the role of intermediaries such as priests and bishops helping individuals make their way to heaven, and on embellishments such as stained-glass windows, incense, and elaborate churches as a way to glorify God, the tenets of John Calvin, Martin Luther, and other prominent Protestant reformers and thinkers emphasized the concept of *Sola Scriptura,* or Scripture alone. Fancy structures such as the soaring gothic cathedrals, jeweled chalices, and other elaborate apparatus, as well as human mediators (priests), were unnecessary and in fact hindered an individual's road to salvation. Each individual through faith and study of the Bible might find God for him- or herself.

Varieties. In 1505, after nearly being struck by a bolt of lightning, Martin Luther, a young German man intending to become a lawyer, chose to become a monk instead. As an Augustinian monk, however, he found the Church rituals such as Mass and confession to lack meaning. Instead inward faith or grace was the means of personal salvation, he argued. Luther rejected the idea that Church officials could help guide others to grace. While this doctrine of justification by faith did not iniially cause the church to be suspicious, his open attacks in 1517 on the sale of indulgences did. Indulgences were purchases of forgiveness, by which an individual might reduce time spent in purgatory and by which the Pope was raising money for the building of St. Peter's in Rome. Luther published his Ninety-five Theses against the sale of indulgences and also urged German princes to take control of religion in their states, in direct defiance of Rome. Another belief system, Calvinism, held great appeal for both uneducated and educated Europeans and would influence the Puritans who settled in Massachusetts beginning in the 1620s. By 1534 the French John Calvin had converted (though not in the formal sense as we think of it today) to a scripture-based form of Christianity. Going to Geneva, Switzerland, to reform religion in 1536, he was forced out by 1538 as the political climate of the city changed and Protestant leaders were no longer welcome. Three years later, reformist advocates were once again invited as the town's politics changed again. Calvin remained there until his death in 1564. Calvin stressed predestination, the tenet that even before an individual was born God had determined if he were to be saved or damned. Calvin placed the reading of Scripture at the center of worship. He also emphasized the primacy of faith: "All we have attempted . . . is to restore the native purity from which [the Christian ordinances] had degenerated" and "to bring . . . faith back to its [biblical] fountainhead." Without faith the Christian could not find lasting benefit from word or sacrament.

Spread of Calvinism. Calvin gained many adherents in Geneva; his system of belief, which he and his students continued to develop, spread to other Swiss cities, such as Zurich, and to other countries, especially England. The ascendancy of the Catholic queen Mary Tudor in 1553 drove many Protestants into exile. Since the late fifteenth century, Protestantism had been growing in strength in England. Henry VIII had created the Church of England in 1534 largely because of his dissatisfaction with the Pope's refusal to grant him a divorce. The Church of England retained many elements of the Catholic Church; what had changed was the confiscation of monasteries and other Church property, to the profit of the Crown and national independence under the Crown as head of the Church in England. Henry's son Edward moved the Church of England in a more Protestant direction, to the satisfaction of many English people who found greater spiritual nourishment in several varieties of reformed religion. The Marian exiles, as those Protestants were known who fled England after Mary became queen and rejoined Rome, studied Calvinism on the Continent. As such, upon their return to England, Genevan Calvinism took a firm hold at both Cambridge and Oxford. The tenets of Calvin and his successors shaped (though by no means exclusively) Church of England doctrine in the late Elizabethan and Jacobean periods. Some of the most prominent reform theologians in Europe, including William Perkins, William Whi-

taker, John Reynolds, and Lawrence Chaderton, were English. They taught generations of students, some of whom in turn became preachers in English parishes and some of whom would bring their theology to new England, formulating varieties of American Puritanism.

Religious Wars. If after Mary's reign Protestantism was able to spread in England with only a limited amount of conflict and with the monarchs' sanction and support, this was not the case in other European countries. The division between Catholic and Protestant not only engendered disagreement but also caused wars and political strife. The example of France between the years 1559 and 1589 illustrates particularly well how extreme religious division might become. The nobility, at odds with the Catholic monarchy over questions of power, took advantage of the three weak sons of Henry II to strengthen their own position. To gain the upper hand, they often cloaked themselves in reformed religion (in this case French Calvinism) so that Huguenots (as French Calvinists were called) would side with them. Both sides encouraged their followers to desecrate the others' sacred property, including churches, religious statues, and stained-glass windows. The violence did not end there; often rioting led to personal injury and death. One of the worst episodes began 24 August 1572, St. Bartholomew's Day. In Paris, as the king's sister was marrying the Protestant Henry of Navarre in an attempt to reconcile the two sides, Huguenot gentry were slaughtered. The St. Bartholomew's Day Massacre, as it has become known, spread from Paris to the provinces, and over the next six weeks perhaps twelve thousand Huguenots were killed. Besides France the Netherlands also experienced severe religious division.

Exploration and Colonization. Those countries that did not experience religious wars were able to focus their resources on exploration. Both for profit and for the glory of God (especially in light of the growth of Protestantism) mainly Catholic countries such as Spain and Portugal set sail for distant lands. Portugal was the first to venture out, beginning with voyages to Africa in the 1420s. It was Columbus, however, who met with the greatest success. The Genoan was supported by Queen Isabella of Spain. He reached the Bahamas in 1492; upon his arrival in the New World, Columbus declared that "God has shown his will." A well-circulated pamphlet he wrote on his return to Spain praising the friendly natives, fertile soil, and rivers overflowing with gold ensured support for Columbus. As a result he would make three more voyages. Several clergymen arrived in the Antilles with Columbus on his second voyage. Five members of the Franciscan order were sent to the New World in 1500 and another seventeen in 1502. Members of the Dominican order began arriving in 1510. Spanish Jesuits and then Dominicans settled in Florida, which Juan Ponce de León had first explored in 1515 and 1521, and Franciscans accompanied voyagers to California and the Southwest. Seeing Spanish success, the French turned their attention to the New World, though not as avidly as the Spanish. French Jesuits were entrusted with missionary activity. Jacques Cartier arrived on the St. Lawrence River first in 1534, but it was not until 1608, led by Samuel de Champlain, that the French would establish a permanent settlement, also in the St. Lawrence Valley. The first Jesuit team arrived in Nova Scotia in 1611. The missionaries baptized more than one hundred Indians. Led by Pierre Biard and Enemond Massé, they catechized the natives in their own language. The French enjoyed slight success for a while, but their most enduring result was making the Indians economically dependent upon them.

English Attempts. Initially Queen Elizabeth I of England did not sponsor much overseas exploration. She was preoccupied with helping other Protestant monarchs, such as the Dutch king, and with fighting Catholic Phillip II of Spain. In 1588 Phillip sent the Spanish Armada—130 ships, 30,000 men, and 2,400 artillery pieces strong—to the coast of England. Despite a weaker fleet, the English defeated the Spanish Armada. This victory solidified Protestantism in England, and with a stalemate in the religious wars England was able to join the exploration race. In the 1580s and 1590s exploration captured the English imagination. For the nobles this was a chance to gain new authority and new lands, for the merchants new markets, and for radical Protestant clergy the opportunity to convert literally millions of heathens. First attempts were unsuccessful, but later they met with greater success. Sir Francis Drake defeated the Spanish in Florida. As the economy worsened and the tide turned against radical Protestantism, more and more English looked to colonization as a way to leave. In time the English gained a more solid foothold and established Protestantism in their colonies more strongly than the Spanish did Catholicism.

Native Americans and Spirituality. The Native Americans were guided by spirits and deities. They did not worship a single god, nor did they hold a single text to be sacred. Though several tribal and language groups lived in the Americas, each possessing its own set of myths, Native American religions were, fundamentally, based on the same idea. As polytheists they believed that the spirit power dwelled throughout nature. Every element in nature was sacred and interconnected. In contrast to Europeans who adhered to the biblical injunction found in Genesis that humans were to reign over the earth and all lesser creatures, Native Americans saw themselves as equal parts of a larger system; it was not for humans to disturb this balance. They regarded plants and animals as gifts to be used wisely. If they misused nature's gifts, they risked retaliation. Animals were thought to have great spiritual power. Thus, rather than killing them excessively for food, Native Americans sought other sources. Different animals possessed different powers: crows, for example, were not to be harmed as these birds brought the gift of grain. Other deities had different powers, and Native Americans believed in a paramount deity, though not in an historical religious sense. As well as singling out deities, Native Americans looked to certain gifted men known as shamans. They were respected for their spirituality and healing powers. Shamans also led ceremonies acknowledging nature's gifts at annual and cyclical festivals such as the harvest.

Encounters. To the European explorers and settlers, Native American belief systems represented not a respect for the power of nature but worship of false gods. Native American practices were to the newcomers at best peculiar and at worst satanic. One Englishman in 1589 noted that he had seen the Devil at an Indian's house. Three years later another Englishman noted that Native Americans in New Spain actually talked to the Devil and made sacrifices to him. The Dominican Tomas Ortiz noted that the natives were "most hostile to religion" and that never had God "created a race more full of vice." Europeans regarded Native American dances and noisy ceremonies that were performed to please the gods as evidence of demonic possession. European settlers made several attempts to convert the native peoples. While the Spanish settler Bartholomé de las Casas noted in 1550–1551 that Indians understood Christianity and were eager to embrace the faith, missionaries, for the most part, met with only limited successes. In many cases the Christian missionaries mistreated the indigenous peoples, including stealing food and raping and murdering those whom they had come to save. Often the missionaries' own infighting made sustained conversion efforts impossible; so too did their unwillingness to try to survive in the New World. Priests often misinterpreted the Native Americans' hospitality toward newcomers—an integral part of the Indians' system of morality—as success in conversion. Indians "converted" not out of new faith or belief but in an effort to understand and take part in the Europeans' culture. In contrast, with few exceptions, Europeans made little effort to understand the natives' language or cultural ways. Though an integral part of the stated goals of exploration and colonization, conversion of the native peoples went largely unfulfilled.

TOPICS IN THE NEWS

RELIGION IN EUROPE: CATHOLICISM

The Universal Church. Until the middle of the fifteenth century the overwhelming majority of Europeans were Christians, and the overwhelming majority of them were Catholics. There had long been calls for reform of the Church. While a few groups might have been discontented with the Church and splintered off to form their own religions, to be Christian in Europe was to be a member of the Catholic Church, adhering to the authority of the Pope in Rome as the Vicar of Christ and to his shepherds spread throughout Western Europe, the cardinals, bishops, parish priests, and nuns. The word *catholic* means universal; the Catholic Church was so named because of its universal membership and authority of the Pope throughout the Continent rather than the sectarian divisions that would characterize Protestantism. Religion had a tremendous influence in everyday life: the calendar, with its saints' days, feasts, and fasts, helped dictate the rhythm of life; so, too, the icons and images of Jesus and the saints gave religion a visual presence in churches and homes alike. However, not all Catholics were content with the Church. Late-medieval critics decried the lackluster papacy and practices such as simony (the selling of spiritual goods) and other forms of abuse as well as the general spiritual poverty. This was followed by a revival of religious practice fortified by the vitality of groups such as the Spiritual Franciscans, Waldensians, and Hussianites.

The Road to Reformation. The mid fifteenth century found many Catholics dissatisfied with what they perceived to be growing corruption and declining spirituality. Many clerical leaders were interested more in their own material gain than in leading their flocks. The sale of indulgences (payments to the Church which shortened the amount of time Catholics or their deceased relatives had to spend in purgatory) and absentee priests (in which priests served more than one parish and were supported by each of those parishes but were not present) led many to call for reforms. Martin Luther and John Calvin were among the most prominent reformers; Calvin in particular drew many Catholics away from the Church. In 1534 Henry VIII, King of England, dealt another blow to the Church. After the Pope refused to grant him a divorce, Henry created the Church of England. The Church of England resembled the Catholic Church except at the head stood the English

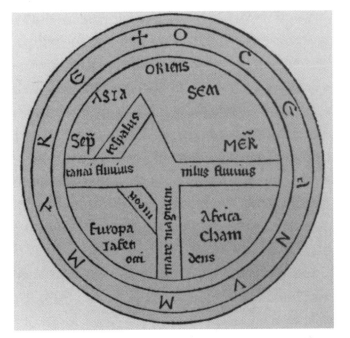

A 1473 theological map of the world from Isidore of Seville's *Etymologiae*. Jerusalem is at the center.

monarch rather than the Pope. The creation of the English church opened the door for reformers. When Mary, Henry's staunchly Catholic daughter, ascended the throne, she not only reconnected with the Church in Rome but also persecuted or forced those in opposition to the Catholic Church into exile on the Continent. England did not remain a Catholic country for long; when Mary's half sister, Elizabeth I, came to the throne in 1558, she did so as a Protestant and helped defend reformed religion not only in her country but also throughout Europe.

The Counter-Reformation. The Catholic Church did not sit idle, watching its numbers diminish. The clergy and laity instituted a series of changes known as the Counter-Reformation. Recognizing the existence of abuses, the Church sought to purify itself. While the Catholic Church stressed that it was not acting only in response to Protestantism but rather was putting into place much-needed reform, it is clear that both the origins of the Reformation and the Counter-Reformation could be found

A 1505 Spanish painting of the Virgin of Navigators offering
her protection to Christopher Columbus, his crew,
and Native Americans

in a shared discontent with the status quo. The Church took up the question of reform primarily at the Council of Trent (1545–1563). The council articulated doctrine on such matters as salvation and grace and defined the seven sacraments. Indeed, the Council of Trent gave the Catholic Church a doctrinal clarity lacking in Protestantism. The Church rededicated itself to the education of priests, establishing several seminaries for that purpose, and gave the Society of Jesus a special role, entrusted with promoting missionary work as well as education. Indeed, establishing missionaries in the New World and Asia was one of the major works of the Catholic Reformation (as the Counter-Reformation is also known). Ultimately the Counter-Reformation helped to revitalize spirituality and change religious culture to recognize the needs of the laity.

Sources:

John Bossy, *Christianity in the West, 1400–1700* (New York: Oxford University Press, 1985);

Richard Mackenney, *Sixteenth-Century Europe: Expansion and Conflict* (New York: St. Martin's Press, 1993).

RELIGION IN EUROPE: CATHOLICISM: THE INQUISITION

Special Tribunals. While the Inquisition stands out among few other events in history as an example of the human capacity for intolerance and cruelty, its motivation was the preservation of doctrinal purity. From the twelfth to the sixteenth centuries the Roman Catholic Church in western Europe employed aspects of Roman legal procedure and appointed clergy to carry out the task of preserving orthodox beliefs from heresy. These tribunals were institutionalized, and the personnel and procedures were termed "inquisitions." In the beginning the inquisitors used persuasion to discover if those Christians suspected of heresy were, indeed, heretics. Over ime, however, as heresy was feared to be increasing, persuasion gave way to coercion.

Spain. In Spain, from the fourteenth century on, economic and social transformations created political and economic upheaval. As a result non-Christians, Muslims, and Jews had new legal disabilities thrust upon them. Many Jews converted toward the end of the fourteenth century; they became known as *conversos*. In all, more than two hundred Jewish communities were destroyed, and 160,000 Jews either fled or converted. Those who fled were not allowed to take gold, arms, horses, or money out of Spain, and they wandered, often starving, in search of new homes. Now the inquisitors subjected conversos to the inquisitors' inspections, and the former Jews were often accused of being false Christians or having gone through invalid conversions. Between 1440 and 1465 anti-Semitism intensified, and Spaniards were particularly hated. Conversos as worse than Jews, for the new Christians now had privileges and positions not available to them before. At the same time Spanish Christians believed their religious practices to be purer and superior.

Ferdinand and Isabella. In this climate the Spanish monarchs Ferdinand and Isabella requested a papal bull establishing an inquisition. In November 1478 Pope Sixtus IV allowed them to appoint inquisitors. The monarchs assigned the task of naming priests to the Dominican Order, and by October 1480 the inquisition was at work. Many conversos fled Spain. After an alleged converso plot to destroy the inquisitors was discovered in Seville in 1481, the conversos were widely attacked, and the first public burning of condemned heretics was carried out.

Gaining Strength. Ferdinand took further measures to control the Inquisition. In 1482 he took the action of joining the inquisitions of two Spanish kingdoms, Castile and Aragon, thereby strengthening his own power. He and Isabella also issued an edict expelling the Jews from Spain in 1492. Thus the monarchy was actively engaged in combating heresy and ensuring religious "purity" in Spain.

Revitalization. The number of heretics had all but dwindled when, in 1520, new Protestant movements had sprung up in the German states to revitalize the Inquisition. The tribunals acted quickly and intensely to combat the offending Lutherans. Tribunals would come to towns harboring suspected heretics. Local preachers would define heresy in sermons and issue Edicts of Grace, in which parishioners could voluntarily confess or point out suspects to the inquisitors. After 1500 it became mandatory to identify suspects to the inquisitors. Those who did not, according to the 1500 Edict of Faith, would be excommunicated. Treatment of the accused became increasingly harsh: land and goods were taken; the suspected heretic was jailed at his own expense until the hearing was completed; and if, despite sufficient evidence, the accused did not confess, the inquisitors permitted torture. Lutherans

were especially persecuted after 1558. Torture occurred relatively infrequently, since the inquisitors sought penitence rather than justice. Spanish territories were fair game for the Board of Inquisitors; both Mexico and Hispaniola, where conversos had fled, had inquisitions in place. The Inquisition was also present in Portugal and Italy. The Spanish Inquisition was particularly long-lived and was not abolished until 1814.

The Black Legend. One historian has suggested that the Spanish Inquisition as we perceive it today—as a single, continuous process replete with torture—is a myth. Protestants from the sixteenth century onward exaggerated its reach to show how brutal the Catholics could be to heretics. This "Black Legend" holds that Spain represented and epitomized repression, brutality, and political and spiritual intolerance. Such intolerance was not limited to Catholics: Protestants in England pursued Catholics, but without the official structure of the Inquisition.

Sources:
Edward Peters, *The Inquisition* (New York: Free Press, 1988);
David Raphael, ed., *The Expulsion 1492 Chronicles* (North Hollywood, Cal.: Carmi House Press, 1992).

THE RETURN OF THE LORD

Most of the prophecies of holy Scripture have already been fulfilled. The Scriptures say this and the Holy Church loudly and unceasingly is saying it, and no other witness is necessary. I will, however, speak of one prophecy in particular because it bears on my argument and gives me support and happiness whenever I think about it. . . .

I have already said that for the voyage to the Indies neither intelligence nor mathematics nor world maps were of any use to me; it was the fulfillment of Isaiah's prophecy. This is what I want to record here in order to remind Your Highnesses and so that you can take pleasure from the things I am going to tell you about Jerusalem on the basis of the same authority. If you have faith in this enterprise, you will certainly have the victory. . . .

The sons of the ones who humbled you will come, bending low to you; and all who disparaged you will worship the traces of your feet and will call you the city of the Lord, Zion of the Holy One of Israel. Although you have been forsaken and hated, with no one passing through, I will make you majestic forever, a joy throughout the ages. You will suck the milk of the people and be nursed at the breasts of kings; and you will know that I, the Lord, am your saviour and your redemptor, the mighty one of Jacob.

Source: *The Book of Prophecies Edited by Christopher Columbus*, edited by Roberto Rusconi (Berkeley: University of California Press, 1997), pp. 75, 203.

A copy of an image found on a five-inch copper plate in northwest Georgia. It probably depicts the appearance of Our Lady of Guadalupe in Mexico City in 1531.

RELIGION IN EUROPE: CATHOLICISM: MISSIONARIES

The Role of Missionaries. European missionaries to the Americas served two primary purposes. The explorers, monarchs financing the voyages, and missionaries themselves would argue that the more important reason was the Christianizing of the native peoples. Many "heathens" awaited conversion. Missionaries not only would help save "savages" from eternal damnation but also would help fulfill the larger project of spreading Christianity throughout the world, thereby helping to effect the Last Days or second coming of Christ. Sending missionaries to the Americas served a second purpose, too. The Catholic Church wanted to send Catholics to spread the faith all over the world and thus check the growth of Protestantism. Likewise, Protestants used missionaries to disseminate their religious beliefs.

Catholic Success. Catholic missionaries were more successful than Protestants in the sixteenth century, for Catholics had the support of the Church and of monarchs. Dominicans, Franciscans, and especially the Jesuits each saw their endeavors become successful even if their work took time. In contrast French Protestants had trouble establishing themselves in South Carolina and Florida. Later, in the seventeenth century, English Puritans, led most notably by minister John Eliot, realized some of the desired results in ministering to the Native Americans.

Dominicans. The Dominican Order of the Catholic Church began as a preaching order in southern France in the early thirteenth century. It was created, in large part, to address the changes resulting from the transforma-

tions of feudal governments to more centralized ones and of economies that were becoming more urban. The Dominicans also responded to the growing impact of lay preachers. Living as mendicant friars according to the rule of St. Augustine, which included dedication to study, the Dominicans stressed the contemplative life and apostolic ministry. To realize the former, they took vows of poverty, chastity, and obedience. For the latter they stressed evangelism and education; indeed, they stressed mobility and the need to be "in the world." The Protestant Reformation did much damage to the Dominican Order. However the brothers compensated for this decimation with overseas expansion. The first Dominican friars came to America in 1510. Dominicans were among the founders, with Antonio de Montesinos, of the colony of San Miguel in 1526, near where Jamestown would later be founded. Montesinos, with the support and encouragement of the Dominicans, was a champion of Indian rights. Life, however, proved too difficult, and ultimately the colony failed. Other Dominicans tried to show a modicum of respect for the Native Americans. Bernadino de Minaya, a Dominican who settled in Peru, obtained a papal bull in 1537 which asserted that the natives were not "dumb brutes," nor were they incapable of learning the Catholic faith. Bartholomé de las Casas, who perhaps more than any other missionary was a champion of charitable treatment of the natives, became a Dominican in 1523. Despite the good work of many Dominicans, others were not as open-minded (and perhaps more typical); one Dominican friar remarked that Indians ate human flesh and were hostile to religion.

Franciscans. The Franciscan Order of the Catholic Church is actually several groups who profess to live ac-

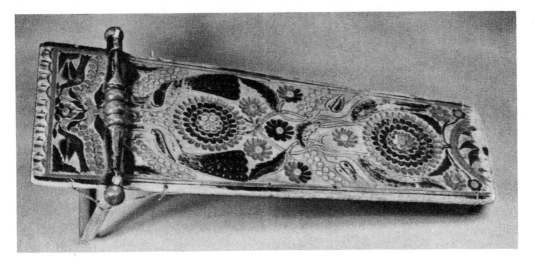

The floral motif on this Mohawk cradleboard, circa 1600, illustrates the influence of European missionaries (Museum of the American Indian, Heye Foundation, New York)

cording to the ideals of St. Francis of Assisi. Taking vows of austerity and poverty, the Franciscans held intellectual dominance until the Reformation. Although this was lost, the Franciscans were still an accomplished order.

Zeal. Reforming impulses led to the reinvigoration of the Franciscan order, especially in Spain. Much of their success came in their ambitious missionary activity, again, especially by the Spanish Franciscans. The Franciscans' imperative was to be "in the world" rather than a cloistered monastic order. Wherever there were Spanish expeditions, so too were there Franciscans. Five Franciscans went to San Domingo with Alvar Núñez Cabeza de Vaca in 1527. In 1539 Franciscans accompanied an expedition to the Gulf of California and another to New Mexico. After the Jesuits' unsuccessful attempts at conversion in Florida, the Franciscans took advantage of the void and stepped in after 1584.

Activity in the New World. By 1635 approximately five Franciscan groups were supporting forty-five missions and shepherding nearly thirty thousand Indian converts. In many instances the Franciscans had attempted to translate the catechism into native languages and offered elementary schooling to the Indians. However, this was not always the case: in northern Mexico the Franciscan missionaries made no attempt to understand either the language or culture of their intended audience. Without a sensitive understanding of the Native Americans the missionaries were unsuccessful, and their activities were often met with resistance and violence.

Jesuits. The Society of Jesus, or Jesuits, an order of the Catholic Church, was founded by St. Ignatius Loyola. Born in Spain, Ignatius Loyola had been educated in the chivalric tradition. After he was severely wounded in the Battle of Pamplona in 1521, Loyola began for the first time to contemplate religious questions. He underwent conversion and was ordained a priest in Paris. Along with fellow students, he created the Society of Jesus. The group made a special vow to God: they would travel anywhere in the world when the Pope so commanded. In this vow they sought to emulate Jesus, who had followed an itinerant life. As missionaries the Jesuits departed from an older view of Catholic orders, which emphasized cloistering, intense study, and reflection and a separation from the world. Christian life, the Jesuits emphasized, was not static. They aimed to effect perfection and salvation in themselves and the general population.

Achieving Their Aims. To achieve this goal the Jesuits placed great importance on teaching, especially through preaching. They believed they were called to preach and thought they could have the most far-reaching effects by preaching in public places. The Jesuits also organized schools; by 1556 they had set up thirty-three schools in Europe. Schools were meant to help "our neighbors," including the poor. They taught the laity as well as the clergy. Teaching and establishing schools gave the Society of Jesus an evangelical bent. Although the Society was not founded to counter the Reformation, the order became tremendously popular in France, and Jesuits played a major role in keeping France from falling completely into Protestant hands.

Efforts Abroad. Obeying their vows to go anywhere in the world, Spanish Jesuits were particularly active as missionaries in the Americas. They went to Florida in 1527, 1539, and 1549. However, it was not until 1565 that they established a colony of even minimal success. They helped found St. Augustine, Florida, but as living conditions were difficult and they disagreed among themselves and with the lay explorers about how to set up the colony, they were soon replaced by the Franciscans. Spanish Jesuits also went to areas in northern Mexico and the American Southwest. French Jesuits met with greater success. French explorers such as Champlain asked for Jesuit assistance in converting Indians in the vast amounts of land to be colonized. In New France

An 1875 engraving of the first mass held at St. Augustine, Florida, on 8 September 1565

(Nova Scotia, Acadia, and the St. Lawrence River Valley) the Jesuits established a solid presence. By 1600 the Jesuits had founded nearly 250 schools around the world. While they might have converted many native peoples, it is difficult to know if the Indians truly understood and believed their teachings or were acting diplomatically. Often the Jesuits' methods included showing the native peoples that their own religious leaders were ineffective and that only the Jesuits could bring about positive change.

Sources:

William A. Hinnebusch, *The History of the Dominican Order* (New York: Alba House, 1973);

Lazaro Iriarte, *Franciscan History: The Three Orders of St. Francis of Assisi,* translated by Patricia Rose (Chicago: Franciscan Herald Press, 1983);

John W. O'Malley, "The Society of Jesus," in *Religious Orders of the Catholic Reformation,* edited by Richard L. DeMoen (New York: Fordham University Press, 1994).

RELIGION IN EUROPE: CATHOLICISM: MISSIONARIES: EFFORTS IN ST. AUGUSTINE

Beginnings. The first mission to the Timuca Indians of St. Augustine took place in 1565 as the Spanish reclaimed Florida from the Huguenots. Spain had first laid claim to the city, which its founder, Juan Ponce de León, believed held the Fountain of Youth, in 1513. In 1564, after the French Protestants established Fort Caroline twenty-five miles to the north, the Spanish became alarmed that the French might take control and that the Huguenots would have the chance to convert the Indi-

ans. Although the Jesuits had tried to convert the natives, they had been unsuccessful, and by 1572 the last of the Jesuits had left Florida. The Jesuits' goal of converting large numbers of natives was hampered by the fact that several Jesuits were killed by the Indians and by the frequent disagreements between the soldiers and friars distracting the missionaries. This did not end the goal of converting the natives. Despite difficult living conditions, the Franciscans wanted to gain a foothold in Florida and continued to send friars. In May 1584 eight Franciscans sailed from Spain, but only three arrived. Three years later another twelve came to St. Augustine, and in 1590 eight more arrived. By 1592 only three remained. Twelve Franciscans arrived in 1595, and at last their missionary efforts began to take off in earnest.

Reasons for the Failure. Missionary efforts in St. Augustine ultimately did not succeed as the Spanish had hoped for several reasons. The Spanish government regarded Florida as a distant frontier and withheld financial and organizational support, and the missionaries themselves, both Jesuits and Franciscans, were unable and unwilling to build support among the native peoples. Rather than being eager and easy objects of conversion, the Indians manipulated the missionaries, often extracting Spanish goods in exchange for religious conversion. If the Spanish were to Christianize the Indians, it was in the settlers' best interests to keep good relations with their neighbors. This was not to be the case. The missionaries exacted tribute—animal skins, corn, and labor—from the Indians. Finally, in the 1610s, missionaries in St. Augustine began to see the fruits of their labors

The execution of Jesuit priests by southeastern Indians
in 1571

as the number of Indian conversions began to increase. Ultimately, however, these efforts were doomed to failure. The Timuca dwindled from six thousand to ten thousand (estimates vary) in 1600 to less than one hundred by the time the Spanish ceded Florida to the United States in 1821.

Sources:
Charles E. Bennett, *Laudonniere and Fort Caroline, History and Documents* (Gainesville: University of Florida Press, 1964);

Jerald T. Milanich, *Florida Indians and the Invasion from Europe* (Gainesville: University of Florida Press, 1995).

RELIGION IN EUROPE: PROTESTANTISM

Importance of Faith. Protestantism developed in response to perceptions that the Catholic Church was departing from matters of faith and spirituality in favor of material concerns. Protestants placed great emphasis on the importance of faith and belief, achieved through a transformation of one's heart. The way to know God was through reading the Bible and listening to sermons. Preaching would assist one in the quest for finding God. Thus the spread of Protestantism led to a rise in literacy as believers took it upon themselves to learn God's word. In contrast to Catholicism, Protestant theology did not find good works, such as the paying of indulgences or the building of lavish altars, a sign of salvation. Good works

were "correlatives of faith, not preludes," as the historian Huston Smith has argued. When one possessed faith, good works would naturally flow. Despite their downplaying of good works, Protestants nonetheless stressed the importance of self-discipline. And Protestants believed in only two sacraments, baptism and communion, of the seven the Catholics revered.

History. Calls for reform are as old as Christianity itself. Sometimes heeded and sometimes not, reforms came in waves, but the basic structure of the Catholic Church remained in place until the Reformation. The Reformation was the most massive and permanent set of reforms. Indeed some historians have argued that Martin Luther, one of the primary architects of the Reformation, did not mean to rend the Church. Luther, Calvin, and their intellectual heirs succeeded because they gained the support of monarchs, nobles, local leaders, and the laity. In some cases rulers joined the Protestant movement because it was politically or economically advantageous; in other cases their faith was genuine. Harbingers of the Reformation were present in the late fourteenth century. John Wyclif, an English theologian, criticized the Church's abuses and late in his life called for appeals to Scripture as the most sound authority. He denied the dogma of transubstantiation as being unscriptural. He called for the stripping of all temporal (and therefore extraneous) possessions held by both Church and king. While the monarchy regarded him as a threat and his ideas as heretical, he gained much popular support and went on to train lay preachers known as the Lollards. In their efforts at purifying the Church the Lollards have been called precursors to the Puritans. From the beginning, several varieties of Protestantism existed. Luther and Calvin advocated different theologies. Some sects, such as the Puritans, argued that the Church of England variety of Protestantism was not pure enough; some groups of Puritans further advocated separating from the Church of England.

Expansion. Protestantism was able to spread in some locales because of political support and its popularity among the people and because of the Church's inability to suppress it. Calvinism, supported by Genevan princes, caught on in Switzerland. Though popular in France, Calvinism was resisted by the monarchies, and only a series of religious wars ensured that Catholicism would prevail. In England, Henry VIII cut the ties between himself and the Pope, but for personal reasons (the Pope refused to grant him a divorce). His children did not agree on religious issues: while Mary persecuted Protestants, Elizabeth, pushed by Parliament, moved England in a more Protestant direction. Other countries, such as Spain, remained firmly Catholic.

Source:
Sidney E. Ahlstrom, *A Religious History of the American People* (New Haven: Yale University Press, 1972).

RELIGION IN EUROPE: PROTESTANTISM: CALVINISM

Theological System. Calvinism is the name given to the theological system of John Calvin and his followers. Calvinism had a tremendous impact in Europe and on the Puritans who came to New England. It has also influenced many aspects of life and culture as well as religion in the United States from the seventeenth century to the present. At the heart of Calvin's system was the idea of *Sola Scriptura,* or Scripture as the sole source of knowledge needed to attain salvation. More important than symbols that were so much a part of Catholic practice was one's understanding of the Bible, which would, in turn, deepen one's faith. Adherence to biblical law would check the depravity that humans had carried with them since Adam. People also needed to have faith, for hearing sermons or receiving the sacraments held little meaning without it. However, faith or grace was not available to all. Calvin proffered the notion of predestination. God had chosen who was predestined to be among the elect, or saved, and who was damned. Members of the elect were a part of the invisible church, and only God knew who they were. Following St. Augustine, the seventh-century Christian thinker, Calvin also believed that a visible church existed, the historical church on Earth. Membership in the visible church, earned by upright, moral behavior, was also important and a goal to be worked toward. It was also evidence that one might be a part of the invisible church.

Social System. Calvinism must also be considered as a social system. Both to achieve and reflect status in the visible church, Christians were to behave in a certain way in daily life, not only on the Sabbath and other holy days. Such uprightness might be a sign of sainthood. Calvin envisioned a model Christian society. Yet because he believed that humans were depraved as a result of Adam's original sin, self-discipline and social control had to be imposed to achieve the desired ends. In Geneva a council of twelve elders was appointed. They instituted rules of discipline. Life was austere: music and incense were forbidden, as were bright colors and decorations, for they were temptations to evil and distractions from godliness. In establishing their new societies the Puritans who immigrated to New England were able to adhere more closely to Calvin's idea of a model Christian community than either Calvin or his followers in Europe ever could. Calvinism, both in the Old and New Worlds, particularly appealed to the emergent middle class. Industrious and pious, they found particularly appealing the tenet that hard work and discipline suggested godliness and election.

Source:
Michael A. Mullett, *Calvin* (New York: Routledge, 1989).

RELIGION IN EUROPE: PROTESTANTISM: THE HUGUENOTS

Background. The Huguenots were French Protestants. As John Calvin was French, the sect he founded spread quickly throughout France. While their numbers were not significant (between 1560 and 1570, the high watermark of their success, twelve hundred churches, or 10 percent of all churches in France, were Protestant), the Huguenots were extremely vocal and uncompromising in their demands. Some were content with local religious rights; others would only be happy with the spread of Protestantism throughout France, if not the world. Although the French monarchy was not closely tied to Rome and, in fact, was frequently at odds with the Pope, kings feared the Huguenots because they threatened the power of the monarch and a national church. Nobles enjoyed the autonomy Protestantism allowed them; many chose to convert since being Huguenot gave them the liberty to listen to their own consciences and follow their own laws rather than those of the Catholic monarch or the Church. Without the support of some powerful and wealthy nobles, the monarch's authority was compromised. In time Protestantism became a power to be reckoned with, and several French kings recognized the wisdom of establishing a good relationship with the Huguenots and extending more rights to them. However, this did not mean the Huguenots were popularly accepted. The persecution of Huguenots began in the 1550s, including burnings at the stake. The violence culminated in the St. Bartholomew's Day Massacre on 24 August 1572. Some Huguenots were even dragged out of bed after midnight; when it was over, about twelve thousand French Protestants had been killed.

The Americas. The Huguenots tried to bring their religion to the New World. In part this was to spread Protestantism and check the growth of Catholicism in the Americas; in part it was to provide a refuge for themselves. In 1562 they established the colony of Fort Caroline near present-day Jacksonville, Florida. However, three years later Pedro Menéndez de Avilés organized an expedition to drive the French out and gain control of Florida. The Spanish colony of St. Augustine was established, and the Huguenot (as well as French) presence in the area was eliminated.

Source:
Mack P. Holt, *The French Wars of Religion, 1562–1629* (Cambridge: Cambridge University Press, 1995).

RELIGION IN EUROPE: PROTESTANTISM: LUTHER'S NINETY-FIVE THESES

Motivations. According to popular lore, Martin Luther nailed his Ninety-five Theses against the sale of indulgences on the door of a church in Wittenberg, Germany, on 31 October 1517. While it now appears improbable that he took hammer in hand, his influence on Christianity in Europe and both indirectly and directly in the Americas is indisputable. Luther protested the sale of indulgences or purchased redemption from sin, which profited both Rome and his local archbishop. Archbishop Albert of Hohenzollern hoped to finance his recent elevation to Archbishop of Mainz, a politically important post, through indulgences. Luther precipitated a popular movement in Germany, capitalizing on widespread anti-Roman and anticlerical sentiment. Ultimately he formulated a new understanding of the Christian faith and helped begin the Reformation.

Impact. Of course the spread of reformed religion had a widespread effect on Europe. Those countries barely affected (such as Spain) took advantage of wars and political strife afflicting countries such as England and France, using the opportunity to move ahead in the colonization race. The initial advantage of Catholic Spain prevailed in New Spain. Ironically, however, reformed religion, embracing that which Luther had advocated in the Ninety-five Theses and other writings, would prevail in North America.

Source:
John Bossy, *Christianity in the West, 1400–1700* (New York: Oxford University Press, 1985).

RELIGION IN EUROPE: RELIGIOUS CONFLICT

Origins and Causes. Wars of religion exemplified the extent to which animosity between Catholics and Protestants had developed in the sixteenth and seventeenth centuries. As Protestantism spread throughout northern Europe, Protestants of different nationalities felt closer to members of their own faith than to their countrymen. The same was true of Catholics. For instance, the Spanish king, ruling over the Netherlands, sent twenty thousand Spanish soldiers to suppress religious and political dissidents in 1567. In 1570 the Pope excommunicated Queen Elizabeth I, thereby freeing English Catholics from owing allegiance to her and giving them the right to overthrow her. Elizabeth tried to assist the Dutch by sending six thousand troops to Holland. The Spanish king, Phillip II, believed that the best way to defeat the English was to send an armada, or fleet, to defeat England's weak navy. However, England defeated the Spanish Armada in 1588 and emerged as a stronghold of Protestantism.

The Case of France. The French witnessed much more horror in the wars of religion. French Protestants, the Huguenots, were radical in their demands: to them, no middle road existed. The Huguenots threatened the monarchy's power, and the king was intent on destroying them. Some monarchs as well as Catherine de Medici, regent for her young son, tried to straddle a middle ground between Catholic and Huguenot. Catherine issued the Edict of St. Germaine in 1562, which proclaimed limited but legal recognition of the Huguenots. This edict led to violence as the Duke of Guise, staunch leader of the Catholic faction, commanded his troops to fire shots at the Protestants. This was the beginning of three generations of violence and took power away from Calvinist clergy, putting it into the hands of nobles. Ultimately, with the Edict of Nantes, issued during the rule of Henry IV (himself a former Protestant) in April 1598, the monarchy reached an agreement with the Huguenots. Unity, not toleration, was the aim. Huguenots were given full civil rights, including admission to college and the ability to hold public office. Their right to worship freely was severely restricted. It was a settlement which pleased neither side and which cost Henry his life; an unhappy Catholic murdered the king in 1610. (Louis XIV would revoke the Edict of Nantes in 1685.) Persecutions, including burnings at the stake, began in the 1530s, and in all there were eight wars. Some Huguenots fled to present-day Florida and South Carolina to escape persecution and build Huguenot havens, though with limited success. The wars of religion lasted for several more decades in France, not ending until 1648.

Effects. The wars of religion did not only affect Europe, where they took place, nor did they influence only matters of faith. They touched economics, politics, and society. They also contributed to the ability of France to participate in overseas exploration and colonization. The more France had to focus its attention and resources on civil wars, the less it had to give to colonization.

Source:
Mack P. Holt, *The French Wars of Religion, 1529–1629* (Cambridge: Cambridge University Press, 1995).

RELIGION IN EUROPE: WOMEN

Place in Society. The Catholic Church venerated women. Although in the Old Testament it was Eve who led Adam into temptation, Mary, the mother of Jesus, and Ann, her mother, were lauded as examples of virtue and godliness. In the Church women's roles were circumscribed; they could become nuns, not priests (although nuns' contributions were valued). Some women, such as Teresa of Ávila, were valued (and feared) for their mystical visions and reform activities during the Counter-Reformation.

A WOMAN SPEAKS OUT

It seemed so funny to me, it made me laugh, because in this matter I was never afraid, it was well known that in matters of the faith, I would die a thousand deaths before I'd go against even the least ceremony of the church, or against any in the Sacred Scriptures. And I said that . . . if I thought there was any reason [to fear the Inquisition], I would go to them myself, and that if such an accusation were raised, the Lord would free me and I would profit from it.

Source: Gillian T. W. Ahlgren, *Teresa of Ávila and the Politics of Sanctity* (Ithaca, N.Y.: Cornell University Press, 1996), p. 44.

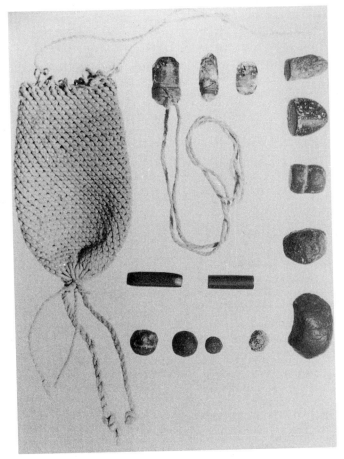

A looped cotton medicine bag and its contents, circa 1100–1300 A.D. (Arizona State Museum, University of Arizona, Tucson, Arizona)

The Reformation. The Protestant Reformation both enlarged and diminished women's opportunities. Often the best time for women was in the few years after a town had adopted the reformed faith. Institutions and structures were somewhat fluid, and women had some opportunity to create a place for themselves. Both women and men participated in the religious wars and riots which characterized the sixteenth century. On the one hand, women's increased activity angered men; many cities prohibited women from gathering to discuss religion. On the other hand, reformers such as Calvin and Luther needed and cultivated relationships with women. Calvin looked for the support of noblewomen, and Luther corresponded with several women. In each case both relied upon female converts to bring their influential male relatives, such as local rulers, to reformed religion.

Changes. Unlike Catholicism, which celebrated women as saints and pious believers, Protestantism aimed to strip away such externals, which were considered unnecessary to faith. Calendar days which honored women were eradicated; so were processions and other activities which allowed women's participation and gave women an active role in religious life. Joining a convent, long an option for women (and one that gave them a de-

gree of autonomy), was no longer a possibility as marriage and motherhood were women's highest callings.

Fear. Protestantism and Catholicism shared a basic fear of women: that they, more than men, might be agents of Satan, as witches. As Protestant teaching spread among the laity, so did popular superstition, including that of the woman as witch. Women without a proper place in society—older women, single women, widows, poor women, and childless women—were especially feared. Without social ties and limits, these women were particularly appealing to the Devil. The changing legal system permitted larger witchcraft trials. Once accusatory, the system became more inquisitorial. Whereas before the accuser had to stand before the accused, the system became more anonymous and official, and legal authorities could bring charges. Curiously, the Roman and Spanish inquisitions acted with lenience on witches, for they pitied those whom they thought bedeviled as mere pawns of Satan.

Witches. Witchcraft was not only a fear in Europe. In 1585 Jean Lery, a French explorer, wrote about how Brazilian native women, like their Christian counterparts, were prone to giving in to the Devil. The Puritans of New England were especially on the lookout for witches, culminating in the Salem trials of 1692 in Massachusetts.

Sources:

Robin Briggs, *Witches and Neighbors: The Social and Cultural Context of European Witchcraft* (New York: Penguin, 1996);

Merry E. Wiesner, *Women and Gender in Early Modern Europe* (Cambridge: Cambridge University Press, 1995).

Christopher Columbus bearing Christ to the New World, an illustration on Juan de la Cosa's 1500 map of the world (New York Public Library)

RELIGION IN THE NEW WORLD: AMERICA AS "VIRGIN LAND"

Origins of an Idea. The idea that the Americas were "virgin lands," untouched and sequestered from the crowding, disease, and other problems plaguing Europe, may be said to have originated with Christopher Columbus. He compiled a book of sayings, opinions, and prophecies using biblical texts that stressed the urgency of recovering Mount Zion and Jerusalem and of converting native peoples in the Indies. Columbus tried to show that the discovery of the Indies was an important step in liberating Jerusalem from Muslim control and would usher in the days of salvation. He also assigned himself a prominent role in these events. In a letter written to Ferdinand and Isabella of Spain from Jamaica in 1503, Columbus noted: "Jerusalem and Mt. Zion will be rebuilt by a Christian; God tells who it will be through the mouth of the Prophet in the fourteenth psalm. The abbot Joachim said that this person would come from Spain."

Raleigh. Sir Walter Raleigh also emphasized the idea of America as virgin land. He organized an expedition to Roanoke Island off the North Carolina coast in 1584. This failed, but he organized and led a second expedition to the Orinoco River in South America. To Raleigh, America held the promise of being an innocent, pure, and virtuous land, but those virtues might be ruined by the explorers coming to take advantage of the land's beauties and resources. Raleigh described the land in both material and sexual terms: Of Guiana, he wrote, "The Ingas [Incas] had a garden of pleasure in an yland . . . where they went to recreat themselves, when they would take the aire of the sea, which had all kinde of garden-hearbs, flowers, and trees of gold and silver." The image took a firm hold in the minds of Europeans. Later generations of English settlers, es-

A circa 1400 wooden deer's head carved by a Calusa Indian in Florida and used in religious ceremonies (University Museum, Philadelphia)

pecially the Puritans who went to New England in the seventeenth century, were no doubt influenced by Columbus and Raleigh. The Puritans regarded New England as a virgin land perfect for creating the New Israel.

Sources:

Sacvan Bercovitch, *The Puritan Origins of the American Self* (New Haven: Yale University Press, 1975);

The Book of Prophecies edited by Christopher Columbus, edited by Roberto Rusconi (Berkeley: University of California Press, 1997).

RELIGION IN THE NEW WORLD: THE HUGUENOTS IN SOUTH CAROLINA

Safe Haven. As an extension of their colonizing Fort Caroline in Florida, Huguenots attempted several times to settle South Carolina. Generations before South Carolina was successfully colonized, French Protestants attempted to make it a safe haven for others facing persecution and destitution as a consequence of their religious beliefs.

AZTEC MYTH

The gods Quetzalcoatl and Tezcatlipoca brought the earth goddess Tlalteuctli down from on high. All the joints of her body were filled with eyes and mouths biting like wild beasts. Before they got down, there was water already below, upon which the goddess then moved back and forth. They did not know who had created it.

They said to each other, "We must make the earth." So saying, they changed themselves into two great serpents, one of whom seized the goddess from the right hand down to the left foot, the other from the left hand down to the right foot. As they tightened their grip, she broke at the middle. The half with the shoulders became the earth. The remaining half they brought to the sky—which greatly displeased the other gods.

Afterward, to compensate the earth goddess for the damage those two had inflicted upon her, all the gods came down to console her, ordaining that all the produce required for human life would issue from her. From her hair they made trees, flowers, and grasses; from her skin, very fine grasses and tiny flowers; from her eyes, wells and fountains, and small caves; from her mouth, rivers and large caves; from her nose, valleys and mountains; from her shoulders, mountains.

Sometimes at night this goddess wails, thirsting for human hearts. She will not be silent until she receives them. Nor will she bear fruit unless she is watered with human blood.

Source: *The Red Swan: Myths and Tales of the American Indians,* edited by John Bierhorst (New York: Farrar, Straus & Giroux, 1976), pp. 50–51.

Difficult Beginnings. In 1562 Jean Ribault and René Goulaine de Laudonnière tried to settle on St. John's River. Unsatisfied there, they moved up the coast to Port Royal Harbor, within the bounds of present-day South Carolina. They constructed Charlesfort on Parris Island. While foundations of a colony were laid, the adventurers were unwilling to endure the hardships and returned to France. Ribaut and Laudonnière returned to Fort Caroline, but as they were defeated by the Spaniards the following year, further efforts to settle South Carolina were not made until 1629. The Huguenots kept their eyes on South Carolina, however. In that year the French Protestants contacted King Charles I of England to establish a colony in South Carolina. He issued a patent to Sir Robert Heath, who had worked with the Duc de Fontenany in conjunction with the Huguenots. Huguenots sailed from England in 1633 but landed in Virginia and ultimately returned to Europe. Finally, a permanent Huguenot colony was begun in South Carolina in 1670.

Source:

The Huguenot Connection: The Edict of Nantes, Its Revocation, and Early French Migration to South Carolina, edited by Richard M. Golden (Boston: Kluwer, 1988).

RELIGION IN THE NEW WORLD: NATIVE AMERICAN MYTHS

Oral Culture. Native American culture has been traditionally oral. Indians did not write down their myths and sacred histories; rather, they told and retold their stories. While the tales would, no doubt, change in each generation's retelling, the fundamental vocabulary, intended moral, and mood remained the same. They gave to a tribe a sense of being and a sense that they had much to learn from the spiritual and natural worlds. The myths' repetitions, through the generations, gave them spiritual power and authority. At the same time, as the historian of religion Mircea Eliade has postulated, by hearing a myth, listeners could put themselves into the spiritual sphere just as their ancestors had so placed themselves.

Creation Myths. One important theme of Native American myth is the creation of the world. Common to all of such stories are the animal and spiritual assistants who helped humans in the creation. Most of the tales relate that people came from Mother Earth. For example, the Cherokee tell the story of the Earth's beginnings as a "great island floating in a sea of water," flat, soft, and wet. Finally, the Earth dried, and the animals waiting between heaven and Earth came down upon the advice of the Great Buzzard. Animals and plants came first, followed by humans. Despite the differences, the myths gave the Native Americans a sense of their history and confirmed their belief in a higher power and in the power of the natural world.

Source:

Bruce G. Trigger, *The Children of Aatenaetsic: A History of the Huron People to 1660,* 2 volumes (Montreal: McGill-Queen's University Press, 1976).

The Huron Feast of the Dead, in which the living carry the deceased to a
common burial pit (engraving, circa 1600)

A circa 1600 engraving of a shamanic ceremony in a Powhatan village

RELIGION IN THE NEW WORLD: NATIVE AMERICAN SPIRITUALITY

Definition. The term "Native American religion" is actually a misnomer if we consider religion in a traditional western sense; that is, a coherent system based on a single text, remaining fairly consistent over many generations. It is more accurate to refer to Native American spirituality. However, Native American spirituality, while possessing certain similarities, differed from tribe to tribe and from region to region. As a whole, Native Americans considered their culture and social structure to be intimately connected to spirituality, which was an integral part of each aspect of community life. Ceremony and ritual were extensions of everyday existence, but often these celebrations held meaning only for a particular tribe.

The Natural World. Each Native American tribe had spiritual relationships with the natural world. The Earth and its fruits were gifts to be appreciated, not taken for granted. Depending on the tribe or language group, different animals held particular powers. For all tribes it was important not to abuse the animals, in order to avoid their wrath. Each Native American tribe worshiped many gods, with one god often possessing superior powers. Some men

A Mide bag of otterskin, circa 1600. Used to carry medicinal charms and herbs, it belonged to a member of the Winnebago Midewiwin Society, a group of healers (Chandler-Pohrt Collection, Buffalo Bill Historical Center, Cody, Wyoming)

A three-thousand-year-old split-twig deer used by prehistoric hunters as a talisman and found in the Grand Canyon, Arizona (Arizona State Museum, University of Arizona, Tucson, Arizona)

also possessed spiritual powers. These were the shamans, who were thought to have supernatural powers as well as the ability to heal others. In this way Native Americans connected body and spirit; an ailing spirit would beget an ailing body. Shamans were also responsible for transmitting myths, which, instead of written texts, served as the Indians' sacred words.

Varieties. A few examples illustrate the varieties of Native American spirituality, gods, and beliefs. The Micmacs, who lived south and west of the gulf of the St. Lawrence River, shared beliefs similar to those of other northern hunting tribes. They especially respected the bear and believed that bears and other animals could become transformed into other species. Gluskap was a mighty warrior who had gone away but would return to help the Micmacs when necessary. The main religious authority among the

In a house in the Sky World, native traditions say, a man and woman lived on opposite sides of a fireplace. The two had great spiritual power because each had been isolated from other people until the age of puberty. Every day after their housemates went out to work, the woman crossed to the other side to comb the man's hair. Through mysterious means, she became pregnant and bore a daughter. Shortly thereafter, the man fell ill and announced that he would soon die. Because no one in the Sky World knew what death was, he had to explain to the woman what would happen to him and instruct her how to preserve his body. After he died, the woman's growing daughter endured fits of weeping that, despite the best efforts of village neighbors to comfort her, could be relieved only by visits to the preserved corpse of the deceased, whose spirit told her that he was her father and taught her many things.

When the daughter, whom the Iroquois called Sky Woman, reached adulthood, her father's spirit instructed her to take a dangerous journey to the village of a man destined to become her spouse. She brought her prospective husband loaves of bread baked with berries and then, enduring great travail, cooked him a potent soup that cured him of a long-troublesome ailment. In exchange he sent her home with a burden of venison that nearly filled her family's house. After Sky Woman returned to her husband, the pair always slept on opposite sides of the fire and refrained from sexual intercourse. Nevertheless, she, like her mother before her, inexplicably became pregnant. Stricken by jealousy, the husband again became ill and dreamed that a great tree near his house must be uprooted so that he and his spouse could look down through the resulting hole to the world below. To cure his sickness, all the people of the village worked together to pull it up. When Sky Woman looked over the edge of the abyss, her husband pushed her down.

As she fell toward the endless waters below, the spirit birds and animals of the sea held a council to decide how to rescue her. Ducks flew up to catch her on their wings and bring her safely down, and the Turtle agreed to provide a place for her to rest on his Back. Meantime, various animals tried to dive to the bottom of the lake and bring up earth on which the woman could walk; only the Muskrat succeeded. The material he placed on the Turtle's Back grew, with Sky Woman's help, into the living dry land of North America. Soon the celestial visitor gave birth to a daughter, who in time became supernaturally pregnant by the spirit of the Turtle. In the younger woman's womb grew male twins, who began arguing over the best way to emerge from her body. The first, the Good Twin (Tharonhiawagon, Upholder of the Heavens, or Sky-Grasper), was born by the normal route. The second, the Evil Twin (Tawiskaron), burst forth from his mother's side and thus killed her. When Sky Woman asked which of her grandsons had slain her daughter, they blamed each other, but the Evil Twin was the more persistent and persuasive. The Grandmother cherished him, whom she loved; she turned the body and the head of the boys' deceased mother into the sun and moon, respectively; and she threw the Good Twin out of her house, assuming he would die.

But he did not perish. Instead, with the aid of his father the Turtle, the Good Twin improved Iroquoia, making various animals, learning the secrets of cultivating maize and other crops, and finally bringing into existence mortal human beings. All of these things he did not create from nothingness; rather, they grew through a process of transformation and infusion of supernatural power from the living earth and from prototypical spirit beings who dwelled in the Sky World and beneath the waters. At each step, Sky Woman and the Evil Twin partially undid the Good Twin's efforts in ways that forever after would make life difficult for humans. When the Good Twin constructed straight rivers that facilitated canoe travel by flowing both ways at once, the Evil Twin introduced rocks and hills to twist the streams and make their frequently obstructed waters fall in only one direction. When the Good Twin grew succulent ears of corn, Sky Woman threw ashes into his cooking pot and decreed that henceforth maize must be parched and ground before it could be eaten. When the Good Twin made animals readily give themselves to humans as food, the Evil Twin sealed them all in a cave, from which Sky-Grasper could rescue only a portion; the rest the Evil Twin turned into enemies of humans.

Finally, the two brothers fought, and the Good Twin triumphed. He could not, however, undo all the evil that his brother and Grandmother had left in the world. Instead he taught humans how to grow corn to support themselves and how to keep harm at bay through ceremonies of thanksgiving and propitiation to the spirit world. To keep these ceremonies, Sky-Grasper assigned roles to various camps of people he arbitrarily designated as clans named after such animals as the Wolf, the Bear, and the Turtle. But he knew that mortals could never keep the rituals adequately.

Source: Daniel Richter, *The Ordeal of the Longhouse: The Peoples of the Iroquois League in the Era of European Colonization* (Chapel Hill: University of North Carolina Press, 1992), pp. 9–11.

A miniature vessel and a nine-inch-long sandstone Kachina (sacred spirit effigy),
circa 1200–1300 A.D., discovered in a crypt near Vernon, Arizona
(Chicago Natural History Museum)

Narragansetts in Rhode Island and Connecticut (they would figure prominently in Puritan New England in the seventeenth century) was the shaman. In each case the shaman, who was always male, had been selected as a result of a dream or vision which may have been induced by herbal infusions. Public rituals, such as those held at harvest time and in midwinter, honored the creator. The North Carolina Algonquians believed in various gods and spirits; the principal god had created lesser gods to create the world. Life after death assured treatment according to one's moral conduct in this world.

Other Beliefs. The Miwoks in northern California believed that all living things belonged to one of two distinct categories. For people this was either land or water, and each category was represented by animals. The South Si-erra Miwok's symbols for land were the blue jay and the grizzly bear; the coyote represented water.

Sources:

Handbook of North American Indians (Washington, D.C.: Smithsonian Institution, 1978–1990);

Daniel K. Richter, *The Ordeal of the Longhouse: The Peoples of the Iroquois League in the Era of European Colonization* (Chapel Hill: University of North Carolina Press, 1992).

RELIGION IN THE NEW WORLD: NATIVE AMERICAN SPIRITUALITY: SHAMANS

Role. Shamans in Native American culture were religious leaders and were believed to have extraordinary powers. Their most important function was not preaching or administering religious rites but healing. Shamans were also the Native Americans' physicians. Indians believed that one's physical condition was linked to his or her spiritual condition. It was up to the shaman to determine the cause of a person's illness—what was missing from that individual's spirit—and then to suggest a cure through prayer, surgery, or other means.

Power. With a greater connection to and understanding of the supernatural world (they were thought to mediate between the human and spirit world), shamans were tremendously respected in Native American societies. After revealing that they possessed shamanistic powers, made evident to them in dreams or visions, shamans went through initiation ceremonies to demonstrate further their powers and their wisdom. They were thought to experience the world more spiritually than did anyone else. As they grew older, shamans' powers were believed to increase. Age was particularly honored, for the elders were the keepers of tradition. In a culture which lacked written texts, older people were the repository of history, knowledge, tradition, wisdom, and memory.

Source:
The Red Swan: Myths and Tales of the American Indians, edited by John Bierhorst (New York: Farrar, Straus & Giroux, 1976).

RELIGION IN THE NEW WORLD: REQUIERIMENTO

The Requirement. Upon arriving on the lands they wished to colonize and claim in the name of the monarchy and in God's name, explorers from Spain and other countries, beginning with Christopher Columbus, were compelled to read aloud the king's summons to the Indians, the *Requierimento,* or Requirement. In essence this was the explorers' way of taking possession of land for the Spanish monarchy and inform the natives of the truth of Christianity. This example was presented by Gov. Pánfilo de Narváez: "On behalf of the Catholic Caesarian Majesty of Don Carlos . . . I . . . notify and cause you to know in the best manner that I can, that God our Lord . . . created the heaven and earth. . . . because of the infinity of offspring that followed in the five thousand years and more since the world was created, it has become necessary that some men should go in one direction and others in another, dividing into many kingdoms and provinces." The governor continued by saying that God required the Pope to be "obeyed and be head of all the human race, wheresoever they might live and be." The Spanish notary recorded the episode and obtained witnesses of signatures. The Spanish took this exercise seriously, "with scrupulous regard for the law." Even though the Indians could not understand what was being said to them, the colonizers repeated this exercise with every arrival in a new land. Only Bartolomé de las Casas ridiculed the practice.

Source:
James Axtell, *Beyond 1492: Encounters in Colonial North America* (New York: Oxford University Press, 1992).

HEADLINE MAKERS

PIERRE BIARD

1576-1622
JESUIT MISSIONARY

Acadia. Pierre Biard, a Jesuit missionary in Acadia, was regarded by the Micmac tribe as a European with shamanistic powers. Born in Grenoble, France, in 1576, he was summoned from his position as professor of scholastic theology and Hebrew at the University of Lyons to head the mission to Acadia. The choice of Biard was controversial: the founder of Acadia and many of its settlers were Huguenots and did not welcome a Catholic in their midst. Finally, after three years of waiting, the Jesuits arrived at Port Royal in May 1611.

Conversion Efforts. In Acadia, Biard and his colleague, Enemond Massé, attempted to catechize the natives in their own language, though this took time. Biard was well-respected and recognized as having shamanistic powers after presiding over the "Grand Sagamore's" son, who had been left for dead as a result of illness. Later, during an Abenaki epidemic, he preached the Gospel and offered crosses to those who were ill. Biard recognized that successful conversion required proving to the Native Americans that Christian healing methods were superior to their own ways. Ultimately, however, Biard's conversion record was poor.

Later Career. French Huguenots remained hostile to Biard and Massé and took the Jesuits hostage on Mount Desert Island in 1613. Biard was exiled to Virginia but was compelled by the English to return to Port Royal in order to participate in an attack on the new French colony. Along with Massé, Biard was forced to take responsibility for the marauding that resulted. Ultimately, Biard was returned to France, where he was blamed for his participation in Port Royal's destruction. Samuel de Champlain vindicated him. He returned to his position as a professor of theology and later became a missionary in the south of France. He died in Avignon, France, in 1622.

Source:

Jesuit Encounters in the New World: Jesuit Chroniclers, Geographers, Educators, and Missionaries in the Americas, 1549–1767, edited by Joseph A. Gagliano and Charles E. Ronan (Rome: Institutum Historicum, 1997).

JOHN CALVIN

1509-1564
THEOLOGIAN

Early Life. John Calvin was one of the primary reformers and theologians of the Protestant Reformation. Born in 1509 in Noyon, France, the son of a notary, attorney for the Church, and secretary for the local bishop, John Calvin was destined for a life in religious service. Noyon was the site of a cathedral and thus had a rich episcopal history. Calvin spent his first university years in Paris, supported by the generosity of the bishop of Noyon. His intellectual life was cultivated by spending time with the large circle of scholars at the court of King Francis I. He was studying for the priesthood until his father argued with the local bishop and sent his son to study law in Orleans. After earning his doctor of laws degree in 1531, Calvin went to Paris to study politics and theology. His humanistic studies led him to look carefully at the Church, and soon after, he joined a reformed religious party. His attitudes toward the Church were also affected by the fact that he could not secure Christian burial for his father, who had been excommunicated upon his death in 1531.

Conversion. Calvin published his first book in 1532, a commentary on Seneca's *On Clemency.* The next year, after helping his friend Nicholas Cop, rector of the University of Paris, compose an address which included Lutheran Reformation ideas, the two had to flee Paris, and the Church instituted heresy proceedings against him. It was perhaps after this that Calvin experienced his conversion to scripture-based religion; the event sent Calvin into exile and a life of supporting Reformation ideals.

Geneva. The year 1536 witnessed two important events in Calvin's life: he published his most significant work and was persuaded to go to Geneva, Switzerland, to reform religion there. *The Institutes of the Christian Religion* forms the principal source for Calvin's thought; it is also a manual on spirituality. Calvin accepted Luther's idea that salvation is by grace alone, through faith. At the core of Calvin's thinking was predestination—the idea that God had long ago determined who would be saved and who would be damned—and that humans were dependent on God for knowledge and faith. In Geneva, where Calvin would remain for the rest of his life (except for three years, when the political climate became less amenable for Protestants and he returned to Strasbourg in France), he transformed the city regarded for its ill repute into one in which a strict moral code prevailed, regulating the lives of everyone, regardless of rank or class. Geneva thus became the model Protestant city, and the University of Geneva was a training ground for Calvinism. Calvin lived out his life developing and refining his ideas on church government. He published the *Ecclesiastical Ordinances* in 1541, which set forth the organization of churches. In his system he placed authority in the laity, assuring that even if a minister left or the church leaders were persecuted (a real fear), the church would continue, as it had leadership in place. When Calvin died in 1564, he left followers in Switzerland and throughout Europe to ensure the survival of his theological system.

Sources:

William Bouwsma, *John Calvin: A Sixteenth-Century Portrait* (New York & Oxford: Oxford University Press, 1988);

Michael A. Mullett, *Calvin* (New York: Routledge, 1989).

CHRISTOPHER COLUMBUS

1451-1506
EXPLORER

Judging the Man. The quincentennial, or 500th anniversary of Christopher Columbus's arrival in America in 1992, raised many new questions about the man. Once nearly universally regarded as a hero, Columbus today also conjures up brutality, violence, and the destruction of Native Americans and their culture. However, rather than rushing to judgment one way or another, we need to consider him in the context of his times.

Background. For a long time historians believed that Columbus was the son of a poor Genoese weaver and that before going to sea he had been a trader of African slaves in Spain. His marriage to the daughter of a prominent Lisbon merchant gave him many connections to the royal court. More recently other scholars have argued that Columbus was too prominent to have come from such humble beginnings.

Gold and Christianity. Part of Columbus's desire to explore was to bring Christianity to the world's peoples. He firmly believed, inspired by the prophecies in the Book of Isaiah, that the second coming of Christ would not be realized until every last individual was converted to Christianity. One of Columbus's goals was to personally deliver the Christian message. Ultimately he strove to bring enough gold back from his voyage to finance the final Crusade, the one that would achieve the Christianization of the whole world. Queen Isabella was convinced by Columbus's reasoning, and even though the Spanish Crown was impoverished, she agreed to fund his first voyage. Of course, gaining wealth, power, and fame was also a part of Columbus's agenda.

First Voyage. Seven weeks after going to sea in three small boats with a crew of about ninety men, Columbus landed in the Bahamas on 12 October 1492. He promptly erected two banners of the Green Cross, one each for Ferdinand and Isabella. He named the land San Salvador, or "Holy Savior." The Indies were, to him, paradise, and he spent the next ten weeks exploring the Caribbean, including parts of present-day Haiti, Cuba, and the Dominican Republic. Columbus returned with spices, slaves, and a small amount of gold. On his return voyage he authored a pamphlet extolling the lands he had found. They were, he exclaimed, filled with amiable natives and vast riches.

Second Voyage. Columbus returned to the New World for a second time in 1494. This second voyage witnessed not the conversion of the Native Americans as much as, in the words of one historian, "the true beginning of the invasion of the Americas." An epidemic hit many of Columbus's crew, and the Grand Admiral of the Ocean Sea also fell ill for months. As he lay sick, despite his personal promise to Ferdinand and Isabella not to be violent toward the natives, many of his soldiers used the opportunity not to proselytize but to wander freely, abusing and killing as many as fifty thousand Native Americans. Violence and murder were a part of Spanish culture; fifteenth-century Spain was a brutal place in which the questioning of heretics—and swift, severe punishment if they were found guilty but did not confess—famine, and disease were parts of normal life. However, Columbus's men no doubt felt justified in their marauding by the fact that their victims were not Christians but "beasts."

Book of Prophecies. Toward the end of his life, in 1500, after returning from his third voyage, Columbus composed the *Book of Prophecies*. This collection of thoughts, commentary, and biblical passages was an appeal to the Spanish monarchy to regain Jerusalem from Muslim control and affirmed that recovering the Holy City and finding and converting the native peoples he had discovered would lead to the second coming of Christ. Columbus placed himself squarely in this holy history which intended to show the schema of the salvation of the human race. Columbus was certain, he wrote Ferdinand and Isabella in 1503 from Jamaica, that Jerusalem would be rebuilt by a Christian and that "this person would come from Spain." He appealed to the monarchs to continue to support his voyages to enable him to find more gold and thus be able to liberate the Holy City.

Legacy. In considering Columbus's legacy, we must also consider that he acted in the name of religion. He believed he was directed by divine guidance on all of his voyages. To Columbus, religion and the less-than-benevolent treatment of the Native Americans were not necessarily mutually exclusive. If such brutality led to greater riches for Spain, it could use this wealth to effect more conversions, according to his thinking.

Sources:

Roberto Rusconi, ed., *The Book of Prophecies edited by Christopher Columbus* (Berkeley: University of California Press, 1997);

Margarita Zamora, *Reading Columbus* (Berkeley: University of California Press, 1993).

TERESA OF ÁVILA

1515-1582
SPANISH SAINT

Beginnings. Teresa of Ávila was a Christian saint, mystic, religious reformer, and author of several religious tracts. Teresa de Ahumeda y Cepeda was born in Ávila, in Castile, Spain, in 1515. As a child she demonstrated deep spirituality. Attending boarding school in a convent as a teenager, she began to think about becoming a nun. In 1535 she entered the Convent of the Incarnation and remained there for twenty-eight years until she founded her own reformed convent. Life in the Convent of the Incarnation was not particularly difficult or demanding. Reading St. Augustine's *Confessions* (400?) led her to desire a more disciplined, rigorous life; in her intense personal prayer she experienced what she called "intellectual visions and locutions."

Founding Convents. Seven years after these visions she left the convent to create a new one. Teresa argued that she had been told to do so in her visions. In her new convent, established with permission of the Pope, she and the other Carmelite nuns kept a much stricter observance. Fasting, silence, and limited contact with outsiders characterized the new order. Now calling herself Teresa of Jesus, she went on to found one convent a year for the next fifteen years, as per the command of the Roman Catholic authorities. Teresa also founded monasteries for Carmelite friars.

Opposition. Despite her fruitful efforts, not everyone was supportive of Teresa. Some Church authorities asserted that her visions might be a sign of witchcraft. As if her spiritual experiences were not sufficiently threatening, the inquisitors were further alarmed by Teresa establishing convents and venturing into the unwomanly financial world. She was threatened with the Inquisition but was never charged.

Legacy. Teresa was also a prolific writer; among her spiritual classics were *Camino de perfección* (The Way of Perfection), published in 1583, and *Libro de la vida* (Book of Life), in 1611. Her four major prose works touched upon prayer, the dimensions of spiritual and mystical growth, and founding convents. She also wrote poetry and letters. She died in 1582. Pope Paul V beati- fied her in 1614; eight years later Gregory XV canonized her. Teresa has been described as a writer of "Christian masterpieces" and one of history's great authorities on mysticism.

Source:
Gillian T. W. Ahlgren, *Teresa of Ávila and the Politics of Sanctity* (Ithaca, N.Y.: Cornell University Press, 1996).

PUBLICATIONS

Pietro Martire d'Anghiera (Peter Martyr), *De Orbe novo* (New York & London: Putnam, 1912)—although Peter Martyr never traveled to the New World, this Italian cleric befriended many explorers while living in Spain. Listening to the stories of Christopher Columbus, Vasco de Gama, Hernando Cortés, and others, Martyr compiled their accounts in *The Eight Decades*, first printed in 1516; it was translated into English and expanded in 1555 by Richard Eden. While few people regarded diversity as the spiritual sign he suggested it to be, Martyr maintained that the variety of skin colors in the world was a source of wonder, one for which people owed gratitude to God. He also asserted that color should not determine the fate of Native Americans;

The Book of Prophecies edited by Christopher Columbus, edited by Roberto Rusconi (Berkeley: University of California Press, 1997)—originally written in 1500, this compilation of essays based on biblical passages asserts among other things that the conversion of Native Americans would lead to the second coming of Christ;

John Calvin, *Institutio Christianae religionis* (Geneva: Excudebat Franciscus Perrinus, 1568)—*The Institutes of the Christian Religion* was originally published in 1536 and is the major treatise on Calvinistic theology;

Michel de Montaigne, *Complete Essays* (Stanford, Cal.: Stanford University Press, 1958)—written between 1572 and 1588, these essays are by a leading skeptic who criticizes European notions of Native American spiritual inferiority.

CHAPTER NINE

SCIENCE, MEDICINE, AND TECHNOLOGY

by DAVID COLEMAN

CONTENTS

CHRONOLOGY

204

OVERVIEW

209

TOPICS IN THE NEWS

Background: An Age of Renaissance
and Recovery................211
The Travels of Marco Polo.......212
Background: Culture and Thought in
Renaissance Italy 213
Background: The Printing Press and
the Spread of Ideas 214
Europe's Place in the World: Classical
Geography and Its Legacy ...214
Europe's Place in the World: Evidence
from Medieval Maps 216
Predictions of Other Lands 216

Europe's Place in the World:
Geographical Speculation in the
Renaissance Era 217
*Columbus's Sense of Religious
Mission*..................218
Exploring the Atlantic: Portuguese
and Spanish Voyages before
Columbus 218
Growth of an Idea: Columbus and the
Enterprise of the Indies 219
Mariners and Their Ships: A Revolu-
tion in Ship Design........220
Mariners and Their Ships: The Tech-
nology of Navigation 221
The Military Revolution and
European Expansion 223
The Black Legend..........224
Power and Patronage: Columbus's
Search for Financial
Support 225
Reconnaissance:
Columbus's Voyages 226
Syphilis in Europe 227

Reconnaissance: The New Continents
and Their Place in
the World...............227
Reconnaissance: Voyages to North
America 228
A Revolution in Cartography:
Mapping the World 229
The Transformation of
Post-Columbian Europe:
The Impact of Contact.....230

HEADLINE MAKERS

Nicolaus Copernicus 232
Prince Henry the Navigator ...233
Bartolomé de las Casas........234

PUBLICATIONS

235

Sidebars and tables are listed in italics.

1200s

- The magnetic compass is first used by European sailors in the Mediterranean Sea.

1298- 1299

- While a prisoner of the Genoese, Venetian traveler Marco Polo writes *Divisament dou monde*, a lengthy account of his adventures in China and other areas of East Asia. His book fascinates European readers for centuries to come.

1348- 1351

- The bubonic plague, also known as the Black Death, ravages Europe, killing as much as one-third of the continent's population.

1410

- Pierre d'Ailly completes his geographical summary titled *Imago Mundi* (Image of the World).
- Florentine scholar Jacopo Angelo de' Scarperia completes his Latin translation of Ptolemy's *Geographia*.

1420s

- Portugal begins the settlement of the Madeira Islands, and sugar plantations there make extensive use of imported African slave labor.

1430?

- Portuguese sailors discover the Azores Islands.

1439

- Greek scholar Gemistus Plethon introduces to Florentine mapmakers the work of the Roman geographer Strabo.

1440s

- The term *caravel* is first applied to a class of small but fast Portuguese sailing ships.
- The Portuguese begin settling the previously uninhabited Azores.

1470s   •   The Spanish initiate a series of military campaigns to conquer the Canary Islands and establish stable colonies. Within twenty years they enslave much of the native Canarian population.

1474   •   Florentine geographer Paolo dal Pozzo Toscanelli writes a letter to the Portuguese king in which he explains that Asia could be easily reached by sailing west into the Atlantic Ocean.

1476   •   Lorenzo Buonincontri predicts that a "fourth continent" (in addition to Asia, Africa, and Europe) might be found across the ocean to Europe's west.

1484-1485   •   Genoese sailor Christopher Columbus proposes to the Portuguese crown a plan to sail west in order to reach Asia. His plan is rejected as unsound by a royal commission of scholars.

1486   •   Columbus submits his plan to the Spanish monarchs Ferdinand and Isabella. As in Portugal a crown-appointed commission rejects his ideas.

1487-1488   •   Portuguese navigator Bartholomeu Dias sails to the Cape of Good Hope at the southern tip of Africa.

1491   •   A second crown-appointed commission in Spain again rejects Columbus's plan.

1492   •   Ferdinand and Isabella ignore their advisors' recommendations and agree to provide financial backing for Columbus's proposed expedition.

1492-1493   •   During his first voyage Columbus travels through the Caribbean Sea, believing all the while that he has discovered new islands near the coast of Asia.

1493   •   The earliest cases of syphilis are reported in Italy and Spain.

1493-1496

- Columbus makes his second voyage to the Caribbean.

1494

- The Treaty of Tordesillas between Spain and Portugal establishes a dividing li in the Atlantic Ocean. Portugal reserves the right to claim all new lands discov ered east of the line, with newly discovered lands west of the line going to Spa

1497

- Florentine sailor Amerigo Vespucci makes his first voyage to the New World. Sailing for Spain, he explores the Caribbean coast of the South American mai land.
- Venetian sailor Giovanni Caboto (John Cabot), sailing for England, makes a voyage along the eastern coast of North America.

1497-1499

- Portuguese navigator Vasco da Gama sails around the southern tip of Africa a reaches India.

1498

- A second voyage by John Cabot ends in disaster as four of his five ships, includ ing the one carrying Cabot himself, are lost at sea.

1498-1500

- Columbus conducts his third voyage, and for the first time he makes landfall o the South American mainland.

1500

- Portuguese sailors begin to use the constellation known as the Southern Cross a navigational aid in the southern hemisphere.
- Juan de la Cosa draws a map of the Caribbean regions explored by Spaniards u to that point. The map is kept a state secret by the Spanish government.

1501

- Amerigo Vespucci returns to the New World on a mapping expedition for Por tugal.

1502-1504

- Columbus makes his fourth and final voyage to the New World.

1506 • Christopher Columbus dies in Valladolid, Spain, still maintaining that the lands he had reached were islands near or extensions of the Asian continent.

1507 • The St. Dié map drawn by Martin Waldseemüller and others first applies the name *America* to the South American continent.

1508 • Amerigo Vespucci is appointed pilot major of Spain.

1508-1509 • Sebastian Cabot, sailing for England, fails to find a northwestern passage to Asia.

1519-1522 • An expedition under Ferdinand Magellan circumnavigates the globe. Magellan does not live to see his achievement, as he is killed by natives in the Philippines.

1523-1524 • Giovanni da Verrazano, sailing for France, explores the eastern coast of North America in search of a northwestern passage to Asia.

1525 • Esteban Gómez, sailing for Spain, explores the eastern coast of North America in search of a northwestern passage to Asia.

• Over the course of the next seven years, Diego Ribeiro draws several detailed maps of the New World.

1534 • Frenchman Jacques Cartier explores the Gulf of St. Lawrence in search of a northwestern passage to Asia.

1535 • Jacques Cartier's second voyage explores the St. Lawrence River valley.

1538 • Flemish cartographer Gerardus Mercator completes his earliest world map, applying for the first time the name *America* to the North American continent.

1543	• Shortly before his death, Nicolaus Copernicus publishes *On the Revolution of the Heavenly Spheres*, in which he outlines his model of a sun-centered universe.
1569-1571	• Spanish physician Nicolás Monardes publishes two books dealing with medicines drawn from plants of American origins. His books are translated into English and published in 1577 as one volume entitled *Joyfull Newes out of the Newe Founde Worlde*.
1595	• Gerardus Mercator's world atlas is published posthumously.

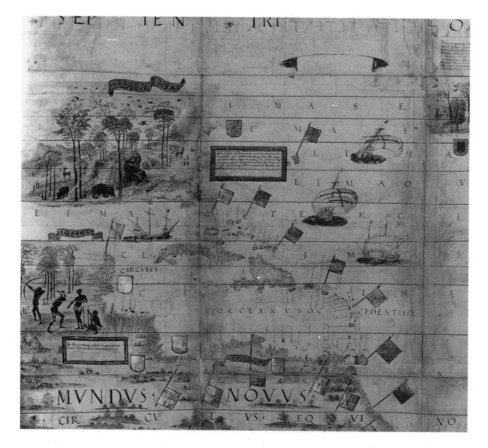

A 1525 map of the Western Hemisphere attributed to Lopo Homem

OVERVIEW

Europe at a Crossroads. In the 1400s and 1500s the major states of Europe took their first steps toward imperialistic domination of much of the globe by exploring, conquering, and colonizing various regions of Africa, Asia, and the Americas. The motives of these nations and the technological innovations that made possible their imperial expansion grew largely from the transformation of European thought and society during the period that historians call the Renaissance (1350–1600). For Europeans the Renaissance was above all a period of recovery. The 1300s had been a particularly disastrous era in European history. Millions had died as a result of successive waves of famine on the one hand and the appearance of the bubonic plague, or Black Death, on the other. Besides causing immeasurable human suffering, these disasters also threw Europe's economy into turmoil and crisis. Moreover, Christian Europe in the early and mid 1400s increasingly found itself threatened by the growing power of the Muslim Ottoman empire, which extended its reach into the Mediterranean Sea and even into southeastern Europe itself. Recovery from these years of crisis came gradually through the course of the 1400s. By the end of the century a new spirit of assertive self-confidence had grown within European culture and civilization—a spirit turned by some toward expansion as they began to build overseas empires.

Changing Worldviews. The Renaissance was also an era during which scholars and sailors began to rethink traditional ideas about the physical globe and Europe's place on it. Contrary to long-standing myths that survive even today in our popular culture, Columbus and his contemporaries were not the first to conclude that the earth was spherical in shape. For at least two thousand years before Columbus, in fact, all educated Europeans had understood that the earth was round. The ancient Greeks had even produced remarkably accurate estimates of the earth's circumference. What was new in Columbus's time was the widespread idea that it might be possible for European ships to sail across oceans to reach other continents. In the early fifteenth century several European misconceptions continued to stand in the way of the possibility of such ocean voyages. Many people had long believed, for instance, that if a ship sailed too close to the equator the intense heat of the tropical sun

not only would prove fatal to crews but also would even begin to melt the ship itself. Two fifteenth-century developments led to the gradual dismissal of such mental obstacles. First, scholars in Italy—the center of much of Europe's cultural innovation in the Renaissance—engaged in lively debates and discussions during which they questioned geographical ideas. Studying long-forgotten books written by ancient Roman geographers, for instance, the Italian scholars of the 1400s learned that the earth's equatorial zone was in fact inhabited, and some of them proposed that it should be possible for Europeans to sail through or even settle in such tropical regions. Second, in contrast to the mere speculation of the scholars, some European navigators of the era actually set out on successive voyages into previously uncharted waters, gaining in the process practical experience against which to test traditional ideas concerning ocean travel. Fifteenth-century Portuguese expeditions along the African coast, for example, eventually managed to sail south through the equatorial zone, disproving conclusively the old ideas concerning the impossibility of such voyages.

The Lure of Asia. By the 1400s many Europeans had long dreamed of the possibility of establishing direct seaborne commercial trade routes to the ports of India, China, and the "Spice Islands" of Indonesia. Since the late Middle Ages wealthy Europeans had developed a taste for a variety of consumer products of East Asian origin, including pepper and other spices as well as silk cloth. Such products, however, could reach European markets only via complicated trade routes that passed through the Islamic lands of the Near and Middle East, where Muslim traders held a monopoly on commerce. Similarly once the products reached the Mediterranean Sea they were transported to European markets by the equally monopolistic merchants of Venice and other Italian cities. Thus by the time they reached Europe, Asian goods were simply too expensive for all but the wealthiest of Europeans. Many Europeans left out of the profitable Asian trade dreamed of finding a direct ocean trade route to Asia in order to bypass the Muslim and Venetian middlemen. One possibility was to sail south from Europe around the southern tip of Africa and east across the Indian Ocean to the ports of Asia. In the early fifteenth century, however, no one in Europe knew whether or not such a voyage was possible since no one knew the southern extent of the African continent. A series of fifteenth-century Portuguese expeditions answered this question by successfully pioneering this southeastern passage to Asia via the Cape of Good Hope at Africa's southern tip. Portuguese efforts culminated in the landmark 1497–1499 voyage of Vasco da Gama all the way around Africa to India and then back to Portugal via the same route. Direct trade with Asia made tiny Portugal one of Europe's leading commercial powers in the sixteenth century.

Columbus. Meanwhile other fifteenth-century Europeans speculated that rounding Africa might not be the quickest and simplest way for European vessels to reach Asia. Some had in fact already proposed that it might be possible for ships to reach Asia by sailing directly west across the Atlantic Ocean and around the globe to Asia. In the fifteenth century the "known world" for Europeans consisted of only three major continental landmasses—Europe itself, Africa, and Asia. No European in 1492 knew that North and South America stood between Europe's western shores and East Asia. In short Columbus did not set out in 1492 with the intent of "discovering America." Instead his explicit goal was to provide a new and quick ocean route to Asia by sailing west. After a long and arduous search for financial backing for his proposed expedition, Columbus finally secured the support of the Spanish monarchs Isabella and Ferdinand. Sailing across the Atlantic in three small vessels with a combined crew of only ninety men, Columbus in October 1492 made landfall on an island in the Bahamas. His expedition then ventured south, visiting Cuba, Hispaniola, and many of the other islands of the Caribbean Sea. Over the coming decades Spain took its first steps toward empire in the Americas by establishing colonies and settlements on these Caribbean islands, often enslaving their native populations. Columbus himself, however, never realized the nature or territorial extent of the lands he had discovered. Even after making a total of four voyages to the Caribbean region, Columbus maintained until his death in 1506 that the lands he had visited were islands near or parts of the Asian mainland. He had no idea that what he had found was an entire new world previously unknown to Europeans.

Technology. European exploration and expansion in the Renaissance would have been impossible without a number of critical technological innovations. From Portugal and Spain, for instance, came new classes of sailing ships, particularly the small caravel and the larger carrack, that were capable of long-distance ocean voyages. European mariners in the age of exploration also improved their ability to find their way in open ocean waters by making use of a variety of navigational tools including the magnetic compass and the astrolabe, an instrument that helped ship pilots calculate latitudinal position at sea. Even with the aid of such devices, however, navigation remained throughout the age of exploration a

highly inexact science. Until the 1700s European navigators remained almost completely baffled, for example, by the problem of calculating longitude at sea. As a result European mariners in the age of exploration occasionally found themselves lost at sea, often resulting in the death of entire crews. Renaissance-era developments in military technology also played an important role in making possible Europe's overseas conquests and the establishment of global empires. Gradual improvements in artillery and handheld firearms, for example, contributed to the military advantage enjoyed by Europeans when they encountered the people of the Americas and other parts of the globe during the age of exploration and expansion.

Naming America. Other European expeditions soon followed the ocean path blazed by Columbus in 1492. Even before Columbus's death in 1506, some of his contemporaries had already begun to speculate that the lands on the other side of the Atlantic were not Asia after all. Among the earliest Europeans to reach this conclusion was the Florentine Amerigo Vespucci, who in 1502 published a highly popular book recounting his travel experiences in what he called the "New World." In 1507 a group of mapmakers in France decided that it would be best to credit Vespucci rather than Columbus with the "discovery" of the New World since it had been Vespucci and not Columbus who had first publicly recognized that these newly found lands were not parts of Asia. As a result their map called the mainland of this New World "America," after Amerigo. Their map sold thousands of copies throughout Europe, and the name America stuck.

Looking for a Passageway. Even as they came to realize that the profitable Asian trade still lay half a world away from the Americas, some Europeans continued the search for Columbus's original objective: a westerly sailing route to Asia. From 1519 to 1522 an expedition led by Ferdinand Magellan succeeded in finding such a route. Magellan led his ships from Spain across the Atlantic and around the southern tip of South America. From there the expedition crossed the Pacific Ocean to the Philippine Islands, where Magellan died in a battle. His remaining crew, however, continued the journey, eventually returning to Spain after having passed across the Indian Ocean and around the tip of Africa. In the process Magellan's crew had become the first expedition ever to circumnavigate the globe. The southwestern passage from Europe to Asia via the tip of South America, pioneered by Magellan's ships, however, proved simply too treacherous to sustain regular commerce. The failure of the Magellan expedition to find a convenient southwestern route encouraged the major states of Europe to target instead the North American Atlantic coastline in search of a more easily navigable northwestern passage to Asia. Throughout the sixteenth century repeated efforts by English, French, and Spanish explorers to locate such a route all proved fruitless. In the process of this search, however, the Europeans learned a great deal about the eography and native populations of North America's eastern coast.

Mapmaking. Sixteenth-century European maps illustrate well Europe's growing knowledge of the world's oceans and continents, including North America. Cartographers not only incorporated the new data brought to them by explorers into their ever-more-comprehensive world maps, but they also devised new and more-accurate ways of representing the three-dimensional globe on a flat, two-dimensional map. Particularly significant in this regard was work of the Flemish cartographer Gerardus Mercator, the inventor of the "Mercator projection" technique preferred among mapmakers and navigators even today. Accurate geographical knowledge was critical to the imperial ambitions of many European states, and many of the best sixteenth-century maps were jealously guarded as state secrets, especially by the Spanish and Portuguese governments. Other maps, however, were published and broadly disseminated, including Mercator's landmark 1595 world atlas, which sold thousands of copies across Europe.

Legacy. Columbus's voyages marked the establishment for the first time of sustained contact between the people and cultures of the Old World (Asia, Africa, and Europe) and those of the New World (the Americas). Perhaps no other event in recorded history has surpassed the overall impact of this development on the world as a whole. For many of the natives of the Americas, for instance, the coming of the Europeans brought subjection to the imperial domination of European states and the introduction of deadly diseases such as smallpox that killed millions. Europeans also introduced into the Americas a variety of plant and animal species. Some of these European introductions, including wheat and the horse, dramatically transformed the cultures and landscapes of the Americas. Yet the impact of sustained contact between the Old World and the New World significantly transformed Europe as well. From the Americas, for example, explorers brought back a variety of plants that would eventually reshape European diets and agriculture. Corn, tomatoes, and potatoes—all originally American crops—have over the centuries since Columbus's voyages become staples in the diets of people not only in Europe but also in many areas of Asia and Africa. In short, contact between the Old World and the New World gradually transformed the lives of people around the globe.

TOPICS IN THE NEWS

BACKGROUND: AN AGE OF RENAISSANCE AND RECOVERY

Medieval Prosperity and Growth, 1000–1300. For centuries before Christopher Columbus's famous 1492 voyage, Europeans were already gaining greater knowledge of the world around them. Beginning around the year 1000 Europe experienced what historians have labeled a commercial revolution of the High Middle Ages—a period of remarkable and unprecedented growth in economy and population. Large cities, mostly absent from the European landscape since the dissolution of the western Roman empire in the fifth century, reappeared and were connected to one another by ever-expanding networks of roads and commerce. Part of the impetus for Europe's dramatic economic expansion in this era came from long-distance trade that brought to Europe's markets the consumer products of Asia. Fueled in large measure by contacts established during the Christian crusades against the Muslim-dominated Holy Land beginning in 1081, Europeans of means developed a taste for spices, silk, and other luxury goods of East Asian origin. Demand for such products was filled through complex patterns of intercontinental trade. Muslim traders brought goods from China, India, the Spice Islands (modern Indonesia), and other parts of South and East Asia to the port cities of the eastern Mediterranean Sea. Italian ships from the maritime city-republics of Venice and Genoa took the goods across the Mediterranean to European markets. From its swampy but strategically advantageous lagoon at the northern tip of the Adriatic Sea, Venice became Europe's dominant medieval commercial power. The Venetian gold coin called the "ducat" became the standard of trade across the continent.

Routes East. Through centuries of armed conflict as well as trade, Venetians and other Europeans became quite familiar with the culture of their Muslim neighbors to their immediate south and east. However, the civilizations and cultures further east, including the technologically advanced Chinese, long remained in the European

THE TRAVELS OF MARCO POLO

During the fifteenth and sixteenth centuries European notions of the wonders and wealth to be found in East Asia continued to be shaped in large part by the extremely popular accounts of the thirteenth-century Venetian traveler Marco Polo. He was only a teenager when he set out from Venice with his father and uncle in 1271 on a journey through Asia which would last twenty-four years. After more than three years of perilous travel, the Polos reached the court of the great Chinese emperor Kublai Khan. The emperor took a special interest in the young Venetian, and soon Polo found himself employed as a diplomat and ambassador in the service of the powerful Chinese empire. Polo remained in this post for seventeen years, traveling on a variety of missions for the emperor and in the process becoming a wealthy and well-respected man among the Chinese elite. When the Polos finally returned to Venice in 1295 ragged and weary from the difficult return journey, their family, who had years earlier given them up for dead, reportedly did not recognize them and refused to have anything to do with them. Family sentiment, however, quickly became more nostalgic and affectionate when the disheveled travelers produced from their threadbare clothing large quantities of rubies and other jewels which they had brought back from Asia.

Through the course of his journeys Polo saw and learned a great deal about the politics, people, and cultures of the Far East. Yet his experiences might have disappeared entirely from the European historical record had it not been for the misfortunes which befell him soon after his return to Venice. In 1298 Polo commanded a warship in a battle against the naval forces of Venice's principal commercial rival, Genoa, and during the battle he was taken prisoner. While in the hands of the Genoese, Polo met Rustichello, a fellow prisoner from the city of Pisa who became fascinated with Polo's tales of his travels in faraway lands. During their long hours of imprisonment together, Rustichello produced detailed written summaries of Polo's stories. Manuscript copies of these accounts circulated across Europe throughout the fourteenth century. After the development of the moveable-type printing press in the mid fifteenth century, dozens of printed editions of Polo's travel stories appeared in all major European languages. His accounts of the people and wealth of the civilizations of East Asia long remained one of the best-sellers of the early print era.

Source: Daniel J. Boorstin, *The Discoverers: A History of Man's Search to Know His World and Himself* (New York: Vintage, 1983).

imagination distant shadows and the subject of fanciful legends. Only a handful of Europeans actually traveled during the High Middle Ages directly to the sources of the coveted East Asian trade. Though few in number, journeys by Europeans to the Far East were facilitated somewhat during the time of the short-lived Mongol dynasty in China. Beginning with the great warrior-emperor Genghis Khan, the Mongols established an empire stretching from Asia's Pacific coast to the steppes of southwestern Russia. The era of *Pax mongolica,* or Mongol dominance, facilitated trade of all sorts across the Eurasian landmass. Some Europeans managed to follow the trade routes eastward, and a few, such as the Venetian traveler Marco Polo, produced written accounts of what they saw in their travels among the people and cultures of Asia. After the fall of the Mongol dynasty in 1368 and the dissolution of their vast empire, however, the lines of contact between Europe and East Asia constricted significantly.

Crisis. In Europe meanwhile a series of cataclysmic disasters brought to an abrupt end the prosperity and growth of the High Middle Ages. The 1300s began with a series of failed harvests and widespread famine across Europe. Then from 1347 to 1351 Europe was ravaged by the Black Death (bubonic plague) that killed as much as

one-third of the continent's population. From a peak of some eighty-four million people in 1300, Europe's population dipped to slightly more than fifty million by 1351, mostly as a result of the waves of famine and pestilence. Population decline was coupled with economic contraction and social unrest, and Europe's tailspin continued into the early decades of the 1400s. The rise of the powerful Muslim Ottoman empire in Asia Minor (modern Turkey) presented in the fifteenth century a new external threat to Europe. The Ottomans conquered much of the Near East and North Africa. After besieging Constantinople in 1453, they began to move into the Balkan peninsula, that is, the southeastern corner of Europe itself. In short the era that historians call the "Renaissance" (approximately 1350 to 1600) was born in the midst of a deep crisis for European civilization.

Growth. Renaissance Europe's economic and demographic recovery came gradually in the middle decades of the fifteenth century, as populations and economies across the continent began slowly to rebound. Throughout the preceding 150 years of crisis, long-distance trade with East Asia had been maintained. The Asian trade that survived the years of crisis had, however, increasingly fallen under the monopolistic stranglehold of the Muslim traders of the Ottoman empire on one hand and

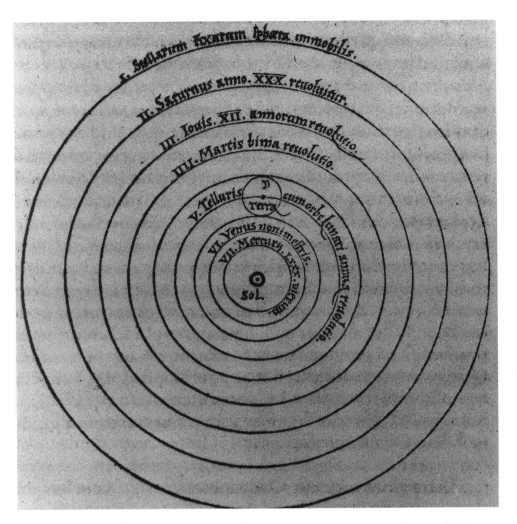

Copernican model of the solar system, in *De revolutionibus orbium coelestium* (1543)

the Venetian ship captains that dominated the Mediterranean Sea on the other. Both the Muslims and the Venetians made as high as 2,000 percent profits from this trade. By the time they reached European markets the spices and silks of Asia were prohibitively expensive for many people. The Genoese sailor Christopher Columbus and others wondered if it would be possible to find an alternative means of access to the legendary and lucrative East Asian trade, a route that bypassed the Muslim and Venetian middlemen.

Source:
William D. Phillips Jr. and Carla Rahn Phillips, *The Worlds of Christopher Columbus* (Cambridge, U.K.: Cambridge University Press, 1992).

BACKGROUND: CULTURE AND THOUGHT IN RENAISSANCE ITALY

Recovery of Ancient Knowledge. Europe's intellectual agenda in the age of exploration and expansion was set largely by the thinkers and scholars of Renaissance Italy. Beginning with the fourteenth-century scholars Francesco Petrarca (better known by his Latinized pen-name "Petrarch") and Giovanni Boccaccio, Italian think-

ers took a special interest in the literature, philosophy, and thought of the ancient cultures of Greece and Rome. Fifteenth-century scholars such as Poggio Bracciolini scoured libraries and monasteries not only in Italy but also across Europe and the Mediterranean basin in search of long-forgotten Greek, Latin, and even translated Arabic manuscript copies of the works of such writers as Plato and Tacitus. It should be noted that many of these works had been "forgotten" only from the point of view of the western European intellectual tradition. Arabic and Byzantine scholars had continued throughout the Middle Ages to study several of the literary and scientific classics of Greece and Rome that the Italians "recovered" only in the fifteenth century. Nonetheless exposure to previously lost ideas and knowledge gleaned from these recovered works opened up fresh lines of intellectual inquiry to the scholars of the Italian Renaissance. Of particular importance in this regard was the recovery of the works of the Roman geographers Ptolemy and Strabo, whose ideas would contribute significantly to fifteenth-century shifts in Europeans' views of the physical globe and of their own place within it. The changing worldviews of the Renaissance would in turn inspire

European navigators to sail out into previously uncharted waters in search of, among other things, new water routes to Asia.

A New "Golden Age"? Coupled with the recovery of much of the thought and knowledge of the Greeks and Romans was a new spirit of assertive self-confidence among the thinkers of the Renaissance. Italian scholar Lorenzo Valla proudly proclaimed this era to be a new "golden age" that might be favorably compared to the most glorious and learned civilizations of history. The word *Renaissance* itself in fact means rebirth, and this label was applied to the era by Italian thinkers themselves, who understood their age to represent a re-emergence of the glories of ancient civilization. Whatever the merits of such claims, the Renaissance was also an era that extolled individualism and often a boastful individual self-confidence. Such haughtiness was perhaps most apparent among artists, including the great sculptor and painter Michelangelo and the famous goldsmith and sculptor Benevenuto Cellini, who penned the following poem in praise of himself:

> My cruel fate hath warred with me in vain:
> Life, glory, worth, and all unmeasured skill,
> Beauty and grace, themselves in me fulfill
> That many I surpass, and to the best attain.

Similar individualism and boastful self-confidence would also be common among many of the famous sailors and explorers of the Renaissance, including Christopher Columbus himself.

Source:
John P. McKay, Bennett D. Hill, and John Buckler, *A History of Western Society*, fourth edition (Boston: Houghton Mifflin, 1991).

BACKGROUND: THE PRINTING PRESS AND THE SPREAD OF IDEAS

Gutenberg. For an invention that so radically transformed history, we know remarkably little about the early development of the moveable-type printing press. All that can be said for certain is that it was a gradual process that culminated in the German city of Mainz sometime between 1445 and 1450, when several people, including a former goldsmith named Johann Gutenberg, contributed to the earliest workable prototype. Although it would be an exaggeration to say that Gutenberg "invented" moveable-type printing, it is true that his press was the first to publish a lengthy, substantial printed book, the famous Gutenberg Bible, 1454–1456. From Mainz the printing press spread rapidly, first through Germany and then into other areas of Europe. By 1500 more than one thousand presses had been established across the continent, and they had collectively produced more than nine million copies of more than forty thousand separate book titles. Europe's commercial center, Venice, likewise became the continent's capital of printing, as the city alone housed nearly one hundred printing shops.

Literacy and the Book Market. The cultural impact of the printing press in late-fifteenth-century Europe was enormous. Widespread availability of standard copies of the works of ancient and modern writers alike meant above all, more rapid transmission and dissemination of ideas than had been possible in previous centuries, when books had been produced and copied only in manuscript form. In addition the explosion in the availability of books made possible by printing responded to and in turn contributed to increasing levels of literacy among the population of Europe. Reacting to the demands of Europe's largely devout reading public, the early book market was dominated by prayer manuals, Bibles, and other religious works. Besides religious books academic readers called for printed copies of the works of ancient Roman and Greek thinkers, including many of those that had only recently been "recovered" by the scholars of the Italian Renaissance.

Availability of Books. As in other fields of inquiry the availability of printed books greatly facilitated dissemination of geographical knowledge and theories. Europe's growing book market in the late fifteenth century provided a critical point of connection between the shifting worldviews of Renaissance intellectuals on the one hand and the enterprises of European sailors such as Christopher Columbus on the other. Spanish and Portuguese navigators, for example, could easily find in the bookstores of major port cities such as Seville and Lisbon copies of the works of both ancient and modern geographers and scientists. Columbus's personal library, for instance, included printed copies of Ptolemy's *Geographia*, Marco Polo's thirteenth-century travel accounts, and the highly influential 1410 geographical summary *Imago Mundi* (Image of the World) written by French clergyman Pierre d'Ailly. Drawing their information from sources such as these, European scholars and sailors alike regularly engaged in lively debates regarding the size of the earth and the relative positions of its landmasses.

Source:
William D. Phillips Jr. and Carla Rahn Phillips, *The Worlds of Christopher Columbus* (Cambridge, U.K.: Cambridge University Press, 1992).

EUROPE'S PLACE IN THE WORLD: CLASSICAL GEOGRAPHY AND ITS LEGACY

A Round Earth. Among the great myths concerning the age of exploration, perhaps none is more powerful and durable than the widespread notion that Christopher Columbus proved to a disbelieving Europe that the earth was in fact round and spherical, not flat. In reality educated Europeans had understood that the earth was spherical for at least two millennia before Columbus's 1492 voyage. As early as 500 B.C. the students of the mathematician Pythagoras were already speaking of the earth's spherical shape. Evidence for the earth's sphericity came from a variety of observations. The ancients noticed, for example, that the hull of a ship sailing away from an observer disappeared before the tip of the mast,

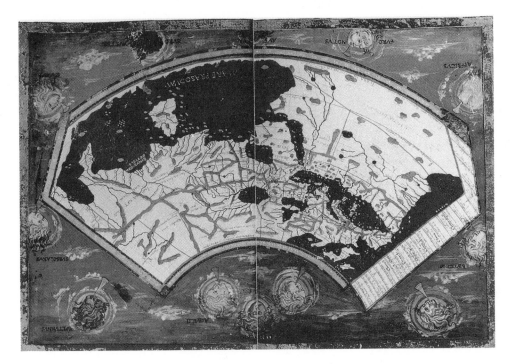

A Ptolemaic map of the world, circa 1490 (University of Valencia)

suggesting that the earth's shape was curved. Similarly the ancients noted that the circular shadow cast by the earth on the surface of the moon during a lunar eclipse further supported the idea of the earth's sphericity. The idea of the round earth was in fact so widely accepted that it became a cornerstone assumption of the cosmological system that would continue to dominate European thought for two thousand years, well into the age of exploration.

Aristotelian Worldview. The vision of the universe and the earth's place within it that continued to shape Renaissance worldviews received its definitive formulation in the work of the ancient Greek philosopher Aristotle. Summarizing received knowledge and adding observations of his own, Aristotle outlined a theory which placed an immobile, spherical earth at the very center of a finite universe which was bounded on its outer edge by the so-called sphere of fixed stars. Nearly all of the stars which we see in the night sky were, according to Aristotle, embedded within this hollow, glasslike globe on the universe's outer edge. This sphere of fixed stars rotated on its axis once daily, explaining the circular motion which we see as the stars move across the sky each night. Between the central earth and the stars were seven other rotating spheres into which were embedded what Aristotle called the "planets." These included, in succession moving away from the earth: the moon, Mercury, Venus, the sun, Mars, Jupiter, and Saturn (Uranus, Neptune, and Pluto are invisible to the naked eye and were discovered only after the invention of the telescope). Until the Renaissance, Europeans accepted Aristotle's model of the universe for two reasons. First, it effectively explained observed phenomena. Second, it had a variety of practical applications including, significantly, in the field of navigation.

Navigation. As a scientific model of the actual universe, Aristotle's cosmology was gradually discredited as a result of the Scientific Revolution of the sixteenth and seventeenth centuries. However, as a theoretical tool it continues to be useful in many ways even today. For example, current navigation handbooks continue to base navigational practices on Aristotelian principles, and most begin with some statement such as this: "For present purposes we shall assume that the earth is a small stationary sphere whose center coincides with a much larger rotating stellar sphere." In short whether in the time of Columbus or in our own day, navigating "by the stars" requires that the navigator make the thoroughly Aristotelian assumption that the earth is a stationary sphere at the center of a much larger sphere of fixed stars. Of particular significance to sailors in the northern hemisphere is, of course, the North Star. Because of its position at one pole of the navigator's assumed sphere of fixed stars, the North Star does not appear to rotate circularly along with the other stars in the night sky. The navigational usefulness of the North Star lies principally in the fact that its position in the sky allows the sailor to calculate latitude. The further north one goes the higher in the sky the North Star will appear. As one moves south the North Star will appear in a lower position in the sky, nearer to the horizon. As one moves south of the equator it disappears completely from view. By 1500 European navigators sailing in waters south of the equator had identified the group of stars called the Southern Cross, the southern hemisphere's equivalent of the North Star. Identification of the constellation allowed European sailors to determine their latitudinal position in southern waters as well. Basing their calculations on an Aristotelian vision of the universe, mariners by the time of Columbus had become quite skillful in determining latitude as they sailed the open ocean.

Eratosthenes. From the modern point of view one of the most startling achievements of ancient scientific thought comes from the Greek geographer Eratosthenes. Based upon observation and speculation Eratosthenes not only knew that the earth was spherical in shape but also provided the amazingly accurate estimate that it was 24,675 miles in circumference at the equator. (We know today that its circumference is about 24,860 miles.) By the third century B.C., then, ancient thinkers not only

understood that the earth was spherical in shape but also had a remarkably accurate idea of its size. Eratosthenes also speculated that it would be possible for a ship to sail from Spain either around the southern tip of Africa or directly west across the Atlantic Ocean to reach India, predicting some 1,700 years before the fact, European voyages in the age of exploration and expansion.

Sources:

Thomas Kuhn, *The Copernican Revolution: Planetary Astronomy in the Development of Western Thought* (Cambridge, Mass.: Harvard University Press, 1957);

John P. McKay, Bennet D. Hill, and John Buckler, *A History of Western Society*, fourth edition (Boston: Houghton Mifflin, 1991).

EUROPE'S PLACE IN THE WORLD: EVIDENCE FROM MEDIEVAL MAPS

Theology and Geography. Throughout the Middle Ages, Europeans' notions of their own place on the globe continued to be shaped not only by observation of the world around them but also by religious considerations. Nowhere is Christian theology's impact on European geographical thought more apparent than in the medieval tradition of the so-called T-O maps. These maps placed the city of Jerusalem, the site of the crucifixion of Jesus Christ, at the center of the world. Their makers customarily aligned these maps such that east was placed at the top since according to Scripture the Garden of Eden had been located at the eastern edge of the world (Genesis 2:8). The T-O maps portrayed the three continents known to medieval Europeans (Europe, Asia, and Africa) as distinct landmasses separated by bodies of water that collectively formed a *T*. This *T* was inscribed within a larger *O*-shaped mass of water that encircled the whole: the great Ocean Sea. Subsequent scholars have often pointed to these T-O maps as evidence of the general ignorance of medieval European civilization and the blindness to scientific truth induced by strict adherence to Christian theology. It is likely, however, that medieval Europeans interpreted these maps in spiritual and allegorical terms rather than as faithful representations of physical reality. Moreover, alongside this essentially theological tradition of cartography ran a more practical medieval tradition of mapmaking based upon observation of minute geographical detail.

Portolans. To medieval navigators in the Mediterranean and elsewhere, the T-O maps provided little practical assistance. In order to protect their crews and cargoes from disaster, shipmasters needed reliable charts that provided notice of dangerous rocks or shallows near the entrances to particular harbors and the proper compass headings to travel from one place to another. Throughout the Middle Ages sailors gradually compiled such empirical data based upon experience and observation of physical reality. Mariners then compiled and summarized such information in charts that they called "portolans," or harbor guides. Venice and the other principal commercial powers of medieval Europe often guarded the vital information contained in their portolans as state

---

PREDICTIONS OF OTHER LANDS

To fifteenth-century Europeans the "known world" included only three major continental landmasses: Asia, Africa, and Europe itself. Accounts in the Norse sagas of the lands visited by Leif Ericsson were scarcely known outside Scandinavia, and even well-educated Europeans in the Renaissance era were completely unaware of the existence of the Americas. With the exception of the Vikings' voyages and perhaps a few other mostly forgotten moments of contact, the peoples of the Old World and the New World lived in complete isolation from one another. Over the centuries preceding Christopher Columbus's accidental encounter with the American coastline, however, at least a few Europeans had actually written about the possibility that there might exist other continents unknown to Europe. As early as the time of Christ, for example, the Roman geographer Strabo wrote: "It is possible that in the same temperate zone (of the northern hemisphere) there are actually two inhabited worlds, or even more, and particularly in the proximity of the parallel that runs through Athens that is drawn across the (Atlantic) Ocean."

In the fifteenth century too there were at least some who believed that other continents, heretofore unknown to Europe, might exist in other parts of the globe. In 1476, for example, the Italian scholar Lorenzo Buonincontri wrote that the existence of a "fourth continent" had to him become a foregone conclusion. Ironically, Columbus, like many late-fifteenth-century Europeans, would prove oblivious to such considerations, maintaining until his 1506 death that the lands he had visited were either islands near or parts of the Asian mainland.

Source: Thomas Goldstein, "Geography in Renaissance Florence," in *The European Opportunity*, edited by Felipe Fernández Armesto (Brookfield, Vt.: Variorum, 1995), pp. 1–22.

---

ecrets. For ships sailing in the well-charted waters of the Mediterranean Sea, rarely if ever leaving sight of land, these portolans provided essential information to assure the safety of their voyages. For Christopher Columbus and other fifteenth- and sixteenth-century sailors who journeyed into unfamiliar regions, however, they were, of course, useless.

Source:

Daniel J. Boorstin, *The Discoverers: A History of Man's Search to Know His World and Himself* (New York: Vintage, 1983);

William D. Phillips Jr. and Carla Rahn Phillips, *The Worlds of Christopher Columbus* (Cambridge, U.K.: Cambridge University Press, 1992).

EUROPE'S PLACE IN THE WORLD: GEOGRAPHICAL SPECULATION IN THE RENAISSANCE ERA

Florence. To Europeans who dreamed of finding a sea route to Asian markets, questions regarding what lay beyond the familiar waters of the Mediterranean and Atlantic coasts of Europe were matters of utmost importance. The size and relative positions of the earth's major landmasses and bodies of water became issues of particularly vigorous discussion and debate among the Renaissance scholars of early-fifteenth-century Italy. In the absence of reliable maps and concrete data, however, such debates drew almost entirely from hearsay, speculation, and the supposedly well-informed writings of ancient Roman geographers. As in many fields of Renaissance cultural achievement, the city of Florence functioned as the center of the fifteenth century's revolution in geographical thought. Interest in such issues among Florentine scholars derived in part from commercial interests and in part from the "recovery" of two critical geographical texts from Roman antiquity. First, in 1400 an Italian scholar brought to Florence from Constantinople a Greek manuscript summarizing Roman geographical knowledge written in the second century A.D. by the renowned geographer and astronomer Claudius Ptolemaeus, better known as Ptolemy. A Latin translation of Ptolemy's *Geographia* was completed in 1410, and copies soon circulated throughout Italy and the rest of western and central Europe. Second, in 1439 the Byzantine scholar Gemistus Plethon arrived in Florence, bringing with him a Greek copy of another key ancient geographical text previously unknown among the Italians: the *Geography* of Strabo, written about the time of Christ. The geographical knowledge contained in Strabo's and Ptolemy's books inspired a generation of Florentine thinkers, including scholars such as Poggio Bracciolini and the future pope Aeneas Silvius Piccolomini, to reconsider long-held notions concerning Europe's place in the world.

The Question of Africa. Strabo's and Ptolemy's ideas added fresh considerations and often contradictory perspectives to a variety of long-standing debates concerning the possibility of using the ocean as a transcontinental waterway to the Far East. For example, Europeans in the early fifteenth century were completely unaware of the southern extent of the African continent. Was it possible to sail from Europe around the southern tip of Africa in order to reach the ports of India, China, and the Spice Islands? Ptolemy's book, in fact, suggested that such a voyage was impossible.

A map of Asia from a 1542 edition of Ptolemy's *Geographia*. Monstrous beings are depicted on both sides.

COLUMBUS'S SENSE OF RELIGIOUS MISSION

Christopher Columbus had several motivations for pursuing his "enterprise of the Indies." To him it was not simply a matter of proving a point for purposes of scholarly debate. Obviously the commercial advantage and personal riches to be found by pioneering a short westerly route to the wealthy Asian markets were important considerations. In addition Columbus always concerned himself greatly with matters of personal glory and fame, the individual acclaim that would befall him as the discoverer of this new route to Asia. Finally, and most important, Columbus's writings reveal that he had an extremely powerful religious notion of the personal role that God had chosen him to play in what he believed was the rapidly approaching end of the world. Pierre d'Ailly's 1410 *Imago Mundi* (Image of the World) had argued, based upon astrological evidence, that the coming century would see the arrival on earth of the anti-Christ followed by the Christian reconquest of the Holy Land from Muslim control and the coming of God's eternal kingdom. The extremely pious and somewhat mystical Columbus strongly believed in d'Ailly's apocalyptic vision and furthermore believed that God had personally entrusted him with a critical role in initiating this process. Columbus believed that his voyage to Asia would be the first step toward a Christian conquest of the Holy Land from the east and the beginning of a process by which God's word would be brought to the "unenlightened" people of southern and eastern Asia in preparation for Christ's return.

Source: Pauline Moffit Watts, "Prophecy and Discovery: On the Spiritual Origins of Christopher Columbus's 'Enterprise of the Indies,'" *American Historical Review*, 90 (1985): 73–102.

Africa and Asia were, according to Ptolemy, joined at their southern tips, leaving the Indian Ocean completely landlocked and inaccessible to European ships. Strabo's picture of the world, however, rejected this idea, correctly claiming that there was no southern point of connection between Asia and Africa. Piccolomini and other Renaissance scholars adopted Strabo's perspective on this issue, and many Europeans gradually came to believe in the possibility of sailing to Asia by rounding the southern tip of Africa.

The Torrid Zone. In a second principal area of debate, however, Strabo's ideas were ultimately rejected by the sailors and scholars of the Renaissance. Many Europeans had believed for centuries that the regions around and south of the equator constituted what they called a sweltering "Torrid Zone," a region too hot for human habitation and a zone in which men and ships might even begin to melt from the intense heat. Strabo's book provided support for this idea. Ptolemy's description of the world, however, suggested to Renaissance scholars that the equatorial zone and southern hemisphere were in fact inhabited and that it was thus possible for Europeans to sail through or even settle in these regions. In short the ideas of Florentine geographers in the Renaissance era (although based upon little more than speculation) played an important role in overcoming a variety of long-standing myths that stood in the way of transoceanic voyages. Moreover, from this tradition of Florentine geographical thought came one scholar, Paolo dal Pozzo Toscanelli, whose ideas would exert direct and profound influence on the thought and plans of Christopher Columbus.

Source:
Thomas Goldstein, "Geography in Renaissance Florence," in *The European Opportunity*, edited by Felipe Fernández Armesto (Brookfield, Vt.: Variorum, 1995), pp. 1–22.

EXPLORING THE ATLANTIC: PORTUGUESE AND SPANISH VOYAGES BEFORE COLUMBUS

African Coast. Portuguese navigators spearheaded Europe's ventures into uncharted waters at the dawn of the age of exploration and expansion. From their homeland at Europe's southwestern tip, early-fifteenth-century Portuguese mariners set out on voyages along the unfamiliar coast of Africa. Eventually these efforts would culminate in the late fifteenth century with two landmark voyages: Bartholomeu Dias's 1487–1488 journey to the Cape of Good Hope at Africa's southern tip and the 1497–1499 expedition of Vasco da Gama, the first European to reach the ports of India by sailing around Africa. It is doubtful, however, that Prince Henry the Navigator and his contemporaries had in mind any such grand scheme to reach India. The earliest fifteenth-century Portuguese voyages appear to have been inspired by more-immediately tangible goals such as religious crusades against Muslim North Africa and securing direct access to the gold of central Africa.

Atlantic Wind Patterns. Fifteenth-century Portuguese expeditions found that it was quite easy to sail southwest from Portugal down the coast of Africa. However, returning to Portugal by backtracking along the same route, they discovered, was nearly impossible. This was because prevailing winds along the coast of northwestern Africa typically blow from the northeast, part of a pattern that meteorologists call the "northeast trade winds." By trial, error, and accident, however, Portuguese vessels through the course of the fifteenth century gradually discovered that the return journey became somewhat easier if instead of returning directly to Portugal along the African coast they ventured far to the northwest out into the Atlantic Ocean. There, in the middle of the North Atlantic, the Portuguese found more convenient winds, the westerlies, that blew strongly from the west and made the return to Portugal a much quicker trip. It is likely that the uninhabited Azores, one-third of the way across the Atlantic Ocean, were in fact first sighted sometime in the 1420s or 1430s by Portuguese sailors taking this rather circular route home from the African coast. By the later decades of the fifteenth century, Portuguese mariners had become familiar with the clockwise wind patterns of the Atlantic: the prevailing northeast trade winds in the tropical latitudes and the dominant westerlies of the North Atlantic. During his years in Portugal in the 1470s and 1480s, Christopher Columbus learned about these wind patterns in his discussions with navigators. For the early-sixteenth-century Spaniards who sailed in Columbus's wake, the clockwise wind patterns of the Atlantic provided an ocean highway—the *carrera de Indias* as the Spanish called it—that carried them to their newly established empire in the Americas and back home again.

Atlantic Islands. Fifteenth-century Portuguese voyages thus led not only to greater familiarity with the African coastline but also to increasing knowledge of the various island groups in nearby ocean waters. The existence of some of these islands such as the Canaries had been known to Europeans for centuries. Others, including the faraway Cape Verde Islands and the Azores, were in fact first discovered by the fifteenth-century expeditions. It was in these Atlantic archipelagoes that Portugal and Spain took their first steps toward global empires, establishing patterns of occupation and colonization that would be followed later in the Americas and elsewhere. In the previously uninhabited Madeira Islands, for example, the Portuguese in the middle decades of the fifteenth century gradually developed a colony centered economically on the production of sugar. The Portuguese sugar plantations in the Madeiras relied heavily upon imported African slave labor. This marked the beginning of a colonial slave trade that would over the coming centuries carry millions of Africans away from their homes to faraway lands, where they would be put to forced labor in the emerging empires of European states. For their part the Spaniards began to stake nominal claims to the Canary Islands in the early 1400s. Unlike the Madeiras, however, the Canaries had long been inhabited, and the native Canarians often resisted Spanish incursions. Beginning in the 1470s various Spanish expeditions launched vigorous attacks to conquer the Canarians and establish stable colonies on the islands. Those natives who resisted were enslaved, foreshadowing later Spanish treatment of native populations in many regions of the Americas.

Source:
J. H. Parry, *The Age of Reconnaissance* (Cleveland: World, 1963).

GROWTH OF AN IDEA: COLUMBUS AND THE ENTERPRISE OF THE INDIES

Genoa. Christopher Columbus spent his childhood in the northern Italian coastal city of Genoa, a commercial power rich in maritime tradition. Columbus's father, Domenico, however, was no sailor. Instead he made a comfortable but by no means wealthy living as a wool weaver. Like his father the young Christopher learned to weave wool, but like many Genoese youth at the time, Columbus dreamed of pursuing glory at sea. Abandoning his father's trade, Columbus in the 1470s ventured out on several Genoese commercial and military expeditions across the Mediterranean Sea. Through the course of his many voyages, Columbus became familiar with the waters of the Mediterranean as well as the practice of navigation. Still in his twenties, Columbus also began to venture out of the Mediterranean on expeditions into the Atlantic Ocean.

Portugal Interlude. On a 1476 voyage along the Portuguese coast on the way to the Low Countries, Columbus's ship was reportedly sunk during a battle. According to a later biography written by his son Hernando, Columbus managed almost miraculously to survive this disaster by swimming many miles to the safety of the Portuguese shore. Whether or not we believe Hernando's dramatic claims, we do know that Columbus took up residence in Portugal around 1476 and lived there for nearly a decade. It was during this time that Columbus gradually came to believe in the possibility of sailing to Asia by going west across the Atlantic. The ideas that lay behind Columbus's "enterprise of the Indies"—his plan to reach Asia by sailing west—were by no means unique to him. Many fifteenth-century scholars had already considered and written about the possibility. Columbus himself retrospectively reported that the thought of two men had proven particularly important in providing scholarly support for his emerging scheme.

D'Ailly. Although Italy was Europe's center of geographical thought and speculation during the Renaissance, an influential voice from outside the area also contributed significantly to the era's growing debates concerning the size of the earth and relative positions of its continents. In 1410 the French clergyman Pierre d'Ailly completed his book *Imago Mundi* (Image of the World), and copies soon circulated throughout Europe. One argument advanced by d'Ailly in this book proved particularly interesting to geographers and sailors across fifteenth-century Europe. Based upon a passage from a book of the Apocrypha (ancient writings considered sacred by some Christians but which had been excluded from the Bible), d'Ailly argued that God had created the earth such that six-sevenths of its surface was covered by land and only one-seventh by water. If that were true and Asia, Africa, and Europe together covered six-sevenths of the earth, then the Atlantic Ocean must be quite small and the spherical globe as a whole much smaller than Eratosthenes and the ancients had imagined. D'Ailly's ideas in this regard inspired a century of speculation concerning the possibility of sailing west from Europe, across a supposedly small Atlantic Ocean, directly to the ports of East Asia. Columbus was particularly fascinated

A map of the New World from Abraham Oertel's *Theatrum orbis terrarum* (1570)

by this idea. His personal copy of d'Ailly's *Imago Mundi,* in fact, survives today in a library in Seville, Spain, and it is filled with notes scribbled in the margins by Columbus himself.

Toscanelli. Along with d'Ailly the Florentine geographer Paolo dal Pozzo Toscanelli proved highly influential in the formulation of Columbus's plan to reach Asia by sailing west. Born to wealthy Florentine parents, Toscanelli spent much of his life working for the powerful Medici banking family that dominated Florence's government. Meanwhile, Toscanelli also became a well-respected scholar in his own right, participating actively in the discussions and debates that were so common in his native city concerning geography, politics, and other matters. Based upon what he had learned in his readings of the works of Ptolemy, Strabo, Marco Polo, and other authorities, Toscanelli speculated that the overall size of Asia was probably much larger than previously realized. In a famous 1474 letter to Portuguese king John II, Toscanelli outlined the implications of this idea for European commerce. His letter suggested to the Portuguese monarch that the wealthy ports of East Asia must lay only a few thousand miles off of Europe's west coast. At the time, the Portuguese had long been engaged in efforts to reach Asia not by sailing west but rather by passing to the south around Africa and then east across the Indian Ocean. Convinced that these attempts would soon lead to success, the Portuguese monarch ignored Toscanelli's advice. However, while living in Portugal in the early 1480s, the young Genoese sailor Columbus heard about this letter and probably obtained a copy. Later biographers' reports that Columbus subsequently engaged in a personal correspondence with Toscanelli are almost certainly a myth, but it is true that the ideas in his 1474 letter provided further scholarly support for Columbus's plan to reach Asia by sailing west.

Source:
Pauline Moffit Watts, "Prophecy and Discovery: On the Spiritual Origins of Christopher Columbus's 'Enterprise of the Indies,'" *American Historical Review,* 90 (1985): 73–102.

MARINERS AND THEIR SHIPS: A REVOLUTION IN SHIP DESIGN

The Galley. Christopher Columbus's "enterprise of the Indies" and subsequent European overseas expansion would have been unthinkable without a variety of ship-building and navigational innovations that made it possible for fifteenth-century Europeans to sail across long stretches of treacherous ocean waters. Throughout the later Middle Ages trade and naval warfare on the Mediterranean and Atlantic coasts of Europe had been dominated by a class of ships called "galleys." They typically employed one square sail set on a central mast. Their principal source of power, however, was not the sail but rather a large number of oars that lined each side of the ship. Reliance on oar power carried both advantages and disadvantages for the captains and owners of galleys. On one hand the ships were not dependent upon the vicissitudes of the wind for their propulsion, and they could thus make forward progress at relatively steady and predictable speeds. For a Venetian merchant, for instance, his meant that a galley could be dispatched from Venice on a trading voyage to the eastern Mediterranean with a reasonable idea of when it would return to the home port. Such dependable scheduling was critical to commerce. On the other hand the galley also required large crews to man the oars. For this rather unpleasant task the Venetians and other commercial powers typically used convicts and prisoners of war. With such a large number of people on board, galley captains had to dedicate a great deal of cargo space to food and water as well as make frequent stops to obtain fresh supplies. For voyages in the Mediterranean or along Europe's Atlantic coast, where ports of call were plentiful, this was not a problem. For lengthy trips across the open ocean, however, the galley was impractical.

Iberian Roundships. Ships better suited for long-distance ocean travel developed gradually from the twelfth through the fifteenth century. The maritime powers of the Iberian peninsula (Portugal and Spain) provided the setting for a variety of technological innovations that contributed to the development of new sorts of vessels called "roundships." Unlike galleys Iberian roundships were propelled entirely by sails. Moreover they employed not only traditional square sails but also lateen (triangular) sails. While the square sail was the most efficient means of harnessing wind power when the wind blew from directly behind a ship, the lateen sail carried the advantage of being more easily rotated to take advantage of all sorts of contrary winds. By combining the two sorts of sails on the same vessel, Iberian roundships proved to be effective in a wide variety of sailing conditions. In addition, since they did not depend on oar power they carried crews that were much smaller than those of the galleys. Having on board fewer mouths to feed, a fully supplied roundship had a sailing range that far exceeded that of the galley. These roundships, as it turned out, generally could store just enough food and water to maintain their relatively small crews for a journey across the Atlantic Ocean to the Americas.

Caravel and Carrack. The earliest of these roundships was the caravel, a small but agile Portuguese vessel. Caravels, which existed in prototype form as early as the thirteenth century, were typically between twenty and thirty-five meters in length and extremely maneuverable. Fifteenth-century Portuguese mariners used these ships in their explorations along the coast of Africa and in lengthy voyages to the Madeira Islands and the faraway Azores. The Portuguese crown considered the caravel's technology an essential state secret, and a Portuguese man was in fact executed in 1454 for selling a ship to an English buyer. Despite their attempts the Portuguese monarchs found it impossible to keep the caravel technology entirely to themselves. Shipbuilders in southern Spain were constructing caravels of their own by the late fifteenth century. The Spanish also began to build a new class of roundships called carracks—ships which were two to three times larger than the Portuguese caravels.

A model of Christopher Columbus's *Santa Maria* (Mariners' Museum, Newport News, Virginia)

Together the caravel and carrack were the most-prominent ships in the early phases of European exploration and expansion in the years around 1500. The three ships used by Columbus in his 1492 voyage, for instance, included two caravels (the *Niña* and *Pinta*) and one carrack (the *Santa María*).

Source:
William D. Phillips Jr. and Carla Rahn Phillips, *The Worlds of Christopher Columbus* (Cambridge, U.K.: Cambridge University Press, 1992).

MARINERS AND THEIR SHIPS: THE TECHNOLOGY OF NAVIGATION

Magnetic Compass. Accurate navigation on the open ocean requires precise knowledge of a ship's direction of travel. Experienced sailors can make reasonably good estimations of travel direction based upon the position of the sun in the daytime sky and the North Star at night. This sort of informed guesswork, however, was often not sufficiently accurate to lead fifteenth-century ships on lengthy journeys across open water to a small point in the middle of the ocean such as the Azores. Moreover in cloudy conditions when the precise positions of the sun and North Star in the sky are indeterminable, even experienced mariners such as Christopher Columbus could find themselves helplessly lost if they depended exclusively on this sort of navigation. Missing one's target in the open ocean could be fatal; ships that became lost at sea often ran out of supplies of food or fresh water before the crews could reorient themselves and find their way

A page from a sixteenth-century astronomy book predicting
a total eclipse of the moon on 29 February 1504
(British Library, London)

the position of the North Star in the night sky as their primary point of reference for determining latitude. The further north one sailed, the higher in the sky (in other words the more distant from the horizon) the North Star would appear. Skillful mariners could make fairly accurate estimations of their latitude by using only naked-eye observations. Precise navigation, however, required precise calculation of the distance between the horizon and the North Star. To ensure the accuracy of their calculations, navigators used a variety of tools, including astrolabes and quadrants. Astrolabes were typically circular in shape with two viewing holes on the circumference. A moving pointer attached to the center of the circle would remain parallel to the horizon as the navigator pointed the instrument at the North Star. Once the viewing holes were aligned with the star, the sailor would read the angle between the viewing holes and the pointer and from this data calculate the latitude of the ship. Quadrants worked in a similar manner except that they were shaped only as quarter circles, and as a result they were much lighter in weight than the bulky astrolabes. Although astrolabes and quadrants enabled mariners to make observations that were more accurate than those made only by the naked eye, they were still far from perfectly dependable. On the deck of a rolling ship tossed by ocean swells, for instance, it was often difficult to maintain the steady hand necessary to make accurate calculations using an astrolabe or quadrant.

"Dead Reckoning." Although fifteenth-century European mariners gradually improved their ability to calculate latitude by using tools such as the astrolabe and quadrant, they remained almost entirely perplexed by the problem of determining longitudinal position while at sea. The problem of discerning how far east or west a ship had sailed continued to vex European navigators throughout the age of exploration and expansion. Only in the eighteenth century, in fact, would an English clockmaker named John Harrison provide an effective solution to the problem of determining longitude in the open ocean. In the meantime Renaissance-era mariners such as Columbus had to depend upon a variety of primitive techniques that collectively constituted a process called "dead reckoning." Dead reckoning required that a

back to land. Because of such dangers fifteenth-century European sailors traveling across ocean waters increasingly depended upon the navigational aid provided by the magnetic compass. The compass was not originally a European invention; the Chinese were already using it as a navigational device by 1000 A.D. The earliest European reference to the magnetic compass dates to the twelfth century. Some historians claim that Muslim traders brought compass technology to the Mediterranean from Asia, while others assert that the Europeans invented their own version independently. Regardless of how they obtained it, some Europeans suspected that the apparently mystical power of the compass needle derived ultimately from black magic or even the devil himself. Pilots at times had to keep their compass needles and the lodestones by which the needles were remagnetized hidden from view in order not to raise suspicion. Nonetheless by the late 1400s the magnetic compass had become an essential tool among European navigators.

Astrolabes and Quadrants. Accurate navigation among fifteenth-century European mariners also depended upon their ability to determine the latitudinal position (the distance north or south of the equator) of their ships. In the northern hemisphere navigators used

Ship's compass, circa 1500 (National Maritime
Museum, London)

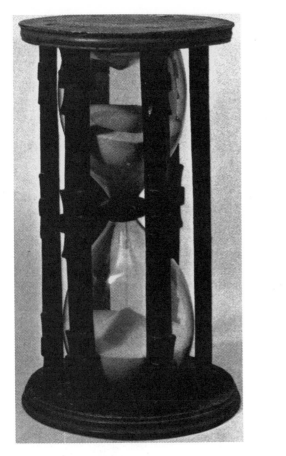

A sandglass and an astrolabe, both used circa 1500 (National Maritime Museum, London)

navigator keep painstakingly careful track not only of a ship's direction of travel but also the speed of that travel and the length of time spent in traveling that direction. The magnetic compass made it possible to keep fairly accurate record of direction of travel. With regard to measuring speed and time, however, fifteenth-century mariners faced debilitating technological limitations. To measure speed, for instance, the best that Columbus and his contemporaries could do was simply to throw into the water at the bow of the ship a rope with knots tied at regular intervals and then observe how quickly the moving ship's hull passed the knots. Measurement of time at sea was similarly primitive. The constant movement and rolling of a ship combined with the corrosive effects of salty ocean air made fifteenth-century European clocks virtually useless on the open sea. As a result most European ships in the age of exploration relied upon the simple, primitive sand hourglass, a device of limited accuracy at best since it required that a crew member attentively turn the glass over each and every hour of the day and night at the precise moment when the sand ran out. Faced with such limitations, determination of longitude was highly inexact and often depended as much upon the instincts of the navigator as it did upon concrete data. As one recent historian has noted, dead reckoning was an appropriate name for this process since it frequently left entire crews for dead, lost at sea.

Sources:

William D. Phillips Jr. and Carla Rahn Phillips, *The Worlds of Christopher Columbus* (Cambridge, U.K.: Cambridge University Press, 1992);

Dava Sobel, *Longitude: The True Story of a Lone Genius Who Solved the Greatest Scientific Problem of His Day* (New York: Walker, 1995).

THE MILITARY REVOLUTION AND EUROPEAN EXPANSION

Constant Warfare. Europeans in the age of exploration and expansion held a significant military advantage over nearly all of the people they encountered when they traveled to other parts of the globe. European military prowess grew largely from technological advances made by the major powers as they fought one another almost incessantly throughout the Renaissance era. Before 1350 Europe's military technology was generally no more advanced than that which could be found among the other major civilizations of the late medieval world. As late as 1415 at the height of the Hundred Years' War, English king Henry V led a highly successful invasion of France with a small army of only about eight thousand men. Moreover the most effective battlefield weapon during Henry's campaign in France that year was the Welsh longbow, an efficient weapon for its time but hardly an engine of mass destruction. In short Europeans at the dawn of the Renaissance may even have been significantly behind the Muslims, Chinese, and other major world civilizations in their ability to make war. Nearly two centuries later, however, late-sixteenth-century European states often fielded armies then numbered in the hundreds of thousands, armed with much more destructive weaponry including artillery and primitive muskets. The dramatic transformation of European warfare in the fifteenth and sixteenth centuries has been said by some historians to have constituted a military revolution. The elements of this revolution provide important clues to an explanation of how European states were able to build far-reaching empires in the Americas and around the globe in the age of exploration and expansion.

Gunpowder and Firearms. Ironically the use of gunpowder and firearms in battle was not originally a European invention. The Chinese had discovered the correct formula for gunpowder as early as the ninth century A.D., and by the mid 1200s Chinese armies were already using metal-barreled cannon in battle. The earliest evidence of such artillery in Europe, by contrast, dates only to the mid 1300s. In addition to cannon European armies in the Renaissance era began to make use of primitive handheld firearms called arquebuses, the bulky precursors of the musket. Whether in China or Europe, however, the military usefulness of early firearms was limited by several factors. First, these early guns were dangerous to use; they were nearly as likely to explode in the faces of those firing them as they were to inflict damage on the enemy. Second, they had extremely limited range and accuracy compared to more-traditional missile weapons such as the longbow. Finally, the usefulness of early firearms was limited by the length of time needed to reload. Whereas a well-trained archer could discharge up to ten arrows a minute, for example, it typically took a fifteenth-century arquebusier several minutes just to load his weapon once. Despite their limited effectiveness on European battlefields, Spanish conquerors in the sixteenth-century Americas always took along at least some firearms on their campaigns. Among the natives of the Americas who had never seen such weaponry, the roar of European cannon and muskets according to many reports frequently inspired fear and dread.

From Castles to Forts. Even if primitive Renaissance-era firearms rarely proved decisive in open battles, their effects on European warfare were nonetheless far-reaching. Over the centuries preceding the Renaissance, for example, the lofty walls of medieval castles had proven largely impenetrable from direct assaults by even the best-equipped European armies. Fifteenth-century cannon, however, could reduce even large and well-defended castles to rubble in a matter of hours. The

THE BLACK LEGEND

Spain was the first European state to establish a territorial empire in the Americas. Through the course of their conquests in the Caribbean, Mexico, and Central and South America, the Spaniards developed a reputation for cruel treatment of conquered Native American populations. Spain's enemies in Europe (the French, Dutch, and English) exploited tales of Spanish atrocities in the New World to build a popular image of Spain as an "evil empire." These stories collectively contributed to what historians call the Black Legend of Spanish cruelty.

Spain's reputation was partly deserved. It is true, for instance, that Spanish conquistadores and colonial settlers often treated conquered populations inhumanely. It is also true that the Native Americans died by the millions in the wake of Spain's imperial expansion. The principal cause of death and suffering was not, however, Spanish weapons but rather the inadvertent introduction of Old World diseases such as smallpox and measles against which the populations of the Americas had no immunity. Far from celebrating the mass slaughter wrought by diseases among the American natives, Spanish authorities took whatever feeble steps they could to stop the epidemics. After all, the Spanish wanted more souls to convert to Christianity and more laborers to put to work,

not more dead bodies. In general, official Spanish crown policies through the 1500s sought to protect the natives of conquered areas from abuse by Spanish settlers. From across the Atlantic Ocean, however, effective enforcement of royal policies proved impossible, and exploitation of conquered populations continued in many areas.

Ironically it was a Spanish critic of these abuses who provided the fuel for the Black Legend as it spread across Europe: the Dominican friar Bartolomé de las Casas. Las Casas wrote a scathing book about his countrymen's cruel treatment of the natives of the Caribbean islands titled *The Devastation of the Indies: A Brief Account* (1552). In the second half of the sixteenth century, his book was translated into French and English, and his stories of Spanish atrocities became the basis for popular disdain of the Spaniards in other areas of Europe. When France and England began to attempt to establish their own permanent colonial settlements in the Americas in the late sixteenth and seventeenth centuries, they often expected to be welcomed by the Native American populations as protectors against the universally despised Spaniards.

Source: Anthony Pagden, *Lords of All the World: Ideologies of Empire in Spain, Britain, and France c. 1500–1800* (New Haven, Conn. & London: Yale University Press, 1995).

advent of artillery in European warfare thus led to a radical transformation in defensive fortifications. Beginning in Italy in the late fifteenth and sixteenth centuries, Europeans began to abandon old medieval castle designs with their tall, thin walls and build instead new styles of fortifications characterized by low, thick walls that could withstand repeated barrages of cannon fire. Moreover the jagged outer works of these new-style forts allowed defending garrisons to fire directly on any attacking army that approached its low walls. By the mid sixteenth century this new style of fortification in Europe had become quite effective in resisting assault. When applied by the Spanish and Portuguese to their growing overseas empires in the sixteenth century, this system of fortification provided bases of colonial operation that proved nearly impregnable. A well-preserved sixteenth-century example of this sort of colonial fortification survives today in San Juan, Puerto Rico.

Sources:

Geoffrey Parker, *The Military Revolution: Military Innovation and the Rise of the West, 1500–1800* (Cambridge, U.K.: Cambridge University Press, 1988);

Brian Tierney and Sidney Painter, *Western Europe in the Middle Ages, 300–1475*, third edition (New York: Knopf, 1978).

POWER AND PATRONAGE: COLUMBUS'S SEARCH FOR FINANCIAL SUPPORT

Searching for a Patron. Driven by his belief in the possibility of quickly reaching Asia by sailing west, as well as by his notion of having a divinely ordained role in preparing the world for the apocalypse, Christopher Columbus in the 1480s actively sought financial support for his ambitious scheme. Columbus first brought his "enterprise of the Indies" to the attention of Portuguese king John II, who was initially excited by the idea. In 1484 or 1485, however, a crown-appointed committee of Portuguese scholars rejected Columbus's plan as unsound. The committee's decision was not, contrary to popular myth, founded upon a rejection of the idea that the earth was round. The committee's decision was based upon three considerations. First, the committee believed that Eratosthenes's ancient estimate of an earth nearly twenty-five thousand miles in circumference was correct. Second, they rejected as misguided Pierre d'Ailly's underestimation of the size of the Atlantic Ocean. Third, they similarly rejected Paolo dal Pozzo Toscanelli's estimation of the size of Asia as exaggerated. In short they argued that if their calculations were correct Asia simply lay too far away to be reached by European vessels sailing west. In fact we retrospectively know that it was the committee members and not Columbus who held the more accurate view of East Asia's location on the globe and its distance from Europe's western shores. Neither the committee nor Columbus, of course, realized that there were actually two large continents heretofore unknown to Europeans standing between Europe and Asia. By being correct, ironically, the committee members' decisions prevented Portugal from becoming the first European state to access the as-yet-unforeseen riches of the Americas. Although disheartened by the Portuguese crown's rejection, Columbus did not simply give up. Instead he left Portugal in 1485 and went to Spain, where he hoped to secure the backing of the powerful monarchs Isabella and Ferdinand.

Rejection in Spain. When Columbus first proposed his plan to the Spanish crown in 1486, Isabella and Ferdinand were engaged in a costly war against the Muslim kingdom of Granada in southern Spain. Financially burdened by the war, the Catholic monarchs had little money to spare to fund expeditions such as the one offered by Columbus. Nonetheless the Genoese mariner's scheme interested them enough to appoint a committee to study his proposal. Like the Portuguese committee before it, however, the assembled group of Spanish scholars rejected Columbus's plans as unsound. Again disheartened, Columbus in 1488 returned briefly to Portugal to present his case anew to the Portuguese king. Unfortunately for Columbus, however, he arrived in Lisbon just as the Portuguese mariner Bartolomeu Dias was returning from his landmark voyage with the news that he had reached the southern tip of the African continent. From the point of view of the Portuguese crown, Columbus's proposed scheme was unnecessary and redundant since Portuguese ships would soon be making regular trips directly to the ports of Asia by rounding Africa.

Reconsideration. Realizing the hopelessness of gaining Portuguese support, Columbus once again returned to Spain in hope that Isabella and Ferdinand would reconsider. A second Spanish royal commission in 1491, however, again rejected Columbus's scheme. Weary from his failures in Iberia, Columbus planned to set off for the north, hoping that the king of France might be more helpful. Fortunately for Columbus, however, Isabella and Ferdinand on 2 January 1492 finally concluded their war with Granada by obtaining a surrender agreement from the city's Muslim emir. Freed from their wartime financial burdens and anxious not to let the Asian trade fall exclusively into the hands of the Portuguese, the Catholic monarchs ignored their advisors and decided to take a chance on Columbus's eccentric scheme. After having visited the king and queen in Granada and heard of the commission's rejection of his idea, however, Columbus had already set off for France by the time Isabella and Ferdinand finally decided to finance the expedition. The crown's messengers caught up with the dejected Columbus some twelve miles north of Granada. From there, as one recent historian has so dramatically put it, Columbus "turned back to Granada and into the pages of history."

Source:

William D. Phillips Jr. and Carla Rahn Phillips, *The Worlds of Christopher Columbus* (Cambridge, U.K.: Cambridge University Press, 1992).

RECONNAISSANCE: COLUMBUS'S VOYAGES

First Voyage. Christopher Columbus left Spain for his epochal journey on 3 August 1492 with only a tiny fleet of three ships—the small caravels *Niña* and *Pinta* and the larger carrack *Santa María*. Together the three vessels carried a total of only ninety men, including Columbus himself. Putting to good use the knowledge of Atlantic wind patterns that he had learned from Portuguese sailors, Columbus chose to begin his journey west by first sailing south to the Canary Islands, where he could pick up the northeast trade winds that would carry him westward across the ocean. On 6 September Columbus's fleet left the Canaries, venturing into the unknown waters of the west. Based upon his own speculations Columbus expected to reach Asia within a few weeks at most if he maintained a steady westerly course. He was, of course, mistaken. A month after their departure from the Canaries, Columbus's ships still had not encountered land, and his crew began to grow restless. At least twice during the early days of October, Columbus faced near mutinies among crew members who insisted that he turn the fleet around and return to Spain. Each time Columbus firmly asserted that Asia must be nearby and that the expedition should continue westward for just a few more days. Finally, on 12 October the three ships and their relieved captain made landfall on a small island in the Bahamas, an island that Columbus believed until his death to have been located near the Asian mainland. The crew celebrated, and Columbus himself went ashore with a landing party to claim the land in the name of the Spanish crown.

Initial Encounters. As Columbus and his men quickly discovered, the island upon which they had landed was not uninhabited. Unfortunately there is no firsthand record of what the natives of this island thought of their strange visitors. Believing that he was near India, Columbus called the natives "Indians," and he described them as generally timid on first contact but later quite friendly and eager to trade with the crew. Yet Columbus and his men found themselves somewhat confused by the fact that the culture of these islanders bore little resemblance to the wealthy and bustling ports of Asia about which they had read in Marco Polo's travel accounts. Even across the almost insurmountable language barrier that separated the islanders from the Europeans, the natives managed to communicate to Columbus that many other lands lay nearby. The mariner thought that these must house the great Asian civilizations of which Marco Polo had spoken. The Spanish ships then spent the next few months continuing their search, wandering through the Bahamas and other islands of the Caribbean, including Cuba and Hispaniola. Nowhere, however, did they find the sorts of wealthy and populous cities that they had expected to find in Asia.

Homeward. On the coast of Hispaniola on Christmas Eve 1492, disaster struck the expedition. Columbus's flagship, the *Santa María*, ran aground and was wrecked Unable to carry his entire crew on the two remaining small caravels, Columbus was forced to leave thirty-nine men behind on Hispaniola in a makeshift fort that became the first European settlement in the Americas since the Vikings' short-lived colony on Newfoundland some five centuries earlier. Columbus gave the settlement the name La Navidad (Spanish for Christmas) in honor of the day on which it was established. After a difficult return journey plagued by navigational mishaps, Columbus and his two ships finally returned to Spain in March 1493. He brought with him not only the startling news of having found many islands that he believed to be near the Asian mainland but he brought also, probably against their will, some natives of those islands. Word of Columbus's voyage spread quickly across Europe, and others would soon follow his path across the Atlantic.

Later Voyages. Columbus subsequently made three more voyages to the Caribbean region, one in 1493–1496, another in 1498–1500, and the last in 1502–1504. In 1493 Columbus returned to the site of La Navidad only to find that the men he had left there a year earlier had mysteriously disappeared. Local natives reported that after Columbus's departure the settlers had quarreled among themselves and aroused the hostility of nearby native groups by forcibly seizing gold and supplies from villages. As a result all the Spaniards had been killed. After the disappearance of La Navidad, however, the Spaniards over the next two decades began to establish more-lasting settlements on the Caribbean islands, first on Hispaniola and later on Cuba and Puerto Rico. The Spaniards then enslaved much of the local populations on these islands and put them to work mining for gold.

Death. By the time Columbus died in 1506 other Europeans had already begun to speculate that the lands he had "discovered" were in fact not parts of or islands near the Asian landmass but rather a "New World" previously unknown to Europe. Despite the fact that none of his voyages revealed anything akin to medieval travelers' descriptions of the legendary civilizations of Asia, Columbus himself remained steadfast in his conviction that he had led Europe to Asia by sailing west. He also continued to assert that his journeys had been missions assigned to him by God in order to prepare the world for the rapidly approaching end of time. In the final years of his life Columbus even published a book in which he cited biblical references that he believed prophesied his voyages and their role as precursors to the apocalypse.

Source:
Pauline Moffit Watts, "Prophecy and Discovery: On the Spiritual Origins of Christopher Columbus's 'Enterprise of the Indies,'" *American Historical Review*, 90 (1985): 73–102.

In addition to plant and animal species a variety of diseases were highly significant aspects of the Columbian Exchange. To the Americas, for instance, the Europeans brought smallpox, a malady native only to the Old World and against which the people of the Americas had no immunity. In the centuries following Christopher Columbus's first voyage in 1492, native populations throughout the Caribbean region as well as North and South American mainlands succumbed by the millions to the deadly disease.

From the Americas, Europeans did not bring back to the Old World anything as wantonly destructive as smallpox. They did, however, bring back syphilis, a sexually transmitted disease native to the Americas and previously unknown in the Old World. It appears that the disease may have been first introduced into Europe by the returning crews of Columbus's early voyages themselves since the earliest reported outbreaks of syphilis in Spain and Italy date to the mid 1490s. From there the disease spread quickly, bringing chronic pain, suffering, and death to hundreds of thousands of victims throughout sixteenth-century Europe.

European doctors at the time had no idea how to cure syphilis. The most-common treatments of the disease in sixteenth-century Europe were not only ineffective but also extremely painful. One common treatment included, for instance, the rubbing of the bodily sores caused by syphilis with mercury. Baffled by the disease, many European physicians and their patients began also to experiment with treatments that involved the use of the wood of a New World tree known as *guayacum,* a plant native to the Caribbean island of Haiti. Despite the fact that the results of such treatment were scarcely more effective than mercury and certainly did not constitute a cure, Europe continued to import shiploads of Haitian guayacum throughout the sixteenth century.

Source: J. S. Cummins, "Pox and Paranoia in Renaissance Europe," *History Today,* 38 (August 1988): 28–35.

RECONNAISSANCE: THE NEW CONTINENTS AND THEIR PLACE IN THE WORLD

The Italian Connection. The Iberian maritime powers, Spain and Portugal, spearheaded European expansion in the era of Columbus, and the French and English crowns soon followed in the sixteenth and seventeenth centuries with colonization attempts of their own. Yet many of the earliest voyages commissioned by the monarchs of these western European states were actually headed by Italian captains. Although his voyages laid the foundations for a Spanish overseas empire, for example, Christopher Columbus had originally come from the Italian city of Genoa. Similarly another Genoese sailor, John Cabot, led a 1497 expedition to the North American coast in the name of English king Henry VII. In addition Renaissance Italy's cultural and intellectual capital, Florence, produced two mariners who headed other significant early voyages of exploration in the service of foreign monarchs. Amerigo Vespucci sailed alternatively in the service of Spain and Portugal, and his compatriot Giovanni da Verrazano made a 1524 voyage in the service of French king Francis I along the eastern coast of North America. The prevalence of Italians among the early European explorers was no mere coincidence. Italy had after all been Europe's center of geographical thought and speculation throughout the fifteenth century. Moreover the Italians also held an interest in maintaining a prominent place in European commerce even as the continent's economic center of gravity was shifting away from their native Mediterranean and toward the Atlantic seaboard.

The Naming of America. Although our popular culture today credits Columbus with the "discovery" of America, he did not receive the honor of having the two continents of the New World named after him; that distinction fell instead upon Vespucci. The naming of the two continents of the western hemisphere North and South "America" rather than North and South "Columbia" aroused heated controversy in the years following the deaths of Columbus and Vespucci in 1506 and 1512, respectively. For instance, the famous Spanish clergyman Bartolomé de las Casas, who admired Columbus greatly even as he criticized the cruel treatment of Caribbean natives by Spanish settlers, angrily charged that Vespucci had unjustly stolen the honor that rightly pertained to Columbus. Vespucci was a wealthy and well-educated man who worked for the powerful Medici banking family. In 1492 he was sent to Spain to oversee Medici business interests there. Between 1499 and 1502 Vespucci made several voyages across the Atlantic exploring the Caribbean region visited by Columbus as well as the coast of mainland South America. On these trips Vespucci gradually came to the conclusion that these lands were nowhere near Asia but instead constituted what he called a previously unknown "New World." His detailed account of his experiences was translated into nearly all major European languages, published in various editions, and circulated throughout early-sixteenth-century western and central Europe. In short the attribution of his name to the newly found continents instead of Columbus's had a great deal to do with superior public relations. Contrary to Las Casas's accusations, however,

Vespucci himself appears to have played no direct, personal role in the application of his own name to the new continents. Instead that connection was first made without Vespucci's knowledge by a group of mapmakers headed by Martin Waldseemüller at the monastery of St. Dié in France. The 1507 map drawn by this group placed the name America only on the South American continent. The mapmakers justified the appellation by claiming that it was Vespucci and not Columbus who had first recognized these lands for what they actually were: a new continent. The landmark 1538 world map of the famous cartographer Gerardus Mercator first extended the usage of the name America to the North American continent.

Passages to Asia. The gradual realization that Columbus's voyages had not reached Asia but rather had accidentally bumped into a New World previously unknown to Europeans did not stop European states from continuing their search for a convenient oceanic trading route to Asia. A 1497–1499 expedition headed by Vasco da Gama finally brought to a successful completion the long Portuguese search for a route around Africa's southern tip to the lucrative markets of India. In the years following da Gama's visit to India, the Portuguese gradually built a commercial empire that included fortified trading posts on the African coast as well as along the shore of India itself. The Portuguese later expanded this commercial empire to include fortified posts in Malaysia near the Spice Islands of Indonesia. As a result of their efforts the Portuguese had finally broken the long-standing Muslim and Venetian stranglehold on Asian trade, and Portugal replaced Venice as Europe's capital of overseas commerce.

Magellan. With substantially less-successful results the Spanish also managed to find their own all-water route to Asia through a 1519–1522 expedition led ironically by a Portuguese captain working for the Spanish crown, Ferdinand Magellan. His expedition pioneered a southwesterly route to Asia by passing through the perilous straits (later named the Straits of Magellan) near South America's southern tip. From there the expedition proceeded directly across the Pacific Ocean to East Asia. Magellan himself died in a 1521 skirmish with some natives of the Philippine Islands. Led by the expedition's senior surviving officer, Juan Sebastian del Cano, the surviving crew members then struggled across the Indian Ocean and around the southern tip of Africa, finally returning to Spain in 1522. In the process del Cano and his crew became the first expedition to circumnavigate the entire globe. This achievement was by itself noteworthy. Their three-year trip, however, had proven deadly for the majority of the crew. Of an original expedition contingent of 4 ships and some 250 men, only 1 ship and 18 surviving crew members managed to complete the journey. Their news that there existed a navigable southwesterly passage to Asia also aroused some excitement, but the dangerous Antarctic waters of South America's southern tip proved too treacherous to provide a practical path for regular trade with Asia.

Sources:

Daniel Boorstin, *The Discoverers: A History of Man's Search to Know His World and Himself* (New York: Vintage, 1983);

Carl Ortwin Sauer, *Sixteenth-Century North America: The Land and Its People as Seen by Europeans* (Berkeley and London: University of California Press, 1971).

RECONNAISSANCE: VOYAGES TO NORTH AMERICA

Cabot. The life and navigational career of John Cabot (Giovanni Caboto) in many ways parallel that of his contemporary and fellow Genoa native Christopher Columbus. Like Columbus, Cabot sought and eventually attained the financial backing of a foreign monarch for a voyage west into the Atlantic in hope of reaching Asia. Also like Columbus, Cabot appears to have believed until his death that the lands he found on his westerly voyage were extensions of the Asian landmass. Cabot left his native Genoa in 1495 and settled in England, where he managed to convince the customarily frugal King Henry VII to fund his plan for a westerly journey to Asia. Cabot's 1497 voyage carried him all the way to the coast of New England from which he sailed northward perhaps as far as Newfoundland and Labrador, claiming the entire region for the English crown. Cabot's expedition

Illustration of a New World plant, the sunflower, from Rembert Dodoens' *Florum et coronariarum odoratarumque nonullarum herbarum historia* (1568)

constituted the first recorded European visit to the North American continental mainland since the time of the Vikings. Cabot himself, however, had no idea of the extent or nature of the continent that he had found, and his attempts at further exploration came to an abrupt end when during a 1498 return voyage his ship was lost at sea.

Northwest Passage. By the 1520s it was clear that the Portuguese dominated the southeastern passage to Asia via Africa's southern tip, and all at the time agreed that Ferdinand Magellan's southwestern passage was commercially impractical. The combination of these facts led Spanish, French, and English expeditions at various times in the sixteenth century to target the North American coastline with the object of locating a supposed northwestern passage through which their ships could sail on their way to Asia. We know today that no such natural waterway through the North American continent exists south of the Arctic circle. To sixteenth-century European mariners, however, the thousands of bays, harbors, and rivers from the Gulf of Mexico in the south to the coast of Labrador in the north offered various intriguing possibilities.

Verrazano and Cartier. By 1523 word arrived in France of the difficulties encountered by the Magellan expedition at the southern tip of South America. In response to the news French king Francis I, always looking for ways to gain the upper hand over his Spanish enemies, financed a voyage to search for a northwestern passage through North America. The expedition, headed by the Florentine navigator Giovanni da Verrazano, made landfall in North America near Cape Hattaras (North Carolina) in 1524. From there Verrazano moved north, charting the coast all the way to the New York harbor and the New England shore before turning back to France. Verrazano returned from this trip with extensive information regarding the geography and native populations of North America's eastern coast but no answer to the question of a northwestern passage. France's search resumed in 1534–1536 when Jacques Cartier led a series of similarly fruitless expeditions in the region of the Gulf of St. Lawrence and St. Lawrence River. Following Cartier, however, French interest in North America subsided.

English and Spanish Attempts. The English and Spanish had no more luck than the French in finding a waterway through North America. Sailing for England in 1508–1509, Sebastian Cabot, the son of John Cabot, made an early attempt to locate a northwestern passage in the icy waters to the north of Newfoundland and the Labrador coast. The details of his course of travel are unclear, but he may even have entered the straits leading into Hudson Bay. After Cabot's voyage, however, the English withdrew for decades from New World exploration. Cabot himself soon left England and settled in Spain, where he managed to obtain a high post in the Spanish colonial administration in Seville. Meanwhile some sixteenth-century Spanish expeditions also sought a pas-

Woodcut of an American bison from Francisco López de Gómara's *La historia general de las Indias* (1554)

sage through North America. By the 1520s the Spanish had concluded that there was no strait leading westward from the Caribbean or Gulf of Mexico. In 1525 Estéban Díaz led a Spanish expedition up the eastern coast of North America in search of a passage, exploring and charting the same regions that had been visited only a year earlier by Verrazano. Despite the fruitlessness of the search, the dream of locating a northwestern passage to Asia would continue to draw explorers to North American waters well into the seventeenth century.

Source:

Carl Ortwin Sauer, *Sixteenth-Century North America: The Land and Its People as Seen by Europeans* (Berkeley and London: University of California Press, 1971).

A REVOLUTION IN CARTOGRAPHY: MAPPING THE WORLD

Clarity. The evolution of sixteenth-century maps clearly reflects the Europeans' expanding knowledge of the world around them. No longer were questions regarding the breadth of the Atlantic Ocean or the size and relative positions of the earth's major continents matters of simple speculation. Nor did sixteenth-century geographers or navigators feel compelled to consult the texts of ancient authorities on such matters. Instead cartographers increasingly based their representations of the world on concrete data and empirical observation. In addition they developed new, more-accurate methods of portraying the three-dimensional globe on flat, two-dimensional surfaces. It is true that problems such as the inability of navigators and chartmakers to measure longitude accurately while at sea continued to lead to some distortion and imprecision in European maps of the era. Nonetheless, in terms of the general outlines and relative positions of the oceans and continents, late-sixteenth-century European world maps began to look similar to those that we produce today with our advanced surveying techniques and satellite technology.

State Secrets. Many of the most-comprehensive sixteenth-century maps were, at the time they were made, accessible only to a small group of government officials. This was because Spain and Portugal held the geographical data collected by their sailors to be critical state secrets. Navigators returning from voyages of exploration in the crown's service were required to report their findings and charts to colonial administrators in charge of collecting such information. From the compiled data cartographers would draw and update secret official maps. These maps would then be kept under lock and key in order to prevent hard-won and strategically significant information from falling into unfriendly hands. One of the most interesting of these secret documents is a representation of the Atlantic world drawn by Spanish royal cartographer Juan de la Cosa in the year 1500, a map whose secrecy was guarded so effectively that historians learned of its existence only in the nineteenth century. De la Cosa almost certainly had personal experience navigating Caribbean waters, and he may even have accompanied Columbus on his first voyage in 1492. The map summarizes official Spanish understanding of the geography of the Caribbean and the Americas. The major Caribbean islands are represented with reasonable accuracy. The map also shows the South American mainland, and the North American mainland is marked with an English flag, indicating that de la Cosa had heard word of the 1497 voyage of John Cabot. Between 1525 and 1532 the cartographer Diego Ribeiro produced another set of official secret charts for the Spanish government. Ribeiro's representation of the world incorporated the data collected by all Spanish voyages up to that point including that of the crew of the Magellan expedition that had circled the globe in 1519–1522. Not surprisingly the strategic and commercial value of secret maps such as these attracted occasional efforts at espionage. While working in Spain's colonial administrative offices in Seville, for instance, Sebastian Cabot attempted to sell secret Spanish charts to the English and the Venetians.

Maps for Public Consumption. As the sixteenth century progressed, however, geographical knowledge could not be kept secret for long. Along with the official secret charts of the Spanish and Portuguese governments, other maps summarizing up-to-date geographical information began to be published and broadly distributed. The 1507 map drawn and published by Martin Waldseemüller and his colleagues at St. Dié, France, quickly sold more than one thousand copies. Ironically, Waldseemüller himself later decided that he had erred in applying Amerigo Vespucci's name to the New World, and in later editions of the map he deleted the name America. Waldseemüller's change of heart, however, counted for little in the face of the power of the printing press. The name America on the original 1507 map was already too broadly disseminated and too widely used to be withdrawn, and the label stuck.

Mercator. The most skillful of all sixteenth-century cartographers was the Flemish scholar Gerardus Merca-

tor. He is best remembered as the inventor of what came to be called the Mercator projection, a method of depicting the curved surface of the earth on a flat, two-dimensional chart without distorting compass-heading directional relationships between any two points on the map. The Mercator projection was particularly useful to navigators, and it remains even today one of the most commonly used projections in modern cartography. Mercator produced his first world map in 1538 and then spent much of the rest of his life working on various mapmaking projects. By the time of his death in 1594 he had nearly completed a comprehensive atlas of maps summarizing the best available geographic data of the day. Following his death, his son put the finishing touches on the work and published the landmark three-volume book in 1595. It was in fact the first printed collection of maps to carry the title atlas. Copies sold quickly, and thirty-one editions of Mercator's atlas were published in the years following its original appearance.

Sources:

Daniel J. Boorstin, *The Discoverers: A History of Man's Search to Know His World and Himself* (New York: Vintage, 1983);

Carl Ortwin Sauer, *Sixteenth-Century North America: The Land and Its People as Seen by Europeans* (Berkeley and London: University of California Press, 1971).

THE TRANSFORMATION OF POST-COLUMBIAN EUROPE: THE IMPACT OF CONTACT

Old and New Worlds. For the first time in recorded history, the voyages of Christopher Columbus established regular, sustained long-term contact between the civilizations and cultures of the American New World on the one hand and those of the Old World of Europe, Africa, and Asia on the other. For the people of the Americas, the arrival of the Europeans obviously had far-reaching consequences that radically transformed their lives. From the point of view of native Americans, the legacy of this contact was largely negative. European conquest and imperialism, the enslavement of native populations in many areas, and outbreaks of Old World diseases such as smallpox against which the Americans had no immunity resulted in widespread death and suffering. Yet the Atlantic Ocean in the age of exploration and expansion was not simply a one-way street. Contact with the Americas also had far-reaching social, cultural, and intellectual implications for the natives of the Old World. In Europe, for example, sustained contact with the Americas substantially transformed fields of thought and endeavor as diverse as agriculture and medicine as well as geography and cartography.

The Columbian Exchange. The voyages of Columbus initiated a massive transhemispheric mutual exchange of plants, animals, and diseases that historians collectively call the Columbian Exchange. Europeans brought to the Americas, for instance, a variety of plant and animal species native to the Old World and previously unknown in the New World. These European introductions into the New World included, for example, wheat and the horse—two

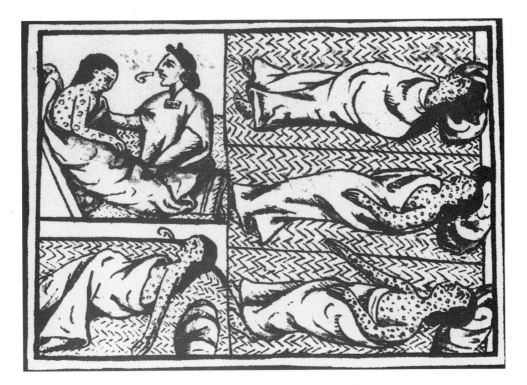

Sixteenth-century engraving of Native American smallpox victims

species that have had enormous impact in reshaping the cultures and landscapes of the Americas. Similarly many species native only to the New World were first introduced to Europeans by travelers returning from the Americas, resulting in a transformation of European agriculture and diets. Today, for instance, it is difficult for us to imagine Italian cuisine without tomato sauce. Yet tomatoes are native to the Americas, and they were introduced to Italy and the rest of Europe only after 1492. Similarly maize, or corn, and many varieties of beans are crops native to the Americas which, after their introduction into Europe during the age of exploration and expansion, gradually came to play significant roles in European agriculture. From Europe many of these New World crops later spread to Asia and Africa, bringing about significant dietary changes among civilizations throughout the Old World. In the long term no American plant species has had greater impact on Old World diets than the potato. Yet when it was first brought back from the Americas in the sixteenth century, many Europeans feared that the potato was poisonous and refused to eat it. By the eighteenth and nineteenth centuries, however, the potato had become an indispensable staple food in many areas of Europe.

European Medicine. American products previously unknown in Europe also changed many aspects of European medical practice in the age of exploration and expansion. In Spain, for instance, a physician named Nicolás Monardes published several books between 1565 and 1574 in which he outlined methods of curing or treating various diseases by making use of newly available plants from the Americas.

His books were quickly translated into all major European languages, and in 1577 a combined English translation of Monardes's books was published in London under the title *Joyfull Newes out of the Newe Founde Worlde*. A principal concern of Monardes and other European physicians of the era was malaria, a disease that had since ancient times been a constant and persistent killer in the Mediterranean region and elsewhere. In his book Monardes proposed that tea made from the American sassafras plant not only constituted an outstanding tonic but also could be used effectively as a treatment for malaria as well as other diseases. As many of Monardes's readers discovered, sassafras tea did little or nothing to help malaria victims, but it remained for centuries a popular tonic among Europeans. Another plant imported by the Europeans from the New World, however, would finally provide European physicians a successful means of curing malaria. As other Spanish doctors discovered in the late 1500s and early 1600s, quinine, an extract from the bark of the South American cinchona tree, effectively cures malaria. The use of quinine not only allowed Europeans gradually to eradicate malaria in Europe itself but also over the coming centuries to send conquering armies into malaria-infested tropical areas without fear of losing most of their soldiers to the deadly disease.

Sources:

Don Beecher, "The Book of Wonders of Nicolás Monardes," *Cahiers Elisabethians*, 51 (1997): 1–13;

Lucile H. Brockway, *Science and Colonial Expansion: The Role of the British Royal Botanical Gardens* (New York: Academic Press, 1979);

Alfred W. Crosby, *The Columbian Exchange: Biological and Cultural Consequences of 1492* (Westport, Conn.: Greenwood Press, 1972).

HEADLINE MAKERS

NICOLAUS COPERNICUS

1473-1543
POLISH ASTRONOMER AND MATHEMATICIAN

Education. Nicolaus Copernicus was born in Poland in 1473. As a young man he excelled in his studies at the University of Cracow, developing in the process a particular fascination with the subjects of astronomy and mathematics. Abandoning his native Poland in 1496, Copernicus traveled to Italy to continue his education. A decade of study at some of Italy's leading universities exposed him to the scientific thought of the ancient Greeks and Romans. A somewhat shy and conservative man, Copernicus at this stage of his life certainly did not appear to be the sort of intellectual whose work would eventually revolutionize astronomy and call into question traditional European conceptions of humankind's place in the universe. After returning from Italy to his Polish homeland, in fact, Copernicus became a Catholic clergyman and led a relatively obscure life at the cathedral in Frauenberg. During his years at Frauenberg, however, Copernicus gradually developed a new system of astronomical thought that proved to be, quite literally, earthmoving.

Aristotle and Ptolemy. In Copernicus's time Europe's view of the universe continued to be based upon the ideas of the Greek philosopher Aristotle. According to Aristotle the earth upon which we live is a stable, motionless sphere located at the very center of the universe. At the outer edge of Aristotle's universe stood a much larger "sphere of fixed stars," a hollow, rotating glass ball into which were embedded the stars that we see circling across the nighttime sky. In the space between the central earth and the outer sphere of fixed stars were several "planets" that orbited circularly around the earth. According to Aris-

totle's scheme the sun was one of these planets that circled the earth each day. In the second century A.D. the geographer and astronomer Ptolemy wrote a highly influential book, the *Almagest*, summarizing Aristotelian astronomical thought and providing observational and mathematical data regarding the motions of the sun and the other planets. Aristotle's conceptual scheme of the universe, combined with the mathematical details provided by Ptolemy, dominated European astronomical thought well into the 1500s.

The Moving Earth. Copernicus was hardly the first scholar to notice that Ptolemy's mathematical descriptions of planetary motion did not match exactly with the actual observed paths of the sun and planets through the sky. Many astronomers throughout the Middle Ages, in fact, proposed minor adjustments to Ptolemy's system but always maintained the basic Aristotelian assumptions that the earth lay motionless at the center of the universe and that the sun revolved around the earth. In the early decades of the sixteenth century, however, the quiet and studious Polish clergyman Copernicus arrived at the radical conclusion that astronomy could more accurately account for the motion of the planets if it abandoned the old idea that the earth was located at the center of the universe. Copernicus instead suggested that it was the sun that occupied the central position and that the earth was simply one of the many planets that revolved around the sun.

The Theory. Copernicus's ideas threatened not only traditional astronomical thought but also other long-held scientific and religious principles. First, the old earth-centered conception of the universe had long appealed to Christian thinkers since it placed humankind at the center of God's creation. As a Catholic clergyman Copernicus understood that his new system, by placing the sun rather than the earth at the center, removed humankind from its special position in God's universe. Second, the stable, motionless earth of the old Aristotelian model had been a key element of medieval physics. If the earth was constantly and rapidly hurtling through the heavens,

Copernicus's Aristotelian critics would ask, then why do objects on the earth's surface not go flying off? Fully aware of the controversy that his sun-centered model would cause, the naturally timid Copernicus kept his radical ideas to himself for most of his life. Only in 1543, the year of his death, was his theory finally published in a book titled *On the Revolution of the Heavenly Spheres*. The publication of Copernicus's theory did not, however, cause an immediate revolution in European astronomical thought. The old Aristotelian system continued to prove convincing to most European intellectuals through the end of the 1500s in part because of religious considerations and in part because it seemed to provide a better common-sense explanation of observed physical reality than did the Copernican model. Only in the 1600s and 1700s, following the work of such noted scientists as Galileo Galilei and Isaac Newton, was Copernicus's idea of a moving earth incorporated into a new and widely accepted modern worldview.

Age of Exploration. Copernicus's revolutionary astronomical ideas were emblematic of the sorts of radical transformations that characterized European intellectual life in the age of exploration and expansion. However, even though European exploration shared with the Copernican revolution common roots in the inquisitive spirit of the Renaissance era, the two movements were in many ways opposed to one another. In fact European navigators in the age of exploration and expansion had particularly strong reasons to reject Copernicus's idea of a moving earth. By the time of Copernicus, European sailors had become highly adept at navigating by the stars on the open sea. Such navigational techniques were based, in fact, on the Aristotelian model of the universe. From their supposedly stationary earth at the center of the universe, navigators measured the position of heavenly bodies on the universe's outer sphere of fixed stars in order to calculate their position on the earth. If the earth were constantly moving as Copernicus suggested, then their navigational calculations would be thrown way off the mark. To European sailors, in other words, common sense and practical experience remained thoroughly Aristotelian. The achievements of European navigation in the age of exploration and expansion illustrate, in fact, the powerful explanatory power of the Aristotelian model of the universe and help to explain why Europeans took so long to abandon it. As a scientific model of the actual universe, the old Aristotelian system has in fact been thoroughly discredited by the achievements of modern science. As a practical basis for navigation, however, the Aristotelian model proved highly effective and useful.

Source:
Thomas Kuhn, *The Copernican Revolution: Planetary Astronomy in the Development of Western Thought* (Cambridge, Mass.: Harvard University Press, 1957).

PRINCE HENRY THE NAVIGATOR

1394-1460
PORTUGUESE STATESMAN

History and Legend. Besides Christopher Columbus, Prince Henry the Navigator of Portugal has been the subject of more mythmaking than any other historical figure of Europe's age of exploration and expansion. Portuguese historians since the 1400s have exalted him as a national hero and credited him with many of the key technological, intellectual, and navigational innovations that during his lifetime made Portugal a leading maritime power. According to the traditional heroic accounts of his life, Henry supposedly attracted to Sagres on Portugal's southwestern tip the leading navigators and thinkers of his day. From Sagres, Henry directed a grand imperial scheme, dispatching his mariners into the unknown waters of the African coast and the islands of the Atlantic. In so doing he laid the foundations for the later 1497–1499 voyage of Vasco da Gama to India and the growth of a global commercial empire that would eventually stretch from India and Malaysia in the east to Brazil in the west. In recent years, however, historians have discovered that much of the legend surrounding the historical figure of Prince Henry is hollow and misleading. Yes, the "real" Prince Henry was one of the leading proponents of Portuguese expansion in the middle decades of the 1400s, and he did in fact play a leading role in organizing the early Portuguese voyages along the African coast. However, the available evidence suggests that Henry's supposed navigational "school" at Sagres may not have existed and that instead of an innovative visionary Henry was a man of his time. In many ways, in fact, the historical Henry that emerges from a careful study of the evidence is even more interesting than the mythical Henry of traditional Portuguese legend.

Royal Family. Henry was born in 1394, the third son of Portuguese king John I. As a younger son Prince Henry was destined never to inherit the throne himself. Yet he remained throughout his adult life one of the key figures in Portuguese politics, at times becoming involved in confrontations and power struggles with his brothers and other members of the royal family. When Henry's nephew Afonso inherited the throne as a young boy in 1538, Henry lost a power struggle with his own elder brother Prince Pedro over who would serve as regent to govern the kingdom until the boy-king reached adulthood. Never at the center of the royal decision-making processes, Henry nonetheless exerted considerable influence, becoming the leading voice in favor of a military offensive against the Muslims of North Africa.

On Campaign. Henry distinguished himself in the 1415 attack on the Muslim city of Ceuta on the Mediterranean coast of Morocco. While his brothers feared that holding the city would spread military resources too thinly and make Portugal itself vulnerable to Muslim or Spanish attacks, Henry advocated not only continued occupation of Ceuta but also new offensives against other North African locales. His grandiose ambitions brought disaster when in 1437 he led a failed assault on the city of Tangier. The fiasco at Tangier discredited Henry in policy-making circles, and in the coming years he was to spend most of his time in the southern coastal city of Sagres, far from the royal court in Lisbon.

Roots of Expansion. Even before taking up residence in Sagres, Henry had already begun to patronize Portuguese maritime expeditions south along the African coast. The goals and motives of these missions were various. They included gaining a military advantage against the Muslims of North Africa, finding allies to help in the struggle against Islam, establishing direct contact with the African gold trade then dominated by the Muslims, and simple curiosity concerning what they might find in these previously uncharted regions. During these early stages of Portuguese exploration, there is no evidence that Henry envisioned sailing directly to India by rounding Africa's southern tip, as Vasco da Gama would later succeed in doing in his 1497–1499 voyage long after Henry's death. A key mental obstacle to these early voyages was the long-held belief among Portuguese mariners that if a ship sailed past Cape Bojador on the African coast, strong currents and unfavorable winds would make it impossible to return to Portugal. It was one of Henry's captains, Gil Eannes, who finally disproved this myth in 1434 by successfully navigating around the cape and returning to Portugal. Subsequent Portuguese voyages, some commissioned by Henry and others financed by private commercial interests, continued to sail further down the African coast. In 1446 Henry received as a grant from his nephew King Afonso a commercial monopoly on all trade south of Cape Bojador. Portuguese expeditions in the later years of Henry's life developed along the African coast a flourishing trade in gold, ivory, and even slaves, many of whom were shipped to Portugal's colonies in the Madeira Islands to work on sugar plantations. By the time of Henry's death in 1460, Portuguese navigators had sailed as far south as the mouth of the Gambia River.

Myth and Reality. Traditional biographies of Henry have credited him with other revolutionary achievements such as the invention of the oceangoing caravel ship and the perfection of the critical navigational instrument called the astrolabe. Both claims are groundless because Henry was no navigator. A politician and soldier, he actually spent little time at sea. Rather than a heroic figure who single-handedly fathered the Portuguese empire, Henry was just one key political advocate of a broad and gradual process of Portuguese expansion that involved the efforts of hundreds of sailors, scholars, and statesmen.

Source:

Bailey W. Diffie and George D. Winius, *Foundations of the Portuguese Empire, 1415–1580* (Minneapolis: University of Minnesota Press, 1977).

BARTOLOMÉ DE LAS CASAS

1484-1566
SPANISH PRIEST

Background in Seville. Bartolomé de las Casas was born in 1484 to a fairly well-to-do merchant family in the bustling Spanish port city of Seville. His family took part in Spain's New World enterprise from its earliest stages. Bartolomé's father, Pedro de las Casas, and three uncles, for instance, sailed with Christopher Columbus on his second voyage. As a reward for his services on this expedition, Pedro received from Columbus a young Indian slave whom he in turn gave to his son Bartolomé as a companion. The young Las Casas reportedly rejected this "gift," returning the Indian boy to Spanish authorities in order that he might be sent back to his home in the Indies. This incident constituted the first expression of Las Casas's lifelong crusade against Spain's exploitation of the natives of the New World.

Early Years in the New World. In 1502 at the age of eighteen, Las Casas went to the Indies for the first time, and in 1512 he became the first priest to be ordained in the New World. He subsequently served as a chaplain on a Spanish military campaign that conquered various regions of the island of Cuba. Like other members of such expeditions Las Casas received in return for his services a grant of land and Indian slave labor. Hardly a typical Spanish settler, however, Las Casas in 1514 shocked the conquistadores by freeing all of his slaves and preaching an inflammatory sermon against the Spaniards' inhumane treatment of the natives. He then began an active campaign of intercession with Spanish authorities on behalf of the rights of conquered Indian populations.

Eyewitness to Atrocities? Over the coming decades Las Casas became the most passionate and vocal critic of Spain's New World policies. In the 1520s he began to publish a series of writings about Spanish massacres of native communities and other atrocities that he claimed to have witnessed. He aimed his writings squarely at the moral consciences of Spanish civic and religious officials, whom he hoped would respond with strict policies preventing mistreatment of New World natives by Spanish settlers. His most famous work, *The Devastation of the Indies: A Brief Account*, was published in its definitive form in Seville in 1552. In this short book Las Casas portrayed Spanish conquerors and settlers in the New World as barbaric murderers of gentle and innocent Indians. He supported his case with dozens of dramatic and horrifying tales of Spanish cruelty. Opponents charged that

Las Casas's work was misleading and inaccurate, and it is true that Las Casas frequently exaggerated the number of Indians directly killed by the Spaniards. Nonetheless his writings attracted a great deal of attention both inside and outside of Spain, contributing significantly to a growing debate about the proper treatment of conquered populations in the New World.

Response. Among the people moved by Las Casas's chilling accounts of Spanish atrocities in the Americas, none was more important than Spanish king and Holy Roman Emperor Charles V. As early as 1520 Charles responded to the pleas of Las Casas and other Native American rights advocates by ordering that New World natives be governed equitably and without force of arms. In 1542 the king's government issued the famous New Laws aimed at eliminating the system of forced labor that had developed in the decades since Columbus's earliest voyages. Pope Paul III, likewise moved by Las Casas's tales of Spanish cruelty, issued a proclamation in 1537 in which he stated that the natives of the New World were rational beings who had souls and that they should thus be governed humanely. Half a world away on the other side of the Atlantic, however, the proclamations of kings and popes in Europe meant little. Spanish settlers in the Americas frequently either disregarded or circumvented such laws, and exploitation of New World natives continued into the seventeenth century.

Legacy. Any portrayal of Las Casas as a human rights advocate must be balanced by the recognition that his campaigns for better treatment of conquered Native American populations included calls for increased use of African slave labor to take the place of the Indians. Although some biographers note that Las Casas also appears to have developed misgivings late in life about the enslavement of Africans, he never publicized such views in print. In addition the image of Spanish cruelty and barbarism fostered ironically by the Spaniard Las Casas continued to shape foreign opinion of Spain well into the twentieth century. Soon after its publication Las Casas's *Devastation of the Indies* was quickly translated into English, French, Dutch, and other major European languages. Las Casas's tales of Spanish barbarism in the New World in turn contributed to the growth of the Black Legend, the image of Spain as a corrupt, evil empire. Even as late as 1898 U.S. officials during the Spanish-American War used stories from Las Casas's *Devastation of the Indies* as propaganda to justify the expulsion of Spain from the vestiges of its New World empire.

Source:
Bill Donovan, "Introduction," in Bartolomé de las Casas, *The Devastation of the Indies: A Brief Account*, translated by Herma Briffault (Baltimore and London: Johns Hopkins University Press, 1992).

PUBLICATIONS

Christopher Columbus, *The Voyage of Christopher Columbus: Columbus's Own Journal of Discovery*, translated by John Cummins (London: Weidenfeld & Nicholson, 1992)—a personal account of the landmark voyage;

Nicolas Copernicus, *On the Revolutions of the Heavenly Spheres*, translated by A. M. Duncan (New York: Barnes & Noble, 1976)—the classic 1543 work that revolutionized astronomical study;

Bartolomé de las Casas, *The Devastation of the Indies: A Brief Account*, translated by Herma Briffault (Baltimore & London: Johns Hopkins University Press, 1992)—a highly influential and at times exaggerated account of Spanish atrocities in the New World written by a Spanish priest who claimed to have witnessed the events that he described;

Marvin Lunenfeld, ed., *1492: Discovery, Invasion, Encounter* (Lexington, Mass. & Toronto: D. C. Heath, 1991)—an outstanding collection of primary source readings pertaining to interactions between Europeans and the native people of the Americas in the age of exploration and expansion;

Nicolás Monardes, *Joyfull Newes out of the Newe Founde Worlde* (New York: Da Capo Press, 1970)—in this translated English text of the highly influential sixteenth-century medical work, Monardes provides an inventory of medicines drawn from New World plants;

Amerigo Vespucci, *Letters from a New World: Amerigo Vespucci's Discovery of America*, edited by Luciano Formisano, translated by David Jacobson (New York: Marsilio, 1992)—a collection of works by the man for whom the North and South American continents were named.

A medicine wheel, circa 1300 A.D., found at Medicine Mountain, Wyoming. The wheel measures eighty feet in diameter, and anthropologists speculate it was used for Sun Dance ceremonies or astronomical sightings

CHAPTER TEN

TRADE AND COMMERCE

by ROBERT J. FLYNN and BRET RIPLEY

CONTENTS

CHRONOLOGY

238

OVERVIEW

242

TOPICS IN THE NEWS

Indigenous Trade:
   The Northeast 243

Cahokia: The Great City of the Mound
   Builders **244**
Grease Trails **245**
Indigenous Trade:
   The Southeast **245**
Wampum....................**246**
Indigenous Trade:
   The Southwest **247**
The Transformation of Indian
   Exchange: The Fur Trade ...**248**

The Western Invasion: Privateers
   and The Settlement of
   North America **249**

HEADLINE MAKERS

Sir Francis Drake **251**

PUBLICATIONS

252

Sidebars and tables are listed in italics.

2000? B.C.

- The indigenous peoples of northeast North America begin trading for copper with Old Copper culture Indians living in the upper Great Lakes region.

300 B.C. - 250 A.D.

- The rise of the Hopewell culture in the central Mississippi, Illinois, and Ohio River valleys leads to a large-scale, thriving trade in luxury goods.

1000?

- Anasazi Indians trade extensively with Mesoamerican civilizations such as the Toltec.
- The rise of Mississippian culture spurs trade in the Southeast.

1250?

- Pueblo Indians living in and near the Rio Grande valley develop a complementary trading relationship with Plains Indians.

1510?

- French, Spanish, Portuguese, Breton, and Basque fisherman initiate the fur trade with the Indians of Nova Scotia and Labrador.
- French privateers begin to attack Spanish treasure ships returning from the New World.

1521-1526

- During the first phase of the Hapsburg-Valois Wars French corsairs under the command of Jean Ango of Dieppe take a heavy toll on Spanish treasure ships.

1524

- While exploring the North American coast from Cape Fear to Nova Scotia for France, the Florentine explorer Giovanni da Verrazano trades with Narraganset and Abenaki Indians.

1525

- The Portuguese navigator Esteban Gómez trades with Native Americans while mapping the North American coast from Florida to Cape Cod.
- The Spanish begin to use convoys to protect their treasure ships from privateers.

1534

- Iroquois Indians' first contact with Europeans occurs at Baie de Gaspé when they meet and barter with Jacques Cartier.

1535

- During Cartier's second voyage Donnacona, the leader of the Stadacona Indians, attempts to monopolize the region's fur trade by preventing the French from exploring further up the St. Lawrence River.

1539-1543

- Hernando de Soto leads an expedition across the American South in search of gold and silver.

1540-1542

- Francisco Vásquez de Coronado leads an expedition into the American Southwest in search of the fabled Seven Cities of Cíbola.

1541

- Jacques Cartier constructs the first French settlement in North America, Charlesbourg-Royal, near the site of present-day Quebec City, in hopes of trading with the Indians and discovering gold.

1542

- Facing constant attacks by the nearby Stadacona Indians, Cartier decides to abandon Charlesbourg-Royal.
- British privateer John Reneger seizes the Spanish ship *San Salvador* off Cape St. Vincent, initiating a lengthy period of poor relations between Spain and England.

1552-1556

- During the Hapsburg-Valois Wars French privateers prey upon Spanish treasure ships returning from the New World. Spain retaliates by attacking French fishing vessels off Newfoundland.

1559

- The Treaty of Cateau-Cambrésis ends the Hapsburg-Valois Wars.

1564

- French Huguenots under the leadership of René Goulaine de Laudonnière found Fort Caroline at the site of present-day Jacksonville, Florida, as a base from which French ships could raid the Spanish treasure fleet.

1565

- A Spanish expedition under the command of Pedro Menéndez de Avilés attacks and captures Fort Caroline.

- Menéndez founds St. Augustine to protect the Spanish treasure fleets from French, British, and Dutch buccaneers.

1567

- Spanish naval forces attack a British fleet commanded by John Hawkins off Vera Cruz, Mexico.

1572

- Francis Drake captures Nombre de Dios in present-day Panama and seizes the annual silver caravan as it arrives from Peru.

1578

- Humphrey Gilbert explores North America for England in a voyage designed, in part, to attack the Spanish fishing fleet off Newfoundland.

1580?

- The fur trade begins to alter the nature of the northeast Indians' trade and economic system.

1581

- French ships begin sailing annually to the Montagnais trading center of Tadoussac on the St. Lawrence River.

1585

- Sir Walter Raleigh establishes the short-lived colony of Roanoke on North Carolina's Outer Banks as a base from which privateers could attack the Spanish treasure fleets.

- En route home from Roanoke, the British ship *Tiger* under the command of Richard Grenville captures the Spanish vessel *Santa Maria de San Vicente*.

1586

- A British raiding fleet under Sir Francis Drake attacks and destroys the Spanish fort at St. Augustine and disrupts Spanish trading in the Caribbean.

1595

- Sir Francis Drake and John Hawkins lead a disastrous raid on Spanish colonies in the New World. Hawkins dies of illness in the Virgin Islands while preparing to attack Puerto Rico.

1596

- Sir Francis Drake dies of dysentery in the West Indies.

1598

- Holland and England agree to coordinate raids on the West Indies and attacks on the Spanish treasure fleet.

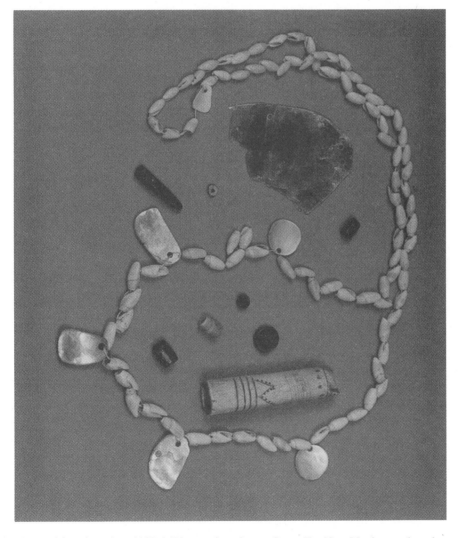

Anasazi jewelry, circa 1100–1400 A.D., found near Santa Fe, New Mexico, and made of mica, turquoise, jet, stone, and bone (School of American Research, Santa Fe, New Mexico)

OVERVIEW

Transformation. Trade in North America began to undergo a sweeping transformation during the fifteenth and sixteenth centuries because of the arrival of European traders, explorers, and fishermen. For thousands of years subsistence-based Native American tribes had engaged in the local, reciprocal exchange of high-prestige luxury items. With the coming of European merchants and explorers in the decades after Christopher Columbus's discovery, however, the Indians of the Northeast began exchanging beaver furs for European manufactured goods. As a result they soon abandoned subsistence activities and became specialized participants in the early modern system of international trade. The Europeans also brought another, more violent form of commercial intercourse with them to the New World: predatory commerce through privateering raids in the waters off North America.

Precontact Trade. Living for the most part in self-sufficient, subsistence-based communities, precontact-era Indians did not need to trade to survive and saw little gain in accumulation. They nonetheless participated extensively in intertribal commerce. They did so, in part, to acquire luxury goods and exotic prestige items that they interred with the dead in keeping with their practice of mortuary ceremonialism. More important, they engaged in the reciprocal exchange of gifts as a way of securing and perpetuating political alliances by linking tribes together. Intertribal trade was thus an important tool for maintaining the peace.

The East. Indian tribes located in the eastern part of North America had traded with one another for thousands of years prior to the arrival of the Europeans. In the northeast tribes such as the Petuns, Hurons, Montagnais, Susquehannocks, and Algonkins exchanged surplus goods and luxury items such as squirrel-skin robes over an extensive trade network. In the Southeast, meanwhile, tribes such as the Chicaza, Catawba, and Cofitachequi took part in a regional trade that occurred largely between coastal and inland tribes. In both areas, Native Americans also participated extensively in informal, continentwide trade through intermediary tribes.

The Southwest. Intertribal commerce among the Indians of the Southwest differed markedly from indigenous trade in eastern North America in terms of its development and nature. Early southwest Indians such as the Anasazi had participated in a pansouthwest trade network with Central American civilizations such as the Toltec Empire. As a result they helped spread Mesoamerican agricultural techniques and pottery styles to the Indians of North America. At the time of first contact, meanwhile, the Pueblo Indians living in and near the Rio Grande valley had developed a complementary commercial relationship with the Plains Indian tribes located to their east that was far more complex and differentiated than the reciprocity-based trade practiced in eastern North America.

Fur Trade. The arrival of European fisherman, explorers, and merchants in the late fifteenth and early sixteenth centuries sparked a dramatic and far-reaching transformation of indigenous trade. Through contact with Europeans, tribes in the Northeast began to exchange beaver pelts for manufactured goods. Initially this trade followed the traditional pattern of reciprocal exchange that had governed Indian trade for centuries. Soon, though, growing participation in the fur trade changed the northeast Indians' system of exchange, altered fundamentally the economic basis of their society, and left them economically dependent on continued European trade for their survival.

Privateering. Before 1600 the nations of western Europe did not engage in normal commercial intercourse with one another in North America. Instead the British, French, and Dutch participated in a form of predatory trade in the waters off North America through privateering raids against Spanish shipping that were destined to play an important part in the early settlement of North America. Both the French and the British, for example, attempted to establish fortified colonies on the continent from which privateers could raid the lucrative Spanish treasure fleet year round. The first permanent European settlement in North America, meanwhile, was an indirect product of privateering: Spain established St. Augustine to defend its Caribbean shipping and to prevent the construction of further privateering bases in Florida.

TOPICS IN THE NEWS

INDIGENOUS TRADE: THE NORTHEAST

Northeastern Indians. The Indian tribes of northeastern North America bartered extensively with one another and with the indigenous peoples of other regions long before Columbus's first voyage to the New World. The Hurons, Iroquois, Susquehannocks, Petuns, Neutrals, Montagnais, and others maintained extensive trade networks over which they exchanged surplus items—largely corn, dried fish, or furs—either with each other for necessities or with more-distant tribes for luxury goods such as tobacco and prized religious items such as sea shells. This complex trade network did more than just supply the Indians of the Northeast with luxury goods, however; it also ensured the peace by extending to intertribal relations the system of personal reciprocity on which harmonious Indian social relations rested.

Early Patterns. Archaeological evidence suggests strongly that Native Americans living in the Northeast traded with each other and with Indians from other regions as early as 2000 B.C. Copper artifacts found at sites in New York and Ontario, for example, were likely acquired through trade with Indians living in the copper-rich upper Great Lakes region. Archaeological evidence also indicates that Middle Woodland-era Indians living in the Northeast traded with the Hopewell culture that dominated the central Mississippi, Ohio, and Illinois River valleys from 300 B.C. to 250 A.D. From these Mound Builders the northeastern Indians obtained luxury goods such as large sea shells that originated in the Gulf of Mexico, pottery figures, pearls, and copper and silver ornaments. Through this trade the northeastern Indians also acquired the Hopewell culture's highly developed pottery styles and agricultural techniques.

Precontact Era. During the centuries prior to first contact with the Europeans, the Indians of the Northeast traded extensively with Native Americans living in other regions. Through indirect trade conducted by intermediary tribes the Hurons, Iroquois, Montagnais, and others

Small brass hawk-bells given to Florida Indians by Spanish explorers in the mid 1500s (Memphis State University)

acquired luxury goods such as gourds, conch shells, and shark teeth that originated in the Southeast and along the Gulf Coast. From the West and the North, meanwhile, these tribes obtained buffalo-skin robes, charms, clothing, and raw copper. The Indians of the Northeast also engaged in a highly developed regional system of exchange. The Susquehannocks who lived in and around present-day Pennsylvania, for instance, exchanged wampum beads for goods produced by more-northerly tribes while the Neutrals of contemporary New York State had a thriving business trading tobacco and black squirrel skins with the Hurons of modern-day southern Ontario. The Hurons, in turn, supplied the seminomadic Algonkin Indians located further north with squirrel-skin coats, nets, ropes, and southern luxury goods such as tobacco, and foodstuffs in exchange for dried fish and skins. St. Lawrence River valley tribes such as the Montagnais Indians, meanwhile, continued to use the well-established Saguenay River trade route to swap foodstuffs for upper Great Lakes copper.

Diplomatic Aspects. Along with its obvious economic role, trade performed a crucial diplomatic function by extending to intertribal relations the system of reciprocity that governed social relations among the northeastern Indians. That system ensured tribal harmony by linking individuals and clans together through the reciprocal exchange of obligations, gifts, and spiritual power. At the intertribal level this resulted in peaceful, friendly relations between tribes that regularly traded goods and hostile relations between those that did not. During the fifteenth and sixteenth centuries, for example, the Hurons enjoyed peaceful ties with the Algonkins

CAHOKIA: THE GREAT CITY OF THE MOUND BUILDERS

The most important precontact trading hub in North America was the Mississippian-tradition city of Cahokia. Located at the confluence of the Mississippi and Missouri Rivers near present-day St. Louis, Cahokia was a political, economic, and religious center with a population of 38,000. From about 1000 A.D. to 1200 A.D. it dominated trade along the Mississippi River, served as an important commercial gateway for tribes living to the north, and occupied a key intermediary position in the extensive-if-informal continental trading network. Evidence suggests strongly, moreover, that Cahokia engaged in direct—if limited—commercial intercourse with Mesoamerican cultures such as the Aztec Indians. Through this trade and its position as an important intermediary the city helped bring high-yield, Mesoamerican corn to the Indians of eastern North America. Ultimately, however, Cahokia's dominance of Mississippi valley trade proved to be short-lived; it began to decline sharply around 1250 and was abandoned entirely not long thereafter.

Sources: Paul D. Welch, *Moundville's Economy* (Tuscaloosa: University of Alabama Press, 1991);

Thomas E. Emerson and R. Barry Lewis, eds., *Cahokia and the Hinterlands: Middle Mississippian Cultures of the Midwest* (Urbana & Chicago: University of Illinois Press, 1991).

A Lakota painting on buffalo skin of warriors armed with muskets and a chief on horseback, circa 1600 (Musée de l'Homme, Paris)

A detail from Pierre Descaliers's 1546 map of the New World, depicting whaling ships off the coast of Canada

GREASE TRAILS

Trade amongst the Indians of the Northwest generally followed the pattern prevalent in the East. The exchange of luxury goods was unique, however, in that it was dominated by a single product: *oolichan,* or grease, fish. Nine to ten inches long and native to the Pacific Northwest, the oily oolichan fish were highly prized for two reasons. First, they provided an abundance of fish oil used to improve the flavor of the Indians' winter diet of dried fish. More important, the grease fish were so oily that the Native Americans could use them as candles simply by lighting them.

No northwestern product was traded as extensively as the oolichan fish. The Tsimshian Indians who controlled the oolichan business by virtue of their location along the Nass River caught the fish during their annual runs in March and April. After cooking the fish down to get the grease, they transported them inland by canoe and then along forest paths known as "grease trails." So desirable were the fish that the Tsimshian people achieved great wealth; they thus became the "envy of the whole coast."

Source: George Woodchuck, *Peoples of the Coast: The Indians of the Pacific Northwest* (Bloomington: Indiana University Press, 1977).

as a result of their regular, reciprocal commerce. At the same time they warred ceaselessly with the Iroquois confederation, with which they did not trade.

The Ritual of Exchange. The diplomatic nature of trade and its basis in the Indians' system of reciprocal social relations powerfully shaped the way it was conducted. The trading itself took place only after several days of feasting, speeches, and the exchange of formal gifts between headmen designed to ease tensions between the parties and to assure continued commercial relations. Reciprocity and the desire to retain good relations also governed the actual bartering. As a result, while northeastern Indians keenly understood the relative market value of a commodity, they refused to haggle for fear of offending their trading partners and destroying the commercial relations on which peace rested.

Sources:
Neal Salisbury, *Manitou and Providence: Indians, Europeans, and the Making of New England, 1500–1643* (New York: Oxford University Press, 1982);

Bruce G. Trigger, *The Children of Aataentsic: A History of the Huron People to 1660,* 2 volumes (Kingston: McGill-Queen's University Press, 1976, 1987);

Trigger, *Handbook of North American Indians,* Volume 15: *Northeast* (Washington, D.C.: Smithsonian Institution, 1988).

INDIGENOUS TRADE: THE SOUTHEAST

Southeastern Tribes. Like the Indians of the Northeast, the indigenous peoples of southeastern North

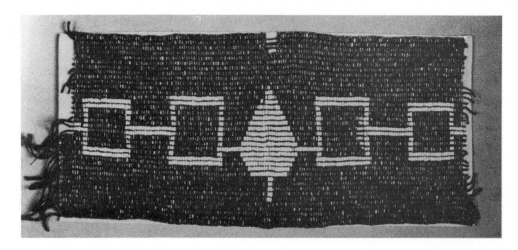

An Iroquoian wampum belt made with cylindrical beads manufactured by Europeans

America had engaged in widespread, long-distance trade for thousand of years before the arrival of Europeans. Tribes such as the Catawbas, Algonkins, Cofitachequi, and Chicaza participated extensively in both regional, intertribal commerce—which centered largely on the exchange of goods between inland and coastal tribes—and in the larger continental trade. Southeastern commerce, however, differed from northeastern bartering in one important regard: during the Mississippian period the South witnessed the rise of several large cities that served as important commercial centers.

Initial Networks. The Indians of the Southeast engaged extensively in intertribal trading as far back as the Woodland period (1000 B.C.). Archaeological evidence suggests strongly that this trade was closely related to the widespread practice of mortuary ceremonialism, wherein luxury goods and prestige items were interred in ossuaries with the dead. To acquire the exotic, high prestige goods desired for their burial rituals, the southeastern Indians exchanged locally produced items with intermediary tribes for such prized rarities as Great Lakes copper, western obsidian, and Rocky Mountain grizzly-bear teeth. The presence of Appalachian Mountain mica and Gulf Coast marine shells at archaeological sites throughout the South also indicates that southeastern tribes bartered goods regularly along a network of regional and local trade routes.

Mississippian Period (1000–1250 A.D.). A new and more elaborate trade system developed around 1000 A.D. in conjunction with the rise of the Mississippian culture. Along with the enormous earthen mounds for which they are still renowned, Indians of the Mississippian tradition built large, impressive cities such as Moundville on the Black Warrior River in present-day Alabama and Cahokia at the confluence of the Mississippi and Missouri Rivers. These cities quickly became important commercial centers in the informal, continentwide trade network. The presence of long-nosed god masks at Mississippian archaeological sites indicates, moreover, that

WAMPUM

Wampum's dramatic transformation in the late sixteenth and early seventeenth centuries demonstrates clearly the effects of the fur trade on the northeast Indians' socioeconomic system. Made of carefully ground whelk and quahog shells found only in Long Island Sound, strings of purple and white wampum did not function as currency in precontact North America. Rather, as the historian William Cronon points out, these high-prestige items served as an important "medium of gift giving" that conformed to the Native Americans' system of reciprocal social relations. So prized were wampum beads, in fact, that they were exchanged as gifts only for important purposes such as paying restitution for a murder, offering tribute to a powerful chief, or consummating an alliance with a foreign tribe.

The arrival of Europeans and the consequent integration of the Indians into the Atlantic economy through the fur trade rapidly transformed wampum's nature and purpose. This occurred, in part, because metal tools of European origin allowed tribes living along Long Island Sound to increase markedly their production of the shells. More important, Dutch, French, and English traders gave wampum an established-if-fluctuating value in terms of pelts and made it available throughout New England after they realized that they could exchange it as currency for beaver furs. As a result, wampum rapidly changed from a high-prestige gift used to cement personal and political relationships to a medium of exchange used to purchase goods.

Source: William Cronon, *Changes in the Land: Indians, Colonists, and the Ecology of New England* (New York: Hill & Wang, 1983).

A 1594 engraving of caravels in port

these cities traded directly with the Aztec Empire, likely through traveling Aztec merchants known as *pochtecas*.

Eve of Contact. Like their northeastern contemporaries, the Mississippian-tradition Indians who dominated the Southeast on the eve of European contact had a subsistence-based economy. While this system allowed the peoples of the Southeast to satisfy their needs independently, they nonetheless engaged extensively in regional intertribal trade and, through intermediaries, in the larger, continentwide trade. Most of the regional commerce involved the exchange of goods that, for ecological reasons, tribes had in abundance; it thus occurred largely between inland and coastal tribes. Interior tribes exchanged flint, cane, mica, pelts, wood, and feather cloaks for salt, dried fish, and *ilex vomitoria* leaves used to make the ritually important black drink. In addition coastal tribes supplied interior Indians with much-sought-after shells used to produce high-prestige items such as necklaces.

Sources:

Charles Hudson, *The Southeastern Indians* (Knoxville: University of Tennessee Press, 1976);

J. Leitch Wright Jr., *The Only Land They Knew: The Tragic Story of the American Indians in the Old South* (New York: Free Press, 1981).

INDIGENOUS TRADE: THE SOUTHWEST

Southwestern Tribes. At the time of first contact, trade among the Indians of the Southwest was similar to that practiced in the rest of North America. Like their eastern counterparts, both the sedentary Pueblo Indians and nearby semisedentary tribes such as the Navajo reciprocally exchanged gifts to cement personal and political relationships. In several important ways, though, trade in the Southwest differed from commercial interactions in the eastern part of North America. First, early southwestern Indians exchanged goods with Mesoamerican civilizations in the pansouthwest commercial network to a far greater degree than they traded with other North American Indians. More important, sedentary pueblo-dwelling Indians such as the Tiwas and semisedentary plains tribes such as the Apaches developed a complementary trading relationship in the centuries prior to the European invasion that was far more complex than the eastern Indians' reciprocity-based commerce.

Anasazi. Around the end of the first millennium A.D., Anasazi Indians living in the Southwest had become fully integrated into the pansouthwest trade network. They supplied highly valued turquoise and, to a lesser extent, obsidian to tribes located along the Gulf of California in exchange for luxury goods such as bracelets and pendants fashioned from Pacific shells. They also traded turquoise with Mesoamerican civilizations such as the Toltec Empire for high-prestige items such as macaw feathers, ornaments, and pottery. This intercourse had important consequences because it helped spread Mesoamerican pottery styles, religious customs, crops, and agricultural techniques to North America.

New Avenues. After the pansouthwest commercial system collapsed between 1200 and 1400, the pueblo-dwelling Indians of the Rio Grande valley began to trade with semisedentary plains tribes such as the Apache. Pueblo tribes such as the Tewas exchanged surplus corn, cotton textiles, ceramics, and turquoise for the Plains Indians' tallow, salt, buffalo meat, and hides. This new commercial intercourse was based, in part, on the same system of reciprocal gift giving that governed trade among the Indians of eastern North America. Commerce between Pueblo and Plains tribes was substantially more complex than reciprocity-based trade, however, because it involved the complementary exchange of surplus goods. It thus allowed the Plains tribes and, to a greater extent, the Pueblo Indians to shift from a simple, subsistence-based economic system to a more complicated one based on specialized production.

Pueblo Indians. Trade among the Pueblo tribes was also becoming more and more specialized in the centuries prior to European contact. Tiwa and Northern Tewa provided fibrolite used in the manufacture of ritual items and axes; Piro and Southern Tiwa exchanged malachite; Tanos Indians supplied turquoise and lead; and Tewas traded obsidian and pedernal chert. Archaeological evidence suggests, meanwhile, that the Pecos Indians had a monopoly in the production of leather goods.

Sources:

Elizabeth H. John, *Storms Brewed in Other Men's Worlds: The Confrontation of Indians, Spanish and French in the Southwest, 1540–1795* (College Station: Texas A&M University Press, 1975);

Alfonso Ortiz, ed., *Handbook of North American Indians,* volumes 9 and 10: *Southwest* (Washington, D.C.: Smithsonian Institution, 1979, 1983);

David R. Wilcox and W. Bruce Masse, eds., *The Protohistoric Period in the North American Southwest, AD 1450–1700* (Tempe: Arizona State University Research Papers, 1981).

THE TRANSFORMATION OF INDIAN EXCHANGE: THE FUR TRADE

Cause of Change. The arrival of Europeans in North America in the late fifteenth and early sixteenth centu-

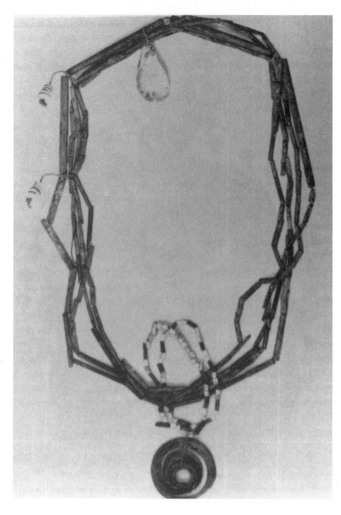

A Seneca brass and shell necklace, circa 1570 (Rochester Museum and Science Center, Rochester, New York)

ries initiated a process that would, over the next 150 years, change forever the eastern Indians' socioeconomic system. During that period tribes living in the Northeast began gradually to exchange beaver furs for European manufactured goods. At first this trade was conducted in a manner consistent with the Native Americans' system of reciprocal gift exchange. As the years passed, however, the northeast Indians' increasing participation in the fur trade radically transformed their traditional system of exchange and the nature of their society, and left them economically dependent on the Europeans.

Origins. The fur trade began as a side business for European fishermen in the late fifteenth and early sixteenth centuries. Breton, French, Basque, Spanish, and Portuguese sailors supplemented the profits they earned fishing off Newfoundland by exchanging manufactured goods for beaver furs, the only valuable commodity the Indians possessed. Early trade was in keeping with the traditional system of reciprocal exchange: Native Americans bartered pelts for decorative trinkets such as earrings and glass beads in order to establish good relations with the Europeans. Soon, though, coastal tribes such as the Micmac and Abenaki were exchanging furs

Illustration of tobacco plant in Nicholas Monardes's *Joyfull Newes out of the Newe Founde Worlde* (1577)

with Europeans not to affirm social and political ties but to acquire utilitarian items such as brass kettles, fishing hooks, and, especially, iron weapons.

Expansion. The fur trade became a major economic activity during the latter half of the sixteenth century. Sharply increasing demand for fashionable beaver-fur hats in Europe, the construction of fish-processing stations on Labrador and Newfoundland, and the institution of regular trade between the French port of St. Malo and the Montagnais settlement of Tadoussac on the St. Lawrence River in the early 1580s combined to spur a dramatic rise in the exchange of pelts for manufactured goods. Seeking the prestige and utility that accompanied the possession of European goods, tribes such as the Micmacs gradually devoted less and less time to subsistence agriculture so that they could concentrate on hunting beavers. The resultant overtrapping of fur-bearing animals soon forced such tribes to war with nearby Indians in order to expand their hunting grounds. Such territorially motivated warfare, in turn, spurred other Indians to participate in the fur trade so that they could acquire the iron weapons needed to defend themselves and restore the balance of power. Military necessity thus played

a critical part in bringing the northeastern Indians into the expanding Atlantic economy.

Specialization and Dependency. Over time the fur trade fundamentally transformed the northeastern Indians' socioeconomic system and the nature of their trade. The growing desire for high-prestige European goods gradually led tribes such as the Micmac, Montagnais, Malecite, and Passamaquoddy to abandon subsistence activities and the manufacture of tools in favor of an exclusive focus on fur trapping. By the early seventeenth century, therefore, these tribes were no longer autonomous, subsistence-based societies that secured personal and political relations through the reciprocal exchange of gifts. Instead they had become specialized participants in an Atlantic economy which depended on continued trade with the Europeans for their survival.

Continuation. By 1600 the fur trade was well on its way to changing irrevocably the material basis of Native American society. The desire for utilitarian, high-prestige European manufactured goods had already transformed the tribes of eastern Canada from autonomous, subsistence-based societies into dependent ones that specialized in trapping. At the end of the sixteenth century this process had not yet affected tribes located in the interior and to the South, though European goods were already moving west along indigenous trade routes. The spreading demand for European goods; the increased penetration of French, Dutch, and British traders; and the need for iron weapons to keep pace with similarly armed hostile neighbors combined, however, to insure that the fur trade would soon alter the economic basis and system of trade among all the tribes located in eastern North America.

Sources:

William Cronon, *Changes in the Land: Indians, Colonists, and the Ecology of New England* (New York: Hill & Wang, 1983);

Neal Salisbury, *Manitou and Providence: Indians, Europeans, and the Making of New England, 1500–1643* (New York: Oxford University Press, 1982);

Bruce G. Trigger, *The Children of Aataentsic: A History of the Huron People to 1660*, 2 volumes (Kingston: McGill-Queen's University Press, 1976, 1987);

Trigger, *Handbook of North American Indians*, volume 15: *Northeast* (Washington, D.C.: Smithsonian Institution, 1988).

THE WESTERN INVASION: PRIVATEERS AND THE SETTLEMENT OF NORTH AMERICA

Predatory Commerce. European powers did not trade with one another in North America during the sixteenth century. In part such commerce failed to develop because the mercantilist economic policies of the day forbade it. More to the point, European states had established only a handful of settlements on the continent with which trade could be conducted, and only one, St. Augustine, survived for more than a year. Through privateering, however, the French, British, and Dutch engaged in a form of predatory commerce against Spanish shipping in

The arrival of Spaniards depicted in a sixteenth-century Navajo pictograph on a wall of Canyon del Muerto, Arizona

the waters off Florida. Small at first but increasing as the century progressed, privateering raids ultimately came to play an important part in shaping the exploration and colonization of North America.

Beginnings. Privateering originated as a way for merchants to settle disputes with foreign governments. Having had a ship or goods expropriated by a foreign nation, a merchant would apply for a letter of reprisal that entitled its bearer to seize on the high seas vessels and merchandise owned by citizens of the offending country. This system thus provided a well-regulated means for traders to redress international commercial grievances without putting governments in conflict. Over time, though, privateering became so profitable that adventurous merchants and gentlemen who had lost no goods began purchasing letters of reprisal from government officials only too happy to look the other way for a bribe or a percentage of the take. Hostilities with Spain, moreover, led the French and then the British governments to view privateering as a cheap tool they could use to chip away at Spanish power.

Wars of the Sixteenth Century. The French were the first to prey upon Spanish shipping in the West Indies. During early hot periods in the collection of conflicts known as the Hapsburg-Valois Wars (1522–1559), French buccaneers cruised the Caribbean alternately trading and plundering in a region Spain considered to be its exclusive sphere. After 1552 the French government began to send large squadrons of ships to attack the Spanish treasure fleets in an effort to interrupt at its source the flow of bullion on which Spanish power rested. Though French Protestants known as Huguenots continued to raid shipping in the Caribbean following the conclusion of the Hapsburg-Valois Wars, Britain rapidly surpassed France as Spanish king Philip II's chief nemesis in the New World. Greed and religious hatred combined initially to motivate daring men such as Sir John Hawkins to plunder Spanish vessels and settle-

ments in the West Indies. When war with Spain broke out in 1585, though, the desire to undermine Philip's financial base spurred the British to organize massive raids such as Sir Francis Drake's devastating 1585–1586 cruise.

Impact on Settlement. Privateering shaped virtually all colonization efforts in North America prior to the seventeenth century. In the 1560s, for example, the French Huguenot leader Adm. Gaspard de Coligny sent a force to establish a privateering base at the site of present-day Port Royal, South Carolina. Though this settlement failed, he also sent René Goulaine de Laudonnière to found Fort Caroline on the Florida coast as a base from which ships could raid the treasure fleet on their return voyage. When war broke out between Spain and Britain in 1585, meanwhile, Queen Elizabeth commissioned Sir Walter Raleigh to construct a settlement at Roanoke Island from which corsairs could raid Spanish shipping year-round.

St. Augustine. Privateering also played an indirect part in the founding of the first permanent European settlement in North America. Following Pedro Menéndez de Avilés's destruction of Fort Caroline in 1565, Philip II concluded that Spain could ensure against another European power building a privateering base in Florida only by maintaining a fortified colony on the peninsula. As a result he ordered Menéndez to turn the temporary base of St. Augustine into a permanent colony.

Sources:

Kenneth R. Andrews, *The Spanish Caribbean: Trade and Plunder, 1530–1630* (New Haven: Yale University Press, 1978);

Karen Ordhal Kupperman, *Roanoke: The Abandoned Colony* (Totowa, N.J.: Rowman & Allandheld, 1984);

Max Savelle, *The Origins of American Diplomacy: The International History of Angloamerica, 1492–1763* (New York: Macmillan, 1967);

J. Leitch Wright Jr., *Anglo-Spanish Rivalry in North America* (Athens: University of Georgia Press, 1971).

HEADLINE MAKERS

SIR FRANCIS DRAKE

1543-1596
ENGLISH ADMIRAL

An English Hero. Sir Francis Drake was the most renowned and successful English privateer of the late sixteenth century. His raids on Spanish settlements and shipping in the New World made him a hero to his countrymen, a man of great wealth, and a thorn in Philip II's side. Most important, his success inspired thousands of British merchants and gentlemen to organize privateering expeditions in the Caribbean as a way both to earn profits and to undercut Spanish power.

A Born Sea Dog. Drake's life at sea began at the age of thirteen when he became a pilot in the North Sea coastal trade. Around the age of twenty he joined his powerful and wealthy cousin, Sir John Hawkins, in the semi-illicit Spanish Caribbean trade. Harsh, heavy-handed treatment at the hands of Spanish officials during his first voyage to the New World (1566) inflamed Drake's already virulent hatred of Catholic Spain. Spanish actions further enraged Drake during his second voyage (1567) when forces under the command of Viceroy Martín Enríquez attacked a five-ship squadron commanded by Hawkins at San Juan de Ulúa. Only the ships commanded by Hawkins and Drake survived the battle.

Fortune and Reputation. Personal, patriotic, and religious motives led Drake to raid Spain's New World possessions three times between 1570 and 1572. The first two expeditions proved unsuccessful, but the third ended with the capture of the annual Peruvian silver caravan at Nombre de Dios in Panama. In 1577 Drake embarked with a small flotilla on an exploratory and predatory voyage up the western side of the Americas. After raiding Spanish shipping and settlements along the South American coast and claiming present-day California for Britain he returned to Plymouth via the Cape of Good Hope, thus becoming the first English captain to circumnavigate the globe. Along with the Nombre de Dios raid, this trip secured Drake's fortune and reputation. More important, the two expeditions inspired hundreds of English merchants and gentlemen to take up privateering along the Spanish Main.

War with Spain. Drake played a pivotal part in the early phase of the Anglo-Spanish War (1585–1604). Following the outbreak of hostilities in 1585, Queen Elizabeth I sent a twenty-three-ship fleet under Drake's command to attack Spanish vessels and colonies in the New World. The yearlong raid was spectacularly effective: Drake sacked Cartagena, Santo Domingo, and St. Augustine and swept the Caribbean of Spanish shipping. In 1587, he led a crushing naval attack on the Spanish port of Cadiz that sank twenty ships and delayed the sailing of the Armada by a year. When the Armada put to sea in 1588, his leadership and daring proved critical in its defeat.

Later Career. Drake's fortunes declined rapidly beginning in 1589. That year he led a 150-ship attack on Lisbon that failed as spectacularly as the raid on Cadiz had succeeded. He consequently lost favor with Elizabeth and was forced into semiretirement. In 1595 he returned to service for a joint raid with Hawkins on Spain's New World possessions. Despite high expectations, the cruise failed to match the success of Drake's earlier Caribbean sweeps because the Spanish had greatly improved their defenses and because Drake and Hawkins clashed over the expedition's objectives. The raid proved to be Drake's last. He died of dysentery on 28 January 1596 and was buried at sea off the coast of Panama.

Sources:

Kenneth R. Andrews, *The Spanish Caribbean: Trade and Plunder, 1530–1630* (New Haven: Yale University Press, 1978);

Karen Ordhal Kupperman, *Roanoke: The Abandoned Colony* (Totowa, N.J.: Rowman & Allandheld, 1984);

James A. Williamson, *Sir Francis Drake* (New York: Colliers Books, 1962);

J. Leitch Wright Jr., *Anglo-Spanish Rivalry in North America* (Athens: University of Georgia Press, 1971).

PUBLICATIONS

Alvar Nuñez Cabeza de Vaca, *Castaways*, edited by Enrique Pupo-Walker, translated by Frances M. López-Morillas (Berkeley: University of California Press, 1993)—the tale of Pánfilio de Narváez's expedition to Florida in 1528 by one of its four survivors. This work contains excellent source material regarding Native American trade in the Southeast and present-day Texas;

Jacques Cartier, *The Voyages of Jacques Cartier*, translated by H. P. Biggar (Ottawa: F. A. Acland, 1924)—the French explorer's story of his three expeditions to North America. This book describes in detail early French commercial relations with the Micmac and Stadaconan Indians;

Sir Francis Drake, *Sir Francis Drake's West Indian Voyage 1585–1586*, edited by Mary Frear Keeler (London: Hakluyt Society, 1981)—Drake's account of his spectacular and devastating raid through the Spanish Caribbean following the outbreak of war between Britain and Spain;

René Laudonnière, *Three Voyages*, translated by Charles E. Bennett (Gainesville: University Presses of Florida, 1975)—a narration of the French effort to establish a privateering base in Florida from which ships could raid the Spanish treasure fleet.

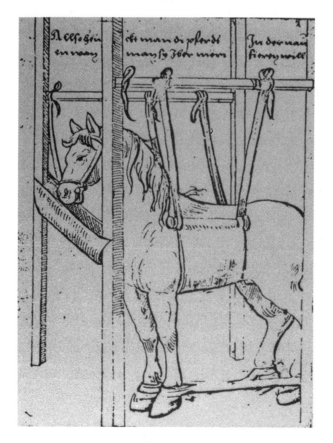

An early-sixteenth-century diagram of how to transport a horse at sea. By suspending the animal several feet off the deck, the sling prevented the horse from sustaining serious leg injuries in rough weather

CHAPTER ELEVEN

WARFARE

by ROBERT J. FLYNN

CONTENTS

CHRONOLOGY
254

OVERVIEW
260

TOPICS IN THE NEWS

Native American Warfare in the
    East: Mourning Wars 262
War Chiefs 263
European Style of War 263
Precontact Indian Weapons 264
Native American Warfare in the West:
    Conflict Among the Southwestern
    Indians 265
The Transformation of Native
    American Warfare: Conflict

and the Emergence of
    Confederations.............266
Disappearance of the St. Lawrence
    Iroquois 266
Animals of War...............268
The Transformation of Native
    American Warfare: Trade and the
    Shift to Economically Motivated
    Conflict 268
Aztec Armor 268
Muskets.....................269
The Western Invasion: Dividing the
    World 269
Treasure Fleet................270
The Western Invasion: Early Spanish
    Expeditions to North
    America, 1513-1562.........271
The Western Invasion: Franco-
    Spanish Conflict in North
    America 273

The Western Invasion:
    Spain's Empire in
    La Florida, 1565-1585 274
The Western Invasion: Warfare
    Between England and Spain
    in North America,
    1585-1604 275

HEADLINE MAKERS

Jacques Cartier.................276
Francisco Vásquez de
    Coronado...............277
Hernando de Soto 278

PUBLICATIONS
280

Sidebars and tables are listed in italics.

1450?– 1550?

- The Huron and Iroquois confederations are formed.

1493

- Pope Alexander VI issues four papal bulls validating Spain's claims to the territories discovered by Christopher Columbus.

1494

- The Spanish and Portuguese crowns agree to the Treaty of Tordesillas, which establishes a line of demarcation one hundred leagues west of the Cape Verde Islands. Spain receives the exclusive right to all territories west of the line not ruled by a Christian prince; Portugal receives similar privileges in territory east of the line.

1506

- Pope Julius II agrees to amend the Treaty of Tordesillas by moving the line to 370 leagues west of the Cape Verde Islands.

1510?

- French, Spanish, Portuguese, and Basque fishermen initiate trade with the Indians of Nova Scotia and Labrador, giving them cloth and iron weapons in exchange for beaver pelts.
- French privateers begin to attack Spanish treasure ships returning from the New World.

1513

- Calusa Indians successfully defeat a Spanish landing party led by Juan Ponce de León at San Carlos Bay in Florida.

1517

- Calusa Indians repulse a second Spanish landing party under the leadership of Hernández de Córdoba.

1519– 1521

- A Spanish force under the command of Hernando Cortés conquers the Aztec empire in Mexico.

1520

- The Portuguese establish a short-lived colony on Cape Breton Island.

1521

- The Calusas defeat the Spanish for the third time at San Carlos Bay. Juan Ponce de León, the leader of the Spanish expedition, dies of wounds inflicted by the Indians.

- Spanish explorer Pedro de Quxós lands at Winyaw Bay in present-day South Carolina, where he enslaves sixty Guale Indians.

1521-1526

- During the first phase of the Hapsburg-Valois Wars, French corsairs under the command of Jean Ango of Dieppe take a heavy toll on Spanish treasure ships.

1526

- The Spanish establish the short-lived colony of San Miguel de Gualdape near the mouth of the Pee Dee River in present-day South Carolina.

1528

- Seeking to copy the success of Cortés, Pánfilo de Narváez leads an expedition of three hundred men to Florida; only four members survive.

1529

- In the Treaty of Saragossa, Spain and Portugal agree to a demarcation of their spheres of control in the Pacific Ocean.

1530?

- Micmac Indians war with the Stadacona branch of the Saint Lawrence Iroquois for control of the Gaspé Peninsula.

1532

- A Spanish expedition under the command of Francisco Pizarro conquers the Incan empire of Peru.

1534

- The Iroquois Indians' first contact with Europeans occurs at Baie de Gaspé when they meet a French expedition under Jacques Cartier.

1535

- During Cartier's second voyage, Donnacona, the leader of the Stadacona Indians, attempts to monopolize the region's fur trade by preventing the French from exploring further up the St. Lawrence River.

1536

- Led by Alvar Núñez Cabeza de Vaca, the four survivors of the Narváez expedition arrive in Mexico after wandering for eight years through present-day Texas and northern Mexico. They report rumors of a wealthy Indian civilization located somewhere northwest of New Spain.

1539-1543

- Hernando de Soto leads an expedition across the present-day southeastern United States in search of gold and silver.

1540-1542

- Francisco Vásquez de Coronado leads an expedition of Spanish cavalry and Mexican foot soldiers into the American southwest in search of the fabled Seven Cities of Cíbola.

1541

- Jacques Cartier constructs the first French settlement in North America, Charlesbourg-Royal, near the site of present-day Quebec City.

1542

- Facing constant attacks by the nearby Stadacona Indians, Cartier decides to abandon Charlesbourg-Royal. Jean François de La Rocque, sieur de Roberval, establishes a new colony called France-Roy near the same site.

- Hernando de Soto dies of disease. His lieutenant, Luis de Moscoso y Alvarado, leads the expedition westward in a failed attempt to link up with Coronado.

1543

- The three hundred survivors of the De Soto expedition escape down the Mississippi River to Mexico on rafts.

- The French abandon France-Roy, in part because of hostile relations with nearby Native Americans.

- In the Reneger Incident, British privateer John Reneger seizes the Spanish ship *San Salvador*, initiating a lengthy period of poor relations between Spain and England.

1549

- Timucuan Indians destroy a Dominican mission on Tampa Bay and kill two priests, including the mission's founder, Luis Cáncer de Barbastro.

1550?

- The musket replaces the crossbow as the principal weapon among conquistadors in Spanish America.

- The Hurons and Iroquois increasingly wage war with each other.

1552–1556

- French vessels continue to prey upon Spanish treasure ships returning from the New World. Spain retaliates by attacking French fishing vessels off Newfoundland.

1555

- A French fleet under Adm. Jacques de Sores captures and sacks Havana.

1559

- The Treaty of Cateau-Cambrésis ends the Hapsburg-Valois Wars between France and Spain.

1559–1561

- Spanish colonists under the command of Tristán de Luna y Arellano fail in their attempt to establish a colony in Florida, largely because a severe hurricane destroys most of the expedition's ships in Pensacola Harbor.

1560

- Fifty Spanish troops under the command of Mateo del Sauz join three hundred Coosa warriors in an attack on the Napochi Indians.

1560–1563

- Three separate Spanish attempts to colonize Florida fail.

1561

- The Spaniard Antonio Velázquez leads the first European ship into Chesapeake Bay. His crew kidnaps the Indian Paquiquineo and inadvertently spreads a major epidemic that kills many of the Native Americans in the region.

1562

- Philip II decrees that Florida is no longer the object of Spanish colonization efforts.

- French admiral Gaspard de Coligny, a Huguenot, sends the navigator Jean Ribault to explore the coast of Florida. Ribault establishes a short-lived, earthen fort on the site of modern Port Royal, South Carolina.

1564
- French Huguenots under the leadership of René Goulaine de Laudonnière found Fort Caroline at the site of present-day Jacksonville, Florida, as a base from which French ships could raid the Spanish treasure fleet.

1565
- A Spanish expedition under the command of Pedro Menéndez de Avilés foun St. Augustine in preparation for an attack on Fort Caroline. After capturing t French stronghold, Menéndez executes the Huguenot survivors for heresy.

1565-1567
- Menéndez establishes a network of forts and blockhouses throughout the sout eastern North America.

1567
- Spanish naval forces attack a British fleet commanded by John Hawkins off Vera Cruz, Mexico.

1567-1569
- Hostile Indians overrun all but the largest of the forts established by Menénde

1568
- A French expedition retaliates for the Spanish attack on Fort Caroline by tem porarily recapturing the fort and hanging the garrison.

1570
- Jesuits establish a mission near the Chesapeake Bay to convert the local Algon quin Indians.

1571
- Algonquins attack and kill the Jesuit missionaries in the Chesapeake Bay regio Spanish forces retaliate the next year by killing thirty-four Indians.

1572
- Francis Drake captures Nombre de Dios in present-day Panama and seizes the annual silver caravan as it arrives from Peru.

1578
- Humphrey Gilbert explores North America for England in a voyage designed, in part, to attack the Spanish fishing fleet off Newfoundland.

1580?

- Increasing European demand for fur begins to change the style of warfare among eastern woodland Indian tribes.

- Seeking slaves to work the rich silver mines at Zacatecas and Santa Bárbara in northern Mexico, Spaniards begin raiding Indian settlements in southern Texas.

1581

- French ships begin sailing annually to the Montagnais trading center of Tadoussac on the St. Lawrence River.

1585

- En route home from Roanoke, the British ship *Tiger* under the command of Richard Grenville captures the Spanish treasure vessel *Santa María de San Vicente*.

1586

- A British raiding fleet under Sir Francis Drake attacks and destroys the Spanish fort at St. Augustine.

1595

- Drake and John Hawkins lead a disastrous raid on Spanish possessions in the New World. Hawkins dies of illness in the Virgin Islands while preparing to attack Puerto Rico.

1596

- Drake dies of dysentery in the West Indies.

1597

- Franciscan missionaries living among the Guale Indians of present-day Georgia attempt to keep Chief Juanillo from becoming tribal *mico*. The Guale respond by massacring five priests.

1598

- Indians from the Pueblo town of Ácoma attack a Spanish force of thirty soldiers commanded by Vicente de Zaldívar, killing thirteen, in response to the Spaniards' demand for food. Juan de Oñate retaliates by destroying Ácoma and enslaving the five hundred survivors.

OVERVIEW

North American Warfare. During the fifteenth and sixteenth centuries, warfare in North America underwent a series of dramatic and far-reaching changes. In part, this transformation was the product of the ongoing political, economic, and social evolution of Native American culture. A more important cause, however, was the arrival of European explorers, missionaries, settlers, and conquerors in the years following Christopher Columbus's "discovery" of the New World. Their presence altered North American warfare in three ways. First, their efforts to plunder easily extractable wealth and found colonies created new conflicts between them and the Indians. Second, they brought with them to the New World Europe's dynastic, economic, and religious conflicts. Finally, they transformed the objectives and style of warfare among the indigenous peoples by bringing the Native Americans into the nascent, early-modern system of international trade.

Mourning Wars. On the eve of first contact with Europeans, warfare in North America differed markedly from fighting in the Old World. Rather than engaging in large-scale, high-casualty, European-style wars aimed at achieving territorial or economic goals, Native Americans fought conflicts known as blood feuds or mourning wars, in which they retaliated for the deaths of their kinsmen by killing or capturing Indians from rival tribes. These conflicts satisfied important cultural, demographic, and religious functions in Indian society. They achieved vengeance, provided an outlet for grief, gave young men the opportunity to gain prestige, secured captives to replace deceased clan members, and assured a supply of victims for important ritual sacrifices. In keeping with these goals, mourning wars were small-scale, low-intensity affairs that involved ambushes rather than set-piece battles and that produced light casualties compared to contemporary European wars. The perception that each murder or captive taken was a fresh attack rather than a legitimate retaliation, however, meant that a single death could initiate a costly, self-perpetuating cycle of violence that was almost impossible to stop once begun.

Rise of Confederations. By the fifteenth and sixteenth centuries, the increasing cost of perpetual warfare spurred Native Americans to find ways to limit mourning wars. At first, culturally and linguistically related bands located nearby joined together to establish large villages that provided better security against their rivals. Later, neighboring settlements formed defensive alliances that offered additional protection against distant enemies and, more important, outlawed local blood feuds. Finally, during the fifteenth and sixteenth centuries, many tribes ended regional mourning wars altogether by joining together to form large, intertribal leagues such as the Iroquois Confederacy. These leagues proved highly effective in curtailing vengeance-motivated warfare between member tribes, but ended neither the individual warrior's desire for military glory nor the tribe's need for sacrificial victims. Rather than ending blood feuds, therefore, the confederations that developed during the fifteenth and sixteenth centuries transformed them from small, local conflicts into large, long-distance affairs between rival leagues.

Beaver Wars. A more dramatic and substantial change in Indian warfare occurred as a consequence of the European discovery of North America. Beginning in the early part of the sixteenth century, Portuguese, Basque, and French fishermen began exchanging European manufactured goods such as cloth, glass, kettles, and iron weapons for a valuable commodity the Indians possessed: beaver pelts. Once established, the fur trade rapidly transformed the Indians' vengeance-motivated blood feuds into new conflicts known as beaver wars. These wars were fought for control of hunting grounds and access to direct trade with Europeans. The Micmac Indians of coastal Canada, for example, took advantage of the technologically superior iron weapons that they had purchased from the Europeans to seize the Etchemin tribe's rich trapping grounds. The Wappinger Indians of the upper Hudson Valley, meanwhile, violently drove the Munsees out of the lower part of the valley in order to gain direct access to coastal trading. At the end of the sixteenth century, the effects of the fur trade were confined largely to tribes living along the coast of northeastern North America, in the St. Lawrence River valley, and in the eastern Great Lakes region. The growing desire for manufactured goods and the need for iron weapons to keep pace with similarly armed neighbors, however, assured that trade with the Europeans would transform the objectives and style of warfare among all the eastern woodland Indians during the seventeenth century.

Warfare in the Southwest. Native American conflict in the Southwest during the fifteenth and sixteenth centuries was similar to warfare among the eastern woodland Indians. Like their eastern counterparts, semisedentary tribes such as the Apache and Navajo waged low-intensity blood feuds to avenge the killing of their kinsmen by members of rival tribes. In several important ways, however, warfare in the Southwest differed from that practiced in the East. First, semisedentary Native Americans raided both other seminomadic tribes and the sedentary Pueblo Indians in an effort to acquire material goods through plunder. More important, the Pueblo Indians engaged in territorial and economic wars that were, in many ways, more similar to contemporary European conflicts than to the woodland Indians' mourning wars.

Franco-Spanish Conflict. The Europeans also changed warfare in North America by bringing to the Americas the existing dynastic and religious conflicts of the Old World. Sixteenth-century European warfare in the Americas centered largely on Britain and France's efforts to undermine Spain by interrupting the transatlantic flow of New World gold on which Spanish power rested. During the on-again, off-again series of struggles between France and Spain known as the Hapsburg-Valois Wars, for example, French privateers sought to weaken Spain indirectly by raiding its New World possessions and by preying upon its treasure fleets. The Treaty of Cateau-Cambrésis ended the Hapsburg-Valois Wars in Europe in 1559 but did not extend to the New World because King Philip II of Spain refused to sanction formally any violation of what he considered to be his nation's exclusive sphere. Unable to come to a formal agreement regarding the Americas, the two states agreed informally that force would settle disputes in the New World and that fighting there would not lead to hostilities in Europe. As a result, the brief, bloody conflict fought between Spanish and French forces for control of Florida in the 1560s did not upset peaceful relations between those nations in the Old World.

Anglo-Spanish Conflict. During the last two decades of the sixteenth century, Britain replaced France as Spain's chief competitor in the New World. Relations between England and Spain had been deteriorating steadily since the 1550s because of religious differences and Spain's refusal to allow British ships to trade in the West Indies. The final break occurred in 1585 when Queen Elizabeth I sent troops to assist Dutch Protestant rebels in their uprising against Spain. Hoping to undermine Philip by attacking the most vulnerable part of his empire, she sent a fleet of ships under the command of Sir Francis Drake to raid Spanish settlements in the West Indies. She also commissioned Sir Walter Raleigh to build a fortified base in North America from which privateers could plunder Philip's treasure fleets. Drake's

raid was spectacular. He sacked various settlements including St. Augustine and swept the Caribbean of Spanish shipping. Raleigh's colony at Roanoke proved less impressive: it failed, as did a second settlement established in 1587. Nonetheless, the conflict between British and Spanish forces in the New World had proven critical to the outcome of the war in Europe.

European vs. Indian. The arrival of Europeans in the New World also changed warfare in North America by giving rise to conflict between Indians and invading Europeans. Fighting between Native Americans and Europeans stemmed from several sources. Often such conflict was the product of the Europeans' heavy-handed actions. Spanish expeditions in the Southeast, for example, antagonized Indians by burning settlements and demanding food. French explorers likewise provoked Native Americans by kidnapping Indians and taking them back to Europe. At other times, conflict stemmed from cultural differences. Native Americans often angered Europeans, for instance, by "stealing" items in keeping with their belief that anything left unattended was free for the taking. The Europeans' custom of establishing settlements on land that Indians claimed as their own likewise inspired hostility, as did the efforts of many tribes to establish exclusive trading monopolies by discouraging the Europeans from contacting rival tribes.

Conquistadors. Beginning in 1513, Spain sent a series of expeditions into the southern part of North America in hopes of discovering and plundering a wealthy Indian civilization similar to the Aztec empire. Early invasions by Juan Ponce de León in 1513 and Pánfilo de Narváez in 1528 failed because of the opposition of powerful Indian tribes. In 1539 Hernando de Soto organized a larger and much stronger expeditionary force equipped with matchlock firearms and armored cavalry. De Soto's force was so overwhelmingly powerful that it was able to roam about the South for four years searching for treasure. Constant Indian attacks nonetheless played an important part in persuading the Spanish to abandon their expedition in 1543. After several other failed incursions, Spanish forces established nominal control of the Southeast in the 1560s by building a series of small forts and blockhouses. Ongoing abuses and demands for food angered the Indians, however; they consequently attacked the garrisons and ejected the invaders from the interior. By the end of the sixteenth century, potent Indian opposition had reduced Spanish territory in the Southeast to the settlement of St. Augustine on Florida's Atlantic coast.

St. Lawrence River Valley. The French crown, meanwhile, sponsored several attempts to found colonies along the St. Lawrence River during the mid 1500s. In 1541, the explorer and navigator Jacques Cartier established a settlement called Charlesbourg-Royal near the site of present-day Quebec City. Unlike de Soto, Cartier had not journeyed to North America with the intention of attacking and plundering the Indians. Cultural conflict, however, along with trade disputes and clashes over land soon sparked hostilities between the French and the nearby Stadacona Indians. By 1542 fighting with the local Indians had proven so costly that Cartier had to abandon Charlesbourg-Royal. Shortly after Cartier departed the St. Lawrence Valley, his superior, Viceroy Jean François de La Rocque, sieur de Roberval, established a new settlement called France-Roy not far from the site of Charlesbourg-Royal. For a variety of reasons the Stadaconas did not war with the new colonists as they had with Cartier's men. Continued cold relations between the French and Native Americans nonetheless contributed to Roberval's decision to abandon France-Roy.

Seventeenth Century. Conflict in North America had thus changed markedly between the mid fifteenth century and 1600. Blood-feud warfare among the Indians had begun to give way gradually to economically motivated fighting over hunting grounds and access to trans-atlantic trade. The Europeans, meanwhile, had extended their traditional dynastic and religious rivalries to the New World. Most important, Europeans and Native Americans had started warring with each other. Such conflicts had been costly for the indigenous peoples because of the Europeans' vast technological and organizational superiority; nonetheless, the Native Americans had proven that they could stand up to the invaders. The Indians had, in fact, forced the Europeans to abandon all of the colonies they had established in North America during the sixteenth century save for the small, tenuous Spanish settlement at St. Augustine. In many ways, however, the end of the sixteenth century marked the high-water mark of Indian resistance to European intrusions. Thereafter, the invaders were able to take advantage of their better weapons and the devastation that disease had wrought among the Native Americans to establish a series of lasting colonies from which they eventually conquered the entire continent.

TOPICS IN THE NEWS

NATIVE AMERICAN WARFARE IN THE EAST: MOURNING WARS

Eve of Contact. Like Europeans, the eastern woodland Indians of North America engaged in near-constant fighting during the centuries prior to first contact. Native American warfare differed dramatically from European hostilities, however, in terms of its roots, aims, and nature. Old World wars of the fifteenth and sixteenth centuries such as the Spanish *Reconquista* or the Hapsburg-Valois Wars were costly, large-scale affairs that had religious or dynastic origins, produced comparatively high casualties, and were fought to achieve territorial or economic gains. The indigenous peoples living throughout the eastern half of North America, in contrast, engaged in low-intensity, low-casualty conflicts known as blood feuds or mourning wars. Through these wars tribes such as the Mahican, Cofitachequi, Susquehannock, Petun, Oneida, and Micmac retaliated for the deaths of relatives and clan members by taking captives or killing Indians from rival bands. Such an approach to war, not surprisingly, rarely resulted in large, bloody battles or in decisive defeats.

Purpose. Indians fought these wars for several reasons. First, blood feuds were a way for Native Americans to avenge the deaths of kin or tribesmen murdered by other Indians. Second, mourning wars gave young men the opportunity to earn the prestige needed to become respected and influential members of their tribe. Third, taking captives satisfied demographic needs by providing a source of replacements for a tribe's deceased members. Fourth, mourning wars fulfilled a spiritual and psychological function by easing grief, by providing a means for coping with death, and by restoring to the community the spiritual strength believed lost through the death of a clan member. Finally, blood feuds provided a steady source of captives for some Native Americans' ritual sacrifices.

Typical Campaign. Centered as they were on ambush and surprise, woodland Indian military operations generally occurred during the warmer months to take advantage of the cover that foliage provided. The typical campaign began when clan matriarchs commissioned a male war chief to avenge the death of a family member. After assembling a raiding party, gaining village approval, and holding a ceremonial feast, the war chief led his men into battle. Upon entering the foe's territory, the war party split into smaller groups of five or six; each group then established ambushes near fields or along paths frequented by the enemy. As ambushing Indians enjoyed surprise and could refuse to give battle to larger forces,

WAR CHIEFS

While superficially similar, Indian war chiefs and European military leaders of the fifteenth and sixteenth centuries fulfilled dramatically different roles and had sharply divergent relationships with their soldiers. European generals had autocratic powers and were able to issue orders to their troops backed by the threat of imprisonment or death. They also enjoyed direct control of their armies through an imprecise but nonetheless effective chain of command. War chiefs, in contrast, lost control of their warriors after their raiding parties entered enemy territory and broke up into smaller, independent groups. More important, Indian military leaders lacked the authority to compel obedience and instead had to win popular approval for their campaigns. A war chief commissioned by a family to avenge a death, for example, had to recruit warriors and build support for the raid by distributing gifts and discussing strategy. The contrasting roles of war chiefs and generals thus reveals not only the difference between styles of war but the contrast between the Europeans' hierarchical culture and the Indians' more open and consensual one.

Sources: Paul Kennedy, *The Rise and Fall of the Great Powers* (New York: Random House, 1987);

Bruce G. Trigger, *The Children of Aataentsic: A History of the Huron People to 1660*, 2 volumes (Montreal: McGill-Queen's University Press, 1976).

engagements were usually one-sided affairs that ended with the taking of captives.

Tactics and Spiritual Beliefs. Aside from increasing the chances of taking captives, ambushes and surprise attacks reflected the woodland Indians' belief system. Native Americans believed that those who died a violent death could not spend their afterlife with other deceased members of their families in the villages of the dead; rather, they had to spend eternity wandering about in search of vengeance. Indian warriors consequently avoided combat when overmatched and generally

EUROPEAN STYLE OF WAR

As with the Indians of North America, the Europeans' style of war reflected their goals. Seeking economic, dynastic, and religious objectives through the acquisition of territory, European princes of the fifteenth and sixteenth centuries undertook military campaigns designed to crush enemy forces in decisive engagements. They consequently employed large armies centered on highly disciplined, massed infantry formations such as the potent Spanish *tercio* that were composed of pikemen and harquebusiers. Supported by smaller contingents of artillery and cavalry, these infantry regiments engaged in large, set-piece battles that resulted in staggering numbers of casualties. Because Europeans sought largely territorial goals, moreover, their wars often involved lengthy and well-organized sieges of fortifications and cities, such as those that occurred during the failed Spanish effort to crush the revolt of the Netherlands in the late sixteenth century.

Source: Paul Kennedy, *The Rise and Fall of the Great Powers* (New York: Random House, 1987).

shunned high-risk assaults on fortified positions in favor of hit-and-run attacks on outnumbered and surprised enemy groups.

Large Battles. Occasionally a war chief would respond to an especially severe attack by besieging an enemy village with a force of several hundred warriors. Such armies did not seek to capture or destroy their rival's settlement but attempted to lure the enemy into battle by placing burning branches against the wooden palisades that surrounded the village. When the foe emerged to douse the flames, the two sides fought a highly ritualized clash that ended after some of the enemy had been killed or taken captive. The besieging force then retreated before reinforcements arrived from nearby settlements. For several reasons, large-scale engagements such as these rarely involved taking or destroying enemy villages. Large settlements were difficult to attack because they were surrounded by stout palisades constructed of several rows of three-to-five-inch diameter wooden poles interweaved with bark and branches. Bigger villages also had watchtowers and galleries built on the insides of the palisades from which defenders could fire arrows at a besieging force. More important, the Indians of eastern North America at the time of first contact fought wars to take vengeance and secure captives rather than to acquire enemy territory; they thus saw little point in capturing or destroying their adversary's settlements.

The Captives' Fate. Enemy Indians taken captive in mourning wars confronted several fates. Women and children who were a burden and enemy warriors perceived to be a threat were, on occasion, scalped and killed immediately. In general, however, prisoners were bound and led back to their captors' home village. Upon arrival the captives were stripped, bound at the hands and feet, and forced to walk a gauntlet of tribe members who repeatedly struck them with clubs, torches, and knives. Later the tribal council assigned each prisoner to a family that had lost relatives to that captive's tribe. In general, women, children, and skilled or especially attractive men were adopted into the family. These captives were given the name, title, and position of the person they replaced, and, over time, became integrated into their new family and became loyal to their new tribe. Their capture thus eased the pain of bereavement, maintained the size of family, clan, and tribe, and restored the spiritual strength that the community had lost through the death of a member.

Ritual Sacrifice. While women and children generally replaced dead family members, most captured warriors were condemned to die through ritual sacrifice. As with women and children, such prisoners were adopted into a family and took the name and title of a recently deceased clan member. After a brief period in which the family treated the prisoner with respect and affection, the clan gave the victim a final feast in anticipation of his death. The next day, the entire village assembled in the primary war chief's longhouse and began torturing the captive in a lengthy, highly ritualized ceremony. After the prisoner's death, the tribe concluded the ceremony by cooking and eating his remains.

Exceptions. While mourning wars generally followed this pattern, there were important exceptions and qualifications. Because young men could gain the prestige needed to become influential and respected members of their tribe only through war, they frequently raided without village or tribal approval. Such attacks often upset delicate peace arrangements and, thereby, restarted recently concluded wars. In addition, relations with foreign tribes were an extension of the Indian's system of social relations. That system rested on reciprocal exchanges of obligations, gifts, and spiritual power wherein kinship groups and individuals bound themselves to-

PRECONTACT INDIAN WEAPONS

The weapons of the precontact period were well suited to the Native Americans' preferred strategies and tactics. Unlike the noisy and smoky firearms used by contemporary Europeans, Indian weapons such as stone-headed axes, wooden clubs, and spears lent themselves well to ambushes and surprise attacks. Bows that fired stone-tipped arrows were likewise employed in such engagements, though they had only a short effective range and were of limited value in the thickly forested eastern part of the continent. For protection, Indian warriors carried bark shields and wore crude wooden armor over their torsos and legs. This protective covering could stop a stone-tipped arrow or deflect an ax blow and proved important in keeping casualties to a minimum during the large battles that occasionally took place outside besieged villages.

Sources: Bruce G. Trigger, ed., *Handbook of North American Indians, Volume 15: Northeast* (Washington, D.C.: Smithsonian Institution, 1988);

Wilcomb E. Washburn, ed., *Handbook of North American Indians, Volume 4: History of Indian-White Relations* (Washington, D.C.: Smithsonian Institution, 1988).

gether by sharing or exchanging goods. At the intertribal level, this meant that eastern Indians generally had peaceful, friendly relations with neighboring tribes with which they engaged in substantial reciprocal commerce and hostile relations with tribes with which they did no trade. Finally, evidence suggests that Indians in the southeastern part of the continent occasionally fought territorially motivated wars.

A French copy of a Seneca pictograph of warriors returning to their village with a captive, circa 1666 (Archives Nationales, Paris)

Figures of warriors, circa 1200, found on the walls of a Utah canyon

Cyclical Warfare. The nature of blood feuds meant that they were almost impossible to stop once they had begun. Native Americans perceived each murder or captive taken not as a legitimate retaliation but as a new attack that demanded vengeance through further bloodshed. As a result, the noted scholar Bruce G. Trigger points out, mourning wars produced "a self-perpetuating cycle of violence that was broken only at irregular intervals so that exchanges of prisoners might be arranged."

Sources:
Charles Hudson, *The Southeastern Indians* (Knoxville: University of Tennessee Press, 1976);

Daniel K. Richter, *The Ordeal of the Longhouse: The Peoples of the Iroquois League in the Era of European Colonization* (Chapel Hill: University of North Carolina Press, 1992);

Bruce G. Trigger, *The Children of Aataentsic: A History of the Huron People to 1660*, 2 volumes (Montreal: McGill-Queen's University Press, 1976);

Trigger, ed., *Handbook of North American Indians, Volume 15: Northeast* (Washington, D.C.: Smithsonian Institution, 1988).

NATIVE AMERICAN WARFARE IN THE WEST: CONFLICT AMONG THE SOUTHWESTERN INDIANS

The Southwest. Indian fighting in the Southwest during the fifteenth and sixteenth centuries followed the mourning-war pattern prevalent among the eastern woodland Indians. Like their eastern counterparts, both sedentary Pueblo Indians and seminomadic tribes such as the Navajo warred to avenge the murder of their kinsmen. In important ways, however, warfare in the Southwest differed from that practiced in the eastern part of North America. First, semisedentary Native Americans raided both other seminomadic tribes and the Pueblo Indians in an effort to acquire material goods through plunder. More importantly, the Pueblo Indians living in and near the Rio Grande valley often fought wars that were more similar to European conflicts than to the woodland Indians' blood feuds.

Semisedentary Tribes. Like their eastern neighbors, tribes such as the Apache and Navajo fought to avenge the deaths of kinsmen rather than to acquire territory. When a clan member was killed by Indians from another tribe, a war leader related to the deceased formed a war party composed of kinsmen and unrelated young men who sought the prestige that came through success in battle. After two nights of war dances and a day of feasting, the war party moved into enemy territory, where it took women and children captive and killed enemy warriors. Because semi-nomadic Indians such as the Navajo had to avenge every clan member killed by a rival tribe, blood-feud warfare was, as in the East, self-perpetuating and never ending. As with eastern woodland Indian conflict, moreover, warfare among the Native Americans of the Southwest produced light casualties in comparison to contemporary European wars.

Raiding Parties. There were, however, important differences between the objectives of eastern Indian warfare and the goals of their southwestern counterparts. While eastern Indians fought almost exclusively to achieve retribution, southwestern Indians clashed with their neighbors both to avenge previous wrongs and to loot them of material possessions. Apaches and Navajos, for example, raided both each other and the sedentary Pueblo Indian tribes in an effort to acquire goods through plunder. Though the distinction was missed by the Pueblo Indians and, later, by the Spanish, raiding parties differed substantially from war parties in terms of their objectives and their approach. While war parties sought to take captives and to achieve vengeance through killing, the smaller raiding parties hoped to avoid fighting and focused instead on taking booty. Raids often spawned blood feuds, though, because a tribe had to avenge the death of a warrior who died either in a raid or in an ensuing battle with pursuers.

Pueblo Indians. The sedentary Pueblo Indians of the Rio Grande valley likewise engaged in the vengeance-

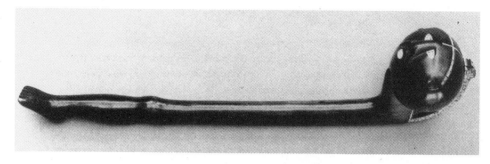

A seventeenth-century wooden ball-headed war club of the Delaware tribe
(Nationalmuseet, Copenhagen)

motivated warfare that was common to kinship-based societies. Pueblo warfare was not, however, limited to blood feuds. Living in and near the densely populated but resource-poor Rio Grande valley, Pueblo tribes such as the Hopis, Zunis, Piros, and Tewas fought with one another to secure control of the region's limited supply of arable land. Such economically and territorially motivated warfare led the Pueblo Indians to make their adobe towns—called pueblos—powerful defensive fortifications. They did so by building their settlements atop steep mesas, by constructing their multistory buildings around a central plaza to form sheer exterior walls, and by limiting access to the main square to a single, narrow, easily defended passageway. Navajo and Apache raiding parties consequently found the Pueblo Indians' settlements to be tempting but formidable targets.

Sources:

George J. Gumerman, ed., *Themes in Southwest Prehistory* (Santa Fe, N.M.: School of American Research Press, 1994);

Elizabeth H. John, *Storms Brewed in Other Men's Worlds: The Confrontation of Indians, Spanish and French in the Southwest, 1540–179* (College Station: Texas A&M University Press, 1975);

Alfonso Ortiz, ed., *Handbook of North American Indians, Volume Southwest* (Washington, D.C.: Smithsonian Institution, 1979);

Ortiz, ed., *Handbook of North American Indians, Volume 10: Southwe* (Washington, D.C.: Smithsonian Institution, 1983).

THE TRANSFORMATION OF NATIVE AMERICAN WARFARE: CONFLICT AND THE EMERGENCE OF CONFEDERATIONS

Indian Political Evolution. The centuries prior t contact with Europeans witnessed an important trans formation in the woodland Indians' political system. I the northeastern and Great Lakes regions of Nort America, nearby groups of linguistically and culturall related Indians underwent a process of political agglom eration wherein smaller bands joined together to forn large villages and tribes. By the fifteenth and sixteent centuries, this process had begun to result in the forma tion of large, populous, intertribal political confedera

DISAPPEARANCE OF THE ST. LAWRENCE IROQUOIS

When the French explorer Samuel de Champlain traveled up the St. Lawrence River in 1603, he discovered to his surprise that the Hochelaga and Stadacona Indians (Iroquoian tribes) visited by Jacques Cartier seventy years earlier had vanished. Over the past four centuries, the disappearance of these tribes has produced a substantial debate among scholars. Some have argued that overhunting of beaver during the mid sixteenth century depleted the valley of the furbearing animals and forced the tribes to relocate to better trapping grounds. Others have asserted that a temporary period of climactic cooling resulted in a series of bad harvests that compelled the Stadacona and Hochelaga to move south.

The best evidence suggests, however, that the disappearance of the St. Lawrence Iroquois was a consequence of the fur-trade-induced transformation of Indian warfare. Surrounded by iron-weapon–armed enemies such as the Susquehan-

nocks and Mahicans and lacking such arms themselves, the Mohawk Indians of present-day upstate New York found themselves at an increasing military disadvantage as the century progressed. By the 1550s, this predicament led them to initiate a new type of commercially motivated warfare against the St. Lawrence Iroquois in which they sought to plunder iron weapons and to acquire territory from which they could trade directly with the French. The Mohawks succeeded in destroying the Hochelaga and Stadacona and thereby restored the balance of power by acquiring substantial quantities of iron weapons. They were unable to dislodge the powerful Montagnais from the key trading post of Tadoussac, however, and thus failed to gain the principal objective of their St. Lawrence campaign: a direct trading relationship with the French.

Source: Bruce G. Trigger, *The Children of Aataentsic: A History of the Huron People to 1660,* 2 volumes (Montreal: McGill-Queen's University Press, 1976).

ions. Under the guidance of Hiawatha, for example, the Seneca, Cayuga, Onondaga, Oneida, and Mohawk tribes joined to create the powerful Iroquois Confederacy. At about the same time, the Attignawantan, Arendarhonon, Attigneenongnahac, and Tahontaenrat tribes came together to form the Huron Confederacy.

Unification. Blood feuds were the principal factor behind the formation of confederations. In many instances, the increasing cost of mourning wars during the late prehistoric period led smaller bands to join together to form bigger, more easily defended villages; other large settlements developed when one band or village absorbed the remnants of a defeated one. Either way, the formation of such settlements forced nearby groups of Indians likewise to form larger villages or suffer the consequences of numerical inferiority. This process continued until a settlement reached the maximum size that the Indians' slash-and-burn agriculture could support. At that point, neighboring villages came together to suppress blood feuds through defensive alliances. By the late fifteenth and early sixteenth centuries, these tribal-sized alliances began to form confederations.

Characteristics. The confederations that emerged during this period were not powerful centralized political organizations. Rather, they were loose, decentralized leagues designed to suppress blood feuds between their constituent members through the establishment of an intertribal council. Composed of civic leaders, confederation councils met periodically to adjudicate disputes, supervise the payment of compensation, and hold ceremonial feasts that reaffirmed the league. Ending blood feuds and ensuring goodwill between the member tribes was the sole purpose of the Indian confederations formed during the fifteenth and sixteenth centuries; they neither coordinated their member tribes' foreign policies—which often worked at cross purposes—nor functioned as defensive alliances.

Conflict. The confederations formed in the centuries prior to contact with the Europeans proved effective in limiting blood feuds between their constituent tribes. Such intertribal leagues did not, however, end the chief underlying causes of war: the tribe's demand for sacrificial victims, the clan's need for a way to cope with death, and the individual warrior's desire for the military glory required to become a respected member of the tribe. Rather than ending woodland Indian warfare, therefore, the rise of confederations transformed its scope. Local, small-scale blood feuds between neighboring tribes became large, long-distance conflicts involving rival leagues such as the Iroquois and Susquehannock or the Erie and Huron. The emergence of confederations during the fifteenth and sixteenth centuries thus changed markedly the scale of Indian warfare, but not its goals or tactics.

Sources:

Daniel K. Richter, *The Ordeal of the Longhouse: The Peoples of the Iroquois League in the Era of European Colonization* (Chapel Hill: University of North Carolina Press, 1992);

Bruce G. Trigger, ed., *Handbook of North American Indians, Volume 15: Northeast* (Washington, D.C.: Smithsonian Institution, 1988).

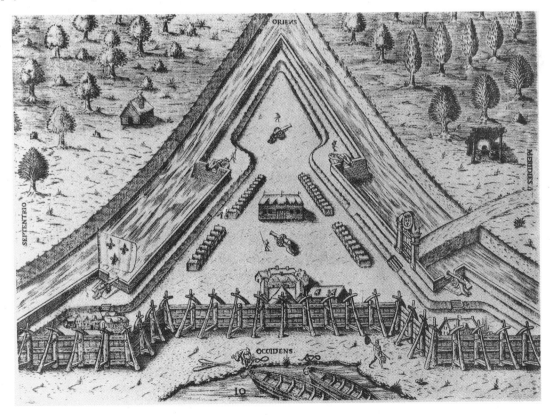

Plan of Fort Caroline in Florida (engraving by Theodor de Bry, after a painting by Jacques le Moyne, 1564)

ANIMALS OF WAR

Much of the military superiority the Spanish enjoyed over the Indians of North America stemmed from their use of two animals: dogs and horses. Trained war dogs proved especially effective in the dense terrain of the Deep South. The savage Irish hounds that accompanied the Hernando de Soto expedition, for example, were able to locate and brutally kill Indian warriors who sought refuge in the near-impenetrable swamps of the Gulf Coast. As valuable as war dogs proved, though, horses constituted the Spaniards' principal military edge in the New World. In part, their advantage was psychological: having never seen horses, Native Americans found the huge creatures terrifying. Horses, however, provided more than just a psychological edge. Riding armored mounts and wearing armor themselves, Spanish cavalrymen equipped with powerful lances were far more mobile than foot-bound Indian warriors and could, by charging, rout virtually any Native American force they encountered in open combat. The only defense sixteenth-century foot soldiers had against cavalry was the pike, which few Indian tribes possessed and which none knew how to use effectively. Without war dogs and, especially, horses, expeditions such as de Soto's would have had a far more difficult time fending off the southeastern Indians' constant attacks.

Sources: Alfred W. Crosby Jr., *The Columbian Exchange: Biological and Cultural Consequences of 1492* (Westport, Conn.: Greenwood Press, 1972);

Charles M. Hudson, *Knights of Spain, Warriors of the Sun: Hernando De Soto and the South's Ancient Chiefdoms* (Athens: University of Georgia Press, 1997).

THE TRANSFORMATION OF NATIVE AMERICAN WARFARE: TRADE AND THE SHIFT TO ECONOMICALLY MOTIVATED CONFLICT

Change. While warfare among the eastern Indians during the fifteenth and sixteenth centuries followed the mourning-war pattern, it was in the process of being altered by a combination of demographic and economic factors. Eastern Indians practiced slash-and-burn agriculture, which quickly depleted the soil and thus forced settlements to move every twenty or thirty years. Combined with a rising continental population during the centuries prior to European contact, this agricultural system was compelling tribes to fight for control of increasingly scarce territory. More important, the rapidly growing exchange of beaver furs for European manufactured goods during the sixteenth century was beginning to transform dramatically the objectives (as well as the nature and style) of eastern woodland Indian warfare.

Origins of the Fur Trade. The fur trade originated during the early sixteenth century as a side business for European fishermen. French, Spanish, Basque, and Portuguese sailors supplemented the profits earned fishing off Newfoundland by exchanging manufactured goods for the Indians' only salable commodity: beaver pelts. Around the middle of the century, the increasing demand for fashionable beaver-fur hats in Europe transformed the pelt trade into a major economic activity in which merchants exchanged brass items, beads, glass, kettles, liquor, cloth, and, especially, iron weapons for furs. By 1581 the beaver trade had become so lucrative that French merchants from the port of St. Malo began sending ships annually to the Montagnais settlement of Tadoussac on the St. Lawrence River. Within three years earnings were so high that they sent five ships; in 1585 they sent ten.

Hunting Grounds. The fur trade quickly transformed the eastern Indians' blood feuds into territorial contests called beaver wars. The ever-increasing desire for European manufactured goods induced Native Americans such as the Micmacs of coastal Canada to begin specializing in fur trapping. Intensive trapping of beaver, in turn, led them to expand their hunting grounds into areas possessed by other tribes. After hunting beaver to the point of extinction in their own territory, for example,

AZTEC ARMOR

The Spanish soldiers that accompanied early conquistadores such as Juan Ponce de León and Pánfilo de Narváez wore traditional, European metal armor. While such armor proved highly effective in Europe, it was unsuited to campaigning in the humid, swampy south because of its weight and its tendency to create easily infected wounds by chafing against the wearer's bare skin. More important, metal back- and breastplates could not stop the flint-tipped arrows that southeastern Indians such as the Aute fired from their powerful longbows. The more-experienced soldiers who accompanied de Soto consequently adopted the style of armor worn by the Aztec Indians. Composed of several inches of quilted cotton covered by thick leather, Aztec armor protected the Spanish troops from Indian arrows while simultaneously allowing them to maneuver quickly and easily. Without this New World invention, de Soto's expedition would doubtless have suffered more substantially from Indian attacks.

Source: Ian K. Steele, *Warpaths: Invasion of North America* (New York: Oxford University Press, 1994).

Micmacs attacked the nearby Etchemin Indians in an effort to take their rich trapping grounds. The superior [ir]on weapons that the Micmacs received in exchange for [b]eaver pelts ensured that they would prevail. By the early [se]venteenth century, in fact, Micmac assaults had forced [th]e Etchemin to relocate permanently to less-valuable [te]rritory north of the St. Lawrence River.

Centers of Trade. The fur trade also led inland tribes [to] clash with coastal Indians over access to European [tr]ade. Such conflicts stemmed from the coastal tribes' ef[fo]rts to establish exclusive trading relations with the [E]uropeans. During the 1580s, for example, the Montag[n]ais used their position on the Saguenay River—a trade [ro]ute long before the arrival of the Europeans—to profit [n]ot by increasing fur trapping as the Micmacs had done, [b]ut by purchasing pelts from other tribes at a discount [an]d then selling them to the French. To maintain their [m]onopoly, the Montagnais periodically clashed with in[la]nd Native Americans who sought to trade directly with [th]e Europeans. Inland tribes responded to such actions [i]n two fashions. Some attacked coastal Indians and [fo]rced them out of their territory. The Wappingers of [th]e upper Hudson River, for instance, violently drove the

Munsee Indians out of the lower part of the valley. Others sought to restore the balance of power by initiating concerted campaigns designed to seize the iron weapons that underlay the coastal tribes' military advantage. The Mohawks apparently conducted such a campaign against the St. Lawrence Iroquois during the latter half of the sixteenth century.

Ongoing Change. By 1600 the fur trade was well on its way to altering irrevocably the nature of the eastern woodland Indians' wars. The desire for the pelts needed to acquire manufactured goods had already transformed warfare in the Northeast from low-intensity blood feuds to far deadlier contests over hunting grounds and trading sites. At the end of the sixteenth century this process had not yet changed the style and objectives of warfare among tribes living in the interior and in the South. The spreading demand for European manufactured goods, however, and the desire for the iron weapons needed to keep pace with similarly armed hostile neighbors ensured that the fur trade would change the nature of warfare among all the eastern woodland Indian tribes. Growing conflict over territory, moreover, compelled small bands and tribes to join together for protection and led victorious tribes to absorb vanquished ones. It thus abetted the rise of confederations that had begun during the prior century.

Sources:

Neal Salisbury, *Manitou and Providence: Indians, Europeans, and the Making of New England, 1500–1643* (New York: Oxford University Press, 1982);

Bruce G. Trigger, *The Children of Aataentsic: A History of the Huron People to 1660*, 2 volumes (Montreal: McGill-Queen's University Press, 1976);

Trigger, ed., *Handbook of North American Indians, Volume 15: Northeast* (Washington, D.C.: Smithsonian Institution, 1988).

MUSKETS

Initially, the matchlock firearms employed by European troops did not lend themselves well to combat in the New World. Muskets proved highly effective in the mass-formation style warfare common in Europe, but were ill suited to the Indians' favored tactics of ambush and surprise attack because the lighted, smoke-producing wick they required revealed the bearer's location. Sixteenth-century matchlock muskets, moreover, were heavy, unreliable weapons that misfired often and would not work in rain or other inclement weather. In addition they were only accurate up to fifty to seventy-five yards.

The musket nonetheless rapidly became the favored weapon of European troops operating in the New World. This occurred, in part, because some matchlock firearms could fire a spray of small, deadly musket balls that could strike several targets at once. More important, muskets required very little training or skill compared to other projectile weapons such as the crossbow. Ease of use, in fact, led Spanish troops in the New World to use matchlocks exclusively after 1550, even while the crossbow remained the dominant weapon among Spain's European armies.

Sources: M. L. Brown, *Firearms in Colonial America: The Impact on History and Technology, 1492–1792* (Washington, D.C.: Smithsonian Institution, 1980);

Ian K. Steele, *Warpaths: Invasion of North America* (New York: Oxford University Press, 1994).

THE WESTERN INVASION: DIVIDING THE WORLD

The Treaty of Tordesillas. Though its consequences were ultimately indirect, the Treaty of Tordesillas between Spain and Portugal had an enormous effect on European warfare in North America during the sixteenth century. The agreement evolved out of the earlier Treaty of Alcaçovas (1479), which had recognized exclusive Spanish and Portuguese spheres of interest in West Africa and the islands of the eastern Atlantic. Christopher Columbus's discovery of the New World in 1492 upset that arrangement, however, because the Alcaçovas accord contained no provision for newly found territories. To resolve the dispute, Spain and Portugal asked for a ruling from Pope Alexander VI. The pontiff responded by issuing a papal bull—a formal directive from the Pope—that divided the non-Christian world into two spheres demarcated by a line running north to south through the Atlantic Ocean. Spain, according to the Pope's decree, acquired a monopoly on trade and exclusive control of all territory not ruled by a Christian prince in the sphere west of the line; Portugal gained identical

Spanish soldiers massacring the inhabitants of a Native American village (from Bartolomé de las Casas's *Narratio regionum indicarum*, 1614)

privileges in all territories to the east. The two Iberian powers formally accepted the Pope's division of the globe by signing the Treaty of Tordesillas in 1494. With papal approval, therefore, Spain and Portugal had divided the world into two absolutely exclusive spheres into which the vessels of other European states were forbidden from sailing.

Challenges. Not surprisingly, the other nations of Western Europe took issue with the Iberian powers' division of the globe. Francis I of France, in particular, disputed the Spanish and Portuguese contention that the Tordesillas agreement barred other European states from trading or colonizing in the New World. Asking "to see the clause in Adam's will that excludes me from a share in the world," he rejected their claims to exclusive spheres and instead advanced the doctrine of freedom of the seas. England likewise took issue with the Hispano-Portugese division of the world, especially after a majority of its citizens became Protestants. British monarchs such as Elizabeth I consequently championed the competing "doctrine of effective occupation," which held that all Europeans could operate freely in any territory not directly controlled by a Christian prince.

"No Peace beyond the Line." The French and British challenge to the Hispano-Portugese division of the world bore fruit through a series of treaties signed in the late sixteenth and early seventeenth centuries. The most important of these was the Treaty of Cateau-Cambrésis

TREASURE FLEET

The Spanish practice of transporting wealth from the New World in an annual treasure fleet emerged out of a combination of mercantilist economic beliefs and the threat of pirate attacks. Each year two flotillas sailed from Seville to the Caribbean. Dubbed the *galeones*, the Tierra Firma fleet sailed to the ports of Cartagena and Portobello in the Viceroyalty of Peru. The other fleet, the *flota*, sailed to Veracruz in the Viceroyalty of New Spain. After exchanging Spanish manufactured goods for the gold and silver of the New World, the two flotillas rendezvoused in Havana for the perilous return trip. The combined fleet that sailed back to Seville each year carried 20 percent of Philip II's royal revenue and transported the wealth on which Spain's military and diplomatic power rested. It consequently was a factor in virtually every military encounter between European nations in North America during the sixteenth century.

Sources: Max Savelle, *The Origins of American Diplomacy: The International History of Angloamerica, 1492–1763* (New York: Macmillan, 1967);

J. Leitch Wright, *Anglo-Spanish Rivalry in North America* (Athens: University of Georgia Press, 1971).

1559), which ended the Hapsburg-Valois Wars and transformed dramatically the nature of the spheres established by the Treaty of Tordesillas. At the outset of the negotiations, the diplomats found themselves at an impasse between France's demand that it enjoy the right to establish colonies and trade in the New World and Spain's adamant refusal to sanction formally any violation of its sphere. The negotiators resolved this dispute through a *modus vivendi* that granted France the right to trade and colonize unoccupied parts of the Spanish sphere and Spain the right to attack French ships or settlements in territories it occupied. Conflict in the New World, the agreement further stipulated, would not upset peaceful relations between the two nations in Europe. The Treaty of Cateau-Cambrésis thus changed the line established in the Treaty of Tordesillas from one that divided exclusive Spanish and Portuguese zones into one that demarcated two spheres governed by radically different international customs, conventions, and laws. More to the point, the agreement between France and Spain established the principle that there was "no peace" in the New World and the doctrine that war "beyond the Line" did not produce hostilities in Europe. The treaty thus largely divorced conflict in North America from war in Europe.

Sources:
Max Savelle, "Colonial Origins of American Diplomatic Principles," *Pacific Historical Review*, 3 (1934): 334–350;

Savelle, *The Origins of American Diplomacy: The International History of Angloamerica, 1492–1763* (New York: Macmillan, 1967).

THE WESTERN INVASION: EARLY SPANISH EXPEDITIONS TO NORTH AMERICA, 1513-1562

La Florida. Spanish interests in North America during the first half of the sixteenth century centered on La Florida. Conquistadores such as Juan Ponce de León and Pánfilo de Narváez launched repeated invasions beginning in 1513 in hopes of finding gold, seizing slaves, and taking control of the strategic peninsula. While their expeditions often included hundreds of soldiers equipped with muskets, horses, and armor, they failed to achieve their objectives because of the opposition of powerful Indian tribes such as the Timucua, Calusa, Aute, and Apalachee. The Native Americans' resistance was so effective, in fact, that it helped persuade King Philip II of Spain to decree in 1562 that Florida would no longer be the object of Spanish colonization efforts.

Early Efforts. Juan Ponce de León led the first Spanish expedition to Florida in 1513. Seeking gold and slaves, he landed on the east coast of the peninsula just south of present-day St. Augustine. His soldiers could not establish a foothold, however, because of formidable opposition from Timucua Indians already angered by earlier Spanish slave raids. Later, bow-armed Calusa warriors defeated de León's attempt to land at San Carlos Bay on Florida's west coast. In 1517 a force commanded by Hernández de Córdoba landed at San Carlos Bay in search of fresh water. Despite the advantage of steel weapons and muskets, the Spanish again had to retreat because of intense resistance from Calusa archers. In 1521 de León was among those killed by the Calusa in a third failed effort to land at San Carlos Bay.

Narváez. Violent Indian resistance and the absence of treasure shifted attention away from Florida. Spanish interest rapidly rekindled, however, after Hernando Cortés's conquest of the fabulously rich Aztec Empire raised the possibility of hidden wealth in inland Florida. As a result, the brutal conqueror of Cuba and Jamaica, Pánfilio de Narváez, led an expedition of four hundred men and forty-two horses to the peninsula in 1528 in search of "other Mexicos." Faced with such a large and well-armed Spanish force, the Timucuas adopted a passive-resistance strategy designed to move the invaders out of their territory with as little bloodshed as possible. They consequently hid food, avoided contact, and, after discovering what the Spanish wanted, repeatedly told the invaders that their traditional enemies, the Apalachee, possessed large quantities of gold.

Demise. Encouraged by the Timucuans, the Spanish force moved north into Apalachee territory where they attacked the first village they came upon. While the assault produced no gold—the Apalachee possessed none—it provoked the bow-armed Indians to begin a guerrilla campaign of hit-and-run attacks. The absence of treasure and the ferocity of the Apalachees' resistance soon spurred Narváez to move westward into Aute territory. After nine days of ambushes and night attacks at the hands of the Apalachee, the Spanish arrived at the Aute's village only to discover that the Indians had torched their settlement to keep the invaders from find-

A 1.75-inch metal tip to a Spanish crossbow dart, circa 1540, found near Tallahassee, Florida (Florida Bureau of Archaeological Research, Tallahassee)

ing any food. Lack of provisions, the death of ten soldiers in Aute ambushes, and a malaria epidemic finally persuaded Narváez to build boats and abandon his expedition. Only four survivors made it back to Mexico.

De Soto. While the failure of the Narváez expedition temporarily diminished Spanish interest in southeastern North America, Francisco Pizarro's conquest of the wealthy Incan Empire in the early 1530s reignited hopes that La Florida held vast stores of hidden treasures. One of Pizarro's lieutenants, Hernando de Soto, consequently landed a powerful expeditionary force of infantry and cavalry at Tampa Bay in 1539. He solved the problems that had plagued the Narváez expedition by brutally extorting food from the Native Americans and by having his men wear lightweight Aztec armor rather than heavy, European-style breastplates. His troops were thus able to spend the next four years roaming about North America bullying Indians and searching for riches. Constant Native American attacks and the failure to discover gold, however, persuaded the Spanish to abandon the expedition and return to New Spain in 1543.

Later Forays. De Soto's failure to find treasure diminished hopes that Florida contained mineral wealth but did not end Spanish interest in the peninsula. In 1549 the Dominican priest Luis Cáncer de Barbastro sought to convert Florida's Indians by establishing a mission among the Timucuas. Still angry at the Spanish because of Narváez and de Soto's depredations, the Timucuans quickly destroyed the mission and killed Cáncer. In the late 1550s Philip II ordered the viceroy of New Spain, Luis de Velasco, to establish a fortified colony on Florida's east coast that could aid shipwrecked sailors and protect the treasure fleet. Commanded by Tristán de Luna y Arellano, this new expedition failed largely because a powerful hurricane sank most of the ships and

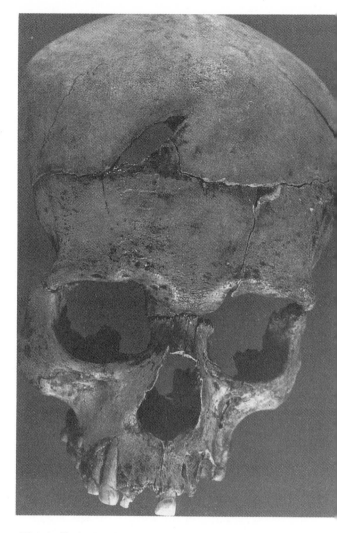

The skull of a Native American male, age 50 and dating from 1540, found in northwest Georgia. The gash above the right eye was caused by a sword stroke (Georgia State University)

The thigh bone of an elderly Native American woman, circa 1540, with three sword cuts (Georgia State University)

Native American warriors shooting poisoned arrows at a French ship (engraving by Theodor de Bry, circa 1594–1596)

killed many of the settlers. Three other efforts to establish a colony in Florida between 1560 and 1563 proved equally unsuccessful, in part because of unremitting Indian hostility. The failure of those expeditions, in turn, led Philip II to stop all efforts to settle Florida. From 1513 to 1562, therefore, the Indians of La Florida had successfully resisted a series of well-organized, large-scale efforts by Europe's most powerful state to subjugate them.

Sources:

Charles Hudson, *The Southeastern Indians* (Knoxville: University of Tennessee Press, 1976);

Ian K. Steele, *Warpaths: Invasion of North America* (New York: Oxford University Press, 1994).

THE WESTERN INVASION: FRANCO-SPANISH CONFLICT IN NORTH AMERICA

Interests. By the early 1560s, Pánfilo de Narváez and Hernando de Soto's failure to discover easily extractable wealth and the hostility of powerful Indian tribes such as the Calusa combined to diminish Spanish interest in the southeastern part of North America. La Florida, however, continued to attract the attention of Spain and other European states because of its strategic position just north of the course the annual Spanish treasure fleet took on its riches-laden return trip to Seville. After the Peace of Cateau-Cambrésis in 1559, the French crown in particular eyed Florida as an ideal location from which privateers could attack the treasure fleet and plunder Spain's New World settlements. France consequently made plans to establish a fort on the peninsula's Atlantic coast. For the Spanish

crown, on the other hand, Florida served as a critical bulwark that protected its Caribbean possessions from raiders. Much of Spain's efforts to defend its New World empire consequently centered on ensuring that a European rival such as France never took possession of the peninsula.

Fort Caroline. Following the failure of the Tristán de Luna y Arellano expedition in 1562, King Philip II of Spain concluded that the Timucua and Calusa Indians were themselves powerful and hostile enough to keep Spain's European competitors out of Florida. That same year, however, French admiral Gaspard de Coligny, a Huguenot, or French Protestant, sent an expedition to establish a short-lived colony on the site of present-day Port Royal, South Carolina. Though that settlement failed, Coligny decided to send a second force of two hundred soldiers and colonists under the command of René Goulaine de Laudonnière to Florida with orders to establish a permanent base. Arriving in June 1564, de Laudonnière's group constructed Fort Caroline near the mouth of the St. John River on Florida's Atlantic coast. Conflict came quickly for them; not long after they built their settlement, they found themselves embroiled in the local Timucua Indians' intertribal wars. More important, de Laudonnière's men were soon raiding Spanish settlements and ships in the Caribbean.

Spanish Response. News of the French settlement soon persuaded Philip to reverse his recent decree against colonizing Florida. He consequently ordered Pedro Menéndez de Avilés, former commander of the Indies fleets, to lead an expedition to Florida, end the French menace, and establish a permanent Spanish settlement that could control the peninsula. Menéndez's powerful force of eight hundred men arrived in Florida in August 1565 only to discover that a French squadron carrying five hundred reinforcements had beaten them to Fort Caroline. Aware that the newly arrived Huguenot infantry made an amphibious assault on the fort impossible, Menéndez decided to sail forty miles to the south and establish a base before undertaking an overland attack on the French stronghold. Shortly after the Spanish came ashore and set up their camp, Timucua Indians hostile to the French informed Menéndez that the French naval commander, Jean Ribault, was stripping Fort Caroline of most of its defenders in order to launch a surprise amphibious assault on the Spaniards. Taking advantage of this information and of a severe storm that dispersed and wrecked Ribault's fleet, Menéndez marched his troops overland and stormed Fort Caroline in a successful dawn attack. In keeping with the savage and unforgiving nature of Reformation warfare, he subsequently charged more than one hundred of the recently surrendered Huguenots with heresy and had them executed on the spot. Most of the survivors of Ribault's fleet—including its commander—received a similar fate. With the help of nature and the Timucua Indians, therefore, Spain had ended the French threat to Florida.

Consequences. The struggle between France and Spain for control of Florida had important consequences both for the colonization of the southeast and for European warfare in the New World. The Spanish victory ended a serious threat to future treasure fleets and greatly limited France's capacity to meddle in Spain's Caribbean territories. The ability of Spain and France to remain at peace in Europe while their forces fought in the New World, meanwhile, reinforced the implicit provisions in the Treaty of Cateau-Cambrésis that war "beyond the Line" did not affect relations in the Old World and that "might makes right" in the Americas. Most important, the conflict led Spain to conclude that it could ensure against another European power establishing a base in Florida only by maintaining a permanent settlement on the peninsula. St. Augustine, the base that Menéndez had established for his overland attack on Fort Caroline, thus became the first permanent European settlement in North America.

Sources:

Eugene Lyon, *The Enterprise of Florida: Pedro Menéndez de Avilés and the Spanish Conquest of 1565–1568* (Gainesville: University Presses of Florida, 1976);

Paul Quattlebaum, *The Land Called Chicora: The Carolinas under Spanish Rule with French Intrusions, 1520–1670* (Gainesville: University Presses of Florida, 1956);

Ian K. Steele, *Warpaths: Invasion of North America* (New York: Oxford University Press, 1994);

J. Leitch Wright, *Anglo-Spanish Rivalry in North America* (Athens: University of Georgia Press, 1971).

THE WESTERN INVASION: SPAIN'S EMPIRE IN LA FLORIDA, 1565-1585

Consolidation. Following his defeat of the French in 1565, Pedro Menéndez de Avilés, Spanish governor of La Florida, moved to establish control over the southeastern

A marine shell gorget, circa 1200–1450 A.D., showing the falcon impersonator, a Mississippian warrior in a falcon costume carrying a mace and a severed head (Museum of the American Indian, Heye Foundation, New York)

part of North America. He began by securing his northern flank through the construction of Fort San Felipe on Parris Island, South Carolina, near the site of the short-lived stronghold the French had built in 1562. Garrisoned with 160 men and six cannon, San Felipe joined St. Augustine and Fort Caroline—renamed San Mateo by the Spanish—as the core of Spain's defenses in La Florida. Menéndez supplemented these larger forts with seven smaller coastal garrisons spread along both sides of the Florida coast. These smaller installations, Menéndez ordered, were to be supplied by tribute extracted from the local Indians. Partly because of the hostility that this supply system inspired among the peninsula's Native Americans, all of the smaller garrisons failed by 1569 save for the Guale mission of San Pedro de Tacatcuru on the coast of present-day Georgia.

Inland Empire. Having established at least nominal command of the coast, Menéndez moved to gain control over the interior of southeastern North America. In 1566 he sent a force of several hundred soldiers under the command of newly arrived Capt. Juan Pardo inland from San Felipe with orders to take food from the Indians and to conquer the interior. In 1567 Pardo again ventured inland, going as far as the foothills of the Blue Ridge Mountains, where his men built the small fort of San Juan de Xuala. After garrisoning the fort with a small force of thirty men under the command of Sgt. Hernando Moyano de Morales, Pardo explored an alternate return route to the coast. Moyano had little interest in defending a static post, however, and consequently became involved in intertribal war-are. Later, Pardo returned from the coast with orders to construct and garrison a series of blockhouses spread across the Southeast. The establishment of these garrisons and the Indians' apparent willingness to accept Spanish rule led Menéndez to conclude in late 1567 that he had pacified the region.

Decline. Menéndez's empire collapsed suddenly in the spring of 1568. As with the installations along the Florida coast, the scattered garrisons that he established to control the interior proved to be simultaneously too small to dominate the Indians and too large for the Native Americans to supply easily with food. Enraged by Spanish abuses and demands for provisions, the Indians rose up against the invaders, destroyed all of their blockhouses, and ejected them from the interior. That same year, the French retaliated for Menéndez's earlier execution of Huguenot prisoners by sacking Fort San Mateo and hanging the survivors. A later French effort to take control of the area failed, however, because of Indian hostility and an untimely shipwreck.

Anglo-Spanish War. The Spanish continued their efforts to establish control over the Southeast during the next few decades, but never had the manpower needed to dominate the Indians of the region. Indeed Native American resistance led the Spanish to abandon temporarily Fort San Felipe in the 1570s; the Cusabo tribe quickly took advantage of their absence by burning the fort to the ground. On the eve of the Anglo-Spanish War, therefore, the Spanish found themselves too weak to overcome the opposition of powerful Indian tribes and, thus, unable to subjugate the Southeast. At the same time, however, they were able to deny Florida to their European rivals and were thereby able to protect the valuable treasure fleets from privateers based on the strategically critical peninsula.

Sources:
Charles Hudson, *The Juan Pardo Expeditions: Exploration of the Carolinas and Tennessee, 1566–1568* (Washington: Smithsonian Institution, 1990);

Eugene Lyon, *The Enterprise of Florida: Pedro Menéndez de Avilés and the Spanish Conquest of 1565–1568* (Gainesville: University Presses of Florida, 1976);

Paul Quattlebaum, *The Land Called Chicora: The Carolinas under Spanish Rule with French Intrusions, 1520–1670* (Gainesville: University Presses of Florida, 1956);

Ian K. Steele, *Warpaths: Invasion of North America* (New York: Oxford University Press, 1994).

THE WESTERN INVASION: WARFARE BETWEEN ENGLAND AND SPAIN IN NORTH AMERICA, 1585-1604

Old World Wars. Following the Peace of Cateau-Cambrésis in 1559, most European crowns accepted the doctrine that fighting "beyond the Line" did not affect peaceful relations in the Old World. The opposite, however, did not hold true: conflict in Europe in the late sixteenth century often extended into the Americas. This occurred, in part, because Spain—by far the dominant power of the day—derived much of its strength from the gold and silver it received from its New World possessions. Aware of both the importance of Spain's New World empire and of its vulnerability, rival powers attacked Philip II's possessions in the Americas and commissioned private ship captains known as privateers to raid Spanish shipping in the Caribbean. Periodically they even sought to establish bases such as Fort Caroline from which their corsairs could prey upon the riches-laden treasure fleets. Spain, meanwhile, worked diligently to protect its New World settlements and the vital sea lanes on which the treasure fleets sailed by sending warships to sweep privateers from the seas and by attacking any European bases that it found on the North American coast.

Origins. The pattern of European conflicts spreading to the New World held true during the Anglo-Spanish War of 1585–1604. Relations between Spain and Britain had been deteriorating steadily since Henry VIII officially broke with Rome and declared England a Protestant nation in the 1530s. Unauthorized trading and privateering in the Spanish territories of the West Indies by men such as Sir John Hawkins and Sir Francis Drake further eroded ties between Queen Elizabeth I of Britain and King Philip of Spain. The final break occurred in 1585 when Elizabeth dispatched troops to help Dutch Protestant rebels in their uprising against Spain. After Philip retaliated by outlawing British trade with Spain and by seizing hundreds of English ships in Iberian ports, the two nations found themselves at war.

War in the New World. From virtually the moment she sent troops to Holland in 1585, Elizabeth pursued two policies that extended the war to the Americas. First, she initiated overt raiding against Spain's New World possessions by sending a 23-ship, 2,000-man fleet under the command of Drake to the West Indies with orders to capture key Spanish ports and to attack the treasure fleets. Second, she commissioned Sir Walter Raleigh to build a fortified settlement on the North American coast

A pair of obsidian blades, circa 200 B.C.–400 A.D., found at a Hopewell Site in Ross County, Ohio (Field Museum of Natural History, Chicago)

to provide British corsairs with a year-round New World base from which to operate against Spanish shipping in the Americas. Sailing first, Drake swept the Caribbean of Spanish merchantmen and sacked the cities of Cartagena, Santo Domingo, and St. Augustine—the latter to ensure the safety of Raleigh's colony. In the meantime, Raleigh's men had established the settlement of Roanoke on North Carolina's Outer Banks. Conflict with the Indians and the failure of reinforcements to arrive, however, led the colonists to abandon the settlement and return home with Drake's fleet. Raleigh again founded a settlement on Roanoke Island in 1587, but it too failed. The Spanish responded to the Drake raid by consolidating their North American garrisons at St. Augustine and reacted to the establishment of the Roanoke colony by sending ships to scout its location in preparation for an attack.

The Treaty of London. Although small-scale British privateering continued in the Caribbean, the Anglo-Spanish War remained a largely European affair after the Spanish Armada of 1588, especially after Drake and Hawkins's failed 1595 raid on the Spanish West Indies. It eventually came to an end in 1604 when the financial and human costs of the war led Spain and Britain to agree to the Treaty of London. As with the earlier Peace of Cateau-Cambrésis, the Treaty of London included an informal agreement that war "beyond the Line" did not produce hostilities in Europe and that there was "no peace" in the Americas. The Treaty of London thus strengthened the two-spheres doctrine that war in the New World did not lead to conflict in Europe. At the same time, the agreement and the war that preceded it reinforced the notion that conflict in the Old World could and would be extended to the Americas.

Sources:

Karen Ordhal Kupperman, *Roanoke: The Abandoned Colony* (Totowa N.J.: Rowman & Allandheld, 1984);

Max Savelle, *The Origins of American Diplomacy: The International History of Angloamerica, 1492–1763* (New York: Macmillan, 1967);

J. Leitch Wright, *Anglo-Spanish Rivalry in North America* (Athens: University of Georgia Press, 1971).

HEADLINE MAKERS

JACQUES CARTIER

1491-1557
FRENCH EXPLORER AND NAVIGATOR

Early Career. Born in 1491, Jacques Cartier was a French mariner who sailed out of the port city of St. Malo. His early life remains a mystery, although we know he undertook voyages of exploration to Newfoundland and Brazil during the early decades of the sixteenth century. His success on those trips brought him to the attention King Francis I of France, who hoped to discover either New World wealth or a passage to the Far East. Francis consequently subsidized two exploratory trips by Cartier to North America in the mid 1530s.

First Voyage. Cartier's first voyage to mainland North America took place in 1534. After crossing the Atlantic and charting the western shore of Newfoundland, he sailed into Chaleur Bay, where he met a party of Micmac Indians in canoes. Already experienced in the fur trade, the Micmacs eagerly swapped their beaver skins for French manufactured goods such as kettles and knives. Later, in Gaspé Bay, Cartier encountered members of the Stadacona tribe, who had traveled down the St. Lawrence River to fish. Cartier initially enjoyed warm relations with the Stadaconans and their leader, Donnacona, but soon upset the Indians by erecting a cross on land the tribe regarded as its own. The Frenchman further antagonized the Stadaconans by kidnapping Donnacona's two sons, Taignoagny and Domagaya, so that they could learn French and serve as interpreters on his next voyage. While these heavy-handed and offensive acts angered Donnacona, his desire for trade and need for allies in the Stadaconans' struggle with the powerful Micmacs compelled him to tolerate the French actions.

Second Voyage. Cartier's second voyage to mainland North America engendered even greater hostility between the French and the Stadaconans. Sailing in 1535, he had Taignoagny and Domagaya guide him up the St. Lawrence River to the Stadaconans' village near the site of present-day Quebec. Happy that Cartier had returned with Donnacona's sons, the Stadaconans welcomed the French warmly and treated them as close allies. Conflicting aims and cultural differences, however, soon resulted in animosity between the Europeans and Stadaconans. Much of this hostility stemmed from Donnacona's desire to establish an exclusive trading relationship that would allow his tribe to monopolize the fur trade in the St. Lawrence valley. Cartier's insistence on traveling upriver to visit the rival Hochelaga Indians consequently angered the Stadaconan headman greatly. The Indians' tendency to carry off items in accordance with their belief that unused articles were free for the taking, along with Cartier's construction of a small fort on tribal land and the outbreak of a deadly disease among the Stadaconans further poisoned relations and left the two sides on the brink of hostilities. Even Cartier's departure generated ill will because of his decision to kidnap Donnacona and nine other Native Americans in hopes that a new Stadaconan leader would be more favorably disposed to the French. None of the abducted Indians ever returned to their native land.

Third Voyage. While relations had become increasingly antagonistic during Cartier's first two visits, the French and the Stadaconans had managed to avoid outright hostilities. Such was not the case when Cartier returned to the St. Lawrence valley in 1541 under orders from Viceroy Jean-François de La Rocque de Roberval to establish a permanent trading settlement. Sailing upriver past the Stadaconan villages, Cartier founded the fortified colony of Charlesbourg-Royal on a hill overlooking the St. Lawrence River. At first the Indians traded with the French settlement. Cartier's appropriation of Stadaconan territory, his failure to return the Native Americans he had taken in 1536, and his decision to deny the tribe a trading monopoly infuriated the Stadaconans, however, and led them to war with the French. Concluding that Charlesbourg-Royal was too strong for a frontal assault, the Stadaconans opted for an Indian-style war of attrition in which they ambushed Frenchmen foraging for food or firewood. Their strategy proved highly effective: during the winter of 1541–1542, they killed thirty-five of Cartier's men. Along with Roberval's failure to arrive with reinforcements, unending Indian hostility persuaded Cartier to abandon Charlesbourg-Royal in June 1542.

France-Roy. Just a month after Cartier departed, Roberval sailed up the St. Lawrence with 150 new colonists and established a fortified hilltop colony called France-Roy near the site of Charlesbourg-Royal. The new French settlement did not face Stadaconan attacks because Roberval kept his men from antagonizing the Indians and because his colony was larger and better armed than Cartier's. Much of the Indians' earlier animosity toward Cartier, moreover, was personal in nature. Continued cold relations with the Indians nonetheless helped persuade Roberval to abandon France-Roy in the spring of 1543.

Temporary End. Unlike Hernando de Soto, neither Cartier nor Roberval ventured to North America expressly looking for conflict with the Indians. They hoped, rather, to avoid hostilities with the Native Americans while they established trading relations and searched for valuable mineral deposits. Sharp cultural differences, French appropriation of lands that the Indians regarded as their own, trade disputes, individual acts of depredation, and the French habit of kidnapping Native Americans nonetheless ensured that, good intentions aside, they ended up warring with the Stadaconans. Such conflicts proved especially costly for the French because they were not strong enough to establish colonies in North America in the face of Indian hostility. France, in fact, was to mount no further attempt to colonize the St. Lawrence valley until after 1600. Once again, therefore, the Indians of North America proved themselves able to defeat a sizable, well-supported European invasion.

Sources:

Bruce G. Trigger, *The Children of Aataentsic: A History of the Huron People to 1660*, 2 volumes (Montreal: McGill-Queen's University Press, 1976);

Wilcomb E. Washburn, ed., *Handbook of North American Indians, Volume 4: History of Indian-White Relations* (Washington, D.C.: Smithsonian Institution, 1988).

FRANCISCO VÁSQUEZ DE CORONADO

1510?-1554

CONQUISTADOR

Expedition. In 1536 Alvar Núñez Cabeza de Vaca and the three other survivors of the Pánfilo de Narváez expedition finally reached Mexico City after wandering through present-day Texas for eight years. Though these men had seen no treasure during the time they spent living among the Indians, they had heard rumors of several large, wealthy cities located to the northwest of Spain's Mexican possessions. Their story of an Indian civilization akin to the Aztec Empire elicited great interest among the Spaniards living in Mexico City, particularly the viceroy of New Spain, Antonio Mendoza. De Vaca's account persuaded Mendoza to send one of his protégés, Francisco Vásquez de Coronado, governor of the province of Nueva Galicia, to locate and take possession of what many Spaniards had concluded were the fabled Seven Cities of Cíbola. Coronado was forbidden from indiscriminately attacking Indians or looting their wealth as Hernando Cortés had during his conquest of the Aztecs, however, because Emperor Charles V's recently promulgated New Laws expressly prohibited such practices.

Zuni and Hopi. Coronado's large expedition of 250 cavalry, 80 infantry, 1,000 Indians, and thousands of horses, cows, and sheep departed from Culiacán, the capital of Nueva Galicia, in the spring of 1540. Moving ahead with a small advanced guard, he reached Háwikuh, a Zuni pueblo, in July. Despite Coronado's peaceful intentions, fighting broke out almost immediately between the Indians and the Spanish. Equipped with muskets, armor, and horses, his men made short work of it: they killed a dozen Zunis and easily occupied the town. An expedition sent north to the Hopi Indians' pueblos likewise resulted in a brief engagement that ended in the Spanish occupying a town. Coronado thus had little trouble dealing with the militarily inferior Pueblo Indians. The economic results of the campaign were disappointing, however; neither the Zunis nor the Hopis possessed precious metals or stones. Coronado nonetheless sent a messenger to New Spain ordering the expedition's main body to join the advanced guard in Pueblo territory.

The Tiguex War. With cold weather approaching, Coronado decided to winter in the part of the Rio Grande valley inhabited by the Tiwa Indians. At first, relations between the Spaniards and the Indians were amicable. Intolerable pressures on the Native Americans' food supply and sexual assaults on Indian women soon antagonized the Tiwas, however, and led them to attack the Spaniards' horses. Believing that he had to crush the Tiwas decisively to intimidate other tribes, Coronado retaliated by savagely sacking the biggest Tiwa settlement and burning thirty Indians to death at the stake. His men then besieged the large and well-defended pueblo of Moho, which capitulated in March 1541 due to lack of food. Coronado enslaved the survivors and distributed them among his men.

Disappointment. Still hoping to find treasure, Coronado sent out small parties in various directions. He led one group eastward into present-day Kansas in 1541 in search of the Quivira Indians, who were rumored to possess large amounts of gold. Coronado succeeded in finding the Quivirans but discovered that they possessed nothing of value. After spending the winter of 1541–1542 in the Rio Grande valley, Coronado led his men back to Mexico. Shortly after his return, Coronado faced charges of having violated the New Laws by abusing Indians and by taking goods from them. He eventually cleared himself of these charges but lost his position as governor of Nueva Galicia. He died soon afterward.

Legacy. Coronado's expedition had important and lasting consequences for both the Spanish and the Pueblo Indians. For the Pueblos, Coronado's invasion demonstrated that the Spanish were a hostile, arrogant people who retaliated viciously for any infraction and who enjoyed a vast military advantage due to their horses, muskets, and iron weapons. For the Spanish, meanwhile, Coronado's foray into the Southwest ended the belief that North America contained a wealthy, easily plundered Indian civilization akin to the Aztec or Incan empires. Spain consequently lost interest in the region until settlers under the leadership of Juan de Oñate established the colony of New Mexico in 1598.

Sources:

Elizabeth H. John, *Storms Brewed in Other Men's Worlds: The Confrontation of Indians, Spanish and French in the Southwest, 1540–1795* (College Station: Texas A&M University Press, 1975);

Alfonso Ortiz, ed., *Handbook of North American Indians*, Volume 9: *Southwest* (Washington, D.C.: Smithsonian Institution, 1979).

HERNANDO DE SOTO

1500?-1542
CONQUISTADOR

Ruthless Ambition. Perhaps no one better exemplified the savage nature of the sixteenth-century Europeans who invaded North America than Hernando de Soto. A captain in the Spanish army at the age of twenty, de Soto had served as Francisco Pizarro's chief military advisor during Spain's ruthless conquest of Peru in the early 1530s. While de Soto had become a wealthy man as a result of that venture, he remained restless and desired to increase his fortune. Evidence of gold in the southeastern part of North America consequently spurred him to organize an expedition in hopes of finding another New World empire to plunder.

Followers. De Soto organized his expedition in the port city of Havana on the island of Cuba. His force consisted of 330 infantrymen equipped with swords, harquebuses, and crossbows, and 270 cavalrymen armed with swords and lances. Primarily veterans of earlier New World expeditions, his men opted for the lighter and more effective Aztec armor over the heavy and ineffective European variety. His force also included about 100 slaves, servants, camp followers, and pig herders. Finally, the expedition took with it mules to carry baggage, a herd of hogs—the ancestors of today's southern razorbacks—to provide a source of food, and a pack of brutal Irish hounds to hunt and kill Indians in the swamps of the Deep South.

Methods. By using the approach pioneered by Hernando Cortés and Pizarro, de Soto hoped to avoid the fate that had befallen the Pánfilo de Narváez expedition a decade earlier. Like his predecessors, de Soto planned to use advanced weapons, armored cavalry, and better tactics to dominate the numerically superior Indians. More important, he aimed to gain information, secure concubines for his men, ensure against attack, and extort the food on which his expedition depended by taking a tribe's leader hostage upon entering its territory. When Indians did attack, moreover, he planned to retaliate savgely by slaughtering any he could find and by burning their settlements.

Early Campaign. Conflict with the Indians began as soon as de Soto's men landed at Tampa Bay in May 1539. Timucuan hit-and-run attacks increased in frequency because de Soto's men ruthlessly torched settlements and mercilessly killed peaceful Indians who approached them. When the Spanish passed into Apalachee territory they stumbled into a large, skillfully laid ambush at a difficult swamp crossing. The Apalachee thereafter constantly harassed de Soto's men—who wintered in their territory—by attacking suddenly and by ambushing small, isolated detachments. De Soto retaliated by killing any Apalachees that his men caught.

Ocute and Cofitachequi. While de Soto's relations with Native Americans were almost universally hostile, he did not war with every tribe he encountered. The Ocute of southern Georgia, in fact, allied with his expedition for an attack on their rivals, the Cofitachequi. The alliance with the Ocute was short-lived, however, and reflected the difference between European and Indian military objectives. The Ocute took vengeance on their traditional foe by killing and taking scalps in the first few Cofitachequi villages they entered. They then returned to their homeland satisfied that they had evened the score with their rivals. The Spanish, in contrast, sought wealth to plunder and food to fuel their expedition; de Soto's men consequently looted pearls and other valuables from the Cofitachequis' temples and forced the Indians to supply them with corn.

Battle of Mabila. De Soto's only major pitched battle occurred later in 1540 in the large trading center of Mabila, located in present-day Alabama. As was their custom, the Spanish seized the Mabilan chief, Tazcaluza, upon meeting him on the outskirts of his chiefdom. Tazcaluza was ingratiating and compliant; he gladly escorted de Soto's men to Mabila, where, he promised, they would find great stores of food and many women. Unbeknownst to de Soto, though, the Mabilan chief had laid an elaborate trap designed to destroy the unsuspecting Spaniards. Shortly after de Soto's men entered the town, Tazcaluza sprang the trap by escaping from his Spanish guards. Suddenly, Indian warriors leapt from hiding, rained arrows on the invaders, and forced them out of the town with heavy casualties. Believing that they had routed de Soto, the Indians pursued the fleeing Spanish into the open fields outside Mabila's fifteen-foot palisades. The Spanish, however, were preparing a trap of their own. After luring the Native Americans away from the protection of Mabila's walls by feigning a disorderly retreat, de Soto's elite, armored cavalry suddenly spun about and launched a devastating counterattack that crushed the Indians' charge. Soon thereafter, the Spanish infantry reentered the town and set it to the torch while de Soto's powerful cavalry prevented any Indians from escaping the conflagration.

Consequences. Native American losses at Mabila were staggering. Between twenty-five hundred and five thousand had died in the battle, most burning to death in the inferno that consumed the town. The Spanish likewise suffered heavily even though they wore Aztec armor and enjoyed the overwhelming advantage of cavalry: hundreds had been injured; more than forty had died; and they had lost some three dozen horses. More important, the battle had eroded seriously the expedition's morale and had led de Soto and his lieutenants to doubt whether they could conquer and control the Indians of North America as they had the Aztec and Incan empires.

Death. Increasingly desperate because he had discovered no gold and because his men were becoming mutinous, de Soto moved northward into Chicaza territory in hopes of finding treasure. That proved to be a poor decision, however, because the Chicaza had developed a new tactic for dealing with the Spanish invaders: night attacks. In one especially effective night assault on de Soto's winter camp, the Chicaza greatly weakened the expedition by killing a dozen Spaniards and slaughtering more than fifty horses. Continued night raids eventually drove the Spanish force westward across the Mississippi, where they destroyed many Indian villages and seized large quantities of corn. Then, while moving south along the Mississippi in the spring of 1542, de Soto suddenly took ill. He died in May and was replaced as commander by one of his lieutenants, Luis de Moscoso y Alvarado.

The End. Having heard rumors of Coronado's expedition in the southwestern part of North America, Moscoso decided to move west through the plains of Texas in hopes of joining his countrymen. His men soon ran low on provisions and began to suffer grievous losses from the Tonkawa Indians' skillfully laid ambushes. Desperate for food and weary from the Native Americans' constant harassing attacks, the Spanish returned to the Mississippi, where they spent the winter of 1542–1543. Deciding to abandon the expedition that spring, Moscoso's men constructed seven barges on which they planned to escape to Mexico. Their conflict with the Indians had not yet ended, however. A coalition of Mississippi valley tribes temporarily put aside their differences and joined together to pursue the Spanish down the river in a flotilla of canoes. Later, javelin-throwing Indians warred with the Spanish as they passed westward along the Gulf Coast. In the end, only about three hundred survivors— half the number that landed with de Soto at Tampa Bay—returned to Spanish Mexico.

Impact. De Soto's expedition had profound ramifications for all the parties involved. It demonstrated that North America lacked easily plundered treasure and that the Indians were still too powerful to conquer. Consequently Spanish authorities lost interest in La Florida for several decades. As for the Native Americans, they were able to drive the Spanish out of North America despite the invaders' superior weapons, better tactics, and irresistible armored cavalry. On the other hand, they had suffered thousands of deaths in battle and had lost tens of thousands more as a result of the diseases that the Spaniards had brought with them. De Soto's invasion thus weakened the southeastern Indians greatly and left them increasingly unable to withstand the European incursions that grew steadily during the seventeenth century.

Sources:

Miguel Albornoz, *Hernando de Soto: Knight of the Americas* (New York Watts, 1986);

Charles M. Hudson, *Knights of Spain, Warriors of the Sun: Hernando d Soto and the South's Ancient Chiefdoms* (Athens: University of Georgia Press, 1997);

Ian K. Steele, *Warpaths: Invasion of North America* (New York: Oxford University Press, 1994).

PUBLICATIONS

René Laudonnière, *Three Voyages,* edited and translated by Charles E. Bennett (Gainesville: University Presses of Florida, 1975)—an account of the failed French effort to establish a base in Florida from which privateers could raid the Spanish treasure fleet. This work contains excellent material on French impressions of Indian warfare, on the 1565 clash with Pedro Menéndez de Avilés's Spaniards, and on Laudonnière's dramatic escape from Fort Caroline;

Alvar Nuñez Cabeza de Vaca, *Castaways,* edited by Enrique Pupo-Walker, translated by Frances M. López-Morillas (Berkeley: University of California Press, 1993)—an eyewitness report of Pánfilio de Narváez's expedition to Florida in 1528 by one of its four survivors. De Vaca's narrative contains a superb description of both the Native Americans' style of war and the Narváez expedition's conflict with the Apalachee and the Aute. In addition, it provides a fascinating description of de Vaca's eight-year overland return trip to Spanish Mexico;

Jacques Cartier, *The Voyages of Jacques Cartier,* edited and translated by H. P. Biggar (Ottawa: F. A. Acland, 1924)—the famous French explorer's record of his three expeditions to North America. This book describes in detail the growing conflict between the Stadacona Indians and the French and contains several fine reproductions of original maps.

A Caddoan stone ax, circa 1200–1350 A.D. (Thomas Gilcrease Institute of American History and Art, Tulsa, Oklahoma)

GENERAL REFERENCES

ARTS

Christian F. Betts, *Native Arts of North America* (New York: Oxford University Press, 1980);

Bernadette Bucher, *Icon and Conquest: A Structural Analysis of the Illustrations of de Bry's* Great Voyages (Chicago, Ill.: University of Chicago Press, 1981);

Bainbridge Bunting, *Early Architecture in New Mexico* (Albuquerque: University of New Mexico Press, 1976);

Alan Gowans, *Building Canada: An Architectural History of Canadian Life* (Toronto: Oxford University Press, 1966);

Hugh Honour, *The New Golden Legend: European Images of America from the Discoveries to the Present Time* (New York: Pantheon, 1975);

George Kubler, *The Religious Architecture of New Mexico in the Colonial Period and since the American Occupation* (Albuquerque: University of New Mexico Press, 1990);

Trent Elwood Sanford, *The Architecture of the Southwest: Indian, Spanish, American* (New York: Norton, 1950).

COMMUNICATIONS

James Axtell, "Babel of Tongues: Communicating with the Indians in Eastern North America," in *The Language Encounter in the Americas, 1492–1800,* edited by G. Gray and Norman Fiering (Providence, R.I.: Berghahn Books, forthcoming);

Peter Bakker, "'The Language of the Coast Tribes is Half Basque': A Basque-American Pidgin in Use between Europeans and Native Americans in North America, ca. 1540–ca. 1640," *Anthropological Linguistics,* 31 (1989): 117–147;

Ives Goddard, ed., *Handbook of North American Indians: Languages* (Washington, D.C.: Smithsonian Institution, 1996);

David B. Quinn, *Set Fair for Roanoke: Voyages and Colonies, 1584–1606* (Chapel Hill: University of North Carolina Press, 1985);

Carroll L. Riley, "Early Spanish-Indian Communication in the Greater Southwest," *New Mexico Historical Review,* 46 (1971): 285–314;

David J. Weber, *The Spanish Frontier in North America* (New Haven, Conn. & London: Yale University Press, 1992);

Lawrence C. Wroth, *The Voyages of Giovanni da Verrazzano, 1524–1528* (New Haven, Conn. & London: Yale University Press for the Pierpont Morgan Library, 1970).

EDUCATION

Linda S. Cordell, *Prehistory of the Southwest* (New York: Academic Press, 1984);

Joseph A. Gagliano and Charles E. Ronan, eds., *Jesuit Encounters in the New World: Jesuit Chroniclers, Geographers, Educators, and Missionaries in the Americas, 1549–1767* (Rome, Italy: Institutum Historicum, 1997);

Charles Hudson, *The Southeastern Indians* (Knoxville: University of Tennessee Press, 1976);

Bonnie G. McEwan, ed., *The Spanish Missions of La Florida* (Gainesville: University Press of Florida, 1993);

Bruce G. Trigger, *The Children of Aataentsic: A History of the Huron People to 1660,* 2 volumes (Montreal: McGill-Queen's University Press, 1976).

GOVERNMENT AND LAW

Patricia Galloway, *Choctaw Genesis, 1500–1700* (Lincoln: University of Nebraska Press, 1995);

L. C. Green and Olive P. Dickason, *The Law of Nations and the New World* (Edmonton: University of Alberta Press, 1989);

Charles Hudson, *The Southeastern Indians* (Knoxville: University of Tennessee Press, 1976);

Alice Kehoe, *North American Indians: A Comprehensive Account* (Englewood Cliffs, N.J.: Prentice-Hall, 1981);

John Philip Reid, *A Law of Blood: The Primitive Law of the Cherokee Nation* (New York: New York University Press, 1970);

Daniel K. Richter, *The Ordeal of the Longhouse: The Peoples of the Iroquois League in the Era of European Colonization* (Chapel Hill: University of North Carolina Press, 1992);

J. R. Strayer, *On the Medieval Origins of the Modern State* (Princeton, N.J.: Princeton University Press, 1970);

Rennard Strickland, *Fire and the Spirits: Cherokee Law from Clan to Court* (Norman: University of Oklahoma Press, 1975);

Robert A. Williams, *The American Indian in Western Legal Thought: The Discourses of Conquest* (Oxford: Oxford University Press, 1990).

LIFESTYLES, SOCIAL TRENDS, AND RECREATION

Charles Hudson, *The Southeastern Indians* (Knoxville: University of Tennessee Press, 1976);

Alfonso Ortiz, ed., *Handbook of North American Indians: Southwest*, 2 volumes (Washington, D.C.: Smithsonian Institution, 1979, 1983);

Timothy R. Pauketat and Thomas E. Emerson, eds., *Cahokia: Domination and Ideology in the Mississippian World* (Lincoln: University of Nebraska Press, 1997);

Daniel K. Richter, *The Ordeal of the Longhouse: The Peoples of the Iroquois League in the Era of European Colonization* (Chapel Hill: University of North Carolina Press, 1992);

Bruce G. Trigger, ed., *Handbook of North American Indians: Northeast* (Washington, D.C.: Smithsonian Institution, 1978).

THE PEOPLE

Linda S. Cordell, *Prehistory of the Southwest* (New York: Academic Press, 1984);

Warren L. D'Azevedo, ed., *Handbook of North American Indians: Great Basin* (Washington, D.C.: Smithsonian Institution, 1986);

James E. Dixon, *Quest for the Origins of the First Americans* (Albuquerque: University of New Mexico Press, 1992);

Robert F. Heizer, ed., *Handbook of the North American Indians: California* (Washington, D.C.: Smithsonian Institution, 1978);

Charles Hudson, *The Southeastern Indians* (Knoxville: University of Tennessee Press, 1976);

Bonnie G. McEwan, ed., *The Spanish Missions of La Florida* (Gainesville: University Press of Florida, 1993);

Donald W. Meinig, *The Shaping of America: A Geographical Perspective on 500 Years of History*, Volume 1: *Atlantic America, 1492–1800* (New Haven, Conn.: Yale University Press, 1986);

Alfonso Ortiz, ed., *Handbook of North American Indians: Southwest*, 2 volumes (Washington, D.C.: Smithsonian Institution, 1979, 1983);

Timothy R. Pauketat and Thomas E. Emerson, eds., *Cahokia: Domination and Ideology in the Mississippian World* (Lincoln: University of Nebraska Press, 1997);

James L. Phillips and James A. Brown, eds., *Archaic Hunters and Gatherers in the American Midwest* (New York: Academic Press, 1983);

David B. Quinn, *Set Fair for Roanoke: Voyages and Colonies, 1584–1606* (Chapel Hill: University of North Carolina Press, 1985);

Karl H. Schlesier, ed., *Plains Indians, A.D. 500–1500: The Archaeological Past of Historic Groups* (Norman: University of Oklahoma Press, 1994);

Wayne Suttles, ed., *Handbook of North American Indians: Northwest Coast* (Washington, D.C.: Smithsonian Institution, 1990);

Bruce G. Trigger, ed., *Handbook of North American Indians: Northeast* (Washington, D.C.: Smithsonian Institution, 1978);

Carl Waldman, *Atlas of North American Indians* (New York: Facts on File Publications, 1985);

David J. Weber, *The Spanish Frontier in North America* (New Haven, Conn.: Yale University Press, 1992).

RELIGION

John Bierhorst, ed., *The Red Swan: Myths and Tales of the American Indians* (New York: Farrar Straus Giroux, 1976);

John Bossy, *Christianity in the West, 1400–1700* (New York: Oxford University Press, 1985);

Joseph A. Gagliano and Charles E. Ronan, eds., *Jesuit Encounters in the New World: Jesuit Chroniclers, Geographers, Educators, and Missionaries in the Americas, 1549–1767* (Rome, Italy: Institutum Historicum, 1997);

Richard M. Golden, ed., *The Huguenot Connection: The Edict of Nantes, Its Revocation, and Early French Migration to South Carolina* (Boston: Kluwer, 1988);

Jerald Milanich, *Florida Indians and the Invasion from Europe* (Gainesville: University of Florida Press, 1995);

Daniel K. Richter, *The Ordeal of the Longhouse: The Peoples of the Iroquois League in the Era of European Colonization* (Chapel Hill: University of North Carolina Press, 1992);

Bruce G. Trigger, *The Children of Aataentsic: A History of the Huron People to 1660,* 2 volumes (Montreal: McGill-Queen's University Press, 1976);

Pauline Moffit Watts, "Prophecy and Discovery: On the Spiritual Origins of Christopher Columbus's 'Enterprise of the Indies,'" *American Historical Review,* 90 (1985): 73-102.

SCIENCE AND MEDICINE

Daniel Boorstein, *The Discoverers: A History of Man's Search to Know His World and Himself* (New York: Vintage, 1983);

Lucille H. Brockway, *Science and Colonial Expansion: The Role of the British Royal Botanical Gardens* (New York: Academic Press, 1979);

Alfred W. Crosby, *The Columbian Exchange: Biological and Cultural Consequences of 1492* (Westport, Conn.: Greenwood Press, 1972);

Bailey W. Diffie and George D. Winius, *Foundations of the Portuguese Empire, 1415–1580* (Minneapolis: University of Minnesota Press, 1977);

Thomas Kuhn, *The Copernican Revolution: Planetary Astronomy in the Development of Western Thought* (Cambridge, Mass.: Harvard University Press, 1957);

Geoffrey Parker, *The Military Revolution: Military Innovation and the Rise of the West, 1500–1800* (Cambridge: Cambridge University Press, 1988);

William D. Phillips and Carla Rahn Phillips, *The Worlds of Christopher Columbus* (Cambridge: Cambridge University Press, 1992);

Dava Sobel, *Longitude: The True Story of a Lone Genius Who Solved the Greatest Scientific Problem of His Day* (New York: Walker, 1995).

TRADE AND COMMERCE

Charles Hudson, *The Juan Pardo Expeditions: Exploration of the Carolinas and Tennessee, 1566–1568* (Washington, D.C.: Smithsonian Institution, 1990);

Hudson, *The Southeastern Indians* (Knoxville: University of Tennessee Press, 1976);

Alfonso Ortiz, ed., *Handbook of North American Indians: Southwest,* 2 volumes (Washington, D.C.: Smithsonian Institution, 1979, 1983);

Daniel K. Richter, *The Ordeal of the Longhouse: The Peoples of the Iroquois League in the Era of European Colonization* (Chapel Hill: University of North Carolina Press, 1992);

William C. Sturtevant and Wilcombe Washburn, eds., *Handbook of North American Indians: History of Indian-White Relations* (Washington, D.C.: Smithsonian Institution, 1988);

Bruce G. Trigger, ed., *Handbook of North American Indians: Northeast* (Washington, D.C.: Smithsonian Institution, 1988).

WARFARE

Charles Hudson, *Knights of Spain, Warriors of the Sun: Hernando de Soto and the South's Ancient Chiefdoms* (Athens: University of Georgia Press, 1997);

Hudson, *The Southeastern Indians* (Knoxville: University of Tennessee Press, 1976);

Elizabeth H. John, *Storms Brewed in Other Men's Worlds: The Confrontation of Indians, Spanish and French in the Southwest, 1540–1795* (College Station: Texas A&M University Press, 1975);

Daniel K. Richter, *The Ordeal of the Longhouse: The Peoples of the Iroquois League in the Era of European Colonization* (Chapel Hill: University of North Carolina Press, 1992);

Max Savelle, *The Origins of American Diplomacy: The International History of Angloamerica, 1492–1763* (New York: Macmillan, 1967);

Ian K. Steele, *Warpaths: Invasion of North America* (Oxford: Oxford University Press, 1994);

Bruce G. Trigger, *The Children of Aataentsic: A History of the Huron People to 1660,* 2 volumes (Montreal: McGill-Queen's University Press, 1976);

Trigger, ed., *Handbook of North American Indians: Northeast* (Washington, D.C.: Smithsonian Institution, 1988).

CONTRIBUTORS

AMERICAS: THE PEOPLE

JAMES CARSON
Queen's University

THE ARTS

CHARLENE VILLASEÑOR BLACK
University of New Mexico

COMMUNICATIONS

NANCY L. HAGEDORN
St. John's University

EDUCATION

JAMES CARSON
Queen's University

GOVERNMENT & LAW

TIMOTHY GARRISON
Portland State University

LIFESTYLES, SOCIAL TRENDS,
& RECREATION

GREG O'BRIEN
University of Kentucky

RELIGION

RACHELLE E. FRIEDMAN
Harvard University

SCIENCE, MEDICINE,
& TECHNOLOGY

DAVID COLEMAN
Eastern Kentucky University

TRADE & COMMERCE

ROBERT J. FLYNN
University of Kentucky

BRET RIPLEY
Lexington Community College

WARFARE

ROBERT J. FLYNN
University of Kentucky

GENERAL INDEX

A

Abenaki tribe 29, 107, 156, 199, 238, 248
Ácoma town 259
Acoma tribe 44, 150, 158
Act of Supremacy (1534) 177
Adena culture 28–29, 117, 136, 137
Adobe architecture 69, 266
Afonso, king of Portugal 233–234
Agona (Stadaconan leader) 97
Ahumeda y Cepeda, Teresa de. *See* Teresa de Ávila.
Ailly, Pierre d' 204, 214, 219, 225
Ajacán mission 42
Alabama settlement 160, 246
Alabama tribe 138
Alaskan land bridge. *See* Land bridge.
Albert of Hohenzollern 191
Alexander VI, pope 39, 104, 110–111, 119, 145, 147, 152, 176, 181, 188, 254, 269
Algonkin tribe 156, 165, 242, 244
Algonquian culture 29–30, 35, 42, 48, 52–53, 80, 88, 94, 158, 168, 171, 173, 198, 246, 258
Algonquian language 87–88
Algonquian tribes 29, 35, 80, 88, 94, 158, 168, 171, 173, 198, 246, 258
Almagest (Ptolemy) 232
Alta California 44
Alvarado, Luis de Moscoso y 256
Americas: The People 21–54
Amerind culture 34
Amerind settlers 26
Anasazi culture 36–37, 56, 117–118, 141, 238, 242, 248
Añasco, Juan de 52
Anglo-Spanish War (1585-1604) 251, 275–276
Ango, Jean 238, 255
Animal hide paintings 71–72
Animal skin clothing 59, 60
Anne of Austria 64
Anthony of Padua, saint 67, 72
Apache tribe 35, 37, 68, 71, 118, 157, 160, 168, 247, 261, 265–266
Apalachee tribe 22, 42, 50–51, 271, 279
Arapaho tribe 35
Arawak tribe 25, 39, 40, 49
Archaic culture 22, 24, 27, 29, 31–35, 37, 107, 135

Arendarhonon tribe 267
Argall, Samuel 63
Aristotle 215, 232
Arizona settlement 59, 66, 145, 160, 167
Armor 268
Armouchiquois tribe 100
Arquebuses 165, 224
Arts, The 55–76
Assumption of the Virgin 72
Astrolabe 210, 222, 234
Athapaskan tribe 26, 35, 37, 118, 160
Athore (Timucuan leader) 75
Atlatl 21–22, 27, 35
Attignawantan tribe 267
Attigneenongnahac tribe 267
Augustine, saint 145
Aute tribe 268, 271
Avonlea culture 35
Ayllón, Lucas Vázquez de 41, 78, 92, 109, 121, 156
Aztec Calmecac school 113
Aztec creation myth 175, 194
Aztec tribe 40–41, 50, 56, 92, 111, 119–120, 244, 247, 261, 268, 271–272, 277–279

B

Balboa, Vasco Núñez de 120
Barbastro, Luis Cáncer de 256, 272
Barlowe, Arthur 48, 52
Bartholomew's Day Massacre 178, 181, 190
Basketry 22, 27, 34, 37, 56, 59, 61, 161–162
Basque-Algonquian pidgin 87
Basque-Indian relations 87
Battle of Mabila 279
Battle of Pamplona 187
Beadwork 59–60
Beaver hunting 266
Beaver wars 260, 268
Benavides, Alonso de 67, 72–73
Beothuk tribe 156
Bering Strait. *See* Land bridge.
Biard, Pierre 182, 199
Biencourt, Jean de 100
Bilingualism 81–82, 87, 92
Birch bark architecture 59
Black Legend 185, 203, 224, 235

Black robes 111
Blackfoot tribe 35
Blacksmithing 113
Blood revenge 125, 140, 142–143, 151–152
Boccaccio, Giovanni 213
Body painting 60
Bone carving 59
Book of Prophecies (Columbus) 201
Bracciolini, Poggio 213, 217
Brief and True Report of the New Found Land of Virginia, A (Harriot) 52–53, 179
Bry, Theodor de 53, 56, 60, 63, 74
Bubonic plague ("Black Death") 204, 209, 212
Buffalo hide painting 60, 67, 70–71
Buffalo hunting 24, 34–35, 107, 116, 159
Buonincontri, Lorenzo 205, 216
Busk (to fast) 164

C

Cabeza de Vaca, Alvar Núñez 41, 50–51, 79, 91–92, 98, 156, 187, 256, 277
Cabot, John 22, 24, 48, 110, 119, 156, 206, 227–230
Cabot, Sebastian 48, 110, 120, 207, 229–230
Cabrillo, Juan Rodríguez 44, 121
Cahokia 31–32, 118, 136, 138, 156, 166, 237, 244, 246
California settlement 33–34, 44, 59, 66, 108, 116, 121, 122, 135, 145, 157, 159, 181, 187, 251
Calusa tribe 22, 32, 41–42, 156–157, 254–255, 271, 273
Calvin, John 45, 127, 177, 180–181, 183, 189–190, 192, 200
Camino de perfección (Teresa de Ávila) 202
Campo santo (burial ground) 70
Canada 106
Caravel 204, 210, 221, 226, 234
Carib tribe 39–40
Carlos (Calusan leader) 42
Carpentry 113
Carrack 210, 221, 226
Carraconny 163
Carrera de Indias 219

Cartier, Jacques   23, 45, 79, 90, 96–97, 110, 121, 156, 163, 182, 207, 229, 239, 255–256, 261, 266, 276–277
Castañeda, Pedro de   167
Castillo de San Marcos (Castle of St. Mark)   73
Castillo, Alonso del   92, 98
Catawba tribe   242, 246
Cathedral of St. Francis   72
Catherine de Medicis   45, 191
Catholic Reformation   180, 183–184, 187, 191
Cayuga tribe   31, 151–152, 164, 267
Cellini, Benevenuto   214
Chaderton, Lawrence   181
Champlain, Samuel de   63, 96, 99, 165, 182, 187, 200, 266
Charlemagne   125, 129
Charles, king of Spain and Holy Roman Emperor   150, 177, 194, 235
Charles V, king of Spain   41, 51, 152, 277
Charles IX, king of France   45
Charlesbourg-Royal colony   45, 239, 256, 261, 277
Charlesfort colony   23, 46, 63, 157, 194
Cherokee tribe   30, 139–140, 163, 167, 169, 172
Chesapeake tribe   173
Cheyenne tribe   35
Chicaza tribe   242, 246, 279
Chickasaw tribe   138, 167, 169
Chicora   25, 41–42, 46, 48–49, 109
Chicora, Francisco de   78, 92
Choctaw tribe   30, 138, 167, 169
Christian imagery in Native American art   72
Chumash culture   33, 44, 116
Church of England   177
Cíbola (Seven Cities of Gold)   25, 43, 99, 156, 167, 239, 256, 277
Cisneros, Francisco Jiménez de   109
Civil law   129–130
Cliff dwellers   37, 56
Clovis culture   24, 26–27, 33–35
Coahuiltican tribe   50
Cochise culture   36
Cofitachequi   42, 242, 246, 262, 279
Cofitachequi, Lady of   51–52, 167
Coles Creek culture   31–32
Coligny, Gaspard de   250, 257, 273
College of Santa Cruz de Tlaltelolco   104, 112
Colorado settlement   167
Columbian Exchange   227, 230
Columbus, Bartolomé   119
Columbus, Christopher   22, 24–25, 35, 39, 48, 85, 89–90, 106, 109, 111, 113, 119–120, 124, 134, 144–145, 156, 181, 193–194, 199–201, 205–207, 210–211, 213–214, 216–222, 225–228, 230, 234, 242–243, 254, 260, 269
Columbus, Domenico   219
Columbus, Hernando   219
Common law   129–130
Communications   77–102
Confessions (St. Augustine)   201
Congregaciones   41
Conversos   185

Coosa tribe   32, 42, 52, 257
Cop, Nicholas   200
Copernicus, Nicolaus   176, 208, 232–233
Coppermaking   27, 56
Córdoba, Hernández de   254, 271
Coronado, Francisco Vásquez de   23–24, 43–44, 65, 67, 80, 93, 99, 110, 121, 157, 167–168, 177, 239, 256, 277, 278–279
Corpus Juris Civilis (code of Justinian)   129
Côrte-Real, Gaspar   78, 90
Cortés, Hernando   40–41, 72, 91, 111, 120, 147, 254–255, 271, 277–278
Cosa, Juan de la   206, 230
Council of Trent (1545–1563)   184
Council oratory   81
Counter-Reformation. *See* Catholic Reformation.
Court of Common Pleas   131
Court of King's Bench   131
Court of the Exchequer   131
Cowichan tribe   158
Cree tribe   60
Creek tribe   138, 140, 164, 166–167
Creoles   87
Croatoan tribe   48–49, 94
Cronon, William   246
Cuba settlement   22
Curia regis (Great council)   129, 131
Cusabo tribe   157, 275

D

Da-nah-wah'uwsdi (little brother of war)   172
Dante   109
Daza, Ignacio   73
De La Rocque, Jean François   96, 256, 262
De Léry, Jean   74
De Niza, Fray Marcos   93
De Orbe Novo (Martyr)   104, 109
De Velasco, Don Luis   90
Decades of the New World or West India, The (Marytr)   178
Decades of the Newe Worlde (Eden)   104, 110
Deganawidah   151, 164
Dehuntshigwa'es (men hit a rounded object)   172
Del Cano, Juan Sebastian   228
Delaune, Etienne   74
Delaware settlement   78, 91
Delaware tribe   60
Desert culture   36
Devastation of the Indies: A Brief Account, The (Las Casas)   224, 234–235
Dias, Bartholomeu   39, 119, 205, 218, 225
Díaz, Estéban   229
Diego, Juan   72, 177
Dietary influences   211, 231
Dios, Nombre de   258
Diseases   170–171
Divers Voyages Touching the Discovery of America (Hakluyt)   105, 110
Divisament dou monde (Marco Polo)   204
Doctrinas   41, 43–44
Domagaya   96–97, 276

Domínguez, Atanasio   67
Don Luis   172–173
Donnacona (Stadaconan leader)   79, 90, 96–97, 156, 239, 255, 276
Dorantes, Andrés   92, 98
Drake, Sir Francis   44, 49, 122, 157, 182, 240–241, 250–251, 258–259, 261, 275
Dry fishing   86
Duc de Fontenany   194
Duke of Guise   191
Duke of Milan   109

E

Eannes, Gil   234
Eastern Woodlands culture   28–29, 31, 56, 60, 117, 141, 259, 261–262, 265–266, 268–269
Ecclesiastical law   130
Ecclesiastical Ordinances (Calvin)   200
Eden, Richard   104, 109–110
Edict of Faith (1500)   185
Edict of Nantes (1598)   191
Edict of St. Germaine (1562)   191
Edicts of Grace (1520s)   185
Education   103–114
Edward I, king of England   131
Eliade, Mircea   194
Eliot, John   186
Elizabeth I, queen of England   44, 46–48, 110, 178–179, 182–183, 191, 250–251, 261, 270, 275
Encomienda   41, 122, 149, 150, 152
English Reformation   47
Engraving   74
Enríquez, Martín   251
Enterprise of the Indies   218–220, 225
Erasmus, Desiderius   109
Eratosthenes   216, 225
Eric the Red   176
Ericsson, Freydis   38
Ericsson, Leif   38, 118, 176, 216
Ericsson, Thorvald   38
Erie tribe   152, 267
Escalante Fontaneda, Hernando de   157
Espejo, Antonio   44, 111, 158
Essays, The (Montaigne)   178
Estates General   132
Estévanico the Moor   79, 92, 98
Etchemin tribe   88, 100, 260, 269
Etowah   138
Euchee tribe   138
European exploration of North America   22, 24, 38–39
European style of war   263
Excommunication   126, 144

F

Face painting   60
Farming   22, 24, 31, 51, 107, 161
Ferdinand II, king of Aragon and Spain   39, 104, 111, 144, 147, 149, 185, 193, 201, 205, 210, 225
Feudalism   125–128
Firearms   224

First Salmon Ceremony 142
Fishing 27
Five Nations. *See* League of the Iroquois.
Florida settlement 22–23, 25, 41–43, 46,
  50, 57, 63, 66, 73–74, 79, 91, 93, 104–
  106, 110–113, 120–123, 137, 145, 150,
  156–157, 160, 170, 176, 178–179, 181–
  182, 186–188, 190–191, 194, 238–239,
  242, 250, 255–258, 261, 271, 273–275,
  279
Flota 270
Foley-Farm culture 28–29
Fort Ancient 29
Fort building 224
Fort Caroline 23, 42, 47, 178, 188, 190,
  194, 239, 250, 258, 273–275
Fort de Buada 63
Fort Raleigh 48
Fort Rémi 63
Fort San Felipe 274–275
Fort San Mateo 275
Fortress churches 66, 67
Fountain of Youth 176, 188
*France Bringing the Law to the Hurons of
  New France* 64
France-Roy colony 256, 262, 277
Francis I, king of France 45, 109–110,
  200, 227, 229, 270, 276
Francis II, king of France 45
Francis of Assisi, saint 111, 187
French fort architecture 63
Fresco paintings 56, 70
Frobisher, Martin 48, 122
Frost Island culture 31
Fuca, Juan de 44, 158
Fur trade 80, 86, 99–100, 238–240, 242,
  246, 248–249, 266, 268–269, 276–277

G

Galeones 270
Galilei, Galileo 109, 233
Gama, Vasco da 39, 206, 210, 218, 228,
  233–234
Geographia (Ptolemy) 204, 214, 217
Geography (Strabo) 217
Georgia settlement 41, 43, 91, 112, 121,
  150, 160, 179, 259, 274
Gilbert, Sir Humphrey 48, 122, 178, 240,
  258
Gluskap (Micmac warrior) 196
Gómara, Francisco Lopez de 104, 109
Gomes, Estevâo 78, 91
Gómez, Esteban 207, 238
Gordillo, Francisco 41
Gosnold, Bartholomew 88
Government and Law 115–154
Great Basin culture 34, 118
Great Voyages (de Bry) 57, 63, 74
Green Corn Ceremony 140, 159, 164
Gregory VII, pope 126
Gregory IX, pope 130
Gregory XV, pope 202
Grenville, Sir Richard 48, 158, 240, 259
Guale tribe 105, 112, 123, 150, 179, 255,
  259, 274
Gunpowder 224

Gutenberg Bible 214
Gutenberg, Johannes 176, 214

H

Hakluyt, Richard 105, 110, 127, 178
Hapsburg-Valois Wars 238–239, 250,
  255, 257, 261–262, 271
Harriot, Thomas 52–53, 94, 171, 173,
  179
Harrison, John 222
Haudenosaunee (Longhouse) 164
Háwikuh (Zuni pueblo) 278
Hawkins, John 240, 250–251, 258–259,
  275
Heath, Sir Robert 194
Heere, Lucas de 109
Henry, Earl of Northumberland 53
Henry II, king of France 45, 131, 181
Henry IV, king of France 126, 191
Henry V, king of England 223
Henry VII, king of England 227–228
Henry VIII, king of England 47, 177,
  181, 183, 189, 275
Henry the Navigator, prince 39, 144, 218,
  233–234
Herjolfsson, Bjarni 38
Hiawatha (Iroquoian leader) 151, 164,
  267
Hidatsa tribe 118, 160
Hispaniola 25, 39–40, 119
Historia general (Gómara) 104, 109
Historiae Canadensis 65
History of New France (Lescarbot) 63
Hitchiti tribe 138
Hochelaga tribe 23, 45, 96–97, 163, 266,
  277
Hoebel, E. Adamson 124
Hohokam culture 36, 56, 117–118, 141
Hopewell culture 28–29, 117, 137, 238,
  243
Hopi tribe 157, 266, 278
Horses 268
Horticulture 22, 24, 27, 29–32, 35–37,
  107, 118, 159, 160, 165, 167
Huguenots 45, 189–193
Humanism 109, 111–112
Hundred Years' War 223
Hunter gatherers 22, 24, 27–29, 31–36,
  50, 96, 107–108, 159
Huret, Grégoire 65
Huron tribe 64, 151–152, 156, 160–161,
  163, 168, 242, 243, 254, 257, 267
Hybrid art 59, 66, 71

I

Illius fulciti praesidio (Pope Julius II) 104,
  111
Images of saints 72
Images of the Virgin Mary 72
Imago Mundi (d'Ailly) 204, 214, 218–219
Inca tribe 40, 255, 272, 278–279
Indigenous trade 242
Indios bravos 39
Indios pacificos 39

Indo-Christian art and terminology 55
Indulgences 127
Informal language 81
Innocent III, pope 111
Innocent IV, pope 146
Innocent VIII, pope 104, 111
Institutes of the Christian Religion, The
  (Calvin) 127, 177, 200
Inter Caetera Divinae (Pope Alexander VI)
  104, 111, 119, 144–145, 149
Intercultural communication 82, 84, 91
Intertribal trade 242, 244, 246
Inuit tribe 26
Iroquoian creation myth 175, 197
Iroquoian language 88
Iroquois Confederacy. *See* League of the
  Iroquois.
Iroquois culture 30, 45, 65, 96, 107, 143,
  151–152, 164, 253, 255, 266, 269
Iroquois longhouse 164
Iroquois tribes 23, 29, 31, 60, 63, 79, 151,
  160, 163, 165, 167, 239, 243, 257, 267
Irrigation systems 118
Isabella (first American settlement) 119
Isabella I, queen of Castile and Spain 39,
  111, 144, 147, 181, 185, 193, 201, 205,
  210, 225
Isleta tribe 141

J

Jamestown colony 25, 49, 94, 186
Jargons 87, 90, 95
Jeune, Paul Le 88
Jewelry making 56
John I, king of Portugal 39, 131, 233
John II, king of Portugal 220, 225
Joyfull Newes out of the Newe Founde Worlde
  (Monardes) 208, 231
Juanillo, Guale chief 259
Julius II, pope 104, 111, 120, 254
Jury system 130

K

Kachina dolls 56, 62
Kanati (The Lucky Hunter) 164
Karankawa tribe 91, 98
Karlesefni, Thorfinn 38
Kepler, Johannes 53
Khan, Genghis 212
Khan, Kublai 212
Kiowa tribe 35
Kivas 37, 62, 69, 108
Kutenai tribe 141

L

La Conquistadora (the Conquering Virgin)
  72
La France Antarctique (Thevet) 104, 109
La republica de los indios 40
La Villa Real de la Santa Fe (The Royal
  City of the Holy Faith) 65

Lacrosse 172
Laguna Santero 70
Lakota (Sioux) tribe 61, 160
Land bridge 22, 25–27, 106, 116
Lane, Ralph 48, 52, 80
Las Casas, Bartolomé de 120, 132, 134, 148–149, 152–153, 182, 186, 199, 224, 227, 234
Las Casas, Pedro de 234
Laudonnière, René Goulaine de 23, 46, 57, 74, 157, 194, 239, 250, 258, 273
Laws of Burgos 120, 149
League of Peace 164
League of the Iroquois 31, 119, 134, 151–152, 254, 260, 267
Leifsburthir settlement 38
Leisure activities 171
Léry, Jean de 74, 192
Lescarbot, Marc 63, 88, 100
Lex talionis (law of retaliation) 142–143
Libro de la vida (Teresa de Ávila) 202
Lifestyles, Social Trends, and Recreation 155–174
Lingua franca 82, 85, 92–93, 95
Locarno Beach culture 36
Louis IX, king of France 129
Louis XIV, king of France 63, 191
Louisiana settlement 160
Loyola, Ignatius, Saint 111, 176, 187
Luis, Don (de Velasco) 47, 80, 157, 178
Luna y Arellano, Tristan de 41, 122, 157, 257, 272–273
Luther, Martin 127, 177, 180, 183, 189–192, 200

M

Mabila tribe 150, 279
Magellan, Ferdinand 120, 207, 210, 228–229
Magna Carta 131
Magnetic compass 204, 210, 221
Mahican (Mohican) tribe 88, 262, 266
Maine settlement 79, 80, 88, 99, 100, 160
Malecite tribe 249
Maliseet-Passamaquoddy language 88
Mandan Robe 60
Mandan tribe 61, 118, 160
Manteo (Croatoan leader) 48–49, 52, 80, 94, 173
Map of the East Coast from Florida to Chesapeake Bay (White) 63
Mapmaking 211
Marchin (Armouchiquois leader) 100
Marcos de Niza, Fray 43, 79–80, 93, 98–99, 156
Martire, Pietro 133
Martyrdom of Jesuit Missionaries, The 65
Mary, queen of England 183, 189
Mary, Queen of Scots 47
Maryland settlement 29, 178
Massachuset tribe 156
Massé, Enemond 182, 199
Mathew 48
Mazaque pueblo 167
Membertou (Souriquois leader) 100
Mendoza, Antonio de 66, 79, 93, 277

Menéndez de Avilés, Pedro 23, 42–43, 47, 73, 110, 112, 122, 157, 170, 172, 190, 240, 250, 258, 273–275
Mercantilism 128
Mercator, Gerardus 207–208, 211, 228, 230
Mercator projection 211, 230
Mesoamerican culture 27, 30, 34
Messamouet (Micmac leader) 80, 87, 99–100
Michael the Archangel, saint 66
Michelangelo 109, 214
Micmac tribe 57, 60, 80, 87–88, 99, 119, 156, 196, 199, 248, 255, 260, 262, 268–269, 276
Mico 259
Minaya, Bernadino de 177, 186
Mingo Hopaii (War-Prophet King) 170
Mission building efforts 56–58, 63, 66, 68–69, 80, 104, 113, 148
Missionary efforts 43–44, 105–106, 111, 113, 188, 256
Mississippi settlement 160
Mississippi tribe 31–32, 41, 46
Mississippian culture 30, 32, 42, 51, 107, 118, 138, 156, 160, 166–167, 246
Miwok tribe 157, 198
Mobile settlement 157
Mogollon culture 36–37, 56, 117
Mohawk tribe 31, 151–152, 164–165, 266–267
Mohegan-Pequot language 88
Monardes, Nicolás 208, 231
Monks Mound 138
Monongahela culture 29
Montagnais tribe 87, 99, 156, 165, 240, 242–243, 249, 259, 268–269
Montaigne, Michel de 178
Montesino, Antón 149
Montesinos, Antonio de 186
Morales, Hernando Moyano de 274
Morgues, Jacques Le Moyne de 57, 74, 122, 157
Mortuary ceremonialism 246
Moscoso y Alvarado, Luis de 279
Mothe, Antoine Laumet de la, Sieur de Cadillac 63
Moundbuilders 24, 28–29, 31, 35, 116–117, 136–137, 156, 160, 166, 176, 237, 243–244
Moundville 138, 246
Mourning wars 143, 260–263, 265, 267–268
Moveable-type printing press 214
Movilla, Gregorio de 113
Munsee tribe 88, 260, 269
Muskogean language 88

N

Na-Déné tribe 26, 37
Nahuatl (Aztec language) 92, 95
Nanticoke language 88
Napochi tribe 157, 257
Narragansett tribe 29, 107, 198, 238

Narváez, Pánfilo de 22, 41, 50–51, 79, 91, 98, 121, 199, 255, 261, 268, 271–273, 277–278
Natchez tribe 138
Nation-state 125, 127–128
Native Americans:
—agricultural techniques 137
—architecture 155, 167
—art 58
—burial customs 28–29, 31, 35–36, 136–137
—chiefdoms 137–138, 141
—clans 165
—clothing 45, 63, 160
—creation myths 30, 194
—death rates 25, 32
—diets 159, 168
—dwellings 24, 29, 31, 36–37, 141, 160, 162, 167
—government 115, 124, 132, 134, 138, 142
—irrigation systems 36, 125, 141
—labor divisions 161, 165
—menstruation rituals 169
—naming patterns 169
—oral culture 194
—populations 25
—spirituality 38, 83, 124, 168, 182, 196
—styles of war 263
—technology 29
—transportation 38
—weapons 217, 219
Natural law 115, 129, 146, 152
Navajo tribe 37, 118, 141, 160, 168, 247, 261, 265–266
Navidad settlement 39, 226
Navigationi et Viaggi (Ramusio) 109
Neutral tribe 243–244
Nevada settlement 34
New France 45
New Galicia 51
New Mexico settlement 25, 59, 65, 70, 106, 110, 113, 122–123, 145, 158, 160, 167, 187
New York settlement 151, 160
Newfoundland, Viking settlement 22
Newton, Isaac 233
Nez Percé tribe 36
Nicholas V, pope 144
Nicotiana rustica 49
Niña 221, 226
Ninety-five Theses (Luther) 127, 177, 181, 190–191
Nonverbal communication 82–85
Nootka tribe 35–36, 44, 158
North Carolina settlement 25, 45, 80, 94, 106, 160, 171, 173, 240, 276
Northern Tewa tribe 248
Northwest Passage 89, 90, 120, 229
Numic language 34

O

Ocute tribe 279
Old Copper culture 27, 238
On Clemency 200

On the Revolution of the Heavenly Spheres
(Copernicus) 208, 233
Oñate, Juan de 23, 44, 65, 71, 111, 113,
123, 150, 158, 168, 259, 278
Oneida tribe 31, 151, 152, 164, 262, 267
Onemechin (Armouchiquois leader) 100
Onondaga tribe 31, 151, 164, 172, 267
Opechancanough (Powhatan leader) 90,
172
Oral communication 81
Order of the Society of Jesus 176
Oregon settlement 34
Ortiz, Juan 79, 93
Ortiz, Tomas 132–133, 182
Ottawa tribe 168
Our Lady of the Angels (*Nuestra Señora de
los Ángeles de Porciúncula*) 66–67
Our Lady of the Immaculate Conception
68
Oviedo, Fernández de 152
Owasco tribe 31

P

Pacific Northwest culture 118
Paiute tribe 34
Palace of the Governors (Santa Fe, New
Mexico) 70–71
Palácios Rubios, Juan López de 148
Paleo-Indian culture 26–27, 29, 36
Papago tribe 172
Papal donation 145, 153
Paquiquineo (Chesapeake Indian) 257
Pardo, Juan 157, 274
Pareja, Francisco 113
Parlement 129
Passamaquoddy tribe 249
Paul III, pope 121, 235
Paul V, pope 202
Pawnee tribe 157
Pax mongolica (Mongol dominance) 212
Peace of Cateau-Cambrésis (1559) 273,
275
Peckham, George 133
Pecos tribe 248
Pedro, prince of Portugal 233
Pennsylvania settlement 151, 244
Peralta, Pedro de 65, 70
Perkins, William 181
Peter Martyr 104, 109, 178
Petrarch 109
Petrarch, Francesco 213
Petrine Mandate 145
Petun tribe 242–243, 262
Philip I, king of Spain 275
Philip II, king of Spain 42, 44, 47, 49, 65,
111, 172, 179, 182, 191, 250–251, 257,
261, 270–273, 275
Philip III, king of Spain 65
Philip IV, king of Spain 132
Piccolomini, Aeneas Silvius 217–218
Pictography 84
Pidgins 78, 80, 87–88, 90, 95
Pima tribe 93, 95
Pineda, Alvarez de 78, 91
Pinta 221, 226
Piracy 110, 254, 270, 273, 275

Piro tribe 248, 266
Pithouses 36–37
Pizarro, Francisco 40–41, 255, 272, 278
Plains Woodlands culture 117
Plaquemine culture 31
Plato 213
Plethon, Gemistus 204, 217
Polo, Marco 204, 212, 214, 220
Pomo tribe 33
Ponce de Léon, Diego de Vargas Zapata
Luján 71
Ponce de León, Juan 22, 41–42, 91, 120,
156, 254, 255, 261, 268, 271
Popé (Pueblo medicine man) 71
Poskita (to fast) 164
Postcontact communication 82
Potlatch ceremony 35–36, 142
Pottery making 22, 27, 29, 33–37, 51, 56,
58–59, 61, 107, 137–138, 161–162,
242–243, 248
Poverty Point, Louisiana 31
Powhatan tribe 29, 48–49, 88, 107, 156,
159, 172, 173, 178
Powhatan (Powhatan leader) 29
Presidios 41, 148
*Principall Navigations . . . of the English
Nation* (Hakluyt) 105, 110
Privateering 238, 242, 249–251
Protestant Reformation 145, 177, 180,
183, 186–187, 189, 191–192, 200
Protestantism 24, 178
Ptolemy 213–214, 217–218, 220
Pueblo architecture 61, 67–69, 266, 278
Pueblo culture 25, 30, 43–45, 61, 66, 69,
71, 113, 118, 158, 160–161, 167–168,
242, 248, 259, 261, 265, 278
Pueblo fresco paintings 61–62
Pueblo Revolt of 1680 66-67, 70–71, 73,
113, 168
Pueblo tribe 23, 25, 155, 167, 238, 247
Pueblo weavings 61
Pythagoras 214

Q

Quadrant 222
Quarai mission 68
Quejo, Pedro de 41, 78, 91
Quetzalcoatl (Aztec god) 194
Quillwork 57, 59, 61
Quivira tribe 25, 43, 278
Quxós, Pedro de 255

R

Raleigh, Sir Walter 48, 52, 63, 80, 94,
122, 158, 171, 173, 193, 240, 250, 261,
275
Ramusio, Giovanni Bautista 109
Rancherias 41
Real Patronato 104, 111
Real, Gaspar Corte 120
Reciprocal learning 91
Reconquista 39, 147, 262
Reformation. *See* Protestant Reformation.
Relations (Jesuits) 63–64

Religion 175–202
Renaissance 58, 106, 108–109, 127,
209–210, 212, 214
Reneger, John 239, 256
Repartimiento 41, 122, 150
Requerimiento (Requirement) 41, 120,
147, 152, 199
Reynolds, John 181
Ribault, Jean 23, 46, 63, 75, 110, 157,
170, 194, 257, 274
Ribeiro, Diego 207, 230
Roanoke colony 23, 25, 48–49, 53, 80,
94, 106, 110, 122, 158, 173, 193, 240,
250, 259, 261, 276
Roanoke tribe 48–49, 80, 94
Roberval, Jean-François de La Rocque
45, 96, 256, 262, 277
Rodríguez, Agustin 43, 111
Romanus Pontifex (Pope Nicholas V) 144
Rubens, Peter Paul 72
Rustichello 212
Rut, John 48

S

Sagard, Gabriel 161, 168
Saguenay 96
St. Augustine colony 23, 42–43, 49, 75,
110, 113, 122, 150, 157, 170, 178–179,
187–188, 190, 240, 242, 249–251,
258–259, 261–262, 271, 274, 276
St. Michael the Archangel mission, New
Mexico 56, 69
St. Steven of Ácoma mission, New Mexico
69
Salem witch trials 192
Salish tribe 35–36
Salmon chief 142
San Esteban del Rey mission, New Mexico
70
San Gabriel mission, New Mexico 113
San Gabriel colony 65, 71
San Juan de los Caballeros 113
San Juan de Xuala 274
San Juan de Yunque 44, 111, 113
San Mateo 170, 274
San Miguel colony 186
San Miguel de Gualdape 41, 255
San Salvador 39, 239, 256
Sangallo, Antonio 73
Sangallo, Giuliano 73
Sanpoil tribe 142
Santa Elena 42–43
Santa María 221, 226
Santa Maria de San Vicente 240, 259
Santo Domingo colony 119
Sapelo Sound, Georgia 41
Saturiwa tribe 157
Saturnia (Timucuan chief) 23, 47
Sauz, Mateo del 257
Scarperia, Jacopo Angelo de' 204
Scholasticism 109
Science, Medicine, and Technology
203–236
Scientific Revolution 215
Sculpting 138
Secotan tribe 48, 94

Secoudon (Etchemin leader)   100
Segura (Jesuit priest)   42
Selu   30, 169
Selu (Corn)   164
Seminole tribe   167
Seneca tribe   31, 151–152, 164, 267
Sepúlveda, Juan Ginés de   132, 152
Seven Cities of Gold. *See* Cíbola.
Serpent Mound   117
Shawnee culture   29
Shell carving   59
Shinny (stickball game)   172
Shipbuilding and navigational innovations   220
Shoemaking   113
Shoshone tribe   34, 35
Sign language   82, 84–85, 93, 95
Siouan-Catawba language   88
Sipapu   37
Síscara, Juan   73
Sixtus IV, pope   185
Skraelings   38
Sky Woman   30, 197
Sky World   197
Slash-and-burn agriculture   267–268
Slavery   36, 41–42, 44, 50, 78, 85, 91, 93, 98, 119–120, 156, 161, 170, 201, 204, 210, 226, 255, 259, 271
Smith, Huston   180, 189
Smith, John   53, 100, 172
Sola Scriptura   180, 190
Songish tribe   158
Sores, Jacques de   257
Sosa, Gaspar Castaño de   158
Soto, Hernando de   23–24, 32, 41, 44, 51–52, 79, 93, 110, 121–122, 150, 156, 166–167, 239, 256, 261, 268, 272–273, 277–279
Souriquois tribe   80, 99
South Carolina settlement   51, 63, 78, 92, 109, 157, 160, 186, 191, 194, 250, 255, 257, 273–274
Southern Tiwa tribe   248
Spanish Armada   94, 179, 182, 191, 251, 276
Spanish colonial architecture   66
Spanish colonial painting   58, 61
Spanish Inquisition   184–185, 191, 201
Spanish Islamic art and architecture   68
Spanish sculpture   72
Spanish-Pueblo architecture   70–71
Stadacona tribe   23, 45, 90, 96, 239, 255–256, 262, 266, 276–277
Staden, Hans   74
Stalo tribe   158
Stare decisis   130
Steatite (soapstone) bowls   56
Stone carving   56, 59
Strabo   204, 213, 216–218, 220
Suárez, Andrés   67
Sublimus Deus   104, 111, 177
Susquehannock tribe   242–244, 262, 266–267
Sweathouse   160

Syphilis   203–205, 227

T

Tacitus   213
Tactacura tribe   157
Tadoussac   240, 249, 259, 266, 268
Tahontaenrat tribe   267
Taignoagny   96–97, 276
Tailoring   113
Tanos tribe   248
Tattoo art   60
Tawiskaron (the Evil Twin)   197
Tazcaluza (Mabilan chief)   279
Tercio   263
Teresa de Ávila   191, 201–202
Tewa tribe   248, 266
Texas settlement   59, 66, 79, 91, 121, 145, 156, 160, 259
Tezcatlipoca (Aztec god)   194
Tharonhiawagon (the Good Twin)   197
Thevet, André   104, 109
Three Sisters (corn, beans, and squash)   27, 29, 30–32, 107, 140, 159, 163, 167
Tiger   240, 259
Tiguex War   278
Timucuan tribe   75, 88, 113, 156–157, 188–189, 256, 271–274, 279
Tiwa tribe   158, 247–248, 278
Tlalteuctli (Aztec earth goddess)   194
T-O maps   217
Tobacco   49
Tohome tribe   157
Tohono O'odham tribe. *See* Papago tribe.
Toka (stickball game)   172
Toltec tribe   238, 242, 248
Tonkawa tribe   279
"Torrid Zone"   218
Toscanelli, Paolo dal Pozzo   205, 218, 220, 225
Trade and Commerce   237–252
Treaties:
—Alcaçovas (1479)   269
—Cateau-Cambrésis (1559)   239, 257, 261, 270, 274
—London (1604)   276
—Saragossa (1529)   255
—Tordesillas (1494)   39–40, 119, 145, 206, 254, 269, 271
Tsimshian tribe   245
Tudor, Mary   177, 181
Tunica tribe   30
Tuscarora tribe   151

U

Ulloa, Francisco de   177
Unami language   88
University of Alcalá de Henares   104, 109, 112
Utah settlement   34

Uto-Aztecan culture   34

V

Valla, Lorenzo   214
Vargas, Diego de   70
Vauban, Sébastien Le Prestre de   73
Velasco, Luis de   42, 80, 90, 178, 272
Velázquez, Antonio   257
Veritas ipsa   104, 111
Verrazano, Giovanni da   22, 29, 45, 109, 120, 156, 207, 227, 229, 238
Vespucci, Amerigo   109, 176, 206–207, 210, 227, 230
Victoria, Franciscus de   121, 152
Viking explorers   22, 24, 26, 29, 38
Vinland   38
Virgin of Guadalupe   72
Virginia settlement   23, 25, 29, 42, 48, 63, 74, 87, 90, 160, 194, 199
Visitadores   150
Voyages (Champlain)   63

W

Wahunsonacock (Powhatan leader)   172
Waldseemüller, Martin   207, 228, 230
Walker, John   80, 88
Wampum   246
Wanchese   48, 52, 80, 94
Wappinger tribe   260, 269
Warfare   253–280
Weaponry   22, 27, 29, 35–36, 53, 95, 162, 165, 223–224, 254, 257, 264, 266, 268–269, 271–272, 278–279
Werowance   31, 48, 53
Whitaker, William   181
White, John   49, 52–53, 57, 63, 74, 80, 94–95, 158, 173
Wichita tribe   157
William the Conqueror   130–131
Wingina (Croatoan leader)   23, 48, 173
Witchcraft   151, 192, 201
Witenagemot   131
Woodcarving   59
Woodcuts   91
Wyclif, John   189

Y

Yokut culture   33

Z

Zaldívar, Vincente de   259
Zuni tribe   79, 99, 157, 167, 266, 278

Index of Photographs

Pierre d'Ailly, *Concordantia astronomiae cum theologia* (1490); an engraving of an astronomer teaching a theologian about the stars   114

An Algonquian pictograph on a cliff overlooking Hegman Lake, Minnesota, circa 1600, of a man, moose, puma, and canoes   92

An Algonquian priest and his family; the daughter is carrying an English doll (British Museum, London)   48

America on a world map drawn by Alberto Catino in 1502 (Biblioteca Estense, Modena)   144

Anasazi culture; section of a wall made circa 1050–1300 A.D. and showing the sophisticated masonry of the period (Pueblo Bonito, Chaco Canyon, New Mexico)   166

Anasazi jewelry, circa 1100–1400 A.D., found near Santa Fe, New Mexico, and made of mica, turquoise, jet, stone, and bone (School of American Research, Santa Fe, New Mexico)   241

Anasazi pueblo village built in 1175-1273 A.D. and called Cliff Palace (Mesa Verde National Park, Colorado)   44

Anasazi striped twill cotton blanket, 1132–1135 A.D. (private collection)   45

An Apache bison-skin cloak (circa 1600) with instructions for carrying out magical cures (from *The Ninth Annual Report of the Bureau of American Ethnology*, 1887–1888)   112

An astrolabe and a sandglass, both used circa 1500 (National Maritime Museum, London)   223

An astronomer teaching a theologian about the stars; engraving from Pierre d'Ailly's *Concordantia astronomiae cum theologia* (1490)   114

St. Augustine, Florida; an 1875 engraving of the first mass held there on 8 September 1565   188

St. Augustine, Florida; plan of the fort, 1593 (Archives of the Indies, Seville)   102

Awatovi, Arizona, kiva mural decoration, circa 1400 A.D.   75

Big Mound, St. Louis; copy of a daguerreotype made in 1852 by Thomas Easterly (Missouri Historical Society)   28

Bird ornaments with golden eyes made by south Florida tribesmen using silver and gold salvaged from Spanish shipwrecks, circa 1500 (South Florida Museum and Bishop Planetarium, Bradenton)   164

Theodor de Bry   74

Theodor de Bry's engraving of Spanish treatment of runaway slaves, 1595   148

Theodor de Bry's engraving of two Virginia *weroans* or chiefs, from Thomas Harriot's *Briefe and True Report of the New Found Land of Virginia* (1588)   32

Theodor de Bry's 1566 engraving of Timucuan men dredging a Florida river bottom for gold nuggets   149

Alvar Núñez Cabeza de Vaca   50

A Caddoan stone ax, circa 1200–1350 A.D. (Thomas Gilcrease Institute of American History and Art, Tulsa, Oklahoma)   280

Calusa Indian wood carving (circa 1400) of a deer's head used in religious ceremonies (University Museum, Philadelphia)   193

John Calvin   200

Canyon del Muerto, Arizona, Navajo pictograph of the arrival of Spaniards   250

Caravels in port; 1594 engraving   247

Jacques Cartier   276

Bartolomé de las Casas   234

Alberto Catino's view of America on a 1502 world map (Biblioteca Estense, Modena)   144

Cliff Palace, a pueblo village built by the Anasazi in 1175-1273 A.D. (Mesa Verde National Park, Colorado)   44

Christopher Columbus   200

Christopher Columbus bearing Christ to the New World, an illustration on Juan de la Cosa's 1500 map of the world (New York Public Library)   192

Christopher Columbus's arrival in the New World, showing imaginary European-style houses on the islands; 1494 woodcut   143

Copernican model of the solar system, in *De revolutionibus orbium coelestium* (1543)   213

Nicolas Copernicus   232

A copy of an image found on a five-inch copper plate in northwest Georgia. It probably depicts the appearance of Our Lady of Guadalupe in Mexico City in 1531   186

Corn grown by Native American farmers in Mexico. By 1000 B.C. the tiny cob and the loose-husked ear shown at top were crossed to produce the hybrid shown at bottom   33

Francisco Vásquez de Coronado   277

Dallas culture, late Mississippian period, 1300–1500 A.D.; human-effigy pipe made of hermatitic stone (Frank H. McClung Museum, University of Tennessee, Knoxville)   76

A detail from Pierre Descaliers's 1546 map of the New World, depicting whaling ships off the coast of Canada   245

Rembert Dodoens, *Florum et coronariarum odoratarumque nonullarum herbarum historia* (1568); illustration of a New World plant, the sunflower   228

Sir Francis Drake   251

Europeans meeting inhabitants of the New World; engraving from Sebastian Münster's *Cosmographia* (1550)   40

The execution of Jesuit priests by southeastern Indians in 1571   189

The falcon impersonator, a Mississippian warrior in a falcon costume carrying a mace and a severed head, on a marine shell gorget, circa 1200–1450 A.D. (Museum of the American Indian, Heye Foundation, New York)   274

The first mass held at St. Augustine, Florida, on 8 September 1565   188

Florida Indians drying meat and fish (engraving by Theodor de Bry, after a painting by Jacques le Moyne, 1564)   162

A four-legged effigy urn, circa 250–800 A.D. (Indian Temple Mound Museum, Fort Walton Beach, Florida)   73

A 1494 woodcut of Christopher Columbus's arrival in the New World, showing imaginary European-style houses on the islands   143

A 1473 theological map of the world from Isidore of Seville's *Etymologiae*. Jerusalem is at the center 183

A French copy of a Seneca pictograph of warriors returning to their village with a captive, circa 1666 (Archives Nationales, Paris) 264

A French drawing of an Iroquois pictograph of the bear and turtle clans in council, circa 1666 (Archives Nationales, Paris) 133

The French sailing into the mouth of the St. John's River, Florida (1564), initially called the River of May because it was discovered on the first of that month (engraving by Theodor de Bry, after a painting by Jacques le Moyne) 47

A German's view of Europeans meeting inhabitants of the New World (engraving from Sebastian Münster's *Cosmographia*, 1550) 40

Grand Gulch, Utah, Anasazi culture; a mummy wrapped in a diamond twill tapestry cotton blanket, 1132–1135 A.D., (American Museum of Natural History, New York) 38

A hand-shaped cutout made of sheet mica, Ohio Hopewell culture, Middle Woodland period, 200 B.C.–400 A.D. (Ohio Historical Society, Columbus) 59

Hegman Lake, Minnesota; an Algonquian pictograph, circa 1600, of a man, moose, puma, and canoes 92

Prince Henry the Navigator 233

A Hohokam child's poncho made of cotton, circa 1100–1400 A.D. (Arizona State Museum, University of Arizona, Tucson, Arizona) 167

Hohokam jewelry made of red argillite, shell, stone, and turquoise (Arizona State Museum, University of Arizona, Tucson, Arizona) 169

Hohokam pottery bowl (circa 600–900 A.D.) found along the banks of the Santa Cruz River in southern Arizona (Arizona State Museum, University of Arizona, Tucson, Arizona) 62

Hohokam seashell decorated by the first known etching process, developed between 1000 and 1200 A.D. from an acid made of fermented cactus juice (Arizona State Museum, University of Arizona, Tucson, Arizona) 66

A Hohokam sunken ball court at Snaketown, Arizona, originally constructed between 600 and 900 A.D. 170

Lopo Homem's 1525 map of the Western Hemisphere 208

A Hopewell Indian wooden figurine of a mother carrying a child, circa 400 B.C.–400 A.D., discovered in western Illinois (Milwaukee Public Museum) 107

Hopewell site, Ross County, Ohio; a pair of obsidian blades, circa 200 B.C.–400 A.D. (Field Museum of Natural History, Chicago) 275

Human-effigy pipe made of hermatitic stone, Dallas culture, late Mississippian period, 1300–1500 A.D. (Frank H. McClung Museum, University of Tennessee, Knoxville) 76

The Huron Feast of the Dead, in which the living carry the deceased to a common burial pit (engraving, circa 1600) 195

Huron village of the seventeenth century, complete with a palisade wall, reconstructed at the University of Western Ontario's Museum of Indian Archaeology and Pioneer Life 64

Hypothetical plan and section of an early-seventeenth-century mission in New Mexico (Arthur LaZar, Albuquerque) 65

An Ice Age needle made from bone (American Museum of Natural History, New York) 161

Illustration of a New World plant, the sunflower, from Rembert Dodoens' *Florum et coronariarum odoratarumque nonullarum herbarum historia* (1568) 228

Illustration of tobacco plant in Nicholas Monardes's *Joyfull Newes out of the Newe Founde Worlde* (1577) 249

An illustration on Juan de la Cosa's 1500 map of the world (New York Public Library); Christopher Columbus bearing Christ to the New World 192

An Iroquoian bowl game made circa 1600. The object of the game was to rap the bowl on the ground and get all the peach pits (one side of each was black, the other white) to turn up the same color (National Museum of Man, National Museums of Canada, Quebec) 171

Iroquoian longhouse engraving; circa 1720 (Newberry Library, Chicago) 136

An Iroquoian wampum belt made with cylindrical beads manufactured by Europeans 246

Iroquois pictograph of the bear and turtle clans in council, circa 1666 (Archives Nationales, Paris) 133

An Iroquois wampum belt (circa 1600 A.D.) celebrating the friendship between colonists and Native Americans (New York State Museum) 29

Isidore of Seville, *Etymologiae* (1473); a theological map with Jerusalem at the center 183

Kiva mural decoration, circa 1400 A.D., from Awatovi, Arizona 75

A Lakota painting on buffalo skin of warriors armed with muskets and a chief on horseback, circa 1600 (Musée de l'Homme, Paris) 244

A late-sixteenth-century Seneca antler comb with human visages that reflect the Iroquois preoccupation with the spirit world (Rochester Museum and Science Center, Rochester, New York) 179

René de Laudonnière meeting the Florida Indian chief Saturnia in 1564 (engraving by Theodor de Bry, after a painting by Jacques le Moyne) 46

A looped cotton medicine bag and its contents, circa 1100–1300 A.D. (Arizona State Museum, University of Arizona, Tucson, Arizona) 192

Francisco López de Gómara, *La historia general de las Indias* (1554); woodcut of an American bison 229

A map of Asia from a 1542 edition of Ptolmey's *Geography*; monstrous beings are depicted on both sides 217

A map of the east coast of North America from Florida to the Chesapeake Bay; drawn by John White in 1585 (British Museum, London) 40

A map of Europe in 1520 20

A map of the New World, made in 1507 by Martin Waldseemüller 26

Santa Maria model (Mariners' Museum, Newport News, Virginia) 221

A marine shell gorget, circa 1200–1450 A.D., showing the falcon impersonator, a Mississippian warrior in a falcon costume carrying a mace and a severed head (Museum of the American Indian, Heye Foundation, New York) 274

Medicine Mountain, Wyoming, medicine wheel, circa 1300 A.D.; it measures eighty feet in diameter, and anthropologists speculate it was used for Sun Dance ceremonies or astronomical sightings 236

A medicine wheel, circa 1300 A.D., found at Medicine Mountain, Wyoming. The wheel measures eighty feet in diameter, and anthropologists speculate it was used for Sun Dance ceremonies or astronomical sightings 236

A Mide bag of otterskin, circa 1600. Used to carry medicinal charms and herbs, it belonged to a member of the Winnebago Midewiwin Society, a group of healers (Chandler-Pohrt Collection, Buffalo Bill Historical Center, Cody, Wyoming) 196

A miniature vessel and a nine-inch-long sandstone Kachina (sacred spirit effigy), circa 1200–1300 A.D., discovered in a crypt near Vernon, Arizona (Chicago Natural History Museum) 198

Mississippian period, 1200–1500 A.D.; a ceramic bear-effigy bottle (University of Arkansas Museum, Fayetteville) 60

A model of Christopher Columbus's *Santa Maria* (Mariners' Museum, Newport News, Virginia) 221

Mogollon culture, a black-on-white painted pottery bowl, circa 1050–1150 A.D., Treasure Hill site, New Mexico (Maxwell Museum of Anthropology, University of New Mexico, Albuquerque) 34

Mogollon pottery bowl, circa 900–1100 A.D., deliberately broken in the center ("killed") before it was placed in the grave of its owner (Arizona State Museum, University of Arizona, Tucson, Arizona) 62

Mohawk cradleboard, circa 1600; the floral motif illustrates the influence of European missionaries (Museum of the American Indian, Heye Foundation, New York)   187

Navajo pictograph on a wall of Canyon del Muerto, Arizona, depicting the arrival of Spaniards in the sixteenth-century   250

Nicholas Monardes, *Joyfull Newes out of the Newe Founde Worlde* (1577); illustration of a tobacco plant   249

A mummy wrapped in a diamond twill tapestry cotton blanket, 1132–1135 A.D., found in Grand Gulch, Utah, Anasazi culture (American Museum of Natural History, New York)   38

Native American hunters, disguised in deerskins, stalking prey (engraving by Theodor de Bry, after a painting by Jacques le Moyne, 1564)   174

Native American petroglyphs inscribed on a boulder in Utah, 900–1700 A.D.   86

Native American warriors shooting poisoned arrows at a French ship (engraving by Theodor de Bry, circa 1594–1596)   273

A nearly intact woven yucca-fiber sandal, made circa 1100 A.D. and found at Mesa Verde, Colorado (Mesa Verde National Park)   162

New World map (1550) with pygmies attacking flamingoes while a unicorn stands in the foreground (British Library, London)   89

A nine-inch-long sandstone Kachina (sacred spirit effigy) and a miniature vessel, circa 1200–1300 A.D., discovered in a crypt near Vernon, Arizona (Chicago Natural History Museum)   198

Ohio Hopewell culture, Middle Woodland period, 200 B.C.– 400 A.D.; bird-claw-shaped cutout made of sheet mica (Ohio Historical Society, Columbus)   64

Ohio Hopewell culture, Middle Woodland period, 200 B.C.–400 A.D.; a hand-shaped cutout made of sheet mica (Ohio Historical Society, Columbus)   59

A 1.75-inch metal tip to a Spanish crossbow dart, circa 1540, found near Tallahassee, Florida (Florida Bureau of Archaeological Research, Tallahassee)   271

Our Lady of Guadalupe in Mexico City, 1531; a copy of an image found on a five-inch copper plate in northwest Georgia   186

A page from a sixteenth-century astronomy book predicting a total eclipse of the moon on 29 February 1504 (British Library, London)   222

A pair of obsidian blades, circa 200 B.C.–400 A.D., found at a Hopewell Site in Ross County, Ohio (Field Museum of Natural History, Chicago)   275

Petroglyphs at the Village of the Great Kivas in New Mexico; Anasazi, circa 1100 A.D.   61

Plan of Fort Caroline in Florida (engraving by Theodor de Bry, after a painting by Jacques le Moyne, 1564)   267

Pomeioc, a typical Algonquian village surrounded by a defensive palisade; drawn by John White in 1585   139

A pottery bowl of the Mogollon culture, circa 900–1100 A.D., deliberately broken in the center ("killed") before it was placed in the grave of its owner (Arizona State Museum, University of Arizona, Tucson, Arizona)   62

Powhatan village, a circa 1600 engraving of a shamanic ceremony   195

Products of Native American craftsmen and farmers of the Southwest, circa 700 A.D.: pottery, a sandal made of yucca fiber, jewelry, a basket of beans, corn, and squash (Southwest Museum, Santa Fe, New Mexico)   108

A Ptolemaic map of the world, circa 1490 (University of Valencia)   215

Ptolmey, *Geography* (1542); a map of Asia with monstrous beings depicted on both sides   217

Pueblo Bonito ruins in Chaco Canyon, New Mexico, built circa 961 A.D. Covering more than three acres, the pueblo housed approximately one thousand people   37

Sir Walter Raleigh's Lost Colony "Roanoac"; map by John White, circa 1585   49

Reconstructed Huron village of the seventeenth century, complete with a palisade wall, at the University of Western Ontario's Museum of Indian Archaeology and Pioneer Life   64

The ruins of Pueblo Bonito in Chaco Canyon, New Mexico, built circa 961 A.D. Covering more than three acres, the pueblo housed approximately one thousand people   37

St. Augustine, Florida, circa 1565, with the fortifications at center (Archives of the Indies, Seville)   43

St. Augustine, Florida, fort plan, 1593 (Archives of the Indies, Seville)   102

St. John's River, Florida (1564), initially called the River of May because it was discovered on the first of that month (engraving by Theodor de Bry, after a painting by Jacques le Moyne)   47

San Esteban del Rey, Acoma, New Mexico, built between 1629 and 1642   70

A sandglass and an astrolabe, both used circa 1500 (National Maritime Museum, London)   223

Saturnia, Florida Indian chief, meeting René de Laudonnière in 1564 (engraving by Theodor de Bry, after a painting by Jacques le Moyne)   46

A seashell decorated by the first known etching process, developed between 1000 and 1200 A.D. by the Hohokam, who probably used an acid made from fermented cactus juice (Arizona State Museum, University of Arizona, Tucson, Arizona)   66

Section of a wall made circa 1050–1300 A.D. by the Anasazi culture, showing the sophisticated masonry of the period (Pueblo Bonito, Chaco Canyon, New Mexico)   166

Seneca antler comb with human visages that reflect the Iroquois preoccupation with the spirit world (Rochester Museum and Science Center, Rochester, New York)   179

A Seneca brass and shell necklace, circa 1570 (Rochester Museum and Science Center, Rochester, New York)   248

Seneca ornamental combs of the mid-sixteenth and late-seventeenth centuries (New York State Museum, Albany)   163

A Seneca pictograph of warriors returning to their village with a captive, circa 1666 (Archives Nationales, Paris)   264

A seventeenth-century engraving of an Algonquian priest and his family; the daughter is carrying an English doll (British Museum, London)   48

A seventeenth-century wooden ball-headed war club of the Delaware tribe (Nationalmuseet, Copenhagen)   266

A shamanic ceremony in a Powhatan village; circa 1600 engraving   195

Shipping diagram from the early-sixteenth-century showing how to transport a horse at sea. By suspending the animal several feet off the deck, the sling prevented the horse from sustaining serious leg injuries in rough weather   252

Ship's compass, circa 1500 (National Maritime Museum, London)   222

A 1683 Huron wampum belt commemorating the erection of the first Jesuit church on tribal lands (McCord Museum, Notman Photographic Archives, University of New Mexico, Albuquerque)   103

Sixteenth-century engraving of Native American smallpox victims   231

The skeleton of a Mississippian woman adorned with strands of two thousand shell beads (Milwaukee Public Museum)   165

The skull of a Native American male, age 50 and dating from 1540, found in northwest Georgia. The gash above the right eye was caused by a sword stroke (Georgia State University)   272

Small brass hawk-bells given to Florida Indians by Spanish explorers in the mid 1500s (Memphis State University)   243

A small seated human figure carved in wood, circa 1480, found near the Tomoka River, Florida (Tomoka State Park, Ormond Beach, Florida)   123

Snaketown, Arizona; a Hohokam sunken ball court originally constructed between 600 and 900 A.D.   170

Hernando de Soto   278

Southeast view of San Esteban del Rey, Acoma, New Mexico, built between 1629 and 1642   70

Spanish cruelty to Caribbean Indians; a 1598 engraving   146

Spanish soldiers massacring the inhabitants of a Native American village (from Bartolomé de las Casas's *Narratio regionum indicarum,* 1614)   270

Striped twill cotton blanket, 1132–1135 A.D.; Anasazi culture (private collection)   45

Teresa of Ávila   201

The thigh bone of an elderly Native American woman, circa 1540, with three sword cuts (Georgia State University)   272

A three-thousand-year-old split-twig deer used by prehistoric hunters as a talisman and found in the Grand Canyon, Arizona (Arizona State Museum, University of Arizona, Tucson, Arizona)   196

Timucuan tribal leaders meeting while women prepare *casina,* an emetic used to purify individuals on important occasions (engraving from Nicholas Le Challeux, *Discours de l'historie de la Floride,* 1566)   135

Title page for Gregor Reisch's *Margarita philosophica* (1503), with representations of the seven liberal arts and philosophy   110

Treasure Hill site, New Mexico, Mogollon culture; a black-on-white painted pottery bowl, circa 1050–1150 A.D., (Maxwell Museum of Anthropology, University of New Mexico, Albuquerque)   34

Two Virginia *weroans* or chiefs, from Thomas Harriot's *Briefe and True Report of the New Found Land of Virginia* (1588); engraving by Theodor de Bry   32

An unusually accurate sixteenth-century map of the region explored by Hernando de Soto   147

Village of the Great Kivas in New Mexico; Anasazi, circa 1100 A.D., petroglyphs   61

The Virgin of Navigators offering her protection to Christopher Columbus, his crew, and Native Americans; 1505 Spanish painting   184

Martin Waldseemüller's 1507 map of the New World   26

Warriors, circa 1200, depicted on the walls of a Utah canyon   265

Western Hemisphere map (1525) attributed to Lopo Homem   208

John White's *A Camp-Fire Ceremony,* 1585–1587   105

John White's 1585 map of the east coast of North America from Florida to the Chesapeake Bay (British Museum, London)   40

John White's map of Sir Walter Raleigh's Lost Colony "Roanoac," circa 1585   49

John White's rendering of Pomeioc, a typical Algonquian village surrounded by a defensive palisade, 1585   139

Woodcut of an American bison from Francisco López de Gómara's *La historia general de las Indias* (1554)   229

Wooden figurine of a mother carrying a child, circa 400 B.C.–400 A.D., discovered in western Illinois; Hopewell culture (Milwaukee Public Museum)   107

Yucca-fiber sandal, made circa 1100 A.D. and found at Mesa Verde, Colorado (Mesa Verde National Park)   162